D1456387

CCNA Data Center
DCICN 640-911
Official Cert Guide

Wendell Odom, CCIE No. 1624
Chad Hintz, CCIE No. 15729

Cisco Press
800 East 96th Street
Indianapolis, IN 46240

CCNA Data Center DCICN 640-911
Official Cert Guide

Wendell Odom, Chad Hintz

Copyright© 2015 Pearson Education, Inc.

Published by:
Cisco Press
800 East 96th Street
Indianapolis, IN 46240 USA

Printed in the United States of America

First Printing November 2014

Library of Congress Control Number: 2014950532

ISBN-13: 978-1-58720-454-8

ISBN-10: 1-58720-454-1

Warning and Disclaimer

This book is designed to provide information about the 640-911 DCICN exam for CCNA Data Center certification. Every effort has been made to make this book as complete and as accurate as possible, but no warranty or fitness is implied.

The information is provided on an "as is" basis. The authors, Cisco Press, and Cisco Systems, Inc. shall have neither liability nor responsibility to any person or entity with respect to any loss or damages arising from the information contained in this book or from the use of the discs or programs that may accompany it.

The opinions expressed in this book belong to the author and are not necessarily those of Cisco Systems, Inc.

Trademark Acknowledgments

All terms mentioned in this book that are known to be trademarks or service marks have been appropriately capitalized. Cisco Press or Cisco Systems, Inc., cannot attest to the accuracy of this information. Use of a term in this book should not be regarded as affecting the validity of any trademark or service mark.

Special Sales

For information about buying this title in bulk quantities, or for special sales opportunities (which may include electronic versions; custom cover designs; and content particular to your business, training goals, marketing focus, or branding interests), please contact our corporate sales department at corpsales@pearsoned.com or (800) 382-3419.

For government sales inquiries, please contact governmentsales@pearsoned.com.

For questions about sales outside the U.S., please contact international@pearsoned.com.

Feedback Information

At Cisco Press, our goal is to create in-depth technical books of the highest quality and value. Each book is crafted with care and precision, undergoing rigorous development that involves the unique expertise of members from the professional technical community.

Readers' feedback is a natural continuation of this process. If you have any comments regarding how we could improve the quality of this book, or otherwise alter it to better suit your needs, you can contact us through email at feedback@ciscopress.com. Please make sure to include the book title and ISBN in your message.

We greatly appreciate your assistance.

Publisher: Paul Boger

Associate Publisher: Dave Dusthimer

Business Operation Manager, Cisco Press: Jan Cornelssen

Executive Editor: Brett Bartow

Managing Editor: Sandra Schroeder

Senior Development Editor: Christopher Cleveland

Senior Project Editor: Tonya Simpson

Copy Editor: Keith Cline

Technical Editors: Frank Dagenhardt, Dave Schulz

Editorial Assistant: Vanessa Evans

Cover Designer: Mark Shirar

Composition: Bronkella Publishing

Indexer: WordWise Publishing Services

Proofreader: Williams Woods Publishing Services

Americas Headquarters
Cisco Systems, Inc.
San Jose, CA

Asia Pacific Headquarters
Cisco Systems (USA) Pte. Ltd.
Singapore

Europe Headquarters
Cisco Systems International BV
Amsterdam, The Netherlands

Cisco has more than 200 offices worldwide. Addresses, phone numbers, and fax numbers are listed on the Cisco Website at **www.cisco.com/go/offices.**

About the Authors

Wendell Odom, CCIE No. 1624, has a long history of writing networking books. He is the author of all the previous books in the Cisco Press *CCNA Official Certification Guide* series, in addition to earlier editions of CCNP certification guides (ROUTE and QoS) and many earlier editions of the *CCIE Routing and Switch Official Certification Guide*. He has written textbooks and produced networking videos. He also contributes to the design and to labs with the popular *CCNA 200-120 Network Simulator* from Pearson. His 30+ year career includes stints at IBM and Cisco and jobs ranging from network engineering, consulting, presale engineering, and teaching. You can find Wendell's books and blogs at www.certskills.com, and find him on Twitter (@WendellOdom).

Chad Hintz, CCIE No. 15729, is a technical solutions architect for the Cisco Commercial East Area focusing on designing enterprise solutions for customers around the Cisco data center technologies. He also holds three CCIEs: Routing and Switching, Security, and Storage. He has more than 10 years of experience in the industry and has held certifications from Novell, VMware, and Cisco. His focus is working with enterprise/commercial customers to address their challenges with comprehensive end-to-end data center architectures. Chad has been with Cisco for eight years, and working as a solution architect has provided unique experiences in building these types of solutions. Chad is a regular speaker at Cisco Live and industry conferences on data center technologies. Chad lives near Buffalo, New York, with his wife and two wonderful children and enjoys golfing in his spare time.

About the Technical Reviewers

Frank Dagenhardt, CCIE No. 42081, is a Systems Engineer for Cisco focusing primarily on data center architectures in Commercial Select accounts. Frank has more than 19 years in information technology and has held certifications from HP, Microsoft, Citrix, and Cisco. A Cisco veteran of more than eight years, he works with customers daily, designing, implementing, and supporting end-to-end architectures and solutions such as workload mobility, business continuity, and cloud/orchestration services. In the recent months, he has been focusing on Tier 1 applications, including but not limited to VDI, Oracle, and SAP. He recently presented on the topic of UCS/VDI at Cisco Live 2013. When not thinking about data center topics, Frank can be found backpacking, kayaking, or at home with his family.

Dave Schulz has more than 30 years of experience with various technologies, ranging from routing and switching to security and voice and data center technologies. Before joining the Skyline Advanced Technology Services, he was involved in network engineering and consulting, project management, and oversight of engineering and maintenance activities for a reseller in the Midwest. He has also been involved in teaching various technologies to customers and engineers, as well as creating various process and procedure methodologies, service pricing, and documentation. Dave created a technical assistance center as a manager and director of professional services and performed installation, support, and consulting for various customer environments. He also had contracting responsibilities at a large global enterprise-level corporation, where duties varied from routing, switching, security, wireless, and project management. Dave currently teaches voice technology classes throughout the United States for Skyline Advanced Technology Services. He also is the author of the Cisco Press book *Cisco Unity Connection and CCNA Voice LiveLessons*.

Dave has three daughters, Amy, Ericka, and Tiffany, and lives in Cincinnati, Ohio with his wife, Peggy.

Dedications

Wendell: Thanks to my wife, Kris, for 16 wonderful years of marriage and of writing books! (Our 16th anniversary fell almost to the day I wrote this sentence.) Thanks to my daughter, Hannah, for teaching dear old Dad how real students write in this day and age. And thanks to Jesus Christ, for the lessons about unity and how that can apply to work and book projects just as much as my walk with Him.

Chad: This booked is dedicated to my loving wife and my two children, Tyler and Evan. You are my inspiration, and without your love and support, I would have never been able to complete this project. This book is also dedicated to my late father, Edward Hintz: You inspire me every day to be a better husband, father, and friend. I miss you every day.

Acknowledgments

It just so happens that Cisco begins its first Data Center certifications with CCNA Data Center. Cisco requires you to pass two exams to achieve CCNA Data Center certification, with this book discussing the first such exam, the Introducing Cisco Data Center Networking (DCICN) exam. As it turns out, the DCICN exam overlaps with the Cisco CCNA Routing and Switch certification quite a bit, with well more than half of the topics in this book also being part of the CCNA Routing and Switching certification. As a result of Cisco's choice to overlap the topics in DCICN and CCNA Routing and Switching, this book uses much material from the two best-selling Cisco Press cert guides for CCNA Routing and Switching.

To begin, we would like to acknowledge those who worked on the original books: the Cisco *CCENT/CCNA ICND1 100-101 Official Cert Guide* and the Cisco *CCNA Routing and Switching ICND2 200-101 Official Cert Guide*. During the writing, Drew Cupp did his usual artful job in guiding these books through the development process, developing standards and keeping the text clear and concise. Elan Beer did his usual amazing job with the technical edits. The figures for the ICND1 and ICND2 books, completely revised for the new editions released in 2013, were the result of some hard work from Laura Robbins and Mike Tanamachi.

Chris Cleveland did his usual superb job of keeping both of us authors on track for book features, style, and organization. And he got to read every word to begin the refining process, as part of his role as development editor. Thanks, Chris, for helping us through the book.

The technical editors for this book, Frank Dagenhardt and Dave Schulz, did an excellent job reviewing the manuscript. Frank's deep skills with Nexus architecture and NX-OS software helped catch those niggling little items; he also made some great big-picture suggestions. Dave's teaching experience was evident in his thoughtfulness about the overall flow, watching the storyline and helping us refine the edges of the content (what to add, what to remove, and what needs more support to make sense). Both technical editors helped improve the book; thanks, guys!

Brett Bartow again served as executive editor on the book. No matter the issue, Brett's always there and ready to help figure out the right course of action. It is great to have his steady hand keeping us on track from the original idea to publication and beyond. Thanks as always, Brett.

The production team deserves some special credit in this book, beyond their usual notices. Sure, as usual, we sent in some Word docs, and out came these beautiful finished products. Thanks for fixing all our grammar, crummy word choices, passive-voice sentences, and then pulling the design and layout together! Particular to this time around, some chapters had a little different path to take, given their origins from the ICND1 and ICND2 cert guides. Thanks to the team for working those elements so well. Also, thanks to Sandra Schroeder for working through the minutia related to final choices for figure design and colors (and credit to Brett Bartow on that task as well); we very much appreciate your going the extra mile.

From Wendell: This is the fourth book on which I have worked with Mike Tanamachi to create the figures early in the writing process. Thanks again, Mike, for taking on the project, making my hand-drawn figures presentable, and tweaking all those little things I cannot seem to make work in Illustrator.

Contents at a Glance

Introduction   xxxi

Getting Started   1

Part I: Networking Fundamentals   9

Chapter 1   The TCP/IP and OSI Networking Models   11

Chapter 2   Fundamentals of Ethernet LANs   39

Chapter 3   Fundamentals of WANs   67

Chapter 4   Fundamentals of IPv4 Addressing and Routing   89

Chapter 5   Fundamentals of TCP/IP Transport and Applications   117

Part I Review   142

Part II: Ethernet LAN Basics   147

Chapter 6   Building Ethernet LANs with Switches   149

Chapter 7   Installing and Operating Nexus Switches   183

Chapter 8   Configuring Ethernet Switching   215

Part II Review   234

Part III: Ethernet Virtual LANs and Spanning Tree   239

Chapter 9   VLAN and Trunking Concepts   241

Chapter 10   VLAN Trunking and Configuration   261

Chapter 11   Spanning Tree Protocol Concepts   283

Chapter 12   Cisco Nexus Spanning Tree Protocol Implementation   311

Part III Review   336

Part IV: IP Addressing and Subnetting   341

Chapter 13   Perspectives on IPv4 Subnetting   343

Chapter 14   Analyzing Classful IPv4 Networks   371

Chapter 15   Analyzing Subnet Masks   389

Chapter 16   Analyzing Existing Subnets   409

Chapter 17   Fundamentals of IP Version 6   437

Part IV Review   466

Part V: IPv4 Routing   471

Chapter 18   IPv4 Routing Concepts   473

Chapter 19   Cisco Nexus IPv4 Routing Configuration   491

Chapter 20   IPv4 Routing Protocol Concepts   505

Chapter 21   Nexus Routing Protocol Configuration   531

Chapter 22   IPv4 Access Control Lists on Cisco Nexus Switches   555

                Part V Review   572

Part VI: Final Preparation   577

Chapter 23   Final Review   579

Part VII: Appendices   593

Appendix A   Answers to the "Do I Know This Already?" Quizzes   595

Appendix B   DCICN Exam Updates   613

Appendix C   Numeric Reference Tables   615

Appendix D   Nexus Lab Guide   623

                Index   636

DVD-only Appendices

Appendix E   Practice for Chapter 14: Analyzing Classful IPv4 Networks

Appendix F   Practice for Chapter 15: Analyzing Subnet Masks

Appendix G   Practice for Chapter 16: Analyzing Existing Subnets

Appendix H   Practice for Chapter 22: IPv4 Access Control Lists on Cisco Nexus
                Switches

Appendix I   Memory Tables

Appendix J   Memory Tables Answer Key

                Glossary

Contents

Introduction   xxxi

Getting Started   1

Part I: Networking Fundamentals   9

Chapter 1   The TCP/IP and OSI Networking Models   11

"Do I Know This Already?" Quiz   11

Foundation Topics   14

Perspectives on Networking   14

TCP/IP Networking Model   15

History Leading to TCP/IP   16

Overview of the TCP/IP Networking Model   17

TCP/IP Application Layer   19

HTTP Overview   19

HTTP Protocol Mechanisms   20

TCP/IP Transport Layer   21

TCP Error Recovery Basics   21

Same-Layer and Adjacent-Layer Interactions   22

TCP/IP Network Layer   22

Internet Protocol and the Postal Service   23

Internet Protocol Addressing Basics   24

IP Routing Basics   25

TCP/IP Link Layer (Data Link Plus Physical)   26

TCP/IP Model and Terminology   28

Comparing the Original and Modern TCP/IP Models   28

Data Encapsulation Terminology   28

Names of TCP/IP Messages   30

OSI Networking Model   30

Comparing OSI and TCP/IP   30

Describing Protocols by Referencing the OSI Layers   31

OSI Layers and Their Functions   32

OSI Layering Concepts and Benefits   33

OSI Encapsulation Terminology   34

Exam Preparation Tasks   36

Review All the Key Topics   36

Definitions of Key Terms   36

Chapter 2   Fundamentals of Ethernet LANs   39

"Do I Know This Already?" Quiz   39

Foundation Topics   42

An Overview of LANs   42

Typical SOHO LANs   42

Typical Enterprise Campus LANs   43

Typical Data Center Ethernet LAN   44

The Variety of Ethernet Physical Layer Standards   45

Consistent Behavior over All Links Using the Ethernet Data Link Layer   46

Building Physical Ethernet Networks with UTP   47

Transmitting Data Using Twisted Pairs   47

Breaking Down a UTP Ethernet Link   48

UTP Cabling Pinouts for 10BASE-T and 100BASE-T   51

Straight-Through Cable Pinout   51

Crossover Cable Pinout   53

Choosing the Right Cable Pinouts   54

UTP Cabling Pinouts for 1000BASE-T   55

Sending Data in Ethernet Networks   55

Ethernet Data-Link Protocols   55

Ethernet Addressing   56

Identifying Network Layer Protocols with the Ethernet Type Field   58

Error Detection with FCS   59

Sending Ethernet Frames with Switches and Hubs   59

Sending in Modern Ethernet LANs Using Full-Duplex   59

Using Half-Duplex with LAN Hubs   60

Exam Preparation Tasks   63

Review All the Key Topics   63

Complete the Tables and Lists from Memory   63

Definitions of Key Terms   64

Chapter 3   Fundamentals of WANs   67

"Do I Know This Already?" Quiz   67

Foundation Topics   70

Leased Line WANs   70

Positioning Leased Lines with LANs and Routers   70

Physical Details of Leased Lines   71

Leased Line Cabling   72

Building a WAN Link in a Lab   73

Data Link Details of Leased Lines   74

HDLC Basics   *74*

How Routers Use a WAN Data Link   *75*

Ethernet as a WAN Technology   77

Ethernet WANs that Create a Layer 2 Service   78

How Routers Route IP Packets Using Ethernet Emulation   79

Accessing the Internet   80

The Internet as a Large WAN   80

Internet Access (WAN) Links   81

Digital Subscriber Line   82

Cable Internet   84

Exam Preparation Tasks   86

Review All the Key Topics   86

Complete the Tables and Lists from Memory   86

Definitions of Key Terms   86

Chapter 4   **Fundamentals of IPv4 Addressing and Routing**   **89**

"Do I Know This Already?" Quiz   89

Foundation Topics   92

Overview of Network Layer Functions   92

Network Layer Routing (Forwarding) Logic   92

Host Forwarding Logic: Send the Packet to the Default Router   *93*

R1 and R2's Logic: Routing Data Across the Network   *94*

R3's Logic: Delivering Data to the End Destination   *94*

How Network Layer Routing Uses LANs and WANs   94

IP Addressing and How Addressing Helps IP Routing   95

Routing Protocols   97

IPv4 Addressing   97

Rules for IP Addresses   98

Rules for Grouping IP Addresses   98

Class A, B, and C IP Networks   *99*

The Actual Class A, B, and C IP Networks   *101*

IP Subnetting   103

IPv4 Routing   105

IPv4 Host Routing   105

Router Forwarding Decisions and the IP Routing Table   106

A Summary of Router Forwarding Logic   *106*

A Detailed Routing Example   *107*

IPv4 Routing Protocols   109

Other Network Layer Features   111

Using Names and the Domain Name System   111

The Address Resolution Protocol   112

ICMP Echo and the ping Command   113

Exam Preparation Tasks   115

Review All the Key Topics   115

Complete the Tables and Lists from Memory   115

Definitions of Key Terms   115

Chapter 5   Fundamentals of TCP/IP Transport and Applications   117

"Do I Know This Already?" Quiz   117

Foundation Topics   120

TCP/IP Layer 4 Protocols: TCP and UDP   120

Transmission Control Protocol   121

Multiplexing Using TCP Port Numbers   *122*

Popular TCP/IP Applications   *125*

Connection Establishment and Termination   *126*

Error Recovery and Reliability   *127*

Flow Control Using Windowing   *130*

User Datagram Protocol   131

TCP/IP Applications   132

QoS Needs and the Impact of TCP/IP Applications   132

Defining Interactive and Batch Applications   *132*

Real-Time Voice and Video Applications   *133*

The World Wide Web, HTTP, and SSL   134

Uniform Resource Locators   *134*

Finding the Web Server Using DNS   *135*

Transferring Files with HTTP   *137*

How the Receiving Host Identifies the Correct Receiving Application   *138*

Exam Preparation Tasks   140

Review All the Key Topics   140

Complete the Tables and Lists from Memory   140

Definitions of Key Terms   140

Part I Review   142

Part II: Ethernet LAN Basics   147

Chapter 6   Building Ethernet LANs with Switches   149

"Do I Know This Already?" Quiz   149

Foundation Topics   152

Ethernet History   152

Early Ethernet with Coaxial Cabling   152

Ethernet Devices   154

Ethernet Repeaters   154

10BASE-T with Hub   155

Ethernet Transparent Bridges   157

Ethernet Switches   158

Ethernet Standards   159

Ethernet Data-Link Protocols   160

Ethernet Physical Layer Standards   161

Ethernet Competition   162

Switching Logic   164

Layer 2 Switching Basics   164

The Forward Versus Filter Decision   165

How Switches Learn MAC Addresses   167

Flooding Frames   167

Avoiding Loops Using Spanning Tree Protocol   168

LAN Switching Summary   169

Design Choices in Ethernet LANs   170

Collision Domains, Broadcast Domains, and VLANs   170

Collision Domains   170

Broadcast Domains   171

Virtual LANs and Broadcast Domains   172

The Impact of Collision and Broadcast Domains on LAN Design   173

Ethernet LAN Media and Cable Lengths   174

Autonegotiation   175

Autonegotiation Results When Only One Node Uses Autonegotiation   176

Autonegotiation and LAN Hubs   178

Exam Preparation Tasks   179

Review All the Key Topics   179

Complete the Tables and Lists from Memory   179

Definitions of Key Terms   180

Chapter 7   **Installing and Operating Nexus Switches   183**

"Do I Know This Already?" Quiz   183

Foundation Topics   186

Accessing the Cisco Nexus 5500 Switch CLI   186

Cisco Nexus Switches and the 5500 Switch   186

Accessing the Cisco NX-OS CLI   186

Cabling the Console Connection   187

Configuring the Terminal Emulator for the Console   188

Accessing the CLI with Telnet and SSH in NX-OS   189

Management Interface   190

Password Security for CLI Access   191

User Settings   192

CLI Help Features   194

The debug and show Commands   196

Introduction to Cisco NX-OS   196

Software Modularity in Cisco NX-OS   197

Service Restart in Cisco NX-OS   198

Software High Availability in Cisco NX-OS   199

In-Service Software Upgrades   199

Cisco NX-OS Licensing   200

Cisco NX-OS and Cisco IOS Comparison   201

Configuring Cisco NX-OS Software   202

Configuration Submodes and Contexts   202

Storing Switch Configuration Files   204

Copying and Erasing Configuration Files   206

Initial Configuration (Setup Mode)   208

NX-OS Version and Other Reload Facts   209

Exam Preparation Tasks   211

Review All the Key Topics   211

Complete the Tables and Lists from Memory   211

Definitions of Key Terms   211

Command References   211

Chapter 8   **Configuring Ethernet Switching   215**

"Do I Know This Already?" Quiz   215

Foundation Topics   217

Configuration of Features in Common on all Nexus Switches   217

Securing the Switch CLI   217

Securing Access with Local Usernames and Passwords   217

Securing Access with External Authentication Servers   218

Configuring Secure Shell   219

Banners   220

History Buffer Commands   221

The logging synchronous and exec-timeout Commands   222

Nexus Switch Configuration and Operation   222

Switch Virtual Interface Concept Inside a Switch   223

Configuring IPv4 on a Cisco Nexus Switch   223

Verifying IPv4 on a Switch   224

Configuring Switch Interfaces   225

Securing Unused Switch Interfaces   226

Predicting the Contents of the MAC Address Table   227

Scenario 1: Communication Between S1 and S2   228

Scenario 2: Communication from S1 to S3   228

Exam Preparation Tasks   230

Review All the Key Topics   230

Complete the Tables and Lists from Memory   230

Definitions of Key Terms   230

Command References   230

Part II Review   234

Part III: Ethernet Virtual LANs and Spanning Tree   239

Chapter 9   VLAN and Trunking Concepts   241

"Do I Know This Already?" Quiz   241

Foundation Topics   244

Virtual LANs and VLAN Trunks   244

Creating Multiswitch VLANs Using Trunking   245

The 802.1Q and ISL VLAN Trunking Protocols   247

Forwarding Data Between VLANs   248

Routing Packets Between VLANs with a Router   249

Routing Packets with a Layer 3 Switch   251

VLAN Trunking Protocol   252

VTP Functions   252

Making VTP Work with VTP Servers and Clients   253

Disabling VTP   256

Summary of VTP Features   257

Exam Preparation Tasks   259

Review All the Key Topics   259

Complete the Tables and Lists from Memory   259

Definitions of Key Terms   259

Chapter 10   VLAN Trunking and Configuration   261

"Do I Know This Already?" Quiz   261

Foundation Topics   264

VLAN Configuration and Verification   264

VLAN Guidelines for Cisco Nexus Switches   264

Creating VLANs and Assigning Access VLANs to an Interface   265

VLAN Configuration Example 1: Full VLAN Configuration   265

VLAN Configuration Example 2: Shorter VLAN Configuration   268

VLAN Trunking Configuration and Verification   268

Controlling Which VLANs Can Be Supported on a Trunk   271

VTP Configuration and Verification   275

Enabling VTP   275

Limiting VTP Using Pruning   278

Exam Preparation Tasks   280

Review All the Key Topics   280

Complete the Tables and Lists from Memory   280

Command Reference to Check Your Memory   280

Chapter 11   Spanning Tree Protocol Concepts   283

"Do I Know This Already?" Quiz   283

Foundation Topics   286

Spanning Tree Protocol (IEEE 802.1D)   286

The Need for Spanning Tree   286

What IEEE 802.1D Spanning Tree Does   288

How Spanning Tree Works   290

The STP Bridge ID and Hello BPDU   291

Electing the Root Switch   292

Choosing Each Switch's Root Port   294

Tiebreakers for Root Port   296

Choosing the Designated Port on Each LAN Segment   296

Influencing and Changing the STP Topology   297

Making Configuration Changes to Influence the STP Topology   *298*

Reacting to State Changes That Affect the STP Topology   *298*

How Switches React to Changes with STP   *299*

Changing Interface States with STP   *300*

Optional STP Features   301

EtherChannel   302

PortFast   303

BPDU Guard   303

Rapid STP (IEEE 802.1w)   304

RSTP and the Alternate (Root) Port   305

RSTP States and Processes   306

RSTP Backup (Designated) Ports   *307*

Exam Preparation Tasks   309

Review All the Key Topics   309

Complete the Tables and Lists from Memory   309

Definitions of Key Terms   309

Chapter 12   Cisco Nexus Spanning Tree Protocol Implementation   311

"Do I Know This Already?" Quiz   311

Foundation Topics   314

STP Configuration and Verification   314

Connecting STP Concepts to STP Configuration Options   315

Per-VLAN Configuration Settings   *315*

The Bridge ID and System ID Extension   *316*

Per-VLAN Port Costs   *317*

STP Configuration Option Summary   *317*

Verifying STP Operation   318

Improving STP Operation   321

Configuring STP Port Costs   321

Configuring Priority to Influence the Root Election   322

Spanning-Tree Port Types   324

Configuring PortFast and BPDU Guard   324

Configuring EtherChannel   326

Configuring a Manual EtherChannel   *326*

Configuring Dynamic EtherChannels   *328*

Troubleshooting EtherChannel   329

Incorrect Options on the channel-group Command   *329*

Configuration Checks Before Adding Interfaces to EtherChannels   *331*

Exam Preparation Tasks   333

Review All the Key Topics   333

Definitions of Key Terms   333

Command Reference to Check Your Memory   333

Part III Review   336

Part IV: IP Addressing and Subnetting   341

Chapter 13   Perspectives on IPv4 Subnetting   343

"Do I Know This Already?" Quiz   343

Foundation Topics   346

Introduction to Subnetting   346

Subnetting Defined Through a Simple Example   346

Operational View Versus Design View of Subnetting   347

Analyze Subnetting and Addressing Needs   348

Rules About Which Hosts Are in Which Subnet   348

Subnet Rules with Layer 3 Switches   349

Determine the Number of Subnets   351

Determine the Number of Hosts per Subnet   353

One Size Subnet Fits All (Or Not)   354

Defining the Size of a Subnet   *354*

One Size Subnet Fits All   *355*

Multiple Subnet Sizes (Variable-Length Subnet Masks)   *356*

Make Design Choices   357

Choose a Classful Network   357

Public IP Networks   *357*

Growth Exhausts the Public IP Address Space   *358*

Private IP Networks   *359*

Choose an IP Network During the Design Phase   *360*

Choose the Mask   360

Classful IP Networks Before Subnetting   *361*

Borrow Host Bits to Create Subnet Bits   *361*

Choose Enough Subnet and Host Bits   *362*

Example Design: 172.16.0.0, 200 Subnets, 200 Hosts 364

Masks and Mask Formats 364

Build a List of All Subnets 365

Plan the Implementation 366

Assign Subnets to Different Locations 367

Choose Static and Dynamic Ranges per Subnet 367

Foundation Topics 369

Review All the Key Topics 369

Complete the Tables and Lists from Memory 369

Definitions of Key Terms 369

Chapter 14   Analyzing Classful IPv4 Networks   371

"Do I Know This Already?" Quiz 371

Foundation Topics 374

Classful Network Concepts 374

IPv4 Network Classes and Related Facts 374

Actual Class A, B, and C Networks 375

Address Formats 376

Default Masks 377

Number of Hosts per Network 377

Deriving the Network ID and Related Numbers 378

Unusual Network IDs and Network Broadcast Addresses 380

Practice with Classful Networks 381

Practice Deriving Key Facts Based on an IP Address 381

Practice Remembering the Details of Address Classes 382

Additional Practice 383

Exam Preparation Tasks 384

Review All the Key Topics 384

Complete the Tables and Lists from Memory 384

Definitions of Key Terms 384

Practice 384

Answers to Earlier Practice Problems 385

Answers to Practice Problem 7 (From Table 14-5) 385

Answers to Practice Problem 8 (From Table 14-5) 386

Answers to Practice Problem 9 (From Table 14-5) 386

Chapter 15   Analyzing Subnet Masks   389

"Do I Know This Already?" Quiz   389

Foundation Topics   392

Subnet Mask Conversion   392

Three Mask Formats   392

Converting Between Binary and Prefix Masks   393

Converting Between Binary and DDN Masks   394

Converting Between Prefix and DDN Masks   396

Practice Converting Subnet Masks   397

Identifying Subnet Design Choices Using Masks   398

Masks Divide the Subnet's Addresses into Two Parts   399

Masks and Class Divide Addresses into Three Parts   400

Classless and Classful Addressing   401

Calculations Based on the IPv4 Address Format   401

Practice Analyzing Subnet Masks   403

Exam Preparation Tasks   405

Review All the Key Topics   405

Complete the Tables and Lists from Memory   405

Definitions of Key Terms   405

Practice   405

Answers to Earlier Practice Problems   406

Chapter 16   Analyzing Existing Subnets   409

"Do I Know This Already?" Quiz   409

Foundation Topics   412

Defining a Subnet   412

An Example with Network 172.16.0.0 and Four Subnets   412

Subnet ID Concepts   414

Subnet Broadcast Address   415

Range of Usable Addresses   415

Analyzing Existing Subnets: Binary   416

Finding the Subnet ID: Binary   416

Finding the Subnet Broadcast Address: Binary   418

Binary Practice Problems   419

Shortcut for the Binary Process   420

Brief Note About Boolean Math   422

Finding the Range of Addresses   422

Analyzing Existing Subnets: Decimal   422

  Analysis with Easy Masks   423

  Predictability in the Interesting Octet   424

  Finding the Subnet ID: Difficult Masks   425

  Resident Subnet Example 1   426

  Resident Subnet Example 2   427

  Resident Subnet Practice Problems   427

  Finding the Subnet Broadcast Address: Difficult Masks   428

  Subnet Broadcast Example 1   428

  Subnet Broadcast Example 2   429

  Subnet Broadcast Address Practice Problems   430

Practice Analyzing Existing Subnets   430

  A Choice: Memorize or Calculate   430

  Additional Practice   431

Exam Preparation Tasks   432

Review All the Key Topics   432

Complete the Tables and Lists from Memory   432

Definitions of Key Terms   432

Practice   432

Answers to Earlier Practice Problems   433

Chapter 17   Fundamentals of IP Version 6   437

"Do I Know This Already?" Quiz   437

Foundation Topics   440

Introduction to IP Version 6   440

  The Need and Effect of a New Internet Protocol   440

  Additional Motivations for IPv6   441

  Many Protocols Updated   442

  Introduction to IPv6 Addresses and Prefixes   442

  Representing Full (Unabbreviated) IPv6 Addresses   443

  Abbreviating IPv6 Addresses   443

  Expanding IPv6 Addresses   444

  Representing the Prefix Length of an Address   445

  Calculating the IPv6 Prefix (Subnet ID)   445

  Assigning Unique IPv6 Prefixes Across the Globe   447

IPv6 Addressing and Subnetting   449

    Global Unicast Addresses and IPv6 Subnetting   449

    IPv6 Subnetting Concepts   450

    Assign Subnets and Addresses   452

    The Actual Global Unicast Addresses   453

    Unique Local Unicast Addresses   453

    Link Local Addresses   454

    IPv6 Multicast Addresses   455

    Miscellaneous IPv6 Addresses   456

Implementing IPv6   457

    IPv6 Address Assignment   457

    Dynamic Assignment of the Interface ID with EUI-64   457

    Discovering the IPv6 Prefix with SLAAC   459

    Dynamic Configuration Using Stateful DHCP   460

    IPv6 Transition and Coexistence   461

    Dual Stack   462

    Tunneling IPv6 Inside IPv4   462

Exam Preparation Tasks   464

Review All the Key Topics   464

Complete the Tables and Lists from Memory   464

Definitions of Key Terms   464

Answers to Earlier Practice Problems   464

Part IV Review   466

Part V: IPv4 Routing   471

Chapter 18   IPv4 Routing Concepts   473

"Do I Know This Already?" Quiz   473

Foundation Topics   475

IP Routing   475

    IPv4 Routing Process Reference   475

    An Example of IP Routing   478

    Host Forwards the IP Packet to the Default Router (Gateway)   478

    Routing Step 1: Decide Whether to Process the Incoming Frame   479

    Routing Step 2: Deencapsulation of the IP Packet   480

    Routing Step 3: Choosing Where to Forward the Packet   480

    Routing Step 4: Encapsulating the Packet in a New Frame   481

    Routing Step 5: Transmitting the Frame   482

Internal Processing on Cisco Routers   482

Potential Routing Performance Issues   483

Cisco Router Fast Switching and CEF   483

Cisco Nexus Switch Operations with Routing   484

Exam Preparation Tasks   488

Review All the Key Topics   488

Complete the Tables and Lists from Memory   488

Definitions of Key Terms   488

Chapter 19   Cisco Nexus IPv4 Routing Configuration   491

"Do I Know This Already?" Quiz   491

Foundation Topics   494

Configuring Connected Routes on Cisco Nexus Switches   494

Direct and Local Routes and the ip address Command   494

Routing Between Subnets on VLANs   497

Configuring Routing to VLANs Using a Layer 3 Switch   497

Configuring Static Routes   499

Static Route Configuration   499

Static Default Routes   501

Exam Preparation Tasks   502

Review All the Key Topics   502

Complete the Tables and Lists from Memory   502

Definitions of Key Terms   502

Command Reference to Check Your Memory   502

Chapter 20   IPv4 Routing Protocol Concepts   505

"Do I Know This Already?" Quiz   505

Foundation Topics   508

Introduction to Routing Protocols   508

History of Interior Gateway Protocols   508

Comparing IGPs   509

Distance Vector Basics   511

The Concept of a Distance and a Vector   511

Full Update Messages and Split Horizon   512

Monitoring Neighbor State with Periodic RIP Updates   513

Split Horizon   513

Route Poisoning   514

RIP Concepts and Operation   515

Features of Both RIPv1 and RIPv2   515

Differences Between RIPv1 and RIPv2   516

EIGRP Concepts and Operation   517

EIGRP Maintains Neighbor Status Using Hello   518

EIGRP Topology and the Metric Calculation   518

EIGRP Convergence   519

EIGRP Summary   521

Understanding the OSPF Link-State Routing Protocol   521

OSPF Comparisons with EIGRP   521

Building the OSPF LSDB and Creating IP Routes   522

Topology Information and LSAs   522

Applying Dijkstra SPF Math and OSPF Metrics to Find the Best Routes   524

Scaling OSPF Through Hierarchical Design   525

Exam Preparation Tasks   528

Review All the Key Topics   528

Definitions of Key Terms   528

Chapter 21   Nexus Routing Protocol Configuration   531

"Do I Know This Already?" Quiz   531

Foundation Topics   533

RIP Version 2 Configuration on NX-OS   536

EIGRP Configuration on NX-OS   541

OSPF Configuration on NX-OS   546

Exam Preparation Tasks   551

Review All the Key Topics   551

Definitions of Key Terms   551

Command Reference to Check Your Memory   551

Chapter 22   IPv4 Access Control Lists on Cisco Nexus Switches   555

"Do I Know This Already?" Quiz   555

Foundation Topics   557

IPv4 Access Control List Basics   557

ACL Location and Direction   557

Matching Packets   558

Taking Action When a Match Occurs   559

Types of IP ACLs   559

List Logic with IP ACLs   560

Matching Logic and Command Syntax   562

Matching TCP and UDP Port Numbers   562

Implementing Cisco Nexus IPv4 ACLs   566

ACL Example 1   566

ACL Example 2   567

Practice Cisco Nexus IPv4 ACLs   568

Practice Building access-list Commands   568

Exam Preparation Tasks   570

Review All the Key Topics   570

Definitions of Key Terms   570

Appendix H Practice Problems   570

Command Reference to Check Your Memory   570

Part V Review   572

Part VI: Final Preparation   577

Chapter 23   Final Review   579

Advice About the Exam Event   579

Learn the Question Types Using the Cisco Certification Exam
Tutorial   579

Think About Your Time Budget Versus Numbers of Questions   580

A Suggested Time-Check Method   581

Miscellaneous Pre-Exam Suggestions   582

Exam-Day Advice   582

Exam Review   583

Practice Subnetting and Other Math-Related Skills   583

Take Practice Exams   585

Practicing Taking the DCICN Exam   585

Advice on How to Answer Exam Questions   586

Taking Other Practice Exams   587

Find Knowledge Gaps Through Question Review   588

Practice Hands-On CLI Skills   591

Review Mind Maps from Part Review   591

Other Study Tasks   591

Final Thoughts   591

Part VII: Appendices   593

Appendix A   **Answers to the "Do I Know This Already?" Quizzes   595**

Appendix B   **DCICN Exam Updates   613**

Appendix C   **Numeric Reference Tables   615**

Appendix D   **Nexus Lab Guide   623**

Index   636

DVD-only Appendices

Appendix E   **Practice for Chapter 14: Analyzing Classful IPv4 Networks**

Appendix F   **Practice for Chapter 15: Analyzing Subnet Masks**

Appendix G   **Practice for Chapter 16: Analyzing Existing Subnets**

Appendix H   **Practice for Chapter 22: IPv4 Access Control Lists on Cisco Nexus Switches**

Appendix I   **Memory Tables**

Appendix J   **Memory Tables Answer Key**

Glossary

Icons Used in This Book

 Layer 2 Switch

 Layer 3 Switch

 Nexus Switch

 Nexus 7000 Switch

 Router

 Printer

 PC

 Laptop

 Server

 IP Phone

 WAN Switch

 Frame Relay Switch

 Cable Modem

 DSLAM

 CSU/DSU

 Access Point

 Hub

 Bridge

 Phone

 PIX Firewall

 ASA

 Network Cloud

 Ethernet Connection

Serial Line

Virtual Circuit

Ethernet WAN

Wireless

Command Syntax Conventions

The conventions used to present command syntax in this book are the same conventions used in the IOS Command Reference. The Command Reference describes these conventions as follows:

- **Boldface** indicates commands and keywords that are entered literally as shown. In actual configuration examples and output (not general command syntax), boldface indicates commands that are manually input by the user (such as a **show** command).
- *Italic* indicates arguments for which you supply actual values.
- Vertical bars (|) separate alternative, mutually exclusive elements.
- Square brackets ([ ]) indicate an optional element.
- Braces ({ }) indicate a required choice.
- Braces within brackets ([{ }]) indicate a required choice within an optional element.

Introduction

About the Exam

Congratulations! If you are reading far enough to look at this book's Introduction, you've probably already decided to go for your Cisco CCNA Data Center certification, and that begins with the Introduction to Cisco Data Center Networking (DCICN 640-911) exam. Cisco dominates the networking marketplace, and in a few short years after entering the data center server marketplace, they have achieved significant market share and become one of the primary vendors of data center server hardware as well. If you want to succeed as a technical person in the networking industry, and in data centers in particular, you need to know Cisco. Getting your CCNA Data Center certification is a great first step to build your skills and become respected by others in the data center field.

The Exams That Help You Achieve CCNA Data Center Certification

The Cisco CCNA Data Center certification is the most basic Cisco Data Center certification, and acts as a prerequisite for the other Cisco Data Center certifications. CCNA Data Center itself has no other prerequisites. To achieve the CCNA Data Center cert, you simply have to pass two exams: Introduction to Cisco Data Center Networking (DCICN) and Introduction to Cisco Data Center Technologies (DCICT), as shown in Figure I-1.

Figure I-1 *Path to Cisco CCNA Data Center Certification*

The DCICN and DCICT differ quite a bit in terms of the topics covered. DCICN focuses on networking technology. In fact, it overlaps quite a bit with the topics in the ICND1 100-101 exam, which leads to the Cisco Certified Entry Network Technician (CCENT) certification. DCICN explains the basics of networking, focusing on Ethernet switching and IP routing. The only data center focus in DCICN happens to be the fact that all the configuration and verification examples use Cisco Nexus switches, which Cisco builds specifically for use in the data center.

The DCICT exam instead focuses on technologies specific to the data center. These technologies include storage networking, Unified Computing (the term used by Cisco for their server products and services), and data networking features unique to the Nexus model series of switches.

Basically, DCICN touches on concepts that you might see in all parts of a corporate network (including the data center), and DCICT then hits the topics specific to data centers.

Types of Questions on the Exams

Cisco certification exams follow the same general format. At the testing center, you sit in a quiet room with a PC. Before the exam timer begins, you have a chance to do a few other tasks on the PC. For instance, you can take a sample quiz just to get accustomed to the PC and the testing engine. Anyone who has user-level skills in getting around a PC should have no problems with the testing environment.

Once the exam starts, the screen shows you question after question. The questions typically fall into one of the following categories:

- Multiple choice, single answer
- Multiple choice, multiple answer
- Testlet
- Drag-and-drop (DND)
- Simulated lab (sim)
- Simlet

The first three items in the list are all actually multiple-choice questions. The multiple-choice format simply requires that you point and click a circle beside the correct answer(s). Cisco traditionally tells you how many answers you need to choose, and the testing software prevents you from choosing too many answers. The testlet asks you several multiple-choice questions, all based on the same larger scenario.

DND questions require you to move some items around on the graphical user interface (GUI). You left-click and hold, move a button or icon to another area, and release the clicker to place the object somewhere else (usually into a list). Or, you might see a diagram, and you have to click and drag the icons in the figure to the correct place to answer a question. For some questions, to get the question correct, you might need to put a list of five things in the proper order.

The last two types, sim and simlet questions, both use a network simulator to ask questions. Interestingly, the two types actually allow Cisco to assess two very different skills. First, sim questions generally describe a problem, and your task is to configure one or more routers and switches to fix the problem. The exam then grades the question based on the configuration you changed or added. Basically, these questions begin with a broken configuration, and you have to fix the configuration to answer the question.

Simlet questions also use a network simulator, but instead of answering the question by changing the configuration, the question includes one or more multiple-choice questions. The questions require that you use the simulator to examine the current behavior of a network, interpreting the output of any **show** commands that you can remember to answer the question. While sim questions require you to troubleshoot problems related to a configuration, simlets require you to analyze both working and broken networks, correlating **show** command output with your knowledge of networking theory and configuration commands.

You can watch and even experiment with these command types using the Cisco Exam Tutorial. To find the Cisco Certification Exam Tutorial, go to www.cisco.com, and search for "exam tutorial."

What's on the DCICN Exam?

Everyone wants to know what is on the test, for any test, ever since the early days of school. Cisco tells the world the topics on each of its exams. Cisco wants the public to know both the variety of topics, and an idea about the kinds of knowledge and skills required for each topic, for every Cisco certification exam. To that end, Cisco publishes a set of exam topics for each exam.

While the exam topics list the specific topics, like IP addressing, OSPF, and VLANs, the verb in the exam topic is just as important. The verb tells us to what degree the topic must be understood and what skills are required. The topic also implies the kinds of skills required for that topic. For example, one topic might start with "Describe...," another with "Configure...," another with "Verify...," and another might begin with "Troubleshoot...." That last topic has the highest required skill level, because to troubleshoot, you must understand the topic, be able to configure it (to see what is wrong with the configuration), and verify it (to find the root cause of the problem). By listing the topics and skill level, Cisco helps us all prepare for its exams.

Cisco's posted exam topics, however, are only guidelines. Cisco's disclaimer language mentions that fact. Cisco makes the effort to keep the exam questions within the confines of the stated exam topics, and I know from talking to those involved that every question is analyzed for whether it fits within the stated exam topics.

DCICN 640-911 Exam Topics

You can easily find exam topics for both the DCICN and DCICT exams with a simple search at Cisco.com. Alternatively, you can go to www.cisco.com/go/ccna, which gets you to the page for CCNA Routing and Switching, and easily navigate to the nearby CCNA Data Center page.

Over time, Cisco has begun making two stylistic improvements to the posted exam topics. In the past, the topics were simply listed as bullets, with some indentation to imply subtopics under a major topic. More and more often today, including for the DCICN and DCICT exam topics, Cisco also numbers the exam topics, making it easier to refer to specific topics. In addition, Cisco lists the weighting for each of the major topic headings. The weighting tells you the percentage of points from your exam that should come from each major topic area. The DCICN contains four major headings, with the weightings shown in Table I-1.

Table I-1   Four Major Topic Areas in the DCICN 640-911 Exam

Number	Exam Topic	Weighting
1.0	Describe How a Network Works	15%
2.0	Configure, Verify, and Troubleshoot a Switch with VLANs and Interswitch Communication Using Nexus	21%
3.0	Implement an IP Addressing Scheme and IP Services to Meet Network Requirements in a Medium-Size Enterprise Branch Office Network Using Nexus	12%
4.0	Configure, Certify, and Troubleshoot Basic Router Operation and Routing on Cisco Devices Using Nexus	52%

Note that while the weighting of each topic area tells you something about the exam, in the authors' opinion, the weighting probably does not change how you study. All four topic areas hold enough weighting so that if you completely ignore one topic, you will likely not pass. Also, networking requires that you put many concepts together, so you need all the pieces before you can understand the whole network. The weightings might tell you where to spend a little more of your time during the last days before taking the exam, but otherwise, plan on studying for all the exam topics.

Tables I-2 through I-5 list the details of the exam topics, with one table for each of the major topic areas, as listed in Table I-1. Note that these tables also list the book chapters that discuss each of the exam topics.

Table I-2 Exam Topics in First Major DCICN Exam Topic Area

Number	Exam Topic		Chapter
1.0	Describe How a Network Works		
1.1	Describe the purpose and functions of various network devices		Most
1.1.a		Interpret a network diagram	1, 2, 3, 4, 6, 7, 13
1.1.b		Define physical network topologies	6
1.2	Select the components required to meet a network specification		Most
1.2.a		Switches	2, 6, 7
1.3	Use the OSI and TCP/IP models and their associated protocols to explain how data flows in a network		All
1.3.a		IP	4, 13–17
1.3.b		TCP	5
1.3.c		UDP	5
1.4	Describe the purpose and basic operation of the protocols in the OSI and TCP models		Most
1.4.a		TCP/IP	1
1.4.b		OSI Layers	1

Table I-3 Exam Topics in Second Major DCICN Exam Topic Area

Number	Exam Topic		Chapter
2.0	Configure, Verify, and Troubleshoot a Switch with VLANs and Interswitch Communication Using Nexus		
2.1	Explain the technology and media access control method for Ethernet networks		2, 6
2.1.a		IEEE 802 protocols	2, 6
2.1.b		CSMA/CD	2, 6

Number	Exam Topic	Chapter
2.2	Explain basic switching concepts and the operation of Cisco switches	2, 6–10
2.2.a	Layer 2 addressing	2
2.2.b	MAC table	6–10
2.2.c	Flooding	6–10
2.3	Describe and configure enhanced switching technologies	9–12
2.3.a	VTP	9, 10
2.3.b	VLAN	9, 10
2.3.c	802.1q	9, 10
2.3.d	STP	11, 12

Table I-4   Exam Topics in Third Major DCICN Exam Topic Area

Number	Exam Topic	Chapter
3.0	Implement an IP Addressing Scheme and IP Services to Meet Network Requirements in a Medium-Size Enterprise Branch Office Network Using Nexus	
3.1	Describe the operation and benefits of using private and public IP addressing	13–17
3.1.a	Classfull IP addressing	13–15
3.1.b	RFC 1918	13, 14
3.1.c	RFC 4193	17
3.2	Describe the difference between IPv4 and IPv6 addressing scheme	13–17
3.2.a	Comparative address space	12–16
3.2.b	Host addressing	17

Table I-5   Exam Topics in Fourth Major DCICN Exam Topic Area

Number	Exam Topic	Chapter
4.0	Configure, Certify, and Troubleshoot Basic Router Operation and Routing on Cisco Devices Using Nexus	
4.1	Describe and Configure basic routing concepts	18–22
4.1.a	Packet forwarding	18–22
4.1.b	Router lookup process (exec mode, exec commands, configuration mode)	18, 19

Number	Exam Topic	Chapter
4.2	Describe the operation of Cisco routers	18–22
4.2.a	Router bootup process	18
4.2.b	POST	18
4.2.c	Router components	18, 20, 21

NOTE   Because it is possible that the exam topics may change over time, it may be worth the time to double-check the exam topics as listed on the Cisco website (www.cisco.com/go/certifications and navigate to the CCNA Data Center page). In the unlikely event that Cisco does happen to add exam topics at a later date, note that Appendix B, "DCICN Exam Updates," describes how to go to www.ciscopress.com and download additional information about those newly added topics.

About the Book

This book discusses the content and skills needed to pass the 640-911 DCICN exam.

Book Features

This book uses several tools to help you discover your weak topic areas, to help you improve your knowledge and skills with those topics, and to prove that you have retained your knowledge of those topics. So, this book does not try to help you pass the exams only by memorization, but by truly learning and understanding the topics. This book helps you pass the DCICN exam by using the following methods:

- Helping you discover which exam topics you have not mastered
- Providing explanations and information to fill in your knowledge gaps
- Supplying exercises that enhance your ability to recall and deduce the answers to test questions
- Providing practice exercises on the topics and the testing process via test questions on the DVD

Chapter Features

To help you customize your study time using these books, the core chapters have several features that help you make the best use of your time:

- **"Do I Know This Already?" Quizzes:** Each chapter begins with a quiz that helps you determine the amount of time you need to spend studying that chapter.
- **Foundation Topics:** These are the core sections of each chapter. They explain the protocols, concepts, and configuration for the topics in that chapter.

■ **Exam Preparation Tasks:** At the end of the "Foundation Topics" section of each chapter, the "Exam Preparation Tasks" section lists a series of study activities that should be done at the end of the chapter. Each chapter includes the activities that make the most sense for studying the topics in that chapter. The activities include the following:

■ **Review Key Topics:** The Key Topic icon is shown next to the most important items in the "Foundation Topics" section of the chapter. The key topics review activity lists the key topics from the chapter and their corresponding page numbers. Although the contents of the entire chapter could be on the exam, you should definitely know the information listed in each key topic.

■ **Complete Tables and Lists from Memory:** To help you exercise your memory and memorize some lists of facts, many of the more important lists and tables from the chapter are included in a document on the DVD. This document lists only partial information, allowing you to complete the table or list.

■ **Define Key Terms:** Although the exams may be unlikely to ask a question like, "Define this term," the CCNA exams require that you learn and know a lot of networking terminology. This section lists the most important terms from the chapter, asking you to write a short definition and compare your answer to the Glossary at the end of this book.

■ **Command Reference Tables:** Some book chapters cover a large amount of configuration and EXEC commands. These tables list the commands introduced in the chapter, along with an explanation. For exam preparation, use it for reference, but also read the table once when performing the exam preparation tasks to make sure that you remember what all the commands do.

Part Review

The part review tasks help you prepare to apply all the concepts in this part of the book. (Each book part contains a number of related chapters.) The part review includes sample test questions that require you to apply the concepts from multiple chapters in that part, uncovering what you truly understood and what you did not quite yet understand. The part review also uses mind map exercises that help you mentally connect concepts, configuration, and verification, so that no matter what perspective a single exam question takes, you can analyze and answer the question.

The part reviews list tasks, along with checklists, so that you can track your progress. The following list explains the most common tasks you will see in the part review; note that not all "Part Review" sections use every type of task:

■ **Review Do I Know This Already? (DIKTA) Questions:** Although you have already seen the DIKTA questions from the chapters in a part, re-answering those questions can be a useful way to review facts. The "Part Review" section suggests that you repeat the DIKTA questions, but also use the Pearson IT Certification Practice Test (PCPT) exam software that comes with the book, for extra practice in answering multiple-choice questions on a computer.

■ **Answer Part Review Questions:** The PCPT exam software includes several exam databases. One exam database holds part review questions, written specifically for part reviews. These questions purposefully include multiple concepts in each question, sometimes from multiple chapters, to help build the skills needed for the more challenging analysis questions on the exams.

■ **Review Key Topics:** Yes, again! They are indeed the most important topics in each chapter.

■ **Create Configuration Mind Maps:** Mind maps are graphical organizing tools that many people find useful when learning and processing how concepts fit together. The process of creating mind maps helps you build mental connections between concepts and configuration commands, in addition to developing your recall of the individual commands. For this task, you may create the mind map on paper or use any mind mapping or graphic organizer software. (For more information about mind maps, see the section "About Mind Maps," later in this Introduction.)

■ **Create Verification Mind Maps:** These mind mapping exercises focus on helping you connect router and switch **show** commands to either networking concepts or to configuration commands. Simply create the mind maps on paper or use any mind mapping or graphic organizer software.

■ **Repeat Chapter Review Tasks:** (Optional) Browse through the chapter review tasks, and repeat any chapter review tasks that you think may help you with review at this point.

Final Prep Tasks

Chapter 23, "Final Review," at the end of this book, lists a series of preparation tasks that you can best use for your final preparation before taking the exam.

Other Features

In addition to the features in each of the core chapters, this book, as a whole, has additional study resources, including the following:

■ **DVD-based practice exam:** The companion DVD contains the powerful PCPT exam engine. You can answer the questions in study mode or take simulated DCICN exams with the DVD and activation code included in this book.

■ **eBook:** If you are interested in obtaining an eBook version of this title, we have included a special offer on a coupon card inserted in the DVD sleeve in the back of the book. This offer enables you to purchase the *CCNA Data Center DCICN 640-911 Official Cert Guide, Premium Edition* eBook and Practice Test at a 70 percent discount off the list price. In addition to three versions of the eBook—PDF (for reading on your computer), EPUB (for reading on your tablet, mobile device, or Nook or other eReader) and Mobi (the native Kindle version)—you will receive additional practice test questions and enhanced practice test features.

■ **Subnetting videos:** The companion DVD contains a series of videos that show you how to calculate various facts about IP addressing and subnetting (in particular, using the shortcuts described in this book).

■ **Subnetting practice:** Four appendices on the companion DVD (Appendices E through H) contain IPv4 subnetting practice problems, with the answers, and with explanations of how the answers were found. This is a great resource to get ready to do subnetting well and quickly.

■ **Companion website:** The website www.ciscopress.com/title/9781587204548 posts up-to-the-minute material that further clarifies complex exam topics. Check this site regularly for new and updated postings written by the authors that provide further insight into the more troublesome topics on the exam.

■ **PearsonITCertification.com:** The website www.pearsonitcertification.com is a great resource for all things IT-certification related. Check out the great CCNA articles, videos, blogs, and other certification preparation tools from the industry's best authors and trainers.

Book Organization, Chapters, and Appendices

This book contains 22 core chapters (Chapters 1 through 22), with Chapter 23 including some suggestions for how to approach the actual exams. Each core chapter covers a subset of the topics on the DCICN exam. The core chapters are organized into sections. The core chapters cover the following topics:

Part I: Networking Fundamentals

■ **Chapter 1, "The TCP/IP and OSI Networking Models":** Introduces the terminology surrounding two different networking architectures, namely Transmission Control Protocol/Internet Protocol (TCP/IP) and Open Systems Interconnection (OSI).

■ **Chapter 2, "Fundamentals of Ethernet LANs":** Covers the concepts and terms used for the most popular option for the data link layer for local-area networks (LAN), namely Ethernet.

■ **Chapter 3, "Fundamentals of WANs":** Covers the concepts and terms used for the most popular options for the data link layer for wide-area networks (WAN), including High-Level Data Link Control (HDLC).

■ **Chapter 4, "Fundamentals of IPv4 Addressing and Routing":** IP is the main network layer protocol for TCP/IP. This chapter introduces the basics of IP Version 4 (IPv4), including IPv4 addressing and routing.

■ **Chapter 5, "Fundamentals of TCP/IP Transport and Applications":** The Transmission Control Protocol (TCP) and User Datagram Protocol (UDP) are the main transport layer protocols for TCP/IP. This chapter introduces the basics of TCP and UDP.

Part II: Ethernet LAN Basics

■ **Chapter 6, "Building Ethernet LANs with Switches":** Deepens and expands the introduction to LANs from Chapter 2, discussing the roles and functions of LAN switches.

■ **Chapter 7, "Installing and Operating Nexus Switches":** Explains how to access, examine, and configure Cisco Nexus switches.

■ **Chapter 8, "Configuring Ethernet Switching":** Shows how to configure a variety of Nexus switch features, including duplex and speed, port security, securing the command-line interface (CLI), and the switch IP address.

Part III: Ethernet Virtual LANs and Spanning Tree

- **Chapter 9, "VLAN and Trunking Concepts":** Explains the concepts and configuration surrounding virtual LANs, including VLAN trunking and VLAN Trunking Protocol (VTP).

- **Chapter 10, "VLAN Trunking and Configuration":** Explains the concepts and configuration surrounding VLANs, including VLAN trunking and VTP.

- **Chapter 11, "Spanning Tree Protocol Concepts":** Discusses the concepts behind the IEEE Spanning Tree Protocol (STP) and how it makes some switch interfaces block frames to prevent frames from looping continuously around a redundant switched LAN.

- **Chapter 12, "Cisco Nexus Spanning Tree Protocol Implementation":** Shows how to configure, verify, and troubleshoot STP implementation on Cisco switches.

Part IV: IP Addressing and Subnetting

- **Chapter 13, "Perspectives on IPv4 Subnetting":** Walks through the entire concept of subnetting, from starting with a Class A, B, or C network, analyzing requirements, making choices, calculating the resulting subnets, assigning those on paper, all in preparation to deploy and use those subnets by configuring the devices.

- **Chapter 14, "Analyzing Classful IPv4 Networks":** IPv4 addresses originally fell into several classes, with unicast IP addresses being in Class A, B, and C. This chapter explores all things related to address classes and the IP network concept created by those classes.

- **Chapter 15, "Analyzing Subnet Masks":** In most jobs, someone else came before you and chose the subnet mask used in a network. What does that mean? What does that mask do for you? This chapter focuses on how to look at the mask (and IP network) to discover key facts, like the size of a subnet (number of hosts) and the number of subnets in the network.

- **Chapter 16, "Analyzing Existing Subnets":** Most troubleshooting of IP connectivity problems starts with an IP address and mask. This chapter takes that paired information and shows you how to find and analyze the subnet in which that IP address resides, including finding the subnet ID, range of addresses in the subnet, and subnet broadcast address.

- **Chapter 17, "Fundamentals of IP Version 6":** Surveys the big concepts, addressing, and routing created by the new version of IP: IP Version 6 (IPv6). This chapter attempts to show the similarities with IPv4, as well as the key differences, in particular the differences in IPv6 addresses.

Part V: IPv4 Routing

- **Chapter 18, "IPv4 Routing Concepts":** Looks at the IPv4 packet forwarding process. It shows how a pure router forwards packets. This chapter also breaks down the multilayer switches (which includes Cisco Nexus switches), including the Layer 3 routing logic in the same device that does Layer 2 Ethernet switching.

- **Chapter 19, "Cisco Nexus IPv4 Routing Configuration":** Discusses how to implement IPv4 on Nexus switches. This chapter includes the details of configuring IPv4 addresses, static IPv4 routes, and multilayer switching.

- **Chapter 20, "IPv4 Routing Protocol Concepts"**: Examines a variety of protocols available to routers and multilayer switches to dynamically learn routes for the IP subnets in an internetwork. This chapter focuses on the routing protocol theory that applies to any routing device, with discussion of RIP, OSPF, and EIGRP.

- **Chapter 21, "Nexus Routing Protocol Implementation"**: Explains how to implement IPv4 routing protocols on Cisco Nexus switches, specifically for RIP, OSPF, and EIGRP.

- **Chapter 22, "IPv4 Access Control Lists on Cisco Nexus Switches"**: Begins from the basic concept of how an Access Control List can filter packets, through the implementation of IPv4 ACLs with Nexus switches.

Part VI: Final Preparation

- **Chapter 23, "Final Review"**: Suggests a plan for final preparation once you have finished the core parts of the book, in particular explaining the many study options available in the book.

Part VII: Appendices (In Print)

- **Appendix A, "Answers to the 'Do I Know This Already?' Quizzes"**: Includes the answers to all the questions from Chapters 1 through 22.

- **Appendix B, "DCICN Exam Updates"**: Covers a variety of short topics that either clarify or expand upon topics covered earlier in the book. This appendix is updated from time to time and posted at www.ciscopress.com/title/9781587204548, with the most recent version available at the time of printing included here as Appendix B. (The first page of the appendix includes instructions on how to check to see whether a later version of Appendix B is available online.)

- **Appendix C, "Numeric Reference Tables"**: Lists several tables of numeric information, including a binary-to-decimal conversion table and a list of powers of 2.

- **Appendix D, "Nexus Lab Guide"**: Gives some advice on options for building hands-on skills with NX-OS, the operating system on Cisco Nexus switches.

Appendices (On the DVD)

The following appendices are available in digital format on the DVD that accompanies this book:

- **Appendix E, "Practice for Chapter 14: Analyzing Classful IPv4 Networks"**: Lists practice problems associated with Chapter 14. In particular, the practice questions ask you to find the classful network number in which an address resides, and all other facts about that network.

- **Appendix F, "Practice for Chapter 15: Analyzing Subnet Masks"**: Lists practice problems associated with Chapter 15. In particular, the practice questions ask you to convert masks between the three formats, and to examine an existing mask, determine the structure of the IP addresses, and calculate the number of hosts/subnet and number of subnets.

- **Appendix G, "Practice for Chapter 16: Analyzing Existing Subnets"**: Lists practice problems associated with Chapter 16. In particular, the practice questions ask you to take an IP address and mask and find the subnet ID, subnet broadcast address, and range of IP addresses in the subnet.

- **Appendix H, "Practice for Chapter 22: IPv4 Access Control Lists on Cisco Nexus Switches":** Lists practice problems associated with Chapter 22. In particular, the practice questions give you a chance to practice working with access control list (ACL) wildcard masks.

- **Appendix I, "Memory Tables":** Holds the key tables and lists from each chapter, with some of the content removed. You can print this appendix and, as a memory exercise, complete the tables and lists. The goal is to help you memorize facts that can be useful on the exams.

- **Appendix J, "Memory Tables Answer Key":** Contains the answer key for the exercises in Appendix I.

- **Appendix K, "Mind Map Solutions":** Shows an image of sample answers for all the part-ending mind map exercises.

- **Appendix L, "Study Planner":** A spreadsheet with major study milestones, where you can track your progress through your study.

- The **Glossary** contains definitions for all of the terms listed in the "Definitions of Key Terms" section at the conclusion of Chapters 1 through 22.

CCNA Data Center and the Other CCNA Certifications

Cisco offers a wide variety of Cisco Certified Network Associate certifications. Cisco first offered CCNA back in 1998, using the name CCNA, with the certification focusing on routing and switching. Since that time, Cisco has added the CCNA certifications for various technology areas, as listed in Figure I-2. Cisco even renamed the original CCNA to CCNA Routing and Switching, so each and every CCNA certification's topic area is part of the name.

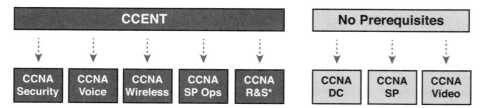

Figure I-2   *Cisco CCNA Certifications: CCENT Prerequisite or Not*

* The CCNA R&S has two different exam paths. One begins with CCENT, whereas the other allows you to get CCNA R&S certified using one exam: the CCNA 200-120 exam. With the single-exam path, CCENT is technically not a prerequisite; however, the single exam includes coverage of the topics in CCENT, so you still need to know CCENT content to achieve CCNA R&S.

Interestingly, Cisco uses the Cisco Certified Entry Networking Technician (CCENT) certification as the minimum prerequisite for some of the CCNA certifications, but not all. As you can see in Figure I-2, CCNA Data Center, along with CCNA Video and CCNA Service Provider, do not require you to first achieve CCENT (or some other more advanced routing and switching certification). Why? All three of these CCNA certifications that have no prerequisites cover the required routing and switching topics within the certification already. For instance, almost all the concepts discussed in this book are included in the scope of the ICND1 100-101 exam.

NOTE   Always check www.cisco.com/go/certifications for current prerequisites. Cisco sometimes changes the prerequisites with the introduction of a new version of an exam or certification.

For Those Studying Routing & Switching

This next short topic gives some advice to those of you who have read, or may soon read, the *Cisco CCENT/CCNA ICND1 100-101 Official Cert Guide* in pursuit of your CCENT certification.

The DCICN exam includes many fundamental networking concepts. It includes Ethernet LANs in depth: cabling, framing, addressing, switching logic, virtual LANs, spanning tree, and the list goes on. It includes IP Version 4 (IPv4) addressing, subnetting, IPv4 routing, and how to dynamically learn IPv4 routes with routing protocols.

The ICND1 100-101 exam covers almost all these same concepts. If you look only at the concepts, ignoring the commands, ICND1 and DCICN overlap by about 75 percent, maybe more. ICND1 includes a little more depth in routing, including more on IP Version 6 (IPv6), compared to DCICN. DCICN includes Spanning Tree Protocol (STP), which happens to be in the scope of the ICND2 200-101 exam instead of the ICND1 100-101 exam.

Basically, DCICN is a routing and switching exam, with the implementation details shown on Cisco Nexus data center switches, instead of the Cisco Catalyst switches featured in the CCNA R&S exams.

This DCICN cert guide was designed in part to help reduce the workload for those of you who are pursuing both CCNA DC and either CCENT or CCNA R&S. Most of the conceptual material in this book is taken from the *Cisco CCENT/CCNA ICND1 100-101 Official Cert Guide* from Cisco Press. If you have already read the ICND1 100-101 Cert Guide, you can reduce the amount of time you take to read this book.

All you have to do is look at the introduction to each chapter in this book. The introduction sits just before the "Do I Know This Already" quiz that's early in the chapter. That introduction, for the chapters that primarily discuss concepts rather than commands, ends with some notes comparing the chapter to the ICND1 100-101 book. Specifically, the notes tell you the following:

- Whether this DCICN chapter is a good candidate for saving time if you already read the ICND1 book
- What headings and topics in this chapter have been added to this DCICN book compared to the ICND1 book, so that you can make sure and read those, even if you ignore the rest of the chapter

Figure I-3 shows the chapters of this book where you might save some reading time, assuming that you have read the ICND1 book.

Note that the other chapters in this book (those not mentioned in Figure I-3) often have some portions taken from either the ICND1 or ICND2 cert guide. However, for the DCICN book chapters not listed in Figure I-3, the chapters differ enough so that you should probably just go ahead and read through the entire chapter.

Figure I-3 *Overview of DCICN Chapters Where You Might Save Some Reading Time*

Reference Information

This short section contains a few topics available for reference elsewhere in the book. You may read these when you first use the book, but you may also skip these topics and refer back to them later. In particular, make sure to note the final page of this Introduction, which lists several contact details, including how to get in touch with Cisco Press.

Install the Pearson IT Certification Practice Test Engine and Questions

The DVD in the book includes the Pearson IT Certification Practice Test (PCPT) engine (software that displays and grades a set of exam-realistic multiple-choice, drag-and-drop, fill-in-the-blank, and testlet questions). Using the PCPT engine, you can either study by going through the questions in Study Mode, or you can take a simulated DCICN exam that mimics real exam conditions.

The installation process requires two major steps. The DVD in the back of this book has a recent copy of the PCPT engine. The practice exam (the database of DCICN exam questions) is not on the DVD. After you install the software, the PCPT software will use your Internet connection and download the latest versions of both the software and the question databases for this book.

> **NOTE** The cardboard DVD case in the back of this book includes both the DVD and a piece of thick paper. The paper lists the activation code for the practice exam associated with this book. *Do not lose the activation code.*

> **NOTE** Also on this same piece of paper, on the opposite side from the exam activation code, you will find a one-time-use coupon code that will give you 70 percent off the purchase of the *CCNA Data Center DCICN Official Cert Guide, Premium Edition eBook and Practice Test.*

Install the Software from the DVD

The software installation process is routine as compared with other software installation processes. If you have already installed the PCPT software from another Pearson product, you do not need to reinstall the software. Simply launch the software on your desktop and proceed to activate the practice exam from this book by using the activation code included in the DVD sleeve. The following steps outline the installation process:

Step 1.   Insert the DVD into your PC.

Step 2.   The software that automatically runs is the Cisco Press software to access and use all DVD-based features, including the exam engine and the DVD-only appendices. From the main menu, click the option to **Install the Exam Engine.**

Step 3.   Respond to windows prompts as with any typical software installation process.

The installation process gives you the option to activate your exam with the activation code supplied on the paper in the DVD sleeve. This process requires that you establish a Pearson website login. You will need this login to activate the exam, so please do register when prompted. If you already have a Pearson website login, there is no need to register again. Just use your existing login.

Activate and Download the Practice Exam

When the exam engine is installed, you should then activate the exam associated with this book (if you did not do so during the installation process) as follows:

Step 1.   Start the PCPT software from the Windows Start menu or from your desktop shortcut icon.

Step 2.   To activate and download the exam associated with this book, from the My Products or Tools tab, click the **Activate** button.

Step 3.   At the next screen, enter the activation key from the paper inside the cardboard DVD holder in the back of the book. When it is entered, click the **Activate** button.

Step 4.   The activation process will download the practice exam. Click **Next,** and then click **Finish.**

When the activation process completes, the My Products tab should list your new exam. If you do not see the exam, make sure that you have selected the **My Products** tab on the menu. At this point, the software and practice exam are ready to use. Just select the exam and click the **Open Exam** button.

To update a particular product's exams that you have already activated and downloaded, simply select the **Tools** tab and click the **Update Products** button. Updating your exams will ensure that you have the latest changes and updates to the exam data.

If you want to check for updates to the PCPT software, select the **Tools** tab and click the **Update Application** button. This will ensure that you are running the latest version of the software engine.

Activating Other Products

The exam software installation process and the registration process only have to happen once. Then for each new product, only a few steps are required. For instance, if you buy another new Cisco Press Official Cert Guide or Pearson IT Certification Cert Guide, extract the activation code from the DVD sleeve in the back of that book; you do not even need the DVD at this point. From there, all you have to do is start PCPT (if not still up and running) and perform Steps 2 through 4 from the previous list.

PCPT Exam Databases with This Book

This book includes an activation code that allows you to load a set of practice questions. The questions come in different exams or exam databases. When you install the PCPT software, and type in the activation code, the PCPT software downloads the latest version of all these exam databases. And with the ICND1 book alone, you get four different "exams," or four different sets of questions, as listed in Figure I-4.

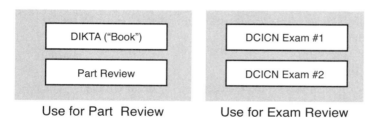

Figure I-4   *PCPT Exams/Exam Databases and When to Use Them*

You can choose to use any of these exam databases at any time, both in Study Mode and Practice Exam Mode. However, many people find it best to save some of the exams until exam review time, after they have finished reading the entire book. Figure I-4 begins to suggest a plan, spelled out here:

- During part review, use PCPT to review the DIKTA questions for that part, using Study Mode.

- During part review, use the questions built specifically for part review (the part review questions) for that part of the book, using Study Mode.

- Save the remaining exams to use with Chapter 23, "Final Review," using Practice Exam Mode.

The two modes inside PCPT give you better options for study versus practicing a timed exam event. In Study Mode, you can see the answers immediately, so you can study the topics more easily. Also, you can choose a subset of the questions in an exam database; for instance, you can view questions from only the chapters in one part of the book.

Practice Exam Mode creates an event somewhat like the actual exam. It gives you a preset number of questions, from all chapters, with a timer event. Practice Exam Mode also gives you a score for that timed event.

How to View Only DIKTA Questions by Part

Each "Part Review" section asks you to repeat the Do I Know This Already (DIKTA) quiz questions from the chapters in that part. Although you could simply scan the book pages to review these questions, it is slightly better to review these questions from inside the PCPT software, just to get a little more practice in how to read questions from the testing software. But you can just read them in the book as well.

To view these DIKTA (book) questions inside the PCPT software, follow these steps:

Step 1. Start the PCPT software.

Step 2. From the main (home) menu, select the item for this product, with a name like **DCICN 640-911 Official Cert Guide**, and click **Open Exam**.

Step 3. The top of the next window that appears should list some exams; select the box beside **DCICN Book Questions**, and deselect the other boxes. This selects the "book" questions (that is, the DIKTA questions from the beginning of each chapter).

Step 4. In this same window, click at the bottom of the screen to deselect all objectives (chapters). Then select the box beside each chapter in the part of the book you are reviewing.

Step 5. Select any other options on the right side of the window.

Step 6. Click **Start** to start reviewing the questions.

How to View Only Part Review Questions by Part

The exam databases you get with this book include a database of questions created solely for study during the part review process. DIKTA questions focus more on facts, with basic application. The part review questions instead focus more on application, and look more like real exam questions.

To view these questions, follow the same process as you did with DIKTA/book questions, but select the part review database instead of the book database, as follows:

Step 1. Start the PCPT software.

Step 2. From the main (home) menu, select the item for this product, with a name like **DCICN 640-911 Official Cert Guide**, and click **Open Exam**.

Step 3. The top of the next window should list some exams; select the box beside **Part Review Questions**, and deselect the other boxes. This selects the questions intended for part-ending review.

Step 4. On this same window, click at the bottom of the screen to deselect all objectives, and then select (check) the box beside the book part you want to review. This tells the PCPT software to give you part review questions from the selected part.

Step 5. Select any other options on the right side of the window.

Step 6. Click **Start** to start reviewing the questions.

About Mind Maps

Mind maps are a type of visual organization tool that can be used for many purposes. For instance, mind maps can be used as an alternative way to take notes.

You can also use mind maps to improve how your brain organizes concepts. Mind maps stress the connections and relationships between ideas. When you spend time thinking about an area of study, and organize your ideas into a mind map, you strengthen existing mental connections and create new connections, all into your own frame of reference.

In short, mind maps help you internalize what you learn.

Mind Map Mechanics

Each mind map begins with a blank piece of paper or blank window in an application. You then add a large central idea, with branches that move out in any direction. The branches contain smaller concepts, ideas, commands, pictures, whatever idea needs to be represented. Any concepts that can be grouped should be put near each other. As need be, you can create deeper and deeper branches, although for this book's purposes, most mind maps will not go beyond a couple of levels.

NOTE   While many books have been written about mind maps, Tony Buzan often gets credit for formalizing and popularizing mind maps. You can learn more about mind maps at his website, www.thinkbuzan.com.

For example, Figure I-5 shows a sample mind map that begins to output some of the IPv6 content from Part IV of this book. The central concept of the mind map is IPv6 addressing, and the part review activity asks you to think of all facts you learned about IPv6 addressing and organize them with a mind map. The mind map allows for a more visual representation of the concepts as compared to just written notes.

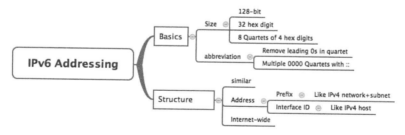

Figure I-5   *Sample Mind Map*

About Mind Maps Used During Part Review

This book suggests mind mapping exercises during part review. This short topic lists some details about the part review mind mapping exercises, listed in one place for reference.

The "Part Review" sections use two main types of mind mapping exercises:

- Configuration exercises ask you to recall the related configuration commands and group them. For instance, in a configuration exercise, related commands that happen to be interface subcommands should be grouped, but shown as being inside interface configuration mode.

- **Verification exercises** ask you to think about the output of **show** commands and link the output to either the configuration commands that cause that output or to the concepts that explain the meaning of some of that output.

Create these configuration mind maps on paper, using any mind mapping software, or even any drawing application. Many mind mapping apps exist as well. Regardless of how you draw them, follow these rules:

- If you have only a little time for this exercise, spend your time making your own mind map, instead of looking at suggested answers. The learning happens when thinking through the problem of making your own mind map.

- When first creating these maps, set aside the book and all your notes and do not look at them. Do as much as you can without looking at the book or your notes (or Google, or anything else).

- Try all the mind maps listed in a "Part Review" section before looking at your notes.

- Afterward, look at your notes to complete all the mind maps.

- Make a note of where you put your final results so that you can find them later during final exam review.

Finally, when learning to use these tools, take two other important suggestions as well. First, use as few words as possible for each node in your mind map. The point is for you to remember the idea and its connections, not to explain the concept to someone else. Just write enough to remind yourself of the concept. Second, if the mind map process just is not working for you, discard the tool. Instead, take freeform notes on a blank piece of paper. Try to do the important part of the exercise (the thinking about what concepts go together) without letting the tool get in the way.

For More Information

If you have any comments about the book, submit them via www.ciscopress.com. Just go to the website, select **Contact Us**, and type your message.

Cisco might make changes that affect the CCNA Data Center certification from time to time. You should always check www.cisco.com/go/certification for the latest details.

The *CCNA Data Center DCICN 640-911 Official Cert Guide* helps you attain the CCNA Data Center certification. This is the DCICN exam prep book from the only Cisco-authorized publisher. We at Cisco Press believe that this book certainly can help you achieve CCNA Data Center certification, but the real work is up to you! We trust that your time will be well spent.

Getting Started

You just got this book. You have probably already read (or quickly skimmed) the Introduction. And you are wondering, is this where I really start reading, or can I skip ahead to Chapter 1?

Stop to read this "Getting Started" section to think about how you will study for this exam. Your study will go much better if you take time (maybe 15 minutes) to think about a few key points about how to study, before starting on this journey that will take you many hours, over many weeks. That's what this "Getting Started" section will help you do.

A Brief Perspective on Cisco Certification Exams

Cisco sets the bar pretty high for passing their exams, including all the exams related to CCNA certifications like CCNA Data Center. Most anyone can study and pass these exams, but it takes more than just a quick read through the book and the cash to pay for the exam.

The challenge of these exams comes from many angles. Each of these exams covers a lot of concepts, in addition to many commands specific to Cisco devices. Beyond knowledge, these Cisco exams also require deep skills. You must be able to analyze and predict what really happens in a network. You must be able to configure Cisco devices to work correctly in those networks. And you must be ready to troubleshoot problems when the network does not work correctly.

The more challenging questions on these exams work a lot like a jigsaw puzzle—but with four out of every five puzzle pieces not even in the room. To solve the puzzle, you have to mentally re-create the missing pieces. To do that, you must know each networking concept and remember how the concepts work together. You also have to match the concepts with what happens on the devices with the configuration commands that tell the devices what to do. You also have to connect the concepts, and the configuration, with the meaning of the output of various troubleshooting commands, to analyze how the network is working and why it is not working right now.

For example, you need to know IP subnetting well, and that topic includes some math. A simple question—one that might be too simple to be a real exam question—would tell you enough of the numbers so that all you have to do is the equivalent of a little addition or multiplication to find a number called a subnet ID.

A more exam-realistic question makes you connect concepts together to set up the math problem. For example, a question might give you a network diagram and ask you to list the subnet ID used in one part of the diagram. But the diagram has no numbers at all. Instead, you have the output of a command from a router, for example, the **show ip ospf database** command, which does list some numbers. But before you can use those numbers, you might need to predict how the devices are configured and what other troubleshooting commands would tell you. So, you end up with a question like a puzzle, as shown in Figure 1. The question puts some pieces in the right place; you have to find other pieces using different commands and by applying your knowledge. And some pieces will just remain unknown for a given question.

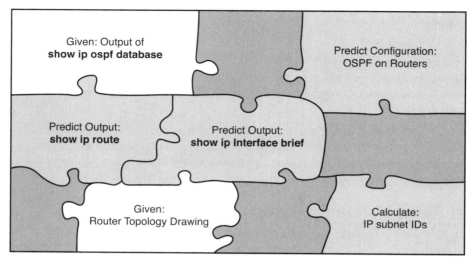

Figure 1   *Filling in Puzzle Pieces with Your Analysis Skills*

These skills require that you prepare by doing more than just reading and memorizing what you read. Of course, you will need to read many pages in this book to learn many individual facts and how these facts are related to each other. But a big part of this book lists exercises beyond reading, exercises that help you build the skills to solve these networking puzzles.

Suggestions for How to Approach Your Study with This Book

These exams are challenging, but many people pass them every day. So, what do you need to do to be ready to pass, beyond reading and remembering all the facts? You need to develop skills. You need to mentally link each idea with other related ideas. Doing that requires additional work. To help you along the way, the next few pages give you five key perspectives about how to use this book to build those skills and make those connections, before you dive into this exciting but challenging world of learning networking on Cisco gear.

Not One Book: 22 Short Read-and-Review Sessions

First, look at your study as a series of read-and-review tasks, each on a relatively small set of related topics.

Each of the core chapters of this book (1 through 22) has around 20 pages of content on average. If you glance around any of those chapters, you will find a heading called "Foundation Topics" on about the fifth page of each chapter. From there to the "Exam Preparation Tasks" section at the end of the chapter, the chapters average about 20 pages.

So, do not approach this book as one big book. Treat the task of your first read of a chapter as a separate task. Anyone can read 20 pages. Having a tough day? Each chapter has two or three major sections, so read just one of them. Or, do some related labs or review something you have already read. This book organizes the content into topics of a more manageable size to give you something more digestible to manage your study time throughout the book.

For Each Chapter, Do Not Neglect Practice

Next, plan to use the practice tasks at the end of each chapter.

Each chapter ends with practice and study tasks under a heading "Exam Preparation Tasks." Doing these tasks, and doing them at the end of the chapter, really does help you get ready. Do not put off using these tasks until later! The chapter-ending "Exam Preparation Tasks" section helps you with the first phase of deepening your knowledge and skills of the key topics, remembering terms, and linking the concepts together in your brain so that you can remember how it all fits together.

The following list describes the majority of the activities you will find in "Exam Preparation Tasks" sections:

- Review key topics
- Complete memory tables
- Define key terms
- Review command summary tables
- Review feature configuration checklists
- Do subnetting exercises

Approach each chapter with the same plan. You can choose to read the entire core ("Foundation Topics") section of each chapter, or you can choose to skim some chapters, based on your score on the Do I Know This Already? (DIKTA) quiz, a pre-chapter self-assessment quiz at the beginning of most chapters. However, regardless of whether you skim or read thoroughly, do the study tasks in the "Exam Preparation Tasks" section at the end of the chapter. Figure 2 shows the overall flow.

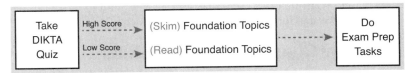

Figure 2 *Suggested Approach to Each Chapter*

Use Book Parts for Major Milestones

Third, view the book as having five major milestones, one for each major topic.

Beyond the more obvious organization into chapters, this book also organizes the chapters into five major topic areas called book parts. Completing each part means that you have completed a major area of study. At the end of each part, take a little extra time. Do the Part Review tasks at the end of each part. Ask yourself where you are weak and where you are strong. And give yourself some reward for making it to a major milestone. Figure 3 lists the five parts in this book.

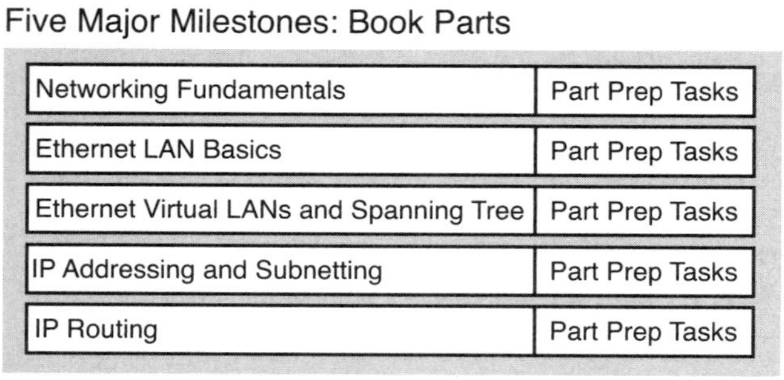

Five Major Milestones: Book Parts

Networking Fundamentals	Part Prep Tasks
Ethernet LAN Basics	Part Prep Tasks
Ethernet Virtual LANs and Spanning Tree	Part Prep Tasks
IP Addressing and Subnetting	Part Prep Tasks
IP Routing	Part Prep Tasks

Figure 3   *Parts as Major Milestones*

The tasks in the "Part Review" sections focus on helping you apply concepts (from that book part) to new scenarios for the exam. Some tasks use sample test questions so that you can think through and analyze a problem. This process helps you refine what you know and to realize what you did not quite yet understand. Some tasks use mind map exercises that help you mentally connect the theoretical concepts with the configuration and verification commands. These part review activities help build these skills.

Note that the part review directs you to use the Pearson Certification Practice Test (PCPT) software to access the practice questions. Each part review tells you to repeat the DIKTA questions, but using the PCPT software. Each part review also directs you how to access a specific set of questions reserved for reviewing concepts at part review. Note that the PCPT software and exam databases with this book give you the rights to additional questions as well; Chapter 23, "Final Review," gives some recommendations on how to best use those questions for your final exam preparation.

Also, consider setting a goal date for finishing each part of the book, and a reward as well! Plan a break, some family time, some time out exercising, eating some good food—whatever helps you get refreshed and motivated for the next part.

Use the Final Review Chapter to Refine Skills

Fourth, do the tasks outlined in the final preparation chapter (Chapter 23) at the end of this book.

The "Final Review" chapter has two major goals. First, it helps you further develop the analysis skills you need to answer the more complicated questions on the exam. Many questions require that you connect ideas about concepts, configuration, verification, and troubleshooting. More reading on your part does not develop all these skills; this chapter's tasks give you activities to further develop these skills.

The tasks in the "Final Review" chapter also help you find your weak areas. This final element gives you repetition with high-challenge exam questions, uncovering any gaps in your knowledge. Many of the questions are purposefully designed to test your knowledge of the most common mistakes and misconceptions, helping you avoid some of the common pitfalls people experience with the actual exam.

Set Goals and Track Your Progress

Finally, before you start reading the book and doing the rest of these study tasks, take the time to make a plan, set some goals, and be ready to track your progress.

While making lists of tasks might or might not appeal to you, depending on your personality, goal setting can help everyone studying for these exams. And to do the goal setting, you need to know what tasks you plan to do.

As for the list of tasks to do when studying, you do not have to use a detailed task list. Although you could list every single task in every chapter-ending "Exam Preparation Tasks" section, every task in the part reviews section, and every task in the final chapter, listing just the major tasks can be enough.

You should track at least two tasks for each typical chapter: reading the "Foundation Topics" section and doing the "Exam Preparation Tasks" section at the end of the chapter. And, of course, do not forget to list tasks for part reviews and the "Final Review" chapter. Table 1 shows a sample for Part I of this book.

Table 1   Sample Excerpt from a Planning Table

Element	Task	Goal Date	First Date Completed	Second Date Completed (Optional)
Chapter 1	Read Foundation Topics			
Chapter 1	Do Exam Prep Tasks			
Chapter 2	Read Foundation Topics			
Chapter 2	Do Exam Prep Tasks			
Chapter 3	Read Foundation Topics			
Chapter 3	Do Exam Prep Tasks			
Chapter 4	Read Foundation Topics			
Chapter 4	Do Exam Prep Tasks			
Chapter 5	Read Foundation Topics			
Chapter 5	Do Exam Prep Tasks			
Part I Review	Do Part Review Activities			

NOTE   Appendix L, "Study Planner," on the DVD that comes with this book, contains a complete planning checklist like Table 1 for the tasks in this book. This spreadsheet allows you to update and save the file to note your goal dates and the tasks you have completed.

Use your goal dates as a way to manage your study, and not as a way to get discouraged if you miss a date. Pick reasonable dates that you can meet. When setting your goals, think about how fast you read and the length of each chapter's "Foundation Topics" section, as listed in the Table of Contents. Then, when you finish a task sooner than planned, move up the next few goal dates.

If you miss a few dates, do not start skipping the tasks listed at the ends of the chapters! Instead, think about what is impacting your schedule—real life, commitments, and so on— and either adjust your goals or work a little harder on your study.

Other Small Tasks Before Getting Started

You will need to do a few overhead tasks to install software, find some PDFs, and so on. You can do these tasks now, or do them in your spare moments when you need a study break during the first few chapters of the book. But do these early, so that if you do stumble upon an installation problem, you have time to work through it before you need a particular tool.

Register (for free) at the Cisco Learning Network (CLN, http://learningnetwork.cisco.com) and join the CCNA Data Center study group. This mailing list allows you to lurk and participate in discussions about CCNA DC topics, for both the DCICN and DCICT exams. Register, join the group, and set up an email filter to redirect the messages to a separate folder. Even if you do not spend time reading all the posts yet, later, when you have time to read, you can browse through the posts to find interesting topics. Or just search the posts from the CLN website.

Find and print a copy of DVD Appendix I, "Memory Tables." Many of the chapter review sections use this tool, in which you take the incomplete tables from the appendix and complete the table to help you remember some key facts.

If you are reading this chapter as part of an eBook version of this book, find and download the media files per the instructions supplied on the last page of the eBook file under the heading "Where Are the Companion Files?"

Install the PCPT exam software and activate the exams. For more details on how to load the software, refer to the Introduction, under the heading "Install the Pearson Certification Practice Test Engine and Questions."

Getting Started—Now

Now dive in to your first of many short, manageable tasks: reading Chapter 1, "The TCP/IP and OSI Networking Models." Enjoy!

Part I of this book introduces you to the most important topics in TCP/IP networking. Chapter 1 introduces the terms, concepts, and protocols for TCP/IP. Chapters 2 and 3 then look at how networking devices send data to each other over a physical link, with Chapter 2 focusing on links between nearby devices (local-area networks [LANs]) and Chapter 3 focusing on links between far away devices (wide-area networks [WANs]).

Chapter 4 focuses on the rules of IP routing, which pulls the LAN and WAN links together by forwarding data all the way from one user device to another. Finally, Chapter 5 looks at several other topics, mostly related to how applications make use of the TCP/IP network.

Part I

Networking Fundamentals

Chapter 1: The TCP/IP and OSI Networking Models

Chapter 2: Fundamentals of Ethernet LANs

Chapter 3: Fundamentals of WANs

Chapter 4: Fundamentals of IPv4 Addressing and Routing

Chapter 5: Fundamentals of TCP/IP Transport and Applications

Part I Review

This chapter covers the following exam topics:

1.1 Describe the purpose and functions of various network devices

1.1.a Interpret a network diagram

1.4 Describe the purpose and basic operation of the protocols in the OSI and TCP models

1.4.a TCP/IP

1.4.b OSI layers

CHAPTER 1

The TCP/IP and OSI Networking Models

This chapter begins Part I, which focuses on the basics of networking. Because networks require all the devices to follow the rules, this part starts with a discussion of networking models, which gives you a big-picture view of the networking rules.

You can think of a networking model as you think of a set of architectural plans for building a house. A lot of different people work on building your house, such as framers, electricians, bricklayers, painters, and so on. The blueprint helps ensure that all the different pieces of the house work together as a whole. Similarly, the people who make networking products, and the people who use those products to build their own computer networks, follow a particular networking model. That networking model defines rules about how each part of the network should work, as well as how the parts should work together, so that the entire network functions correctly.

The DCICN exam includes detailed coverage of one networking model: Transmission Control Protocol/Internet Protocol (TCP/IP). TCP/IP is the most pervasively used networking model in the history of networking. You can find support for TCP/IP on practically every computer operating system (OS) in existence today, from mobile phones to mainframe computers. Every network built using Cisco products today supports TCP/IP.

The DCICN exam also covers a second networking model, called the Open Systems Interconnection (OSI) reference model. Historically, OSI was the first large effort to create a vendor-neutral networking model. Because of that timing, many of the terms used in networking today come from the OSI model, so this chapter's section on OSI discusses OSI and the related terminology.

NOTE   As promised in the Introduction, this note is meant to help those of you who have already read the *ICND1 100-101 Official Cert Guide*. This chapter has the exact same material as the ICND1 book. See the Introduction's section, "For Those Studying Routing & Switching."

"Do I Know This Already?" Quiz

Use the "Do I Know This Already?" quiz to help decide whether you might want to skim this chapter, or a major section, moving more quickly to the "Exam Preparation Tasks" section near the end of the chapter. You can find the answers at the bottom of the page following the quiz. For thorough explanations, see Appendix A, "Answers to the 'Do I Know This Already?' Quizzes."

Table 1-1   "Do I Know This Already?" Foundation Topics Section-to-Question Mapping

Foundation Topics Section	Questions
Perspectives on Networking	None
TCP/IP Networking Model	1–6
OSI Networking Model	7–9

1. Which of the following protocols are examples of TCP/IP transport layer protocols? (Choose two answers.)

    a. Ethernet

    b. HTTP

    c. IP

    d. UDP

    e. SMTP

    f. TCP

2. Which of the following protocols are examples of TCP/IP data link layer protocols? (Choose two answers.)

    a. Ethernet

    b. HTTP

    c. IP

    d. UDP

    e. SMTP

    f. TCP

    g. PPP

3. The process of HTTP asking TCP to send some data and making sure that it is received correctly is an example of what?

    a. Same-layer interaction

    b. Adjacent-layer interaction

    c. OSI model

    d. All of these answers are correct.

4. The process of TCP on one computer marking a TCP segment as segment 1, and the receiving computer then acknowledging the receipt of TCP segment 1 is an example of what?

    a. Data encapsulation

    b. Same-layer interaction

    c. Adjacent-layer interaction

    d. OSI model

    e. All of these answers are correct.

5. The process of a web server adding a TCP header to the contents of a web page, followed by adding an IP header and then adding a data link header and trailer, is an example of what?

   a. Data encapsulation

   b. Same-layer interaction

   c. OSI model

   d. All of these answers are correct.

6. Which of the following terms is used specifically to identify the entity created when encapsulating data inside data link layer headers and trailers?

   a. Data

   b. Chunk

   c. Segment

   d. Frame

   e. Packet

7. Which OSI layer defines the functions of logical network-wide addressing and routing?

   a. Layer 1

   b. Layer 2

   c. Layer 3

   d. Layer 4

   e. Layer 5, 6, or 7

8. Which OSI layer defines the standards for cabling and connectors?

   a. Layer 1

   b. Layer 2

   c. Layer 3

   d. Layer 4

   e. Layer 5, 6, or 7

9. Which of the following terms are not valid terms for the names of the seven OSI layers? (Choose two answers.)

   a. Application

   b. Data link

   c. Transmission

   d. Presentation

   e. Internet

   f. Session

Foundation Topics

This chapter introduces some of the most basic ideas about computer networking, while also defining the structure of two networking models: TCP/IP and OSI. The chapter begins with a brief introduction of how most people view a network, which hopefully connects with where you are to start your CCNA Data Center journey. The middle of this chapter introduces networking by explaining some of the key features of TCP/IP. The chapter closes with some additional concepts and terminology related to the OSI model.

Perspectives on Networking

So, you are new to networking. Like many people, your perspective about networks might be that of a user of the network, as opposed to the network engineer who builds networks. For some, your view of networking might be based on how you use the Internet, from home, using a high-speed Internet connection like DSL or cable TV, as shown in Figure 1-1.

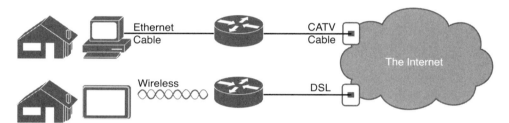

Figure 1-1   *End-User Perspective on High-Speed Internet Connections*

The top part of the figure shows a typical high-speed cable Internet user. The PC connects to a cable modem using an Ethernet cable. The cable modem then connects to a cable TV (CATV) outlet in the wall using a round coaxial cable—the same kind of cable used to connect your TV to the CATV wall outlet. Because cable Internet services provide service continuously, the user can just sit down at the PC and start sending email, browsing websites, making Internet phone calls, and using other tools and applications as well.

The lower part of the figure uses two different technologies. First, the tablet computer uses wireless technology that goes by the name wireless local-area network (wireless LAN), or Wi-Fi, instead of using an Ethernet cable. In this example, the router uses a different technology, digital subscriber line (DSL), to communicate with the Internet.

Although the technologies included in the DCICN (640-911) exam can be used to build a small home network, the exam focuses more on networking technology used inside a company. The Information Technology (IT) world refers to a network created by one corporation, or enterprise, for the purpose of allowing its employees to communicate, as an *enterprise network*. The smaller networks at home, when used for business purposes, often go by the name small office home office (SOHO) networks.

Users of enterprise networks have some idea about the enterprise network at their company or school. People realize that they use a network for many tasks. PC users might realize that their PC connects through an Ethernet cable to a matching wall outlet, as shown at the top of Figure 1-2. Those same users might use wireless LANs with their laptop when going to a meeting in the conference room as well. Figure 1-2 shows these two end-user perspectives on an enterprise network.

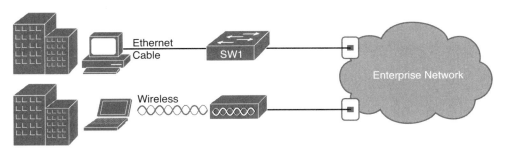

Figure 1-2 *Example Representation of an Enterprise Network*

NOTE In networking diagrams, a cloud represents a part of a network whose details are not important to the purpose of the diagram. In this case, Figure 1-2 ignores the details of how to create an enterprise network.

Some users might not even have a concept of the network at all. Instead, these users just enjoy the functions of the network—the ability to post messages to social media sites, make phone calls, search for information on the Internet, listen to music, and download countless apps to their phones—without caring about how it works or how their favorite device connects to the network.

Regardless of how much you already know about how networks work, this book, and the related certifications, help you learn how networks do their job. That job is simply this: moving data from one device to another. The rest of this chapter, and the rest of this first part of the book, reveals the basics of how to build both SOHO and enterprise networks so that they can deliver data between two devices.

In the building business, much work happens before you nail the first boards together. The process starts with some planning, an understanding of how to build a house, and some architectural blueprints of how to build that specific house. Similarly, the journey toward building any computer network does not begin by installing devices and cables, but instead by looking at the architectural plans for those modern networks: the TCP/IP model.

TCP/IP Networking Model

A *networking model*, sometimes also called either a *networking architecture* or *networking blueprint*, refers to a comprehensive set of documents. Individually, each document describes one small function required for a network; collectively, these documents define everything that should happen for a computer network to work. Some documents define a *protocol*, which is a set of logical rules that devices must follow to communicate. Other documents define some physical requirements for networking. For example, a document could define the voltage and current levels used on a particular cable when transmitting data.

You can think of a networking model as you think of an architectural blueprint for building a house. Sure, you can build a house without the blueprint. However, the blueprint can ensure that the house has the right foundation and structure so that it will not fall down, and it has the correct hidden spaces to accommodate the plumbing, electrical, gas, and so on. Also, the many different people that build the house using the blueprint—such as framers, electricians, bricklayers, painters, and so on—know that if they follow the blueprint, their part of the work should not cause problems for the other workers.

Similarly, you could build your own network—write your own software, build your own networking cards, and so on—to create a network. However, it is much easier to simply buy and use products that already conform to some well-known networking model or blueprint. Because the networking product vendors build their products with some networking model in mind, their products should work well together.

History Leading to TCP/IP

Today, the world of computer networking uses one networking model: TCP/IP (Transmission Control Protocol/Internet Protocol). However, the world has not always been so simple. Once upon a time, networking protocols didn't exist, including TCP/IP. Vendors created the first networking protocols; these protocols supported only that vendor's computers. For example, IBM published its Systems Network Architecture (SNA) networking model in 1974. Other vendors also created their own proprietary networking models. As a result, if your company bought computers from three vendors, network engineers often had to create three different networks based on the networking models created by each company, and then somehow connect those networks, making the combined networks much more complex. The left side of Figure 1-3 shows the general idea of what a company's enterprise network might have looked back in the 1980s, before TCP/IP became common in enterprise internetworks.

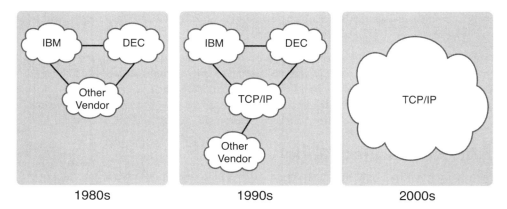

Figure 1-3 *Historical Progression: Proprietary Models to the Open TCP/IP Model*

Although vendor-defined proprietary networking models often worked well, having an open, vendor-neutral networking model would aid competition and reduce complexity. The International Organization for Standardization (ISO) took on the task to create such a model, starting as early as the late 1970s, beginning work on what would become known as the Open Systems Interconnection (OSI) networking model. ISO had a noble goal for the OSI model: to standardize data networking protocols to allow communication between all computers across the entire planet. ISO worked toward this ambitious and noble goal, with participants from most of the technologically developed nations on Earth participating in the process.

A second, less formal effort to create an open, vendor-neutral, public networking model sprouted forth from a U.S. Department of Defense (DoD) contract. Researchers at various universities volunteered to help further develop the protocols surrounding the original DoD work. These efforts resulted in a competing open networking model called TCP/IP.

During the 1990s, companies began adding OSI, TCP/IP, or both to their enterprise networks. However, by the end of the 1990s, TCP/IP had become the common choice, and OSI fell away. The center part of Figure 1-3 shows the general idea behind enterprise networks in that decade—still with networks built upon multiple networking models, but including TCP/IP.

Here in the twenty-first century, TCP/IP dominates. Proprietary networking models still exist, but they have mostly been discarded in favor of TCP/IP. The OSI model, whose development suffered in part because of a slower formal standardization process as compared with TCP/IP, never succeeded in the marketplace. And TCP/IP, the networking model originally created almost entirely by a bunch of volunteers, has become the most prolific network model ever, as shown on the right side of Figure 1-3.

In this chapter, you will read about some of the basics of TCP/IP. Although you will learn some interesting facts about TCP/IP, the true goal of this chapter is to help you understand what a networking model or networking architecture really is and how it works.

Also in this chapter, you will learn about some of the jargon used with OSI. Will any of you ever work on a computer that is using the full OSI protocols instead of TCP/IP? Probably not. However, you will often use terms relating to OSI. Also, the ICND1 exam covers the basics of OSI, so this chapter also covers OSI to prepare you for questions about it on the exam.

Overview of the TCP/IP Networking Model

The TCP/IP model both defines and references a large collection of protocols that allow computers to communicate. To define a protocol, TCP/IP uses documents called Requests for Comments (RFC). (You can find these RFCs using any online search engine.) The TCP/IP model also avoids repeating work already done by some other standards body or vendor consortium by simply referring to standards or protocols created by those groups. For example, the Institute of Electrical and Electronic Engineers (IEEE) defines Ethernet LANs; the TCP/IP model does not define Ethernet in RFCs, but refers to IEEE Ethernet as an option.

An easy comparison can be made between telephones and computers that use TCP/IP. You go to the store and buy a phone from one of a dozen different vendors. When you get home and plug in the phone to the same cable in which your old phone was connected, the new phone works. The phone vendors know the standards for phones in their country and build their phones to match those standards.

Similarly, when you buy a new computer today, it implements the TCP/IP model to the point that you can usually take the computer out of the box, plug in all the right cables, turn it on, and it connects to the network. You can use a web browser to connect to your favorite website. How? Well, the OS on the computer implements parts of the TCP/IP model. The Ethernet card, or wireless LAN card, built into the computer implements some LAN standards referenced by the TCP/IP model. In short, the vendors that created the hardware and software implemented TCP/IP.

To help people understand a networking model, each model breaks the functions into a small number of categories called *layers*. Each layer includes protocols and standards that relate to that category of functions. TCP/IP actually has two alternative models, as shown in Figure 1-4.

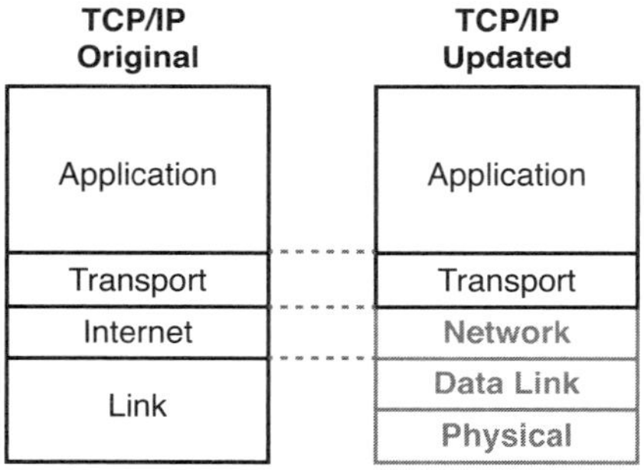

Figure 1-4 *Two TCP/IP Networking Models*

The model on the left shows the original TCP/IP model listed in RFC 1122, which breaks TCP/IP into four layers. The top two layers focus more on the applications that need to send and receive data. The bottom layer focuses on how to transmit bits over each individual link, with the internet layer focusing on delivering data over the entire path from the original sending computer to the final destination computer.

The TCP/IP model on the right is a common method used today to refer to the layers formed by expanding the original model's link layer on the left into two separate layers: data link and physical (similar to the lower two layers of the OSI model). Note that the model on the right is used more often today.

NOTE   The original TCP/IP model's link layer has also been referred to as the *network access* and *network interface* layer.

Many of you will have already heard of several TCP/IP protocols, like the examples listed in Table 1-2. Most of the protocols and standards in this table will be explained in more detail as you work through this book. Following the table, this section takes a closer look at the layers of the TCP/IP model.

Table 1-2   TCP/IP Architectural Model and Example Protocols

TCP/IP Architecture Layer	Example Protocols
Application	HTTP, POP3, SMTP
Transport	TCP, UDP
Internet	IP
Link	Ethernet, Point-to-Point Protocol (PPP), T1

TCP/IP Application Layer

TCP/IP application layer protocols provide services to the application software running on a computer. The application layer does not define the application itself, but it defines services that applications need. For example, application protocol HTTP defines how web browsers can pull the contents of a web page from a web server. In short, the application layer provides an interface between software running on a computer and the network itself.

Arguably, the most popular TCP/IP application today is the web browser. Many major software vendors either have already changed or are changing their application software to support access from a web browser. And thankfully, using a web browser is easy: You start a web browser on your computer and select a website by typing the name of the website, and the web page appears.

HTTP Overview

What really happens to allow that web page to appear on your web browser?

Imagine that Bob opens his browser. His browser has been configured to automatically ask for web server Larry's default web page, or *home page*. The general logic looks like Figure 1-5.

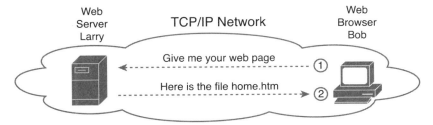

Figure 1-5   *Basic Application Logic to Get a Web Page*

So, what really happened? Bob's initial request actually asks Larry to send his home page back to Bob. Larry's web server software has been configured to know that the default web page is contained in a file called home.htm. Bob receives the file from Larry and displays the contents of the file in Bob's web-browser window.

HTTP Protocol Mechanisms

Taking a closer look, this example shows how applications on each endpoint computer—specifically, the web-browser application and web-server application—use a TCP/IP application layer protocol. To make the request for a web page and return the contents of the web page, the applications use the Hypertext Transfer Protocol (HTTP).

HTTP did not exist until Tim Berners-Lee created the first web browser and web server in the early 1990s. Berners-Lee gave HTTP functions to ask for the contents of web pages, specifically by giving the web browser the ability to request files from the server, and giving the server a way to return the content of those files. The overall logic matches what was shown in Figure 1-5; Figure 1-6 shows the same idea, but with details specific to HTTP.

> **NOTE**   The full version of most web addresses—also called Uniform Resource Locators (URL)—begins with the letters "http," which means that HTTP is used to transfer the web pages.

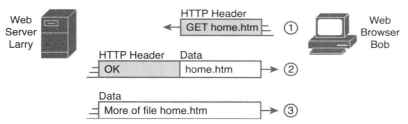

Figure 1-6   *HTTP Get Request, HTTP Reply, and One Data-Only Message*

To get the web page from Larry, at Step 1, Bob sends a message with an HTTP header. Generally, protocols use headers as a place to put information used by that protocol. This HTTP header includes the request to "get" a file. The request typically contains the name of the file (home.htm, in this case), or if no filename is mentioned, the web server assumes that Bob wants the default web page.

Step 2 in Figure 1-6 shows the response from web server Larry. The message begins with an HTTP header, with a return code (200), which means something as simple as "OK" returned in the header. HTTP also defines other return codes so that the server can tell the browser whether the request worked. (Here is another example: If you ever looked for a web page that was not found, and then received an HTTP 404 "not found" error, you received an HTTP return code of 404.) The second message also includes the first part of the requested file.

Step 3 in Figure 1-6 shows another message from web server Larry to web browser Bob, but this time without an HTTP header. HTTP transfers the data by sending multiple messages, each with a part of the file. Rather than wasting space by sending repeated HTTP headers that list the same information, these additional messages simply omit the header.

TCP/IP Transport Layer

Although many TCP/IP application layer protocols exist, the TCP/IP transport layer includes a smaller number of protocols. The two most commonly used transport layer protocols are the *Transmission Control Protocol (TCP)* and the *User Datagram Protocol (UDP)*.

Transport layer protocols provide services to the application layer protocols that reside one layer higher in the TCP/IP model. How does a transport layer protocol provide a service to a higher-layer protocol? This section introduces that general concept by focusing on a single service provided by TCP: error recovery. Later chapters examine the transport layer in more detail, and discuss more functions of the transport layer.

TCP Error Recovery Basics

To appreciate what the transport layer protocols do, you must think about the layer above the transport layer, the application layer. Why? Well, each layer provides a service to the layer above it, like the error-recovery service provided to application layer protocols by TCP.

For example, in Figure 1-5, Bob and Larry used HTTP to transfer the home page from web server Larry to Bob's web browser. But what would have happened if Bob's HTTP GET request had been lost in transit through the TCP/IP network? Or, what would have happened if Larry's response, which included the contents of the home page, had been lost? Well, as you might expect, in either case, the page would not have shown up in Bob's browser.

TCP/IP needs a mechanism to guarantee delivery of data across a network. Because many application layer protocols probably want a way to guarantee delivery of data across a network, the creators of TCP included an error-recovery feature. To recover from errors, TCP uses the concept of acknowledgments. Figure 1-7 outlines the basic idea behind how TCP notices lost data and asks the sender to try again.

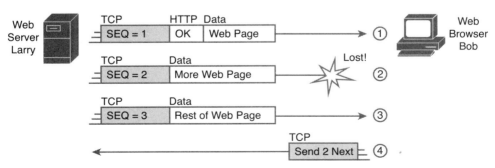

Figure 1-7   *TCP Error-Recovery Services as Provided to HTTP*

Figure 1-7 shows web server Larry sending a web page to web browser Bob, using three separate messages. Note that this figure shows the same HTTP headers as Figure 1-6, but it also shows a TCP header. The TCP header shows a sequence number (SEQ) with each message. In this example, the network has a problem, and the network fails to deliver the TCP message (called a segment) with sequence number 2. When Bob receives messages with sequence numbers 1 and 3, but does not receive a message with sequence number 2, Bob realizes that message 2 was lost. That realization by Bob's TCP logic causes Bob to send a TCP segment back to Larry, asking Larry to send message 2 again.

Same-Layer and Adjacent-Layer Interactions

The example in Figure 1-7 also demonstrates a function called *adjacent-layer interaction*, which refers to the concepts of how adjacent layers in a networking model, on the same computer, work together. In this example, the higher-layer protocol (HTTP) wants error recovery, and the higher layer uses the next lower-layer protocol (TCP) to perform the service of error recovery; the lower layer provides a service to the layer above it.

Figure 1-7 also shows an example of a similar function called *same-layer interaction*. When a particular layer on one computer wants to communicate with the same layer on another computer, the two computers use headers to hold the information that they want to communicate. For example, in Figure 1-7, Larry set the sequence numbers to 1, 2, and 3 so that Bob could notice when some of the data did not arrive. Larry's TCP process created that TCP header with the sequence number; Bob's TCP process received and reacted to the TCP segments. This process through which two computers set and interpret the information in the header used by that layer is called *same-layer interaction*, and it occurs between computers that are communicating over a network.

Table 1-3 summarizes the key points about how adjacent layers work together on a single computer and how one layer on one computer works with the same networking layer on another computer.

Table 1-3   Summary: Same-Layer and Adjacent-Layer Interactions

Concept	Description
Same-layer interaction on different computers	The two computers use a protocol (an agreed-to set of rules) to communicate with the same layer on another computer. The protocol defined by each layer uses a header that is transmitted between the computers to communicate what each computer wants to do. Header information added by a layer of the sending computer is processed by the same layer of the receiving computer.
Adjacent-layer interaction on the same computer	On a single computer, one layer provides a service to a higher layer. The software or hardware that implements the higher layer requests that the next lower layer perform the needed function.

TCP/IP Network Layer

The application layer includes many protocols. The transport layer includes fewer, most notably, TCP and UDP. The TCP/IP network layer includes a small number of protocols, but only one major protocol: the *Internet Protocol (IP)*. In fact, the name *TCP/IP* is simply the names of the two most common protocols (TCP and IP) separated by a /.

IP provides several features, most importantly, addressing and routing. This section begins by comparing IP's addressing and routing with another commonly known system that uses addressing and routing: the postal service. Following that, this section introduces IP addressing and routing. (More details follow in Chapter 4, "Fundamentals of IPv4 Addressing and Routing.")

Internet Protocol and the Postal Service

Imagine that you just wrote two letters: one to a friend on the other side of the country and one to a friend on the other side of town. You addressed the envelopes and put on the stamps, so both are ready to give to the postal service. Is there much difference in how you treat each letter? Not really. Typically, you would just put them in the same mailbox and expect the postal service to deliver both letters.

The postal service, however, must think about each letter separately, and then make a decision of where to send each letter so that it is delivered. For the letter sent across town, the people in the local post office probably just need to put the letter on another truck.

For the letter that needs to go across the country, the postal service sends the letter to another post office, then another, and so on, until the letter gets delivered across the country. At each post office, the postal service must process the letter and choose where to send it next.

To make it all work, the postal service has regular routes for small trucks, large trucks, planes, boats, and so on, to move letters between postal service sites. The service must be able to receive and forward the letters, and it must make good decisions about where to send each letter next, as shown in Figure 1-8.

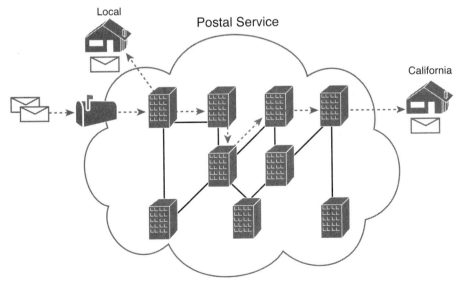

Figure 1-8 *Postal Service Forwarding (Routing) Letters*

Still thinking about the postal service, consider the difference between the person sending the letter and the work that the postal service does. The person sending the letters expects that the postal service will deliver the letter most of the time. However, the person sending the letter does not need to know the details of exactly what path the letters take. In contrast, the postal service does not create the letter, but they accept the letter from the customer. Then, the postal service must know the details about addresses and postal codes that group addresses into larger groups, and it must have the ability to deliver the letters.

The TCP/IP application and transport layers act like the person sending letters through the postal service. These upper layers work the same way regardless of whether the endpoint host computers are on the same LAN or are separated by the entire Internet. To send a message, these upper layers ask the layer below them, the network layer, to deliver the message.

The lower layers of the TCP/IP model act more like the postal service to deliver those messages to the correct destinations. To do so, these lower layers must understand the underlying physical network because they must choose how to best deliver the data from one host to another.

So, what does this all matter to networking? Well, the network layer of the TCP/IP networking model, primarily defined by the *Internet Protocol (IP)*, works much like the postal service. IP defines that each host computer should have a different IP address, just as the postal service defines addressing that allows unique addresses for each house, apartment, and business. Similarly, IP defines the process of routing so that devices called routers can work like the post office, forwarding packets of data so that they are delivered to the correct destinations. Just as the postal service created the necessary infrastructure to deliver letters—post offices, sorting machines, trucks, planes, and personnel—the network layer defines the details of how a network infrastructure should be created so that the network can deliver data to all computers in the network.

> **NOTE**   TCP/IP defines two versions of IP: IP Version 4 (IPv4) and IP Version 6 (IPv6). The world still mostly uses IPv4, so this introductory part of the book uses IPv4 for all references to IP. Later in this book, Part VII, "IP Version 6," discusses this newer version of the IP protocol.

Internet Protocol Addressing Basics

IP defines addresses for several important reasons. First, each device that uses TCP/IP—each TCP/IP *host*—needs a unique address so that it can be identified in the network. IP also defines how to group addresses together, just like the postal system groups addresses based on postal codes (like ZIP codes in the United States).

To understand the basics, examine Figure 1-9, which shows the familiar web server Larry and web browser Bob; but now, instead of ignoring the network between these two computers, part of the network infrastructure is included.

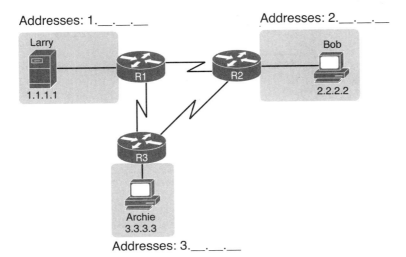

Figure 1-9   *Simple TCP/IP Network: Three Routers with IP Addresses Grouped*

First, note that Figure 1-9 shows some sample IP addresses. Each IP address has four numbers, separated by periods. In this case, Larry uses IP address 1.1.1.1, and Bob uses 2.2.2.2. This style of number is called a *dotted-decimal notation (DDN)*.

Figure 1-9 also shows three groups of address. In this example, all IP address that begin with 1 must be on the upper left, as shown in shorthand in the figure as 1.__.__.__. All addresses that begin with 2 must be on the right, as shown in shorthand as 2.__.__.__. Finally, all IP addresses that begin with 3 must be at the bottom of the figure.

Additionally, Figure 1-9 also introduces icons that represent IP routers. Routers are networking devices that connect the parts of the TCP/IP network together for the purpose of routing (forwarding) IP packets to the correct destination. Routers do the equivalent of the work done by each post office site: They receive IP packets on various physical interfaces, make decisions based on the IP address included with the packet, and then physically forward the packet out some other network interface.

IP Routing Basics

The TCP/IP network layer, using the IP protocol, provides a service of forwarding IP packets from one device to another. Any device with an IP address can connect to the TCP/IP network and send packets. This section shows a basic IP routing example for perspective.

> **NOTE**   The term *IP host* refers to any device, regardless of size or power, that has an IP address and connects to any TCP/IP network.

Figure 1-10 repeats the familiar case in which web server Larry wants to send part of a web page to Bob, but now with details related to IP. On the lower left, note that server Larry has the familiar application data, HTTP header, and TCP header ready to send. Additionally, the message now also contains an IP header. The IP header includes a source IP address of Larry's IP address (1.1.1.1) and a destination IP address of Bob's IP address (2.2.2.2).

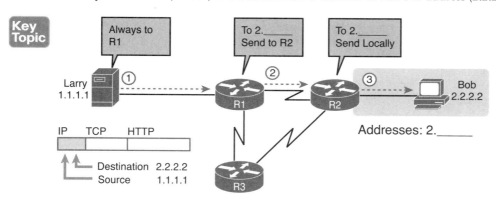

Figure 1-10   *Basic Routing Example*

Step 1, on the left of Figure 1-10, begins with Larry being ready to send an IP packet. Larry's IP process chooses to send the packet to some router—a nearby router on the same LAN—with the expectation that the router will know how to forward the packet. (This logic is much like you or me sending all our letters by putting them in a nearby post office box.) Larry doesn't need to know anything more about the topology or the other routers.

At Step 2, router R1 receives the IP packet, and R1's IP process makes a decision. R1 looks at the destination address (2.2.2.2), compares that address to its known IP routes, and chooses to forward the packet to router R2. This process of forwarding the IP packet is called *IP routing* (or simply *routing*).

At Step 3, router R2 repeats the same kind of logic used by router R1. R2's IP process will compare the packet's destination IP address (2.2.2.2) to R2's known IP routes and make a choice to forward the packet to the right, on to Bob.

Practically half the chapters in this book discuss some feature that relates to addressing, IP routing, and how routers perform routing.

TCP/IP Link Layer (Data Link Plus Physical)

The TCP/IP model's original link layer defines the protocols and hardware required to deliver data across some physical network. The term *link* refers to the physical connections, or links, between two devices and the protocols used to control those links.

Just like every layer in any networking model, the TCP/IP link layer provides services to the layer above it in the model. When a host's or router's IP process chooses to send an IP packet to another router or host, that host or router then uses link-layer details to send that packet to the next host/router.

Because each layer provides a service to the layer above it, take a moment to think about the IP logic related to Figure 1-10. In that example, host Larry's IP logic chooses to send the IP packet to a nearby router (R1), with no mention of the underlying Ethernet. The Ethernet network, which implements link-layer protocols, must then be used to deliver that packet from host Larry over to router R1. Figure 1-11 shows four steps of what occurs at the link layer to allow Larry to send the IP packet to R1.

> **NOTE**   Figure 1-11 depicts the Ethernet as a series of lines. Networking diagrams often use this convention when drawing Ethernet LANs, in cases where the actual LAN cabling and LAN devices are not important to some discussion, as is the case here. The LAN would have cables and devices, like LAN switches, which are not shown in this figure.

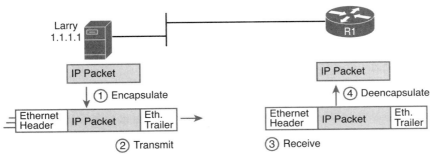

Figure 1-11   *Larry Using Ethernet to Forward an IP Packet to Router R1*

Figure 1-11 shows four steps. The first two occur on Larry, and the last two occur on router R1, as follows:

Step 1.   Larry encapsulates the IP packet between an Ethernet header and Ethernet trailer, creating an Ethernet *frame*.

Step 2.   Larry physically transmits the bits of this Ethernet frame, using electricity flowing over the Ethernet cabling.

Step 3.   Router R1 physically receives the electrical signal over a cable, and re-creates the same bits by interpreting the meaning of the electrical signals.

Step 4.   Router R1 deencapsulates the IP packet from the Ethernet frame by removing and discarding the Ethernet header and trailer.

By the end of this process, the link-layer processes on Larry and R1 have worked together to deliver the packet from Larry to router R1.

> **NOTE**   Protocols define both headers and trailers for the same general reason, but headers exist at the beginning of the message and trailers exist at the end.

The link layer includes a large number of protocols and standards. For example, the link layer includes all the variations of Ethernet protocols, along with several other LAN standards that were more popular in decades past. The link layer includes wide-area network (WAN) standards for different physical media, which differ significantly compared to LAN standards because of the longer distances involved in transmitting the data. This layer also includes the popular WAN standards that add headers and trailers as shown generally in

Figure 1-11—protocols such as the Point-to-Point Protocol (PPP) and Frame Relay. Chapter 2, "Fundamentals of Ethernet LANs," and Chapter 3, "Fundamentals of WANs," further develop these topics for LANs and WANs, respectively.

In short, the TCP/IP link layer includes two distinct functions: functions related to the physical transmission of the data, plus the protocols and rules that control the use of the physical media. The five-layer TCP/IP model simply splits out the link layer into two layers (data link and physical) to match this logic.

TCP/IP Model and Terminology

Before completing this introduction to the TCP/IP model, this section examines a few remaining details of the model and some related terminology.

Comparing the Original and Modern TCP/IP Models

The original TCP/IP model defined a single layer—the link layer—below the internetwork layer. The functions defined in the original link layer can be broken into two major categories: functions related directly to the physical transmission of data and those only indirectly related to the physical transmission of data. For example, in the four steps shown in Figure 1-11, Steps 2 and 3 were specific to sending the data, but Steps 1 and 4—encapsulation and deencapsulation—were only indirectly related. This division will become clearer as you read about additional details of each protocol and standard.

Today, most documents use a more modern version of the TCP/IP model, as shown in Figure 1-12. Comparing the two, the upper layers are identical, except a name change from "internet" to "network." The lower layers differ in that the single link layer in the original model is split into two layers to match the division of physical transmission details from the other functions. Figure 1-12 shows the two versions of the TCP/IP model again, with emphasis on these distinctions.

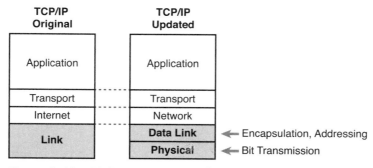

Figure 1-12 *Link Versus Data Link and Physical Layers*

Data Encapsulation Terminology

As you can see from the explanations of how HTTP, TCP, IP, and Ethernet do their jobs, each layer adds its own header (and for data-link protocols, also a trailer) to the data supplied by the higher layer. The term *encapsulation* refers to the process of putting headers (and sometimes trailers) around some data.

Many of the examples in this chapter show the encapsulation process. For example, web server Larry encapsulated the contents of the home page inside an HTTP header in Figure 1-6. The TCP layer encapsulated the HTTP headers and data inside a TCP header in Figure 1-7. IP encapsulated the TCP headers and the data inside an IP header in Figure 1-10. Finally, the Ethernet link layer encapsulated the IP packets inside both a header and a trailer in Figure 1-11.

The process by which a TCP/IP host sends data can be viewed as a five-step process. The first four steps relate to the encapsulation performed by the four TCP/IP layers, and the last step is the actual physical transmission of the data by the host. In fact, if you use the five-layer TCP/IP model, one step corresponds to the role of each layer. The steps are summarized in the following list:

Step 1. **Create and encapsulate the application data with any required application layer headers.** For example, the HTTP OK message can be returned in an HTTP header, followed by part of the contents of a web page.

Step 2. **Encapsulate the data supplied by the application layer inside a transport layer header.** For end-user applications, a TCP or UDP header is typically used.

Step 3. **Encapsulate the data supplied by the transport layer inside a network layer (IP) header.** IP defines the IP addresses that uniquely identify each computer.

Step 4. **Encapsulate the data supplied by the network layer inside a data link layer header and trailer.** This layer uses both a header and a trailer.

Step 5. **Transmit the bits.** The physical layer encodes a signal onto the medium to transmit the frame.

The numbers in Figure 1-13 correspond to the five steps in this list, graphically showing the same concepts. Note that because the application layer often does not need to add a header, the figure does not show a specific application layer header.

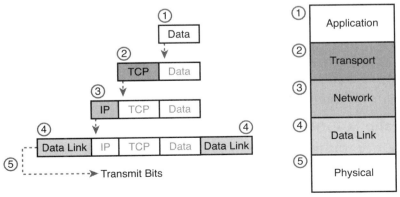

Figure 1-13 *Five Steps of Data Encapsulation: TCP/IP*

Names of TCP/IP Messages

Finally, take particular care to remember the terms *segment*, *packet*, and *frame* and the meaning of each. Each term refers to the headers (and possibly trailers) defined by a particular layer and the data encapsulated following that header. Each term, however, refers to a different layer: segment for the transport layer, packet for the network layer, and frame for the link layer. Figure 1-14 shows each layer along with the associated term.

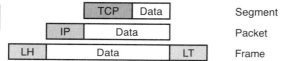

Figure 1-14   *Perspectives on Encapsulation and "Data"**

* The letters LH and LT stand for link header and link trailer, respectively, and refer to the data link layer header and trailer.

Figure 1-14 also shows the encapsulated data as simply "data." When focusing on the work done by a particular layer, the encapsulated data typically is unimportant. For example, an IP packet can indeed have a TCP header after the IP header, an HTTP header after the TCP header, and data for a web page after the HTTP header. However, when discussing IP, you probably just care about the IP header, so everything after the IP header is just called "data." So, when drawing IP packets, everything after the IP header is typically shown simply as "data."

OSI Networking Model

At one point in the history of the OSI model, many people thought that OSI would win the battle of the networking models discussed earlier. If that had occurred, instead of running TCP/IP on every computer in the world, those computers would be running with OSI.

However, OSI did not win that battle. In fact, OSI no longer exists as a networking model that could be used instead of TCP/IP, although some of the original protocols referenced by the OSI model still exist.

So, why is OSI even in this book? Terminology. During those years in which many people thought the OSI model would become commonplace in the world of networking (mostly in the late 1980s and early 1990s), many vendors and protocol documents started using terminology from the OSI model. That terminology remains today. So, while you will never need to work with a computer that uses OSI, to understand modern networking terminology, you need to understand something about OSI.

Comparing OSI and TCP/IP

The OSI model has many similarities to the TCP/IP model from a basic conceptual perspective. It has (seven) layers, and each layer defines a set of typical networking functions. As with TCP/IP, the OSI layers each refer to multiple protocols and standards that implement the functions specified by each layer. In other cases, just as for TCP/IP, the OSI committees did not create new protocols or standards, but instead referenced other protocols that were already defined. For example, the IEEE defines Ethernet standards, so the OSI committees did not waste time specifying a new type of Ethernet; it simply referred to the IEEE Ethernet standards.

Today, the OSI model can be used as a standard of comparison to other networking models. Figure 1-15 compares the seven-layer OSI model with both the four-layer and five-layer TCP/IP models.

	OSI		TCP/IP		TCP/IP
7	Application				
6	Presentation		Application	5 - 7	Application
5	Session				
4	Transport		Transport	4	Transport
3	Network		Internet	3	Network
2	Data Link		Link	2	Data Link
1	Physical			1	Physical

Figure 1-15   *OSI Model Compared to the Two TCP/IP Models*

Next, this section will examine two ways in which we still use OSI terminology today: to describe other protocols and to describe the encapsulation process. Along the way, the text will briefly examine each layer of the OSI model.

Describing Protocols by Referencing the OSI Layers

Even today, networking documents often describe TCP/IP protocols and standards by referencing OSI layers, both by layer number and layer name. For example, a common description of a LAN switch is "layer 2 switch," with "layer 2" referring to OSI layer 2. Because OSI did have a well-defined set of functions associated with each of its seven layers, if you know those functions, you can understand what people mean when they refer to a product or function by its OSI layer.

For another example, TCP/IP's original internet layer, as implemented mainly by IP, equates most directly to the OSI *network* layer. So, most people say that IP is a *network layer protocol*, or a *Layer 3 protocol*, using OSI terminology and numbers for the layer. Of course, if you numbered the TCP/IP model, starting at the bottom, IP would be either Layer 2 or 3, depending on what version of the TCP/IP model you care to use. However, even though IP is a TCP/IP protocol, everyone uses the OSI model layer names and numbers when describing IP or any other protocol for that matter.

The claim that a particular TCP/IP layer is similar to a particular OSI layer is a general comparison, but not a detailed comparison. The comparison is a little like comparing a car to a truck: Both can get you from point A to point B, but they have many specific differences, like the truck having a truck bed in which to carry cargo. Similarly, both the OSI and TCP/IP network layers define logical addressing and routing. However, the addresses have a different size, and the routing logic even works differently. So the comparison of OSI layers to other protocol models is a general comparison of major goals, and not a comparison of the specific methods.

OSI Layers and Their Functions

The exam requires a basic understanding of the functions defined by each OSI layer, as well as remember the names of the layers. It is also important that, for each device or protocol referenced throughout the book, you understand which layers of the OSI model most closely match the functions defined by that device or protocol.

Today, because most people happen to be much more familiar with TCP/IP functions than with OSI functions, one of the best ways to learn about the function of different OSI layers is to think about the functions in the TCP/IP model and to correlate those with the OSI model. If you use the five-layer TCP/IP model, the bottom four layers of OSI and TCP/IP map closely together. The only difference in these bottom four layers is the name of OSI Layer 3 (network) compared to the original TCP/IP model (internet). The upper three layers of the OSI reference model (application, presentation, and session—Layers 7, 6, and 5) define functions that all map to the TCP/IP application layer. Table 1-4 defines the functions of the seven layers.

Table 1-4   OSI Reference Model Layer Definitions

Layer	Functional Description
7	**Application layer.** This layer provides an interface between the communications software and any applications that need to communicate outside the computer on which the application resides. It also defines processes for user authentication.
6	**Presentation layer.** This layer's main purpose is to define and negotiate data formats, such as ASCII text, EBCDIC text, binary, BCD, and JPEG. Encryption is also defined by OSI as a presentation layer service.
5	**Session layer.** This layer defines how to start, control, and end conversations (called sessions). This includes the control and management of multiple bidirectional messages so that the application can be notified if only some of a series of messages are completed. This allows the presentation layer to have a seamless view of an incoming stream of data.
4	**Transport layer.** This layer's protocols provide a large number of services, as described in Chapter 5, "Fundamentals of TCP/IP Transport and Applications." Although OSI Layers 5 through 7 focus on issues related to the application, Layer 4 focuses on issues related to data delivery to another computer (for example, error recovery and flow control).
3	**Network layer.** This layer defines three main features: logical addressing, routing (forwarding), and path determination. Routing defines how devices (typically routers) forward packets to their final destination. Logical addressing defines how each device can have an address that can be used by the routing process. Path determination refers to the work done by routing protocols to learn all possible routes and choose the best route.

Layer	Functional Description
2	**Data link layer.** This layer defines the rules that determine when a device can send data over a particular medium. Data link protocols also define the format of a header and trailer that allows devices attached to the medium to successfully send and receive data.
1	**Physical layer.** This layer typically refers to standards from other organizations. These standards deal with the physical characteristics of the transmission medium, including connectors, pins, use of pins, electrical currents, encoding, light modulation, and the rules for how to activate and deactivate the use of the physical medium.

Table 1-5 lists a sampling of the devices and protocols covered in this book and their comparable OSI layers. Note that many network devices must actually understand the protocols at multiple OSI layers, so the layer listed in Table 1-5 actually refers to the highest layer that the device normally thinks about when performing its core work. For example, routers need to think about Layer 3 concepts, but they must also support features at both Layers 1 and 2.

Table 1-5   OSI Reference Model—Example Devices and Protocols

Layer Name	Protocols and Specifications	Devices
Application, presentation, session (Layers 5–7)	Telnet, HTTP, FTP, SMTP, POP3, VoIP, SNMP	Hosts, firewalls
Transport (Layer 4)	TCP, UDP	Hosts, firewalls
Network (Layer 3)	IP	Router
Data link (Layer 2)	Ethernet (IEEE 802.3), HDLC	LAN switch, wireless access point, cable modem, DSL modem
Physical (Layer 1)	RJ-45, Ethernet (IEEE 802.3)	LAN hub, LAN repeater, cables

Besides remembering the basics of the features of each OSI layer (as in Table 1-4), and some example protocols and devices at each layer (as in Table 1-5), you should also memorize the names of the layers. You can simply memorize them, but some people like to use a mnemonic phrase to make memorization easier. In the following three phrases, the first letter of each word is the same as the first letter of an OSI layer name, in the order specified in parentheses:

- All People Seem To Need Data Processing (Layers 7 to 1)
- Please Do Not Take Sausage Pizzas Away (Layers 1 to 7)
- Pew! Dead Ninja Turtles Smell Particularly Awful (Layers 1 to 7)

OSI Layering Concepts and Benefits

While networking models use layers to help humans categorize and understand the many functions in a network, networking models use layers for many reasons. For example, consider another postal service analogy. A person writing a letter does not have to think about how the postal service will deliver a letter across the country. The postal worker in the middle of the country does not have to worry about the contents of the letter. Likewise, networking models that divide functions into different layers enable one software package or hardware device to implement functions from one layer, and assume that other software/hardware will perform the functions defined by the other layers.

The following list summarizes the benefits of layered protocol specifications:

- **Less complex:** Compared to not using a layered model, network models break the concepts into smaller parts.

- **Standard interfaces:** The standard interface definitions between each layer allow multiple vendors to create products that fill a particular role, with all the benefits of open competition.

- **Easier to learn:** Humans can more easily discuss and learn about the many details of a protocol specification.

- **Easier to develop:** Reduced complexity allows easier program changes and faster product development.

- **Multivendor interoperability:** Creating products to meet the same networking standards means that computers and networking gear from multiple vendors can work in the same network.

- **Modular engineering:** One vendor can write software that implements higher layers—for example, a web browser—and another vendor can write software that implements the lower layers—for example, Microsoft's built-in TCP/IP software in its OSs.

OSI Encapsulation Terminology

Like TCP/IP, each OSI layer asks for services from the next lower layer. To provide the services, each layer makes use of a header and possibly a trailer. The lower layer encapsulates the higher layer's data behind a header. The final topic of this chapter explains some of the terminology and concepts related to OSI encapsulation.

The TCP/IP model uses terms such as *segment*, *packet*, and *frame* to refer to various layers and their respective encapsulated data (refer to Figure 1-13). OSI uses a more generic term: *protocol data unit (PDU)*.

A PDU represents the bits that include the headers and trailers for that layer, as well as the encapsulated data. For example, an IP packet, as shown in Figure 1-14, using OSI terminology, is a PDU. In fact, an IP packet is a *Layer 3 PDU* (abbreviated L3PDU) because IP is a Layer 3 protocol. So, rather than use the terms *segment*, *packet*, or *frame*, OSI simply refers to the "Layer x PDU" (LxPDU), with "x" referring to the number of the layer being discussed.

Figure 1-16 represents the typical encapsulation process, with the top of the figure showing the application data and application layer header and the bottom of the figure showing the L2PDU that is transmitted onto the physical link.

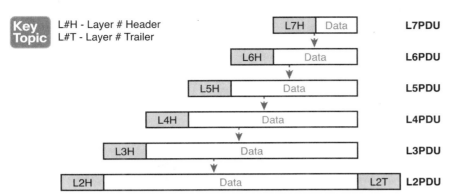

Figure 1-16 *OSI Encapsulation and Protocol Data Units*

Exam Preparation Tasks

Review All the Key Topics

Review the most important topics from this chapter, noted with the Key Topic icon. Table 1-6 lists these key topics and where each is discussed.

Table 1-6   Key Topics for Chapter 1

Key Topic Elements	Description	Page Number
Table 1-3	Provides definitions of same-layer and adjacent-layer interaction	22
Figure 1-10	Shows the general concept of IP routing	26
Figure 1-11	Depicts the data link services provided to IP for the purpose of delivering IP packets from host to host	27
Figure 1-13	Five steps to encapsulate data on the sending host	29
Figure 1-14	Shows the meaning of the terms *segment*, *packet*, and *frame*	30
Figure 1-15	Compares the OSI and TCP/IP network models	31
List	Lists the benefits of using a layered networking model	34
Figure 1-16	Terminology related to encapsulation	35

Definitions of Key Terms

After your first reading of the chapter, try to define these key terms, but do not be concerned about getting them all correct at that time. Chapter 23 directs you in how to use these terms for late-stage preparation for the exam.

adjacent-layer interaction, deencapsulation, encapsulation, frame, networking model, packet, protocol data unit (PDU), same-layer interaction, segment

This chapter covers the following exam topics:

1.1 Describe the purpose and functions of various network devices

1.1.a Interpret a network diagram

1.2 Select the components required to meet a network specification

1.2.a Switches

1.4 Describe the purpose and basic operation of the protocols in the OSI and TCP models

2.1 Explain the technology and media access control method for Ethernet networks

2.1.a IEEE 802 protocols

2.1.b CSMA/CD

2.2 Explain basic switching concepts and the operation of Cisco switches

2.2.a Layer 2 addressing

CHAPTER 2

Fundamentals of Ethernet LANs

Most every enterprise computer network can be separated into two general types of technology: local-area networks (LAN) and wide-area networks (WAN). LANs typically connect nearby devices: devices in the same room (whether a large data center or a small office), in the same building, or in a campus of buildings. In contrast, WANs connect devices that are typically relatively far apart. Together, LANs and WANs create a complete enterprise computer network, working together to do the job of a computer network: delivering data from one device to another.

Many types of LANs have existed over the years, but today's networks use two general types of LANs: Ethernet LANs and wireless LANs. Ethernet LANs happen to use cables for the links between nodes, and because many types of cables use copper wires, Ethernet LANs are often called *wired LANs*. In comparison, wireless LANs do not use wires or cables, instead using radio waves to communicate between nodes.

Data center networks make extensive use of Ethernet LAN technology. For example, most individual servers today have multiple Ethernet connections to Ethernet LAN switches. This chapter begins laying your foundation of Ethernet knowledge that can be applied to all uses of Ethernet LAN technology, with the chapters in Parts II and III of this book adding many more details.

"Do I Know This Already?" Quiz

Use the "Do I Know This Already?" quiz to help decide whether you might want to skim this chapter, or a major section, moving more quickly to the "Exam Preparation Tasks" section near the end of the chapter. You can find the answers at the bottom of the page following the quiz. For thorough explanations, see Appendix A, "Answers to the 'Do I Know This Already?' Quizzes."

Table 2-1 "Do I Know This Already?" Foundation Topics Section-to-Question Mapping

Foundation Topics Section	Questions
An Overview of LANs	1, 2
Building Physical Ethernet Networks	3, 4
Sending Data in Ethernet Networks	5–8

1. In the LAN for a small office, some user devices connect to the LAN using a cable, while others connect using wireless technology (and no cable). Which of the following is true regarding the use of Ethernet in this LAN?

    a. Only the devices that use cables are using Ethernet.

    b. Only the devices that use wireless are using Ethernet.

    c. Both the devices using cables and those using wireless are using Ethernet.

    d. None of the devices are using Ethernet.

2. Which of the following Ethernet standards defines Gigabit Ethernet over UTP cabling?

    a. 10GBASE-T

    b. 100BASE-T

    c. 1000BASE-T

    d. None of the other answers is correct.

3. Which of the following is true about Ethernet crossover cables for Fast Ethernet?

    a. Pins 1 and 2 are reversed on the other end of the cable.

    b. Pins 1 and 2 on one end of the cable connect to pins 3 and 6 on the other end of the cable.

    c. Pins 1 and 2 on one end of the cable connect to pins 3 and 4 on the other end of the cable.

    d. The cable can be up to 1000 meters long to cross over between buildings.

    e. None of the other answers is correct.

4. Each answer lists two types of devices used in a 100BASE-T network. If these devices were connected with UTP Ethernet cables, which pairs of devices would require a straight-through cable? (Choose three answers.)

    a. PC and router

    b. PC and switch

    c. Hub and switch

    d. Router and hub

    e. Wireless access point (Ethernet port) and switch

5. Which of the following is true about the CSMA/CD algorithm?

    a. The algorithm never allows collisions to occur.

    b. Collisions can happen, but the algorithm defines how the computers should notice a collision and how to recover.

    c. The algorithm works with only two devices on the same Ethernet.

    d. None of the other answers is correct.

6. Which of the following is true about the Ethernet FCS field?

   a. Ethernet uses FCS for error recovery.

   b. It is 2 bytes long.

   c. It resides in the Ethernet trailer, not the Ethernet header.

   d. It is used for encryption.

7. Which of the following are true about the format of Ethernet addresses? (Choose three answers.)

   a. Each manufacturer puts a unique OUI code into the first 2 bytes of the address.

   b. Each manufacturer puts a unique OUI code into the first 3 bytes of the address.

   c. Each manufacturer puts a unique OUI code into the first half of the address.

   d. The part of the address that holds this manufacturer's code is called the MAC.

   e. The part of the address that holds this manufacturer's code is called the OUI.

   f. The part of the address that holds this manufacturer's code has no specific name.

8. Which of the following terms describe Ethernet addresses that can be used to send one frame that is delivered to multiple devices on the LAN? (Choose two answers.)

   a. Burned-in address

   b. Unicast address

   c. Broadcast address

   d. Multicast address

Foundation Topics

An Overview of LANs

The term *Ethernet* refers to a family of LAN standards that together define the physical and data link layers of the world's most popular wired LAN technology. The standards, defined by the Institute of Electrical and Electronics Engineers (IEEE), define the cabling, the connectors on the ends of the cables, the protocol rules, and everything else required to create an Ethernet LAN.

Typical SOHO LANs

To begin, first think about a small office/home office (SOHO) LAN today, specifically a LAN that uses only Ethernet LAN technology. First, the LAN needs a device called an *Ethernet LAN switch*, which provides many physical ports into which cables can be connected. An Ethernet uses *Ethernet cables*, which is a general reference to any cable that conforms to any of several Ethernet standards. The LAN uses Ethernet cables to connect different Ethernet devices or nodes to one of the switch's Ethernet ports.

Figure 2-1 shows a drawing of a SOHO Ethernet LAN. The figure shows a single LAN switch, five cables, and five other Ethernet nodes: three PCs, a printer, and one network device called a *router*. (The router connects the LAN to the WAN, in this case to the Internet.)

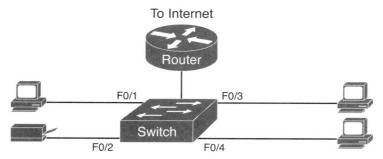

Figure 2-1   *Typical Small Ethernet-Only SOHO LAN*

Although Figure 2-1 shows a simple Ethernet LAN, many SOHO Ethernet LANs today combine the router and switch into a single device. Vendors sell consumer-grade integrated networking devices that work as a router and Ethernet switch, as well as doing other functions. These devices usually have "router" on the packaging, but many models also have four-port or eight-port Ethernet LAN switch ports built in to the device.

Typical SOHO LANs today also support wireless LAN connections. Ethernet defines wired LAN technology only; in other words, Ethernet LANs use cables. However, you can build one LAN that uses both Ethernet LAN technology as well as wireless LAN technology, which is also defined by the IEEE. Wireless LANs, defined by the IEEE using standards that begin with 802.11, use radio waves to send the bits from one node to the next.

Most wireless LANs rely on yet another networking device: a wireless LAN access point (*AP*). The AP acts somewhat like an Ethernet switch, in that all the wireless LAN nodes communicate with the Ethernet switch by sending and receiving data with the wireless AP. Of course, as a wireless device, the AP does not need Ethernet ports for cables, other than for a single Ethernet link to connect the AP to the Ethernet LAN, as shown in Figure 2-2.

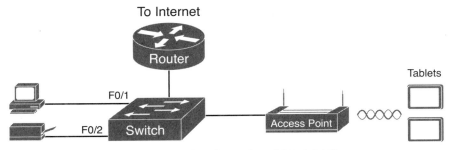

Figure 2-2 *Typical Small Wired and Wireless SOHO LAN*

Note that this drawing shows the router, Ethernet switch, and wireless LAN AP as three separate devices so that you can better understand the different roles. However, most SOHO networks today would use a single device, often labeled as a *wireless router*, that does all these functions.

Typical Enterprise Campus LANs

Companies (enterprises) need to support the devices used by their employees at the enter-prise's business sites. Each site used by the enterprise might be only a few floors in an office building, or it might be the entire building, or even a campus with many buildings. Regardless, the term *campus* LAN refers to the LAN created to support the devices used by the people in an enterprise at a particular site.

Campus networks have similar needs compared to a SOHO network, but on a much larger scale. For example, enterprise Ethernet LANs begin with LAN switches installed in a wiring closet behind a locked door on each floor of a building. The electricians install the Ethernet cabling from that wiring closet to cubicles and conference rooms where devices might need to connect to the LAN. At the same time, most enterprises also support wireless LANs in the same space, to allow people to roam around and still work and to support a growing number of devices that do not have an Ethernet LAN interface.

Figure 2-3 shows a conceptual view of a typical enterprise LAN in a three-story building. Each floor has an Ethernet LAN switch and a wireless LAN AP. To allow communication between floors, each per-floor switch connects to one centralized distribution switch. For example, PC3 can send data to PC2, but it would first flow through switch SW3 to the first floor to the distribution switch (SWD) and then back up through switch SW2 on the second floor.

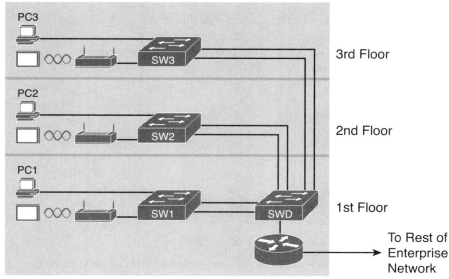

Building

Figure 2-3 *Single-Building Enterprise Wired and Wireless LAN*

The figure also shows the typical way to connect a LAN to a WAN using a router. LAN switches and wireless APs work to create the LAN itself. Routers connect to both the LAN and the WAN. To connect to the LAN, the router simply uses an Ethernet LAN interface and an Ethernet cable, as shown on the lower right of Figure 2-3.

Typical Data Center Ethernet LAN

Data center Ethernet LANs use many of the same Ethernet technologies and concepts used in SOHO and campus LANs. However, the networking needs for data centers differ enough from SOHO and campus LANs for Cisco to offer an entirely different certification track (routing and switching) for core networking functions in the rest of the enterprise, as compared to the data center certification track that begins with the DCICN exam.

Whereas a campus or SOHO LAN connects to end-user devices, a data center LAN connects to servers that users never see with their own eyes. The data center holds a number of servers in a relatively small space, with the servers often sitting in equipment racks. Each server then connects to an Ethernet switch, with the switches connecting together so that the servers can communicate with each other, as well as with end-user devices. Figure 2-4 shows the general idea.

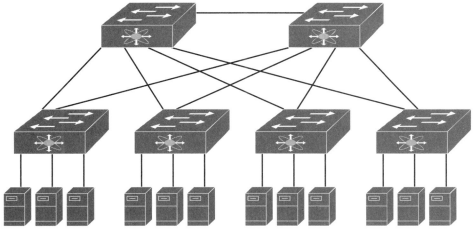

Figure 2-4 *Typical Data Center LAN Design with Four Racks*

NOTE Note that Figure 2-4 uses a slightly different switch icon than the previous figures. Cisco supplies a large variety of standard icons to use when drawing network diagrams. Figures 2-2 and 2-3 show the typical icon for a generic switch. The icons in Figure 2-4 show an icon for any model of Cisco Nexus switch, with the Nexus switch product line being specifically built for data centers.

No matter whether the Ethernet LAN is a single-room small office, a large data center, or some campus LAN, almost all LANs today use Ethernet as the primary LAN technology.

The rest of this chapter focuses on Ethernet in particular.

The Variety of Ethernet Physical Layer Standards

The term *Ethernet* refers to an entire family of standards. Some standards define the specifics of how to send data over a particular type of cabling and at a particular speed. Other standards define protocols, or rules, that the Ethernet nodes must follow to be a part of an Ethernet LAN. All these Ethernet standards come from the IEEE and include the number 802.3 as the beginning part of the standard name.

Ethernet supports a large variety of options for physical Ethernet links given its long history over the past 40 or so years. Today, Ethernet includes many standards for different kinds of optical and copper cabling, and for speeds from 10 megabits per second (Mbps) up to 100 gigabits per second (Gbps). The standards also differ as far as the types of cabling and the allowed length of the cabling.

The most fundamental cabling choice has to do with the materials used inside the cable for the physical transmission of bits: either copper wires or glass fibers. The use of unshielded twisted-pair *(UTP)* cabling saves money compared to optical fibers, with Ethernet nodes using the wires inside the cable to send data over electrical circuits. Fiber-optic cabling, the more expensive alternative, allows Ethernet nodes to send light over glass fibers in the center of the cable. Although more expensive, optical cables typically allow longer cabling distances between nodes.

To be ready to choose the products to purchase for a new Ethernet LAN, a network engineer must know the names and features of the different Ethernet standards supported in Ethernet products. The IEEE defines Ethernet physical layer standards using a couple of naming conventions. The formal name begins with 802.3 followed by some suffix letters. The IEEE also uses more meaningful shortcut names that identify the speed, in addition to a clue about whether the cabling is UTP (with a suffix that includes *T*) or fiber (with a suffix that includes *X*).

Table 2-2 lists a few Ethernet physical layer standards. First, the table lists enough names so that you get a sense of the IEEE naming conventions. It also lists the four most common standards that use UTP cabling, because this book's discussion of Ethernet focuses mainly on the UTP options.

Table 2-2   Examples of Types of Ethernet

Speed	Common Name	Informal IEEE Standard Name	Formal IEEE Standard Name	Cable Type, Maximum Length
10 Mbps	Ethernet	10BASE-T	802.3	Copper, 100 m
100 Mbps	Fast Ethernet	100BASE-T	802.3u	Copper, 100 m
1000 Mbps	Gigabit Ethernet	1000BASE-LX	802.3z	Fiber, 5000 m
1000 Mbps	Gigabit Ethernet	1000BASE-T	802.3ab	Copper, 100 m
10 Gbps	10 Gig Ethernet	10GBASE-T	802.3an	Copper, 100 m

NOTE   Fiber-optic cabling contains long, thin strands of fiberglass. The attached Ethernet nodes send light over the glass fiber in the cable, encoding the bits as changes in the light.

Consistent Behavior over All Links Using the Ethernet Data Link Layer

Although Ethernet includes many physical layer standards, Ethernet acts like a single LAN technology because it uses the same data link layer standard over all types of Ethernet physical links. That standard defines a common Ethernet header and trailer. (As a reminder, the header and trailer are bytes of overhead data that Ethernet uses to do its job of sending data over a LAN.) No matter whether the data flows over a UTP cable, or any kind of fiber cable, and no matter the speed, the data-link header and trailer use the same format.

Whereas the physical layer standards focus on sending bits over a cable, the Ethernet data-link protocols focus on sending an *Ethernet frame* from source to destination Ethernet node. From a data-link perspective, nodes build and forward frames. As first defined in Chapter 1, "The TCP/IP and OSI Networking Models," the term *frame* specifically refers to the header and trailer of a data-link protocol, plus the data encapsulated inside that header and trailer.

The various Ethernet nodes simply forward the frame, over all the required links, to deliver the frame to the correct destination.

Figure 2-5 shows an example of the process. In this case, PC1 sends an Ethernet frame to PC3. The frame travels over a UTP link to Ethernet switch SW1, then over fiber links to Ethernet switches SW2 and SW3, and finally over another UTP link to PC3. Note that the bits actually travel at four different speeds in this example: 10 Mbps, 1 Gbps, 10 Gbps, and 100 Mbps, respectively.

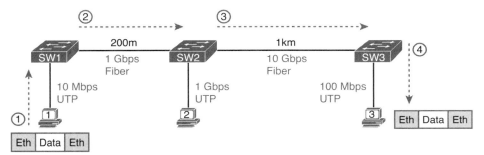

Figure 2-5 *Ethernet LAN Forwards a Data-Link Frame over Many Types of Links*

So, what is an Ethernet LAN? It is a combination of user devices, LAN switches, and different kinds of cabling. Each link can use different types of cables, at different speeds. However, they all work together to deliver Ethernet frames from the one device on the LAN to some other device.

The rest of this chapter takes these concepts a little deeper, first looking at the details of building the physical Ethernet network, followed by some discussion of the rules for forwarding an Ethernet frame from source to destination Ethernet node.

Building Physical Ethernet Networks with UTP

This second of three major sections of this chapter focuses on the individual physical links between any two Ethernet nodes. Before the Ethernet network as a whole can send Ethernet frames between user devices, each node must be ready and able to send data over an individual physical link. This section looks at some of the particulars of how Ethernet sends data over these links.

This section focuses on the three most commonly used Ethernet standards: 10BASE-T (Ethernet), 100BASE-T (Fast Ethernet, or FE), and 1000BASE-T (Gigabit Ethernet, or GE). Specifically, this section looks at the details of sending data in both directions over a UTP cable. It then examines the specific wiring of the UTP cables used for 10-Mbps, 100-Mbps, and 1000-Mbps Ethernet.

Transmitting Data Using Twisted Pairs

Although it is true that Ethernet sends data over UTP cables, the physical means to send the data uses electricity that flows over the wires inside the UTP cable. To better understand how Ethernet sends data using electricity, break the idea down into two parts: how to create an electrical circuit and then how to make that electrical signal communicate 1s and 0s.

First, to create one electrical circuit, Ethernet defines how to use the two wires inside a single twisted pair of wires, as shown Figure 2-6. The figure does not show a UTP cable between two nodes, but instead shows two individual wires that are inside the UTP cable. An electrical circuit requires a complete loop, so the two nodes, using circuitry on their Ethernet ports, connect the wires in one pair to complete a loop, allowing electricity to flow.

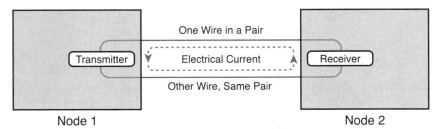

Figure 2-6 *Creating One Electrical Circuit over One Pair to Send in One Direction*

To send data, the two devices follow some rules called an *encoding scheme*. The idea works a lot like when two people talk, using the same language: The speaker says some words in a particular language, and the listener, because she speaks the same language, can understand the spoken words. With an encoding scheme, the transmitting node changes the electrical signal over time, while the other node, the receiver, using the same rules, interprets those changes as either 0s or 1s. (For example, 10BASE-T uses an encoding scheme that encodes a binary 0 as a transition from higher voltage to lower voltage during the middle of a 1/10,000,000th-of-a-second interval.)

Note that in an actual UTP cable, the wires will be twisted together and not parallel, as shown in Figure 2-6. The twisting helps solve some important physical transmission issues. When electrical current passes over any wire, it creates electromagnetic interference (EMI) that interferes with the electrical signals in nearby wires, including the wires in the same cable. (EMI between wire pairs in the same cable is called *crosstalk*.) Twisting the wire pairs together helps cancel out most of the EMI, so most networking physical links that use copper wires use twisted pairs.

Breaking Down a UTP Ethernet Link

The term *Ethernet link* refers to any physical cable between two Ethernet nodes. To learn about how a UTP Ethernet link works, it helps to break down the physical link into those basic pieces, as shown in Figure 2-7: the cable itself, the connectors on the ends of the cable, and the matching ports on the devices into which the connectors will be inserted.

First, think about the UTP cable itself. The cable holds some copper wires, grouped as twisted pairs. The 10BASE-T and 100BASE-T standards require two pairs of wires, and the 1000BASE-T standard requires four pairs. Each wire has a color-coded plastic coating, with the wires in a pair having a color scheme. For example, for the blue wire pair, one wire's coating is all blue; the other wire's coating is blue and white striped.

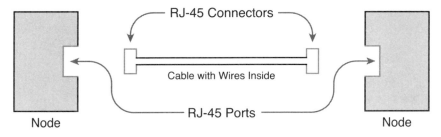

Figure 2-7   *Basic Components of an Ethernet Link*

Many Ethernet UTP cables use an RJ-45 connector on both ends. The RJ-45 connector has eight physical locations into which the eight wires in the cable can be inserted, called *pin positions*, or simply *pins*. These pins create a place where the ends of the copper wires can touch the electronics inside the nodes at the end of the physical link so that electricity can flow.

> **NOTE**   If available, find a nearby Ethernet UTP cable and examine the connectors closely. Look for the pin positions and the colors of the wires in the connector.

To complete the physical link, the nodes each need an RJ-45 *Ethernet port* that matches the RJ-45 connectors on the cable so that the connectors on the ends of the cable can connect to each node. PCs often include this RJ-45 Ethernet port as part of a network interface card (NIC), which can be an expansion card on the PC or can be built in to the system itself. Switches typically have many RJ-45 ports because switches give user devices a place to connect to the Ethernet LAN.

Figure 2-8 shows photos of the cables, connectors, and ports.

> **NOTE**   The RJ-45 connector is slightly wider than, but otherwise similar to, the RJ-11 connectors commonly used for telephone cables in homes in North America.

The figure shows a connector on the left and ports on the right. The left shows the eight pin positions in the end of the RJ-45 connector. The upper right shows an Ethernet NIC that is not yet installed in a computer. The lower-right part of the figure shows the side of a Cisco 2960 switch, with multiple RJ-45 ports, allowing multiple devices to easily connect to the Ethernet network.

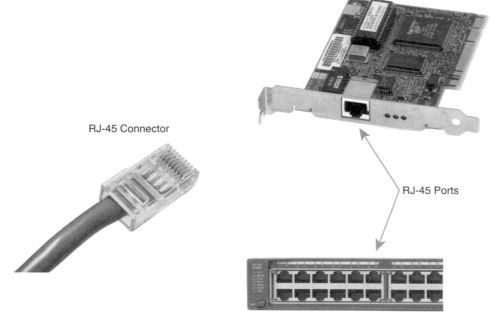

RJ-45 Connector

RJ-45 Ports

Figure 2-8   *RJ-45 Connectors and Ports (Ethernet NIC © Mark Jansen, LAN Cable © Mikko Pitkänen)*

Finally, while RJ-45 connectors with UTP cabling can be common, Cisco LAN switches often support other types of connectors as well. When you buy one of the many models of Cisco switches, you need to think about the mix and numbers of each type of physical ports you want on the switch.

To give its customers flexibility as to the type of Ethernet links, even after the customer has bought the switch, Cisco switches include some physical ports whose port hardware can be changed later, after you purchase the switch. One type of port is called a *gigabit interface converter* (GBIC), which happened to first arrive on the market around the same time as Gigabit Ethernet, so it was given the same "gigabit" name. More recently, improved and smaller types of removable interfaces, called *small form-factor pluggables* (SFP), provide the same function of enabling users to swap hardware and change the type of physical link. Figure 2-9 shows a photo of a Cisco switch with an SFP sitting slightly outside the SFP slot.

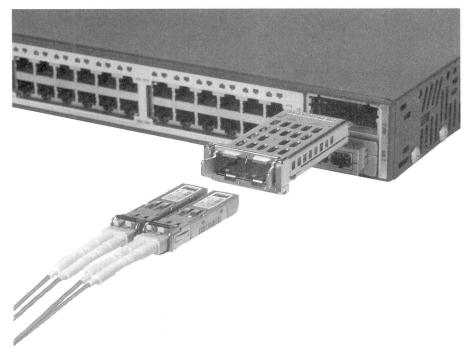

Figure 2-9   *Gigabit Fiber SFP Sitting Just Outside a Switch SFP Port*

UTP Cabling Pinouts for 10BASE-T and 100BASE-T

So far in this section, you have learned about the equivalent of how to drive a truck on a 1000-acre ranch, but you do not know the equivalent of the local traffic rules. If you worked the ranch, you could drive the truck all over the ranch, any place you wanted to go, and the police would not mind. However, as soon as you get on the public roads, the police want you to behave and follow the rules. Similarly, so far this chapter has discussed the general principles of how to send data, but it has not yet detailed some important rules for Ethernet cabling: the rules of the road so that all the devices send data using the right wires inside the cable.

This next topic discusses conventions for 10BASE-T and 100BASE-T together because they use UTP cabling in similar ways (including the use of only two wire pairs). A short comparison of the wiring for 1000BASE-T (Gigabit Ethernet), which uses four pairs, follows.

Straight-Through Cable Pinout

10BASE-T and 100BASE-T use two pair of wires in a UTP cable, one for each direction, as shown in Figure 2-10. The figure shows four wires, all of which sit inside a single UTP cable that connects a PC and a LAN switch. In this example, the PC on the left transmits using the top pair, and the switch on the right transmits using the bottom pair.

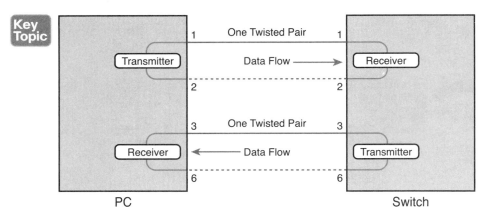

Figure 2-10 *Using One Pair for Each Transmission Direction with 10-Mbps and 100-Mbps Ethernet*

For correct transmission over the link, the wires in the UTP cable must be connected to the correct pin positions in the RJ-45 connectors. For example, in Figure 2-10, the transmitter on the PC on the left must know the pin positions of the two wires it should use to transmit. Those two wires must be connected to the correct pins in the RJ-45 connector on the switch so that the switch's receiver logic can use the correct wires.

To understand the wiring of the cable—which wires need to be in which pin positions on both ends of the cable—you need to first understand how the NICs and switches work. As a rule, Ethernet NIC transmitters use the pair connected to pins 1 and 2; the NIC receivers use a pair of wires at pin positions 3 and 6. LAN switches, knowing those facts about what Ethernet NICs do, do the opposite: Their receivers use the wire pair at pins 1 and 2, and their transmitters use the wire pair at pins 3 and 6.

To allow a PC NIC to communicate with a switch, the UTP cable must also use a *straight-through cable pinout*. The term *pinout* refers to the wiring of which color wire is placed in each of the eight numbered pin positions in the RJ-45 connector. An Ethernet straight-through cable connects the wire at pin 1 on one end of the cable to pin 1 at the other end of the cable; the wire at pin 2 needs to connect to pin 2 on the other end of the cable; pin 3 on one end connects to pin 3 on the other, and so on, as shown in Figure 2-11. Also, it uses the wires in one wire pair at pins 1 and 2, and another pair at pins 3 and 6.

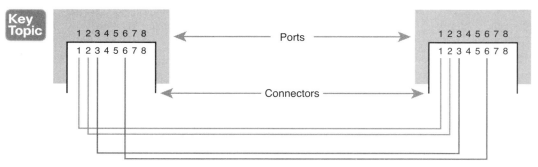

Figure 2-11 *10BASE-T and 100BASE-T Straight-Through Cable Pinout*

Figure 2-12 shows one final perspective on the straight-through cable pinout. In this case, PC Larry connects to a LAN switch. Note that the figure again does not show the UTP cable, but instead shows the wires that sit inside the cable, to emphasize the idea of wire pairs and pins.

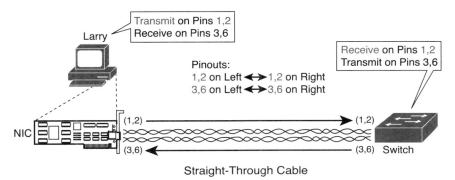

Figure 2-12   *Ethernet Straight-Through Cable Concept*

Crossover Cable Pinout

A straight-through cable works correctly when the nodes use opposite pairs for transmitting data. However, when two like devices connect to an Ethernet link, they both transmit over the same pins. In that case, you then need another type of cabling pinout called a *crossover cable*. The crossover cable pinout crosses the pair at the transmit pins on each device to the receive pins on the opposite device.

That previous sentence is true, but this concept is much clearer with a figure such as Figure 2-13. The figure shows what happens on a link between two switches. The two switches both transmit on the pair at pins 3 and 6, and they both receive on the pair at pins 1 and 2. So, the cable must connect a pair at pins 3 and 6 on each side to pins 1 and 2 on the other side, connecting to the other node's receiver logic. The top of the figure shows the literal pinouts, and the bottom half shows a conceptual diagram.

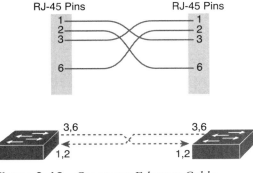

Figure 2-13   *Crossover Ethernet Cable*

Choosing the Right Cable Pinouts

For the exam, be well prepared to choose which type of cable (straight-through or crossover) is needed in each part of the network. The key is to know whether a device acts like a PC NIC, transmitting at pins 1 and 2, or like a switch, transmitting at pins 3 and 6. Then, just apply the following logic:

Crossover cable: If the endpoints transmit on the same pin pair

Straight-through cable: If the endpoints transmit on different pin pairs

Table 2-3 lists the devices mentioned in this book and the pin pairs they use, assuming that they use 10BASE-T and 100BASE-T.

Table 2-3 10BASE-T and 100BASE-T Pin Pairs Used

Transmits on Pins 1,2	Transmits on Pins 3,6
PC NICs	Hubs
Routers	Switches
Wireless AP (Ethernet interface)	—

For example, Figure 2-14 shows a campus LAN in a single building. In this case, several straight-through cables are used to connect PCs to switches. In addition, the cables connecting the switches require crossover cables.

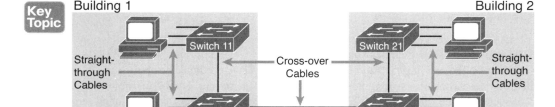

Figure 2-14 *Typical Uses for Straight-Through and Crossover Ethernet Cables*

NOTE If you have some experience with installing LANs, you might be thinking that you have used the wrong cable before (straight-through or crossover), but the cable worked. Cisco switches have a feature called *auto-mdix* that notices when the wrong cable is used and automatically changes its logic to make the link work. However, for the exams, be ready to identify whether the correct cable is shown in the figures.

UTP Cabling Pinouts for 1000BASE-T

1000BASE-T (Gigabit Ethernet) differs from 10BASE-T and 100BASE-T as far as the cabling and pinouts. First, 1000BASE-T requires four wire pairs. Second, it uses more advanced electronics that allow both ends to transmit and receive simultaneously on each wire pair. However, the wiring pinouts for 1000BASE-T work almost identically to the earlier standards, adding details for the additional two pairs.

The straight-through cable connects each pin with the same numbered pin on the other side, but it does so for all eight pins—pin 1 to pin 1, pin 2 to pin 2, up through pin 8. It keeps one pair at pins 1 and 2 and another at pins 3 and 6, just like in the earlier wiring. It adds a pair at pins 4 and 5 and the final pair at pins 7 and 8 (refer to Figure 2-13).

The Gigabit Ethernet crossover cable crosses the same two-wire pairs as the crossover cable for the other types of Ethernet (the pairs at pins 1,2 and 3,6). It also crosses the two new pairs as well (the pair at pins 4,5 with the pair at pins 7,8).

Sending Data in Ethernet Networks

Although physical layer standards vary quite a bit, other parts of the Ethernet standards work the same way, regardless of the type of physical Ethernet link. Next, this final major section of this chapter looks at several protocols and rules that Ethernet uses regardless of the type of link. In particular, this section examines the details of the Ethernet data link layer protocol, plus how Ethernet nodes, switches, and hubs forward Ethernet frames through an Ethernet LAN.

Ethernet Data-Link Protocols

One of the most significant strengths of the Ethernet family of protocols is that these protocols use the same data-link standard. In fact, the core parts of the data-link standard date back to the original Ethernet standards.

The Ethernet data-link protocol defines the Ethernet frame: an Ethernet header at the front, the encapsulated data in the middle, and an Ethernet trailer at the end. Ethernet actually defines a few alternate formats for the header, with the frame format shown in Figure 2-15 being commonly used today.

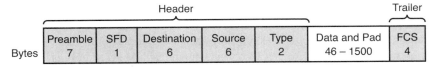

Figure 2-15 *Commonly Used Ethernet Frame Format*

All the fields in the frame matter, but some matter more to the topics discussed in this book. Table 2-4 lists the fields in the header and trailer, and provides a brief description for reference, with the upcoming pages including more detail about a few of these fields.

Table 2-4 IEEE 802.3 Ethernet Header and Trailer Fields

Field	Field Length in Bytes	Description
Preamble	7	Synchronization
Start Frame Delimiter (SFD)	1	Signifies that the next byte begins the Destination MAC Address field
Destination MAC Address	6	Identifies the intended recipient of this frame
Source MAC Address	6	Identifies the sender of this frame
Type	2	Defines the type of protocol listed inside the frame; today, most likely identifies IP version 4 (IPv4) or IP version 6 (IPv6)
Data and Pad*	46–1500	Holds data from a higher layer, typically an L3PDU (usually an IPv4 or IPv6 packet). The sender adds padding to meet the minimum length requirement for this field (46 bytes).
Frame Check Sequence (FCS)	4	Provides a method for the receiving NIC to determine whether the frame experienced transmission errors

* The IEEE 802.3 specification limits the data portion of the 802.3 frame to a minimum of 46 and a maximum of 1500 bytes. The term *maximum transmission unit* (MTU) defines the maximum Layer 3 packet that can be sent over a medium. Because the Layer 3 packet rests inside the data portion of an Ethernet frame, 1500 bytes is the largest IP MTU allowed over an Ethernet.

Ethernet Addressing

The source and destination Ethernet address fields play a big role in much of the Ethernet logic included in the CCENT and CCNA certifications. The general idea for each is relatively simple: The sending node puts its own address in the source address field and the intended Ethernet destination device's address in the destination address field. The sender transmits the frame, expecting that the Ethernet LAN, as a whole, will deliver the frame to that correct destination.

Ethernet addresses, also called *Media Access Control (MAC)* addresses, are 6-byte-long (48-bit-long) binary numbers. For convenience, most computers list MAC addresses as 12-digit hexadecimal numbers. Cisco devices typically add some periods to the number for easier readability as well; for example, a Cisco switch might list a MAC address as 0000.0C12.3456.

Most MAC addresses represent a single NIC or other Ethernet port, so these addresses are often called a *unicast* Ethernet address. The term *unicast* is simply a formal way to refer to the fact that the address represents one interface to the Ethernet LAN. (This term also contrasts with two other types of Ethernet addresses, *broadcast* and *multicast*, which are defined later in this section.)

The entire idea of sending data to a destination unicast MAC address works well, but it works only if all the unicast MAC addresses are unique. If two NICs try to use the same MAC address, there could be confusion. (The problem is like the confusion caused to the postal service if you and I both try to use the same mailing address. Would the postal service deliver mail to your house or to mine?) If two PCs on the same Ethernet try to use the same MAC address, to which PC should frames sent to that MAC address be delivered?

Ethernet solves this problem using an administrative process so that, at the time of manufacture, all Ethernet devices are assigned a universally unique MAC address. Before a manufacturer can build Ethernet products, it must ask the IEEE to assign the manufacturer a universally unique 3-byte code, called the *organizationally unique identifier* (OUI). The manufacturer agrees to give all NICs (and other Ethernet products) a MAC address that begins with its assigned 3-byte OUI. The manufacturer also assigns a unique value for the last 3 bytes, a number that manufacturer has never used with that OUI. As a result, the MAC address of every device in the universe is unique.

> **NOTE**   The IEEE also calls these universal MAC addresses global MAC addresses.

Figure 2-16 shows the structure of the unicast MAC address, with the OUI.

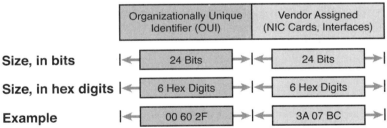

Figure 2-16   *Structure of Unicast Ethernet Addresses*

Ethernet addresses go by many names: LAN address, Ethernet address, hardware address, burned-in address, physical address, universal address, or MAC address. For example, the term *burned-in address* (BIA) refers to the idea that a permanent MAC address has been encoded (burned into) the ROM chip on the NIC. As another example, the IEEE uses the term *universal address* to emphasize the fact that the address assigned to a NIC by a manufacturer should be unique among all MAC addresses in the universe.

In addition to unicast addresses, Ethernet also uses group addresses. *Group addresses* identify more than one LAN interface card. A frame sent to a group address might be delivered to a small set of devices on the LAN, or even to all devices on the LAN. In fact, the IEEE defines two general categories of group addresses for Ethernet:

Broadcast address: Frames sent to this address should be delivered to all devices on the Ethernet LAN. It has a value of FFFF.FFFF.FFFF.

Multicast addresses: Frames sent to a multicast Ethernet address will be copied and forwarded to a subset of the devices on the LAN that volunteers to receive frames sent to a specific multicast address.

Table 2-5 summarizes most of the details about MAC addresses.

Table 2-5   LAN MAC Address Terminology and Features

LAN Addressing Term or Feature	Description
MAC	Media Access Control. 802.3 (Ethernet) defines the MAC sublayer of IEEE Ethernet.
Ethernet address, NIC address, LAN address	Other names often used instead of MAC address. These terms describe the 6-byte address of the LAN interface card.
Burned-in address	The 6-byte address assigned by the vendor making the card.
Unicast address	A term for a MAC address that represents a single LAN interface.
Broadcast address	An address that means "all devices that reside on this LAN right now."
Multicast address	On Ethernet, a multicast address implies some subset of all devices currently on the Ethernet LAN.

Identifying Network Layer Protocols with the Ethernet Type Field

While the Ethernet header's address fields play an important and more obvious role in Ethernet LANs, the Ethernet Type field plays a much less obvious role. The Ethernet Type field, or EtherType, sits in the Ethernet data link layer header, but its purpose is to directly help the network processing on routers and hosts. Basically, the Type field identifies the type of network layer (Layer 3) packet that sits inside the Ethernet frame.

First, think about what sits inside the data part of the Ethernet frame shown earlier in Figure 2-15. Typically, it holds the network layer packet created by the network layer protocol on some device in the network. Over the years, those protocols have included IBM Systems Network Architecture (SNA), Novell NetWare, Digital Equipment Corporation's DECnet, and Apple Computer's AppleTalk. Today, the most common network layer protocols are both from TCP/IP: IP version 4 (IPv4) and IP version 6 (IPv6).

The original host has a place to insert a value (a hexadecimal number) to identify the type of packet encapsulated inside the Ethernet frame. However, what number should the sender put in the header to identify an IPv4 packet as the type? Or an IPv6 packet? As it turns out, the IEEE manages a list of EtherType values, so that every network layer protocol that needs a unique EtherType value can have a number. The sender just has to know the list. (Anyone can view the list; just go to www.ieee.org and search for *EtherType*.)

For example, a host can send one Ethernet frame with an IPv4 packet and the next Ethernet frame with an IPv6 packet. Each frame would have a different Ethernet Type field value, using the values reserved by the IEEE, as shown in Figure 2-17.

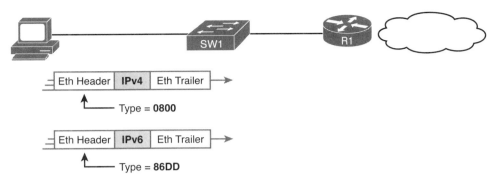

Figure 2-17   *Use of Ethernet Type Field*

Error Detection with FCS

Ethernet also defines a way for nodes to find out whether a frame's bits changed while cross-ing over an Ethernet link. (Usually, the bits could change because of some kind of electrical interference or a bad NIC.) Ethernet, like most every other data-link protocol covered on the CCNA exams, uses a field in the data-link trailer for the purpose of error detection.

The Ethernet Frame Check Sequence (FCS) field in the Ethernet trailer—the only field in the Ethernet trailer—gives the receiving node a way to compare results with the sender, to discover whether errors occurred in the frame. The sender applies a complex math formula to the frame before sending it, storing the result of the formula in the FCS field. The receiver applies the same math formula to the received frame. The receiver then compares its own results with the sender's results. If the results are the same, the frame did not change; other-wise, an error occurred, and the receiver discards the frame.

Note that *error detection* does not also mean *error recovery*. Ethernet does error detection so that if a frame's content has changed, the Ethernet device can simply discard the frame. Ethernet does not attempt to recover the lost frame. Other protocols, notably TCP, recover the lost data by noticing that it is lost and sending the data again.

Sending Ethernet Frames with Switches and Hubs

Ethernet LANs behave slightly differently depending on whether the LAN has mostly mod-ern devices (in particular, LAN switches instead of some older LAN devices called *LAN hubs*). Basically, the use of more modern switches allows the use of full-duplex logic, which is much faster and simpler than half-duplex logic, which is required when using hubs. The final topic in this chapter looks at these basic differences.

Sending in Modern Ethernet LANs Using Full-Duplex

Modern Ethernet LANs use a variety of Ethernet physical standards, but with standard Ethernet frames that can flow over any of these types of physical links. Each individual link can run at a different speed, but each link allows the attached nodes to send the bits in the frame to the next node. They must work together to deliver the data from the sending Ethernet node to the destination node.

The process is relatively simple, on purpose; the simplicity lets each device send a large number of frames per second. Figure 2-18 shows an example in which PC1 sends an Ethernet frame to PC2.

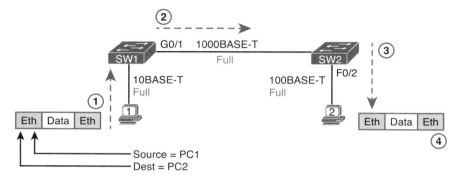

Figure 2-18   *Example of Sending Data in a Modern Ethernet LAN*

Following the steps in the figure:

1. PC1 builds and sends the original Ethernet frame, using its own MAC address as the source address and PC2's MAC address as the destination address.

2. Switch SW1 receives and forwards the Ethernet frame out its G0/1 interface (short for Gigabit interface 0/1) to SW2.

3. Switch SW2 receives and forwards the Ethernet frame out its F0/2 interface (short for Fast Ethernet interface 0/2) to PC2.

4. PC2 receives the frame, recognizes the destination MAC address as its own, and processes the frame.

The Ethernet network in Figure 2-18 uses full-duplex on each link, but the concept might be difficult to see. Full-duplex means that the NIC or switch port has no half-duplex restrictions. So, to understand full-duplex, you need to understand half-duplex, as follows:

Half-duplex: Logic in which a port sends data only when it is not also receiving data; in other words, it cannot send and receive at the same time.

Full-duplex: The absence of the half-duplex restriction.

So, with all PCs and LAN switches, and no LAN hubs, all the nodes can use full-duplex. All nodes can send and receive on their port at the same instant in time. For example, in Figure 2-18, PC1 and PC2 could send frames to each other simultaneously, in both directions, without any half-duplex restrictions.

Using Half-Duplex with LAN Hubs

To understand the need for half-duplex logic in some cases, you have to understand a little about an older type of networking device called a LAN hub. When the IEEE first introduced 10BASE-T in 1990, the Ethernet did not yet include LAN switches. Instead of switches, vendors created LAN hubs. The LAN hub provided a number of RJ-45 ports as a place to connect links to PCs, just like a LAN switch, but it used different rules for forwarding data.

LAN hubs forward data using physical layer standards, and are therefore considered to be Layer 1 devices. When an electrical signal comes in one hub port, the hub repeats that electrical signal out all other ports (except the incoming port). By doing so, the data reaches all the rest of the nodes connected to the hub, so the data hopefully reaches the correct destination. The hub has no concept of Ethernet frames, of addresses, and so on.

The downside of using LAN hubs is that if two or more devices transmitted a signal at the same instant, the electrical signal collides and becomes garbled. The hub repeats all received electrical signals, even if it receives multiple signals at the same time. For example, Figure 2-19 shows the idea, with PCs Archie and Bob sending an electrical signal at the same instant of time (at Steps 1A and 1B) and the hub repeating both electrical signals out toward Larry on the left (Step 2).

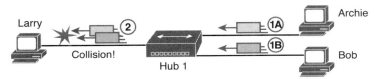

Figure 2-19 *Collision Occurring Because of LAN Hub Behavior*

NOTE For completeness, note that the hub floods each frame out all other ports (except the incoming port). So, Archie's frame goes to both Larry and Bob; Bob's frame goes to Larry and Archie.

If you replace the hub in Figure 2-19 with a LAN switch, the switch prevents the collision on the left. The switch operates as a Layer 2 device, meaning that it looks at the data-link header and trailer. A switch would look at the MAC addresses, and even if the switch needed to forward both frames to Larry on the left, the switch would send one frame and queue the other frame until the first frame was finished.

Now back to the issue created by the hub's logic: collisions. To prevent these collisions, the Ethernet nodes must use half-duplex logic instead of full-duplex logic. A problem only occurs when two or more devices send at the same time; half-duplex logic tells the nodes that if someone else is sending, wait before sending.

For example, back in Figure 2-19, imagine that Archie began sending his frame early enough so that Bob received the first bits of that frame before Bob tried to send his own frame. Bob, at Step 1B, would notice that he was receiving a frame from someone else, and using half-duplex logic, would simply wait to send the frame listed at Step 1B.

Nodes that use half-duplex logic actually use a relatively well-known algorithm called *carrier sense multiple access with collision detection* (CSMA/CD). The algorithm takes care of the obvious cases but also the cases caused by unfortunate timing. For example, two nodes could check for an incoming frame at the exact same instant, both realize that no other node is sending, and both send their frames at the exact same instant, causing a collision. CSMA/CD covers these cases as well, as follows:

Step 1.   A device with a frame to send listens until the Ethernet is not busy.

Step 2.   When the Ethernet is not busy, the sender begins sending the frame.

Step 3.   The sender listens while sending to discover whether a collision occurs; collisions might be caused by many reasons, including unfortunate timing. If a collision occurs, all currently sending nodes do the following:

   A. They send a jamming signal that tells all nodes that a collision happened.

   B. They independently choose a random time to wait before trying again, to avoid unfortunate timing.

   C. The next attempt starts again at Step 1.

Although most modern LANs do not often use hubs, and therefore do not need to use half-duplex, enough old hubs still exist in enterprise networks so that you need to be ready to understand duplex issues. Each NIC and switch port has a duplex setting. For all links between PCs and switches, or between switches, use full-duplex. However, for any link connected to a LAN hub, the connected LAN switch and NIC port should use half-duplex. Note that the hub itself does not use half-duplex logic, instead just repeating incoming signals out every other port.

Figure 2-20 shows an example, with full-duplex links on the left and a single LAN hub on the right. The hub then requires SW2's F0/2 interface to use half-duplex logic, along with the PCs connected to the hub.

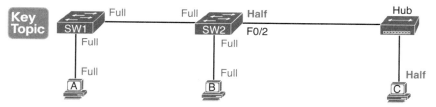

Figure 2-20   *Full- and Half-Duplex in an Ethernet LAN*

Exam Preparation Tasks

Review All the Key Topics

Review the most important topics from this chapter, noted with the Key Topic icon. Table 2-6 lists these key topics and where each is discussed.

Table 2-6 Key Topics for Chapter 2

Key Topic Element	Description	Page Number
Figure 2-3	Drawing of a typical wired and wireless enterprise LAN	44
Figure 2-4	Drawing of a typical data center LAN	45
Table 2-2	Several types of Ethernet LANs and some details about each	46
Figure 2-10	Conceptual drawing of transmitting in one direction each over two different electrical circuits between two Ethernet nodes	52
Figure 2-11	10- and 100-Mbps Ethernet straight-through cable pinouts	52
Figure 2-13	10- and 100-Mbps Ethernet crossover cable pinouts	53
Table 2-3	List of devices that transmit on wire pair 1,2 and pair 3,6	54
Figure 2-14	Typical uses for straight-through and crossover Ethernet cables	54
Figure 2-16	Format of Ethernet MAC addresses	57
List	Definitions of half-duplex and full-duplex	60
Figure 2-20	Examples of which interfaces use full-duplex and which interfaces use half-duplex	62

Complete the Tables and Lists from Memory

Print a copy of DVD Appendix I, "Memory Tables," or at least the section for this chapter, and complete the tables and lists from memory. DVD Appendix J, "Memory Tables Answer Key," includes completed tables and lists for you to check your work.

Definitions of Key Terms

After your first reading of the chapter, try to define these key terms, but do not be concerned about getting them all correct at that time. Chapter 23, "Final Review," directs you in how to use these terms for late-stage preparation for the exam.

Ethernet, IEEE, wired LAN, Ethernet frame, 10BASE-T, 100BASE-T, 1000BASE-T, Fast Ethernet, Gigabit Ethernet, Ethernet link, RJ-45, Ethernet port, network interface card (NIC), straight-through cable, crossover cable, Ethernet address, MAC address, unicast address, broadcast address, Frame Check Sequence

This chapter covers the following exam topics:

1.1 Describe the purpose and functions of various network devices

1.1.a Interpret a network diagram

CHAPTER 3

Fundamentals of WANs

Cisco begins its Data Center certification track with the DCICN exam. This exam focuses on the data center to some extent, but it also provides a broad view of networking technologies. This chapter introduces a function in networking that typically sits outside the data center, connecting multiple sites together: the Wide Area Network (WAN).

Most Layer 1 and 2 networking technology falls into one of two primary categories: WANs and LANs. Because both WANs and LANs match OSI Layers 1 and 2, they have many similarities: Both define cabling details, transmission speeds, encoding, and how to send data over physical links, as well as data link frames and forwarding logic.

Of course, WANs and LANs have many differences as well, most notably the distances between nodes and the business model for paying for the network. First, in terms of the distance, the terms *local* and *wide* give us a small hint: LANs typically include nearby devices, while WANs connect devices that can be far apart, potentially hundreds or thousands of miles apart.

The other big difference between the two is this: You own LANs, but you lease WANs. With LANs, you buy the cables and LAN switches and install them in spaces you control. WANs physically pass through other people's property, and you do not have the right to put your cables and devices there. So, a few companies, like a telephone company or cable company, install and own their own devices and cables, creating their own networks, and lease the right to send data over their networks.

This chapter introduces WANs in three major sections. The first introduces leased line WANs, a type of WAN link that has been part of enterprise networks since the 1960s. The second part shows how Ethernet can be used to create WAN services by taking advantage of the longer cable length possibilities of modern fiber-optic Ethernet standards. The last part of the chapter takes a survey of common WAN technology used to access the Internet.

NOTE As promised in the Introduction's section, "For Those Studying Routing & Switching": This chapter's content mirrors the content in the *ICND1 100-101 Official Cert Guide*'s Chapter 3, with no additional information hidden here.

"Do I Know This Already?" Quiz

Use the "Do I Know This Already?" quiz to help decide whether you might want to skim this chapter, or a major section, moving more quickly to the "Exam Preparation Tasks" section near the end of the chapter. You can find the answers at the bottom of the page following the quiz. For thorough explanations, see Appendix A, "Answers to the 'Do I Know This Already?' Quizzes."

Table 3-1   "Do I Know This Already?" Foundation Topics Section-to-Question Mapping

Foundation Topics Section	Questions
Leased Line WANs	1–4
Ethernet as a WAN Technology	5
Accessing the Internet	6, 7

1. Which of the following best describes the main function of OSI Layer 1 as used in WANs?

   a. Framing

   b. Delivery of bits from one device to another

   c. Addressing

   d. Error detection

2. In the cabling for a leased line, which of the following typically connects to a four-wire line provided by a telco?

   a. Router serial interface without internal CSU/DSU

   b. CSU/DSU

   c. Router serial interface with internal transceiver

   d. Switch serial interface

3. Which of the following is an accurate speed at which a leased line can operate in the United States?

   a. 100 Mbps

   b. 100 Kbps

   c. 256 Kbps

   d. 6.4 Mbps

4. Which of the following fields in the HDLC header used by Cisco routers does Cisco add, beyond the ISO standard HDLC?

   a. Flag

   b. Type

   c. Address

   d. FCS

5. Two routers, R1 and R2, connect using an Ethernet over MPLS service. The service provides point-to-point service between these two routers only, as a Layer 2 Ethernet service. Which of the following are the most likely to be true about this WAN? (Choose two answers.)

   a. R1 will connect to a physical Ethernet link, with the other end of the cable connected to R2.

   b. R1 will connect to a physical Ethernet link, with the other end of the cable connected to a device at the WAN service provider point of presence.

   c. R1 will forward data link frames to R2 using an HDLC header/trailer.

   d. R1 will forward data link frames to R2 using an Ethernet header/trailer.

6. Which of the following Internet access technologies, used to connect a site to an ISP, offers asymmetric speeds? (Choose two answers.)

   a. Leased lines

   b. DSL

   c. Cable Internet

   d. BGP

7. Fred has just added DSL service at his home, with a separate DSL modem and consumer-grade router with four Ethernet ports. Fred wants to use the same old phone he was using before the installation of DSL. Which is most likely true about the phone cabling and phone used with his new DSL installation?

   a. He uses the old phone, cabled to one of the router/switch device's Ethernet ports.

   b. He uses the old phone, cabled to the DSL modem's ports.

   c. He uses the old phone, cabled to an existing telephone port, and not to any new device.

   d. The old phone must be replaced with a digital phone.

Foundation Topics

Leased Line WANs

Imagine that you are the primary network engineer for an enterprise TCP/IP internetwork. Your company is building a new building at a site 100 miles away from your corporate headquarters. You will of course install a LAN throughout the new building, but you also need to connect that new remote LAN to the rest of the existing enterprise TCP/IP network.

To connect the new building's LAN to the rest of the existing corporate network, you need some kind of a WAN. At a minimum, that WAN needs to be able to send data from the remote LAN back to the rest of the existing network and vice versa. Leased line WANs do exactly that, forwarding data between two routers.

From a basic point of view, a leased line WAN works a lot like an Ethernet crossover cable connecting two routers, but with few distance limitations. Each router can send at any time (full-duplex) over the leased line, for tens, hundreds, or even thousands of miles.

This section begins by giving some perspective about where leased lines fit with LANs and routers, because one main goal for a WAN is to move data between LANs. The rest of this first section explains the physical details about leased lines, followed with information about data link protocols.

Positioning Leased Lines with LANs and Routers

The vast majority of end-user devices in an enterprise or SOHO network connect directly into a LAN. Many PCs use an Ethernet NIC that connects to a switch. More and more, devices use 802.11 wireless LANs, with some devices like phones and tablets supporting only wireless LAN connections.

Now think about a typical company that has many different locations. From a human resources perspective, it might have lots of employees that work at many locations. From a facilities perspective, the company might have a few large sites, with hundreds or even thousands of individual branch offices, stores, or other small locations. However, from a networking perspective, think of each site as being one or more LANs that need to communicate with each other, and to communicate, those LANs need to be connected to each other using a WAN.

To connect LANs together using a WAN, the internetwork uses a router connected to each LAN, with a WAN link between the routers. First, the enterprise's network engineer would order some kind of WAN link. A router at each site connects to both the WAN link and the LAN, as shown in Figure 3-1. Note that a crooked line between the routers is the common way to represent a leased line when the drawing does not need to show any of the physical details of the line.

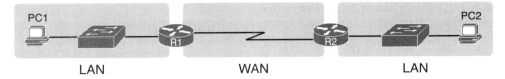

Figure 3-1   *Small Enterprise Network with One Leased Line*

The world of WAN technologies includes many different options in addition to the leased line shown in the figure. WAN technology includes a large number of options for physical links, as well as the data link protocols that control those links. By comparison, the wired LAN world basically has one major option today—Ethernet—because Ethernet won the wired LAN battle in the marketplace back in the 1980s and 1990s.

Physical Details of Leased Lines

The leased line service delivers bits in both directions, at a predetermined speed, using full-duplex logic. In fact, conceptually it acts as if you had a full-duplex crossover Ethernet link between two routers, as shown in Figure 3-2. The leased line uses two pairs of wires, one pair for each direction of sending data, which allows full-duplex operation.

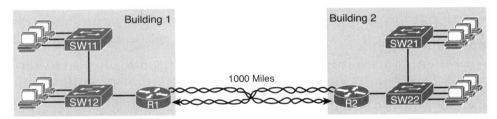

Figure 3-2   *Conceptual View of the Leased Line Service*

Of course, leased lines have many differences compared to an Ethernet crossover cable. To create such possibly long links, or circuits, a leased line does not actually exist as a single long cable between the two sites. Instead, the telco installs a large network of cables and specialized switching devices to create its own computer network. The telco network creates a service that acts like a crossover cable between two points, but the physical reality is hidden from the customer.

Leased lines come with their own set of terminology as well. First, the term *leased line* refers to the fact that the company using the leased line does not own the line, but instead pays a monthly lease fee to use it. However, many people today use the generic term *service provider* to refer to a company that provides any form of WAN connectivity, including Internet services.

Given their long history, leased lines have had many names. Table 3-2 lists some of those names, mainly so that in a networking job, you have a chance to translate from the terms each person uses with a basic description as to the meaning of the name.

Table 3-2 Different Names for a Leased Line

Name	Meaning or Reference
Leased circuit, Circuit	The words *line* and *circuit* are often used as synonyms in telco terminology; *circuit* makes reference to the electrical circuit between the two endpoints.
Serial link, Serial line	The words *link* and *line* are also often used as synonyms. *Serial* in this case refers to the fact that the bits flow serially, and that routers use serial interfaces.
Point-to-point link, Point-to-point line	Refers to the fact that the topology stretches between two points, and two points only. (Some older leased lines allowed more than two devices.)
T1	A specific type of leased line that transmits data at 1.544 megabits per second (1.544 Mbps).
WAN link, Link	Both these terms are very general, with no reference to any specific technology.
Private line	Refers to the fact that the data sent over the line cannot be copied by other telco customers, so the data is private.

Leased Line Cabling

To create a leased line, some physical path must exist between the two routers on the ends of the link. The physical cabling must leave the buildings where each router sits. However, the telco does not simply install one cable between the two buildings. Instead, it uses what is typically a large and complex network that creates the appearance of a cable between the two routers.

Figure 3-3 gives a little insight into the cabling that could exist inside the telco for a short leased line. Telcos put their equipment in buildings called central offices (CO). The telco installs cables from the CO to most every other building in the city, expecting to sell services to the people in those buildings one day. The telco would then configure its switches to use some of the capacity on each cable to send data in both directions, creating the equivalent of a crossover cable between the two routers.

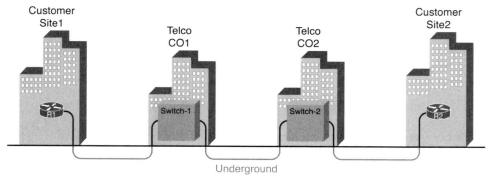

Figure 3-3 *Possible Cabling Inside a Telco for a Short Leased Line*

Although what happens inside the telco is completely hidden from the telco customer, enterprise engineers do need to know about the parts of the link that exist inside the customer's building at the router.

First, each site has *customer premises equipment (CPE)*, which includes the router, serial interface card, and CSU/DSU. Each router uses a serial interface card that acts somewhat like an Ethernet NIC, sending and receiving data over the physical link. The physical link requires a function called a channel service unit/data service unit (CSU/DSU). The CSU/DSU can either be integrated into the serial interface card in the router or sit outside the router as an external device. Figure 3-4 shows the CPE devices, along with the cabling.

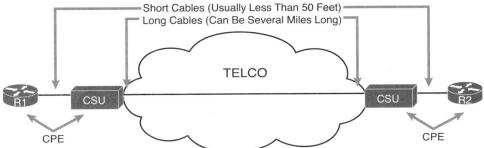

Figure 3-4 *Point-to-Point Leased Line: Components and Terminology*

The cabling includes a short serial cable (only if an external CSU/DSU is used) plus the cable installed by the telco for the leased line itself. The serial cable connects the router serial interface to the external CSU/DSU. (Many cable options exist; the cable just needs to match the connector of the serial interface on one end and the CSU/DSU on the other end.) The four-wire cable from the telco plugs into the CSU/DSU, typically using an RJ-48 connector that has the same size and shape as an RJ-45 connector (as seen in Chapter 2's Figure 2-8).

Telcos offer a wide variety of speeds for leased lines. However, you cannot pick the exact speed you want; instead, you must pick from a long list of predefined speeds. Slower-speed links run at multiples of 64 kbps (kilobits per second), while faster links run at multiples of about 1.5 Mbps (megabits per second).

Building a WAN Link in a Lab

As a brief aside, if you do study routing as an end to itself while also studying for the DCICN exam, you can choose to buy some (relatively cheap) used router hardware for hands-on practice. If you do, you can create the equivalent of a leased line without a real leased line from a telco, and without CSU/DSUs, just using a cabling trick. This short topic tells you enough information to create a WAN link in your home lab.

First, the serial cables normally used between a router and an external CSU/DSU are called *data terminal equipment (DTE) cables*. To create a physical WAN link in a lab, you need two serial cables: one serial DTE cable, plus a similar but slightly different matching *data communications equipment (DCE) cable*. The DCE cable has a female connector, while the DTE cable has a male connector, which allows the two cables to be attached directly. The DCE cable also does the equivalent task of an Ethernet crossover cable by swapping the transmit and receive wire pairs, as shown in Figure 3-5.

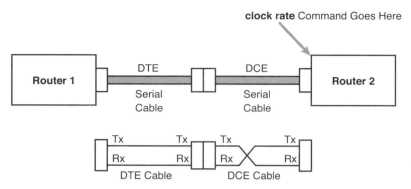

Figure 3-5   *Serial Cabling Uses a DTE Cable and a DCE Cable*

The figure shows the cable details at the top, with the wiring details inside the cable at the bottom. In particular, at the bottom of the figure, note that the DTE serial cable acts as a straight-through cable, and does not swap the transmit and receive pair, while the DCE cable does swap the pairs.

Finally, to make the link work, the router with the DCE cable installed must do one function normally done by the CSU/DSU. The CSU/DSU normally provides a function called *clocking*, in which it tells the router exactly when to send each bit through signaling over the serial cable. A router serial interface can provide clocking, but the router does not do so unless configured with the **clock rate** command.

Data Link Details of Leased Lines

A leased line provides a Layer 1 service. In other words, it promises to deliver bits between the devices connected to the leased line. However, the leased line itself does not define a data link layer protocol to be used on the leased line.

Because leased lines define only the Layer 1 transmission service, many companies and standards organizations have created data link protocols to control and use leased lines. Today, the two most popular data link layer protocols used for leased lines between two routers are High-Level Data Link Control (HDLC) and Point-to-Point Protocol (PPP). This next topic takes a brief look at HDLC, just to show one example, plus a few comments about how routers use WAN data link protocols.

HDLC Basics

All data link protocols perform a similar role: to control the correct delivery of data over a physical link of a particular type. For example, the Ethernet data link protocol uses a destination address field to identify the correct device that should receive the data, and an FCS field that allows the receiving device to determine whether the data arrived correctly. HDLC provides similar functions.

HDLC has less work to do because of the simple point-to-point topology of a point-to-point leased line. When one router sends an HDLC frame, it can only go one place: to the other end of the link. So, while HDLC has an address field, the destination is implied. The idea is sort of like when I have lunch with my friend Gary, and only Gary. I do not need to start every sentence with "Hey Gary"—he knows I am talking to him.

> **NOTE**   In case you wonder why HDLC has an address field at all, in years past, the telcos offered multidrop circuits. These circuits included more than two devices, so there was more than one possible destination, requiring an address field to identify the correct destination.

HDLC has other fields and functions similar to Ethernet as well. Table 3-3 lists the HDLC fields, with the similar Ethernet header/trailer field, just for the sake of learning HDLC based on something you have already learned about (Ethernet).

Table 3-3   Comparing HDLC Header Fields to Ethernet

HDLC Header or Trailer Field	Ethernet Equivalent	Description
Flag	Preamble	Lists a recognizable bit pattern so that the receiving nodes realize that a new frame is arriving
Address	Destination Address	Identifies the destination device
Control	Type	Identifies the type of Layer 3 packet encapsulated inside the frame
FCS	FCS	A field used by the error detection process; it is the only trailer field in this table

HDLC exists today as a standard of the International Organization for Standardization (ISO), the same organization that brought us the OSI model. However, ISO standard HDLC does not have a Type field, and routers need to know the type of packet inside the frame. So, Cisco routers use a Cisco-proprietary variation of HDLC that adds a Type field, as shown in Figure 3-6.

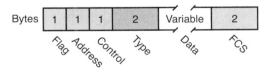

Figure 3-6   *HDLC Framing*

How Routers Use a WAN Data Link

Today, most leased lines connect to routers, and routers focus on delivering packets to a destination host. However, routers physically connect to both LANs and WANs, with those LANs and WANs requiring that data be sent inside data link frames. So, now that you know a little about HDLC, it helps to think about how routers use the HDLC protocol when sending data.

First, the TCP/IP network layer focuses on forwarding IP packets from the sending host to the destination host. The underlying LANs and WANs just act as a way to move the packets to the next router or end-user device. Figure 3-7 shows that network layer perspective.

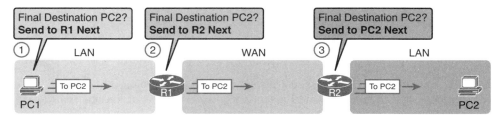

Figure 3-7   *IP Routing Logic over LANs and WANs*

Following the steps in the figure, for a packet sent by PC1 to PC2's IP address:

1. PC1's network layer (IP) logic tells it to send the packet to a nearby router (R1).

2. Router R1's network layer logic tells it to forward (route) the packet out the leased line to router R2 next.

3. Router R2's network layer logic tells it to forward (route) the packet out the LAN link to PC2 next.

While Figure 3-7 shows the network layer logic, the PCs and routers must rely on the LANs and WANs in the figure to actually move the bits in the packet. Figure 3-8 shows the same figure, with the same packet, but this time showing some of the data link layer logic used by the hosts and routers. Basically, three separate data link layer steps encapsulate the packet, inside a data link frame, over three hops through the internetwork: from PC1 to R1, from R1 to R2, and from R2 to PC2.

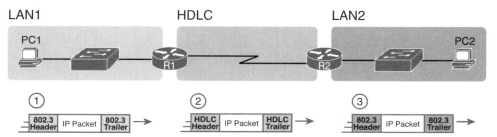

Figure 3-8   *General Concept of Routers Deencapsulating and Reencapsulating IP Packets*

Following the steps in the figure, again for a packet sent by PC1 to PC2's IP address:

1. To send the IP packet to router R1 next, PC1 encapsulates the IP packet in an Ethernet frame that has the destination MAC address of R1.

2. Router R1 deencapsulates (removes) the IP packet from the Ethernet frame, encapsulates the packet into an HDLC frame using an HDLC header and trailer, and forwards the HDLC frame to router R2 next.

3. Router R2 deencapsulates (removes) the IP packet from the HDLC frame, encapsulates the packet into an Ethernet frame that has the destination MAC address of PC2, and forwards the Ethernet frame to PC2.

In summary, a leased line with HDLC creates a WAN link between two routers so that they can forward packets for the devices on the attached LANs. The leased line itself provides the physical means to transmit the bits, in both directions. The HDLC frames provide the means to encapsulate the network layer packet correctly so that it crosses the link between routers.

Leased lines have many benefits that have led to their relatively long life in the WAN marketplace. These lines are simple for the customer, are widely available, are of high quality, and are private. However, they do have some negatives as well compared to newer WAN technologies, including a higher cost and typically longer lead times to get the service installed. The next section looks at an alternative WAN technology used in some examples in this book: Ethernet.

Ethernet as a WAN Technology

For the first several decades of the existence of Ethernet, Ethernet was only appropriate for LANs. The restrictions on cable lengths and devices might allow a LAN that stretched a kilometer or two, to support a campus LAN, but that was the limit.

As time passed, the IEEE improved Ethernet standards in ways that made Ethernet a reasonable WAN technology. For example, the 1000BASE-LX standard uses single-mode fiber cabling, with support for a 5-km cable length; the 1000BASE-ZX standard supports an even longer 70-km cable length. As time went by, and as the IEEE improved cabling distances for fiber Ethernet links, Ethernet became a reasonable WAN technology.

Today, in this second decade of the twenty-first century, many WAN service providers (SP) offer WAN services that take advantage of Ethernet. SPs offer a wide variety of these Ethernet WAN services, with many different names. But all of them use a similar model, with Ethernet used between the customer site and the SP's network, as shown in Figure 3-9.

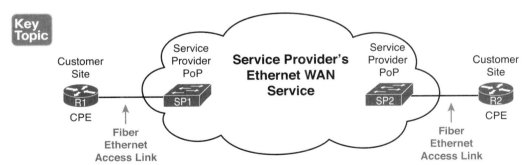

Figure 3-9   *Fiber Ethernet Link to Connect a CPE Router to a Service Provider's WAN*

The model shown in Figure 3-9 has many of the same ideas of how a telco creates a leased line, as seen earlier in Figure 3-3, but now with Ethernet links and devices. The customer connects to an Ethernet link using a router interface. The (fiber) Ethernet link leaves the customer building and connects to some nearby SP location called a point of presence (POP). Instead of a telco switch as seen in Figure 3-3, the SP uses an Ethernet switch. Inside the SP's network, the SP uses any technology that it wants to create the specific Ethernet WAN services.

Ethernet WANs that Create a Layer 2 Service

The WAN services implied by Figure 3-9 include a broad number of services, with a lot of complex networking concepts needed to understand those services. Interestingly, Ethernet began life as purely a LAN technology, with Ethernet growing to be the only commonly used wired LAN technology used today. Over those same years, Ethernet standards improved to support long enough cabling distances for Ethernet to be as effective as a WAN technology as well. This book focuses on one specific Ethernet WAN service that can be easily understood if you understand how Ethernet LANs work.

> **NOTE**   For perspective about the broad world of the service provider network shown in Figure 3-9, consider the Cisco certification paths for a moment. Cisco has CCNA, CCNP, and CCIE certifications in many areas: data center routing and switching, voice, and so on. Two paths—Service Provider and Service Provider Operations—focus on technologies and tasks in the service provider arena. See www.cisco.com/go/certifications for more details.

The one Ethernet WAN service example goes by two names: Ethernet emulation and Ethernet over MPLS (EoMPLS). Ethernet emulation is a general term, meaning that the service acts like one Ethernet link. EoMPLS refers to Multiprotocol Label Switching (MPLS), which is one technology that can be used inside the SP's cloud. This book will refer to this specific service either as Ethernet emulation or EoMPLS.

The type of EoMPLS service discussed in this book gives the customer an Ethernet link between two sites. In other words, the EoMPLS service provides

■ A point-to-point connection between two customer devices

■ Behavior as if a fiber Ethernet link existed between the two devices

So, if you can imagine two routers, with a single Ethernet link between the two routers, you understand what this particular EoMPLS service does.

Figure 3-10 shows the idea. In this case, the two routers, R1 and R2, connect with an EoMPLS service instead of a serial link. The routers use Ethernet interfaces, and they can send data in both directions at the same time. Physically, each router actually connects to some SP PoP, as shown earlier in Figure 3-9, but logically, the two routers can send Ethernet frames to each other over the link.

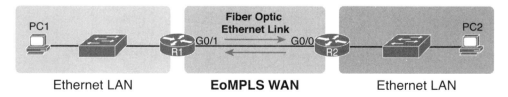

Figure 3-10   *EoMPLS Acting Like a Simple Ethernet Link Between Two Routers*

How Routers Route IP Packets Using Ethernet Emulation

WANs, by their very nature, give IP routers a way to forward IP packets from a LAN at one site, over the WAN, and to another LAN at another site. Routing over an EoMPLS WAN link still uses the WAN like a WAN, as a way to forward IP packets from one site to another. However, the WAN link happens to use the same Ethernet protocols as the Ethernet LAN links at each site.

The EoMPLS link uses Ethernet for both Layer 1 and Layer 2 functions. That means the link uses the same familiar Ethernet header and trailer, as seen in the middle of Figure 3-11.

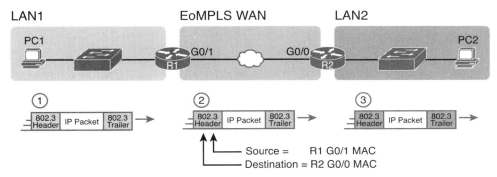

Figure 3-11   *Routing over an EoMPLS Link*

NOTE   This book shows EoMPLS connections as a familiar single black line, like other Ethernet links, but with a small cloud overlaid to note that this particular Ethernet link is through an Ethernet WAN service.

The figure shows the same three routing steps as shown with the serial link in the earlier Figure 3-8. In this case, all three routing steps use the same Ethernet (802.3) protocol. However, note that each frame's data link header and trailer are different. Each router discards the old data link header/trailer and adds a new set, as described in these steps. Focus mainly on Step 2, because compared to the similar example shown in Figure 3-8, Steps 1 and 3 are unchanged:

1. To send the IP packet to router R1 next, PC1 encapsulates the IP packet in an Ethernet frame that has the destination MAC address of R1.

2. Router R1 deencapsulates (removes) the IP packet from the Ethernet frame and encapsulates the packet into a new Ethernet frame, with a new Ethernet header and trailer. The destination MAC address is R2's G0/0 MAC address, and the source MAC address is R1's G0/1 MAC address. R1 forwards this frame over the EoMPLS service to R2 next.

3. Router R2 deencapsulates (removes) the IP packet from the Ethernet frame, encapsulates the packet into an Ethernet frame that has the destination MAC address of PC2, and forwards the Ethernet frame to PC2.

Accessing the Internet

Many people begin their Cisco studies never having heard of leased lines, but many people have heard of two other WAN technologies used to gain access to the Internet: digital subscriber line (DSL) and cable. These two WAN technologies do not replace leased lines in all cases, but they do play an important role in the specific case of creating a WAN connection between a home or office and the Internet.

This last major section of the chapter begins by introducing the basic networking concepts behind the Internet, followed with some specifics of how DSL and cable provide a way to send data to/from the Internet.

The Internet as a Large WAN

The Internet is an amazing cultural phenomenon. Most of us use it every day. We post messages on social media sites, we search for information using a search engine like Google, and we send emails. We use apps on our phones to pull down information, like weather reports, maps, and movie reviews. We use the Internet to purchase physical products and to buy and download digital products like music and videos. The Internet has created completely new things to do and changed the old ways of living life compared to a generation ago.

However, if you instead focus on the networking technology that creates the Internet, the Internet is simply one huge TCP/IP network. In fact, the name "Internet" comes from the core network layer protocol: Internet Protocol. The Internet includes many LANs, and because the Internet spans the globe, it of course needs WAN links to connect different sites.

As a network of networks, the Internet is actually owned by countless companies and people. The Internet includes most every enterprise TCP/IP network and a huge number of home-based networks, as well as a huge number of individuals from their phones and other wireless devices, as shown in Figure 3-12.

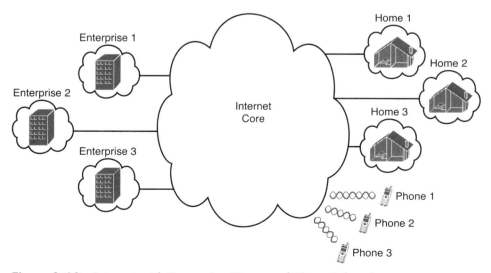

Figure 3-12 *Internet with Enterprise, Home, and Phone Subscribers*

The middle of the Internet, called the *Internet core*, exists as LANs and WANs owned and operated by Internet service providers (ISP). (Figure 3-12 shows the Internet core as a cloud, because network diagrams show a cloud when hiding the details of a part of the network.) ISPs cooperate to create a mesh of links between each other in the Internet core, so that no matter through which ISP a particular company or person connects, some path exists to every device.

Figure 3-13 shows a slightly different version of Figure 3-12, in this case showing the concept of the Internet core: ISP networks that connect to both their customers, as well as each other, so that IP packets can flow from every customer of every ISP to every other customer of every other ISP.

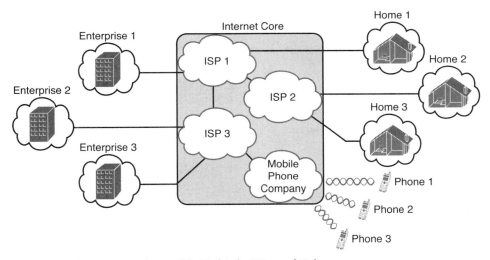

Figure 3-13   *Internet Core with Multiple ISPs and Telcos*

Internet Access (WAN) Links

The Internet also happens to use a huge number of WAN links. All of those lines connecting an enterprise or home to one of the ISPs in Figure 3-13 represent some kind of WAN link that uses a cable, while the phones create their WAN link using wireless technology. These links usually go by the name *Internet access link*.

Historically, businesses tend to use one set of WAN technologies as Internet access links, while home-based consumers use others. Businesses often use leased lines, connecting a router at the business to a router at the ISP. The top of Figure 3-14 shows just such an example.

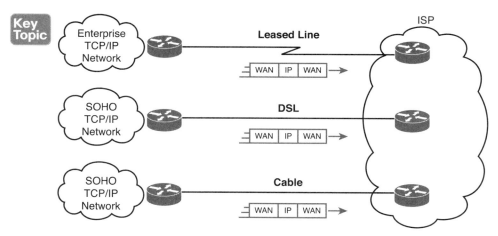

Figure 3-14 *Three Examples of Internet Access Links*

Consumers often use technologies like DSL and cable for Internet access links. These technologies use cabling that is already installed in most homes, making these services somewhat inexpensive for home users. DSL uses the analog phone lines that are already installed in homes, while cable Internet uses the cable TV (CATV) cable.

NOTE While mostly home-based consumers use DSL and cable, there is no restriction against businesses using them as well.

All three of the Internet access technologies in Figure 3-14 happen to use a pair of routers: one at the customer side of the WAN link and one at the ISP side. The routers will continue to think about network layer logic, of sending IP packets to their destination by forwarding the packets to the next router. However, the physical and data link layer details on the WAN link differ as compared to leased lines. The next few pages examine both DSL and cable Internet to show some of those differences.

Digital Subscriber Line

Digital subscriber line (DSL) creates a relatively short (miles long, not tens of miles) high-speed link WAN between a telco customer and an ISP. To do so, it uses the same single-pair telephone line used for a typical home phone line. DSL, as a technology, does not try to replace leased lines, which run between any two sites, for potentially very long distances. DSL instead just provides a short physical link from a home to the telco's network, allowing access to the Internet.

First, to get an idea about the cabling, think about typical home telephone service in the United States, before adding DSL service. Each home has one phone line that runs from a nearby telco CO to the home. As shown on the left side of Figure 3-15, the telephone wiring splits out and terminates at several wall plates, often with RJ-11 ports that are a slightly skinnier cousin of the RJ-45 connector.

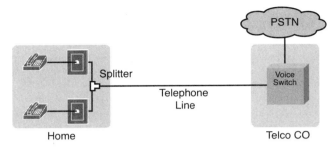

Figure 3-15   *Typical Voice Cabling Concepts in the United States*

Next, think about the telephone line and the equipment at the CO. Sometime in the past, the telco installed all the telephone lines from its local CO to each neighborhood, apartment, and so on. At the CO, each line connects to a port on a telco switch. This switch supports the ability to set up voice calls, take them down, and forward the voice through the worldwide voice network, called the public switched telephone network, or PSTN.

To add DSL service at the home in Figure 3-15, two changes need to be made. First, you need to add DSL-capable devices at the home. Second, the telco has to add DSL equipment at the CO. Together, the DSL equipment at each side of the local telephone line can send data while still supporting the same voice traffic.

The left side of Figure 3-16 shows the changes. A new *DSL modem* now connects to a spare phone outlet. The DSL modem follows the DSL physical and data link layer standards to send data to/from the telco. The home now has a small LAN, implemented with a consumer-grade router, which often includes an Ethernet switch and possibly a wireless LAN access point.

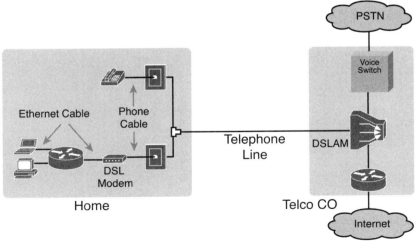

Figure 3-16   *Wiring and Devices for a Home DSL Link*

The home-based router on the left needs to be able to send data to/from the Internet. To make that happen, the telco CO uses a product called a DSL Access Multiplexer (DSLAM). The DSLAM splits out the data over to the router on the lower right, which completes the connection to the Internet. The DSLAM also splits out the voice signals over to the voice switch on the upper right.

DSL gives telcos a useful high-speed Internet service to offer their customers. Telcos have had other offerings that happen to use the same telephone line for data, but these options ran much slower than DSL. DSL supports asymmetric speeds, meaning that the transmission speed from the ISP toward the home (downstream) is much faster than the transmissions toward the ISP (upstream). Asymmetric speeds work better for consumer Internet access from the home, because clicking a web page sends only a few hundred bytes upstream into the Internet, but can trigger many megabytes of data to be delivered downstream to the home.

Cable Internet

Cable Internet creates an Internet access service which, when viewed generally rather than specifically, has many similarities to DSL. Like DSL, cable Internet takes full advantage of existing cabling, using the existing cable TV (CATV) cable to send data. Like DSL, cable Internet uses asymmetric speeds, sending data faster downstream than upstream, which works better than symmetric speeds for most consumer locations. And like DSL, cable Internet does not attempt to replace long leased lines between any two sites, instead focusing on the short WAN links from a customer to an ISP.

Cable Internet also uses the same basic in-home cabling concepts as does DSL. Figure 3-17 shows a figure based on the earlier DSL Figure 3-16, but with the DSL details replaced with cable Internet details. The telephone line has been replaced with coaxial cable from the CATV company, and the DSL modem has been replaced by a cable modem. Otherwise, the details in the home follow the same overall plan.

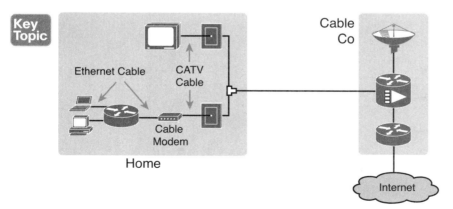

Figure 3-17   *Wiring and Devices for a Home Cable Internet Link*

On the CATV company side of the cable Internet service, the CATV company has to split out the data and video, as shown on the right side of the figure. Data flows to the lower right, through a router, while video comes in from video dishes for distribution out to the TVs in people's homes.

Cable Internet service and DSL directly compete for consumer and small-business Internet access. Generally speaking, while both offer high speeds, cable Internet typically runs at faster speeds than DSL, with DSL providers keeping their prices a little lower to compete. Both support asymmetric speeds, and both provide an "always on" service, in that you can communicate with the Internet without the need to first take some action to start the Internet connection.

3

Exam Preparation Tasks

Review All the Key Topics

Review the most important topics from this chapter, noted with the Key Topic icon. Table 3-4 lists these key topics and where each is discussed.

Table 3-4   Key Topics for Chapter 3

Key Topic Element	Description	Page Number
Figure 3-4	Typical cabling diagram of CPE for a leased line	73
Figure 3-9	Ethernet over MPLS—physical connections	77
Figure 3-14	Common Internet access links	82
Figure 3-16	Typical DSL cabling at home	83
Figure 3-17	Typical cable Internet cabling at home	84

Complete the Tables and Lists from Memory

Print a copy of DVD Appendix I, "Memory Tables," or at least the section for this chapter, and complete the tables and lists from memory. DVD Appendix J, "Memory Tables Answer Key," includes completed tables and lists to check your work.

Definitions of Key Terms

After your first reading of the chapter, try to define these key terms, but do not be concerned about getting them all correct at that time. Chapter 23 directs you in how to use these terms for late-stage preparation for the exam.

leased line, wide-area network (WAN), telco, serial interface, HDLC, DSL, cable Internet, DSL modem, Ethernet over MPLS

This chapter covers the following exam topics:

1.1 Describe the purpose and functions of various network devices

1.1.a Interpret a network diagram

1.3 Use the OSI and TCP/IP models and their associated protocols to explain how data flows in a network

1.3.a IP

CHAPTER 4

Fundamentals of IPv4 Addressing and Routing

The TCP/IP network layer (Layer 3) defines how to deliver IP packets over the entire trip, from the original device that creates the packet to the device that needs to receive the packet. That process requires cooperation between several different jobs and concepts on a number of devices.

This chapter begins with an overview of all these cooperating functions, and then it dives into more detail about each area. These areas include IP routing, IP addressing, and IP routing protocols, all of which play a vital role in data center networks.

IP addressing and routing matters quite a bit to data center networking as well. You can think of the end users of the servers as sitting out in the network somewhere—on the other side of the Internet, at another WAN site in the same enterprise, and so on. The data center part of the network must be connected to the rest of the enterprise and to the Internet; otherwise, the servers will not be accessible to the users. IPv4 defines the rules that enable users to connect to the servers and for traffic to flow back out to the users' devices.

NOTE As promised in the Introduction's section, "For Those Studying Routing & Switching": This chapter's content mirrors the content in the *ICND1 100-101 Official Cert Guide*'s Chapter 4, with no additional information hidden here.

"Do I Know This Already?" Quiz

Use the "Do I Know This Already?" quiz to help decide whether you might want to skim this chapter, or a major section, moving more quickly to the "Exam Preparation Tasks" section near the end of the chapter. You can find the answers at the bottom of the page following the quiz. For thorough explanations, see Appendix A, "Answers to the 'Do I Know This Already?' Quizzes."

Table 4-1 "Do I Know This Already?" Foundation Topics Section-to-Question Mapping

Foundation Topics Section	Questions
Overview of Network Layer Functions	1, 2
IPv4 Addressing	3–5
IPv4 Routing	6–8
IPv4 Routing Protocols	9
Network Layer Utilities	10

1. Which of the following are functions of OSI Layer 3 protocols? (Choose two answers.)

    a. Logical addressing

    b. Physical addressing

    c. Path selection

    d. Arbitration

    e. Error recovery

2. Imagine that PC1 needs to send some data to PC2, and PC1 and PC2 are separated by several routers. Both PC1 and PC2 sit on different Ethernet LANs. What are the largest entities (in size) that make it from PC1 to PC2? (Choose two answers.)

    a. Frame

    b. Segment

    c. Packet

    d. L5 PDU

    e. L3 PDU

    f. L1 PDU

3. Which of the following is a valid Class C IP address that can be assigned to a host?

    a. 1.1.1.1

    b. 200.1.1.1

    c. 128.128.128.128

    d. 224.1.1.1

4. What is the assignable range of values for the first octet for Class A IP networks?

    a. 0 to 127

    b. 0 to 126

    c. 1 to 127

    d. 1 to 126

    e. 128 to 191

    f. 128 to 192

5. PC1 and PC2 are on two different Ethernet LANs that are separated by an IP router. PC1's IP address is 10.1.1.1, and no subnetting is used. Which of the following addresses could be used for PC2? (Choose two answers.)

    a. 10.1.1.2

    b. 10.2.2.2

    c. 10.200.200.1

    d. 9.1.1.1

    e. 225.1.1.1

    f. 1.1.1.1

6. Imagine a network with two routers that are connected with a point-to-point HDLC serial link. Each router has an Ethernet, with PC1 sharing the Ethernet with Router1 and PC2 sharing the Ethernet with Router2. When PC1 sends data to PC2, which of the following is true?

   a. Router1 strips the Ethernet header and trailer off the frame received from PC1, never to be used again.

   b. Router1 encapsulates the Ethernet frame inside an HDLC header and sends the frame to Router2, which extracts the Ethernet frame for forwarding to PC2.

   c. Router1 strips the Ethernet header and trailer off the frame received from PC1, which is exactly re-created by Router2 before forwarding data to PC2.

   d. Router1 removes the Ethernet, IP, and TCP headers and rebuilds the appropriate headers before forwarding the packet to Router2.

7. Which of the following does a router normally use when making a decision about routing TCP/IP packets?

   a. Destination MAC address

   b. Source MAC address

   c. Destination IP address

   d. Source IP address

   e. Destination MAC and IP address

8. Which of the following are true about a LAN-connected TCP/IP host and its IP routing (forwarding) choices? (Choose two answers.)

   a. The host always sends packets to its default gateway.

   b. The host sends packets to its default gateway if the destination IP address is in a different class of IP network than the host.

   c. The host sends packets to its default gateway if the destination IP address is in a different subnet than the host.

   d. The host sends packets to its default gateway if the destination IP address is in the same subnet as the host.

9. Which of the following are functions of a routing protocol? (Choose two answers.)

   a. Advertising known routes to neighboring routers

   b. Learning routes for subnets directly connected to the router

   c. Learning routes, and putting those routes into the routing table, for routes advertised to the router by its neighboring routers

   d. Forwarding IP packets based on a packet's destination IP address

10. A company implements a TCP/IP network, with PC1 sitting on an Ethernet LAN. Which of the following protocols and features requires PC1 to learn information from some other server device?

   a. ARP

   b. ping

   c. DNS

   d. None of the other answers are correct

Foundation Topics

Overview of Network Layer Functions

While many protocol models have existed over the years, today the TCP/IP model dominates. And at the network layer of TCP/IP, two options exist for the main protocol around which all other network layer functions revolve: IP version 4 (IPv4) and IP version 6 (IPv6). Both IPv4 and IPv6 define the same kinds of network layer functions, but with different details. This chapter introduces these network layer functions for IPv4.

> **NOTE**   All references to IP in this chapter refer to the older and more established IPv4.

IP focuses on the job of routing data, in the form of IP packets, from the source host to the destination host. IP does not concern itself with the physical transmission of data, instead relying on the lower TCP/IP layers to do the physical transmission of the data. Instead, IP concerns itself with the logical details, instead of physical details, of delivering data. In particular, the network layer specifies how packets travel end to end over a TCP/IP network, even when the packet crosses many different types of LAN and WAN links.

This first section of the chapter begins a broad discussion of the TCP/IP network layer by looking at IP routing and addressing. The two topics work together, because IP routing relies on the structure and meaning of IP addresses, and IP addressing was designed with IP routing in mind. Following that, this overview section looks at routing protocols, which let routers learn the information they need to know to do routing correctly.

Network Layer Routing (Forwarding) Logic

Routers and end-user computers (called *hosts* in a TCP/IP network) work together to perform IP routing. The host operating system (OS) has TCP/IP software, including the software that implements the network layer. Hosts use that software to choose where to send IP packets, oftentimes to a nearby router. Those routers make choices of where to send the IP packet next. Together, the hosts and routers deliver the IP packet to the correct destination, as seen in the example in Figure 4-1.

The IP packet, created by PC1, goes from the top of the figure all the way to PC2 at the bottom of the figure. The next few pages discuss the network layer routing logic used by each device along the path.

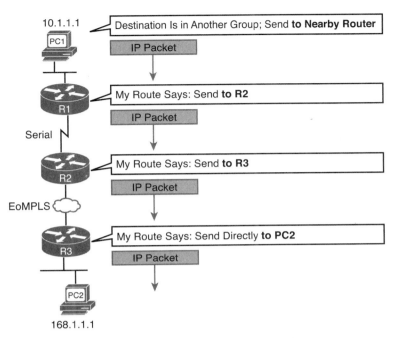

Figure 4-1   *Routing Logic: PC1 Sending an IP Packet to PC2*

> **NOTE**   The term *path selection* is sometimes used to refer to the routing process shown in Figure 4-1. At other times, it refers to routing protocols, specifically how routing protocols select the best route among the competing routes to the same destination.

Host Forwarding Logic: Send the Packet to the Default Router

In this example, PC1 does some basic analysis, and then chooses to send the IP packet to the router so that the router will forward the packet. PC1 analyzes the destination address and realizes that PC2's address (168.1.1.1) is not on the same LAN as PC1. So PC1's logic tells it to send the packet to a device whose job it is to know where to route data: a nearby router, on the same LAN, called PC1's default router.

To send the IP packet to the default router, the sender sends a data link frame across the medium to the nearby router; this frame includes the packet in the data portion of the frame. That frame uses data link layer (Layer 2) addressing in the data link header to ensure that the nearby router receives the frame.

NOTE   The *default router* is also referred to as the *default gateway*.

R1 and R2's Logic: Routing Data Across the Network

All routers use the same general process to route the packet. Each router keeps an *IP routing table*. This table lists IP address *groupings*, called *IP networks* and *IP subnets*. When a router receives a packet, it compares the packet's destination IP address to the entries in the routing table and makes a match. This matching entry also lists directions that tell the router where to forward the packet next.

In Figure 4-1, R1 would have matched the destination address (168.1.1.1) to a routing table entry, which in turn told R1 to send the packet to R2 next. Similarly, R2 would have matched a routing table entry that told R2 to send the packet, over an Ethernet over MPLS (EoMPLS) link, to R3 next.

The routing concept works a little like driving down the freeway when approaching a big interchange. You look up and see signs for nearby towns, telling you which exits to take to go to each town. Similarly, the router looks at the IP routing table (the equivalent of the road signs) and directs each packet over the correct next LAN or WAN link (the equivalent of a road).

R3's Logic: Delivering Data to the End Destination

The final router in the path, R3, uses almost the same logic as R1 and R2, but with one minor difference. R3 needs to forward the packet directly to PC2, not to some other router. On the surface, that difference seems insignificant. In the next section, when you read about how the network layer uses LANs and WANs, the significance of the difference will become obvious.

How Network Layer Routing Uses LANs and WANs

While the network layer routing logic ignores the physical transmission details, the bits still have to be transmitted. To do that work, the network layer logic in a host or router must hand off the packet to the data link layer protocols, which, in turn, ask the physical layer to actually send the data. And as was described in Chapter 2, "Fundamentals of Ethernet LANs," the data link layer adds the appropriate header and trailer to the packet, creating a frame, before sending the frames over each physical network.

The routing process forwards the network layer packet from end to end through the network, while each data link frame only takes a smaller part of the trip. Each successive data link layer frame moves the packet to the next device that thinks about network layer logic. In short, the network layer thinks about the bigger view of the goal, like "Send this packet to the specified next device...," while the data link layer thinks about the specifics, like "Encapsulate the packet in a data link frame and transmit it." Figure 4-2 points out the key encapsulation logic on each device, using the same examples as shown in Figure 4-1.

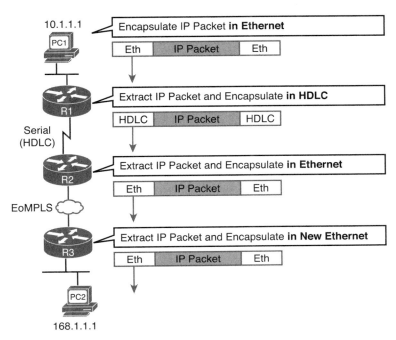

Figure 4-2 *Network Layer and Data Link Layer Encapsulation*

Because the routers build new data link headers and trailers, and because the new headers contain data link addresses, the PCs and routers must have some way to decide what data link addresses to use. An example of how the router determines which data link address to use is the IP Address Resolution Protocol (ARP). *ARP dynamically learns the data link address of an IP host connected to a LAN.* For example, at the last step, at the bottom of Figure 4-2, router R3 would use ARP once to learn PC2's MAC address before sending any packets to PC2.

Routing as covered so far has two main concepts:

- The process of routing forwards Layer 3 packets, also called *Layer 3 protocol data units (L3 PDU)*, based on the destination Layer 3 address in the packet.

- The routing process uses the data link layer to encapsulate the Layer 3 packets into Layer 2 frames for transmission across each successive data link.

IP Addressing and How Addressing Helps IP Routing

IP defines network layer addresses that identify any host or router interface that connects to a TCP/IP network. The idea basically works like a postal address: Any interface that expects to receive IP packets needs an IP address, just like you need a postal address before receiving mail from the postal service.

TCP/IP groups IP addresses together so that IP addresses used on the same physical network are part of the same group. IP calls these address groups an *IP network* or an *IP subnet*. Using that same postal service analogy, each IP network and IP subnet works like a postal code (or in the United States, a ZIP code). All nearby postal addresses are in the same postal code (ZIP code), while all nearby IP addresses must be in the same IP network or IP subnet.

NOTE   IP defines the word *network* to mean a very specific concept. To avoid confusion when writing about IP addressing, this book (and others) often avoids using the term *network* for other uses. In particular, this book uses the term *internetwork* to refer more generally to a network made up of routers, switches, cables, and other equipment.

IP defines specific rules about which IP address should be in the same IP network or IP subnet. Numerically, the addresses in the same group have the same value in the first part of the addresses. For example, Figures 4-1 and 4-2 could have used the following conventions:

■ Hosts on the top Ethernet: Addresses start with 10

■ Hosts on the R1-R2 serial link: Addresses start with 168.10

■ Hosts on the R2-R3 EoMPLS link: Addresses start with 168.11

■ Hosts on the bottom Ethernet: Addresses start with 168.1

It's similar to the USPS ZIP code system and how it requires local governments to assign addresses to new buildings. It would be ridiculous to have two houses, next door to each other, whose addresses had different ZIP codes. Similarly, it would be silly to have people who live on opposite sides of the country to have addresses with the same ZIP code.

Similarly, to make routing more efficient, network layer protocols group addresses, both by their location and by the actual address values. A router can list one routing table entry for each IP network or subnet, instead of one entry for every single IP address.

The routing process also makes use of the IPv4 header, as shown in Figure 4-3. The header lists a 32-bit source IP address, as well as a 32-bit destination IP address. The header of course has other fields, a few of which matter for other discussions in this book. The book will refer back to this figure as needed, but otherwise, be aware of the 20-byte IP header and the existence of the source and destination IP address fields.

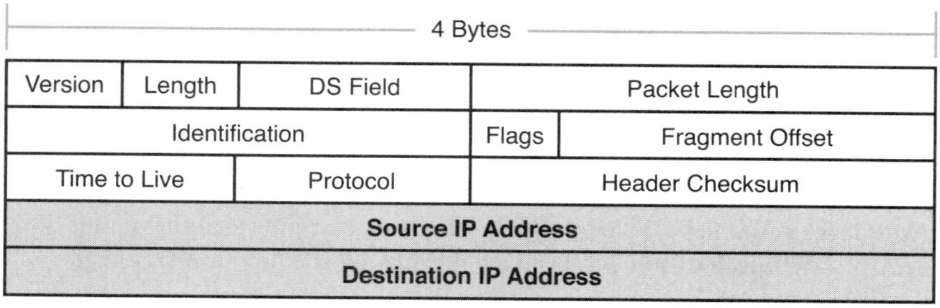

4 Bytes			
Version	Length	DS Field	Packet Length
Identification		Flags	Fragment Offset
Time to Live		Protocol	Header Checksum
Source IP Address			
Destination IP Address			

Figure 4-3   *IPv4 Header, Organized as Four Bytes Wide for a Total of 20 Bytes*

Routing Protocols

For routing logic to work on both hosts and routers, each needs to know something about the TCP/IP internetwork. Hosts need to know the IP address of their default router so that hosts can send packets to remote destinations. Routers, however, need to know routes so that routers know how to forward packets to each and every IP network and IP subnet.

Although a network engineer could configure (type) all the required routes, on every router, most network engineers instead simply enable a routing protocol on all routers. If you enable the same routing protocol on all the routers in a TCP/IP internetwork, with the correct settings, the routers will send routing protocol messages to each other. As a result, all the routers will learn routes for all the IP networks and subnets in the TCP/IP internetwork.

Figure 4-4 shows an example, using the same diagram as in Figures 4-1 and 4-2. In this case, IP network 168.1.0.0, which consists of all addresses that begin with 168.1, sits on the Ethernet at the bottom of the figure. R3, knowing this fact, sends a routing protocol message to R2 (Step 1). R2 learns a route for network 168.1.0.0 as a result, as shown on the left. At Step 2, R2 turns around and sends a routing protocol message to R1 so that R1 now has a route for that same IP network (168.1.0.0).

R1 Routing Table

Subnet	Interface	Next Hop
168.1.0.0	Serial0	R2

R2 Routing Table

Subnet	Interface	Next Hop
168.1.0.0	F0/0	R3

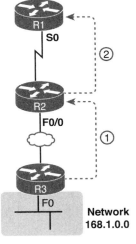

Figure 4-4   *Example of How Routing Protocols Advertise About Networks and Subnets*

This concludes the overview of how the TCP/IP network layer works. The rest of this chapter reexamines the key components in more depth.

IPv4 Addressing

By the time you have finished reading this book, you should be comfortable and confident in your understanding of IP addresses, their formats, the grouping concepts, how to subdivide groups into subnets, how to interpret the documentation for existing networks' IP addressing, and so on. Simply put, you had better know addressing and subnetting!

This section introduces IP addressing and subnetting and also covers the concepts behind the structure of an IP address, including how it relates to IP routing. In Part IV of this book, you will read more about the concepts and math behind IPv4 addressing and subnetting.

Rules for IP Addresses

If a device wants to communicate using TCP/IP, it needs an IP address. When the device has an IP address and the appropriate software and hardware, it can send and receive IP packets. Any device that has at least one interface with an IP address can send and receive IP packets and is called an *IP host*.

IP addresses consist of a 32-bit number, usually written in *dotted-decimal notation (DDN)*. The "decimal" part of the term comes from the fact that each byte (8 bits) of the 32-bit IP address is shown as its decimal equivalent. The four resulting decimal numbers are written in sequence, with "dots," or decimal points, separating the numbers—hence the name *dotted-decimal*. For example, 168.1.1.1 is an IP address written in dotted-decimal form; the actual binary version is 10101000 00000001 00000001 00000001. (You almost never need to write down the binary version, but you can use the conversion chart in Appendix A to easily convert from DDN to binary or vice versa.)

Each DDN has four decimal *octets*, separated by periods. The term *octet* is just a vendor-neutral term for *byte*. Because each octet represents an 8-bit binary number, the range of decimal numbers in each octet is between 0 and 255, inclusive. For example, the IP address of 168.1.1.1 has a first octet of 168, the second octet of 1, and so on.

Finally, note that each network interface uses a unique IP address. Most people tend to think that their computer has an IP address, but actually their computer's network card has an IP address. For example, if your laptop has both an Ethernet network interface card (NIC) and a wireless NIC, with both working at the same time, both will have an IP address. Similarly, routers, which typically have many network interfaces that forward IP packets, have an IP address for each interface.

Rules for Grouping IP Addresses

The original specifications for TCP/IP grouped IP addresses into sets of consecutive addresses called *IP networks*. The addresses in a single IP network have the same numeric value in the first part of all addresses in the network. Figure 4-5 shows a simple internetwork that has three separate IP networks.

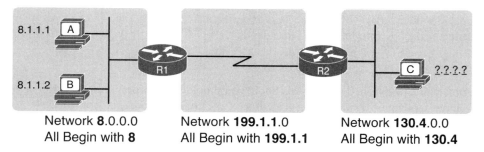

Figure 4-5 *Sample TCP/IP Internetwork Using IPv4 Network Numbers*

The figure lists a network identifier (network ID) for each network, as well as a text description of the DDN values in each network. For example, the hosts in the Ethernet LAN on the far left use IP addresses that begin with a first octet of 8; the network ID happens to be 8.0.0.0. As another example, the serial link between R1 and R2 consists of only two interfaces—a serial interface on each router—and uses an IP address that begins with the three octets 199.1.1.

Figure 4-5 also provides a good figure with which to discuss two important facts about how IPv4 groups IP addresses:

- All IP addresses in the same group must not be separated from each other by a router.
- IP addresses separated from each other by a router must be in different groups.

Take the first of the two rules, and look at hosts A and B on the left. Hosts A and B are in the same IP network and have IP addresses that begin with 8. Per the first rule, hosts A and B cannot be separated from each other by a router (and they are indeed not separated from each other by a router).

Next, take the second of the two rules and add host C to the discussion. Host C is separated from host A by at least one router, so host C cannot be in the same IP network as host A. Host C's address cannot begin with 8.

NOTE This example assumes the use of IP networks only, and no subnets, simply because the discussion has not yet dealt with the details of subnetting.

As mentioned earlier in this chapter, IP address grouping behaves similarly to ZIP codes. Everyone in my ZIP code lives in a little town in Ohio. If some addresses in my ZIP code were in California, some mail might be delivered to the wrong local post office, because the postal service delivers the letters based on the postal (ZIP) codes. The post system relies on all addresses in one postal code being near to each other.

Likewise, IP routing relies on all addresses in one IP network or IP subnet to be in the same location, specifically on a single instance of a LAN or WAN data link. Otherwise, the routers might deliver IP packets to the wrong locations.

For any TCP/IP internetwork, each LAN and WAN link will use either an IP network or an IP subnet. Next, this chapter looks more closely at the concepts behind IP networks, followed by IP subnets.

Class A, B, and C IP Networks

The IPv4 address space includes all possible combinations of numbers for a 32-bit IPv4 address. Literally 2^{32} different values exist with a 32-bit number, for more than 4 billion different numbers. With DDN values, these numbers include all combinations of the values 0 through 255 in all four octets: 0.0.0.0, 0.0.0.1, 0.0.0.2, and all the way up to 255.255.255.255.

IP standards first subdivide the entire address space into classes, as identified by the value of the first octet. Class A gets roughly half of the IPv4 address space, with all DDN numbers that begin with 1–126, as shown in Figure 4-6. Class B gets one-fourth of the address space, with all DDN numbers that begin with 128–191 inclusive, while Class C gets one-eighth of the address space, with all numbers that begin with 192–223.

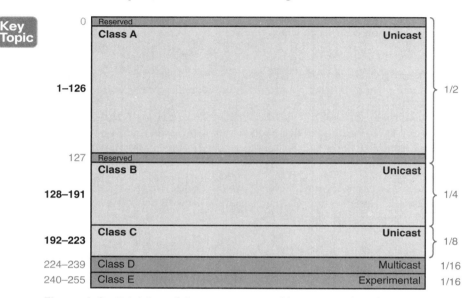

Figure 4-6   *Division of the Entire IPv4 Address Space by Class*

Figure 4-6 also notes the purpose for the five address classes. Classes A, B, and C define unicast IP addresses, meaning that the address identifies a single host interface. Class D defines multicast addresses, used to send one packet to multiple hosts, while Class E defines experimental addresses.

IPv4 standards also subdivide the Class A, B, and C unicast classes into predefined IP networks. Each IP network makes up a subset of the DDN values inside the class.

IPv4 uses three classes of unicast addresses so that the IP networks in each class can be different sizes, and therefore meet different needs. Class A networks each support a very large number of IP addresses (over 16 million host addresses per IP network). However, because each Class A network is so large, Class A holds only 126 Class A networks. Class B defines IP networks that have 65,534 addresses per network, but with space for over 16,000 such networks. Class C defines much smaller IP networks, with 254 addresses each, as shown in Figure 4-7.

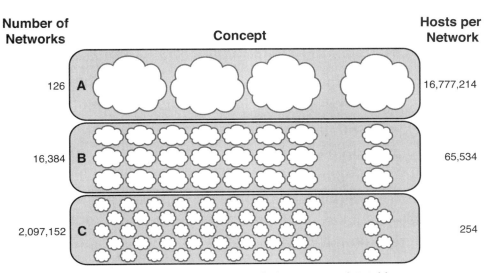

Figure 4-7 *Size of Network and Host Parts of Class A, B, and C Addresses*

Figure 4-7 shows a visual perspective, as well as the literal numbers, for all the Class A, B, and C IPv4 networks in the entire world. The figure shows clouds for IP networks. It of course does not show one cloud for every possible network, but shows the general idea, with a small number of large clouds for Class A and a large number of small clouds for Class C.

The Actual Class A, B, and C IP Networks

Figure 4-7 shows the number of Class A, B, and C IP networks in the entire world. Eventually, you need to actually pick and use some of these IP networks to build a working TCP/IP internetwork, so you need to be able to answer the question: What are the specific IP networks?

First, you must be able to identify each network briefly using a *network identifier* (network ID). The network ID is just one reserved DDN value per network that identifies the IP network. (The network ID cannot be used by a host as an IP address.) For example, Table 4-2 shows the network IDs that match the earlier Figure 4-5.

Table 4-2 Network IDs Used in Figure 4-5

Concept	Class	Network ID
All addresses that begin with 8	A	8.0.0.0
All addresses that begin with 130.4	B	130.4.0.0
All addresses that begin with 199.1.1	C	199.1.1.0

NOTE Many people use the term *network ID*, but others use the terms *network number* and *network address*. Be ready to use all three terms.

So, what are the actual Class A, B, and C IP networks, and what are their network IDs? First, consider the Class A networks. Per Figure 4-7, only 126 Class A networks exist. As it turns out, they consist of all addresses that begin with 1, all addresses that begin with 2, all addresses that begin with 3, and so on, up through the 126th such network of "all addresses that begin with 126." Table 4-3 lists a few of these networks.

Table 4-3   Sampling of IPv4 Class A Networks

Concept	Class	Network ID
All addresses that begin with 8	A	8.0.0.0
All addresses that begin with 13	A	13.0.0.0
All addresses that begin with 24	A	24.0.0.0
All addresses that begin with 125	A	125.0.0.0
All addresses that begin with 126	A	126.0.0.0

Class B networks have a first octet value between 128 and 191, inclusive, but in a single Class B network, the addresses have the same value in the first two octets. For example, Figure 4-5 uses Class B network 130.4.0.0. The DDN value 130.4.0.0 must be in Class B, because the first octet is between 128 and 191, inclusive. However, the first two octets define the addresses in a single Class B network. Table 4-4 lists some sample IPv4 Class B networks.

Table 4-4   Sampling of IPv4 Class B Networks

Concept	Class	Network ID
All addresses that begin with 128.1	B	128.1.0.0
All addresses that begin with 172.20	B	172.20.0.0
All addresses that begin with 191.191	B	191.191.0.0
All addresses that begin with 150.1	B	150.1.0.0

Class C networks can also be easily identified, with a first octet value between 192 and 223, inclusive. With Class C networks and addresses, the first three octets define the group, with addresses in one Class C network having the same value in the first three octets. Table 4-5 shows some samples.

Table 4-5   Sampling of IPv4 Class C Networks

Concept	Class	Network ID
All addresses that begin with 199.1.1	C	199.1.1.0
All addresses that begin with 200.1.200	C	200.1.200.0
All addresses that begin with 223.1.10	C	223.1.10.0
All addresses that begin with 209.209.1	C	209.209.1.0

Listing all the Class A, B, and C networks would of course take too much space. For study review, Table 4-6 summarizes the first octet values that identify the class and summarizes the range of Class A, B, and C network numbers available in the entire IPv4 address space.

Table 4-6   All Possible Valid Network Numbers

Class	First Octet Range	Valid Network Numbers
A	1 to 126	1.0.0.0 to 126.0.0.0
B	128 to 191	128.0.0.0 to 191.255.0.0
C	192 to 223	192.0.0.0 to 223.255.255.0

NOTE   The term *classful IP network* refers to any Class A, B, or C network, because it is defined by Class A, B, and C rules.

IP Subnetting

Subnetting is one of the most important topics in the world of networking. You need to know how subnetting works and how to "do the math" to figure out issues when subnetting is in use, both in real life and on the exam. Part IV of this book covers the details of subnetting concepts, motivation, and math, but you should have a basic understanding of the concepts before covering the topics between here and Part IV.

Subnetting defines methods of further subdividing the IPv4 address space into groups that are smaller than a single IP network. IP subnetting defines a flexible way for anyone to take a single Class A, B, or C IP network and further subdivide it into even smaller groups of consecutive IP addresses. In fact, the name *subnet* is just shorthand for *subdivided network*. Then, in each location where you used to use an entire Class A, B, or C network, you can use a smaller subnet, wasting fewer IP addresses.

To make it clear how an internetwork can use both classful IPv4 networks as well as subnets of classful IPv4 networks, the next two figures show the same internetwork, one with classful networks only and one with subnets only. Figure 4-8 shows the first such example, which uses five Class B networks, with no subnetting.

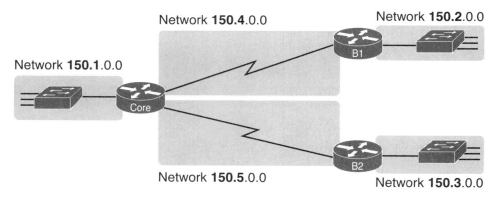

Figure 4-8 *Example That Uses Five Class B Networks*

The design in Figure 4-8 requires five groups of IP addresses, each of which is a Class B network in this example. Specifically, the three LANs each use a single Class B network, and the two serial links each use a Class B network.

Figure 4-8 wastes many IP addresses, because each Class B network has $2^{16} - 2$ host addresses—far more than you will ever need for each LAN and WAN link. For example, the Ethernet on the left uses an entire Class B network, which supports 65,534 IP addresses that begin with 150.1. However, a single LAN seldom grows past a few hundred devices, so many of the IP addresses in Class B network 150.1.0.0 would be wasted. Even more waste occurs on the point-to-point serial links, which only need two IP addresses.

Figure 4-9 illustrates a more common design today, one that uses basic subnetting. As in the previous figure, this figure needs five groups of addresses. However, in this case, the figure uses five subnets of Class B network 150.9.0.0.

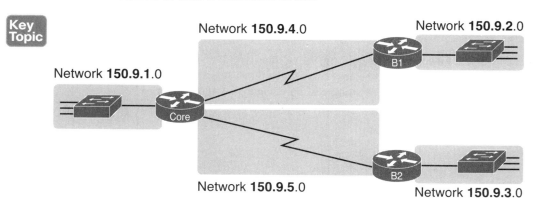

Figure 4-9 *Using Subnets for the Same Design as the Previous Figure*

Subnetting allows the network engineer for the TCP/IP internetwork to choose to use a longer part of the addresses that must have the same value. Subnetting allows quite a bit of flexibility, but Figure 4-9 shows one of the simplest forms of subnetting. In this case, each subnet includes the addresses that begin with the same value in the first three octets, as follows:

- One group of the 254 addresses that begin with 150.9.1
- One group of the 254 addresses that begin with 150.9.2
- One group of the 254 addresses that begin with 150.9.3
- One group of the 254 addresses that begin with 150.9.4
- One group of the 254 addresses that begin with 150.9.5

As a result of using subnetting, the network engineer has saved many IP addresses. First, only a small part of Class B network 150.9.0.0 has been used so far. Each subnet has 254 addresses, which should be plenty of addresses for each LAN, and more than enough for the WAN links.

> **NOTE**   All chapters of Part IV of this book explain the details of IP addressing, including the methods to choose an IP network and subnet it into smaller subnets.

In summary, you now know some of the details of IP addressing, with a focus on how it relates to routing. Each host and router interface will have an IP address. However, the IP addresses will not be randomly chosen, but will instead be grouped together to aid the routing process. The groups of addresses can be an entire Class A, B, or C network number or it can be a subnet.

IPv4 Routing

In the first section of this chapter ("Overview of Network Layer Functions"), you read about the basics of IPv4 routing using a network with three routers and two PCs. Armed with more knowledge of IP addressing, you now can take a closer look at the process of routing IP. This section begins with the simple two-part routing logic on the originating host, and then moves on to discuss how routers choose where to route or forward packets to the final destination.

IPv4 Host Routing

Hosts actually use some simple routing logic when choosing where to send a packet. If you assume that the design uses subnets (which is typical), this two-step logic is as follows:

Step 1.   If the destination IP address is in the same IP subnet as I am, send the packet directly to that destination host.

Step 2.   Otherwise, send the packet to my *default gateway*, also known as a *default router*. (This router has an interface on the same subnet as the host.)

For example, consider Figure 4-10 and focus on the Ethernet LAN on the left. When PC1 sends an IP packet to PC11 (150.9.1.11), PC1 first considers some match related to subnetting. PC1 concludes that PC11's IP address is in the same subnet as PC1, so PC1 ignores its default router (Core, 150.9.1.1), sending the packet directly to PC11, as shown in Step 1 of the figure.

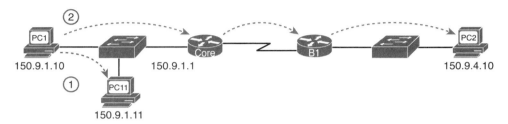

Figure 4-10   *Host Routing: Forwarding to a Host on the Same Subnet*

Alternatively, when PC1 sends a packet to PC2 (150.9.4.10), PC1 does the same kind of subnetting math, and realizes that PC2 is not on the same subnet as PC1. So, PC1 forwards the packet (Step 2) to its default gateway, 150.9.1.1, which then routes the packet to PC2.

Router Forwarding Decisions and the IP Routing Table

Earlier in this chapter, Figure 4-1 shows the network layer concepts of routing, while Figure 4-2 shows the data link encapsulation logic related to routing. This next topic dives a little deeper into that same process, using an example with three routers forwarding (routing) one packet. But before looking at the example, the text first summarizes how a router thinks about forwarding a packet.

A Summary of Router Forwarding Logic

First, when a router receives a data link frame addressed to that router's data link address, the router needs to think about processing the contents of the frame. When such a frame arrives, the router uses the following logic on the data link frame:

Step 1.   Use the data link Frame Check Sequence (FCS) field to ensure that the frame had no errors; if errors occurred, discard the frame.

Step 2.   Assuming that the frame was not discarded at Step 1, discard the old data link header and trailer, leaving the IP packet.

Step 3.   Compare the IP packet's destination IP address to the routing table, and find the route that best matches the destination address. This route identifies the outgoing interface of the router, and possibly the next-hop router IP address.

Step 4.   Encapsulate the IP packet inside a new data link header and trailer, appropriate for the outgoing interface, and forward the frame.

With these steps, each router forwards the packet to the next location, inside a data link frame. With each router repeating this process, the packet reaches its final destination.

While the router does all the steps in the list, Step 3 is the main routing or forwarding step. The packet has a destination IP address in the header, whereas the routing table lists slightly different numbers, typically a list of networks and subnets. To match a routing table entry, the router thinks like this:

Network numbers and subnet numbers represent a group of addresses that begin with the same prefix. Think about those numbers as groups of addresses. In which of the groups does this packet's destination address reside?

The next example shows specific examples of matching the routing table.

A Detailed Routing Example

The routing example uses Figure 4-11. In this example, all routers happen to use the Open Shortest Path First (OSPF) routing protocol, and all routers know routes for all subnets. In particular, PC2, at the bottom, sits in subnet 150.150.4.0, which consists of all addresses that begin with 150.150.4. In the example, PC1 sends an IP packet to 150.150.4.10, PC2's IP address.

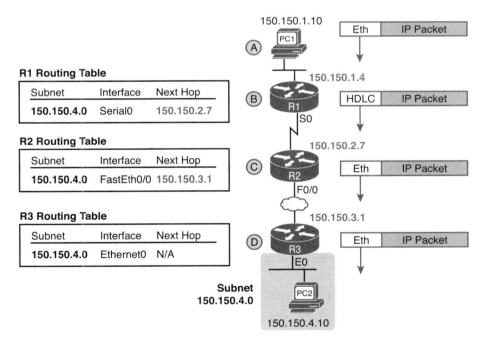

Figure 4-11 *Simple Routing Example, with IP Subnets*

> **NOTE**   Note that the routers all know in this case that "subnet 150.150.4.0" means "all addresses that begin with 150.150.4."

The following list explains the forwarding logic at each step in the figure. (Note that the text refers to Steps 1, 2, 3, and 4 of the routing logic shown in the previous section.)

Step A. **PC1 sends the packet to its default router.** PC1 first builds the IP packet, with a destination address of PC2's IP address (150.150.4.10). PC1 needs to send the packet to R1 (PC1's default router) because the destination address is on a different subnet. PC1 places the IP packet into an Ethernet frame, with a destination Ethernet address of R1's Ethernet address. PC1 sends the frame onto the Ethernet. (Note that the figure omits the data link trailers.)

Step B. **R1 processes the incoming frame and forwards the packet to R2.** Because the incoming Ethernet frame has a destination MAC of R1's Ethernet MAC, R1 copies the frame off the Ethernet for processing. R1 checks the frame's FCS, and no errors have occurred (Step 1). R1 then discards the Ethernet header and trailer (Step 2). Next, R1 compares the packet's destination address (150.150.4.10) to the routing table and finds the entry for subnet 150.150.4.0—which includes addresses 150.150.4.0 through 150.150.4.255 (Step 3). Because the destination address is in this group, R1 forwards the packet out interface Serial0 to next-hop router R2 (150.150.2.7) after encapsulating the packet in a High-Level Data Link Control (HDLC) frame (Step 4).

Step C. **R2 processes the incoming frame and forwards the packet to R3.** R2 repeats the same general process as R1 when R2 receives the HDLC frame. R2 checks the FCS field and finds that no errors occurred (Step 1). R2 then discards the HDLC header and trailer (Step 2). Next, R2 finds its route for subnet 150.150.4.0—which includes the address range 150.150.4.0–150.150.4.255—and realizes that the packet's destination address 150.150.4.10 matches that route (Step 3). Finally, R2 sends the packet out interface Fast Ethernet 0/0 to next-hop router 150.150.3.1 (R3) after encapsulating the packet in an Ethernet header (Step 4).

Step D. **R3 processes the incoming frame and forwards the packet to PC2.** Like R1 and R2, R3 checks the FCS, discards the old data link header and trailer, and matches its own route for subnet 150.150.4.0. R3's routing table entry for 150.150.4.0 shows that the outgoing interface is R3's Ethernet interface, but there is no next-hop router, because R3 is connected directly to subnet 150.150.4.0. All R3 has to do is encapsulate the packet inside a new Ethernet header and trailer, with a destination Ethernet address of PC2's MAC address, and forward the frame.

Next, this chapter briefly introduces the concepts behind IP routing protocols.

IPv4 Routing Protocols

The routing (forwarding) process depends heavily on having an accurate and up-to-date IP routing table on each router. This section takes another look at routing protocols, considering the goals of a routing protocol, the methods routing protocols use to teach and learn routes, and an example based on the same internetwork shown in the routing example around Figure 4-10.

First, consider the goals of a routing protocol, regardless of how the routing protocol works:

- To dynamically learn and fill the routing table with a route to each subnet in the internetwork.

- If more than one route to a subnet is available, to place the best route in the routing table.

- To notice when routes in the table are no longer valid, and to remove them from the routing table.

- If a route is removed from the routing table and another route through another neighboring router is available, to add the route to the routing table. (Many people view this goal and the preceding one as a single goal.)

- To work quickly when adding new routes or replacing lost routes. (The time between losing the route and finding a working replacement route is called *convergence* time.)

- To prevent routing loops.

Routing protocols all use some similar ideas to allow routers to learn routing information from each other. Of course, each routing protocol works differently; otherwise, you would not need more than one routing protocol. However, many routing protocols use the same general steps for learning routes:

Step 1.   Each router, independent of the routing protocol, adds a route to its routing table for each subnet directly connected to the router.

Step 2.   Each router's routing protocol tells its neighbors about the routes in its routing table, including the directly connected routes, and routes learned from other routers.

Step 3.   After learning a new route from a neighbor, the router's routing protocol adds a route to its IP routing table, with the next-hop router of that route typically being the neighbor from which the route was learned.

For example, Figure 4-12 shows the same sample network as in Figure 4-11, but now with a focus on how the three routers each learned about subnet 150.150.4.0. Note that routing protocols do more work than is implied in the figure; this figure just focuses on how the routers learn about subnet 150.150.4.0.

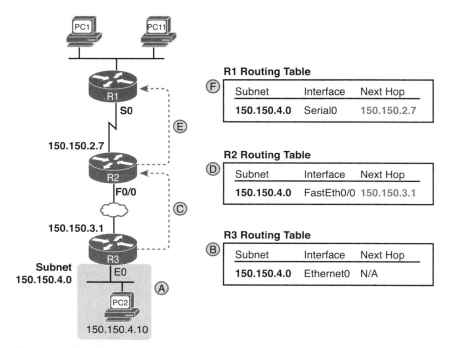

Figure 4-12   *Router R1 Learning About Subnet 150.150.4.0*

Follow items A through F shown in the figure to see how each router learns its route to 150.150.4.0. All references to Steps 1, 2, and 3 refer to the list just before Figure 4-12.

Step A.   Subnet 150.150.4.0 exists as a subnet at the bottom of the figure, connected to router R3.

Step B.   R3 adds a connected route for 150.150.4.0 to its IP routing table (Step 1); this happens without help from the routing protocol.

Step C.   R3 sends a routing protocol message, called a *routing update*, to R2, causing R2 to learn about subnet 150.150.4.0 (Step 2).

Step D.   R2 adds a route for subnet 150.150.4.0 to its routing table (Step 3).

Step E.   R2 sends a similar routing update to R1, causing R1 to learn about subnet 150.150.4.0 (Step 2).

Step F.   R1 adds a route for subnet 150.150.4.0 to its routing table (Step 3). The route lists R1's own Serial0 as the outgoing interface and R2 as the next-hop router IP address (150.150.2.7).

Chapter 20, "IPv4 Routing Protocol Concepts," covers routing protocols in more detail. Next, the final major section of this chapter introduces several additional functions related to how the network layer forwards packets from source to destination through an internetwork.

Other Network Layer Features

The TCP/IP network layer defines many functions beyond the function defined by the IPv4 protocol. Sure, IPv4 plays a huge role in networking today, defining IP addressing and IP routing. However, other protocols and standards, defined in other RFCs, play an important role for network layer functions as well. For example, routing protocols like OSPF exist as separate protocols, defined in separate RFCs.

This last short section of the chapter introduces three other network layer features that should be helpful to you when reading through the rest of this book. These last three topics just help fill in a few holes, helping to give you some perspective, and helping you make sense of later discussions as well. The three topics are

- Domain Name System (DNS)
- Address Resolution Protocol (ARP)
- Ping

Using Names and the Domain Name System

Can you imagine a world in which every time you used an application, you had to think about the other computer and refer to it by IP address? Instead of using easy names like google.com or facebook.com, you would have to remember and type IP addresses, like 74.125.225.5. Certainly, that would not be user friendly and could drive some people away from using computers at all.

Thankfully, TCP/IP defines a way to use *host names* to identify other computers. The user either never thinks about the other computer or refers to the other computer by name. Then, protocols dynamically discover all the necessary information to allow communications based on that name.

For example, when you open a web browser and type in the host name **www.google.com**, your computer does not send an IP packet with destination IP address www.google.com; it sends an IP packet to an IP address used by the web server for Google. TCP/IP needs a way to let a computer find the IP address used by the listed host name, and that method uses the *Domain Name System (DNS)*.

Enterprises use the DNS process to resolve names into the matching IP address, as shown in the example in Figure 4-13. In this case, PC11, on the left, needs to connect to a server named Server1. At some point, the user either types in the name Server1 or some application on PC11 refers to that server by name. At Step 1, PC11 sends a DNS message—a DNS query—to the DNS server. At Step 2, the DNS server sends back a DNS reply that lists Server1's IP address. At Step 3, PC11 can now send an IP packet to destination address 10.1.2.3, the address used by Server1.

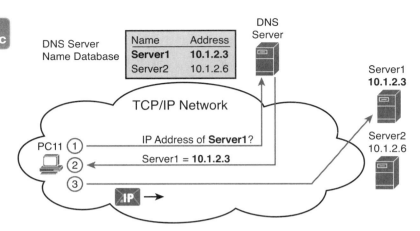

Figure 4-13 *Basic DNS Name Resolution Request*

Note that the example in Figure 4-13 shows a cloud for the TCP/IP network because the details of the network, including routers, do not matter to the name resolution process. Routers treat the DNS messages just like any other IP packet, routing them based on the destination IP address. For example, at Step 1 in the figure, the DNS query will list the DNS server's IP address as the destination address, which any routers will use to forward the packet.

Finally, DNS defines much more than just a few messages. DNS defines protocols, as well as standards for the text names used throughout the world, and a worldwide set of distributed DNS servers. The domain names that people use every day when web browsing, which look like www.example.com, follow the DNS naming standards. Also, no single DNS server knows all the names and matching IP addresses, but the information is distributed across many DNS servers. So, the DNS servers of the world work together, forwarding queries to each other, until the server that knows the answer supplies the desired IP address information.

The Address Resolution Protocol

IP routing logic requires that hosts and routers encapsulate IP packets inside data link layer frames. In fact, Figure 4-11 shows how every router deencapsulates each IP packet and encapsulates the IP packet inside a new data link frame.

On Ethernet LANs, whenever a host or router needs to encapsulate an IP packet in a new Ethernet frame, the host or router knows all the important facts to build that header— except for the destination MAC address. The host knows the IP address of the next device, either another host IP address or the default router IP address. A router knows the IP route used for forwarding the IP packet, which lists the next router's IP address. However, the hosts and routers do not know those neighboring devices' MAC addresses beforehand.

TCP/IP defines the *Address Resolution Protocol (ARP)* as the method by which any host or router on a LAN can dynamically learn the MAC address of another IP host or router on the same LAN. ARP defines a protocol that includes the *ARP Request*, which is a message that asks the simple request "if this is your IP address, please reply with your MAC address." ARP also defines the *ARP Reply* message, which indeed lists both the original IP address and the matching MAC address.

Figure 4-14 shows an example that uses the same router and host from the bottom part of the earlier Figure 4-11. The figure shows the ARP Request on the left as a LAN broadcast, so all hosts receive the frame. On the right, at Step 2, host PC2 sends back an ARP Reply, identifying PC2's MAC address. The text beside each message shows the contents inside the ARP message itself, which lets PC2 learn R3's IP address and matching MAC address, and R3 learn PC2's IP address and matching MAC address.

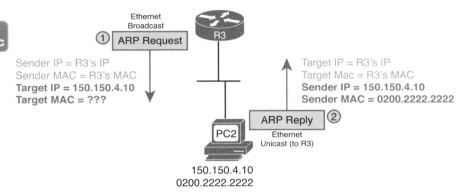

Figure 4-14 *Sample ARP Process*

Note that hosts remember the ARP results, keeping the information in their *ARP cache* or *ARP table*. A host or router only needs to use ARP occasionally, to build the ARP cache the first time. Each time a host or router needs to send a packet encapsulated in an Ethernet frame, it first checks its ARP cache for the correct IP address and matching MAC address. Hosts and routers will let ARP cache entries time out to clean up the table, so occasional ARP Requests can be seen.

> **NOTE**   You can see the contents of the ARP cache on most PC operating systems by using the **arp -a** command from a command prompt.

ICMP Echo and the ping Command

After you have implemented a TCP/IP internetwork, you need a way to test basic IP connectivity without relying on any applications to be working. The primary tool for testing basic network connectivity is the **ping** command.

Ping (Packet Internet Groper) uses the *Internet Control Message Protocol (ICMP)*, sending a message called an *ICMP echo request* to another IP address. The computer with that IP address should reply with an *ICMP echo reply*. If that works, you successfully have tested the IP network. In other words, you know that the network can deliver a packet from one host to the other and back. ICMP does not rely on any application, so it really just tests basic IP connectivity—Layers 1, 2, and 3 of the OSI model. Figure 4-15 outlines the basic process.

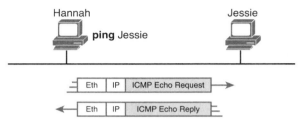

Figure 4-15   *Sample Network,* ping *Command*

Note that while the **ping** command uses ICMP, ICMP does much more. ICMP defines many messages that devices can use to help manage and control the IP network.

Exam Preparation Tasks

Review All the Key Topics

Review the most important topics from this chapter, noted with the Key Topic icon. Table 4-7 lists these key topics and where each is discussed.

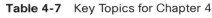 **Table 4-7**   Key Topics for Chapter 4

Key Topic Element	Description	Page Number
List	Two statements about how IP expects IP addresses to be grouped into networks or subnets	99
Figure 4-6	Breakdown of IPv4 address space	100
Figure 4-7	Sizes of Class A, B, and C Networks	101
Table 4-6	List of the three types of unicast IP networks and the size of the network and host parts of each type of network	103
Figure 4-9	Conceptual view of how subnetting works	104
List	Two-step process of how hosts route (forward) packets	105
List	Four-step process of how routers route (forward) packets	106
List	Goals of IP routing protocols	109
Figure 4-13	Example that shows the purpose and process of DNS name resolution	112
Figure 4-14	Example of the purpose and process of ARP	113

Complete the Tables and Lists from Memory

Print a copy of DVD Appendix I, "Memory Tables," or at least the section for this chapter, and complete the tables and lists from memory. DVD Appendix J, "Memory Tables Answer Key," includes completed tables and lists for you to check your work.

Definitions of Key Terms

After your first reading of the chapter, try to define these key terms, but do not be concerned about getting them all correct at that time. Chapter 23 directs you in how to use these terms for late-stage preparation for the exam.

default router (default gateway), routing table, IP network, IP subnet, IP packet, routing protocol, dotted-decimal notation (DDN), IPv4 address, unicast IP address, subnetting, host name, DNS, ARP, ping

This chapter covers the following exam topics:

1.3 Use the OSI and TCP/IP models and their associated protocols to explain how data flows in a network

1.3.b TCP

1.3.c UDP

Fundamentals of TCP/IP Transport and Applications

The DCICN exam focuses mostly on how IP network can send data between servers, and between clients and servers, using Ethernet and IP. This chapter explains the basics of a few topics that receive less attention on the exams: the TCP/IP transport layer and the TCP/IP application layer. The functions of
these higher layers play a big role in real TCP/IP networks, so it helps to have some basic understanding before moving into the rest of the book, where you go deeper into LANs and IP routing.

This chapter begins by examining the functions of two transport layer protocols: Transmission Control Protocol (TCP) and User Datagram Protocol (UDP). The second major section of the chapter examines the TCP/IP application layer, including some discussion of how Domain Name System (DNS) name resolution works.

> **NOTE** As promised in the Introduction's section, "For Those Studying Routing & Switching": This chapter's content covers slightly more information than the *ICND1 100-101 Official Cert Guide*. This chapter adds the topics with the headings "Error Recovery and Reliability," "Flow Control Using Windowing," and "How the Receiving Host Identifies the Correct Receiving Application."

"Do I Know This Already?" Quiz

Use the "Do I Know This Already?" quiz to help decide whether you might want to skim this chapter, or a major section, moving more quickly to the "Exam Preparation Tasks" section near the end of the chapter. You can find the answers at the bottom of the page following the quiz. For thorough explanations, see Appendix A, "Answers to the 'Do I Know This Already?' Quizzes."

Table 5-1 "Do I Know This Already?" Foundation Topics Section-to-Question Mapping

Foundation Topics Section	Questions
TCP/IP Layer 4 Protocols: TCP and UDP	1–5
TCP/IP Applications	6, 7

1. Which of the following is not a feature of a protocol that is considered to match OSI Layer 4?

   a. Error recovery

   b. Flow control

   c. Segmenting of application data

   d. Conversion from binary to ASCII

2. Which of the following header fields identify which TCP/IP application gets data received by the computer? (Choose two answers.)

   a. Ethernet Type

   b. SNAP Protocol Type

   c. IP Protocol

   d. TCP Port Number

   e. UDP Port Number

3. Which of the following are typical functions of TCP? (Choose four answers.)

   a. Flow Control (windowing)

   b. Error recovery

   c. Multiplexing using port numbers

   d. Routing

   e. Encryption

   f. Ordered data transfer

4. Which of the following functions is performed by both TCP and UDP?

   a. Windowing

   b. Error recovery

   c. Multiplexing using port numbers

   d. Routing

   e. Encryption

   f. Ordered data transfer

5. What do you call data that includes the Layer 4 protocol header, and data given to Layer 4 by the upper layers, not including any headers and trailers from Layers 1 to 3? (Choose two answers.)

   a. L3PDU

   b. Chunk

   c. Segment

   d. Packet

   e. Frame

   f. L4PDU

6. In the URL http://www.certskills.com/ICND1, which part identifies the web server?

   a. http

   b. www.certskills.com

   c. certskills.com

   d. http://www.certskills.com

   e. The file name.html includes the host name.

7. When comparing VoIP with an HTTP-based mission-critical business application, which of the following statements are accurate about the quality of service needed from the network? (Choose two answers.)

   a. VoIP needs better (lower) packet loss.

   b. HTTP needs less bandwidth.

   c. HTTP needs better (lower) jitter.

   d. VoIP needs better (lower) delay.

5

Foundation Topics

TCP/IP Layer 4 Protocols: TCP and UDP

The OSI transport layer (Layer 4) defines several functions, the most important of which are error recovery and flow control. Likewise, the TCP/IP transport layer protocols also implement these same types of features. Note that both the OSI model and the TCP/IP model call this layer the transport layer. But as usual, when referring to the TCP/IP model, the layer name and number are based on OSI, so any TCP/IP transport layer protocols are considered Layer 4 protocols.

The key difference between TCP and UDP is that TCP provides a wide variety of services to applications, whereas UDP does not. For example, routers discard packets for many reasons, including bit errors, congestion, and instances in which no correct routes are known. As you have read already, most data link protocols notice errors (a process called *error detection*) but then discard frames that have errors. TCP provides retransmission (error recovery) and helps to avoid congestion (flow control), whereas UDP does not. As a result, many application protocols choose to use TCP.

However, do not let UDP's lack of services make you think that UDP is worse than TCP. By providing fewer services, UDP needs fewer bytes in its header compared to TCP, resulting in fewer bytes of overhead in the network. UDP software does not slow down data transfer in cases where TCP can purposefully slow down. Also, some applications, notably today Voice over IP (VoIP) and video over IP, do not need error recovery, so they use UDP. So, UDP also has an important place in TCP/IP networks today.

Table 5-2 lists the main features supported by TCP and/or UDP. Note that only the first item listed in the table is supported by UDP, whereas all items in the table are supported by TCP.

Table 5-2   TCP/IP Transport Layer Features

Function	Description
Multiplexing using ports	Function that allows receiving hosts to choose the correct application for which the data is destined, based on the port number.
Error recovery (reliability)	Process of numbering and acknowledging data with Sequence and Acknowledgment header fields.
Flow control using windowing	Process that uses window sizes to protect buffer space and routing devices from being overloaded with traffic.

Function	Description
Connection establishment and termination	Process used to initialize port numbers and Sequence and Acknowledgment fields.
Ordered data transfer and data segmentation	Continuous stream of bytes from an upper-layer process that is "segmented" for transmission and delivered to upper-layer processes at the receiving device, with the bytes in the same order.

Next, this section describes the features of TCP, followed by a brief comparison to UDP.

Transmission Control Protocol

Each TCP/IP application typically chooses to use either TCP or UDP based on the application's requirements. For example, TCP provides error recovery, but to do so, it consumes more bandwidth and uses more processing cycles. UDP does not perform error recovery, but it takes less bandwidth and uses fewer processing cycles. Regardless of which of these two TCP/IP transport layer protocols the application chooses to use, you should understand the basics of how each of these transport layer protocols works.

TCP, as defined in RFC 793, accomplishes the functions listed in Table 5-2 through mechanisms at the endpoint computers. TCP relies on IP for end-to-end delivery of the data, including routing issues. In other words, TCP performs only part of the functions necessary to deliver the data between applications. Also, the role that it plays is directed toward providing services for the applications that sit at the endpoint computers. Regardless of whether two computers are on the same Ethernet, or are separated by the entire Internet, TCP performs its functions the same way.

Figure 5-1 shows the fields in the TCP header. Although you don't need to memorize the names of the fields or their locations, the rest of this section refers to several of the fields, so the entire header is included here for reference.

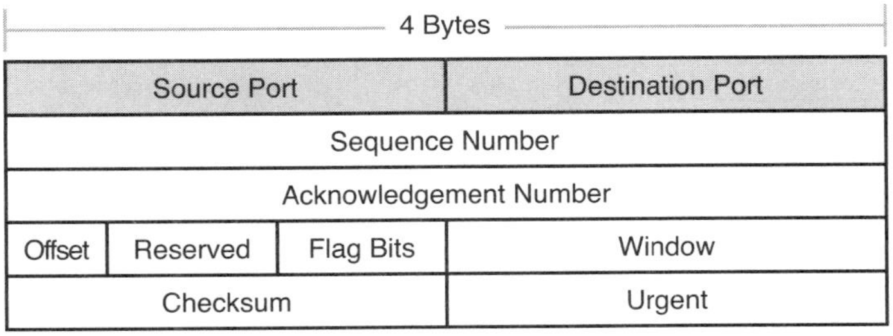

4 Bytes		
Source Port		Destination Port
Sequence Number		
Acknowledgement Number		
Offset	Reserved	Flag Bits	Window
Checksum		Urgent

Figure 5-1 *TCP Header Fields*

The message created by TCP that begins with the TCP header, followed by any application data, is called a *TCP segment*. Alternately, the more generic term *Layer 4 PDU*, or *L4PDU*, can also be used.

Multiplexing Using TCP Port Numbers

TCP and UDP both use a concept called *multiplexing*. Therefore, this section begins with an explanation of multiplexing with TCP and UDP. Afterward, the unique features of TCP are explored.

Multiplexing by TCP and UDP involves the process of how a computer thinks when receiving data. The computer might be running many applications, such as a web browser, an email package, or an Internet VoIP application (for example, Skype). TCP and UDP multiplexing tells the receiving computer to which application to give the received data.

Some examples will help make the need for multiplexing obvious. The sample network consists of two PCs, labeled Hannah and Jessie. Hannah uses an application that she wrote to send advertisements that appear on Jessie's screen. The application sends a new ad to Jessie every 10 seconds. Hannah uses a second application, a wire-transfer application, to send Jessie some money. Finally, Hannah uses a web browser to access the web server that runs on Jessie's PC. The ad application and wire-transfer application are imaginary, just for this example. The web application works just like it would in real life.

Figure 5-2 shows the sample network, with Jessie running three applications:

- A UDP-based ad application
- A TCP-based wire-transfer application
- A TCP web server application

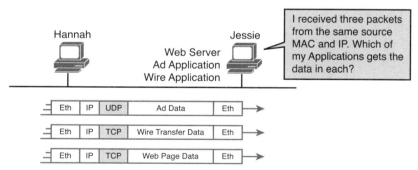

Figure 5-2   *Hannah Sending Packets to Jessie, with Three Applications*

Jessie needs to know which application to give the data to, but *all three packets are from the same Ethernet and IP address*. You might think that Jessie could look at whether the packet contains a UDP or TCP header, but as you see in the figure, two applications (wire transfer and web) are using TCP.

TCP and UDP solve this problem by using a port number field in the TCP or UDP header, respectively. Each of Hannah's TCP and UDP segments uses a different *destination port number* so that Jessie knows which application to give the data to. Figure 5-3 shows an example.

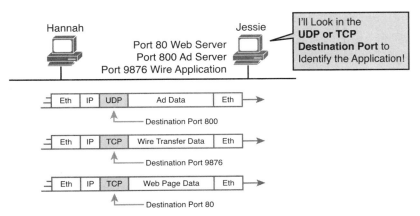

Figure 5-3 *Hannah Sending Packets to Jessie, with Three Applications Using Port Numbers to Multiplex*

Multiplexing relies on a concept called a *socket*. A socket consists of three things:

- An IP address
- A transport protocol
- A port number

So, for a web server application on Jessie, the socket would be (10.1.1.2, TCP, port 80) because, by default, web servers use the well-known port 80. When Hannah's web browser connects to the web server, Hannah uses a socket as well—possibly one like this: (10.1.1.1, TCP, 1030). Why 1030? Well, Hannah just needs a port number that is unique on Hannah, so Hannah sees that port 1030 is available and uses it. In fact, hosts typically allocate *dynamic port numbers* starting at 1024 because the ports below 1024 are reserved for well-known applications.

In Figure 5-3, Hannah and Jessie use three applications at the same time—hence, three socket connections are open. Because a socket on a single computer should be unique, a connection between two sockets should identify a unique connection between two computers. This uniqueness means that you can use multiple applications at the same time, talking to applications running on the same or different computers. Multiplexing, based on sockets, ensures that the data is delivered to the correct applications. Figure 5-4 shows the three socket connections between Hannah and Jessie.

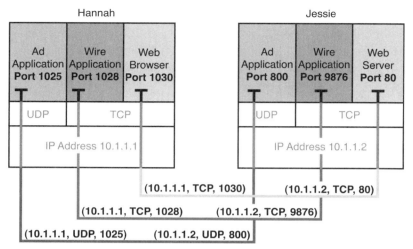

Figure 5-4 *Connections Between Sockets*

Port numbers are a vital part of the socket concept. Well-known port numbers are used by servers; other port numbers are used by clients. Applications that provide a service, such as FTP, Telnet, and web servers, open a socket using a well-known port and listen for connection requests. Because these connection requests from clients are required to include both the source and destination port numbers, the port numbers used by the servers must be well-known. Therefore, each service uses a specific well-known port number. The well-known ports are listed at www.iana.org/assignments/service-names-port-numbers/ service-names-port-numbers.txt.

On client machines, where the requests originate, any locally unused port number can be allocated. The result is that each client on the same host uses a different port number, but a server uses the same port number for all connections. For example, 100 web browsers on the same host computer could each connect to a web server, but the web server with 100 clients connected to it would have only one socket and, therefore, only one port number (port 80, in this case). The server can tell which packets are sent from which of the 100 clients by looking at the source port of received TCP segments. The server can send data to the correct web client (browser) by sending data to that same port number listed as a destination port. The combination of source and destination sockets allows all participating hosts to distinguish between the data's source and destination. Although the example explains the concept using 100 TCP connections, the same port-numbering concept applies to UDP sessions in the same way.

NOTE   You can find all RFCs online at http://www.rfc-editor.org/rfc/rfcxxxx.txt, where *xxxx* is the number of the RFC. If you do not know the number of the RFC, you can try searching by topic at www.rfc-editor.org.

Popular TCP/IP Applications

Throughout your preparation for the DCICN exam, you will come across a variety of TCP/IP applications. You should at least be aware of some of the applications that can be used to help manage and control a network.

The World Wide Web (WWW) application exists through web browsers accessing the content available on web servers. Although it is often thought of as an end-user application, you can actually use WWW to manage a router or switch. You enable a web server function in the router or switch and use a browser to access the router or switch.

The Domain Name System (DNS) allows users to use names to refer to computers, with DNS being used to find the corresponding IP addresses. DNS also uses a client/server model, with DNS servers being controlled by networking personnel and DNS client functions being part of most any device that uses TCP/IP today. The client simply asks the DNS server to supply the IP address that corresponds to a given name.

Simple Network Management Protocol (SNMP) is an application layer protocol used specifically for network device management. For example, Cisco supplies a large variety of network management products, many of them in the Cisco Prime network management software product family. They can be used to query, compile, store, and display information about a network's operation. To query the network devices, Cisco Prime software mainly uses SNMP protocols.

Traditionally, to move files to and from a router or switch, Cisco used Trivial File Transfer Protocol (TFTP). TFTP defines a protocol for basic file transfer—hence the word *trivial*. Alternatively, routers and switches can use File Transfer Protocol (FTP), which is a much more functional protocol, to transfer files. Both work well for moving files into and out of Cisco devices. FTP allows many more features, making it a good choice for the general end-user population. TFTP client and server applications are very simple, making them good tools as embedded parts of networking devices.

Some of these applications use TCP, and some use UDP. For example, Simple Mail Transfer Protocol (SMTP) and Post Office Protocol version 3 (POP3), both used for transferring mail, require guaranteed delivery, so they use TCP. Regardless of which transport layer protocol is used, applications use a well-known port number so that clients know which port to attempt to connect to. Table 5-3 lists several popular applications and their well-known port numbers.

Table 5-3   Popular Applications and Their Well-Known Port Numbers

Port Number	Protocol	Application
20	TCP	FTP data
21	TCP	FTP control
22	TCP	SSH
23	TCP	Telnet

5

Port Number	Protocol	Application
25	TCP	SMTP
53	UDP, TCP	DNS
67, 68	UDP	DHCP
69	UDP	TFTP
80	TCP	HTTP (WWW)
110	TCP	POP3
161	UDP	SNMP
443	TCP	SSL

Connection Establishment and Termination

TCP connection establishment occurs before any of the other TCP features can begin their work. Connection establishment refers to the process of initializing sequence and acknowledgment fields and agreeing on the port numbers used. Figure 5-5 shows an example of connection establishment flow.

Figure 5-5   *TCP Connection Establishment*

This three-way connection establishment flow (also called a three-way handshake) must complete before data transfer can begin. The connection exists between the two sockets, although the TCP header has no single socket field. Of the three parts of a socket, the IP addresses are implied based on the source and destination IP addresses in the IP header. TCP is implied because a TCP header is in use, as specified by the protocol field value in the IP header. Therefore, the only parts of the socket that need to be encoded in the TCP header are the port numbers.

TCP signals connection establishment using 2 bits inside the flag fields of the TCP header. Called the SYN and ACK flags, these bits have a particularly interesting meaning. SYN means "synchronize the sequence numbers," which is one necessary component in initialization for TCP.

Figure 5-6 shows TCP connection termination. This four-way termination sequence is straightforward and uses an additional flag, called the *FIN bit*. (FIN is short for "finished," as you might guess.) One interesting note: Before the device on the right sends the third TCP segment in the sequence, it notifies the application that the connection is coming down. It then waits on an acknowledgment from the application before sending the third segment in the figure. Just in case the application takes some time to reply, the PC on the right sends the second flow in the figure, acknowledging that the other PC wants to take down the connection. Otherwise, the PC on the left might resend the first segment repeatedly.

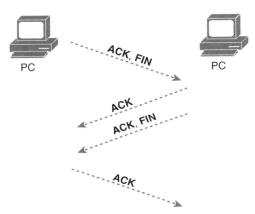

Figure 5-6 *TCP Connection Termination*

TCP establishes and terminates connections between the endpoints, whereas UDP does not. Many protocols operate under these same concepts, so the terms *connection-oriented* and *connectionless* are used to refer to the general idea of each. More formally, these terms can be defined as follows:

- **Connection-oriented protocol:** A protocol that requires an exchange of messages before data transfer begins, or that has a required preestablished correlation between two endpoints.

- **Connectionless protocol:** A protocol that does not require an exchange of messages and that does not require a preestablished correlation between two endpoints.

Error Recovery and Reliability

TCP provides for reliable data transfer, which is also called *reliability* or *error recovery*, depending on what document you read. To accomplish reliability, TCP numbers data bytes using the Sequence and Acknowledgment fields in the TCP header. TCP achieves reliability in both directions, using the Sequence Number field of one direction combined with the Acknowledgment field in the opposite direction.

Figure 5-7 shows an example of how the TCP Sequence and Acknowledgment fields enable the PC to send 3000 bytes of data to the server, with the server acknowledging receipt of the data. The TCP segments in the figure occur in order, from top to bottom. For simplicity's sake, all messages have 1000 bytes of data in the data portion of the TCP segment. The first sequence number is a nice round number (1000), again for simplicity's sake. The top of the figure shows three segments, with each sequence number being 1000 more than the previous, identifying the first of the 1000 bytes in the message. (That is, in this example, the first segment holds bytes 1000–1999; the second holds bytes 2000–2999; and the third holds bytes 3000–3999.)

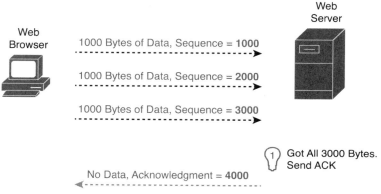

Figure 5-7 *TCP Acknowledgment Without Errors*

The fourth TCP segment in the figure—the only one flowing back from the server to the web browser—acknowledges the receipt of all three segments. How? The acknowledgment value of 4000 means "I received all data with sequence numbers up through one less than 4000, so I am ready to receive your byte 4000 next." (Note that this convention of acknowledging by listing the next expected byte, rather than the number of the last byte received, is called *forward acknowledgment*.)

This first example does not recover from any errors, however—it simply shows the basics of how the sending host uses the sequence number field to identify the data, with the receiving host using forward acknowledgments to acknowledge the data. The more interesting discussion revolves around how to use these same tools to do error recovery. TCP uses the sequence and acknowledgment fields so that the receiving host can notice lost data, ask the sending host to resend, and then acknowledge that the re-sent data arrived.

Many variations exist for how TCP does error recovery. Figure 5-8 shows just one such example, with similar details compared to the previous figure. The web browser again sends three TCP segments, again 1000 bytes each, again with easy-to-remember sequence numbers. However, in this example, the second TCP segment fails to cross the network.

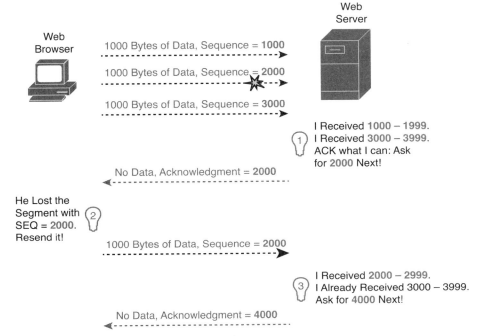

Web
Browser

Web
Server

1000 Bytes of Data, Sequence = **1000**

1000 Bytes of Data, Sequence = **2000**

1000 Bytes of Data, Sequence = **3000**

1 I Received **1000 – 1999**.
I Received **3000 – 3999**.
ACK what I can: Ask
for **2000** Next!

No Data, Acknowledgment = **2000**

He Lost the
Segment with
SEQ = **2000**.
Resend it!

2

1000 Bytes of Data, Sequence = **2000**

3 I Received **2000 – 2999**.
I Already Received 3000 – 3999.
Ask for **4000** Next!

No Data, Acknowledgment = **4000**

Figure 5-8   *TCP Acknowledgment with Errors*

The figure points out three sets of ideas behind how the two hosts think. First, on the right, the server realizes that it did not receive all the data. The two received TCP segments contain bytes numbered 1000–1999 and 3000–3999. Clearly, the server did not receive the bytes numbered in between. The server then decides to acknowledge all the data up to the lost data; that is, to send back a segment with the acknowledgment field equal to 2000.

The receipt of an acknowledgment that does not acknowledge all the data sent so far tells the sending host to resend the data. The PC on the left might wait a few moments to make sure no other acknowledgments arrive (using a timer called the retransmission timer), but will soon decide that the server means, "I really do need 2000 next: resend it." The PC on the left does so, as shown in the fifth of the six TCP segments in the figure.

Finally, note that the server can acknowledge not only the re-sent data, but any earlier data that had been received correctly. In this case, the server received the re-sent second TCP segment (the data with sequence numbers 2000–2999), but the server had already received the third TCP segment (the data numbered 3000–3999). The server's next acknowledgment field acknowledges the data in both those segments, with an acknowledgment field of 4000.

Flow Control Using Windowing

TCP implements flow control by using a window concept that is applied to the amount of data that can be outstanding and awaiting acknowledgment at any one point in time. The window concept lets the receiving host tell the sender how much data it can receive right now, giving the receiving host a way to make the sending host slow down or speed up. The receiver can slide the window size up and down—called a *sliding window* or *dynamic window*—to change how much data the sending host can send.

The sliding window mechanism makes much more sense with an example. The example, shown in Figure 5-9, uses the same basic rules as the examples in the previous few figures. In this case, none of the TCP segments have errors, and the discussion begins one TCP segment earlier than in the previous two figures.

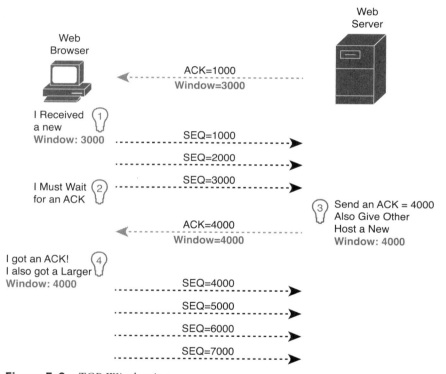

Figure 5-9 *TCP Windowing*

Begin with the first segment, sent by the server to the PC. The acknowledgment field should be familiar by now: It tells the PC that the server expects a segment with sequence number 1000 next. The new field, the window field, is set to 3000. Because the segment flows to the PC, this value tells the PC that the PC can send no more than 3000 bytes over this connection before receiving an acknowledgment. So, as seen on the left, the PC realizes it can send only 3000 bytes, and it stops sending, waiting on an acknowledgment, after sending three 1000-byte TCP segments.

Continuing the example, the server not only acknowledges receiving the data (without any loss), but the server decides to slide the window size a little higher. Note the second message flowing right to left in the figure, this time with a window of 4000. When the PC receives this TCP segment, the PC realizes it can send another 4000 bytes—a slightly larger window than the previous value—with those four 1000-byte segments shown at the bottom of the figure.

Note that although the last few figures show examples for the purpose of explaining how the mechanisms work, the examples might give you the impression that TCP makes the hosts sit there and wait for acknowledgments a lot. TCP does not want to make the sending host have to wait to send data. For example, if an acknowledgment is received before the window is exhausted, a new window begins and the sender continues sending data until the current window is exhausted. Often, in a network that has few problems, few lost segments, and little congestion, the TCP windows stay relatively large with hosts seldom waiting to send.

User Datagram Protocol

UDP provides a service for applications to exchange messages. Unlike TCP, UDP is connectionless and provides no reliability, no windowing, no reordering of the received data, and no segmentation of large chunks of data into the right size for transmission. However, UDP provides some functions of TCP, such as data transfer and multiplexing using port numbers, and it does so with fewer bytes of overhead and less processing required than TCP.

UDP data transfer differs from TCP data transfer in that no reordering or recovery is accomplished. Applications that use UDP are tolerant of the lost data, or they have some application mechanism to recover lost data. For example, VoIP uses UDP because if a voice packet is lost, by the time the loss could be noticed and the packet retransmitted, too much delay would have occurred, and the voice would be unintelligible. Also, DNS requests use UDP because the user will retry an operation if the DNS resolution fails. As another example, the Network File System (NFS), a remote file system application, performs recovery with application layer code, so UDP features are acceptable to NFS.

Figure 5-10 shows the UDP header format. Most importantly, note that the header includes source and destination port fields, for the same purpose as TCP. However, the UDP has only 8 bytes, in comparison to the 20-byte TCP header shown in Figure 5-1. UDP needs a shorter header than TCP simply because UDP has less work to do.

4 Bytes	
Source Port	Destination Port
Length	Checksum

Figure 5-10 *UDP Header*

TCP/IP Applications

The whole goal of building an enterprise network, or connecting a small home or office network to the Internet, is to use applications—applications such as web browsing, text messaging, email, file downloads, voice, and video. This section examines a few issues related to network design in light of the applications expected in an internetwork. This is followed by a much deeper look at one particular application—web browsing using Hypertext Transfer Protocol (HTTP).

QoS Needs and the Impact of TCP/IP Applications

Applications need to send data over a TCP/IP internetwork. However, they need more than the ability to move the data from one application on one device to another application on another device. That communication has different characteristics, or qualities, and the networking world refers to these qualities as quality of service (QoS).

QoS in general defines the quality of the data transfer between two applications and in the network as a whole. QoS often breaks down these qualities into four competing characteristics:

Bandwidth: The volume of bits per second needed for the application to work well; it can be biased with more volume in one direction, or balanced.

Delay: The amount of time it takes one IP packet to flow from sender to receiver.

Jitter: The variation in delay.

Loss: The percentage of packets discarded by the network before they reach the destination, which when using TCP, requires a retransmission.

Today's TCP/IP internetworks support many types of applications, and each type has different QoS requirements. The next few pages look at the QoS requirements for three general categories of applications: batch, interactive, and real-time.

Defining Interactive and Batch Applications

TCP/IP networks began in the 1970s and 1980s with data applications only, with no widely used voice and video applications. Data applications send bits, and the bits represent data: text to be displayed for a user, graphical images to be displayed for a user, customer information, and so on.

Data applications have different QoS requirements depending on whether they are interactive or batch. Interactive data applications usually have a human user at one end of a flow, and the IP packets must flow in both directions for meaningful work to happen. For example, the user takes some action, sending a packet to a server; before the user sees more data on the screen, the server must send a packet back. So, the delay and jitter have a big impact on the user experience.

Batch applications focus more on the bandwidth between two software processes. Batch applications often do not even have a human in the picture. For example, you can have an application on your device that backs up your device data overnight, copying it to some server in the network. You personally might not care how long it takes, but the IT department cares how much bandwidth (how many bits/second) is needed. Why? The IT department might need to support thousands of devices that need to do their backups between 2 a.m. and 5 a.m. each day, so it has to build a network with enough bandwidth to meet that need.

Real-Time Voice and Video Applications

Most modern enterprise TCP/IP internetworks support voice applications as well. Most commonly, the network includes IP phones, which are telephones that connect to the TCP/IP network using an Ethernet or wireless LAN connection. The phone sends the voice as bits inside IP packets, as shown in Figure 5-11.

Figure 5-11   *IP Packet Sent by a Voice Call*

> **NOTE**   Sending voice traffic as bits inside an IP packet is generally called *Voice over IP (VoIP)*, while the use of telephones that connect to LANs as shown in Figure 5-11 is called *IP telephony*.

While a phone call between two IP phones has similar kinds of QoS requirements as an interactive data application, because the QoS requirements are much higher, voice is considered to be a real-time application instead of an interactive application. For example, a one-way network delay of 1 second works well for most web-browsing experiences. However, for a quality voice call, that same one-way delay needs to be less than 0.2 seconds. Also, interactive applications do not suffer much when packets are lost in transit, but a real-time voice call does suffer, with less voice quality.

The QoS requirements for video are similar to those for voice. Like voice, two-way video applications, like videoconferencing, require low delay, low jitter, and low loss.

Table 5-4 compares the QoS requirements of three example applications: interactive web browsing, real-time voice, and real-time video. Use the table to review the comparisons between data applications versus voice and video, as opposed to using it as a set of random facts to memorize.

Table 5-4 *Comparing Interactive and Real-Time Application Requirements*

Category of Application	Delay	Jitter	Loss
Web browsing (interactive)	Medium	Medium	Medium
VoIP phone call	Low	Low	Low
Videoconferencing	Low	Low	Low

To support the QoS requirements of the various applications, routers and switches can be configured with a wide variety of QoS tools. They are beyond the scope of the this exam (but are covered on several of the Cisco professional-level certifications). However, the QoS tools must be used for a modern network to be able to support high-quality VoIP and video over IP.

Next, we examine the most popular application layer protocol for interactive data applications today—HTTP and the World Wide Web (WWW). The goal is to show one example of how application layer protocols work.

The World Wide Web, HTTP, and SSL

The *World Wide Web (WWW)* consists of all the Internet-connected web servers in the world, plus all Internet-connected hosts with web browsers. *Web servers*, which consist of web server software running on a computer, store information (in the form of *web pages*) that might be useful to different people. A web browser, which is software installed on an end user's computer, provides the means to connect to a web server and display the web pages stored on the web server.

> **NOTE** Although most people use the term *web browser*, or simply *browser*, web browsers are also called *web clients*, because they obtain a service from a web server.

For this process to work, several specific application layer functions must occur. The user must somehow identify the server, the specific web page, and the protocol used to get the data from the server. The client must find the server's IP address, based on the server's name, typically using DNS. The client must request the web page, which actually consists of multiple separate files, and the server must send the files to the web browser. Finally, for electronic commerce (e-commerce) applications, the transfer of data, particularly sensitive financial data, needs to be secure. The following sections address each of these functions.

Uniform Resource Locators

For a browser to display a web page, the browser must identify the server that has the web page, plus other information that identifies the particular web page. Most web servers have many web pages. For example, if you use a web browser to browse www.cisco.com and you click around that web page, you'll see another web page. Click again, and you'll see another web page. In each case, the clicking action identifies the server's IP address and the specific web page, with the details mostly hidden from you. (These clickable items on a web page, which in turn bring you to another web page, are called *links*.)

The browser user can identify a web page when you click something on a web page or when you enter a *Uniform Resource Locator (URL)* (often called a *web address* and sometimes a universal resource locator) in the browser's address area. Both options—clicking a link and entering a URL—refer to a URL, because when you click a link on a web page, that link actually refers to a URL.

> **NOTE** Most browsers support some way to view the hidden URL referenced by a link. In several browsers, hover the mouse pointer over a link, right-click, and select **Properties**. The pop-up window should display the URL to which the browser would be directed if you clicked that link.

Each URL defines the protocol used to transfer data, the name of the server, and the particular web page on that server. The URL can be broken into three parts:

■ The protocol is listed before the //.

■ The host name is listed between the // and the /.

■ The name of the web page is listed after the /.

For example, consider the following:

    http://www.certskills.com/ICND1

In this case, the protocol is *Hypertext Transfer Protocol (HTTP)*, the host name is www.certskills.com, and the name of the web page is ICND1.

Finding the Web Server Using DNS

As mentioned in Chapter 4, "Fundamentals of IPv4 Addressing and Routing," a host can use DNS to discover the IP address that corresponds to a particular host name. Although URLs can include the IP address of the web server instead of the name of the web server, URLs typically list the host name. So, before the browser can send a packet to the web server, the browser typically needs to resolve the name in the URL to that name's corresponding IP address.

To pull together several concepts, Figure 5-12 shows the DNS process as initiated by a web browser, as well as some other related information. From a basic perspective, the user enters the URL (http://www.cisco.com/go/learningnetwork), resolves the www.cisco.com name into the correct IP address, and starts sending packets to the web server.

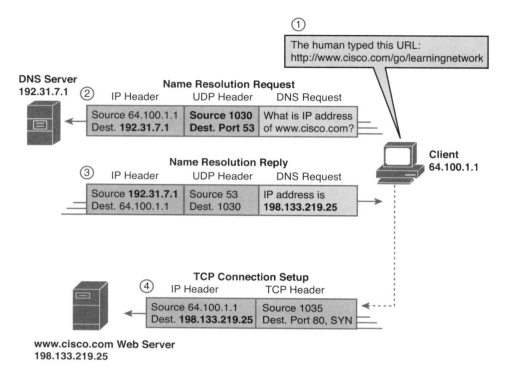

Figure 5-12 *DNS Resolution and Requesting a Web Page*

The steps shown in the figure are as follows:

1. The user enters the URL, http://www.cisco.com/go/learningnetwork, into the browser's address area.

2. The client sends a DNS request to the DNS server. Typically, the client learns the DNS server's IP address through DHCP. Note that the DNS request uses a UDP header, with a destination port of the DNS well-known port of 53. (See Table 5-3, earlier in this chapter, for a list of popular well-known ports.)

3. The DNS server sends a reply, listing IP address 198.133.219.25 as www.cisco.com's IP address. Note also that the reply shows a destination IP address of 64.100.1.1, the client's IP address. It also shows a UDP header, with source port 53; the source port is 53 because the data is sourced, or sent by, the DNS server.

4. The client begins the process of establishing a new TCP connection to the web server. Note that the destination IP address is the just-learned IP address of the web server. The packet includes a TCP header, because HTTP uses TCP. Also note that the destination TCP port is 80, the well-known port for HTTP. Finally, the SYN bit is shown, as a reminder that the TCP connection establishment process begins with a TCP segment with the SYN bit turned on (binary 1).

At this point in the process, the web browser is almost finished setting up a TCP connection to the web server. The next section picks up the story at that point, examining how the web browser then gets the files that comprise the desired web page.

Transferring Files with HTTP

After a web client (browser) has created a TCP connection to a web server, the client can begin requesting the web page from the server. Most often, the protocol used to transfer the web page is HTTP. The HTTP application layer protocol, defined in RFC 2616, defines how files can be transferred between two computers. HTTP was specifically created for the purpose of transferring files between web servers and web clients.

HTTP defines several commands and responses, with the most frequently used being the HTTP GET request. To get a file from a web server, the client sends an HTTP GET request to the server, listing the filename. If the server decides to send the file, the server sends an HTTP GET response, with a return code of 200 (meaning "OK"), along with the file's contents.

> **NOTE**   Many return codes exist for HTTP requests. For example, when the server does not have the requested file, it issues a return code of 404, which means "file not found." Most web browsers do not show the specific numeric HTTP return codes, instead displaying a response such as "page not found" in reaction to receiving a return code of 404.

Web pages typically consist of multiple files, called *objects*. Most web pages contain text as well as several graphical images, animated advertisements, and possibly voice or video. Each of these components is stored as a different object (file) on the web server. To get them all, the web browser gets the first file. This file can (and typically does) include references to other URLs, so the browser then also requests the other objects. Figure 5-13 shows the general idea, with the browser getting the first file and then two others.

In this case, after the web browser gets the first file—the one called "/go/ccna" in the URL—the browser reads and interprets that file. Besides containing parts of the web page, the file refers to two other files, so the browser issues two additional HTTP get requests. Note that, even though it isn't shown in the figure, all these commands flow over one (or possibly more) TCP connection between the client and the server. This means that TCP would provide error recovery, ensuring that the data was delivered.

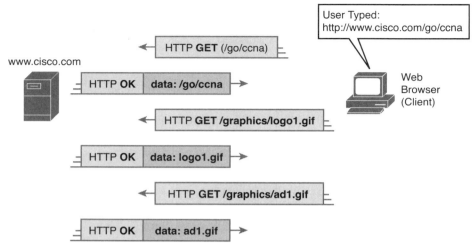

Figure 5-13   *Multiple HTTP Get Requests/Responses*

How the Receiving Host Identifies the Correct Receiving Application

This chapter closes with a discussion that pulls several concepts together from several chapters in Part I of this book. The concept revolves around the process by which a host, when receiving any message over any network, can decide which of its many application programs should process the received data.

As an example, consider host A shown on the left side of Figure 5-14. The host happens to have three different web browser windows open, each using a unique TCP window. Host A also has an email client and a chat window open, both of which use TCP. Each of these applications uses a unique TCP port number on host A as well (1027 and 1028), as shown in the figure.

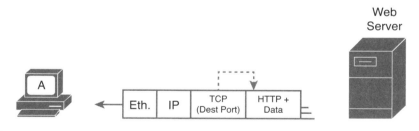

Browser: TCP port 1024
Browser: TCP port 1025
Browser: TCP port 1026
Email: TCP port 1027
Chat: TCP port 1028

Figure 5-14   *Dilemma: How Host A Chooses the App That Should Receive This Data*

This chapter has shown several examples of how transport layer protocols use the destination port number field in the TCP or UDP header to identify the receiving application. For example, if the destination TCP port value in Figure 5-14 is 1024, host A will know that the data is meant for the first of the three web browser windows.

Before a receiving host can even examine the TCP or UDP header and find the destination port field, it must first process the outer headers in the message. If the incoming message is an Ethernet frame, which encapsulates an IPv4 packet, the headers look like the details in Figure 5-15.

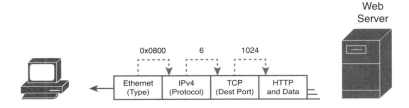

Browser: TCP port 1024
Browser: TCP port 1025
Browser: TCP port 1026
Email: TCP port 1027
Chat: TCP port 1028

Figure 5-15   *Three Key Fields with Which to Identify the Next Header*

The receiving host must look at multiple fields, one per header, to identify the next header or field in the received message. For example, host A uses an Ethernet NIC to connect to the network, so the received message is an Ethernet frame. As first shown back in Figure 2-17 in Chapter 2, the Ethernet Type field identifies the type of header that follows the Ethernet header—in this case, with a value of hex 0800, an IPv4 header.

The IPv5 header has a similar field called the IP Protocol field. The IPv4 Protocol field has a standard list of values that identify the next header, with decimal 6 used for TCP and decimal 17 used for UDP. In this case, the value of 6 identifies the TCP header that follows the IPv4 header.

When the receiving host realizes a TCP header exists, it can process the destination port field as described earlier in this chapter, and identify the correct application. In this case, the destination port of 1024 happens to be used by one of the web browser windows.

Exam Preparation Tasks

Review All the Key Topics

Review the most important topics from this chapter, noted with the Key Topic icon. Table 5-5 lists these key topics and where each is discussed.

Table 5-5   Key Topics for Chapter 5

Key Topic Element	Description	Page Number
Table 5-2	Functions of TCP and UDP	120
Table 5-3	Well-known TCP and UDP port numbers	125
Figure 5-5	Example of TCP connection establishment	126
List	Definitions of connection-oriented and connectionless	127

Complete the Tables and Lists from Memory

Print a copy of DVD Appendix I, "Memory Tables," or at least the section for this chapter, and complete the tables and lists from memory. DVD Appendix J, "Memory Tables Answer Key," includes completed tables and lists for you to check your work.

Definitions of Key Terms

After your first reading of the chapter, try to define these key terms, but do not be concerned about getting them all correct at that time. Chapter 23 directs you in how to use these terms for late-stage preparation for the exam.

connection establishment, error detection, error recovery, flow control, forward acknowledgment, HTTP, ordered data transfer, port, segment, sliding windows, URL, VoIP, web server

Part I Review

Keep track of your part review progress with the checklist shown in Table P1-1. Details on each task follow the table.

Table P1-1   Part I Review Checklist

Activity	First Date Completed	Second Date Completed
Repeat All DIKTA Questions		
Answer Part Review Questions		
Review Key Topics		
Create Terminology Mind Map		

Repeat All DIKTA Questions

For this task, answer the "Do I Know This Already?" questions again for the chapters in this part of the book, using the PCPT software. Refer to the Introduction to this book, heading "How to View Only DIKTA Questions by Part," for help with how to make the PCPT software show you DIKTA questions for this part only.

Answer Part Review Questions

For this task, answer the Part Review questions for this part of the book, using the PCPT software. Refer to the Introduction to this book, heading "How to View Only Part Review Questions by Part," for help with how to make the PCPT software show you Part Review questions for this part only.

Review Key Topics

Browse back through the chapters and look for the Key Topic icons. If you do not remember some details, take the time to reread those topics.

Create Terminology Mind Maps

The first part of this book introduces a large amount of terminology. The sheer number of terms can be overwhelming. But more and more, while you work through each new chapter, you will become more comfortable with the terms. And the better you can remember the core meaning of a term, the easier your reading will be going forward.

For your first mind map exercise in this book, without looking back at the chapters or your notes, you will create six mind maps. The mind maps will each list a number in the center, 1 through 6, to match the numbers shown in Figure P1-1. Your job is as follows:

- Think of every term that you can remember from Part I of the book.
- Think of each of the six mind maps as being about the item next to the number in Figure P1-1. For example, number 1 is about the user PC, number 2 is about an Ethernet cable that connects PC1 to a switch, and so on.

- Add each term that you can recall to all mind maps to which it applies. For example, *leased line* would apply to mind map number 5.

- If a term seems to apply to multiple places, add it to all those mind maps.

- After you have written every term you can remember into one of the mind maps, review the Key Topics lists at the end of Chapters 1 through 5. Add any terms you forgot to your mind maps.

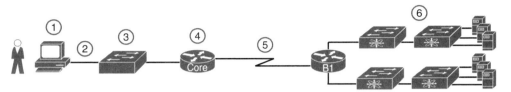

Figure P1-1   *Sample Network to Use with Mind Map Exercise*

The goal of these minds maps is to help you recall the terms with enough meaning to associate the terms with the right part of a simple network design. On your first review of Part I, do not be concerned if you cannot fully explain each term, because you will learn many of these terms more fully just by reading the rest of the book.

> **NOTE**   For more information on mind mapping, refer to the Introduction, in the section "About Mind Maps."

Create the mind maps in Table P1-2 on paper, using any mind-mapping software (or even any drawing application). If you use an application, note the filename and location where you saved the file, for later reference. Sample answers are listed in DVD Appendix K, "Mind Map Solutions."

Table P1-2   Configuration Mind Maps for Part I Review

Map	Description	Where You Saved It
1	Client PC	
2	Ethernet Link	
3	LAN Switch	
4	Router	
5	Leased Line	
6	Data Center	

Data center network technologies can be broken into two broad categories: data networking and storage networking. The data network allows user devices to communicate with the servers, or servers to communicate with each other. The storage network allows a server to communicate with storage devices.

The DCICN exam ignores storage networking, focusing on data networking.

Today's data centers typically build the data networking components using Ethernet technology. Specifically, the physical links, the data-link protocols, and the networking devices, like Ethernet LAN switches, follow Ethernet standards.

Parts II and III dive into detail about Ethernet. Part II begins with Chapter 6, which provides some historical perspectives on Ethernet, while focusing on the logic of how a Layer 2 switch forwards Ethernet frames. Chapters 7 and 8 each look specifically at Cisco Nexus data center switches—how to access the user interface, how to configure administrative features, how to configure the devices to perform LAN switching, and how to make the devices perform many basic functions necessary to a data center LAN.

Part III then moves on to discuss two specific larger topics about how a Layer 2 data center LAN works: virtual LANs (VLANs) and Spanning Tree Protocol (STP).

Part II

Ethernet LAN Basics

Chapter 6: Building Ethernet LANs with Switches

Chapter 7: Installing and Operating Nexus Switches

Chapter 8: Configuring Ethernet Switching

Part II Review

This chapter covers the following exam topics:

1.1 Describe the purpose and functions of various network devices

1.1.a Interpret a network diagram

1.1.b Define physical network topologies

1.2 Select the components required to meet a network specification

1.2.a Switches

2.1 Explain the technology and media access control method for Ethernet networks

2.1.a IEEE 802 protocols

2.1.b CSMA/CD

2.2 Explain basic switching concepts and the operation of Cisco switches

2.2.b MAC table

2.2.c Flooding

CHAPTER 6

Building Ethernet LANs with Switches

IEEE 802.3 Ethernet dominates the wired LAN market today; as a result, data center networks use a large amount of Ethernet technology. In fact, Ethernet is used so much that many people do not even bother to mention Ethernet when discussing networks. For instance, a data center LAN uses servers with Ethernet network interface cards (NICs) connected with Ethernet cables to Ethernet switch ports, but most network engineers would leave out the word *Ethernet* because it is implied.

This chapter takes the next step in building your knowledge of Ethernet as an end to itself. This chapter begins by looking over the history of Ethernet, in addition to some competitive older LAN technology, for perspective. The major sections describe Layer 2 LAN switching, probably one of the most important fundamental processes to know as someone new to networking. The end of the chapter discusses some design issues with Ethernet LANs, showing some basic ideas about how to build a data center LAN.

> **NOTE** As promised in the Introduction's section, "For Those Studying Routing & Switching": Read this entire chapter. This chapter contains many topics not in the *ICND1 100-101 Official Cert Guide.*

"Do I Know This Already?" Quiz

Use the "Do I Know This Already?" quiz to help decide whether you might want to skim this chapter, or a major section, moving more quickly to the "Exam Preparation Tasks" section near the end of the chapter. You can find the answers at the bottom of the page following the quiz. For thorough explanations, see Appendix A, "Answers to the 'Do I Know This Already?' Quizzes."

Table 6-1 "Do I Know This Already?" Foundation Topics Section-to-Question Mapping

Foundation Topics Section	Questions
Ethernet History	1–2
LAN Switching Concepts	3–5
LAN Design Considerations	6–9

1. Which of the following answers is true about the topology of the older 10BASE-2 and 10BASE-5 Ethernet LANs?

   a. Physical star topology

   b. Logical ring topology

   c. Logical bus topology

   d. Physical bus topology

2. Which of the following is true about transparent bridges but not about hubs?

   a. After receiving incoming bits/frame, it regenerates and sends a new signal out all other ports, without delay.

   b. It separates the LAN into multiple collision domains.

   c. It does not forward the bits/frame out the same port the bits/frame arrived.

   d. It uses CSMA/CD to decide when it should forward the bits/frame out some other interface.

3. Which of the following statements describes part of the process of how a switch decides to forward a frame destined for a known unicast MAC address?

   a. It compares the unicast destination address to the bridging, or MAC address, table.

   b. It compares the unicast source address to the bridging, or MAC address, table.

   c. It forwards the frame out all interfaces in the same VLAN except for the incoming interface.

   d. It compares the destination IP address to the destination MAC address.

   e. It compares the frame's incoming interface to the source MAC entry in the MAC address table.

4. Which of the following comparisons does a switch make when deciding whether a new MAC address should be added to its MAC address table?

   a. It compares the unicast destination address to the bridging, or MAC address, table.

   b. It compares the unicast source address to the bridging, or MAC address, table.

   c. It compares the VLAN ID to the bridging, or MAC address, table.

   d. It compares the destination IP address's ARP cache entry to the bridging, or MAC address, table.

5. PC1, with MAC address 1111.1111.1111, is connected to switch SW1's Fa0/1 interface. PC2, with MAC address 2222.2222.2222, is connected to SW1's Fa0/2 interface. PC3, with MAC address 3333.3333.3333, connects to SW1's Fa0/3 interface. The switch begins with no dynamically learned MAC addresses, followed by PC1 sending a frame with a destination address of 2222.2222.2222. If the next frame to reach the switch is a frame sent by PC3, destined for PC2's MAC address of 2222.2222.2222, which of the following are true? (Choose two answers.)

   a. The switch forwards the frame out interface Fa0/1.

   b. The switch forwards the frame out interface Fa0/2.

   c. The switch forwards the frame out interface Fa0/3.

   d. The switch discards (filters) the frame.

6. Which of the following devices would be in the same collision domain as PC1?

   a. PC2, which is separated from PC1 by an Ethernet hub

   b. PC3, which is separated from PC1 by a transparent bridge

   c. PC4, which is separated from PC1 by an Ethernet switch

   d. PC5, which is separated from PC1 by a router

7. Which of the following devices would be in the same broadcast domain as PC1? (Choose three answers.)

   a. PC2, which is separated from PC1 by an Ethernet hub

   b. PC3, which is separated from PC1 by a transparent bridge

   c. PC4, which is separated from PC1 by an Ethernet switch

   d. PC5, which is separated from PC1 by a router

8. Which of the following Ethernet standards support a maximum cable length of longer than 100 meters? (Choose two answers.)

   a. 100BASE-T

   b. 1000BASE-LX

   c. 1000BASE-T

   d. 100BASE-FX

9. A Cisco LAN switch connects to three PCs (PC1, PC2, and PC3), each directly using a cable that supports Ethernet UTP speeds up through 1000 Mbps (1 Gbps). PC1 uses a NIC that supports only 10BASE-T, while PC2 has a 10/100 NIC, and PC3 has a 10/100/1000 NIC. Assuming that the PCs and switch use IEEE autonegotiation, which PCs will use half-duplex?

   a. PC1

   b. PC2

   c. PC3

   d. None of the PCs will use half-duplex.

Foundation Topics

Ethernet History

Here in the decade of the 2010s, Ethernet LANs follow a long-established pattern of how to create a LAN. Endpoint devices, like user PCs and servers, use an Ethernet NIC connected via a cable to some Ethernet switch. The switches connect together with additional cables. Figure 6-1 shows the general idea, with the campus LAN on the left and the data center LAN on the right.

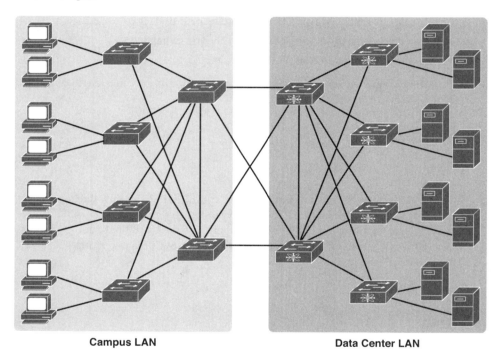

Campus LAN   **Data Center LAN**

Figure 6-1   *Campus LAN and Data Center LAN, Conceptual Drawing*

This book was first published around 40 years after the invention of Ethernet. Ethernet technology has been improved many times over since the original Ethernet specifications, so a modern Ethernet LAN would not look much like the original technology. However, many concepts and terms with modern Ethernet LANs have their origins in some of that history. This first of three major sections of the chapter reviews some of the long history of Ethernet to introduce some terminology that comes from the history of Ethernet.

Early Ethernet with Coaxial Cabling

The earliest Ethernet networks, back in the 1970s and into the 1980s, used a long coaxial cable that ran near each device on the LAN. This early technology, which came to be called 10BASE-5, used a thick coaxial cable that ran through the space in which the LAN was needed. Then, each device used a short cable to tap into the LAN cable (called a *LAN segment*), attaching to 10BASE-5 NIC to the end of the cable. The end result was a LAN, with a single electrical circuit connected to all the NICs connected to the LAN. Figure 6-2 shows the general idea.

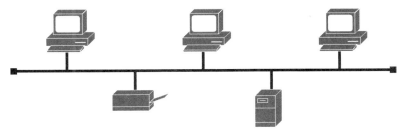

Figure 6-2   *10BASE-5 Conceptual Drawing (Thicknet)*

The next big leap in Ethernet technology, in the 1980s, used a similar overall physical design, as shown in Figure 6-3. This newer type Ethernet, called *10BASE-2*, ran to each device, without the need for the short cables to connect to the central cable, as shown in Figure 6-3. It also ran at 10 Mbps, and used the same Ethernet framing (header and trailer) as 10BASE-5.

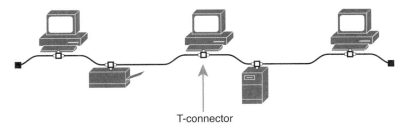

T-connector

Figure 6-3   *10BASE-2 Conceptual Drawing*

The 10BASE-2 LANs actually created the long Ethernet cable as a series of shorter cables with *T-connectors*. The connector, shaped roughly like a capital letter *T*, used the sides of the T to connect to the main cable. The bottom of the T had a round connector (called a *BNC connector*) that connected to the Ethernet NIC. Figure 6-4 shows a T-connector.

Connects to
Co-axial Cables

BNC Connects
to NIC

Figure 6-4   *Photo of BNC Connectors Used with 10BASE-2 (T-branch box for network cable © Devyatkin)*

10BASE-2 became more popular than the older 10BASE-5 for a couple of reasons. 10BASE-2 used thinner, cheaper, and more flexible coaxial than 10BASE-5, making 10BASE-2 cheaper than 10BASE-5. 10BASE-5 had one notable advantage: It supported a distance of 500 meters for the Ethernet cable segment, whereas 10BASE-2 supported only 185 meters. (Note that the 5 and 2 in the names represent the approximate maximum cable length of around 500 meters for 10BASE-5 and around 200 meters for 10BASE-2.)

Finally, both of these early Ethernet technologies used the same topologies. Network engineers describe a LAN's physical topology based on the cabling, and both 10BASE-5 and 10BASE-2 are considered to have a bus topology, because the cable itself passes by each addressable device. Each type of LAN also has a logical LAN topology, based on the media access control logic. With both types of early Ethernet, the carrier sense multiple access collision detect (CSMA/CD) logic required to access the LAN, in which the transmitted frame actually arrives at every device, causes both types to be considered to have a logical bus topology as well. (Note that the CSMA/CD algorithm was introduced back in Chapter 2, "Fundamentals of Ethernet LANs.") Table 6-2 summarizes these key comparison points.

Table 6-2   Comparisons of 10BASE-5 and 10BASE-2

Name	Nickname	Speed	Maximum Distance	Physical Topology	Logical Topology	Requires Half-Duplex (CSMA/CD)?
10BASE-5	Thicknet	10 Mbps	500 m	Bus	Bus	Yes
10BASE-2	Thinnet	10 Mbps	185 m	Bus	Bus	Yes

Ethernet Devices

10BASE-5 and 10BASE-2 did not use a networking device or hardware other than the NICs in the end-user devices. That is, the Ethernet consists of the NICs and the cable. Later Ethernet LAN technologies, including today's current technology, use several types of devices to create the Ethernet LAN. The next few topics examine some of the device types used to create different types of Ethernet LANs over the history of Ethernet, specifically repeaters, hubs, bridges, and switches.

Ethernet Repeaters

Any network designer has to think about maximum cabling distances. Each Ethernet physical standard today defines a maximum distance for a single cable. The designer should not try to use a particular cable, per a particular standard, if the cable would have to be longer than the standard allows.

The maximum cabling distance can be extended using various types of devices, with the first such device being called a *repeater*. Thinking back to the earlier Ethernet technologies, two 10BASE-5 or 10BASE-2 segments could connect to a two-port repeater, as shown in Figure 6-5. The repeater somehow forwards the bits from one cable to the other. Each cable can be as long as the maximum allowed cabling distance, extending the length of the LAN.

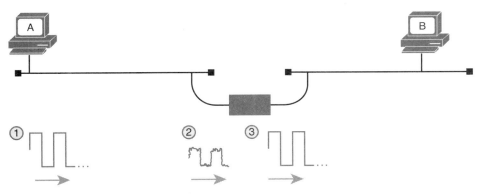

Figure 6-5 *Ethernet Repeater Concepts*

The figure shows the concepts of how a repeater works below the diagram of the repeater and two LAN segments as well. Repeaters work with OSI Layer 1 concepts. Specifically, a repeater regenerates a new clean electrical signal. For instance, following the numbers in the figure:

Step 1. Host A sends an Ethernet frame. From a physical layer (electrical) perspective, the signal is strong, with a clear edge to where the signal levels change.

Step 2. By the time the signal reaches the repeater in the center, the signal has degraded. (That signal degradation is one reason for the limit on cabling lengths, by the way.)

Step 3. The repeater processes the received (poor) signal, interprets it as 1s and 0s, and re-generates the same original good signal sent by host A. The repeater sends that quality electrical signal on to the right-side LAN cable.

Repeaters work well, even with some modern types of Ethernet standards, but within limits. The biggest limitation is that repeaters cannot be used to create ridiculously long Ethernet LANs; each standard states the number of repeaters that could be used and still have the LAN work. For instance, with 10BASE-5 and 10BASE-2, at most four repeaters could be used between a series of Ethernet segments (a great advantage, but with limits).

10BASE-T with Hub

10BASE-T, introduced in 1990, significantly changed the design of Ethernet LANs, more like the designs seen today. 10BASE-T introduced the cabling model similar to today's Ethernet LANs, with each device connecting to a centralized device using an unshielded twisted-pair (UTP) cable. However, 10BASE-T did not originally use LAN switches; instead, the early 10BASE-T networks used a device called an *Ethernet hub*. (The technology required to build even a basic LAN switch was not yet available at the time.)

The left side of Figure 6-6 depicts the typical cabling diagram for 10BASE-T with a hub, with six PCs connected to a central hub. Note that the physical topology looks a little like a child's drawing of a star, as shown on the right side of Figure 6-6. As a result, 10BASE-T networks with a hub are considered to have a *physical star topology*.

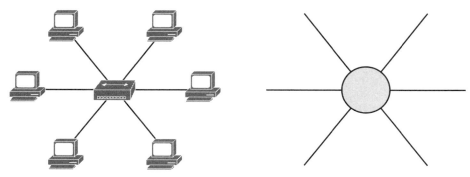

Figure 6-6   *Physical Star Topology with 10BASE-T Hubs*

> **NOTE**   Modern networks with switches use the same general cabling concept, so they are also considered to use a physical star topology.

An Ethernet hub uses physical layer processing to forward data. In effect, a hub acts like a repeater, just with lots of ports. When a repeater receives an incoming electrical signal, it immediately *forwards a regenerated signal out all the other ports except the incoming port*. For instance, in Figure 6-7, Larry sends an Ethernet frame. The hub receives the electrical signal, interprets it as a series of 1s and 0s, and sends a regenerated electrical signal out the ports toward both Archie and Bob.

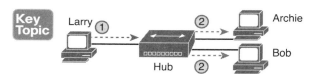

Figure 6-7   *10BASE-T (With a Hub)*

Note that the hub does not use CSMA/CD logic to make itself wait, so collisions can occur. So, all the devices on the LAN must continue to use CSMA/CD when connected to a hub, avoiding sending frames at the same time and reacting when a collision does occur. Summarizing the key points about hubs:

- The hub acts a multiport repeater, blindly regenerating and repeating any incoming electrical signal out all other ports, even ignoring CSMA/CD rules.

- When two or more devices send at the same time, the hub's actions cause an electrical collision, making both signals corrupt.

- The connected devices must take turns by using carrier sense multiple access with collision detection (CSMA/CD) logic, so the devices share the bandwidth.

- Hubs create a physical star topology, but a logical bus topology.

NOTE Although 10BASE-T with a hub physically creates a star topology, it is considered to have a logical bus topology because the hub requires the use of CSMA/CD, just like the older types of Ethernet.

Ethernet Transparent Bridges

10BASE-T became popular relatively quickly. However, it still required that all the devices use CSMA/CD. CSMA/CD basically makes the devices attached to the LAN take turns because no two devices could send at the same time without causing a collision. If Ethernet could support a way for multiple devices to send at the same time without causing a collision, Ethernet performance could be improved.

Ethernet transparent bridges were the first such device. Ethernet *transparent bridges*, or simply *bridges*, made these improvements:

- Bridges separated devices into groups called *collision domains*, because a frame sent by a device on one side of the bridge did not collide with a frame sent by a device on the other side of the bridge.
- Bridges increase the capacity of the entire Ethernet, because each collision domain can have one sender at a time.

Figure 6-8 shows the effect of migrating from using a 10BASE-T hub without a bridge to adding a bridge to the same figure. The top of the figure shows a single hub with four devices, which creates a single collision domain, with a capacity for 10 Mbps of data transfer. The bottom of the figure shows a bridge separating two hubs, with the same number of devices. The resulting two collision domains each support 10 Mbps of traffic, with a total LAN capacity of 20 Mbps in this case.

The Layer 2 forwarding logic of bridges creates these multiple collision domains. In some cases, the bridge does not even need to forward the frame from one side to the other (for instance, when Fred sends a frame to Barney). When the bridge does need to forward a frame, a bridge (unlike a hub) does not blindly forward the frame. Instead, a bridge buffers or queues the frame in memory, waiting until the outgoing interface is available. Unlike a hub, the bridge uses CSMA/CD to help avoid collisions as well. For example, Fred and Betty can both send a frame to Barney at the same time, and the bridge will queue the frame sent by Betty, waiting to forward it on to the collision domain on the left until the collision domain on the left is not busy.

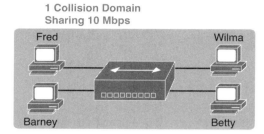

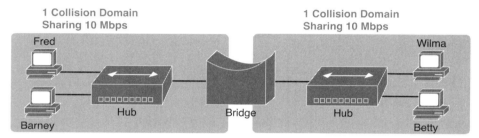

Figure 6-8 *Bridge Creates Two Collision Domains and Two Shared Ethernets*

Ethernet Switches

LAN switches perform the same basic core functions as bridges but at much faster speeds and with many enhanced features. Like bridges, switches segment a LAN into separate collision domains, each with its own capacity. And if the network does not have a hub, each single link is considered its own collision domain, even if no collisions can actually occur in that case.

For example, Figure 6-9 shows a simple LAN with a switch and four PCs. The switch creates four collision domains, with the ability to send at 100 Mbps in this case on each of the four links. And with no hubs, each link can run at full-duplex, doubling the capacity of each link.

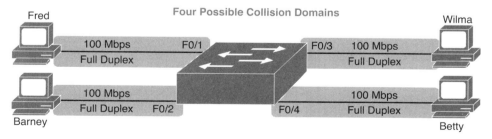

Figure 6-9 *Switch Creates Four Collision Domains and Four Ethernet Segments*

The majority of Parts II and III of this book discuss Ethernet switches in one way or another, so watch for much more detail about switches. The following list summarizes some of the key facts about the Ethernet devices in this section:

- Ethernet repeaters extend the distances supported by a LAN, operating at Layer 1, by regenerating a new clean electrical signal.

- Ethernet hubs, introduced with 10BASE-T, provide the same benefits as a repeater, with the same Layer 1 function. Hubs also provide a central connection point for Ethernet cabling.

- Ethernet bridges also extend LAN distances, but they primarily improve performance of the LAN by creating multiple collision domains, increasing overall capacity of the LAN.

- Ethernet switches provide the same benefits as a bridge, but with many ports on the same device.

Now that you have learned a little more about the components of Ethernet LANs over the years, the next few pages take a look back at the history of Ethernet standards. Those standards define the data link frame, in addition to the types of physical links used to build Ethernet LANs.

Ethernet Standards

Like most computing technologies of those days, Ethernet began as technology developed by a company (Xerox). Xerox then teamed with two other companies, Intel and Digital Equipment Corp. (DEC), to further develop chips, products, a vendor standard, and to promote Ethernet technology. The final vendor-created Ethernet standard came to be known as Ethernet Version II, or as DIX Ethernet (per the names of the companies).

In February 1980, the IEEE took on the job of standardizing Ethernet and two other emerging LAN technologies. The IEEE formed several working groups (committees), each to build a separate standard. The IEEE assigned a number to each working group, with their standards having the same name. The early working groups included one group each for three different types of emerging LAN technologies (Ethernet, Token Bus, and Token Ring), plus the 802.2 working group, which defined features in common to all three new types of LANs. Figure 6-10 shows the names and numbers of the working groups on the left.

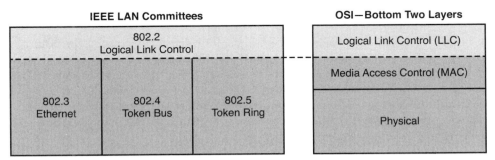

Figure 6-10 *IEEE Standards Committees for the Original Types of LANs*

NOTE   The term *MAC address* comes from the fact that the 802.3 standard, which defines the MAC sublayer, defines the Address field.

The IEEE's organization required two new terms for a subdivision of the work done at OSI Layer 2, as noted on the right side of the figure. The IEEE put some of Ethernet's data link functions into the 802.3 standard, and some into the 802.2 standard. The IEEE named the data link features in the 802.3 standard the *Media Access Control* (MAC) sublayer, with the data link features defined in 802.2 named the *Logical Link Control* (LLC) sublayer.

The next few pages first look at some of the details at the data link layer of IEEE standard Ethernet, as split into the MAC and LLC sublayers, followed by a discussion of the Ethernet physical layer.

Ethernet Data-Link Protocols

When the IEEE standardized Ethernet, they made changes to the original DIX Ethernet framing. The first big change was to actually create two headers instead of one, to match the data-link functions in the MAC and LLC sublayers, rather than the single original Ethernet header. Figure 6-11 shows a comparison of this fundamental difference, with the original IEEE standard Ethernet frame format at the top of the figure.

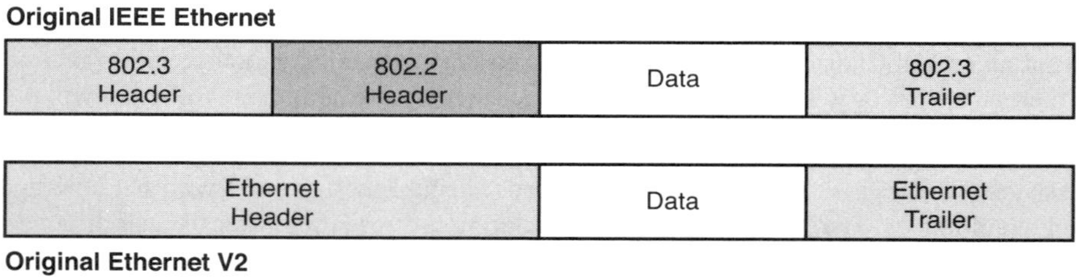

Original IEEE Ethernet

802.3 Header	802.2 Header	Data	802.3 Trailer

Ethernet Header	Data	Ethernet Trailer

Original Ethernet V2

Figure 6-11 *Comparing Overall Structure of IEEE Ethernet Frame to DIXv2 Frame*

Comparing the fields in the DIX frame with the original IEEE frame, you can see both similarities and differences. First, both start with an 8-byte field that simply identifies the beginning of the frame, although with slightly different wording for the names of the fields. Both have a Destination and Source Address field as well.

The biggest change the IEEE made was the field the IEEE defined to use as a Type field. (The Type field identifies the next header found in the Ethernet Data field.) The 802.3 header did not keep the original DIX header's Type field. Instead, the IEEE required that an 802.2 header always follow the 802.3 header. Next, the 802.2 header needed some kind of Type field to identify the next header that follows the 802.2 header, so the IEEE created an 802.2 field called the *Destination Service Access Point* (DSAP) field for that purpose. Figure 6-12 shows the headers with some details, for perspective.

NOTE DIX's preamble and the IEEE's preamble plus start frame delimiter (SFD) had the same binary values; the IEEE just split the DIX preamble into two fields instead of one.

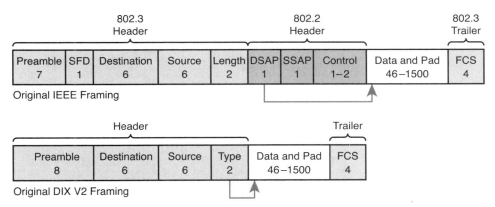

Figure 6-12 *Original IEEE Ethernet Frame Details*

Oddly enough, the story does not end here. Figure 6-12 and the associated text describe the original IEEE frame. However, two notable additions occurred after that, both related to the function of identifying the protocol type.

First, the DSAP field (1 byte) was too short in practice (it did not have enough values to identify all the possible next headers), so the IEEE needed a 2-byte replacement. Rather than change the 802.2 header, the IEEE 802.2 working group added another frame format to the standard, using an extra header after the 802.2 header (called a Sub-Network Access Protocol header, or *SNAP header*). The SNAP header has yet another Type field, this time a 2-byte equivalent of the DIX Type field. (The SNAP format was commonly used with TCP/IP traffic.)

After a few more years, it became clear that for many uses of Ethernet, the original DIX frame's Type field would work well and that all the extra bytes in the 802.2 and SNAP headers often had no purpose. So, the IEEE added support for yet another frame, a frame format that looks almost just like the original DIX frame. The only difference is a trivial naming difference in the first 8 bytes of the frame: The IEEE names these as a 7-byte preamble and a 1-byte SFD.

Ethernet Physical Layer Standards

The IEEE has done an amazing job developing Ethernet standards in such a way to make Ethernet incredibly successful in the marketplace. Many factors have played a part, but two themes in particular have helped Ethernet grow over the long term:

- The IEEE has developed many additional 802.3 standards for different types of cabling, different cable lengths, and for faster speeds.

- No matter what physical standard, all Ethernet devices use the same standard frame formats. That means that one Ethernet LAN can use many types of physical links to meet distance, budget, and cabling needs.

Figure 6-13 shows some insight into Ethernet speed improvements introduced through updated 802.3 standards over the years. The early standards up through the early 1990s ran at 10Mbps, with steadily-improving cabling and topologies. Then, with the introduction of

Fast Ethernet (100 Mbps) in 1995, the IEEE began ramping up the speeds steadily over the next few decades, continuing even until today.

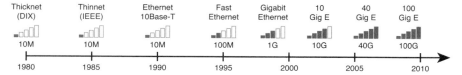

Figure 6-13   *Ethernet Standards Timeline*

NOTE   Often, the IEEE first introduces support for the next higher speed using some form of fiber optic cabling, and later, sometimes many years later, the IEEE completes the work to develop standards to support the same speed on UTP cabling. Figure 6-13 shows the earliest standards for each speed, no matter what cabling.

When the IEEE introduces support for a new type of cabling, or a faster speed, they create a new standard as part of 802.3. These new standards have a few letters behind the name. So, when speaking of the standards, sometimes you might refer to the standard name (with letters). For instance, the IEEE standardized Gigabit Ethernet support using inexpensive UTP cabling is standard 802.3ab. However, more often, engineers refer to that same standard as 1000BASE-T or simply Gigabit Ethernet. Table 6-3 lists some of the IEEE 802.3 physical layer standards and related names for perspective.

Table 6-3   IEEE Physical Layer Standards

Original IEEE Standard	Shorthand Name	Informal Names	Speed	Typical Cabling
802.3i	10BASE-T	Ethernet	10 Mbps	UTP
802.3u	100BASE-T	Fast Ethernet	100 Mbps	UTP
802.3z	1000BASE-X	Gigabit Ethernet, GigE	1000 Mbps (1 Gbps)	Fiber
802.3ab	1000BASE-T	Gigabit Ethernet, GigE	1000 Mbps (1 Gbps)	UTP
802.3ae	10GBASE-X	10 GigE	10 Gbps	UTP
802.3ba	40GBASE-X	40 GigE	40 Gbps	Fiber
802.3ba	100GBASE-X	100 GigE	100 Gbps	Fiber

Ethernet Competition

Today, Ethernet has no significant competition as a wired LAN technology. When a network engineer builds a wired LAN, the technology choices revolve around which Ethernet products to use and the related Ethernet standards, supported cabling, maximum distances, and so on. The challenge is in choosing between competing Ethernet-based options.

However, Ethernet took a three-decade journey before becoming the wired LAN technology of choice, as shown in Figure 6-14. From the point at which the IEEE took over the standardization process for Ethernet in 1980, the IEEE also began standardizing Token Bus and Token Ring, which had its origins in IBM, the dominant computer company at the time. Also, PCs were not commonly used inside companies until the 1980s. The 1980s saw the beginnings of change inside businesses to replace old computer terminals (which could not use LANs) with newer LAN-attached PCs, opening up a huge marketplace for LAN technologies.

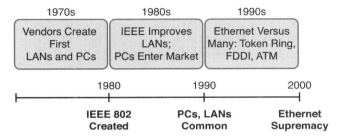

Figure 6-14   *The History of LAN Technologies*

Token Ring became the biggest direct competition to Ethernet as a LAN technology. Token Ring used a physical star topology, with a cable from each device into a central Token Ring hub, as shown on the left side of Figure 6-15.

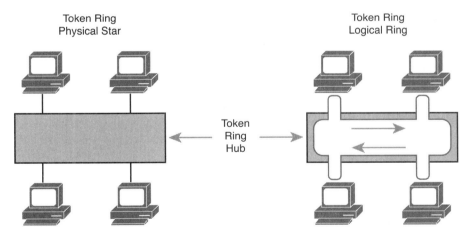

Figure 6-15   *Token Ring Concepts*

However, Token Ring media access logic worked much differently than Ethernet's CSMA/CD, instead creating a logical ring (or loop) with a token. As shown on the right side of the figure, the electrical signal flowed around a loop by passing out to the attached device and then back in to the hub. To control access, a token flowed around the ring. To send, a device had to claim the token first, then send the frame, and then release the token so that another device could send a frame. The token passing logic completely avoided collisions.

Other LAN technologies competed with Ethernet as well. For instance, Fiber Distributed Data Interchange (FDDI) was another LAN technology that also used physical star wiring topology, a logical ring, with a token process to control access to the LAN. FDDI rings were notable as the first common LAN technology to support 100 Mbps. It used more expensive fiber cabling than the slower (at the time) 10BASE-T (10 Mbps) and Token Ring (4 and 16 Mbps). However, for a few years, FDDI products sold well due to its superior speed.

During the 1990s, however, Ethernet surpassed other LAN technologies for a variety of reasons. Ethernet supported the cheaper, easier-to-install UTP cabling much earlier than its competitors. Ethernet had the least expensive hardware, often one-third or so the price of equivalent Token Ring products. Once Ethernet standards for Fast Ethernet (100 Mbps) and Gigabit Ethernet (1000 Mbps) came out, the competition fell away quickly.

This ends the historical perspectives about Ethernet technology. The next major section examines one of the most important topics when learning networking: the logic used by LAN switches when forwarding Ethernet frames.

Switching Logic

LAN switches offer many functions and features, but the most basic features are to connect devices to create the LAN and to forward data through the LAN. This second of three major headings, although short, discusses how a LAN switch forwards data.

Note that most modern LAN switches, including most in the Cisco Nexus model series, support two general types of forwarding: *Layer 2 switching* and *Layer 3 switching* (also known as *multilayer switching*). Layer 2 switching means that the switch uses OSI Layer 2 (data link) logic when forwarding data, whereas Layer 3 switching means that the switch uses OSI Layer 3 (network) logic. In effect, Layer 3 switching is just IP routing as done on a device that also happens to be a LAN switch.

All LAN switches can perform Layer 2 switching, and typically do so by default, without any specific configuration. To enable Layer 3 switching, LAN switches usually require additional configuration. This chapter discusses how switches act at Layer 2, using Layer 2 switching. Chapters 9, "VLAN and Trunking Concepts," 18, "IPv4 Routing Concepts," and 19, "Cisco Nexus IPv4 Routing Configuration," discuss Layer 3 switching.

Layer 2 Switching Basics

Ultimately, the role of a LAN switch (as a Layer 2 switch) is to forward Ethernet frames. To achieve that goal, switches use logic—logic based on the source and destination MAC address in each frame's Ethernet header.

This book discusses how switches forward unicast frames and broadcast frames, ignoring multicast Ethernet frames. Unicast frames have a unicast address as a destination; these addresses represent a single device. A broadcast frame has a destination MAC address of FFFF.FFFF.FFFF; this frame should be delivered to all devices on the LAN.

LAN switches receive Ethernet frames and then make a switching decision: either forward the frame out some other port(s) or ignore the frame. To accomplish this primary mission, switches perform three actions:

1. Deciding when to forward a frame or when to filter (not forward) a frame, based on the destination MAC address

2. Learning MAC addresses by examining the source MAC address of each frame received by the switch

3. Creating a (Layer 2) loop-free environment with other switches by using Spanning Tree Protocol (STP)

The first action is the switch's primary job, whereas the other two items are overhead functions. The next sections examine each of these steps in order.

> **NOTE** Throughout this book's discussion of LAN switches, the terms *switch port* and *switch interface* are synonymous.

The Forward Versus Filter Decision

To decide whether to forward a frame, a switch uses a dynamically built table that lists MAC addresses and outgoing interfaces. Switches compare the frame's destination MAC address to this table to decide whether the switch should forward a frame or simply ignore it. For example, consider the simple network shown in Figure 6-16, with Fred sending a frame to Barney.

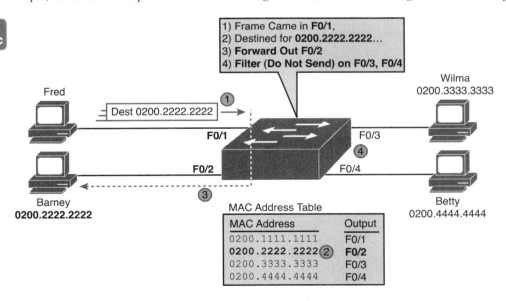

Figure 6-16 *Sample Switch Forwarding and Filtering Decision*

In this figure, Fred sends a frame with destination address 0200.2222.2222 (Barney's MAC address). The switch compares the destination MAC address (0200.2222.2222) to the MAC address table, matching the bold table entry. That matched table entry tells the switch to forward the frame out port F0/2, and only port F0/2.

> **NOTE**   A switch's MAC address table is also called the *switching table*, or *bridging table*, or even the *Content Addressable Memory (CAM) table*, in reference to the type of physical memory used to store the table.

A switch's MAC address table lists the location of each MAC relative to that one switch. In LANs with multiple switches, each switch makes an independent forwarding decision based on its own MAC address table. Together, they forward the frame so that it eventually arrives at the destination.

For example, Figure 6-17 shows the same four PCs as in Figure 6-16, but now with two LAN switches. In this case, Fred sends a frame to Wilma, with destination MAC 0200.3333.3333. Switch SW1 sends the frame out its G0/1 port, per SW1's MAC address table. Then at Step 2, switch SW2 forwards the frame out its F0/3 port, based on SW2's MAC address table.

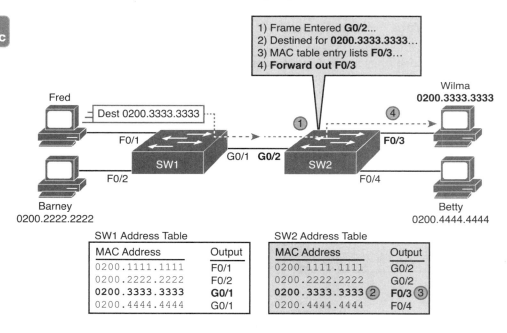

Figure 6-17   *Forwarding Decision with Two Switches*

> **NOTE**   The forwarding choice by a switch was formerly called a *forward versus filter decision* because the switch also chooses to not forward (to filter) frames, not sending the frame out some ports.

How Switches Learn MAC Addresses

The second main function of a switch is to learn the MAC addresses and interfaces to put into its address table. With a full and accurate MAC address table, the switch can make accurate forwarding and filtering decisions.

Switches build the address table by listening to incoming frames and examining the *source MAC address* in the frame. If a frame enters the switch and the source MAC address is not in the MAC address table, the switch creates an entry in the table. That table entry lists the interface from which the frame arrived. Switch learning logic is that simple.

Figure 6-18 depicts the same network as Figure 6-16, but before the switch has built any address table entries. The figure shows the first two frames sent in this network—first a frame from Fred, addressed to Barney, and then Barney's response, addressed to Fred.

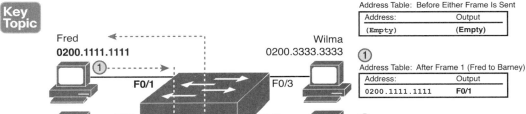

Figure 6-18 *Switch Learning: Empty Table and Adding Two Entries*

As shown in the figure, after Fred sends his first frame (labeled 1) to Barney, the switch adds an entry for 0200.1111.1111, Fred's MAC address, associated with interface F0/1. When Barney replies in Step 2, the switch adds a second entry, this one for 0200.2222.2222, Barney's MAC address, along with interface F0/2, which is the interface in which the switch received the frame. Learning always occurs by looking at the source MAC address in the frame.

Switches keep a timer for each entry in the MAC address table, called an *inactivity timer*. The switch sets the timer to 0 for new entries. Each time the switch receives another frame with that same source MAC address, the timer is reset to 0. The timer counts upward, so the switch can tell which entries have gone the longest time since receiving a frame from that device. The switch then removes entries from the table when they become old. Or, if the switch ever runs out of space for entries in the MAC address table, the switch can then remove table entries with the oldest (largest) inactivity timers.

Flooding Frames

Now again turn your attention to the forwarding process, using Figure 6-18. What do you suppose the switch does with Fred's first frame in Figure 6-18, the one that occurred when there were no entries in the MAC address table? As it turns out, when there is no matching entry in the table, switches forward the frame out all interfaces (except the incoming interface) using a process called *flooding*.

Switches flood *unknown unicast frames* (frames whose destination MAC addresses are not yet in the address table). Flooding means that the switch forwards copies of the frame out all ports, except the port on which the frame was received. If the unknown device receives the frame and sends a reply, the reply frame's source MAC address will allow the switch to build a correct MAC table entry for that device.

Switches also forward LAN broadcast frames because this process helps deliver a copy of the frame to all devices in the LAN.

For example, Figure 6-18 shows the first frame, sent to Barney's MAC address, just going to Barney. However, in reality, the switch floods this frame out F0/2, F0/3, and F0/4, even though 0200.2222.2222 (Barney) is only off F0/2. The switch does not forward the frame back out F0/1 because a switch never forwards a frame out the same interface on which it arrived.

Avoiding Loops Using Spanning Tree Protocol

The third primary feature of LAN switches is loop prevention, as implemented by Spanning Tree Protocol (STP). Without STP, any flooded frames would loop for an indefinite period of time in Ethernet networks with physically redundant links. To prevent looping frames, STP blocks some ports from forwarding frames so that only one active path exists between any pair of LAN segments.

The result of STP is good: Frames do not loop infinitely, which makes the LAN usable. However, STP has negative features as well, including the fact that it takes some work to balance traffic across the redundant alternate links.

A simple example makes the need for STP more obvious. Remember, switches flood frames sent to both unknown unicast MAC addresses and broadcast addresses. Figure 6-19 shows an unknown unicast frame, sent by Larry to Bob, which loops forever because the network has redundancy but no STP.

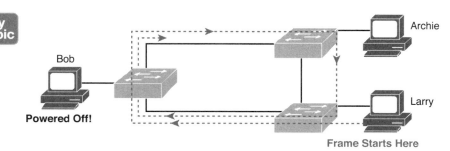

Figure 6-19 *Network with Redundant Links but Without STP: The Frame Loops Forever*

Because none of the switches list Bob's MAC address in their address tables, each switch floods the frame. A physical loop exists through the three switches. The switches keep forwarding the frame out all ports, and copies of the frame go around and around.

To avoid Layer 2 loops, all switches need to use STP. STP causes each interface on a switch to settle into either a blocking state or a forwarding state. *Blocking* means that the interface cannot forward or receive data frames, while *forwarding* means that the interface can send and receive data frames. If a correct subset of the interfaces is blocked, only a single currently active logical path exists between each pair of LANs.

> **NOTE**   STP behaves identically for a transparent bridge and a switch. Therefore, the terms *bridge*, *switch*, and *bridging device* all are used interchangeably when discussing STP.

Part III of this book includes chapters about STP concepts and configuration.

LAN Switching Summary

Switches provide many additional features not offered by older LAN devices such as hubs and bridges. In particular, LAN switches provide the following benefits:

- Switch ports connected to a single device microsegment the LAN, providing dedicated bandwidth to that single device.
- Switches allow multiple simultaneous conversations between devices on different ports.
- Switch ports connected to a single device support full-duplex, in effect doubling the amount of bandwidth available to the device.
- Switches support rate adaptation, which means that devices that use different Ethernet speeds can communicate through the switch (hubs cannot).

Switches use Layer 2 logic, examining the Ethernet data-link header to choose how to process frames. In particular, switches make decisions to forward and filter frames, learn MAC addresses, and use STP to avoid loops, as follows:

Step 1.   Switches forward frames based on the destination address:

    A. If the destination address is a broadcast, multicast, or unknown destination unicast (a unicast not listed in the MAC table), the switch floods the frame.

    B. If the destination address is a known unicast address (a unicast address found in the MAC table):

        i. If the outgoing interface listed in the MAC address table differs from the interface in which the frame was received, the switch forwards the frame out the outgoing interface.

        ii. If the outgoing interface is the same as the interface in which the frame was received, the switch filters the frame, meaning that the switch simply ignores the frame and does not forward it.

Step 2.   Switches use the following logic to learn MAC address table entries:

    A. For each received frame, examine the source MAC address and note the interface from which the frame was received.

6

> **B.** If it is not already in the table, add the MAC address and interface it was learned on, setting the inactivity timer to 0.
>
> **C.** If it is already in the table, reset the inactivity timer for the entry to 0.

Step 3.   Switches use STP to prevent loops by causing some interfaces to block, meaning that they do not send or receive frames.

Design Choices in Ethernet LANs

By this point in your reading, you should know enough to look at a drawing of a small LAN and predict the basic functions that occur in that Ethernet LAN. You know how the common devices (repeater, hub, bridge, and switch) work. You know the frame formats. And most importantly, you know how an Ethernet switch forwards Ethernet frames based on the destination MAC address.

This third major section of the chapter takes a look at Ethernet technology from a design perspective instead of simply defining what happens in the network. This section examines design choices about what devices to use, and how that defines where collisions happen (collision domains), and where Ethernet broadcast frames flow (broadcast domains). The section goes on to discuss some design terminology for both data center and campus LAN designs, and then closes with a discussion of Ethernet autonegotiation.

Collision Domains, Broadcast Domains, and VLANs

When creating any Ethernet LAN today, you use LAN switches and routers. You also have to think about older legacy devices like hubs and bridges, just in case some still exist. The different parts of an Ethernet LAN can behave differently, in terms of function and performance, depending on which types of devices are used. These differences then affect a network engineer's decision when choosing how to design a LAN.

The terms *collision domain* and *broadcast domain* define two important effects of the process of segmenting LANs using various devices. This section defines these terms to explain how hubs, switches, and routers impact collision domains and broadcast domains.

Collision Domains

Originally, the term *collision domain* referred to an Ethernet concept of all ports whose transmitted frames would cause a collision with frames sent by other devices in the collision domain. To review the core concept, Figure 6-20 illustrates collision domains.

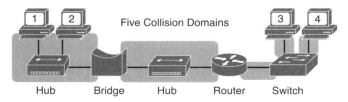

Figure 6-20   *Collision Domains*

NOTE The LAN design in Figure 6-20 is not a typical design today. Instead, it simply provides enough information to help you compare hubs, switches, and routers.

First, pay attention to the devices in the figure. Of the four types of networking devices in the figure, only the hub allows a collision domain to spread from one side of the device to the other. The rest of the networking devices (routers, switches, bridges) all separate the LAN into separate collision domains. For example, frames sent by hosts 1 and 2 would collide, because they are in the same collision domain. Frames sent by hosts 1, 3, and 4, all at the same instant, would not collide, because they are in different collision domains.

Broadcast Domains

Take any Ethernet LAN, and pick any device. Then think of that device sending an Ethernet broadcast (that is, a frame) with destination MAC address FFFF.FFFF.FFFF. An Ethernet *broadcast domain* is the set of devices to which that broadcast is delivered.

Of all the network devices shown in Figure 6-20, routers always separate LANs into multiple broadcast domains. Switches may create multiple broadcast domains based on their configuration, but repeaters, hubs, and bridges do not. The Layer 3 routing logic used on routers simply does not forward Ethernet broadcast frames, either ignoring the frames or processing and then discarding some broadcast from some overhead protocols used by routers.

Figure 6-21 shows the two broadcast domains created when using a router, with the switch on the right using all default configuration with regard to broadcast domains.

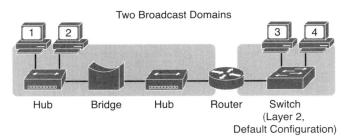

Figure 6-21 *Broadcast Domains*

By definition, broadcasts sent by a device in one broadcast domain are not forwarded to devices in another broadcast domain. In this example, the router does not forward a LAN broadcast sent by a PC on the left to the network segment on the right.

General definitions for a collision domain and a broadcast domain are as follows:

- A *collision domain* is a set of NICs for which a frame sent by one NIC could result in a collision with a frame sent by any other NIC in the same collision domain.
- A *broadcast domain* is a set of NICs for which a broadcast frame sent by one NIC is received by all other NICs in the same broadcast domain.

Virtual LANs and Broadcast Domains

A LAN switch may or may not create multiple broadcast domains, depending on the switch's configuration. By default, a switch does not separate the network into multiple broadcast domains, and the switch's Layer 2 forwarding logic forwards frames between all ports. However, with some simple configuration, a LAN switch can put some ports into one broadcast domain, and others into another broadcast domain, using the concept of virtual LANs (VLAN).

Before understanding VLANs, you must have a very specific understanding of the definition of a LAN. Although you can think about and define the term *LAN* from many perspectives, one perspective in particular will help you understand VLANs:

A LAN consists of all devices in the same broadcast domain.

With VLANs configured, a switch groups interfaces into different VLANs (broadcast domains) based on configuration, with each interface in a specific VLAN. Essentially, the switch creates multiple broadcast domains by putting some interfaces into one VLAN and other interfaces into other VLANs. So, instead of all ports on a switch forming a single broadcast domain, the switch separates them into many, based on configuration. It's really that simple.

The next two figures compare two LANs for the purpose of explaining a little more about VLANs. First, before VLANs existed, if a design needed two separate broadcast domains, two switches could be used (one for each broadcast domain), as shown in Figure 6-22.

Figure 6-22 *Network with Two Broadcast Domains and No VLANs*

With the ability to configure VLANs, that same design could use one physical switch, and simply use configuration to create the needed broadcast domains. Figure 6-23 shows the same two broadcast domains as in Figure 6-22, now implemented as two different VLANs on a single switch.

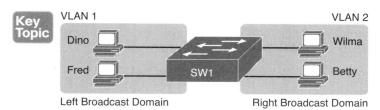

Figure 6-23 *Network with Two VLANs Using One Switch*

The Layer 2 switching logic in a switch purposefully keeps the VLANs separate, at least from a forwarding perspective. For example, in Figure 6-23, the switch would forward frames between Dino and Fred (in the same VLAN), but not from Dino to Wilma (in different VLANs). A device that performs routing (that is, a router or a Layer 3 switch) must be used to forward data between multiple VLANs. Chapter 9, "VLAN and Trunking Concepts," discusses VLANs in more depth, including showing how to route between VLANs with both routers and Layer 3 switches.

The Impact of Collision and Broadcast Domains on LAN Design

When designing a LAN, keep in mind the trade-offs when choosing the number of devices in each collision domain and broadcast domain. First, consider the devices in a single collision domain for a moment. For a single collision domain:

■ The devices share the available bandwidth.

■ The devices might inefficiently use that bandwidth because of the effects of collisions, particularly under higher utilization.

For perspective on the impact of collision domains, it helps to compare an old design using LAN hubs to a newer design that uses the same speeds for each link but instead uses a LAN switch. Consider a design with ten PCs, with each link using 100BASE-T. With a hub, only one PC can send at a time, for a theoretical maximum capacity of 100 Mbps for the entire LAN. Replace the hub with a switch, and you get the following:

■ 100 Mbps per link, times ten PCs, for a total of 1000 Mbps (1 Gbps)

■ The ability to use full-duplex on each link, effectively doubling the capacity to 2000 Mbps (1 Gigabit per direction, times two directions, totaling 2 Gbps)

The example of using hubs versus switches is admittedly a little old, but it shows one reason why no one chooses to use hubs, and why vendors now sell switches instead of hubs.

Now consider the issue of broadcasts. When a host receives a broadcast, the host must process the received frame. This means that the NIC must interrupt the computer's CPU, and the CPU must spend time thinking about the received broadcast frame. All hosts need to send some broadcasts to function properly. (For example, IP ARP messages are LAN broadcasts, as mentioned in Chapter 4, "Fundamentals of IPv4 Addressing and Routing.") So, broadcasts happen, which is good, but broadcasts do require all the hosts to spend time processing each broadcast frame.

NOTE   Using smaller broadcast domains can also improve security, because of limiting broadcasts and because of robust security features in routers.

Table 6-4 lists some of the key comparison points between hubs, a switch acting as a Layer 2 switch, and a router. The features in the table should be interpreted within the following context: "Which of the following benefits are gained by using a hub/switch/router between Ethernet devices?"

Table 6-4   Benefits of Segmenting Ethernet Devices Using Hubs, Switches, and Routers

Feature	Hub	Layer 2 Switch	Router
Greater cabling distances are allowed.	Yes	Yes	Yes
Creates multiple collision domains.	No	Yes	Yes
Increases bandwidth/capacity.	No	Yes	Yes
Creates multiple broadcast domains.	No	With VLANs	Always
The device forwards data between broadcast domains.	—	No	Yes

Ethernet LAN Media and Cable Lengths

When designing a LAN, an engineer must consider the length of each cable run and then find the best type of Ethernet and cabling type that supports that length of cable. For example, inside a data center, the cables often only run inside a rack to a switch at the top of the rack (often called a *top-of-rack* or *ToR switch*). In contrast, if a company leases space in five buildings in the same office park, the campus LAN links might have to run several hundred or even thousands of meters. The network engineer needs to be able to figure out how long the cables between the buildings need to be and then pick the right type of Ethernet.

The IEEE has kept the UTP Ethernet standards consistent in terms of cable length supported, although the particulars of the quality of cable have increased to support the faster speeds. The IEEE UTP standards from 10 Mbps through 10 Gbps all support a 100-meter cable length, which is typically plenty of length to connect a server to a ToR switch in a rack. As of this writing, servers commonly used 1-Gbps (1000BASE-T) and 10-Gbps (10GBASE-T) NICs with UTP cabling to connect to the data center LAN.

Several types of Ethernet define the use of fiber-optic cables. UTP cables include copper wires over which electrical currents can flow, whereas optical cables include ultra-thin strands of glass through which light can pass. To send bits, the switches can alternate between sending brighter and dimmer light to encode 0s and 1s on the cable.

Optical cables have some advantages, but two stand out: distance and speed. The longer distances supported across IEEE 803.3 physical layer standards all use fiber-optic cabling. In addition, to reach the next faster speed for Ethernet, much real scientific research must often be done in labs to create a working new technology. The IEEE has been much faster at developing the newer, faster Ethernet speeds using fiber optics. So, to get the faster speeds, often a fiber-based Ethernet standard is used.

Table 6-5 lists the more common types of Ethernet and their cable types and length limitations.

Table 6-5   Ethernet Types, Media, and Segment Lengths (Per IEEE)

Ethernet Type	Media	Maximum Segment Length
10BASE-T	TIA Category 3 or better, 2 pair	100 m (328 feet)
100BASE-T	TIA Category 5 UTP or better, 2 pair	100 m (328 feet)
1000BASE-T	TIA Category 5e UTP or better, 4 pair	100 m (328 feet)
1000BASE-SX	Multimode fiber	550 m (1804.5 feet) for 50-micron fiber
1000BASE-LX	Multimode fiber	550 m (1804.5 feet) for 50- and 62.5-micron fiber
1000BASE-LX	9-micron single-mode fiber	5 km (3.1 miles)
10GBASE-T	TIA Category 6a or better, 4 pair	100 m
10GBASE-CX4	Twinax (low power)	15 m

Autonegotiation

Ethernet devices on the ends of a link must use the same standard; otherwise, they cannot correctly send data. For example, a NIC cannot use 100BASE-T, which uses a two-pair UTP cable with a 100-Mbps speed, while the switch port on the other end of the link uses 1000BASE-T. Even if you used a cable that works with Gigabit Ethernet, the link would not work with one end trying to send at 100 Mbps while the other tried to receive the data at 1000 Mbps.

Upgrading to new and faster Ethernet standards becomes a problem because both ends have to use the same standard. For example, if you replace an old PC with a new one, the old one might have been using 100BASE-T while the new one uses 1000BASE-T. The switch port on the other end of the link needs to now use 1000BASE-T, so you upgrade the switch. If that switch had ports that would only use 1000BASE-T, you would need to upgrade all the other PCs connected to the switch.

The IEEE gives us a nice solution to this migration problem: IEEE autonegotiation. IEEE autonegotiation (IEEE standard 802.3u) defines a protocol that lets the two UTP-based Ethernet nodes on a link negotiate so that they each choose to use the same speed and duplex settings. The protocol messages flow outside the normal Ethernet electrical frequencies as out-of-band signals over the UTP cable. Basically, each node states what it can do, and then each node picks the best options that both nodes support: the fastest speed and the best duplex setting, with full-duplex being better than half-duplex.

NOTE   Autonegotiation relies on the fact that the IEEE uses the same wiring pinouts for 10BASE-T and 100BASE-T and that faster standards simply add to those pinouts, adding two pair.

Many networks use autonegotiation every day, particularly between user devices and the access layer LAN switches, as shown in Figure 6-24. The company installed four-pair cabling to be ready to support Gigabit Ethernet, so the wiring works for the 10-, 100-, and 1000-Mbps Ethernet options. Both nodes on each link send autonegotiation messages to each other. The switch in this case has all 10/100/1000 ports, while the PC NICs support different options.

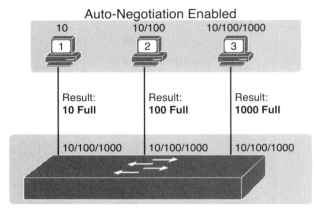

Figure 6-24   *IEEE Autonegotiation Results with Both Nodes Working Correctly*

The following list breaks down the logic, one PC at a time:

PC1: The switch port claims it can go as fast as 1000 Mbps, but PC1's NIC claims a top speed of 10 Mbps. Both the PC and switch choose the best speed both support (10 Mbps) and the best duplex (full).

PC2: PC2 claims a best speed of 100 Mbps, which means that it can use 10BASE-T or 100BASE-T. The switch port and NIC negotiate to use the best speed of 100 Mbps and full-duplex.

PC3: It uses a 10/100/1000 NIC, supporting all three speeds and standards, so both the NIC and switch port choose 1000 Mbps and full-duplex.

Autonegotiation Results When Only One Node Uses Autonegotiation

Figure 6-24 shows the IEEE autonegotiation results when both nodes use the process. However, most Ethernet devices can disable autonegotiation, so it is just as important to know what happens when a node tries to use autonegotiation but the node gets no response.

Disabling autonegotiation is not always a bad idea, but generally you should either use it on both ends of the link or disable it on both ends of the link. For example, many network engineers disable autonegotiation on links between switches and simply configure the desired speed and duplex on both switches. If enabled on both ends of the link, the nodes should pick the best speed and duplex. However, when enabled on only one end, many issues can arise: The link might not work at all, or it might just work poorly.

IEEE autonegotiation defines some rules (defaults) that nodes should use when autonegotiation fails, as follows:

- **Speed:** Use your slowest supported speed (often 10 Mbps).
- **Duplex:** If your speed = 10 or 100, use half-duplex; otherwise, use full-duplex.

Cisco switches also add to the base IEEE logic because Cisco switches can actually sense the speed used by other nodes, even without IEEE autonegotiation. As a result, Cisco switches use this slightly different logic when autonegotiation fails:

- **Speed:** Sense the speed (without using autonegotiation), or if that fails, use the IEEE default (slowest supported speed, often 10 Mbps).
- **Duplex:** Use the IEEE defaults: If speed = 10 or 100, use half-duplex; otherwise, use full-duplex.

Figure 6-25 shows three examples in which three users change their NIC settings and disable autonegotiation. The switch has all 10/100/1000 ports, with autonegotiation enabled. The top of the figure shows the configured settings on each PC NIC, with the choices made by the switch listed next to each switch port.

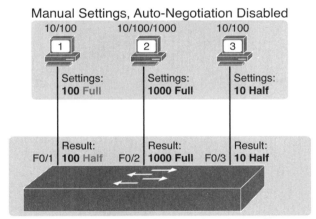

Figure 6-25 *IEEE Autonegotiation Results with Autonegotiation Disabled on One Side*

Reviewing each link, left to right:

- **PC1:** The switch receives no autonegotiation messages, so it senses the electrical signal to learn that PC1 is sending data at 100 Mbps. The switch uses the IEEE default duplex based on the 100 Mbps speed (half-duplex).
- **PC2:** The switch uses the same steps and logic as with the link to PC1, except that the switch chooses to use full-duplex, because the speed is 1000 Mbps.
- **PC3:** The user picks poorly, choosing the slower speed (10 Mbps) and the worse duplex setting (half). However, the Cisco switch senses the speed without using IEEE autonegotiation and then uses the IEEE duplex default for 10-Mbps links (half-duplex).

PC1 shows a classic and unfortunately common end result: a *duplex mismatch*. The two nodes (PC1 and SW1's port F0/1) both use 100 Mbps, so they can send data. However, PC1, using full-duplex, does not attempt to use CSMA/CD logic and sends frames at any time. Switch port F0/1, with half-duplex, does use CSMA/CD. As a result, switch port F0/1 will believe collisions occur on the link, even if none physically occur. The switch port will stop transmitting, back off, resend frames, and so on. As a result, the link is up, but it performs poorly, or may flap between an up and down state.

Autonegotiation and LAN Hubs

LAN hubs also impact how autonegotiation works. Basically, hubs do not react to autonegotiation messages, and they do not forward the messages. As a result, devices connected to a hub must use the IEEE rules for choosing default settings, which often results in the devices using 10 Mbps and half-duplex.

Figure 6-26 shows an example of a small Ethernet LAN that uses a 20-year-old 10BASE-T hub. In this LAN, all devices and switch ports are 10/100/1000 ports. The hub supports only 10BASE-T.

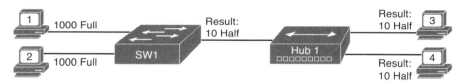

Figure 6-26   *IEEE Autonegotiation with a LAN Hub*

Note that the devices on the right need to use half-duplex because the hub requires the use of the CSMA/CD algorithm to avoid collisions.

Exam Preparation Tasks

Review All the Key Topics

Review the most important topics from this chapter, noted with the Key Topic icon. Table 6-6 lists these key topics and where each is discussed.

Table 6-6   Key Topics for Chapter 6

Key Topic Element	Description	Page Number
Table 6-2	Comparisons of 10BASE-5 and 10BASE-2	154
Figure 6-7	10BASE-T with a hub	156
List	Comparisons of repeaters, hubs, bridges, and switches	159
List	LAN switch actions	165
Figure 6-16	Example of switch forwarding logic	165
Figure 6-17	Example of switch filtering logic	166
Figure 6-18	Example of how a switch learns MAC addresses	167
Figure 6-19	Example of the need for Spanning Tree Protocol (STP)	168
List	Some of the benefits of switching	169
List	Summary of logic used to forward and filter frames and to learn MAC addresses	169
List	Definitions of collision domain and broadcast domain	171
Figure 6-23	Illustration of the concept of a VLAN	172
Table 6-4	Four LAN design feature comparisons with hubs, switches, and routers	174
List	Default autonegotiation actions with added Cisco switch logic to sense the speed	177

Complete the Tables and Lists from Memory

Print a copy of Appendix I, "Memory Tables" (found on the DVD), or at least the section for this chapter, and complete the tables and lists from memory. Appendix J, "Memory Tables Answer Key," also on the DVD, includes completed tables and lists for you to check your work.

Definitions of Key Terms

After your first reading of the chapter, try to define these key terms, but do not be concerned about getting them all correct at that time. Chapter 23, "Final Review," directs you in how to use these terms for late-stage preparation for the exam.

repeater, hub, bridge, switch, autonegotiation, broadcast domain, broadcast frame, collision domain, flooding, Spanning Tree Protocol (STP), unknown unicast frame, virtual LAN

This chapter covers the following exam topics:

1.0 Describe how a network works

1.1 Describe the purpose and functions of various network devices

1.1.a Interpret a network diagram

1.2 Select the components required to meet a network specification

1.2.a Switches

CHAPTER 7

Installing and Operating Nexus Switches

When you buy a Cisco Nexus switch, you can take it out of the box, power on the switch by connecting the power cable to the switch and a power outlet, and connect hosts to the switch using the correct UTP cables, and the switch works. You do not have to do anything else, and you certainly do not have to tell the switch to start forwarding Ethernet frames. The switch uses default settings so that all interfaces will work, assuming that the right cables and devices connect to the switch, and the switch forwards frames in and out of each interface.

However, most enterprises will want to be able to check on the switch's status, look at information about what the switch is doing, and possibly configure specific features of the switch. Engineers will also want to enable security features that allow them to securely access the switches without being vulnerable to malicious people breaking into the switches. To perform these tasks, a network engineer needs to connect to the switch's user interface.

This chapter explains the details of how to access a Cisco switch's user interface, how to use commands to find out how the switch is currently working, and how to configure the switch to tell it what to do. This chapter focuses on the processes, introducing several commands while introducing the process. The remaining chapters in Part II of the book focus on commands to do particular tasks.

"Do I Know This Already?" Quiz

Use the "Do I Know This Already?" quiz to help decide whether you might want to skim this chapter, or a major section, moving more quickly to the "Exam Preparation Tasks" section near the end of the chapter. You can find the answers at the bottom of the page following the quiz. For thorough explanations, see Appendix A, "Answers to the 'Do I Know This Already?' Quizzes."

Table 7-1 "Do I Know This Already?" Foundation Topics Section-to-Question Mapping

Foundation Topics Section	Questions
Accessing the Cisco Nexus 5500 Switch CLI	1–3
Configuring Cisco NX-OS Software	4–6

1. In what modes can you execute the command **show mac address-table**?

   a. EXEC command mode

   b. Subinterface configuration command mode

   c. Global configuration mode

   d. All of the other answers are correct.

2. In which user role can you issue the command reload to reboot the switch?

   a. Network-operator

   b. Network-admin

   c. Test user

   d. Interface user

3. Which of the following is a difference between Telnet and SSH as supported by a Cisco switch?

   a. SSH encrypts the passwords used at login, but not other traffic; Telnet encrypts nothing.

   b. SSH encrypts all data exchange, including login passwords; Telnet encrypts nothing.

   c. Telnet is used from Microsoft operating systems, and SSH is used from UNIX and Linux operating systems.

   d. Telnet encrypts only password exchanges; SSH encrypts all data exchanges.

4. What type of switch memory is used to store the running configuration?

   a. RAM

   b. ROM

   c. Flash

   d. NVRAM

   e. Bubble

5. What command copies the configuration from RAM into NVRAM?

   a. **copy running-config tftp**

   b. **copy tftp running-config**

   c. **copy running-config start-up-config**

   d. **copy start-up-config running-config**

   e. **copy startup-config running-config**

   f. **copy running-config startup-config**

6. A switch user is currently in console line configuration mode. Which of the following would place the user in EXEC mode? (Choose two answers.)

   a. Using the **exit** command once

   b. Using the **end** command once

   c. Pressing the Ctrl+Z key sequence once

   d. Using the **quit** command

7

Foundation Topics

Accessing the Cisco Nexus 5500 Switch CLI

Cisco uses the concept of a command-line interface (CLI) with its router products and most of its Nexus data center switch products. The CLI is a text-based interface in which the user, typically a network engineer, enters a text command and presses Enter. Pressing Enter sends the command to the switch, which tells the device to do something. The switch does what the command says, and in some cases, the switch replies with some messages stating the results of the command.

This book discusses only Cisco Nexus data center enterprise-class switches, and in particular, how to use the Cisco CLI to monitor and control these switches. This first major section of the chapter first examines these Nexus switches in more detail, and then explains how a network engineer can get access to the CLI to issue commands.

Cisco Nexus Switches and the 5500 Switch

Within the Cisco Nexus brand of data center switches, Cisco produced multiple product families to meet a variety of customer needs. For example, there are four series of Nexus switches: the Nexus 7000 and 7700 core and aggregation switches; the Nexus 5500, 5600, and 6000 core, aggregation, and access switches; the Nexus 3000 aggregation, access, and low-latency switches; and the Nexus 2000 fabric extenders.

Figure 7-1 shows a photo of the Nexus 5548 switch series from Cisco, which we will use as our main reference in this chapter.

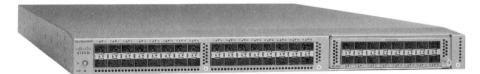

Figure 7-1 *Cisco 5500 Nexus Switch Series*

Cisco refers to a switch's physical connectors as either *interfaces* or *ports*. Each interface has a number in the style x/y, where x and y are two different numbers. On a Nexus 5500 series switch, the numbering of 1/10 gigabit interfaces starts at 1/1, the second is 1/2, and so on. With the Nexus series of switches, unlike the Catalyst series switches, which use descriptions for interfaces such as Gigabit 1/1 or 10 Gigabit 1/1, Nexus uses a generic Ethernet naming convention regardless of the interface speed. For example, the first Ethernet interface on a Nexus 5500 switch would be interface Ethernet 1/1. The Nexus series of switches support 100-MB, 1-GB, 10-GB, 40-GB, and 100-GB interfaces based on the model chosen.

Accessing the Cisco NX-OS CLI

Like any other piece of computer hardware, Cisco switches need some kind of operating system (OS) software. Cisco calls this OS the Nexus Operating System (NX-OS).

Cisco NX-OS software for Nexus switches implements and controls logic and functions performed by a Cisco switch. Besides controlling the switch's performance and behavior, Cisco NX-OS also defines an interface for humans called the *command-line interface* (CLI). The Cisco NX-OS CLI allows the user to use a terminal emulation program, which accepts text entered by the user. When the user presses Enter, the terminal emulator sends that text to the switch. The switch processes the text as if it is a command, does what the command says, and sends text back to the terminal emulator.

The switch CLI can be accessed through three popular methods: the console, Telnet, and Secure Shell (SSH). Two of these methods (Telnet and SSH) use the IP network in which the switch resides to reach the switch. The console is a physical port built specifically to allow access to the CLI. Figure 7-2 depicts the options.

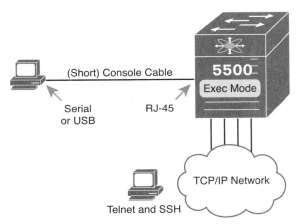

Figure 7-2   *CLI Access*

Console access requires both a physical connection between a PC (or other user device) and the switch's console port, in addition to some software on the PC. Telnet and SSH require software on the user's device, but they rely on the existing TCP/IP network to transmit data. The next few pages detail how to connect the console and set up the software for each method to access the CLI.

Cabling the Console Connection

The physical console connection, both old and new, uses three main components: the physical console port on the switch, a physical serial port on the PC, and a cable that works with the console and serial ports. However, the physical cabling details have changed slowly over time, mainly because of advances and changes with PC hardware.

Older console connections use a PC serial port, a console cable, and an RJ-45 connector on the switch. The PC serial port typically has a D-shell connector (roughly rectangular) with nine pins (often called a *DB-9*). Older switches, as well as some current models, use an RJ-45 connector for the console port. Figure 7-3 shows the cabling on the left.

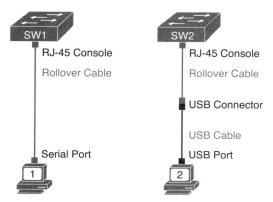

Figure 7-3   *Console Connection to a Switch*

You can use either a purpose-built console cable (which ships with new Cisco switches and routers) or make your own console cable using UTP cables and a standard RJ-45-to-DB-9 converter plug. You can buy the converter plug at most computer stores. Then, for the UTP cabling, the cable uses rollover cable pinouts, rather than any of the standard Ethernet cabling pinouts. Instead, it uses eight wires, rolling the wire at pin 1 to pin 8, pin 2 to pin 7, pin 3 to pin 6, and so on.

PCs have migrated away from using serial ports to instead use Universal Serial Bus (USB) ports for serial communications. Cisco has also begun building newer routers and switches with USB ports for console access as well.

The right side of the figure shows yet another common option. Many PCs no longer have serial ports, but many existing Cisco routers and switches have only an RJ-45 console port and no USB console port. To connect such a PC to a router or switch console, you need some kind of converter that converts from the older console cable to a USB connector, as shown in the middle of Figure 7-3.

NOTE   When using the USB options, you typically also need to install a software driver so that your PC's OS knows that the device on the other end of the USB connection is the console of a Cisco device.

Configuring the Terminal Emulator for the Console

After the PC is physically connected to the console port, a terminal emulator software package must be installed and configured on the PC. The terminal emulator software treats all data as text. It accepts the text typed by the user and sends it over the console connection to the switch. Similarly, any bits coming into the PC over the console connection are displayed as text for the user to read.

The emulator must be configured to use the PC's serial port to match the settings on the switch's console port settings. The default console port settings on a switch are as follows. Note that the last three parameters are referred to collectively as *8N1*:

- 9600 bits/second
- No hardware flow control
- 8-bit ASCII
- No parity bits
- 1 stop bit

Figure 7-4 shows one such terminal emulator, Zterm Pro. The image shows the window created by the emulator software in the background, with some output of a **show** command. The foreground, in the upper left, shows a settings window that lists the default console settings as listed just before this paragraph.

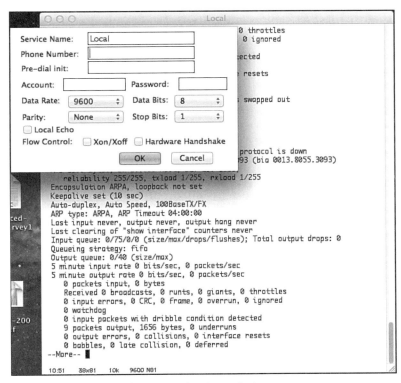

Figure 7-4 *Terminal Settings for Console Access*

Accessing the CLI with Telnet and SSH in NX-OS

The TCP/IP Telnet application allows a terminal emulator to communicate with another willing device. The process works much like what happens with an emulator on a PC connected to the console, except that the data flows over a TCP/IP network instead of over a console cable. However, Telnet uses an IP network to send and receive the data rather than a specialized cable and physical port on the device. The Telnet application protocols call the terminal emulator a Telnet client and the device that listens for commands and replies to them a Telnet server. Telnet is a TCP-based application layer protocol that uses well-known port 23.

To use Telnet, users must install a Telnet client software package on their PC. (As mentioned earlier, most terminal emulator software packages today include both Telnet and SSH client functions.) The Nexus switch disables Telnet server software by default, but the switch does need to have an IP address configured so that it can send and receive IP packets and be enabled for Telnet. (Chapter 8, "Configuring Ethernet Switching," covers switch IP address configuration in greater detail.) In addition, the network between the PC and switch needs to be up and working so that the PC and switch can exchange IP packets.

Many network engineers habitually use a Telnet client to monitor switches. Engineers can sit at their desks without having to walk to another part of the building (or go to another state or country) and still get into the CLI of that device.

While Telnet works well, many network engineers instead use SSH to overcome a serious security problem with Telnet. Telnet sends all data (including any username and password for login to the switch) as clear-text data. SSH encrypts the contents of all messages, including the passwords, avoiding the possibility of someone capturing packets in the network and stealing the password to network devices.

SSH does the same basic things as Telnet, but with added security. The user uses a terminal emulator that supports SSH. Like Telnet, SSH uses TCP, using well-known port 22 instead of Telnet's 23. As with Telnet, the SSH server (on the switch) receives the text from each SSH client, processes the text as a command, and sends messages back to the client. SSH is the default enabled way to access a Cisco Nexus switch.

Management Interface

A Cisco Nexus switch has a dedicated management interface referred to as the *management 0* interface used for out-of-band management of any series of Cisco Nexus switches. Another characteristic to this interface as compared to other interfaces on the switch is it has by default been put in its own virtual routing and forwarding (VRF) instance called the *management VRF*. To access the switch for management via Telnet or SSH you must assign an IP address, default mask, and default route to the Mgmt0 interface, as shown in Example 7-1.

Nexus switches use two VRFs by default for the purpose of separating management traffic from traffic between the servers in the data center and the rest of the network. By default, Nexus places the management interface into the management VRF and places all other interfaces into the default VRF. The Nexus switch does not forward frames between the management interface and the interfaces in the default VRF.

For the switch to communicate out of its management interface, it needs two things to be configured. First, you need to choose an IP address and subnet mask to apply to this interface from your management network. Second, you need to inform the switch of the default route to get to the rest of the network by applying an **ip route** statement under the VRF context for management to tell it what the next-hop Layer 3 device is. Figure 7-5 shows what VRF each interface is in by default on a Nexus switch.

Nexus Switch Internals: VRFs

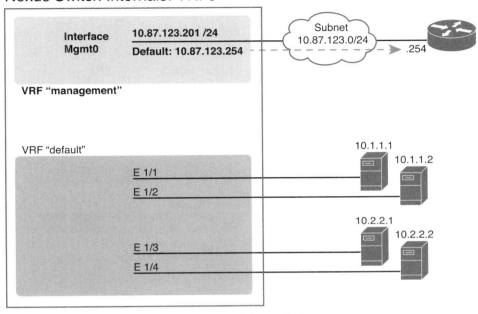

Figure 7-5   *VRF Settings on Nexus Switch by Default*

Example 7-1   *Configuration of the Management Interface and Context Default Route*

```
Certskills1# configure terminal
Enter configuration commands, one per line.  End with CNTL/Z.
Certskills1(config)# interface mgmt0
Certskills1(config-if)# ip address 10.87.123.201/24

Certskills1# configure terminal
Enter configuration commands, one per line.  End with CNTL/Z.
Certskills1(config)# vrf context management
Certskills1(config-vrf)# ip route 0.0.0.0/0 10.87.123.254
```

Password Security for CLI Access

A Cisco Nexus switch with default settings has a default Network-admin role with a user-name of admin; the default user cannot be deleted or changed at any time. This default user does not have a password and should be explicitly defined using a strong password. If the password is basic and easy to decipher, the switch will not accept the password, and you will be asked for a stronger password.

Be sure to configure a strong password for each user account. A strong password has the following characteristics:

- At least eight characters long
- Does not contain many consecutive characters (such as abcd)
- Does not contain many repeating characters (such as aaabbb)
- Does not contain dictionary words
- Does not contain proper names
- Contains both uppercase and lowercase characters
- Contains numbers

Table 7-2 outlines CLI password configuration from the console.

Table 7-2   CLI Password Configuration: Console and Telnet

Access From	Password Type	Sample Configuration
Console, SSH, or Telnet (vty)	Console, SSH, or vty password	Username admin password Cisco123 role (network-operator/network-admin)
Feature	Feature to enable Telnet or SSH	Feature SSH or Telnet

Cisco switches refer to the console as a *console line* (specifically, console line 0). Similarly, switches support 16 concurrent Telnet sessions, referenced as virtual terminal (vty) lines 0 through 15. (The term *vty* refers to an old name for terminal emulators.) The **line vty** configuration command tells the switch that the commands that follow apply to all 16 possible concurrent virtual terminal connections to the switch (0 through 15), which includes Telnet and SSH access.

To enable user, role, and password authentication for SSH and Telnet, you have to use the **feature telnet** or **feature ssh** command for enabling the protocol you would like to use to communicate with for managing your Cisco Nexus switch. Console authentication, by default, is enabled to user authentication. After adding the configuration shown in Table 7-2, a user connecting to the console, Telnet, or SSH is prompted for a username and password, and the user must use **Cisco123** for the password with **admin** as the username in this case.

User Settings

All three CLI access methods covered so far (console, Telnet, and SSH) place the user in an area of the CLI called user EXEC command mode. The *EXEC mode* part of the name refers to the fact that in this mode, when you enter a command, the switch executes the command and then displays messages that describe the command's results.

Cisco NX-OS supports restricting users from executing commands in EXEC mode based on their user role. For example, you can use the **reload** command, which tells the switch to reinitialize or reboot Cisco NX-OS, from network-admin role but not from network-operator mode.

> **NOTE** Unlike IOS, Cisco NX-OS does not store or use an enable-secret in the configuration. Each user account is created with its own password (stored locally or through AAA), and authorization levels are dictated by the role assigned to the account. It is important to secure all accounts by assigning the correct privileged access with the network-admin or vdc-admin roles. Using this method simplifies password management in NX-OS. Table 7-3 shows the predefined roles that can be assigned to a given username in NX-OS

Table 7-3 NX-OS Predefined User Roles

Role Name	Description
Network-admin (super user)	Complete read and write access to the entire switch
Network-operator	Complete read access to the switch
San-admin	Complete read and write access to Fibre Channel and Fibre Channel over Ethernet (FCoE) administrative tasks using SNMP or CLI

Example 7-2 shows the output that you could see in a Telnet window. In this case, the user connects with Telnet and tries the **reload** command. The **reload** command tells the switch to reinitialize or reboot Cisco NX-OS. NX-OS allows this powerful command, so in the example, NX-OS rejects the **reload** command if the user does not have the privileges to execute the **reload** command (for example, the network-operator role).

Example 7-2 *Executing the* reload *Command in Different User Roles on Switch Certskills1*

```
Certskills1(config)# username test password Cisco123 role network-operator
Certskills1(config)# username admin password Cisco123 role network-admin


Nexus 5000 Switch
login: test
Password:
Cisco Nexus Operating System (NX-OS) Software
Certskills1# reload
% Permission denied for the role
Certskills1#



Nexus 5000 Switch
login: admin
Password:
Cisco Nexus Operating System (NX-OS) Software
Certskills1# reload
WARNING: There is unsaved configuration!!!
WARNING: This command will reboot the system
Do you want to continue? (y/n) [n] y
```

> **NOTE**   The commands that can be used in either user (EXEC) mode or enable (EXEC) mode are called *EXEC commands*.

This example is the first instance of this book showing you the output from the CLI, so it is worth noting a few conventions. The bold text represents what the user typed, and the non-bold text is what the switch sent back to the terminal emulator. Also, for security purposes, the typed passwords do not show up on the screen. Finally, note that this switch has been preconfigured with a hostname of Certskills1, so the command prompt on the left shows that host name on each line.

So far, this chapter has pointed out some of the first things you should know when unpacking and installing a switch. The Nexus switch will work with a basic configuration; just plug in the power and Ethernet cables, enable the interfaces, and it works. However, you should at least connect to the switch console port and configure passwords for each user role. Next, this chapter examines some of the CLI features that exist regardless of how you access the CLI.

CLI Help Features

If you printed the Cisco NX-OS Command Reference documents, you would end up with a stack of paper several feet tall. No one should expect to memorize all the commands (and no one does). You can use several very easy, convenient tools to help remember commands and save time typing. As you progress through your Cisco certifications, the exams will cover progressively more commands. However, you should know the methods of getting command help.

Table 7-4 summarizes command-recall help options available at the CLI. Note that in the first column *command* represents any command. Likewise, *parm* represents a command's parameter. For example, the second row lists *command* **?**, which means that commands such as **show ?** and **copy ?** would list help for the **show** and **copy** commands, respectively.

Table 7-4   Cisco NX-OS Software Command Help

What You Enter	What Help You Get
?	Help for all commands available in this mode.
command **?**	Text help describing all the first parameter options for the command.
com?	A list of commands that start with com.
*command parm***?**	This style of help lists all parameters beginning with the parameter typed so far. (Notice that there is no space between *parm* and the **?**.)
command parm<**Tab**>	If you press the Tab key midword, the CLI either spells the rest of this parameter at the command line or does nothing. If the CLI does nothing, it means that this string of characters represents more than one possible next parameter, so the CLI does not know which one to spell out.
command parm1 **?**	If a space is inserted before the question mark, the CLI lists all the next parameters and gives a brief explanation of each.

When you enter the ?, the Cisco NX-OS CLI reacts immediately; that is, you don't need to press the Enter key or any other keys. The device running Cisco NX-OS also redisplays what you entered before the ? to save you some keystrokes. If you press Enter immediately after the ?, Cisco NX-OS tries to execute the command with only the parameters you have entered so far.

The information supplied by using help depends on the CLI mode. For example, when ? is entered in EXEC mode, the commands allowed in EXEC mode are displayed, but commands available only in global configuration mode are not displayed. Also, note that NX-OS enables you to run commands from less-specific modes in more-specific modes, but you cannot run commands from more-specific modes in less-specific modes. For example, you can run EXEC commands in global configuration mode, interface mode, or subinterface mode, but you are not allowed to run global, interface, or subinterface commands in EXEC mode.

Cisco NX-OS stores the commands that you enter in a history buffer, storing ten commands by default. The CLI allows you to move backward and forward in the historical list of commands and then edit the command before reissuing it. These key sequences can help you use the CLI more quickly on the exams. Table 7-5 lists the commands used to manipulate previously entered commands.

Table 7-5   Key Sequences for Command Edit and Recall

Keyboard Command	What Happens
Up arrow or Ctrl+P	This displays the most recently used command. If you press it again, the next most recent command appears, until the history buffer is exhausted. (The *P* stands for previous.)
Down arrow or Ctrl+N	If you have gone too far back into the history buffer, these keys take you forward to the more recently entered commands. (The *N* stands for next.)
Left arrow or Ctrl+B	This moves the cursor backward in the currently displayed command without deleting characters. (The *B* stands for back.)
Right arrow or Ctrl+F	This moves the cursor forward in the currently displayed command without deleting characters. (The *F* stands for forward.)
Backspace	This moves the cursor backward in the currently displayed command, deleting characters.
Ctrl+A	This moves the cursor directly to the first character of the currently displayed command.
Ctrl+E	This moves the cursor directly to the end of the currently displayed command.
Ctrl+R	This redisplays the command line with all characters. It is useful when messages clutter the screen.
Ctrl+D	This deletes a single character.
Ctrl+Shift+6	Interrupts the current command.

7

The debug and show Commands

By far, the single most popular Cisco NX-OS command is the **show** command. The **show** command has a large variety of options, and with those options, you can find the status of almost every feature of Cisco NX-OS. Essentially, the **show** command lists the currently known facts about the switch's operational status. The only work the switch does in reaction to **show** commands is to find the current status and list the information in messages sent to the user.

The **debug** command has a similar role as compared with the **show** command. Like the **show** command, **debug** has many options. However, instead of just listing messages about the current status, the **debug** command asks the switch to continue monitoring different processes in the switch. The switch then sends ongoing messages to the user when different events occur.

The effects of the **show** and **debug** commands can be compared to a photograph (**show** command) and a movie (**debug** command). A **show** command shows what's true at a single point in time, and it takes less effort. A **debug** command shows what's true over time, but it requires more effort. As a result, the **debug** command requires more CPU cycles, but it lets you watch what is happening in a switch while it is happening.

Cisco NX-OS handles the messages from the **show** and **debug** commands very differently. NX-OS sends the output of **show** commands to the user that issued the **show** command, and to no other users. However, NX-OS reacts to **debug** commands by creating log messages related to that **debug** command's options. Any user logged in can choose to view the log messages just by using the **terminal monitor** command from EXEC mode.

NX-OS also treats the **show** command as a very short-lived event and the **debug** command as an ongoing task. The options enabled by a single **debug** command are not disabled until the user takes action or until the switch is reloaded. A **reload** of the switch disables all currently enabled debug options. To disable a single debug option, repeat the same **debug** command with those options, prefaced by the word **no**. For example, if the **debug spanning-tree** command had been issued earlier, issue the **no debug spanning-tree** command to disable that same debug. Also, the **no debug all** and **undebug all** commands disable all currently enabled debugs.

Introduction to Cisco NX-OS

Cisco Nexus switches were created to provide the next generation of data center class features and functionality. To enable these features and functionalities, Cisco created a new OS called Cisco NX-OS. Cisco NX-OS was designed to support modularity, serviceability, and high availability, which are all required in today's data centers.

You gain several advantages when you use the Cisco NX-OS, as highlighted in the brief list that follows:

- Modularity in software
- Virtualization features
- Resiliency

- IPv4 and IPv6 feature-rich routing and multicast functionality
- Data center security, serviceability, and availability features
- Unified Fabric

Cisco NX-OS is a purpose-built OS for data centers of today. Cisco NX-OS is a combination of two well-known operating systems: SAN-OS and Internetwork Operating System (IOS). SAN-OS is the operating system that was used in the Fibre Channel storage-area network (SAN) switches known as the *Cisco MDS*. IOS is the original operating system used and adapted over the years that runs on Cisco routers and Catalyst local-area network (LAN) switches. IOS and SAN-OS merged to create Cisco NX-OS. Figure 7-6 shows the merger of the two operating systems that created NX-OS. Figure 7-7 shows the platforms on which NX-OS is supported.

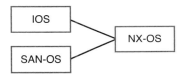

Figure 7-6 *NX-OS OS Merger*

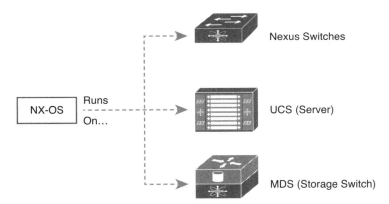

Figure 7-7 *NX-OS Platforms*

Software Modularity in Cisco NX-OS

The first step to understanding how Cisco NX-OS was built and provides an improvement for data center networks is to explore the software modularity that is provided. Cisco NX-OS was built with a mindset to provide the highest level of availability for data center networks. To provide this, the team that created Cisco NX-OS focused on providing modular processes as a foundation to the operating system. When a feature is enabled in Cisco NX-OS, a process is started and system resources are then allocated to the given process. Each individual feature is enabled on demand and given its own protected memory space. Cisco NX-OS then uses a real-time preemptive scheduler that helps ensure the timely processing of critical functions. Example 7-3 shows enabling a feature on a Cisco NX-OS platform and the output before the enablement and after.

Example 7-3   *Enabling VTP Feature Before and After*

```
Certskills1# show vtp
% Incomplete command at '^' marker.
Certskills1# show feature | include vtp
vtp                    1            disabled
Certskills1# configure terminal
Enter configuration commands, one per line.  End with CNTL/Z.
Certskills1(config)# feature vtp
Certskills1(config)# exit

Certskills1# show feature | include vtp
vtp                    1            enabled

Certskills1# show vtp ?
  counters   VTP statistics
  interface  VTP interface status and configuration
  internal   Show internal information
  password   VTP password
  status     VTP domain status

Certskills1# show vtp status
VTP Status Information
----------------------
VTP Version                     : 2 (capable)
Configuration Revision          : 0
Maximum VLANs supported locally : 1005
Number of existing VLANs        : 6
VTP Operating Mode              : Server
VTP Domain Name                 : <VTP domain not acquired/configured yet>
VTP Pruning Mode                : Disabled (Operationally Disabled)
VTP V2 Mode                     : Disabled
VTP Traps Generation            : Disabled
MD5 Digest                      : 0x83 0x35 0xB0 0xD0 0x44 0x8B 0x5E 0x86
Configuration last modified by 10.87.123.230 at 0-0-00 00:00:00

Local updater ID is 10.87.123.230 on interface mgmt0 (first L3 interface found)
VTP version running             : 1
```

Service Restart in Cisco NX-OS

The Cisco NX-OS service restart feature enables you to restart a faulty service without restarting the supervisor. A system manager is in control of the overall function of the system; it monitors the services and system health. The system manager is in charge of instructing the system and service to take an action when an action is needed, such as instructing a service to do a stateful or stateless restart. A service can undergo either a stateful or stateless restart.

Not all services are designed for stateful restart. For example, Cisco NX-OS does not store run-time state information for all Layer 3 routing protocols. Some Layer 3 routing protocols rely on functions such as graceful restart (NSF).

Cisco NX-OS allows services to store run-time state information and messages for a stateful restart. In a stateful restart, the service can retrieve this stored state information and resume operations from the last checkpoint service state. In a stateless restart, the service can initialize and run as if it had just been started with no prior state. Stateful restarts of process use a service enabled in Cisco NX-OS called *Persistent Storage Service* (PSS). PSS is used in many Cisco NX-OS services as a database to store and manage their run-time state information. This allows the services to create checkpoints of their state, and in case of a failure the service can use the checkpoint to recover to its last known operating manner statefully.

Software High Availability in Cisco NX-OS

Along with the service restart functionality of Cisco NX-OS, the software offers what are called *high availability (HA) policies*. Cisco NX-OS allows for each service to have an associated set of HA policies that specify what restart methodology will be used for a failed service. NX-OS supports HA policies that define how NX-OS restarts a service if it fails. The policies can be simple, like the default policy on a single supervisor Nexus switch: The switch simply resets the supervisor, restarting NX-OS. (On a dual-supervisor switch, the default HA policy causes a failover from the current supervisor to the standby supervisor, which does not cause an outage.)

NOTE Supervisor modules are particular to modular switches with multiple line card slots. For example, the Cisco Nexus 7000/7700/9000 and the Cisco MDS 9500/9700 series have the capability to have multiple supervisor modules. Fixed form factor switches, such as the Cisco Nexus 3000, 5500, and 6000, have built-in single supervisor modules.

In-Service Software Upgrades

With the modular architecture that Cisco NX-OS provides, it allows for a unique feature known as *in-service software upgrades* (ISSU). ISSUs enable the Nexus switching system to do a complete system software upgrade without disruption to the data plane. This functionality allows for complete system software upgrades to happen while the system will continue to forward packets. Figure 7-8 shows the process the system takes when performing an ISSU.

NOTE ISSU is done when dual supervisor modules are available in the systems. In special cases, it can be done across physical systems. It should only be done when the network is stable, and a change control window is recommended.

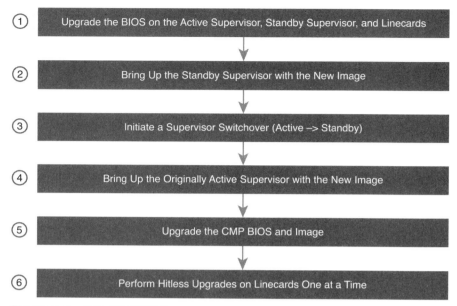

Figure 7-8   *NX-OS ISSU Steps*

Cisco NX-OS Licensing

So far in this chapter, we have discussed how Cisco NX-OS has been architected from its foundation to provide data center class software modularity and HA. Now that you are familiar with the NX-OS features, this section describes how the software licensing model supports the modular software architecture.

Cisco NX-OS is composed of two different images, the kickstart image and the system image. When doing software upgrades, networking administrators must download and install both of these images for the appropriate version they want to install or upgrade to. Note that administrators do not have to upgrade software or purchase a particular level of the operating system, because Cisco NX-OS is a universal image. Therefore, all the features available in a particular version are available in the operating system images they download. For certain features or functionality, they will have to purchase feature licenses, which are loaded into the system's flash and enabled for the system's use. Example 7-4 displays output that results from installing a license file on a Nexus switch.

Example 7-4   *Displaying and Installing an NX-OS License File*

```
Certskills1# show license host-id
License hostid: VDH=TBM14299862


Certskills1# dir bootflash:
        342     Mar 12 15:53:30 2012   LAN_ENT.lic
! some output omitted


Certskills1# install license bootflash:LAN_ENT.lic
Installing license ..done
```

NOTE Cisco NX-OS offers a 120-day grace period to test certain features. The grace period license can be enabled for a customer to test a feature license without purchase. To enable the grace period licensing, you issue the command Certskills1(config)# **license grace-period**.

After you have installed the appropriate license files needed for your Nexus switch, you issue the feature commands to enable their processes and start configuration of your Nexus switch.

Cisco NX-OS and Cisco IOS Comparison

To finish up this introduction to Cisco NX-OS, this section describes how Cisco NX-OS and Cisco IOS differ. Cisco IOS and NX-OS are similar in many ways. From a feature and functionality and also from a configurations standpoint, many of the same commands' structures are the same for working in both IOS and NX-OS command-line interfaces. It is important to understand some of the differences between them, though, which will help you to navigate inside each operating system and lead to less confusion when switching between the two operating systems. The main points to be aware of include the following:

- Interfaces in NX-OS are all listed as Ethernet interfaces (for data interfaces). In contrast, IOS uses a description based on speed, such as Gigabit or 10 Gigabit.

- When you log in to IOS, you are prompted for an enable password to move from user EXEC mode into enable (also called privileged) EXEC mode. NX-OS does not have a user or enable mode, nor an **enable** command. Instead, NX-OS associates a privilege level for each user based on a username/password combination, with all users considered to be in EXEC mode.

- NX-OS uses a universal image, and features are unlocked using license keys and feature enablement commands. Cisco IOS originally required you to purchase, download, and install an operating system image that had the appropriate feature set for your enterprise needs. As of a couple of years ago, IOS has also adopted the universal image concept with license key enablement.

- NX-OS has a management Virtual Routing and Forwarding (VRF) instance per Nexus switch as well as a default VRF that all other interfaces belong to. To get access to remotely manage a Nexus switch, you must configure the Management interface (as covered later in this book).

- NX-OS uses two binary images per version of the operating system to be downloaded and installed (kickstart and system). Cisco IOS is a single binary image that is downloaded and installed by the network administrator.

- To enable features in NX-OS, the **feature** command is used per feature, such as **feature ospf** or **feature eigrp** to enable these Layer 3 routing protocols. In Cisco IOS, the command **ip routing** enables all the processes for every routing protocol a given operating system image will support.

There are also command differences between the two operating systems, but there are too many to list here. To compare the command differences, see this website, which lists each command in Cisco IOS and how you can use it in NX-OS: http://docwiki.cisco.com/wiki/Cisco_NX-OS/IOS_Software_Default_Configuration_Differences.

Configuring Cisco NX-OS Software

You must understand how to configure a Cisco switch to succeed on the exam and in real networking jobs. This section covers the basic configuration processes, including the concept of a configuration file and the locations in which the configuration files can be stored. Although this section focuses on the configuration process, and not on the configuration commands themselves, you should know all the commands covered in this chapter for the exams, in addition to the configuration processes.

Commands entered in configuration mode update the active configuration file. These changes to the configuration occur immediately each time you press the Enter key at the end of a command. Be careful when you enter a configuration command!

Configuration Submodes and Contexts

Configuration mode itself contains a multitude of subcommand modes. Context-setting commands move you from one configuration subcommand mode, or context, to another. These context-setting commands tell the switch the topic about which you will enter the next few configuration commands.

> **NOTE**   *Context setting* is not a Cisco term; it is just a term used here to help make sense of configuration mode. As mentioned earlier in the chapter, NX-OS enables you to enter commands that might be at a less-specific command mode with the **?**. For instance, you can be in interface command mode, enter (config-if)# **spanning-tree vlan ?**, and it will list the help for this global configuration command.

The **interface** command is one of the most commonly used context-setting configuration commands. For example, the CLI user could enter interface configuration mode by entering the **interface Ethernet 1/1** configuration command. Asking for help in interface configuration mode displays only commands that are useful when configuring Ethernet interfaces. Commands used in this context are called *subcommands* (or, in this specific case, *interface subcommands*). When you begin practicing with the CLI with real equipment, the navigation between modes can become natural. For now, consider Example 7-5, which shows the following:

- Movement from EXEC mode to global configuration mode by using the **configure terminal** EXEC command

- Using a **hostname Fred** global configuration command to configure the switch's name

- Movement from console configuration mode to interface configuration mode (using the **interface** command)

- Setting the speed to 10 Gigabit for interface Ethernet1/1 (using the **speed 10000** interface subcommand)

- Movement from interface configuration mode back to global configuration mode (using the exit command)

Example 7-5   *Navigating Between Different Configuration Modes*

```
Switch# configure terminal
Switch(config)# hostname Fred
Fred(config)# interface Ethernet 1/1
Fred(config-if)# speed 10000
Fred(config-if)# exit
Fred(config)#
```

The text inside parentheses in the command prompt identifies the configuration mode. For example, the first command prompt after you enter configuration mode lists (config), meaning global configuration mode. After the **interface Ethernet 1/1** command, the text expands to (config-if), meaning line configuration mode. Table 7-6 shows the most common command prompts in configuration mode, the names of those modes, and the context-setting commands used to reach those modes. NX-OS also has a command **where** that you can use from any mode to tell you what configuration modes you have gone through to get to the current configuration mode and which configuration mode you are currently in.

Table 7-6   Common Switch Configuration Modes

Prompt	Name of Mode	Context-Setting Commands to Reach This Mode
hostname(config)#	Global	None (first mode after configure terminal)
hostname(config-line)#	Line	**line console**, **line vty**
hostname(config-if)#	Interface	**interface** *type number*

You should practice until you become comfortable moving between the different configuration modes, back to EXEC mode, and then back into the configuration modes. However, you can learn these skills just doing labs about the topics in later chapters of the book. For now, Figure 7-9 shows most of the navigation between global configuration mode and the three configuration submodes listed in Table 7-6.

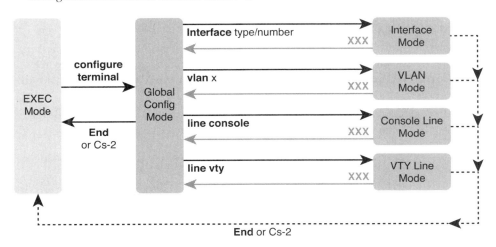

Figure 7-9   *Navigation In and Out of Switch Configuration Modes*

NOTE   You can also move directly from one configuration submode to another without first using the **exit** command to move back to global configuration mode. Just use the commands listed in bold in the center of the figure. To go directly back to enabled mode, you can type the **end** command from any submode.

No set rules exist for what commands are global commands or subcommands. Generally, however, when multiple instances of a parameter can be set in a single switch, the command used to set the parameter is likely a configuration subcommand. Items that are set once for the entire switch are likely global commands. For example, the **hostname** command is a global command because there is only one host name per switch. Conversely, the **duplex** command is an interface subcommand to allow the switch to use a different setting on the different interfaces.

Storing Switch Configuration Files

When you configure a switch, it needs to use the configuration. It also needs to be able to retain the configuration in case the switch loses power. Cisco Nexus switches contain random-access memory (RAM) to store data while Cisco NX-OS is using it, but RAM loses its contents when the switch loses power. To store information that must be retained when the switch loses power, Cisco switches use several types of more permanent memory, none of which has any moving parts. By avoiding components with moving parts (such as traditional disk drives), switches can maintain better uptime and availability.

The following list details the four main types of memory found in Cisco switches and the most common use of each type:

- **RAM:** Sometimes called DRAM, for dynamic random-access memory, RAM is used by the switch just as it is used by any other computer: for working storage. The running (active) configuration file is stored here.

- **ROM:** Read-only memory stores a bootstrap (or boothelper) program that is loaded when the switch first powers on. This bootstrap program then finds the full Cisco NX-OS image and manages the process of loading Cisco NX-OS into RAM, at which point Cisco NX-OS takes over operation of the switch.

- **Flash memory:** Either a chip inside the switch or a removable memory card, flash memory stores fully functional Cisco NX-OS images and is the default location where the switch gets its Cisco NX-OS at boot time. Flash memory also can be used to store any other files, including backup copies of configuration files.

- **NVRAM:** Nonvolatile RAM (NVRAM) stores the initial or startup configuration file that is used when the switch is first powered on and when the switch is reloaded.

Figure 7-10 summarizes this same information in a more convenient form for memorization and study.

Figure 7-10 *Cisco Switch Memory Types*

Cisco NX-OS stores the collection of configuration commands in a configuration file. In fact, switches use multiple configuration files—one file for the initial configuration used when powering on, and another configuration file for the active, currently used running configuration as stored in RAM. Table 7-7 lists the names of these two files, their purpose, and their storage location.

Table 7-7   Names and Purposes of the Two Main Cisco NX-OS Configuration Files

Configuration Filename	Purpose	Where It Is Stored
Startup config	Stores the initial configuration used anytime the switch reloads Cisco NX-OS.	NVRAM
Running config	Stores the currently used configuration commands. This file changes dynamically when someone enters commands in configuration mode.	RAM

Essentially, when you use configuration mode, you change only the running config file. This means that the configuration example earlier in this chapter (Example 7-2) updates only the running config file. However, if the switch were to lose power right after you complete the configuration shown in Example 7-2, all that configuration would be lost. If you want to keep that configuration, you have to copy the running config file into NVRAM, overwriting the old startup config file.

Example 7-6 demonstrates that commands used in configuration mode change only the running configuration in RAM. The example shows the following concepts and steps:

Step 1.   The original **hostname** command on the switch, with the startup config file matching the running config file.

Step 2.   The **hostname** command changes the hostname, but only in the running config file.

Step 3.   The **show running-config** and **show startup-config** commands are shown, with only the **hostname** commands displayed for brevity, to make the point that the two configuration files are now different.

Example 7-6 *How Configuration Mode Commands Change the Running Config File, Not the Startup Config File*

```
! Step 1 next (two commands)
!
hannah# show running-config
! (lines omitted)
hostname hannah
! (rest of lines omitted)

hannah# show startup-config
! (lines omitted)
hostname hannah
! (rest of lines omitted)
! Step 2 next. Notice that the command prompt changes immediately after
! the hostname command.
hannah# configure terminal
hannah(config)# hostname jessie
jessie(config)# exit
! Step 3 next (two commands)
!
jessie# show running-config
! (lines omitted)
hostname jessie
! (rest of lines omitted - notice that the running configuration reflects the
!  changed hostname)
jessie# show startup-config
! (lines omitted)
hostname hannah
! (rest of lines omitted - notice that the changed configuration is not
! shown in the startup config)
```

NOTE Cisco uses the term *reload* to refer to what most PC operating systems call rebooting or restarting. In each case, it is a reinitialization of the software. The **reload** EXEC command causes a switch to reload.

Copying and Erasing Configuration Files

If you want to keep the new configuration commands you add in configuration mode (so that the changes are present the next time the system is rebooted), like the **hostname jessie** command in Example 7-6, you need to use the command **copy running-config startup-config**. This command overwrites the current startup config file with what is currently in the running configuration file.

You can use the **copy** command to copy files in a switch, most typically a configuration file or a new version of Cisco NX-OS software. The most basic method for moving configuration files in and out of a switch is to use the **copy** command to copy files between RAM or NVRAM on a switch and a TFTP server. You can copy the files between any pair, as shown in Figure 7-11.

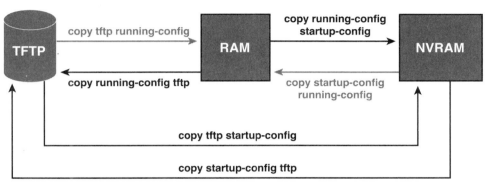

Figure 7-11   *Locations for Copying and Results from Copy Operations*

The commands for copying Cisco NX-OS configurations can be summarized as follows:

```
copy {tftp | running-config | startup-config} {tftp | running-config |
  startup-config}
```

The first set of parameters enclosed in braces ({ }) is the "from" location; the next set of parameters is the "to" location.

The **copy** command always replaces the existing file when the file is copied into NVRAM or into a TFTP server. In other words, it acts as if the destination file was erased and the new file completely replaced the old one. However, when the **copy** command copies a configuration file into the running config file in RAM, the configuration file in RAM is not replaced, but is merged instead. Effectively, any **copy** into RAM works just as if you entered the commands in the "from" configuration file in the order listed in the config file.

Who cares? Well, we do. If you change the running config and then decide that you want to revert to what's in the startup config file, the result of the **copy startup-config running-config** command might not cause the two files to actually match. One way to guarantee that the two configuration files match is to issue the **reload** command, which reloads, or reboots, the switch, which erases RAM and then copies the startup config into RAM as part of the reload process.

You can use the **write erase** command to erase the contents of NVRAM. Of course, if the switch is reloaded at this point, there is no initial configuration. Note that Cisco NX-OS does not have a command that erases the contents of the running config file. To clear out the running config file, simply erase the startup config file and then **reload** the switch.

NOTE   Making a copy of all current switch and router configurations should be part of any network's overall security strategy, mainly so that you can replace a device's configuration if an attack changes the configuration.

Initial Configuration (Setup Mode)

Cisco NX-OS software supports two primary methods of giving a switch an initial basic configuration: configuration mode, which has already been covered in this chapter; and setup mode. Setup mode leads a switch administrator by asking questions that prompt the administrator for basic configuration parameters. After the administrator answers the questions, NX-OS builds a configuration file, saves it as the startup config, and also loads it as the running config to start using the new configuration.

When a Cisco switch or router initializes, but the startup config file is empty, the switch or router asks the console user if he wants to use setup. Figure 7-12 shows the branches in the process. The left side of the figure, moving down, brings the user to the point at which NX-OS asks the user questions about what should be added to the configuration.

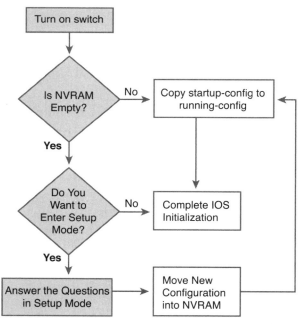

Figure 7-12   *Getting into Setup Mode*

Frankly, most network engineers never use setup mode, mainly because setup supports only a small percentage of modern switch configuration settings. However, you will still see some evidence of setup, because when you reload a switch or router that has no configuration, NX-OS will ask you whether you want to enter the "initial configuration dialog" (the official term for setup mode). Just answer **no** (which is the default), as shown in Example 7-7, and use configuration mode to configure the device.

Example 7-7   *Initial Configuration Dialog (Setup): Rejected*

```
--- System Configuration Dialog ---

Would you like to enter the initial configuration dialog? [yes/no]: no

Switch>
```

NX-OS Version and Other Reload Facts

To finish this first chapter about how Cisco NX-OS works, with the NX-OS CLI, this last topic looks at the switch **show version** command.

When a switch loads the NX-OS, it must do many tasks. The NX-OS software itself must be loaded into RAM. The NX-OS must become aware of the hardware available (for example, all the different interfaces on the switch). After the software is loaded, the NX-OS keeps track of some statistics related to the current operation of the switch, like the amount of time since the NX-OS was last loaded and the reason why the NX-OS was most recently loaded.

The **show version** command lists these facts, plus many others. As you might guess from the command itself, the **show version** command does list information about the NX-OS, including the version of NX-OS software. As highlighted in Example 7-8, however, this command lists many other interesting facts as well.

Example 7-8   *Example of a* **show version** *Command on a Cisco Nexus Switch*

```
SW1# show version


Cisco Nexus Operating System (NX-OS) Software
TAC support: http://www.cisco.com/tac
Documents: http://www.cisco.com/en/US/products/ps9372/tsd_products_support_
  series_home.html
Copyright (c) 2002-2013, Cisco Systems, Inc. All rights reserved.
The copyrights to certain works contained herein are owned by
other third parties and are used and distributed under license.
Some parts of this software are covered under the GNU Public
License. A copy of the license is available at
http://www.gnu.org/licenses/gpl.html.


Software
  BIOS:      version 3.6.0
  loader:    version N/A
  kickstart: version 6.0(2)N2(2)
  system:    version 6.0(2)N2(2)
  Power Sequencer Firmware:
             Module 1: version v1.0
             Module 2: version v1.0
```

```
            Module 3: version v5.0
   Microcontroller Firmware:          version v1.2.0.1
   SFP uC:     Module 1: v1.0.0.0
    QSFP uC:   Module not detected
    BIOS compile time:       05/09/2012
    kickstart image file is: bootflash:///n5000-uk9-kickstart.6.0.2.N2.2.bin
    kickstart compile time:  10/4/2013 12:00:00 [10/04/2013 16:04:23]
    system image file is:    bootflash:///n5000-uk9.6.0.2.N2.2.bin
    system compile time:     10/4/2013 12:00:00 [10/04/2013 18:23:49]


Hardware
   cisco Nexus5548 Chassis ("O2 32X10GE/Modular Universal Platform Supervisor")
    Intel(R) Xeon(R) CPU        with 8253856 kB of memory.
    Processor Board ID FOC153662P2

    Device name: 5K-L3-A
    bootflash:    2007040 kB

Kernel uptime is 32 day(s), 12 hour(s), 37 minute(s), 33 second(s)

Last reset
    Reason: Unknown
    System version: 6.0(2)N2(2)
    Service:

plugin
   Core Plugin, Ethernet Plugin, Fc Plugin, Virtualization Plugin
```

Working through the highlighted parts of the example, top to bottom, this command lists the following:

- The NX-OS kickstart and system image versions
- Hardware version and number of base interfaces
- Switch device name
- Time since last load of the NX-OS
- Reason for last load of the NX-OS

Exam Preparation Tasks

Review All the Key Topics

Review the most important topics from this chapter, noted with the Key Topic icon. Table 7-8 lists these key topics and where each is discussed.

Table 7-8   Key Topics for Chapter 7

Key Topic Element	Description	Page Number
List	Default switch console port settings	189
Table 7-6	Common switch configuration modes	203
Table 7-7	Names and purposes of the two main Cisco NX-OS configuration files	205

Complete the Tables and Lists from Memory

Print a copy of DVD Appendix I, "Memory Tables," or at least the section for this chapter, and complete the tables and lists from memory. DVD Appendix J, "Memory Tables Answer Key," includes completed tables and lists for you to check your work.

Definitions of Key Terms

After your first reading of the chapter, try to define these key terms, but do not be concerned about getting them all correct at that time. Chapter 23, "Final Review," directs you in how to use these terms for late-stage preparation for the exam.

command-line interface (CLI), Telnet, Secure Shell (SSH), EXEC mode, global configuration mode, startup config file, running config file

Command References

Table 7-9 lists and briefly describes the configuration commands used in this chapter.

Table 7-9   Chapter 7 Configuration Commands

Command	Mode and Purpose
line console	Global command that changes the context to console configuration mode.
line vty	Global command that changes the context to vty configuration mode.
interface *ethernet port-number*	Global command that changes the context to interface mode (for example, interface Ethernet 1/1).

Command	Mode and Purpose
hostname *name*	Global command that sets this switch's hostname, which is also used as the first part of the switch's command prompt.
exit	Moves back to the next higher mode in configuration mode.
end	Exits configuration mode and goes back to EXEC mode from any of the configuration submodes.
Ctrl+Z	This is not a command, but rather a two-key combination (pressing the Ctrl key and the letter Z) that together do the same thing as the **end** command.
interface mgmt0	Management interface. Using the command will enter you into interface command mode for the management interface.
vrf context management	Management Virtual Routing and Forwarding context. Using this command will allow you to enter and configure parameters of the management VRF.
install license *license file location and name*	Installs a license file for features a network admin would use on a Nexus switch.

Table 7-10 lists and briefly describes the EXEC commands used in this chapter.

Table 7-10   Chapter 7 EXEC Command Reference

Command	Purpose
no debug all undebug all	Disables all currently enabled debugs.
terminal monitor	Tells Cisco NX-OS to send a copy of all syslog messages, including debug messages, to the Telnet or SSH user who issues this command.
reload	Reboots the switch or router.
copy from-location to-location	Copies files from one file location to another. Locations include the startup config and running config files in RAM, TFTP and RCP servers, and flash memory.
copy running-config startup-config	Saves the active config, replacing the startup config file used when the switch initializes.
copy startup-config running-config	Merges the startup config file with the currently active config file in RAM.
show running-config	Lists the contents of the running config file.
exit	Disconnects the user from the CLI session.
show startup-config	Lists the contents of the startup config (initial config) file.

Command	Purpose
configure terminal	Moves the user into configuration mode.
show license host-id	Displays the serial number (host ID) of the switch chassis to use for licensing.
show feature	Lists all the features available for use on a Cisco Nexus switch. Shows which features have been enabled or disabled.
show vtp status	Shows the status of VLAN Trunking Protocol (VTP) on a Nexus switch.

7

This chapter covers the following exam topics:

1.2 Select the components required to meet a network specification

1.3 Use the OSI and TCP/IP models and their associated protocols to explain how data flows in a network

2.2 Explain basic switching concepts and the operation of Cisco switches

2.2.b MAC table

2.2.c Flooding

CHAPTER 8

Configuring Ethernet Switching

Cisco Nexus switches are designed to have both robust Layer 2 Ethernet switching features in addition to feature-rich Layer 3 routing functionality. This product family is known as a multilayer type of switch because they have the hardware and software capable of using both forwarding methods exclusively (Layer 2 only switch or Layer 3 only router) or as a Layer 3 router and Layer 2 switch at the same time.

This chapter explains a large variety of Layer 2 switching features, broken into two halves of the chapter. The first half of the chapter explains many switch administrative features that happen to work the same way on all models of Nexus switches; this chapter keeps these common features together so that you can easily refer to them later when working with the different models within the Nexus product family. The second half of the chapter shows how to configure some switch-specific features on the Nexus 5500 series switch, many of which impact how a switch forwards frames.

"Do I Know This Already?" Quiz

Use the "Do I Know This Already?" quiz to help decide whether you might want to skim this chapter, or a major section, moving more quickly to the "Exam Preparation Tasks" section near the end of the chapter. You can find the answers at the bottom of the page following the quiz. For thorough explanations, see Appendix A, "Answers to the 'Do I Know This Already?' Quizzes."

Table 8-1   "Do I Know This Already?" Foundation Topics Section-to-Question Mapping

Foundation Topics Section	Questions
Configuration of Features in Common across all Nexus Models	1–3
Nexus Switch Configuration and Operation on the Nexus 5500	4–5

1. Which command enables you to configure a user named Fred to have read-only access to the Nexus switch CLI?

   a. username Fred read-only

   b. username Fred password Cisco123 role network-admin

   c. username Fred password Cisco123 role network-operator

   d. user Fred password Cisco123 role read-only

2. An engineer had formerly configured a Cisco Nexus 5500 switch to allow Telnet access so that the switch expected a password of mypassword from the Telnet user admin with role of network-admin. The engineer then changed the configuration to support Secure Shell. Which of the following commands could have been part of the new configuration? (Choose two answers.)

a. A **username** *name* **password** *password* vty mode subcommand

b. A **username** *name* **password** *password* global configuration command

c. A **login local** vty mode subcommand

d. None of these answers are correct.

3. The following command was copied and pasted into configuration mode when a user was telnetted into a Cisco switch:

```
banner motd  #this is the login banner #
```

Which of the following is true about what occurs the next time a user logs in from the console?

a. No banner text is displayed.

b. The banner text "this is" is displayed.

c. The banner text "this is the login banner" is displayed.

d. The banner text "Login banner configured, no text defined" is displayed.

4. Which of the following describes what VRF context the management interface (mgmt0) is in on a Nexus switch by default?

a. In the Management Virtual Routing and Forwarding (VRF) instance

b. In the Default Virtual Routing and Forwarding (VRF) instance

c. Not in a Virtual Routing and Forwarding (VRF) instance

d. None of the answers are correct.

5. In which of the following modes of the CLI could you configure the speed setting for interface Ethernet 1/5?

a. User mode

b. Enable mode

c. Global configuration mode

d. VLAN mode

e. Interface configuration mode

Foundation Topics

Configuration of Features in Common on all Nexus Switches

This first of the two major sections of this chapter examines the configuration of several features that are configured the exact same way on all Nexus switches. In particular, this section examines how to secure access to the command-line interface (CLI) and also covers various settings for the console. Note that this section refers to only switches, and not routers, but the commands apply to both.

Securing the Switch CLI

The first step to securing a switch is to secure access to the CLI. Securing the CLI includes protecting access to Cisco Nexus switches' network-admin role, because from the network-admin role, an attacker could reload the switch or change the configuration.

For example, consider a user who accesses a switch from the console. The default console configuration settings allow a console user to access the Nexus switch with a default username of admin in the network-admin role, with no password required. These defaults make some sense, because when you use the console, you are typically sitting near or next to the switch. If you can touch the switch, even if the console had all the available password protections, you could still perform the switch password recovery/reset procedure in 5 minutes anyway and get into the switch. So, by default, console access is open; however, most network engineers add login security to the switch for all access methods by providing a strong password for the admin account. A strong password is one that is not easy to decipher.

> **NOTE**   To see the password recovery/reset procedures, go to Cisco.com and search for the phrase "password recovery procedure for Cisco NX-OS."

This section examines many of the configuration details related to accessing EXEC mode on a Cisco Nexus switch. Management interface IP configuration was covered in Chapter 7, "Installing and Operating Nexus Switches," in the section "Management Interface."

In particular, this section covers the following topics:

- Secure Shell (SSH)
- Basics of secure access with authentication servers

Securing Access with Local Usernames and Passwords

Cisco Nexus switches support other login authentication methods that use a username and password so that each user has unique login details that do not have to be shared. One method configures the username/password pairs locally on the switch, and the other relies on an external server called an authentication, authorization, and accounting (AAA) server. (The server could be the same server used for logins for other servers in the network.) This book covers the configuration using locally configured usernames/passwords.

In addition to the username and password, each user can be assigned to a role, as discussed in Chapter 7. Based on the username and password provided and the role assigned by the administrator, the user is given access to entire switch configuration and verification commands or a subset.

When a Telnet or SSH user connects to the switch configured as shown in Figure 8-1, the user is prompted first for a username and then for a password. The username/password pair must be from the list of local usernames; otherwise, the login is rejected.

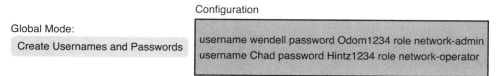

Configuration

Global Mode:

Create Usernames and Passwords

username wendell password Odom1234 role network-admin
username Chad password Hintz1234 role network-operator

Figure 8-1 *Configuring Switches to Use Local Username Login Authentication*

NOTE The default admin username cannot be deleted or modified and always belongs to the network-admin role.

Securing Access with External Authentication Servers

Using a local list of usernames and passwords on a switch or router works well in small networks. However, using locally configured username/password pairs means that every switch and router needs the configuration for all users who might need to log in to the devices. Then, when any changes need to happen, like an occasional change to the passwords, the configuration of all devices must be changed.

Cisco switches and routers support an alternative way to keep track of valid usernames and passwords by using an external AAA server. When using a AAA server for authentication, the switch (or router) simply sends a message to the AAA server asking whether the username and password are allowed, and the AAA server replies. Figure 8-2 shows an example, with the user first supplying his username/password, the switch asking the AAA server, and the server replying to the switch stating that the username/password is valid.

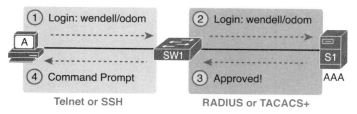

Figure 8-2 *Basic Authentication Process with an External AAA Server*

While the figure shows the general idea, note that the information flows with a couple of different protocols. On the left, the connection between the user and the switch or router uses Telnet or SSH. On the right, the switch and AAA server typically use either the

RADIUS or TACACS+ protocol, both of which encrypt the passwords as they traverse the network.

Configuring Secure Shell

First, the switch already runs an SSH server by default, accepting incoming SSH connections from SSH clients. In addition, the switch is already configured with a cryptography key, used to encrypt the data. Because the Nexus switch is already configured for SSH, recommended practice dictates that you provide a strong password to the default admin user and create any additional usernames and roles that are needed to access the Cisco Nexus switch. The following list details the steps for a Cisco Nexus switch to change any of the default SSH configuration using local usernames.

Step 1. Configure the switch with local usernames, passwords, and role on a AAA server.

Step 2. Disable the SSH feature:

```
(config)# no feature ssh
```

Step 3. Configure the switch to generate a matched public and private key pair to use for encryption, using one command in config mode:

```
ssh key (dsa | rsa (bits) (force)
```

Step 4. Enable the SSH feature:

```
(config)# feature ssh
```

Seeing the configuration happen in configuration mode, step by step, can be particularly helpful with SSH. Note in particular that the **ssh key** command actually prompts the user for more information and generates some messages while the key is being generated. Example 8-1 shows the commands being configured, with the encryption key as the final step.

Example 8-1 *SSH Configuration Process*

```
Emma# configure terminal
Enter configuration commands, one per line.  End with CNTL/Z.
! Step 1's username command happens next
Emma(config)# username admin passwordCisc0123 role Network-admin
Emma(config)# username chad passwordCisc0123 role Network-operator
!
! Step 2's feature commands happen next
   Emma(config)# no feature ssh
XML interface to system may become unavailable since ssh is disabled
!
   ! Step 3's key command happens next
  Emma(config)# ssh key rsa ?
    <CR>
    <1024-2048>  Enter number of bits (in multiples of 8)
   Emma(config)# ssh key rsa 2048
generating rsa key(2048 bits).....
```

8

```
....
    generated rsa key
!
! Step 4's feature command happens next
    Emma(config)# feature ssh
    Emma(config)# exit
```

Two key commands give some information about the status of SSH on the switch. First, the **show ssh server** command lists status information about the SSH server itself. The **show ssh** command then lists information about each SSH client currently connected into the switch. Example 8-2 shows samples of each, with user Wendell currently connected to the switch.

Example 8-2 *Displaying SSH Status*

```
    Emma# show ssh server
    ssh version 2 is enabled

Emma# show ssh key
*************************************
rsa Keys generated:Thu Jan 30 00:08:15 2014

ssh-rsa AAAAB3NzaC1yc2EAAAADAQABAAABAQDICL7II0e18J4pEbgJZ2LnXrKG7xakmhKnIlwf5SRM
lYc3++H5ysdD7dVY2oYYV7lpEjmeAn1lATcn/pvRX+DmqJhl+u9ExQPx9IFVx5fKDQh8MTEKKxIGaISC
ihRYDQFGKGYS3vB1y6uWagXre177XBQKEL9yZ5KXgnYHk9z2OVhE7xa/6mZBUXqb40Id0rheU4GAib5R
TW8S+SFbM59UUXea/09Z4a8v6nSvz7pbSuWzbTfKHieqF5HQSGNb40NJcZUD38jhNq8HnEY1/Y1QhT1i
DoPHnqrkh6h0Dyit8DEWY5Y0aDLA/dTOKP9wQ0/7Uy7DPRNP9nYPdtZB4sEL

bitcount:2048
fingerprint:
ad:0d:54:95:ea:5e:f8:94:ae:28:3e:4d:37:a8:c7:47
```

Note that this example is using SSH Version 2 rather than Version 1; it is the only version of SSH that NX-OS supports. SSH v2 improves the underlying security algorithms over SSH v1 and adds some other small advantages, like banner support.

Banners

Cisco Nexus switches can display a banner to notify users they are attempting to log in to a device. This banner appears prior to the user authentication process and serves as a warning to deter unauthorized users from attempting to log in. A banner is simply some text that appears on the screen for the user. You can configure a Cisco Nexus switch to display a banner for use with all login methods (vty, console), before login.

The **banner motd** global configuration command can be used to configure a banner to be displayed before login for all login types. NX-OS only provides one banner type called Message of the Day (MOTD). IOS has three different types for different login types: console, SSH, and Telnet. The first nonblank character after the banner type is called a *beginning delimiter character*. The banner text can span several lines, with the CLI user pressing

Enter at the end of each line. The CLI knows that the banner has been configured as soon as the user enters the same delimiter character again.

Example 8-3 shows the configuration process for banner MOTD on a Cisco Nexus switch. The banner example in Example 8-3 uses a **Z** as the delimiter character to start and end the message. It is important to know that any character can be used with the exception of the " (quote) or % (percentage) character. Also, the last **banner** command shows multiple lines of banner text.

Example 8-3 *Banner MOTD Configuration*

```
7K-B# configure terminal
Enter configuration commands, one per line.  End with CNTL/Z.
7K-B(config)# banner motd Z
Enter TEXT message. End with the character 'Z'.
> Authorized Access Only!
> Z

! Below, the user of this Nexus switch exits the Telnet connection, and logs back in,
! seeing the MOTD banner, then the password prompt,
     7K-B# exit
Connection closed by foreign host.
telnet 1.1.1.1
Authorized Access Only!
login: admin
Password:
Cisco Nexus Operating System (NX-OS) Software
TAC support: http://www.cisco.com/tac
Copyright (c) 2002-2013, Cisco Systems, Inc. All rights reserved.
The copyrights to certain works contained in this software are
owned by other third parties and used and distributed under
license. Certain components of this software are licensed under
the GNU General Public License (GPL) version 2.0 or the GNU
Lesser General Public License (LGPL) Version 2.1. A copy of each
such license is available at
http://www.opensource.org/licenses/gpl-2.0.php and
http://www.opensource.org/licenses/lgpl-2.1.php
7K-B#
```

History Buffer Commands

When you enter commands from the CLI, the last several commands are saved in the history buffer. As mentioned in Chapter 7, you can use the up-arrow key, or press Ctrl+P, to move back in the history buffer stack to retrieve a command you entered a few commands ago. This feature makes it very easy and fast to use a set of commands repeatedly. Table 8-2 lists some of the key commands related to the history buffer.

Table 8-2   Commands Related to the History Buffer

Command	Description
show cli history	Lists the commands currently held in the history buffer
show cli history X	Lists the last number of commands held in history buffer
show cli history unformatted	Shows how to display unformatted command history

The logging synchronous and exec-timeout Commands

The next short section looks at a couple of ways to make using the console a little more user friendly, by asking the switch to not interrupt with log messages, and to control how long you can be connected to the console before getting forced out.

The console automatically receives copies of all unsolicited syslog messages on a switch. The idea is that if the switch needs to tell the network administrator some important and possibly urgent information, the administrator might be at the console and might notice the message.

The display of these messages at the console can be disabled and enabled with the **no logging console** and **logging console** global commands. For example, when working from the console, if you want to temporarily not be bothered by log messages, you can disable the display of these messages with the **no logging console** global configuration command, and then when finished, enable them again.

Another way to improve the user experience at the console is to control timeouts from the console. By default, the Cisco Nexus switch sets the timeout to 0, which means it never times out. The **exec-timeout** *minutes seconds* line subcommand lets you set the length of that inactivity timer.

Example 8-4 shows the syntax for these two commands, both on the console line. Note that both can be applied to the vty lines as well, for the same reasons.

Example 8-4   *Defining Console Inactivity Timeouts and When to Display Log Messages*

```
line console
 exec-timeout 5
```

Nexus Switch Configuration and Operation

Cisco switches work very well when received from the factory, without any configuration added. Cisco Nexus 5500 switches leave the factory with default settings, with all interfaces enabled (a default configuration of **no shutdown**), and with autonegotiation enabled for ports that can use it (a default configuration of **duplex auto** and **speed auto**). All interfaces default to be part of VLAN 1 (**switchport access vlan 1**). All you have to do with a new Cisco switch is make all the physical connections—Ethernet cables and power cord—and the switch starts working.

In most enterprise networks, you will want the switch to operate with some different settings as compared with the factory defaults. The second half of this chapter discusses some of those settings, with Chapter 10, "VLAN and Trunking Configuration," discussing more. (Also note that the details in this section differ from the configuration on a router.) In particular, this section covers the following:

- Switched virtual interface (SVI)
- Interface configuration (including speed and duplex)
- Securing unused switch interfaces
- Predicting the contents of the MAC address table

Switch Virtual Interface Concept Inside a Switch

A typical Layer 2 Cisco Nexus 5500 switch can use only one Layer 3 VLAN interface (SVI) without a Layer 3 module or license, but the network engineer can choose which VLAN interface to enable this on (typically VLAN 1). All interfaces on a Cisco Nexus switch belong to a Virtual Routing and Forwarding (VRF) instance called Default, except for the management interface, which belongs to the Management VRF. Within the "default" VRF, the network engineer can configure a single Layer 3 interface called a *switched virtual interface* (SVI). Example 8-5 shows the configuration of an SVI on VLAN 1.

> **NOTE**   Some Cisco switches, called Layer 2 switches, forward Ethernet frames, as discussed in depth in Chapter 6, "Building Ethernet LANs with Switches." Other Cisco switches, called multilayer switches or Layer 3 switches, can also route IP packets using the Layer 3 logic normally used by routers. Layer 3 switches configure IP addresses on more than one VLAN interface at a time. This chapter assumes all switches are Layer 2 switches. Chapter 9, "VLAN and Trunking Concepts," further defines the differences between these types of Nexus switches.

8

Configuring IPv4 on a Cisco Nexus Switch

A switch configures its IPv4 address and mask on this special NIC-like *VLAN interface*. The following steps list the commands used to configure IPv4 on a switch, assuming that the IP address is configured to be in VLAN 1, with Example 8-5 that follows showing a configuration example.

Step 1.   Enable the SVI feature on the switch using the **feature interface-vlan** command.

Step 2.   Enter VLAN 1 configuration mode using the **interface vlan 1** global configuration command.

Step 3.   Assign an IP address and mask using the **ip address** *ip-address mask* interface subcommand.

Step 4.   If not already enabled, enable the VLAN 1 interface using the **no shutdown** interface subcommand.

Step 5. (Optional) Add the **ip name-server** *ip-address1 ip-address2...* global command to configure the switch to use DNS to resolve names into their matching IP address.

Example 8-5   *Switch Static IP Address Configuration*

```
Emma# configure terminal
Emma(config)# feature interface-vlan
Emma(config)# interface vlan 1
Emma(config-if)# ip address 192.168.1.200 255.255.255.0
  or...
Emma(config-if)# ip address 192.168.1.200/24
Emma(config-if)# no shutdown
00:25:07: %LINK-3-UPDOWN: Interface Vlan1, changed state to up
00:25:08: %LINEPROTO-5-UPDOWN: Line protocol on Interface Vlan1, changed
  state to up
Emma(config-if)# exit
```

On a side note, this example shows a particularly important and common command: the **[no] shutdown** command. To administratively enable an interface on a switch, use the **no shutdown** interface subcommand; to disable an interface, use the **shutdown** interface subcommand. The messages shown in Example 8-5, immediately following the **no shutdown** command, are syslog messages generated by the switch stating that the switch did indeed enable the interface.

Verifying IPv4 on a Switch

The switch IPv4 configuration can be checked in several places. First, you can always look at the current configuration using the **show running-config** command. Second, you can look at the IP address and mask information using the **show interface vlan** *x* command, which shows detailed status information about the VLAN interface in VLAN *x*. Example 8-6 shows sample output from these commands to match the configuration in Example 8-5.

Example 8-6   *Verifying DHCP-Learned Information on a Switch*

```
Emma# show interface vlan 1
Vlan1 is up, line protocol is up
  Hardware is EtherSVI, address is  0026.980b.55c1
  Internet Address is 192.168.1.200/24
  MTU 1500 bytes, BW 1000000 Kbit, DLY 10 usec,
    reliability 255/255, txload 1/255, rxload 1/255
! lines omitted for brevity
```

The output of the **show interfaces vlan 1** command lists two very important details related to switch IP addressing. First, this **show** command lists the interface status of the VLAN 1 interface—in this case, up and up. If the VLAN 1 interface is not up, the switch cannot use its IP address to send and receive traffic. Notably, if you forget to issue the **no shutdown** command, the VLAN 1 interface remains in its default shutdown state and is listed as administratively down in the **show** command output.

Second, note that the output lists the interface's IP address on the third line. If you statically configure the IP address, as in Example 8-5, the IP address will always be listed.

Configuring Switch Interfaces

NX-OS uses the term *interface* to refer to physical ports used to forward data to and from other devices. Each interface can be configured with several settings, each of which might differ from interface to interface.

NX-OS uses interface subcommands to configure these settings. For example, interfaces can be configured to use the **duplex** and **speed** interface subcommands to configure those settings statically, or an interface can use autonegotiation (the default). Example 8-7 shows how to configure duplex and speed, as well as the **description** command, which is simply a text description that can be configured by the administrator.

Example 8-7 *Interface Configuration Basics*

```
Emma# configure terminal
Enter configuration commands, one per line.  End with CNTL/Z.
Emma(config)# interface Ethernet 1/2
Emma(config-if)# duplex full
Emma(config-if)# speed 10000
Emma(config-if)# description Server1 connects here
Emma(config-if)# exit
Emma(config)# interface Ethernet 1/11 - 20
Emma(config-if-range)# description end-users connect_here
Emma(config-if-range)# duplex full
Emma(config-if-range)# speed 10000
Emma(config-if-range)# ^Z
Emma#
Emma# show interface status

Port            Name              Status   Vlan    Duplex  Speed  Type
--------------------------------------------------------------------------------
Eth1/1          --                connected f-path  full    10G    SFP-H10GB-C
Eth1/2          Server1 connects here  connected 1     full    10G     10Gbase-SR
Eth1/3          --                sfpAbsent 1       full    10G    --
Eth1/4          --                sfpAbsent 1       full    10G    --
Eth1/5          --                sfpAbsent 1       full    10G    --
Eth1/6          --                sfpAbsent 1       full    10G    --
Eth1/7          --                sfpAbsent 1       full    10G    --
Eth1/8          --                sfpAbsent 1       full    10G    --
Eth1/9          --                sfpAbsent trunk   full    10G    --
Eth1/10         --                sfpAbsent 1       full    10G    --
Eth1/11         servers-connect-here sfpAbsent 1     full    10G     --
Eth1/12         servers-connect-here sfpAbsent 1     full    10G     --
Eth1/13         servers-connect-here sfpAbsent 1     full    10G     --
```

8

```
Eth1/14        servers-connect-here sfpAbsent 1      full   10G   --
Eth1/15        servers-connect-here vpcPeerLn t      full   10G   SFP-H10GB-C
Eth1/16        servers-connect-here vpcPeerLn        full   10G   SFP-H10GB-C
Eth1/17        servers-connect-here connected        full   10G   SFP-H10GB-C
Eth1/18        servers-connect-here connected        full   10G   SFP-H10GB-C
Eth1/19        servers-connect-here sfpAbsent 1      full   10G   --
Eth1/20        servers-connect-here sfpAbsent 1      full   10G   --
! lines omitted for brevity
```

You can see some of the details of interface configuration with both the **show running-config** command (not shown in the example) and the handy **show interfaces status** command. This command lists a single line for each interface, the first part of the interface description, and the speed and duplex settings. Several of the early entries in the output purposefully show some differences, as follows:

Ethernet 1/2 (Eth1/2): This output lists the configured speed of 100 and duplex full; however, it lists a status of connected. The connected status means that the physical link is currently working, which means it has been enabled with a cable connection and the **no shutdown** command.

Also, note that for the sake of efficiency, you can configure a command on a range of interfaces at the same time using the **interface** command. In the example, the **interface Ethernet 1/11 - 20** command tells NX-OS that the next subcommand(s) apply to interfaces Eth1/11 through Eth1/20. You can also use a range of interfaces that are not contiguous, such as interface Ethernet 1/11, 2/20, 2/22.

> **NOTE** Configuring both the speed and duplex on a Cisco switch interface disables autonegotiation.

Securing Unused Switch Interfaces

The default settings on Cisco switches work great if you want to buy a switch, unbox it, plug it in, and have it immediately work without any other effort. Those same defaults have an unfortunate side effect for worse security. With all default configuration, unused interfaces might be used by an attacker to gain access to the LAN. So, Cisco makes some general recommendations to override the default interface settings to make the unused ports more secure, as follows:

- Administratively disable the interface using the **shutdown** interface subcommand.
- Prevent VLAN trunking by making the port a nontrunking interface using the **switchport mode access** interface subcommand.
- Assign the port to an unused VLAN using the **switchport access vlan** *number* interface subcommand.
- Set the native VLAN to not be VLAN 1, but to instead be an unused VLAN, using the **switchport trunk native vlan** *vlan-id interface* subcommand. (The native VLAN is discussed in Chapter 10.)

Frankly, if you just shut down the interface, the security exposure goes away, but the other tasks prevent any immediate problems if someone else comes around and enables the interface by configuring a **no shutdown** command.

Predicting the Contents of the MAC Address Table

As explained in Chapter 6, switches learn MAC addresses and then use the entries in the MAC address table to make a forwarding/filtering decision for each frame. To know exactly how a particular switch will forward an Ethernet frame, you need to examine the MAC address table on a Cisco Nexus switch. To derive how this is done, we will use Figure 8-3 and manually build what we believe to be a MAC address table for each switch. It is important to understand how the switch will utilize the MAC address table to forward flows. Your task is to take out a piece of paper and try to build what you believe to be the MAC address table on each Nexus switch.

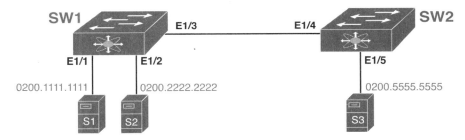

Figure 8-3   *Predicting the MAC Address Table*

Now that we have built our MAC address tables manually, you need to validate whether you got it right. The best way to validate what your MAC address tables contain is to use the command **show mac-address table**. Figure 8-4 shows the MAC address table for each switch. Let's break this down to understand how it was built and how the switch will use it to forward on a Layer 2 network between the servers in the figure.

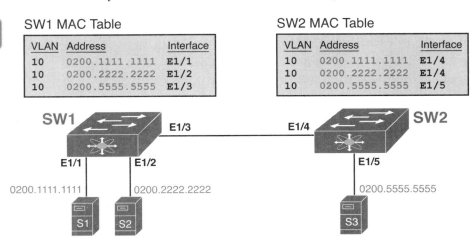

Figure 8-4   *Contents of the MAC Address Table*

The MAC table entries you predict in this case define where you think frames will flow. Even though this sample network in Figure 8-3 shows only one physical path through the Ethernet LAN, the exercise should be worthwhile because it forces you to correlate what you would expect to see in the MAC address table with how the switches forward frames. Figure 8-4 shows the resulting MAC table entries for servers. Let's work through some scenarios where we want to understand how the switch will forward frames between S1 and S2 as well as S1 and S3.

Scenario 1: Communication Between S1 and S2

When S1 sends a frame destined to the MAC address of S2, the frame will be received in on interface Ethernet 1/1 on Switch 1. The list that follows outlines the steps that the switch will take to get the frame to its destination of S2 on the same network (VLAN 10):

Step 1. Switch 1 will do a lookup for the destination MAC address of 0200.2222.2222 in its MAC address table.

Step 2. Switch 1 sees that the destination address of S2 is learned through its Ethernet 1/2.

Step 3. Switch 1 forwards the frame sourced from S1 to the destination of S2 out of the interface of Ethernet 1/2, which is where the MAC address of S2 has been learned.

Step 4. S2 receives the frame from S1.

In this scenario, one lookup is done on the Switch 1 MAC address table and is sent to the output interface where the destination MAC address was learned.

Scenario 2: Communication from S1 to S3

The list that follows outlines the detailed steps that happen across the communication path between S1 and S3 on VLAN 10 when S1 sends a frame into interface Ethernet 1/1:

Step 1. Switch 1 will do a lookup for the destination MAC address of 0200.5555.5555 of S3 in its MAC address table.

Step 2. Switch 1 sees that the destination address of S3 is learned through its Ethernet 1/3.

Step 3. Switch 1 forwards the frame sourced from S1 to the destination of S3 out of the interface of Ethernet 1/3, which is where Switch 1 has learned the MAC address of S3.

Step 4. Switch 2 receives the frame from Switch 1 on its Ethernet 1/4 interface with a source address of S1's MAC address and a destination address of S3's MAC address.

Step 5. Switch 2 will do a lookup for the destination MAC address of 0200.5555.5555 of S3 in its MAC address table and see that it has learned this MAC address on interface Ethernet 1/5.

Step 6.   Switch 2 will forward the frame sourced from S1 to S3 out of interface Ethernet 1/5 to reach S3.

Step 7.   S3 will receive the frame from S1.

As you can see in the table outputs created by learning the MAC addresses of the servers across the data center LAN in Figure 8-3, switches will always make their forwarding decision based on the destination address. Switches will learn the address of host or servers (in our case, across their interswitch links) and label this interface between the switches and the path to get to the remote MAC addresses.

8

Exam Preparation Tasks

Review All the Key Topics

Review the most important topics from this chapter, noted with the Key Topic icon. Table 8-3 lists these key topics and shows where each is discussed.

> **NOTE**   There is no need to memorize any configuration step list referenced as a key topic; these lists are just study aids.

Table 8-3   Key Topics for Chapter 8

Key Topic Element	Description	Page Number
Example 8-1	SSH configuration process	219
Example 8-3	Configuring banner MOTD	221
Example 8-5	Switch static IP address configuration	224
Figure 8-4	Contents of the MAC address table	227
Scenario 1	Communication between S1 and S2	228
Scenario 2	Communication between S1 and S3	228

Complete the Tables and Lists from Memory

Print a copy of DVD Appendix I, "Memory Tables," or at least the section for this chapter, and complete the tables and lists from memory. DVD Appendix J, "Memory Tables Answer Key," includes completed tables and lists for you to check your work.

Definitions of Key Terms

After your first reading of the chapter, try to define these key terms, but do not be concerned about getting them all correct at that time. Chapter 23, "Final Review," directs you in how to use these terms for late-stage preparation for the exam.

Telnet, SSH, local username, VLAN interface

Command References

Tables 8-4 through 8-7 list the configuration commands used in this chapter, by general topic. Table 8-8, at the very end of the chapter, lists the EXEC commands from this chapter.

Table 8-4   Console, Telnet, and SSH Login Commands

Command	Mode/Purpose/Description
line console	Changes the context to console configuration mode.
line vty	Changes the context to vty configuration mode for the range of vty lines listed in the command.
(no)feature ssh	Enables or disables the SSH feature on a Cisco Nexus switch.
username *name* **password** *pass-value* **role** *role-value*	Global command. Defines one of possibly multiple usernames and associated passwords, used for user authentication. Used when the **login local** line configuration command has been used.
ssh key rsa/ dsa key value (1024-2048)	Global command. Creates and stores (in a hidden location in flash memory) the keys required by SSH.

Table 8-5   Switch IPv4 Configuration

Command	Mode/Purpose/Description
(no) feature interface-vlan	Enables or disables the feature interface VLAN (SVI) on a Cisco Nexus switch.
interface vlan *number*	Changes the context to VLAN interface mode. For VLAN 1, allows the configuration of the switch's IP address.
ip address *ip-address subnet-mask*	VLAN interface mode. Statically configures the switch's IP address and mask.
ip name-server *server-ip-1 server-ip-2 ...*	Global command. Configures the IP addresses of DNS servers, so any commands when logged in to the switch will use the DNS for name resolution.

Table 8-6   Switch Interface Configuration

Command	Mode/Purpose/Description
interface *Ethernet port-number*	Changes context to interface mode.. The possible port numbers vary depending on the model of switch (for example, Eth1/1, Eth1/2).
shutdown no shutdown	Interface mode. Disables or enables the interface, respectively.
speed {1000 | 10000 | auto}	Interface mode. Manually sets the speed to the listed speed or, with the **auto** setting, automatically negotiates the speed.
duplex {auto | full | half}	Interface mode. Manually sets the duplex to half or full, or to autonegotiate the duplex setting.

8

Command	Mode/Purpose/Description
description *text*	Interface mode. Lists any information text that the engineer wants to track for the interface, such as the expected device on the other end of the cable.

Table 8-7   Other Switch Configuration

Command	Mode/Purpose/Description
hostname *name*	Global command. Sets this switch's hostname, which is also used as the first part of the switch's command prompt.
exec-timeout *minutes* [*seconds*]	Console or vty mode. Sets the inactivity timeout, so that after the defined period of no action, NX-OS closes the current user login session.
switchport access vlan *vlan-number*	Interface subcommand that defines the VLAN in which the interface resides.
banner motd *delimiter banner-text delimiter*	Global command that defines a banner that is displayed at different times when users log in to the Cisco Nexus switch.

Table 8-8   Chapter 8 EXEC Command Reference

Command	Purpose
show running-config	Lists the currently used configuration
show running-config | begin line vty	Pipes (sends) the command output to the **begin** command, which only lists output beginning with the first line that contains the text "line vty"
show mac address-table dynamic	Lists the dynamically learned entries in the switch's address (forwarding) table
show ssh key rsa	Lists the public and shared key created for use with SSH using the **ssh key rsa** global configuration command
show ssh server	Lists status information for the SSH server, including the SSH version
show ssh key	Lists the key enabled by SSH
show interfaces status	Lists one output line per interface, noting the description, operating state, and settings for duplex and speed on each interface
show interfaces vlan 1	Lists the interface status, the switch's IP address and mask, and much more
show cli history {x/unformatted}	Lists the commands in the current history buffer
(no) logging console	Enables or disables logging messages to the console interface

Part II Review

Keep track of your part review progress with the checklist shown in Table P2-1. Details on each task follow the table.

Table P2-1 Part II Review Checklist

Activity	First Date Completed	Second Date Completed
Repeat All DIKTA Questions		
Answer Part Review Questions		
Review Key Topics		
Create Command Mind Map by Category		

Repeat All DIKTA Questions

For this task, answer the "Do I Know This Already?" questions again for the chapters in this part of the book, using the PCPT software. Refer to the Introduction to this book, heading "How to View Only DIKTA Questions by Part," for help with how to make the PCPT software show you DIKTA questions for this part only.

Answer Part Review Questions

For this task, answer the Part Review questions for this part of the book, using the PCPT software. Refer to the Introduction to this book, heading "How to View Only Part Review Questions by Part," for help with how to make the PCPT software show you Part Review questions for this part only.

Review Key Topics

Browse back through the chapters and look for the Key Topic icons. If you do not remember some details, take the time to reread those topics.

Create Command Mind Map by Category

Part II of this book introduces the Cisco command-line interface (CLI) and a large number of configuration and EXEC commands. The sheer number of commands can be a bit overwhelming.

For the exam, you do not necessarily have to memorize every command and every parameter. However, you should be able to remember all the categories of topics that can be configured in Nexus data center switches, and at least remember the first word or two of most of the commands. This mind map exercise is designed to help you work on organizing these commands in your mind.

Create a mind map with the following categories of commands from this part of the book:

console and VTY, SSH, switch IPv4 support, switch interfaces, other switch administration, other interface subcommands

For each category, think of all configuration commands and all EXEC commands (mostly **show** commands). For each category, group the configuration commands separately from the EXEC commands. Figure P2-1 shows a sample for the switch IPv4 support branch of the commands.

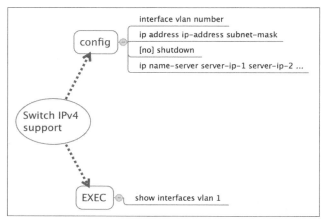

Figure P2-1 *Sample Mind Map from the Switch IPv4 Branch*

> **NOTE** For more information on mind mapping, refer to the Introduction, in the section "About Mind Maps."

Finally, keep the following points in mind when working on this project:

- Learning happens when creating the mind map. Make an attempt; it truly does help your own brain organize the information.
- Make your first attempt without notes and without looking at the book.
- After your first attempt, then you can review notes, the book, and especially the command summary tables at the end of some chapters. Note which commands you did not remember so that you can focus on those commands when you review later.
- Do not bother to record every single parameter of every command; just write down enough of the command to remember it.
- Note which commands you feel you understand well, and which you feel less sure about.
- Repeat this exercise later when you have 10 spare minutes, as a way to find out how much you recall.

DVD Appendix K, "Mind Map Solutions," shows a sample answer, but your mind map will likely differ.

Today's data centers typically build the data networking components using Ethernet technology. Specifically, the physical links, the data-link protocols, and the networking devices (such as Ethernet LAN switches) follow Ethernet standards.

Once built, engineers can then separate traffic into different LAN broadcast domains using the concept of virtual local-area networks (VLANs). VLANs allow data center design engineers to place some servers in the same broadcast domain (VLAN) and keep others separate, as needed for a given design.

Data center networks also typically use many redundant links to achieve the goal of higher network availability. That redundancy, left unchecked, can also cause problems. Spanning Tree Protocol (STP) happens to be the oldest tool for preventing the problems caused by the redundancy, so you can receive the benefits of the redundancy while avoiding the problems.

Part III contains four chapters: a pair of concept and config chapters for VLAN technologies (Chapters 9 and 10) and a pair of chapters for the Spanning Tree Protocol (Chapters 11 and 12).

Part III

Ethernet Virtual LANs and Spanning Tree

Chapter 9: VLAN and Trunking Concepts

Chapter 10: VLAN Trunking and Configuration

Chapter 11: Spanning Tree Protocol Concepts

Chapter 12: Cisco Nexus Spanning Tree Protocol Implementation

Part III Review

This chapter covers the following exam topics:

2.2 Explain basic switching concepts and the operation of Cisco switches

2.2.b MAC table

2.2.c Flooding

2.3 Describe and Configure enhanced switching technologies

2.3.a VTP

2.3.b VLAN

2.3.c 802.1Q

CHAPTER 9

VLAN and Trunking Concepts

At their heart, the Layer 2 switching logic on Ethernet switches receives Ethernet frames, makes decisions, and then forwards (switches) those Ethernet frames. That core logic revolves around MAC addresses, the interface in which the frame arrives, and the interfaces out which the switch forwards the frame.

Several switch features have some impact on an individual switch's decisions about where to forward frames, but of all the topics in this book, virtual LANs (VLAN) easily have the biggest impact on those choices.

This chapter examines the concepts and configuration of VLANs. The first major section of the chapter explains the basics of VLANs and how to forward VLAN traffic over links called *trunks*. This first section explains Layer 2 forwarding that includes considering the existence of VLANs. Next, the chapter adds the logic of how to forward data between two VLANs by using some form of routing, whether that routing is done by a device called a router or whether it is done by a switch that has the ability to also route packets.

The final section of the chapter explains VLAN Trunking Protocol (VTP), which gives network engineers a tool to configure some VLAN configuration settings on one LAN switch, and have that configuration be pushed to the rest of the LAN switches.

> **NOTE** As promised in the Introduction's section "For Those Studying Routing & Switching": If you have already read ICND1's Chapter 9, "Implementing Ethernet Virtual LANs," you can skip the first half of this chapter. However, make sure you read this chapter's major section beginning with "VLAN Trunking Protocol" through the end of the chapter.

"Do I Know This Already?" Quiz

Use the "Do I Know This Already?" quiz to help decide whether you might want to skim this chapter, or a major section, moving more quickly to the "Exam Preparation Tasks" section near the end of the chapter. You can find the answers at the bottom of the page following the quiz. For thorough explanations, see Appendix A, "Answers to the 'Do I Know This Already?' Quizzes."

Table 9-1 "Do I Know This Already?" Foundation Topics Section-to-Question Mapping

Foundation Topics Section	Questions
Virtual LANs and VLAN Trunks	1–4
VLAN and VLAN Trunking Configuration and Verification	5–7

1. In a LAN, which of the following terms best equates to the term *VLAN*?

   a. Collision domain

   b. Broadcast domain

   c. Subnet

   d. Single switch

   e. Trunk

2. Imagine a switch with three configured VLANs. How many IP subnets are required, assuming that all hosts in all VLANs want to use TCP/IP?

   a. 0

   b. 1

   c. 2

   d. 3

   e. You can't tell from the information provided.

3. Switch SW1 sends a frame to switch SW2 using 802.1Q trunking. Which of the answers describes how SW1 changes or adds to the Ethernet frame before forwarding the frame to SW2?

   a. Inserts a 4-byte header and does change the MAC addresses

   b. Inserts a 4-byte header and does not change the MAC addresses

   c. Encapsulates the original frame behind an entirely-new Ethernet header

   d. None of the other answers are correct.

4. For an 802.1Q trunk between two Ethernet switches, which answer most accurately defines which frames do not include an 802.1Q header?

   a. Frames in the native VLAN (only one)

   b. Frames in extended VLANs

   c. Frames in VLAN 1 (not configurable)

   d. Frames in all native VLANs (multiple allowed)

5. A Nexus switch has some ports assigned to VLAN 11, and some to VLAN 12. Which of the following devices, acting as described in the answers, can forward data between ports in different VLANs? (Choose two answers.)

   a. The Nexus switch when acting as a Layer 2 switch

   b. The Nexus switch when acting as a Layer 3 switch

   c. An external router

   d. An external bridge

6. A network engineer wants to use VTP to distribute VLAN configuration information to all switches in a data center so that all switches learn new VLAN configuration when a VLAN configuration change is made. Which of the following modes cannot be used on any of the switches? (Choose two answers.)

    a. Server

    b. Off

    c. Transparent

    d. Client

7. Which of the following answers lists configuration information that VTP distributes? (Choose two answers.)

    a. VLAN name

    b. VLAN assigned to a switch port

    c. Ports on which 802.1Q is enabled

    d. VLAN ID

9

Foundation Topics

Virtual LANs and VLAN Trunks

Before understanding VLANs, you must first have a specific understanding of the definition of a LAN. For example, from one perspective, a LAN includes all the user devices, servers, switches, routers, cables, and wireless access points in one location. However, an alternative narrower definition of a LAN can help in understanding the concept of a virtual LAN:

A LAN includes all devices in the same broadcast domain.

A broadcast domain includes the set of all LAN-connected devices, so that when any of the devices sends a broadcast frame, all the other devices get a copy of the frame. So, from one perspective, you can think of a LAN and a broadcast domain as being basically the same thing.

Without VLANs, a switch considers all its interfaces to be in the same broadcast domain. That is, for one switch, when a broadcast frame entered one switch port, the switch forwarded that broadcast frame out all other ports. With that logic, to create two different LAN broadcast domains, you had to buy two different Ethernet LAN switches, as shown in Figure 9-1.

Figure 9-1   *Creating Two Broadcast Domains with Two Physical Switches and No VLANs*

With support for VLANs, a single switch can accomplish the same goals of the design in Figure 9-1—to create two broadcast domains—with a single switch. With VLANs, a switch can configure some interfaces into one broadcast domain and some into another, creating multiple broadcast domains. These individual broadcast domains created by the switch are called *virtual LANs* (VLAN).

For example, in Figure 9-2, the single switch creates two VLANs, treating the ports in each VLAN as being completely separate. The switch would never forward a frame sent by Dino (in VLAN 1) over to either Wilma or Betty (in VLAN 2).

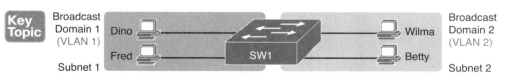

Figure 9-2   *Creating Two Broadcast Domains Using One Switch and VLANs*

Designing campus LANs to use more VLANs, each with a smaller number of devices, often helps improve the LAN in many ways. For example, a broadcast sent by one host in a VLAN will be received and processed by all the other hosts in the VLAN—but not by hosts in a different VLAN. Limiting the number of hosts that receive a single broadcast frame reduces the number of hosts that waste effort processing unneeded broadcasts. It also reduces security risks, because fewer hosts see frames sent by any one host. These are just a few reasons for separating hosts into different VLANs. The following list summarizes the most common reasons for choosing to create smaller broadcast domains (VLANs):

- To reduce CPU overhead on each device by reducing the number of devices that receive each broadcast frame
- To reduce security risks by reducing the number of hosts that receive copies of frames that the switches flood (broadcasts, multicasts, and unknown unicasts)
- To improve security for hosts that send sensitive data by keeping those hosts on a separate VLAN
- To create more flexible designs that group users by department, or by groups that work together, instead of by physical location
- To solve problems more quickly, because the failure domain for many problems is the same set of devices as those in the same broadcast domain
- To reduce the workload for the Spanning Tree Protocol (STP) by limiting a VLAN to a single access switch

This chapter does not examine all the reasons for VLANs in more depth. However, know that most enterprise networks use VLANs quite a bit. The rest of this chapter looks closely at the mechanics of how VLANs work across multiple Cisco switches. To that end, the next section examines VLAN trunking, a feature required when installing a VLAN that exists on more than one LAN switch.

Creating Multiswitch VLANs Using Trunking

Configuring VLANs on a single switch requires only a little effort: You simply configure each port to tell it the VLAN number to which the port belongs. With multiple switches, you have to consider additional concepts about how to forward traffic between the switches.

When using VLANs in networks that have multiple interconnected switches, which, of course, is typical in a data center LAN, the switches need to use *VLAN trunking* on the links between the switches. VLAN trunking causes the switches to use a process called *VLAN tagging*, by which the sending switch adds another header to the frame before sending it over the trunk. This extra trunking header includes a VLAN identifier (VLAN ID) field so that the sending switch can associate the frame with a particular VLAN ID, and the receiving switch can then know in what VLAN each frame belongs.

Figure 9-3 shows an example that demonstrates VLANs that exist on multiple switches, but it does not use trunking. First, the design uses two VLANs: VLAN 10 and VLAN 20. Each switch has two ports assigned to each VLAN, so each VLAN exists in both switches. To forward traffic in VLAN 10 between the two switches, the design includes a link between switches, with that link fully inside VLAN 10. Likewise, to support VLAN 20 traffic between switches, the design uses a second link between switches, with that link inside VLAN 20.

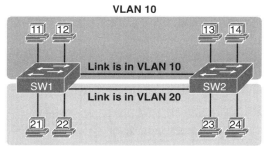

Figure 9-3   *Multiswitch VLAN Without VLAN Trunking*

The design in Figure 9-3 functions perfectly. For example, PC11 (in VLAN 10) can send a frame to PC14. The frame flows into SW1, over the top link (the one that is in VLAN 10), and over to SW2.

The design shown in Figure 9-3 works, but it simply does not scale very well. It requires one physical link between switches to support every VLAN. If a design needed 10 or 20 VLANs, you would need 10 or 20 links between switches, and you would use 10 or 20 switch ports (on each switch) for those links.

VLAN trunking creates one link between switches that supports as many VLANs as you need. As a VLAN trunk, the switches treat the link as if it were a part of all the VLANs. At the same time, the trunk keeps the VLAN traffic separate, so frames in VLAN 10 would not go to devices in VLAN 20, and vice versa, because each frame is identified by VLAN number as it crosses the trunk. Figure 9-4 shows the idea, with a single physical link between the two switches.

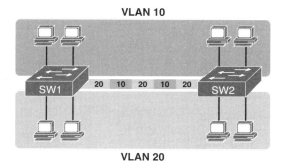

Figure 9-4   *Multiswitch VLAN with Trunking*

The use of trunking allows switches to pass frames from multiple VLANs over a single physical connection by adding a small header to the Ethernet frame. For example, Figure 9-5 shows PC11 sending a broadcast frame on interface Fa0/1 at Step 1. To flood the frame, switch SW1 needs to forward the broadcast frame to switch SW2. However, SW1 needs to let SW2 know that the frame is part of VLAN 10, so that after the frame is received, SW2 will flood the frame only into VLAN 10, and not into VLAN 20. So, as shown at Step 2, before sending the frame, SW1 adds a VLAN header to the original Ethernet frame, with the VLAN header listing a VLAN ID of 10 in this case.

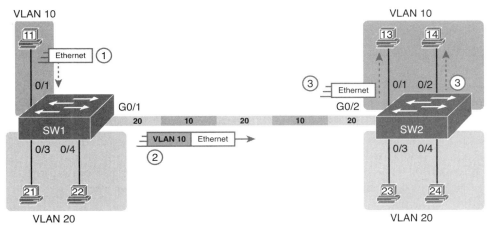

Figure 9-5   *VLAN Trunking Between Two Switches*

When SW2 receives the frame, it understands that the frame is in VLAN 10. SW2 then removes the VLAN header, forwarding the original frame out its interfaces in VLAN 10 (Step 3).

For another example, consider the case when PC21 (in VLAN 20) sends a broadcast. SW1 sends the broadcast out port Fa0/4 (because that port is in VLAN 20) and out Gi0/1 (because it is a trunk, meaning that it supports multiple different VLANs). SW1 adds a trunking header to the frame, listing a VLAN ID of 20. SW2 strips off the trunking header after noticing that the frame is part of VLAN 20, so SW2 knows to forward the frame out only ports Fa0/3 and Fa0/4, because they are in VLAN 20, and not out ports Fa0/1 and Fa0/2, because they are in VLAN 10.

The 802.1Q and ISL VLAN Trunking Protocols

Cisco has supported two different trunking protocols over the years: Inter-Switch Link (ISL) and IEEE 802.1Q. Cisco created the ISL long before 802.1Q, in part because the IEEE had not yet defined a VLAN trunking standard. Years later, the IEEE completed work on the 802.1Q standard, which defines a different way to do trunking. Today, 802.1Q has become the more popular trunking protocol; in fact, the Nexus series of switches supports only 802.1Q, and not ISL.

Both ISL and 802.1Q tag each frame with the VLAN ID, but the details differ. 802.1Q inserts an extra 4-byte 802.1Q VLAN header into the original frame's Ethernet header, as shown at the top of Figure 9-6. As for the fields in the 802.1Q header, only the 12-bit VLAN ID field inside the 802.1Q header matters for topics discussed in this book. This 12-bit field supports a theoretical maximum of 2^{12} (4096) VLANs, while in practice, it supports a maximum of 4094. (Both 802.1Q and ISL use 12 bits to tag the VLAN ID, with two reserved values [0 and 4095].)

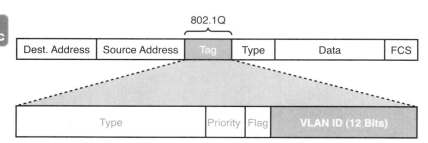

Figure 9-6 *802.1Q Trunking*

802.1Q also defines one special VLAN ID on each trunk as the *native VLAN* (defaulting to use VLAN 1). By definition, 802.1Q simply does not add an 802.1Q header to frames in the native VLAN. When the switch on the other side of the trunk receives a frame that does not have an 802.1Q header, the receiving switch knows that the frame is part of the native VLAN. Note that because of this behavior, both switches must agree on which VLAN is the native VLAN.

The 802.1Q native VLAN provides some interesting functions, mainly to support connections to devices that do not understand trunking. For example, a Cisco switch could be cabled to a switch that does not understand 802.1Q trunking. The Cisco switch could send frames in the native VLAN—meaning that the frame has no trunking header—so that the other switch would understand the frame. The native VLAN concept gives switches the capability of at least passing traffic in one VLAN (the native VLAN), which can allow some basic functions, like reachability to telnet into a switch.

Forwarding Data Between VLANs

If you create a LAN that contains many VLANs, you typically still need all devices to be able to send data to all other devices; however, Layer 2 switching logic purposefully does not forward Ethernet frames between VLANs. The solution? Routing, which is a Layer 3 function. This next topic discusses some concepts about how to route data between VLANs.

First, it helps to know a few terms about some categories of LAN switches. Most of the Ethernet switch functions described in this book so far use the details and logic defined by OSI Layer 2 protocols. For example, Chapter 6, "Building Ethernet LANs with Switches," discussed how LAN switches receive Ethernet frames (a Layer 2 concept), look at the destination Ethernet MAC address (a Layer 2 address), and forward the Ethernet frame out some other interface. This chapter has already discussed the concept of VLANs as broadcast domains, which is yet another Layer 2 concept.

Some switches, including many in the Cisco Nexus series of data center switches, combine Layer 2 switching features with Layer 3 routing features. These basically route IP packets and use IP routing protocols, as introduced back in Chapter 4, "Fundamentals of IPv4 Addressing and Routing." Switches that can also route packets go by the name *multilayer switch*, or *Layer 3 switch*. The next few pages discuss the options for routing packets between VLANs, first with a router, and then with a multilayer switch.

Routing Packets Between VLANs with a Router

When including VLANs in a campus LAN design, the devices in a VLAN need to be in the same subnet. Following the same design logic, devices in different VLANs need to be in different subnets. For example, in Figure 9-7, the two PCs on the left sit in VLAN 10, in subnet 10. The two PCs on the right sit in a different VLAN (20), with a different subnet (20).

Figure 9-7   *Layer 2 Switch Does Not Route Between the VLANs*

NOTE   The figure refers to subnets somewhat generally, like subnet 10, just so the subnet numbers do not distract. Also, note that the subnet numbers do not have to be the same number as the VLAN numbers.

Layer 2 switches will not forward data between two VLANs. In fact, one goal of VLANs is to separate traffic in one VLAN from another, preventing frames in one VLAN from leaking over to other VLANs. For example, when Dino (in VLAN 10) sends any Ethernet frame, if SW1 is a Layer 2 switch, that switch will not forward the frame to the PCs on the right in VLAN 20.

The network as a whole needs to support traffic flowing into and out of each VLAN, even though the Layer 2 switch does not forward frames outside a VLAN. The job of forwarding data into and out of a VLAN falls to routers. Instead of switching Layer 2 Ethernet frames between the two VLANs, the network must route Layer 3 packets between the two subnets.

That previous paragraph has some very specific wording related to Layers 2 and 3, so take a moment to reread and reconsider it. The Layer 2 logic does not let the Layer 2 switch forward the Layer 2 protocol data unit (L2PDU), the Ethernet frame, between VLANs. However, routers can route Layer 3 PDUs (L3PDU) (packets) between subnets as their normal job in life.

For example, Figure 9-8 shows a router that can route packets between subnets 10 and 20. The figure shows the same Layer 2 switch as shown in Figure 9-7, with the same PCs and with the same VLANs and subnets. Now router R1 has one LAN physical interface connected to the switch and assigned to VLAN 10, and a second physical interface connected to the switch and assigned to VLAN 20. With an interface connected to each subnet, the Layer 2 switch can keep doing its job (forwarding frames inside a VLAN) while the router can do its job (routing IP packets between the subnets).

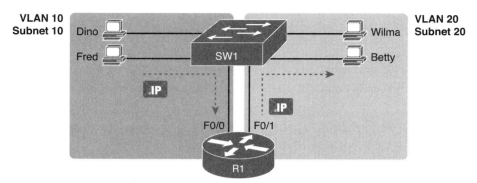

Figure 9-8   *Routing Between Two VLANs on Two Physical Interfaces*

The figure shows an IP packet being routed from Fred, which sits in one VLAN/subnet, to Betty, which sits in the other. The Layer 2 switch forwards two different Layer 2 Ethernet frames: one in VLAN 10, from Fred to R1's F0/0 interface, and the other in VLAN 20, from R1's F0/1 interface to Betty. From a Layer 3 perspective, Fred sends the IP packet to its default router (R1), and R1 routes the packet out another interface (F0/1) into another subnet where Betty resides.

The design shown in Figure 9-8 works, but it uses too many physical interfaces, one per VLAN. A much less-expensive (and much preferred) option uses a VLAN trunk between the switch and router, requiring only one physical link between the router and switch, while supporting all VLANs. Trunking can work between any two devices that choose to support it: between two switches, between a router and a switch, or even between server hardware and a switch.

Figure 9-9 shows the same design idea as Figure 9-8, with the same packet being sent from Fred to Betty, except now R1 uses VLAN trunking instead of a separate link for each VLAN.

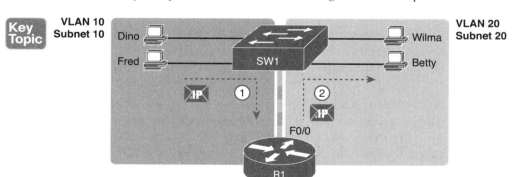

Figure 9-9   *Routing Between Two VLANs Using a Trunk on the Router*

NOTE   Because the router has a single physical link connected to the LAN switch, this design is sometimes called a *router-on-a-stick* or a *one-armed router*.

As a brief aside about terminology, many people describe the concept in Figures 9-8 and 9-9 as "routing packets between VLANs." You can use that phrase, and people know what you mean. However, for exam preparation purposes, note that this phrase is not literally true, because it refers to routing packets (a Layer 3 concept) and VLANs (a Layer 2 concept). It just takes fewer words to say something like "routing between VLANs" rather than the literally true but long "routing Layer 3 packets between Layer 3 subnets, with those subnets each mapping to a different Layer 2 VLAN."

Routing Packets with a Layer 3 Switch

Routing packets using a physical router, even with the VLAN trunk in the router-on-a-stick model shown in Figure 9-9, still has one significant problem: performance. The physical link puts an upper limit on how many bits can be routed, and less-expensive routers tend to be less powerful, and might not be able to route a large enough number of packets per second (pps) to keep up with the traffic volumes.

The ultimate solution moves the routing functions inside the LAN switch hardware. Vendors long ago started combining the hardware and software features of their Layer 2 LAN switches, plus their Layer 3 routers, creating products called *Layer 3 switches* (also known as *multilayer switches*). Layer 3 switches can be configured to act only as a Layer 2 switch, or they can be configured to do both Layer 2 switching as well as Layer 3 routing.

Today, many data centers, as well as medium- to large-sized enterprise campus LANs, use Layer 3 switches to route packets between subnets (VLANs).

In concept, a Layer 3 switch works a lot like the original two devices on which the Layer 3 switch is based: a Layer 2 LAN switch and a Layer 3 router. In fact, if you take the concepts and packet flow shown in Figure 9-8, with a separate Layer 2 switch and Layer 3 router, and then imagine all those features happening inside one device, you have the general idea of what a Layer 3 switch does. Figure 9-10 shows that exact concept, repeating many details of Figure 9-8, but with an overlay that shows the one Layer 3 switch doing the Layer 2 switch functions and the separate Layer 3 routing function.

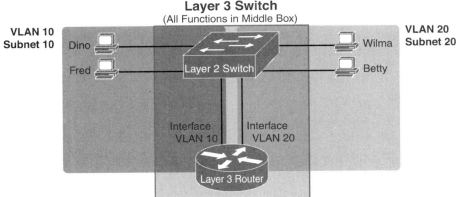

Figure 9-10 *Multilayer Switch: Layer 2 Switching with Layer 3 Routing in One Device*

This chapter introduces the core concepts of routing IP packets between VLANs (or more accurately, between the subnets on the VLANs). Chapter 18, "IPv4 Routing Concepts," discusses routing and Layer 3 switching in more depth, after you have read more about IPv4 addressing and subnetting.

VLAN Trunking Protocol

VLAN Trunking Protocol (VTP) gives engineers a convenient way to distribute some VLAN configuration information among switches. VTP defines a messaging protocol and related processes, so that VLAN configuration made on one switch is then advertised to other switches.

For instance, if a LAN had 40 switches, and VLAN 11 needed to be supported on those switches, the configuration to create and name VLAN 11 could be done on one switch only. Then, VTP, running on all the switches, would send messages so that the other 39 switches could dynamically learn the configuration using VTP.

> **NOTE**   Even though the *T* in VTP is *trunk*, VTP is not a trunking protocol like 802.1Q.

This final of three major sections in this chapter discusses the main concepts behind VTP. This section begins with a discussion of exactly what functions VTP provides, before moving on to show how VTP messages and processes advertise VLAN configuration information. This section ends with a discussion of how to avoid using VTP by using either VTP transparent mode or by disabling VTP.

VTP Functions

In Nexus switches and in Catalyst switches, a VLAN must exist in the switch's configuration before the switch can do any work with that VLAN. Specifically, the VLAN must exist on a switch before that switch can forward frames in that VLAN. Once a VLAN is configured, the switch can assign access interfaces to that VLAN, support that VLAN on trunk interfaces, and forward frames in that VLAN.

VTP distributes some VLAN configuration information from one switch to the rest of the switches in a VTP domain. Specifically, the configuration includes the following:

- The VLAN ID
- The VLAN name

Note that VTP does advertise about each VLAN, but does not advertise the VLAN associated with each access port. For example, VTP does advertise the existence of a VLAN 11, named Payroll; however, VTP does not advertise the configuration that switch SW1's E1/2 port has been assigned to VLAN 11.

VTP can group switches together as well using a concept called *VTP domains*. For instance, a data center might separate the LAN to support accounting functions in one part of the network and sales functions in another. VTP can be configured to use VTP domains with different names (for example, Accounting or Sales) so that VLANs configured in the Sales domain are learned only by other switches inside that domain and are not learned by the Accounting domain's switches, as shown in Figure 9-11.

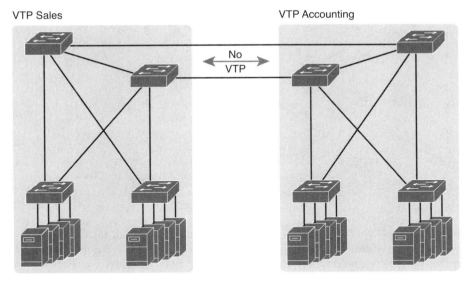

Figure 9-11   *VTP Domains Remain Separate*

VTP can be a powerful tool, but it is also a potentially dangerous tool. It does reduce the configuration effort, and it reduces the chances of making a typo in the VLAN name, because it is only typed once. However, a configuration mistake, such as deleting a VLAN that is still in use, automatically deletes the VLAN from all the switches in the same VTP domain. Once deleted, each switch can no longer forward frames in that VLAN. Other less-obvious mistakes can also lead to unintentionally deleting VLANs as well, so some installations simply avoid the dangers of VTP by just not using VTP.

This section next looks at how VTP works when using VTP, followed by a discussion of a few different ways to disable VTP.

Making VTP Work with VTP Servers and Clients

To use VTP, a network engineer must make a few design choices, such as the following:

■ Which switches to put in the same VTP domain; that is, which switches need to know the same set of VLANs.

■ A text name for the domain.

■ A VTP password for the domain. (Switches ignore incoming VTP messages unless both the domain name and password match with the local switch's configuration.)

■ Which switches will act as VTP servers and which will act as VTP clients.

For example, imagine a small network as shown in Figure 9-12. In this case, the engineer chose to put them all in the same VTP domain, using a domain name of MyCompany and a password of MyPassw0rd. The engineer also chooses to make the two switches at the top of the figure (EoR1 and EoR2) VTP servers, and the other switches VTP clients.

9

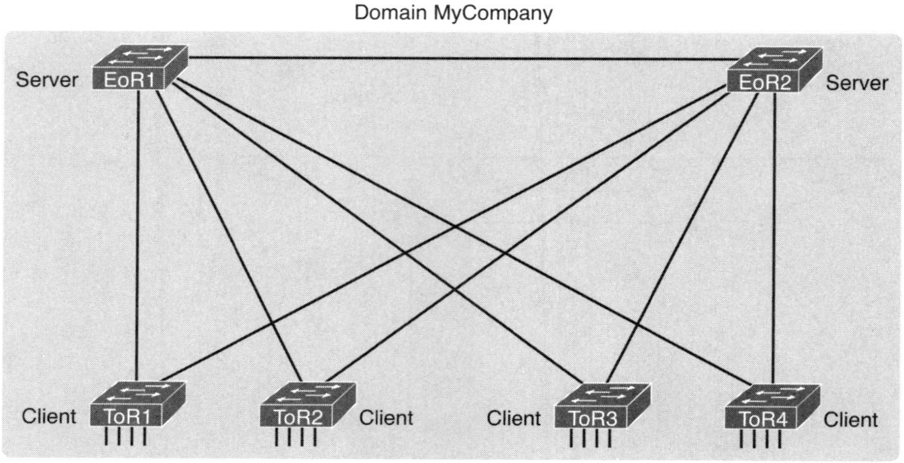

Domain MyCompany

Figure 9-12   *VTP Domain MyCompany with Two VTP Servers*

Most of the choices shown in Figure 9-12 relate to the business needs, but the choice of VTP server and client relates more to the features of VTP. VTP defines several modes of operation, including server mode and client mode. The VTP mode determines how the switch acts with VTP, with VTP servers and clients being active participants in VTP.

VTP servers and clients can both learn about updated configuration by listening for VTP messages, processing the message, and then forwarding the message. However, only VTP servers can be used to configure VLANs—that is, creating a VLAN, giving it a name, and deleting it—whereas VTP client switches do not. VTP client switches literally reject the configuration commands to create a VLAN because of the fact that the switch is a VTP client.

Figure 9-13 shows the process of what happens on a smaller LAN than shown in Figure 9-12. This updated LAN drawing has a different topology, but fewer links, just so the VTP features are more obvious; the design in Figure 9-13 is not a typical design. In this scenario, new VLAN configuration is added to EoR1, which then sends VTP messages to inform the other switches about the new VLAN.

Following the steps in the figure:

Step 1.   An engineer configures VLAN 11 on EoR1.

Step 2.   EoR1 sends a new VTP update out its trunks to ToR1 and EoR2.

Step 3.   ToR1 receives the VTP update, and learns about new VLAN 11, adding VLAN 11 to its local configuration.

Step 4.   EoR2 also receives the VTP update, learns about new VLAN 11, adding VLAN 11 to its local configuration.

Step 5.   EoR2 forwards the VTP update to ToR4.

Step 6.   ToR4 then learns about VLAN 11.

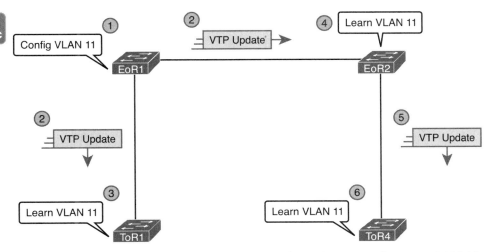

Figure 9-13 *A VTP Example of Configuring and Synchronizing for New VLAN 11*

This example shows the basic process. The switches forward the VTP messages so they reach all the switches, following the spanning-tree path, as discussed in upcoming chapters. Both the VTP client and VTP server switches react, updating their configuration. By the end of the process, all four switches once again have a consistent configuration of the VLAN IDs and VLAN names.

The example shown in Figure 9-13 shows the basics, but VTP does more than what is shown in that example. To round out the discussion, note that the VTP update actually holds the *VLAN database*, which is the entire list of VLAN IDs and names. That is, when a configuration change is made, the server sends the entire database. Once the process has completed, each switch has an updated copy of the database.

The VTP process also makes use of a VTP revision number, which is a revision number for the VLAN database. Each VTP update message lists the revision number of the current database. When a configuration change occurs, the VTP server adds one to the revision number, and sends a new VTP update. The other switches can notice the change to the revision number, and know that the VLAN database has changed.

As an example, suppose that the VTP update message in Figure 9-13 were revision 7. Then imagine the following process happening over the next few days:

Step 1.   For 3 days, no one changes the VLAN configuration. So, EoR1 and EoR2 independently send VTP updates every 5 minutes, with revision number 7.

Step 2.   The engineer makes a VLAN configuration change on EoR1. The resulting VTP update, sent by EoR1 as shown in Figure 9-13, lists revision 8.

Step 3.   All the other switches in the domain receive the VTP update with revision 8, know that the previous message listed revision 7, so each switch uses VTP messages to learn about the VLAN configuration changes and to update their local copy of the VLAN database.

Step 4.   Both VTP servers now have a copy of the VLAN database based on revision 8.

Step 5.   Another day passes with no configuration changes; EoR1 and EoR2 independently send VTP updates, every 5 minutes, with revision 8.

Step 6.   Next, the engineer happens to make a configuration change from EoR2 instead of EoR1. EoR2 sends a VTP update with revision 9.

Step 7.   All the other switches process the revision 9 update, realizing that a configuration change happened because of the revision number change from 8 to 9.

Step 8.   Both VTP servers (EoR1 and EoR2) now have a copy of the database based on revision 9.

As you can see, all the clients and servers track the revision number of the VLAN database as a way to synchronize, so that all switches use the same version of the VLAN database—in other words, the same version of the VLAN configuration.

Disabling VTP

VTP supports two other modes that provide different levels of disabling VTP:

- VTP transparent mode works in subtle ways, and is most useful when an engineer wants to use VTP for some switches, and not use VTP for others.

- VTP off mode is straightforward, disabling VTP completely, and makes more sense when the engineer does not want to use VTP on any of the switches in the LAN.

VTP off mode disables *all* VTP processes on the switch. The switch does not originate VTP messages, process received VTP messages, and importantly, it does not forward VTP messages. In designs that simply want to avoid VTP on all switches, use off mode.

VTP transparent mode disables *most* VTP processing, but not all, making a switch be transparent to the working (server and client) switches. To see how transparent mode is useful, consider the following requirements for a design:

- Use VTP for some switches in the data center.

- Purposefully do not use VTP on one switch, preferring to configure VLANs directly on that switch.

- The switches all have trunks connected to each other, so it is useful for the VTP traffic to be able to pass through the transparent mode switch to other VTP servers and clients.

Figure 9-14 shows just such an example, using the same initial action as shown in Figure 9-13. In this case, the engineer wants to make switch EoR2 not use VTP, but the other three switches will use VTP. With EoR2 configured in VTP transparent mode, the engineer adds VLAN 11 configuration at EoR1, with the behavior of EoR2 differing from the example in Figure 9-13.

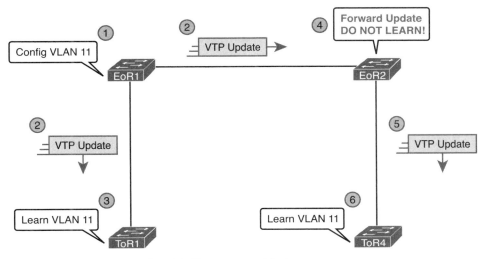

Figure 9-14 *The Need for VTP Transparent Mode*

With EoR2 in VTP transparent mode, the switch acts just like VTP off mode, except that it can forward the VTP update sent by EoR1. As shown in Steps 4 and 5, EoR2 (in transparent mode) ignores the contents of the VTP update, other than to forward the update to ToR4. If EoR2 had been in VTP off mode, it would not have forwarded the VTP update.

NOTE   VTP transparent mode switches must also be configured with matching VTP domain name and password to be willing to forward the VTP updates for a given domain.

VTP transparent and off mode switches also have the added advantage of supporting more VLANs than VTP servers and clients. Servers and clients support VLANs 1–1005 only (called *normal* or *standard VLANs*). On Nexus switches, VTP transparent and off switches support extended VLANs 1006–4094. (Note that 3968–4047 and 4094 are reserved and cannot be deleted.)

Summary of VTP Features

Table 9-2 summarizes the key comparison points of the different VTP modes. Using VTP with server and client mode has some great advantages for ease of configuration; however, it limits the VLANs that can be used in each switch, and it creates a potential danger when misused.

VTP off mode works very well for simply avoiding VTP altogether for all switches, enabling the use of many more switches, and is the preferred method to disable VTP when the design chooses to completely avoid using VTP. VTP transparent mode should be used as a tactic to support designs that call for use of VTP in some but not all switches.

Table 9-2   Comparisons of VTP Modes

	Server	Client	Transparent	Off
Can be used to configure a VLAN	Yes	No	Yes	Yes
Supports VLAN IDs	1–1005	1–1005	1–4094[1]	1–4094[1]
Originates VTP updates	Yes	No	No	No
Forwards VTP updates[2]	Yes	Yes	Yes	No
Synchronizes its VLAN database based on the received VTP updates	Yes	Yes	No	No

[1] VLANs 3968–4047, and 4094, are reserved for internal use.

[2] When configured with a matching VTP domain name and password

Exam Preparation Tasks

Review All the Key Topics

Review the most important topics from this chapter, noted with the Key Topic icon. Table 9-3 lists these key topics and where each is discussed.

Table 9-3   Key Topics for Chapter 9

Key Topic Element	Description	Page Number
Figure 9-2	Basic VLAN concept	244
List	Reasons for using VLANs	245
Figure 9-5	Diagram of VLAN trunking	247
Figure 9-6	802.1Q header	248
Figure 9-9	Routing between VLANs with router-on-a-stick	250
Figure 9-10	Routing between VLANs with Layer 3 switch	251
Figure 9-13	Basic VTP Synchronization Example	255
Table 9-2	VTP mode comparisons	258

Complete the Tables and Lists from Memory

Print a copy of DVD Appendix I, "Memory Tables," or at least the section for this chapter, and complete the tables and lists from memory. DVD Appendix J, "Memory Tables Answer Key," includes completed tables and lists to check your work.

Definitions of Key Terms

After your first reading of the chapter, try to define these key terms, but do not be concerned about getting them all correct at that time. Chapter 23, "Final Review," directs you in how to use these terms for late-stage preparation for the exam.

802.1Q, trunk, trunking administrative mode, trunking operational mode, VLAN, VTP, VTP client mode, VTP server mode, VTP transparent mode, Layer 3 switch, access interface, trunk interface

9

This chapter covers the following exam topics:

2.3 Describe and Configure enhanced switching technologies

2.3a VTP

2.3b VLAN

2.4c 802.1Q

2.5d STP

CHAPTER 10

VLAN Trunking and Configuration

As you learned in Chapter 9, "VLAN and Trunking Concepts," VLANs are a way for us to segment different networks and decrease the size of our broadcast and collision domains. This chapter delves into how to enable VLANs from a configuration perspective on our Nexus datacenter switches.

This chapter examines the configuration of VLANs. The major section of the chapter explains how to configure VLANs and VLAN trunks: how to statically assign interfaces to a VLAN. This chapter also provides detailed information about VLAN Trunking Protocol (VTP) configuration and verification in the last part of the chapter.

> **NOTE** As promised in the Introduction's section, "For Those Studying Routing & Switching": We suggest reading this entire chapter. Although the *ICND1 100-101 Official Cert Guide* also discusses VLAN and VLAN trunking configuration, and the NX-OS commands are often identical or similar, this chapter includes enough differences that it is worth the time to read and review the chapter in full.

"Do I Know This Already?" Quiz

Use the "Do I Know This Already?" quiz to help decide whether you might want to skim this chapter, or a major section, moving more quickly to the "Exam Preparation Tasks" section near the end of the chapter. You can find the answers at the bottom of the page following the quiz. For thorough explanations, see DVD Appendix A, "Answers to the 'Do I Know This Already?' Quizzes."

Table 10-1 "Do I Know This Already?" Foundation Topics Section-to-Question Mapping

Foundation Topics Section	Questions
VLAN Configuration and Verification	1–2
VLAN Trunking Configuration and Verification	3–4
VTP Configuration and Verification	5

1. Imagine that on Switch 1 you are told to configure port Ethernet 1/1 to participate in VLAN 10. Which command would enable interface Ethernet 1/1 to participate in VLAN 10? (Choose two answers.)

   a. switchport mode trunk

   b. switchport access vlan 10

   c. no shutdown

   d. access vlan 10

   e. None of the answers are correct.

2. A Nexus switch has just arrived from Cisco. The switch has never been configured with any VLANs, but VTP has been disabled. An engineer gets into configuration mode and issues the **vlan 22** command, followed by the **name Evans-VLAN** command. Which of the following are true? (Choose two answers.)

   a. VLAN 22 is listed in the output of the **show vlan brief** command.

   b. VLAN 22 is listed in the output of the **show running-config** command.

   c. VLAN 22 is not created by this process.

   d. VLAN 22 does not exist in that switch until at least one interface is assigned to that VLAN.

3. Which of the following commands identify switch interfaces as being trunking interfaces: interfaces that currently operate as VLAN trunks? (Choose two answers.)

   a. show interface

   b. show interface switchport

   c. show interface trunk

   d. show trunks

4. Imagine that you are told that switch 1 is configured with the **switchport mode trunk** parameter for trunking on its Eth1/5 interface, which is connected to switch 2. You have to configure switch 2. Which of the following settings for trunking could allow trunking to work? (Choose two answers.)

   a. switchport mode trunk

   b. shutdown

   c. no shutdown

   d. access

   e. None of the answers are correct.

5. A Nexus switch has just arrived from Cisco. The switch has never been configured. An engineer would like to configure VLAN Trunking Protocol (VTP) in client mode. Which two commands would he enter in configuration mode to do this? (Choose two answers.)

   a.   feature vtp

   b.   vlan 33 mode client

   c.   vtp client

   d.   vtp mode client

Foundation Topics

Cisco Nexus switches require minimal configuration to work, as you have seen in the previous chapters. When you purchase Cisco Nexus switches, install devices with the correct cabling, and turn on the switches, the switch defaults all the interfaces into a single VLAN, known as VLAN 1. You would never need to configure the switch with any more details than the base configuration if all devices were in a single VLAN 1, and it would work fine until you needed more than one VLAN. But if you want to use VLANs—and most every enterprise network does—you need to add some configuration.

This chapter separates the VLAN configuration details into three major sections.

- The first looks at how to configure access interfaces, interfaces used for host connections generally.

- The second part shows how to configure interfaces that do use VLAN trunking between multiple switches to extend VLANs beyond a single switch.

- The third will describe the VLAN Trunking Protocol (VTP), which is a Layer 2 messaging protocol use to distribute the VLAN information between multiple switches .

VLAN Configuration and Verification

This section provides an overview of VLAN support on Nexus switches, including guidelines for VLAN numbering, creating VLANs and assigning access VLANs to an interface, and two VLAN configuration examples for demonstration.

VLAN Guidelines for Cisco Nexus Switches

Cisco Nexus switches support 4094 VLANs, by default; however, VLANs 3968–4094 are considered reserved for system use. When creating VLANs on Nexus switches, it is important not to use one in this reserved range. Table 10-2 outlines some other considerations that are important to note when creating or configuring VLANs on a Nexus switch.

Table 10-2   Considerations for Creating/Configuring VLANs on a Nexus Switch

VLAN Numbers	Range	Usage
1	Normal	Cisco default. You can use this VLAN, but you cannot modify or delete it.
2–1005	Normal	You can create, use, modify, and delete these VLANs.
1006–4094	Extended	You can create, name, and use these VLANs. You cannot change the following parameters: State is always active. VLAN is always enabled. You cannot shut down these VLANs.
3968–4047 and 4094	Internally allocated	These 80 VLANs, plus VLAN 4094, are allocated for internal use. You cannot create, delete, or modify any VLANs within the block reserved for internal use.

Creating VLANs and Assigning Access VLANs to an Interface

This section shows how to create a VLAN, give the VLAN a name, and assign interfaces to a VLAN. To focus on these basic details, this section shows examples using a single switch, so VLAN trunking is not needed.

For a Cisco Nexus switch to forward frames in a particular VLAN, the switch must be configured to believe that the VLAN exists. In addition, the switch must have nontrunking interfaces (called *access interfaces*) assigned to the VLAN, and/or trunks that support the VLAN. The configuration steps for access interfaces are as follows, with the trunk configuration shown later in the section "VLAN Trunking Configuration":

Step 1. To configure a new VLAN, follow these steps:

  A. From configuration mode, use the **vlan** *vlan-id* global configuration command to create the VLAN and to move the user into VLAN configuration mode.

  B. (Optional) Use the **name** *name* VLAN subcommand to list a name for the VLAN. If not configured, the VLAN name is VLAN*ZZZZ*, where *ZZZZ* is the 4-digit decimal VLAN ID.

Step 2. For each access interface (each interface that does not trunk, but instead belongs to a single VLAN), follow these steps:

  A. Use the **interface** command to move into interface configuration mode for each desired interface.

  B. Use the **switchport access vlan** *id-number* interface subcommand to specify the VLAN number associated with that interface.

  C. (Optional) To disable trunking on that same interface, so that the interface does not negotiate to become a trunk, use the **switchport mode access** interface subcommand.

While the list might look a little daunting, the process on a single switch is actually pretty simple. For example, if you want to put the switch's ports in three VLANs—11, 12, and 13—you just add three **vlan** commands: **vlan 11**, **vlan 12**, and **vlan 13**. Then, for each interface, add a **switchport access vlan 11** (or **12** or **13**) command to assign that interface to the proper VLAN.

VLAN Configuration Example 1: Full VLAN Configuration

Example 10-1 shows the configuration process of adding a new VLAN and assigning access interfaces to that VLAN. Figure 10-1 shows the network used in the example, with one LAN switch (SW1) and two hosts in each of three VLANs (1, 2, and 3). The example shows the details of the two-step process for VLAN 2 and the interfaces in VLAN 2, with the configuration of VLAN 3 deferred until the next example.

10

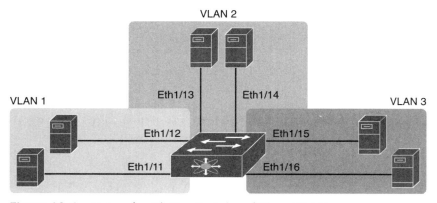

Figure 10-1   *Network with One Switch and Three VLANs*

Example 10-1   *Configuring VLANs and Assigning VLANs to Interfaces*

```
SW1# show vlan brief
VLAN Name                             Status    Ports
---- -------------------------------- --------- ------------------------------
1    default                          active    Eth1/1, Eth1/2, Eth1/3, Eth1/4
                                                Eth1/5, Eth1/6, Eth1/7, Eth1/8
                                                Eth1/9, Eth1/10, Eth1/11, Eth1/12
                                                Eth1/13, Eth1/14, Eth1/15, Eth1/16
                                                Eth1/17, Eth1/18, Eth1/19, Eth1/20
                                                Eth1/21, Eth1/22, Eth1/23, Eth1/24
                                                Eth1/25, Eth1/26, Eth1/27, Eth1/28,
                                                Eth1/29, Eth1/30, Eth1/31, Eth1/32
! Above, VLANs 2 and 3 do not yet exist. Below, VLAN 2 is added, with name Freds-vlan,
! with two interfaces assigned to VLAN 2.

SW1# configure terminal
Enter configuration commands, one per line.  End with CNTL/Z.
SW1(config)# vlan 2
SW1(config-vlan)# name Freds-vlan
SW1(config-vlan)# exit
SW1(config)# interface Ethernet 1/13 - 14
SW1(config-if)# switchport access vlan 2
SW1(config-if)# end

! Below, the show running-config command lists the interface subcommands on
! interfaces Eth1/13 and Eth1/14.
SW1# show running-config
! Many lines omitted for brevity
! Early in the output:
vlan 2
  name Freds-vlan
```

```
!
! more lines omitted for brevity
interface Ethernet1/13
 switchport access vlan 2
 switchport mode access
!
interface Ethernet1/14
 switchport access vlan 2
 switchport mode access
!

SW1# show vlan brief

VLAN Name                     Status    Ports
---- -------------------- --------- -------------------------------
1    default              active    Eth1/1, Eth1/2, Eth1/3, Eth1/4
                                     Eth1/5, Eth1/6, Eth1/7, Eth1/8
                                     Eth1/9, Eth1/10, Eth1/11, Eth1/12
                                     Eth1/15, Eth1/16, Eth1/17, Eth1/18
                                     Eth1/19, Eth1/20, Eth1/21, Eth1/22
                                     Eth1/23, Eth1/24, Eth1/25, Eth1/26,
                                     Eth1/27, Eth1/28, Eth1/29, Eth1/30,
                                     Eth1/31, Eth1/32
2    Freds-vlan           active    Eth1/13, Eth1/14

SW1# show vlan id 2
VLAN Name                         Status    Ports
---- ------------------------------ --------- -------------------------------
2    Freds-vlan                   active    Eth1/13, Eth1/14

VLAN Type  Vlan-mode
---- ----- ----------
2          enet      CE
```

After the configuration has been added, to list the new VLAN, the example repeats the **show vlan brief** command (highlighted in gray). Note that this command lists VLAN 2, named Freds-vlan, and the interfaces assigned to that VLAN (Eth1/13 and Eth1/14).

The example surrounding Figure 10-1 uses six switch ports, all of which need to operate as access ports. That is, each port should not use trunking, but instead should be assigned to a single VLAN, as assigned by the **switchport access vlan** *vlan-id* command.

For ports that should always act as access ports, add the optional interface subcommand **switchport mode access**. This command tells the switch to only allow the interface to be an access interface. The upcoming section "VLAN Trunking Configuration" discusses more details about the commands that allow a port to negotiate whether it should use trunking.

VLAN Configuration Example 2: Shorter VLAN Configuration

Example 10-1 shows several of the optional configuration commands, with a side effect of being a bit longer than is required. Example 10-2 shows a much briefer alternative configuration, picking up the story where Example 10-1 ended and showing the addition of VLAN 3 (as shown in Figure 10-1). Note that SW1 does not know about VLAN 3 at the beginning of this example.

Example 10-2 *Shorter VLAN Configuration Example (VLAN 3)*

```
SW1# configure terminal
Enter configuration commands, one per line.  End with CNTL/Z.
SW1(config)# interface Ethernet 1/15 - 16
SW1(config-if-range)# switchport access vlan 3
% Access VLAN does not exist. Creating vlan 3
SW1(config-if-range)# ^Z


SW1# show vlan brief

VLAN Name                             Status    Ports
---- -------------------------------- --------- ------------------------------
1    default                          active    Eth1/1, Eth1/2, Eth1/3, Eth1/4
                                                Eth1/5, Eth1/6, Eth1/7, Eth1/8
                                                Eth1/9, Eth1/10, Eth1/11, Eth1/12
                                                Eth1/17, Eth1/18, Eth1/19, Eth1/20
                                                Eth1/21, Eth1/22, Eth1/23, Eth1/24
                                                Eth1/25, Eth1/26, Eth1/27, Eth1/28,
                                                Eth1/29, Eth1/30, Eth1/31, Eth1/32
2    Freds-vlan                       active    Eth1/13, Eth1/14
3    VLAN0003                         active    Eth1/15, Eth1/16
```

Example 10-2 shows how a switch can dynamically create a VLAN—the equivalent of the **vlan** *vlan-id* global config command—when the **switchport access vlan** interface subcommand refers to a currently unconfigured VLAN. This example begins with SW1 not knowing about VLAN 3. When the **switchport access vlan 3** interface subcommand was used, the switch realized that VLAN 3 did not exist, and as noted in the shaded message in the example, the switch created VLAN 3, using a default name (VLAN0003). No other steps are required to create the VLAN. At the end of the process, VLAN 3 exists in the switch, and interfaces Eth1/15 and Eth1/16 are in VLAN 3, as noted in the shaded part of the **show vlan brief** command output.

VLAN Trunking Configuration and Verification

So far, we have discussed configuring a single switch with multiple VLANs. The next step is to see how we can extend a single or multiple VLANs between multiple switches using VLAN trunking. Trunking configuration between two Cisco switches can be very simple if you just statically configure trunking. NX-OS trunking requires only some straightfor-ward configuration. Because Cisco Nexus switches support only the more modern trunk-ing option (802.1Q), NX-OS does not need a configuration command to define the type of trunking. You could literally add one interface subcommand for the switch interface on each side of the link (**switchport mode trunk**), and you would create a VLAN trunk that sup-ported all the VLANs known to each switch.

> **NOTE**   Some IOS switches support DOT1Q and ISL trunking encapsulation methodol-ogy; they can be configured using the **switchport trunk encapsulation** command. Because NX-OS only supports the standards-based DOT1Q trunking encapsulation, this command is not available in NX-OS.

However, trunking configuration on Cisco Nexus switches includes many more options, including several options for what VLANs can be carried across the trunk, whether the trunk would be going to an end host such as a virtualized server that might need VLANs trunked down to it or to another switch.

Cisco Nexus switches support only 802.1Q trunking, as previously mentioned, and so in the configurations of a Cisco Nexus switch, there is not an **encapsulation** command, only a **mode trunk** command to enable 802.1Q trunking. It's important to note this difference from other switches where we would have to configure trunking encapsulation methodology like with Cisco Catalyst switches. Table 10-3 references the two switchport administrative mode commands available in Cisco Nexus switches.

Table 10-3   Trunking Administrative Mode Options with the **switchport mode** Command

Command Option	Description
access	Always act as an access (nontrunk) port
trunk	Always act as a trunk port

> **NOTE**   For you CCNA R&S folks: Unlike IOS on Catalyst switches, NX-OS does not dynamically negotiate whether to trunk. As a result, the NX-OS **switchport trunk** command does not have options that tell the Nexus switch to negotiate the trunking state.

For example, consider the two switches shown in Figure 10-2. This figure shows an expan-sion of the network of Figure 10-1, with a trunk to a new switch (SW2) and with parts of VLANs 1 and 3 on ports attached to SW2. The two switches use Ethernet link for the trunk. In this case, the trunk has been enabled because both (5548) switches default to an administrative mode of *access*, meaning that neither switch initiates the trunk negotiation process. By changing both switches to use *trunk* mode, which does initiate the negotiation, the switches negotiate to use trunking, specifically 802.1Q because the 5548s support only 802.1Q. This is done on Interface Ethernet 1/1 in Figure 10-2.

10

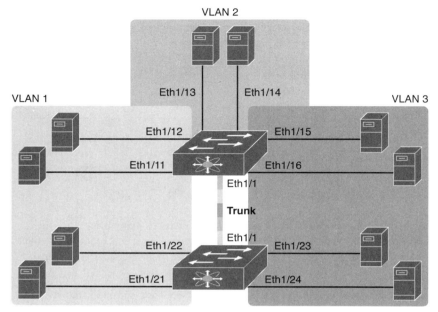

Figure 10-2 *Network with Two Switches and Three VLANs*

Example 10-3 show the basic configuration of setting up a trunk on Interface Ethernet 1/1 based on Figure 10-2.

Example 10-3 *Trunk Configuration and Verification*

```
SW1# show running-config interface Ethernet 1/1

--some lines omitted--

interface Ethernet 1/1
  switchport mode trunk

SW1# show interface Ethernet 1/1 switchport
Name: Ethernet 1/1
  Switchport: Enabled
  Switchport Monitor: Not enabled
  Operational Mode: trunk
  Access Mode VLAN: 1 (default)
  Trunking Native Mode VLAN: 1 (default)
  Trunking VLANs Allowed: 1-4094
  Voice VLAN: none
  Extended Trust State : not trusted [COS = 0]
  Administrative private-vlan primary host-association: none
  Administrative private-vlan secondary host-association: none
  Administrative private-vlan primary mapping: none
  Administrative private-vlan secondary mapping: none
```

```
Administrative private-vlan trunk native VLAN: none
Administrative private-vlan trunk encapsulation: dot1q
Administrative private-vlan trunk normal VLANs: none
Administrative private-vlan trunk private VLANs: none
Operational private-vlan: none
Unknown unicast blocked: disabled
Unknown multicast blocked: disabled
```

As you can see in the output of Example 10-3 the configuration is pretty simple, we get into interface configuration mode and use the command **switchport mode trunk** under Ethernet 1/1. This command will enable trunking on Ethernet 1/1 for all vlan enabled on SW1 to traverse this link. You verify using the **show interface Ethernet 1/1 switchport** command to look at the interface's trunking characteristics. By looking at the output of this command, you see a couple of key things to note:

- The operational mode is trunk.
- Trunking with a native VLAN of 1 (more on native VLAN in the note that follows)

If you use only the **switchport mode trunk** command, the switch, by default, will send all or allow any and all VLANs that have been configured on the switch. You see this in the output highlighted in gray that the allowed VLANs are 1–4094, which means that all are allowed.

> **NOTE**   Native VLAN is by default 1 on all Cisco switches, including Nexus. Native VLAN frames are not encapsulated with any method and are known as *untagged*, which means that any host on this VLAN can see these frames. Cisco Discovery Protocol (CDP), VTP, and other control plane messaging are always sent on the native VLAN 1 by default. You can configure the native VLAN as another VLAN if you want, and in this case, all the frames would be untagged. If you do change the native from its default of 1, it is best practice to do so on other switches as well.

Controlling Which VLANs Can Be Supported on a Trunk

Now that you know how to configure an interface to trunk VLANs from one switch to another, it is important to understand how to control which VLANs are allowed between them. The *allowed VLAN list* feature provides a mechanism for engineers to administratively disable a VLAN from a trunk. By default, switches include all possible VLANs (1–4094) in each trunk's allowed VLAN list. However, the engineer can then limit the VLANs allowed on the trunk by using the following interface subcommand:

```
switchport trunk allowed vlan {add | all | except | remove|none} vlan-list
```

This command provides a way to easily add and remove VLANs from the list. For example, the **add** option permits the switch to add VLANs to the existing allowed VLAN list, and the **remove** option permits the switch to remove VLANs from the existing list. The **all** option means all VLANs, so you can use it to reset the switch to its original default setting (permitting VLANs 1–4094 on the trunk). The **except** option is rather tricky; it adds all VLANs to the list that are not part of the command. For example, the **switchport trunk allowed vlan except 100-200** interface subcommand adds VLANs 1 through 99 and 201 through 4094 to the existing allowed VLAN list on that trunk.

In addition to the allowed VLAN list, a switch has other reasons to prevent a particular VLAN's traffic from crossing a trunk. All five reasons are summarized in the following list:

■ A VLAN has been removed from the trunk's *allowed VLAN* list.

■ A VLAN does not exist in the switch's configuration (as seen with the **show vlan** command).

■ A VLAN does exist, but has been administratively disabled (**shutdown**).

■ A VLAN has been automatically pruned by VTP. (VTP is discussed later in this chapter.)

■ A VLAN's STP instance has placed the trunk interface into a blocking state.

This section has already discussed the first reason (the allowed VLAN list), so let's consider the next two reasons in the list. If a switch does not know that a VLAN exists—for example, if the switch does not have a **vlan** *vlan-id* command configured, as confirmed by the output of the **show vlan** command—the switch will not forward frames in that VLAN over any interface. In addition, a VLAN can exist in a switch's configuration, but also be administratively shut down either by using the **shutdown vlan** *vlan-id* global configuration command, or by using the **shutdown** command in VLAN configuration mode. When disabled, a switch will no longer forward frames in that VLAN, even over trunks. So, switches do not forward frames in nonexistent VLANs or a shutdown VLAN over any of the switch's trunks.

This book has a motive for listing the reasons for limiting VLANs on a trunk: The **show interface trunk** command lists VLAN ID ranges as well, based on these same reasons. This command includes a progression of three lists of the VLANs supported over a trunk. These three lists are as follows:

■ VLANs allowed on the trunk, 1–4094 by default

■ VLANs from the first group that are also in an RSTP forwarding state

■ VLANs from the second group that are not VTP pruned and not STP blocked

To get an idea of these three lists inside the output of the **show interfaces trunk** command, Example 10-4 shows how VLANs might be disallowed on a trunk for various reasons. The command output is taken from SW1 in Figure 10-2, after the completion of the configuration as shown in all the earlier examples in this chapter. In other words, VLANs 1 through 3 exist in SW1's configuration, and are not shut down. Trunking is operational between SW1 and SW2. Then, during the example, the following items are configured on SW1:

Step 1.   VLAN 4 is configured.

Step 2.   VLAN 2 is shut down, which causes RSTP to use a disabled state for all ports in VLAN 2.

Step 3.   VLAN 3 is removed from the trunk's allowed VLAN list.

Example 10-4   *Allowed VLAN List and the List of Active VLANs*

```
! The three lists of VLANs in the next command list allowed VLANs (1-4094),
! Allowed and active VLANs (1-3), and allowed/active/not pruned/STP forwarding
! VLANs (1-3)
SW1# show interfaces trunk

------------------------------------------------------------------------------
Port          Native        Status        Port
              Vlan                                      Channel
------------------------------------------------------------------------------
Eth1/1        1             trunking         -


      ------------------------------------------------------------------------
Port          Vlans Allowed on Trunk
------------------------------------------------------------------------------
Eth1/1        1-4094



------------------------------------------------------------------------------
Port          Vlans Err-disabled on Trunk
------------------------------------------------------------------------------
Eth1/1        none



------------------------------------------------------------------------------
Port          STP Forwarding
------------------------------------------------------------------------------
Eth1/1        1-3



------------------------------------------------------------------------------
Port          Vlans in spanning tree forwarding state and not pruned
------------------------------------------------------------------------------
Eth1/1        1-3


--Some Lines Omitted for Brevity--


! Next, the switch is configured with new VLAN 4; VLAN 2 is shutdown;
! and VLAN 3 is removed from the allowed VLAN list on the trunk.
SW1# configure terminal
Enter configuration commands, one per line.  End with CNTL/Z.
SW1(config)# vlan 4
SW1(config-vlan)# vlan 2
SW1(config-vlan)# shutdown
SW1(config-vlan)# interface Eth1/1
```

```
SW1(config-if)# switchport trunk allowed vlan remove 3
SW1(config-if)# ^Z

! The three lists of VLANs in the next command list allowed VLANs (1-2, 4-4094),
! allowed and active VLANs (1,4), and allowed/active/not pruned/STP forwarding
! VLANs (1,4)
SW1# show interfaces trunk


-------------------------------------------------------------------------------
Port            Native       Status      Port
                Vlan                     Channel
-------------------------------------------------------------------------------
Eth1/1          1            trunking       -

! VLAN 3 is omitted next, because it was removed from the allowed VLAN list.
  -----------------------------------------------------------------------------
Port            Vlans Allowed on Trunk
-------------------------------------------------------------------------------
Eth1/1          1-2,4-4094



-------------------------------------------------------------------------------
Port            Vlans Err-disabled on Trunk
-------------------------------------------------------------------------------
Eth1/1          none

! Since VLAN 2 is shutdown, RSTP considers all ports to be in a disabled state, so the
! switch omits VLAN 2 from the "STP Forwarding" List. VLANs 5-4094 are omitted below
! because SW1 does not have them configured.
-------------------------------------------------------------------------------
Port            STP Forwarding
-------------------------------------------------------------------------------
Eth1/1          1,4



-------------------------------------------------------------------------------
Port            Vlans in spanning tree forwarding state and not pruned
-------------------------------------------------------------------------------
Eth1/1          1,4


--Some Lines Omitted for Brevity--
```

VTP Configuration and Verification

Now that you know how to enable and control the extension of VLANs between switches, let's explore a tool created to help ease the pain of configuring VLANs across every switch of your data center; this older Cisco protocol and tool is called the VLAN Trunking Protocol (VTP). VTP is a Cisco proprietary tool on Cisco switches that advertises each VLAN configured in one switch (with the **vlan** *number* command) so that all the other switches learn about that VLAN. However, for various reasons, many enterprises choose not to use VTP. If you do choose to use VTP we want you to understand how to utilize it best for your datacenter, so we explore what it is and how to use it with your Cisco Nexus switches.

VTP is a Layer 2 messaging protocol that maintains VLAN consistency by managing the addition, deletion, and renaming of VLANs within a VTP domain. A VTP domain is made up of one or more network devices that share the same VTP domain name and that are connected with trunk interfaces. Each network device can be in only one VTP domain. Figure 10-3 shows how VTP is used in a switch network.

 VTP Features

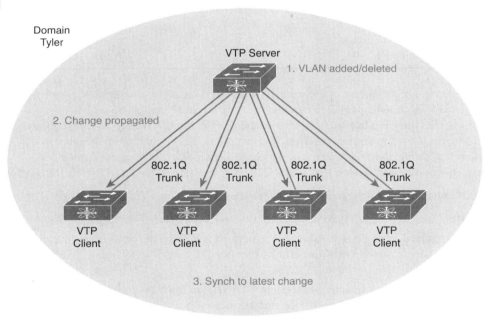

Figure 10-3 *VTP Operation*

Enabling VTP

The VTP is disabled by default on the device. You can enable and configure VTP using the command-line interface (CLI). When VTP is disabled, the device does not relay any VTP protocol packets. To enable VTP on a Nexus switch, use the command **feature vtp**. By default, the switch will then be in VTP server mode. Example 10-5 shows the enabling and verification of VTP.

Example 10-5 *VTP Enablement and Verification*

```
SW1# show vtp
% Invalid command at '^' marker.
SW1# configure terminal
SW1(config)# feature vtp
SW1(config)# show vtp status
VTP Status Information
----------------------
VTP Version                    : 2 (capable)
Configuration Revision         : 0
Maximum VLANs supported locally : 1005
Number of existing VLANs       : 3
VTP Operating Mode             : Server
VTP Domain Name                : <VTP domain not acquired/configured yet>
VTP Pruning Mode               : Disabled (Operationally Disabled)
VTP V2 Mode                    : Disabled
VTP Traps Generation           : Disabled
MD5 Digest                     : 0xB2 0xCC 0x45 0x18 0x7F 0x01 0xCD 0xD7
Configuration last modified by 10.0.128.203 at 0-0-00 00:00:00
Local updater ID is 10.0.128.203
VTP version running            : 1
```

As you can see in the output of Example 10-5, VTP is disabled by default, so there are no associated VTP commands available to you to verify its configuration. To enable VTP, you must use the command **feature vtp**. After enabling VTP, you can see the default settings by using the **show vtp status** command. You can see in the output that by default you are in server mode and currently running in version 1. Let's look at some of the differences between version 2 and version 1 of VTP.

VTP Version 2 supports the following features not supported in VTP Version 1:

■ **Token Ring support:** VTP Version 2 supports Token Ring LAN switching and VLANs.

■ **Unrecognized Type-Length-Value (TLV) support:** A VTP server or client propagates configuration changes to its other trunks, even for TLVs that it is not able to parse. The unrecognized TLV is saved in NVRAM.

■ **Version-dependent transparent mode:** In VTP Version 1, a VTP transparent network device inspects VTP messages for the domain name and version and forwards a message only if the version and domain name match. Because only one domain is supported, VTP Version 2 forwards VTP messages in transparent mode without checking the version.

■ **Consistency checks:** In VTP Version 2, VLAN consistency checks (such as VLAN names and values) are performed only when you enter new information through the CLI or SNMP. Consistency checks are not performed when new information is obtained from a VTP message or when information is read from NVRAM. If the digest on a received VTP message is correct, its information is accepted without consistency checks.

Each switch can use one of three VTP modes: server, client, or transparent (mentioned earlier). Switches use either VTP server or client mode when the switch wants to use VTP for its intended purpose of dynamically advertising VLAN configuration information. Figure 10-4 describes each mode and its properties.

VTP Features

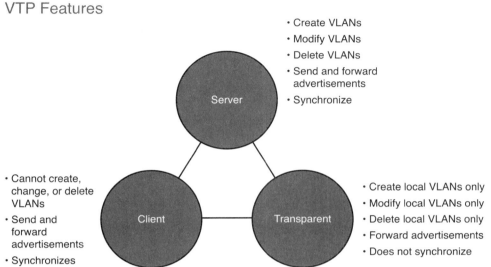

Figure 10-4 *VTP Modes and Descriptions*

It is always a best practice to configure a domain and password pair for your VTP environment to protect against rogue devices attaching to the network with the same domain name and a higher revision number, which would rewrite the VLANs already distributed with whatever was configured on the switch. Example 10-6 shows how to change the domain and password for your VTP environment. Also you can configure the switch to use VTP Version 1 or 2. By default, it runs in Version 1.

Example 10-6 *VTP Version, Domain, and Password Configuration*

```
SW1# configure terminal
SW1(config)# vtp domain Tyler
SW1(config)# vtp password Evan
SW1(config)# vtp version 2
SW1(config)# show vtp status
VTP Status Information
----------------------
VTP Version                     : 2 (capable)
Configuration Revision          : 1
Maximum VLANs supported locally : 1005
Number of existing VLANs        : 3
VTP Operating Mode              : Server
VTP Domain Name                 : Tyler
VTP Pruning Mode                : Disabled (Operationally Disabled)
VTP V2 Mode                     : Enabled
```

10

```
VTP Traps Generation         : Disabled
MD5 Digest                   : 0x46 0xE0 0x71 0x5A 0x6E 0x2D 0x2C 0x4B
Configuration last modified by 10.0.128.203 at 6-9-14 23:13:21
Local updater ID is 10.0.128.203
VTP version running          : 2
```

Limiting VTP Using Pruning

Because you now have a tool to distribute the VLANs across multiple different switches, you also need a tool to control and minimize the risks associated with doing so. This tool is VTP pruning. VTP pruning optimizes the usage of network bandwidth by restricting the flooded traffic to only those trunk ports that can reach all the active network devices. When this protocol is in use, a trunk port does not receive the flooded traffic that is meant for a certain VLAN unless an appropriate join message is received. Figure 10-5 demonstrates how VTP pruning works.

> **NOTE**   VTP maintains a list of trunk ports in the Spanning Tree Protocol (STP) forwarding state by querying STP at boot and listening to the notifications that are generated by STP. VTP sets a trunk port into the pruned or joined state by interacting with STP. STP notifies VTP when a trunk port goes to the blocking or forwarding state. VTP notifies STP when a trunk port becomes pruned or joined.

 VTP Pruning

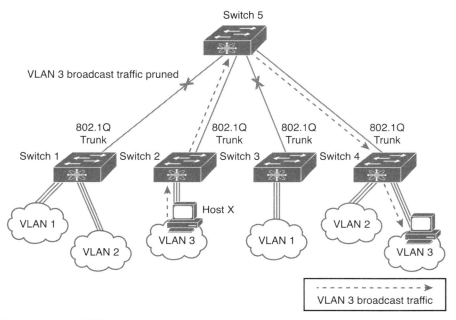

Figure 10-5   *VTP Pruning*

VTP pruning, as shown in Figure 10-5, is a way to determine which VLANs are present and being used on a particular switch (have active hosts). If an active host is not present, you can prune the VLANs off of the trunk links to avoid these switches from having to process flooded traffic from any unused VLANs. This helps from both a bandwidth and CPU perspective. To enable VTP pruning, use the **vtp pruning** command in global configuration mode.

NOTE   VTP pruning is a way to use VTP to determine whether VLANs are active then remove them if needed. Another and more popular way of doing this is by using the **switch-port trunk allowed vlan** command. Using the allowed VLAN solution hard codes what VLANs are allowed on a trunk link and in turn does not send flooded traffic on a trunk for VLANs that are not allowed. VTP pruning is currently supported only on the Nexus 7000s.

10

Exam Preparation Tasks

Review All the Key Topics

Review the most important topics from this chapter, noted with the Key Topic icon. Table 10-4 lists these key topics and where each is discussed.

Table 10-4   Key Topics for Chapter 10

Key Topic Element	Description	Page Number
Table 10-2	VLAN creation guidelines	264
List	VLAN creation and assignment	265
Table 10-3	Trunking administrative mode options with the **switchport mode** command	269
Figure 10-3	VTP operation	275
Example 10-5	VTP enablement and verification	276
Figure 10-4	VTP modes and descriptions	277
Figure 10-5	VTP pruning	278

Complete the Tables and Lists from Memory

Print a copy of DVD Appendix I, "Memory Tables," or at least the section for this chapter, and complete the tables and lists from memory. DVD Appendix J, "Memory Tables Answer Key," includes completed tables and lists to check your work.

Command Reference to Check Your Memory

While you should not necessarily memorize the information in the tables in this section, this section does include a reference for the configuration and EXEC commands covered in this chapter. Practically speaking, you should memorize the commands as a side effect of reading the chapter and doing all the activities in this exam preparation section. To check and see how well you have memorized the commands as a side effect of your other studies, cover the left side of the table with a piece of paper, read the descriptions in the right side, and see whether you remember the command.

Table 10-5   Chapter 10 Configuration Command Reference

Command	Description
vlan *vlan-id*	Global config command that both creates the VLAN and puts the CLI into VLAN configuration mode
name *vlan-name*	VLAN subcommand that names the VLAN
[**no**] **shutdown**	VLAN mode subcommand that enables (**no shutdown**) or disables (**shutdown**) the VLAN

Command	Description
[no] shutdown vlan *vlan-id*	Global config command that has the same effect as the [no] shutdown VLAN mode subcommands
feature vtp	Enables VTP on a Cisco Nexus switch
vtp mode {server | client | transparent | off}	Global config command that defines the VTP mode
switchport mode {access | trunk}	Interface subcommand that configures the trunking administrative mode on the interface
switchport trunk allowed vlan {add | all | except | remove | none} *vlan-list*	Interface subcommand that defines the list of allowed VLANs
switchport access vlan *vlan-id*	Interface subcommand that statically configures the interface into that one VLAN
switchport trunk native vlan *vlan-id*	Interface subcommand that defines the native VLAN for a trunk port
vtp pruning	Enables VTP pruning on a Cisco Nexus switch (Nexus 7x00)

Table 10-6   Chapter 10 EXEC Command Reference

Command	Description
show interface *interface-id* switchport	Lists information about any interface regarding administrative settings and operational state
show interface *interface-id* trunk	Lists information about all operational trunks (but no other interfaces), including the list of VLANs that can be forwarded over the trunk
show vlan [brief | id *vlan-id* | name *vlan-name* | summary]	Lists information about the VLAN
show vlan name [*vlan*]	Displays VLAN information
show vtp status	Lists VTP configuration and status information

10

This chapter covers the following exam topics:

1.1 Describe the purpose and functions of various network devices

2.3 Describe and Configure enhanced switching technologies

2.3d STP

CHAPTER 11

Spanning Tree Protocol Concepts

Spanning Tree Protocol (STP) allows Ethernet LANs to have the added benefits of installing redundant links in a LAN, while overcoming the known problems that occur when adding those extra links. Using redundant links in a LAN design allows the LAN to keep working even when some links fail or even when some entire switches fail. Proper LAN design should add enough redundancy so that no single point of failure crashes the LAN; STP allows the design to use redundancy without causing some other problems.

This chapter discusses the concepts behind STP. In particular, it discusses why LANs need STP, what STP does to solve certain problems in LANs with redundant links, and how STP does its work.

This chapter breaks the STP discussions into three major sections. The first examines the oldest version of STP as defined by the IEEE, based on the 802.1D standard, and generally referred to as *STP*. The second major section looks at various improvements to 802.1D STP over the years, including Etherchannels and Portfast.

> **NOTE** As promised in the Introduction's section "For Those Studying Routing & Switching": Do read this chapter. This chapter's content is not found in the ICND1 book. This chapter ends with a discussion of 802.1w Rapid Spanning Tree Protocol (RSTP).

"Do I Know This Already?" Quiz

Use the "Do I Know This Already?" quiz to help decide whether you might want to skim this chapter, or a major section, moving more quickly to the "Exam Preparation Tasks" section near the end of the chapter. You can find the answers at the bottom of the page following the quiz. For thorough explanations, see Appendix A, "Answers to the 'Do I Know This Already?' Quizzes."

Table 11-1 "Do I Know This Already?" Foundation Topics Section-to-Question Mapping

Foundation Topics Section	Questions
Spanning Tree Protocol (IEEE 802.1D)	1–3
Optional STP Features	5
Rapid STP (IEEE 802.1w)	6, 7

1. Which of the following IEEE 802.1D port states are stable states used when STP has completed convergence? (Choose three answers.)

   a. Blocking

   b. Forwarding

   c. Listening

   d. Learning

   e. Discarding

2. Which of the following are transitory IEEE 802.1D port states used only during the process of STP convergence? (Choose two answers.)

   a. Blocking

   b. Forwarding

   c. Listening

   d. Learning

   e. Discarding

3. Which of the following bridge IDs win election as root, assuming that the switches with these bridge IDs are in the same network?

   a. 32769:0200.1111.1111

   b. 32769:0200.2222.2222

   c. 4097:0200.1111.1111

   d. 4097:0200.2222.2222

   e. 40961:0200.1111.1111

4. Which of the following facts determines how often a nonroot switch sends an 802.1D STP hello BPDU message?

   a. The hello timer as configured on that switch.

   b. The hello timer as configured on the root switch.

   c. It is always every 2 seconds.

   d. The switch reacts to BPDUs received from the root switch by sending another BPDU 2 seconds after receiving the root BPDU.

5. What STP feature causes an interface to be placed in the forwarding state as soon as the interface is physically active?

   a. STP

   b. EtherChannel

   c. Root Guard

   d. PortFast

6. Switch S1 sits in a LAN that uses RSTP. SW1's E1/1 port is its root port, with E1/2 as the only other port connected to other switches. SW1 knows that it will use E1/2 as its root port if E1/1 fails. If SW1's E1/1 interface fails, which of the following is true?

   a. SW1 waits 10 times the hello timer (default 10 × 2 = 20 seconds) before reacting.

   b. SW1 waits 3 times the hello timer (default 3 × 2 = 6 seconds) before reacting.

   c. SW1 does not wait, but makes E1/2 the root port, and puts it in a learning state.

   d. SW1 does not wait, but makes E1/2 the root port, and puts it in a forwarding state.

7. Switch SW1 sits in a LAN that uses RSTP. SW1 has 24 RSTP edge ports, and is also receiving hello BPDUs on two point-to-point ports, E1/1 and E1/2. SW1 chooses E1/1 as its root port. Which of the following about the RSTP port role of E1/2 is true?

   a. Backup role

   b. Blocking role

   c. Discarding role

   d. Alternate role

11

Foundation Topics

Spanning Tree Protocol (IEEE 802.1D)

A LAN with redundant links would cause Ethernet frames to loop for an indefinite period of time unless some other mechanism stops the frames from looping. The fundamental frame-forwarding logic in a switch does not prevent such loops.

Historically, Spanning Tree Protocol (STP) was the first loop-prevention mechanism for Ethernet networks that used bridges and later switches. With STP enabled, some switches block ports so that these ports do not forward frames. In effect, the LAN can have redundant links for backup purposes, but STP logically stops using some links to remove the loops from the network.

STP intelligently chooses which ports to block, with two goals in mind:

■ All devices in a VLAN can send frames to all other devices. In other words, STP does not block too many ports, cutting off some parts of the LAN from other parts.

■ Frames have a short life and do not loop around the network indefinitely.

STP strikes a balance, allowing frames to be delivered to each device, without causing the problems that occur when frames loop through the network over and over again.

STP prevents looping frames by adding an additional check on each interface before a switch uses it to send or receive user traffic. That check: If the port is in STP forwarding state in that VLAN, use it as normal; if it is in STP blocking state, however, block all user traffic and do not send or receive user traffic on that interface in that VLAN.

Note that these STP states do not change the other information you already know about switch interfaces. The interface's state of connected/notconnect does not change. The interface's operational state as either an access or trunk port does not change. STP adds this additional STP state, with the blocking state basically disabling the interface.

In many ways, those last two paragraphs sum up what STP does. However, the details of how STP does its work can take a fair amount of study and practice. This first major section of the chapter begins by explaining the need for STP and the basic ideas of what STP does to solve the problem of looping frames. The majority of this section then looks at how STP goes about choosing which switch ports to block to accomplish STP's goals.

The Need for Spanning Tree

STP prevents three common problems in Ethernet LANs that would occur if the LAN were to have redundant links and STP were not used. All three problems are actually side effects of the fact that without STP, some Ethernet frames would loop around the network for a long time (hours, days, literally forever if the LAN devices and links never failed).

Just one frame that loops around a network causes what is called a *broadcast storm*. Broadcast storms happen when broadcast frames, multicast frames, or unknown-destination unicast frames loop around a LAN indefinitely. Broadcast storms can saturate all the links with copies of that one single frame, crowding out good frames, as well as significantly impacting end-user PC performance by making the PCs process too many broadcast frames.

To help you understand how this occurs, Figure 11-1 shows a sample network in which Bob sends a broadcast frame. The dashed lines show how the switches forward the frame when STP does not exist.

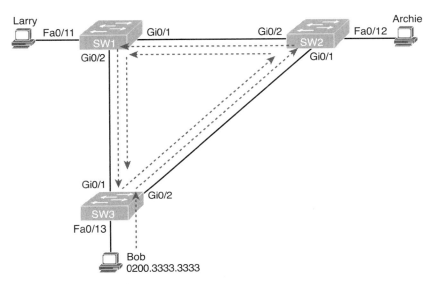

Figure 11-1   *Broadcast Storm*

NOTE   Bob's original broadcast would also be forwarded around the other direction as well, with SW3 sending a copy of the original frame out its Gi0/1 port. The figure does not show that frame just to reduce the clutter.

Remember the LAN switching logic from back in Chapter 6, "Building Ethernet LANs with Switches"? That logic tells switches to flood broadcasts out all interfaces in the same VLAN except the interface in which the frame arrived. In the figure, that means SW3 forwards Bob's frame to SW2, SW2 forwards the frame to SW1, SW1 forwards the frame back to SW3, and SW3 forwards it back to SW2 again.

When broadcast storms happen, frames like the one in Figure 11-1 keep looping until something changes—someone shuts down an interface, reloads a switch, or does something else to break the loop. Also note that the same event happens in the opposite direction. When Bob sends the original frame, SW3 also forwards a copy to SW1, SW1 forwards it to SW2, and so on.

Looping frames also cause a *MAC table instability* problem. MAC table instability means that the switches' MAC address tables keep changing the information listed for the source MAC address of the looping frame. For example, SW3 begins Figure 11-1 with a MAC table entry for Bob, at the bottom of the figure, as follows:

0200.3333.3333   Fa0/13   VLAN 1

11

However, now think about the switch-learning process that occurs when the looping frame goes to SW2, then SW1, and then back into SW3's Gi0/1 interface. SW3 thinks, "Hmm... the source MAC address is 0200.3333.3333, and it came in my Gi0/1 interface... update my MAC table!" resulting in the following entry on SW3:

   0200.3333.3333   Gi0/1   VLAN 1

At this point, SW3 itself cannot correctly deliver frames to Bob's MAC address. At that instant, if a frame arrives at SW3 destined for Bob—a different frame than the looping frame that causes the problems—SW3 incorrectly forwards the frame out Gi0/1 to SW1.

The looping frames also cause a third problem: Multiple copies of the frame arrive at the destination. Consider a case in which Bob sends a frame to Larry but none of the switches know Larry's MAC address. Switches flood frames sent to unknown destination unicast MAC addresses. When Bob sends the frame destined for Larry's MAC address, SW3 sends a copy to both SW1 and SW2. SW1 and SW2 also flood the frame, causing copies of the frame to loop. SW1 also sends a copy of each frame out Fa0/11 to Larry. As a result, Larry gets multiple copies of the frame, which may result in an application failure, if not more pervasive networking problems.

Table 11-2 summarizes the main three classes of problems that occur when STP is not used in a LAN with redundancy.

Table 11-2   Three Classes of Problems Caused by Not Using STP in Redundant LANs

Problem	Description
Broadcast storms	The forwarding of a frame repeatedly on the same links, consuming significant parts of the links' capacities
MAC table instability	The continual updating of a switch's MAC address table with incorrect entries, in reaction to looping frames, resulting in frames being sent to the wrong locations
Multiple frame transmission	A side effect of looping frames in which multiple copies of one frame are delivered to the intended host, confusing the host

What IEEE 802.1D Spanning Tree Does

STP prevents loops by placing each switch port in either a forwarding state or a blocking state. Interfaces in the forwarding state act as normal, forwarding and receiving frames. However, interfaces in a blocking state do not process any frames except STP messages (and some other overhead messages). Interfaces that block do not forward user frames, do not learn MAC addresses of received frames, and do not process received user frames.

Figure 11-2 shows a simple STP tree that solves the problem shown in Figure 11-1 by placing one port on SW3 in the blocking state.

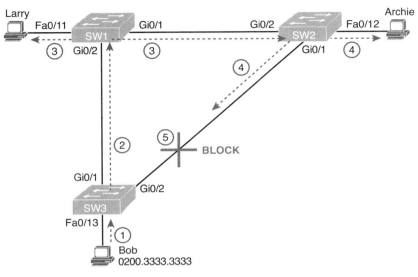

Figure 11-2   *What STP Does: Blocks a Port to Break the Loop*

Now when Bob sends a broadcast frame, the frame does not loop. As shown in the steps in the figure:

Step 1.   Bob sends the frame to SW3.

Step 2.   SW3 forwards the frame only to SW1, but not out Gi0/2 to SW2, because SW3's Gi0/2 interface is in a blocking state.

Step 3.   SW1 floods the frame out both Fa0/11 and Gi0/1.

Step 4.   SW2 floods the frame out Fa0/12 and Gi0/1.

Step 5.   SW3 physically receives the frame, but it ignores the frame received from SW2 because SW3's Gi0/2 interface is in a blocking state.

With the STP topology in Figure 11-2, the switches simply do not use the link between SW2 and SW3 for traffic in this VLAN, which is the minor negative side effect of STP. However, if either of the other two links fails, STP converges so that SW3 forwards instead of blocks on its Gi0/2 interface.

> **NOTE**   The term *STP convergence* refers to the process by which the switches collectively realize that something has changed in the LAN topology and so the switches might need to change which ports block and which ports forward.

That completes the description of what STP does, placing each port into either a forwarding or blocking state. The more interesting question, and the one that takes a lot more work to understand, is the question of how and why STP makes its choices. How does STP manage to make switches block or forward on each interface? And how does it converge to change state from blocking to forwarding to take advantage of redundant links in response to network outages? The following sections answer these questions.

How Spanning Tree Works

The STP algorithm creates a spanning tree of interfaces that forward frames. The tree structure of forwarding interfaces creates a single path to and from each Ethernet link, just like you can trace a single path in a living, growing tree from the base of the tree to each leaf.

NOTE STP was created before LAN switches even existed. In those days, Ethernet bridges used STP. Today, switches play the same role as bridges, implementing STP. However, many STP terms still refer to *bridge*. For the purposes of STP and this chapter, consider the terms *bridge* and *switch* synonymous.

The process used by STP, sometimes called the *spanning-tree algorithm* (STA), chooses the interfaces that should be placed into a forwarding state. For any interfaces not chosen to be in a forwarding state, STP places the interfaces in blocking state. In other words, STP simply picks which interfaces should forward, and any interfaces left over go to a blocking state.

STP uses three criteria to choose whether to put an interface in forwarding state:

- STP elects a *root switch*. STP puts all working interfaces on the root switch in forwarding state.

- Each nonroot switch considers one of its ports to have the least administrative cost between itself and the root switch. The cost is called that switch's *root cost*. STP places its port that is part of the least root cost path, called that switch's *root port* (RP), in forwarding state.

- Many switches can attach to the same Ethernet segment, but in modern networks, normally two switches connect to each link. The switch with the lowest root cost, as compared with the other switches attached to the same link, is placed in forwarding state. That switch is the designated switch, and that switch's interface, attached to that segment, is called the *designated port* (DP).

NOTE The real reason the root switches place all working interfaces in a forwarding state is that all its interfaces will become DPs, but it is easier to just remember that all the root switches' working interfaces will forward frames.

All other interfaces are placed in blocking state. Table 11-3 summarizes the reasons STP places a port in forwarding or blocking state.

Table 11-3   STP: Reasons for Forwarding or Blocking

Characterization of Port	STP State	Description
All the root switch's ports	Forwarding	The root switch is always the designated switch on all connected segments.
Each nonroot switch's root port	Forwarding	The port through which the switch has the least cost to reach the root switch (lowest root cost).
Each LAN's designated port	Forwarding	The switch forwarding the hello on to the segment, with the lowest root cost, is the designated switch for that segment.
All other working ports	Blocking	The port is not used for forwarding user frames, nor are any frames received on these interfaces considered for forwarding.

NOTE   STP only considers working interfaces (those in a connected state). Failed interfaces (for example, interfaces with no cable installed) or administratively shutdown interfaces are instead placed into an STP disabled state. So, this section uses the term *working ports* to refer to interfaces that could forward frames if STP placed the interface into a forwarding state.

The STP Bridge ID and Hello BPDU

STP begins with an election of one switch to be the root switch. To better understand this election process, you need to understand the STP messages sent between switches as well as the concept and format of the identifier used to uniquely identify each switch.

The STP bridge ID (BID) is an 8-byte value unique to each switch. The BID consists of a 2-byte priority field and a 6-byte system ID, with the system ID being based on a universal (burned-in) MAC address in each switch. Using a burned-in MAC address ensures that each switch's BID will be unique.

STP defines messages called *bridge protocol data units* (BPDU), which switches use to exchange information with each other. The most common BPDU, called a hello BPDU, lists many details, including the sending switch's BID. By listing its own unique BID, switches can tell which switch sent which hello BPDU. Table 11-4 lists some of the key information in the hello BPDU.

11

Table 11-4   Fields in the STP Hello BPDU

Field	Description
Root BID	The BID of the switch the sender of this hello currently believes to be the root switch
Sender's BID	The BID of the switch sending this hello BPDU
Sender's root cost	The STP cost between this switch and the current root
Timer values on the root switch	Includes the hello timer, MaxAge timer, and forward delay timer

For the time being, just keep the first three items from Table 11-4 in mind as the following sections work through the three steps in how STP chooses the interfaces to place into a forwarding state. Next, the text examines the three main steps in the STP process.

Electing the Root Switch

Switches elect a root switch based on the BIDs in the BPDUs. The root switch is the switch with the lowest numeric value for the BID. Because the two-part BID starts with the priority value, essentially the switch with the lowest priority becomes the root. For example, if one switch has priority 4096, and another switch has priority 8192, the switch with priority 4096 wins, regardless of what MAC address was used to create the BID for each switch.

If a tie occurs based on the priority portion of the BID, the switch with the lowest MAC address portion of the BID is the root. No other tiebreaker should be needed because switches use one of their own universal (burned-in) MAC addresses as the second part of their BIDs. So if the priorities tie, and one switch uses a MAC address of 0200.0000.0000 as part of the BID and the other uses 0911.1111.1111, the first switch (MAC 0200.0000.0000) becomes the root switch.

STP elects a root switch in a manner not unlike a political election. The process begins with all switches claiming to be the root by sending hello BPDUs listing their own BID as the root BID. If a switch hears a hello that lists a better (lower) BID, that switch stops advertising itself as root and starts forwarding the superior hello. The hello sent by the better switch lists the better switch's BID as the root. It works like a political race in which a less-popular candidate gives up and leaves the race, throwing his support behind the more popular candidate. Eventually, everyone agrees which switch has the best (lowest) BID, and everyone supports the elected switch—which is where the political race analogy falls apart.

> **NOTE**   A better hello, meaning that the listed root's BID is better (numerically lower), is called a *superior hello*; a worse hello, meaning that the listed root's BID is not as good (numerically higher), is called an *inferior hello*.

Figure 11-3 shows the beginning of the root election process. In this case, SW1 has advertised itself as root, as have SW2 and SW3. However, SW2 now believes that SW1 is a better root, so SW2 is now forwarding the hello originating at SW1. So, at this point, the figure shows SW1 is saying hello, claiming to be root; SW2 agrees, and is forwarding SW1's hello that lists SW1 as root; but, SW3 is still claiming to be best, sending his own hello BPDUs, listing SW3's BID as the root.

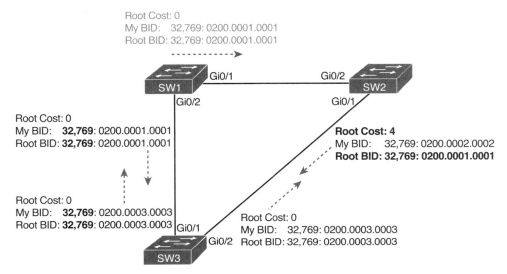

Root Cost: 0
My BID: 32,769: 0200.0001.0001
Root BID: 32,769: 0200.0001.0001

Gi0/1   Gi0/2

SW1   SW2

Gi0/2   Gi0/1

Root Cost: 0
My BID: **32,769**: 0200.0001.0001
Root BID: **32,769**: 0200.0001.0001

Root Cost: 4
My BID: 32,769: 0200.0002.0002
Root BID: 32,769: 0200.0001.0001

Root Cost: 0
My BID: **32,769**: 0200.0003.0003
Root BID: **32,769**: 0200.0003.0003

Root Cost: 0
My BID: 32,769: 0200.0003.0003
Root BID: 32,769: 0200.0003.0003

Gi0/1
Gi0/2

SW3

Figure 11-3   *Beginnings of the Root Election Process*

Two candidates still exist in Figure 11-3: SW1 and SW3. So who wins? Well, from the BID, the lower-priority switch wins; if a tie occurs, the lower MAC address wins. As shown in the figure, SW1 has a lower BID (32769:0200.0001.0001) than SW3 (32769:0200.0003.0003), so SW1 wins, and SW3 now also believes that SW1 is the better switch. Figure 11-4 shows the resulting hello messages sent by the switches.

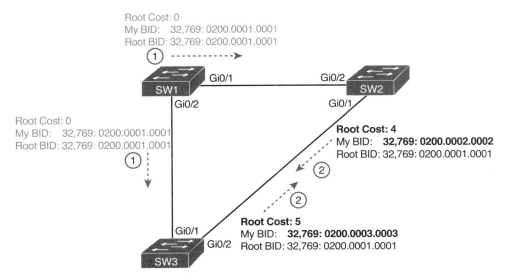

Root Cost: 0
My BID: 32,769: 0200.0001.0001
Root BID: 32,769: 0200.0001.0001

①

Gi0/1   Gi0/2

SW1   SW2

Gi0/2   Gi0/1

Root Cost: 0
My BID: 32,769: 0200.0001.0001
Root BID: 32,769: 0200.0001.0001

①

Root Cost: 4
My BID: **32,769: 0200.0002.0002**
Root BID: 32,769: 0200.0001.0001

②

②

Gi0/1
Gi0/2

Root Cost: 5
My BID: **32,769: 0200.0003.0003**
Root BID: 32,769: 0200.0001.0001

SW3

Figure 11-4   *SW1 Wins the Election*

After the election is complete, only the root switch continues to originate STP hello BPDU messages. The other switches receive the hellos, update the sender's BID field (and root cost field), and forward the hellos out other interfaces. The figure reflects this fact, with SW1 sending hellos at Step 1, and SW2 and SW3 independently forwarding the hello out their other interfaces at Step 2.

Summarizing, the root election happens through each switch claiming to be root, with the best switch being elected based on the numerically lowest BID. Breaking down the BID into its components, the comparisons can be made as

- The lowest priority
- If that ties, the lowest switch MAC address

Choosing Each Switch's Root Port

The second part of the STP process occurs when each nonroot switch chooses its one and only root port. A switch's RP is its interface through which it has the least STP cost to reach the root switch (least root cost).

The idea of a switch's cost to reach the root switch can be easily seen for humans. Just look at a network diagram that shows the root switch, lists the STP cost associated with each switch port, and the nonroot switch in question. Switches use a different process than looking at a network diagram, of course, but using a diagram can make it easier to learn the idea.

Figure 11-5 shows just such a figure, with the same three switches shown in the last several figures. SW1 has already won the election as root, and the figure considers the cost from SW3's perspective.

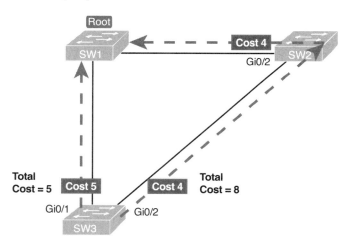

Figure 11-5 *How a Human Might Calculate STP Cost from SW3 to the Root (SW1)*

SW3 has two possible physical paths to send frames to the root switch: the direct path to the left, and the indirect path to the right through switch SW2. The cost is the sum of the costs of all the *switch ports the frame would exit* if it flowed over that path. (The calculation ignores the inbound ports.) As you can see, the cost over the direct path out SW3's

G0/1 port has a total cost of 5, and the other path has a total cost of 8. SW3 picks its G0/1 port as root port because it is the port that is part of the least-cost path to send frames to the root switch.

Switches come to the same conclusion, but using a different process. Instead, they add their local interface STP cost to the root cost listed in each received hello BPDU. The STP port cost is simply an integer value assigned to each interface, per VLAN, for the purpose of providing an objective measurement that allows STP to choose which interfaces to add to the STP topology. The switches also look at their neighbor's root cost, as announced in hello BPDUs received from each neighbor.

Figure 11-6 shows an example of how switches calculate their best root cost and then choose their root port, using the same topology and STP costs as shown in Figure 11-5. STP on SW3 calculates its cost to reach the root over the two possible paths by adding the advertised cost (in hello messages) to the interface costs listed in the figure.

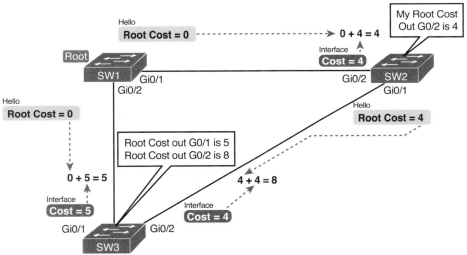

Figure 11-6 *How STP Actually Calculates the Cost from SW3 to the Root*

Focus on the process for a moment. The root switch sends hellos, with a listed root cost of 0. The idea is that the root's cost to reach itself is 0.

Next, look on the left of the figure. SW3 takes the received cost (0) from the hello sent by SW1, adds the interface cost (5) of the interface on which that hello was received. SW3 calculates that the cost to reach the root switch, out that port (G0/1), is 5.

On the right side, SW2 has realized its best cost to reach the root is cost 4. So, when SW2 forwards the hello toward SW3, SW2 lists a root cost 4. SW3's STP port cost on port G0/2 is 4, so SW3 determines a total cost to reach root out its G0/2 port of 8.

As a result of the process depicted in Figure 11-6, SW3 chooses Gi0/1 as its RP, because the cost to reach the root switch through that port (5) is lower than the other alternative (Gi0/2, cost 8). Similarly, SW2 chooses Gi0/2 as its RP, with a cost of 4 (SW1's advertised cost of 0 plus SW2's Gi0/2 interface cost of 4). Each switch places its root port into a forwarding state.

11

Tiebreakers for Root Port

In some cases, a switch must use a tiebreaker when choosing its root port. The reason is simple: The root cost might be equal over more than one path to the root.

In most cases, the first tiebreaker solves the problem—the lowest neighbor BID. For instance, if you refer to Figure 11-6 in the previous section, imagine that SW3's root cost tied over both paths to reach the root (SW1). SW3 then looks at the BIDs of its two neighbors (SW1 and SW2), and picks the one that is lowest. In Figure 11-6, SW1's BID is lowest, so SW3 would choose as root port its port connected to that neighbor, namely SW3's G0/1 port.

In some other cases, STP needs even more tiebreakers. Specifically, when two switches connect with multiple links, as shown in Figure 11-7, the neighbor's BID will be equal.

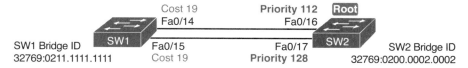

Figure 11-7 *The Need for Additional Root Port Tiebreakers*

In this particular example, SW2 becomes the root, and SW1 needs to choose its RP. SW1's port costs tie, at 19 each, so SW1's root cost ties over each path at cost 19. SW2 sends hellos over each link to SW1, so SW1 cannot break the tie based on the neighbor BID, because both neighbor BIDs list SW2's BID. So, SW1 has to consider the other two tiebreakers, in order: the neighboring switch ports' port priority, and if that ties, the neighboring switch ports' internal port number (with lowest being best).

In Figure 11-7, SW1 would see that the hello that entered its F0/14 port has a neighbor's port priority of 112, better than the other port's priority of 128, so SW1 would choose F0/14 as its root port.

The following list summarizes the criteria for choosing a root port, with all the tiebreakers listed:

1. Choose based on the least cost path to the root. If a tie…
2. Choose based on the lowest BID of the neighboring bridge. If a tie…
3. Choose based on the lowest port priority of the neighboring switch ports. If a tie…
4. Choose based on the lowest internal port number on the neighboring switch ports.

Choosing the Designated Port on Each LAN Segment

STP's final step to choose the STP topology is to choose the designated port on each LAN segment. The designated port (DP) on each LAN segment is the switch port that advertises the lowest-cost hello on to a LAN segment. When a nonroot switch forwards a hello, the nonroot switch sets the root cost field in the hello to that switch's cost to reach the root. In effect, the switch with the lower cost to reach the root, among all switches connected to a segment, becomes the DP on that segment.

For example, earlier Figure 11-4 shows in bold text the parts of the hello messages from both SW2 and SW3 that determine the choice of DP on that segment. Note that both SW2 and SW3 list their respective cost to reach the root switch (cost 4 on SW2 and cost 5 on SW3). SW2 lists the lower cost, so SW2's Gi0/1 port is the designated port on that LAN segment.

All DPs are placed into a forwarding state; so in this case, SW2's Gi0/1 interface will be in a forwarding state.

If the advertised costs tie, the switches break the tie by choosing the switch with the lower BID. In this case, SW2 would also have won, with a BID of 32769:0200.0002.0002 versus SW3's 32769:0200.0003.0003.

> **NOTE**   Two additional tiebreakers are needed in some cases, although these would be unlikely today. A single switch can connect two or more interfaces to the same collision domain by connecting to a hub. In that case, the one switch hears its own BPDUs. So, if a switch ties with itself, two additional tiebreakers are used: the lowest interface STP priority on the local switch and, if that ties, the lowest internal interface number on the local switch.

The only interface that does not have a reason to be in a forwarding state on the three switches in the examples shown in Figures 11-3 through 11-6 is SW3's Gi0/2 port. So, the STP process is now complete. Table 11-5 outlines the state of each port and shows why it is in that state.

Table 11-5   State of Each Interface

Switch Interface	State	Reason for That Interface State
SW1, Gi0/1	Forwarding	The interface is on the root switch, so it becomes the DP on that link.
SW1, Gi0/2	Forwarding	The interface is on the root switch, so it becomes the DP on that link.
SW2, Gi0/2	Forwarding	The root port of SW2.
SW2, Gi0/1	Forwarding	The designated port on the LAN segment to SW3.
SW3, Gi0/1	Forwarding	The root port of SW3.
SW3, Gi0/2	Blocking	Not the root port and not the designated port.

11

Influencing and Changing the STP Topology

Switches do not just use STP once and never again. The switches continually watch for changes. Those changes can be because a link or switch fails or it can be a new link that can now be used. The configuration can change in a way that changes the STP topology. This section briefly discusses the kinds of things that change the STP topology, either through configuration or through changes in the status of devices and links in the LAN.

Making Configuration Changes to Influence the STP Topology

The network engineers can choose to change the STP settings to then change the choices STP makes in a given LAN. Two main tools available to the engineer are to configure the BID and to change STP port costs.

Switches have a way to create a default BID, by taking a default priority value and adding a universal MAC address that comes with the switch hardware. However, engineers typically want to choose which switch becomes the root. Chapter 12, "Cisco Nexus Spanning Tree Protocol Implementation," shows how to configure a Cisco switch to override its default BID setting to make a switch become root.

Port costs also have default values, per port, per VLAN. You can configure these port costs, or you can use the default values. Table 11-6 lists the default port costs defined by IEEE; Cisco uses these same defaults.

Table 11-6   Default Port Costs According to IEEE

Ethernet Speed	IEEE Cost
10 Mbps	100
100 Mbps	19
1 Gbps	4
10 Gbps	2

With STP enabled, all working switch interfaces will settle into an STP forwarding or blocking state, even access ports. For switch interfaces connected to hosts or routers, which do not use STP, the switch still forwards hellos on to those interfaces. By virtue of being the only device sending a hello on to that LAN segment, the switch is sending the least-cost hello on to that LAN segment, making the switch become the designated port on that LAN segment. So, STP puts working access interfaces into a forwarding state as a result of the designated port part of the STP process.

Reacting to State Changes That Affect the STP Topology

After the engineer has finished all STP configuration, the STP topology should settle into a stable state and not change, at least until the network topology changes. This section examines the ongoing operation of STP while the network is stable, and then it covers how STP converges to a new topology when something changes.

The root switch sends a new hello BPDU every 2 seconds by default. Each nonroot switch forwards the hello on all DPs, but only after changing items listed in the hello. The switch sets the root cost to that local switch's calculated root cost. The switch also sets the "sender's bridge ID" field to its own BID. (The root's BID field is not changed.)

By forwarding the received (and changed) hellos out all DPs, all switches continue to receive hellos every 2 seconds. The following steps summarize the steady-state operation when nothing is currently changing in the STP topology:

Step 1. The root creates and sends a hello BPDU, with a root cost of 0, out all its working interfaces (those in a forwarding state).

Step 2. The nonroot switches receive the hello on their root ports. After changing the hello to list their own BID as the sender's BID, and listing that switch's root cost, the switch forwards the hello out all designated ports.

Step 3. Steps 1 and 2 repeat until something changes.

Each switch relies on these periodic received hellos from the root as a way to know that its path to the root is still working. When a switch ceases to receive the hellos, or receives a hello that lists different details, something has failed, so the switch reacts and starts the process of changing the spanning-tree topology.

How Switches React to Changes with STP

For various reasons, the convergence process requires the use of three timers. Note that all switches use the timers as dictated by the root switch, which the root lists in its periodic hello BPDU messages. Table 11-7 describes the timers.

Table 11-7   STP Timers

Timer	Description	Default Value
Hello	The time period between hellos created by the root.	2 seconds
MaxAge	How long any switch should wait, after ceasing to hear hellos, before trying to change the STP topology.	10 times hello
Forward delay	Delay that affects the process that occurs when an interface changes from blocking state to forwarding state. A port stays in an interim listening state, and then an interim learning state, for the number of seconds defined by the forward delay timer.	15 seconds

If a switch does not get an expected hello BPDU within the hello time, the switch continues as normal. However, if the hellos do not show up again within MaxAge time, the switch reacts by taking steps to change the STP topology. With default settings, MaxAge is 20 seconds (10 times the default hello timer of 2 seconds). So, a switch would go 20 seconds without hearing a hello before reacting.

After MaxAge expires, the switch essentially makes all its STP choices again, based on any hellos it receives from other switches. It reevaluates which switch should be the root switch. If the local switch is not the root, it chooses its RP. And it determines whether it is DP on each of its other links. The best way to describe STP convergence is to show an example using the same familiar topology. Figure 11-8 shows the same familiar figure, with SW3's Gi0/2 in a blocking state, but SW1's Gi0/2 interface has just failed.

11

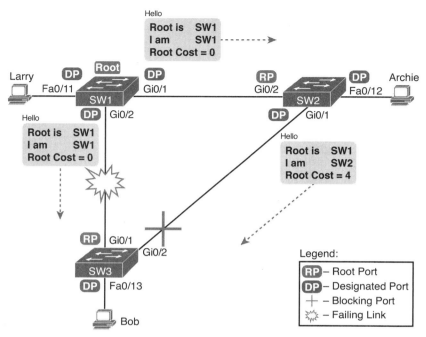

Figure 11-8   *Initial STP State Before SW1-SW3 Link Fails*

SW3 reacts to the change because SW3 fails to receive its expected hellos on its Gi0/1 interface. However, SW2 does not need to react because SW2 continues to receive its periodic hellos in its Gi0/2 interface. In this case, SW3 reacts either when MaxAge time passes without hearing the hellos, or as soon as SW3 notices that interface Gi0/1 has failed. (If the interface fails, the switch can assume that the hellos will not be arriving in that interface anymore.)

Now that SW3 can act, it begins by reevaluating the choice of root switch. SW3 still receives the hellos from SW2, as forwarded from the root (SW1). SW1 still has a lower BID than SW3; otherwise, SW1 would not have already been the root. So, SW3 decides that SW1 is still the best switch and that SW3 is not the root.

Next, SW3 reevaluates its choice of RP. At this point, SW3 is receiving hellos on only one interface: Gi0/2. Whatever the calculated root cost, Gi0/2 becomes SW3's new RP. (The cost would be 8, assuming the STP costs had no changes since Figures 11-5 and 11-6.)

SW3 then reevaluates its role as DP on any other interfaces. In this example, no real work needs to be done. SW3 was already DP on interface Fa0/13, and it continues to be the DP because no other switches connect to that port.

Changing Interface States with STP

STP uses the idea of roles and states. Roles, like root port and designated port, relate to how STP analyzes the LAN topology. States, like forwarding and blocking, tell a switch whether to send or receive frames. When STP converges, a switch chooses new port roles, and the port roles determine the state (forwarding or blocking).

Switches can simply move immediately from forwarding to blocking state, but they must take extra time to transition from blocking state to forwarding state. For instance, when a switch formerly used port G0/1 as its RP (a role), that port was in a forwarding state. After convergence, G0/1 might be neither an RP nor DP; the switch can immediately move that port to a blocking state.

When a port that formerly blocked needs to transition to forwarding, the switch first puts the port through two intermediate interface states. These temporary states help prevent temporary loops:

- **Listening:** Like the blocking state, the interface does not forward frames. The switch removes old stale (unused) MAC table entries for which no frames are received from each MAC address during this period. These stale MAC table entries could be the cause of the temporary loops.

- **Learning:** Interfaces in this state still do not forward frames, but the switch begins to learn the MAC addresses of frames received on the interface.

STP moves an interface from blocking to listening, then to learning, and then to forwarding state. STP leaves the interface in each interim state for a time equal to the forward delay timer, which defaults to 15 seconds. As a result, a convergence event that causes an interface to change from blocking to forwarding requires 30 seconds to transition from blocking to forwarding. In addition, a switch might have to wait MaxAge seconds before even choosing to move an interface from blocking to forwarding state.

For example, follow what happens with an initial STP topology as shown in Figures 11-3 through 11-6, with the SW1-to-SW3 link failing as shown in Figure 11-8. If SW1 simply quit sending hello messages to SW3, but the link between the two did not fail, SW3 would wait MaxAge seconds before reacting (20 seconds by default). SW3 would actually quickly choose its ports' STP roles, but then wait 15 seconds each in listening and learning states on interface Gi0/2, resulting in a 50-second convergence delay.

Table 11-8 summarizes spanning tree's various interface states for easier review.

Table 11-8   IEEE 802.1D Spanning-Tree States

State	Forwards Data Frames?	Learns MACs Based on Received Frames?	Transitory or Stable State?
Blocking	No	No	Stable
Listening	No	No	Transitory
Learning	No	Yes	Transitory
Forwarding	Yes	Yes	Stable
Disabled	No	No	Stable

Optional STP Features

The first major section of this chapter defines STP has standardized in IEEE standard 802.1D. STP as described in that first section has been around for about 30 years. Cisco switches

11

today still support and use STP. And other than changes to the default cost values, the description of STP in this chapter so far works like the original STP as created all those years ago.

Even with such an amazingly long life, STP has gone through several changes over these decades, some small, some large. For instance, Cisco added proprietary features to make improvements to STP. In some cases, the IEEE added these same improvements, or something like them, to later IEEE standards, whether as a revision of the 802.1D standard or as an additional standard. And STP has gone through one major revision that improves convergence, called the Rapid Spanning Tree Protocol (RSTP), as originally defined in IEEE 802.1w.

This final of three major sections of this chapter briefly discusses the basics of several of these optional features that go beyond the base 802.1D STP concepts, including EtherChannel, PortFast, and BPDU Guard.

> **NOTE** Even though STP has enjoyed a long life, many data center LANs have moved past STP to alternative protocols and technologies. The DCICN exam includes the details of STP, while the DCICT exam covers a wide variety of alternatives in the data center. These include Fabric Extension, Fabric Path, and virtual port channels (vPCs), to name a few.

EtherChannel

One of the best ways to lower STP's convergence time is to avoid convergence altogether. EtherChannel provides a way to prevent STP convergence from being needed when only a single port or cable failure occurs.

EtherChannel combines multiple parallel segments of equal speed between the same pair of switches, bundled into an EtherChannel. The switches treat the EtherChannel as a single interface with regard to STP. As a result, if one of the links fails, but at least one of the links is up, STP convergence does not have to occur. For example, Figure 11-9 shows the familiar three-switch network, but now with two Gigabit Ethernet connections between each pair of switches.

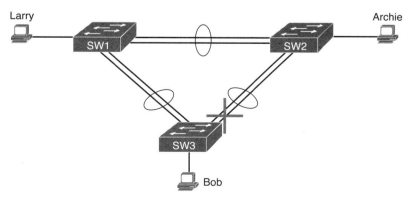

Figure 11-9 *Two-Segment EtherChannels Between Switches*

With each pair of Ethernet links configured as an EtherChannel, STP treats each EtherChannel as a single link. In other words, both links to the same switch must fail for a switch to need to cause STP convergence. Without EtherChannel, if you have multiple parallel links between two switches, STP blocks all the links except one. With EtherChannel, all the parallel links can be up and working at the same time, while reducing the number of times STP must converge, which in turn makes the network more available.

When a switch makes a forwarding decision to send a frame out an EtherChannel, the switch then has to take an extra step in logic: Out which physical interface does it send the frame? The switches have load-balancing logic that let it pick an interface for each frame, with a goal of spreading the traffic load across all active links in the channel. As a result, a LAN design that uses EtherChannels makes much better use of the available bandwidth between switches, while also reducing the number of times that STP must converge.

PortFast

PortFast allows a switch to immediately transition from blocking to forwarding, bypassing listening and learning states. However, the only ports on which you can safely enable PortFast are ports on which you know that no bridges, switches, or other STP-speaking devices are connected. Otherwise, using PortFast risks creating loops, the very thing that the listening and learning states are intended to avoid.

PortFast is most appropriate for connections to end-user devices. If you turn on PortFast on ports connected to end-user devices, when an end-user PC boots, the switch port can move to an STP forwarding state and forward traffic as soon as the PC NIC is active. Without PortFast, each port must wait while the switch confirms that the port is a DP, and then wait while the interface sits in the temporary listening and learning states before settling into the forwarding state.

BPDU Guard

STP opens up the LAN to several different types of possible security exposures. For example:

- An attacker could connect a switch to one of these ports, one with a low STP priority value, and become the root switch. The new STP topology could have worse performance than the desired topology.

- The attacker could plug into multiple ports, into multiple switches, become root, and actually forward much of the traffic in the LAN. Without the networking staff realizing it, the attacker could use a LAN analyzer to copy large numbers of data frames sent through the LAN.

- Users could innocently harm the LAN when they buy and connect an inexpensive consumer LAN switch (one that does not use STP). Such a switch, without any STP function, would not choose to block any ports and would likely cause a loop.

The Cisco BPDU Guard feature helps defeat these kinds of problems by disabling a port if any BPDUs are received on the port. So, this feature is particularly useful on ports that should be used only as an access port and never connected to another switch.

11

In addition, the BPDU Guard feature helps prevent problems with PortFast. PortFast should be enabled only on access ports that connect to user devices, not to other LAN switches. Using BPDU Guard on these same ports makes sense because if another switch connects to such a port, the local switch can disable the port before a loop is created.

Rapid STP (IEEE 802.1w)

As mentioned earlier in this chapter, the IEEE defines STP in the 802.1D IEEE standard. The IEEE has improved the 802.1D protocol with the definition of Rapid Spanning Tree Protocol (RSTP), as defined in standard 802.1w.

RSTP (802.1w) works just like STP (802.1D) in several ways:

- It elects the root switch using the same parameters and tiebreakers.
- It elects the root port on nonroot switches with the same rules.
- It elects designated ports on each LAN segment with the same rules.
- It places each port in either forwarding or blocking state, although RSTP calls the blocking state the discarding state.

RSTP can be deployed alongside traditional 802.1D STP switches, with RSTP features working in switches that support it, and traditional 802.1D STP features working in the switches that support only STP.

With all these similarities, you might be wondering why the IEEE bothered to create RSTP in the first place. The overriding reason is convergence. STP takes a relatively long time to converge (50 seconds with the default settings when all the wait times must be followed). RSTP improves network convergence when topology changes occur, usually converging within a few seconds, or in poor conditions, in about 10 seconds.

IEEE 802.1w RSTP changes and adds to IEEE 802.1D STP in ways that avoid waiting on STP timers, resulting in quick transitions from forwarding to blocking state and vice versa. Specifically, RSTP, compared to STP

- Defines more cases in which the switch can avoid waiting for a timer to expire, such as
  - Adds a new mechanism to replace the root port without any waiting to reach a forwarding state (in some conditions)
  - Adds a new mechanism to replace a designated port, without any waiting to reach a forwarding state (in some conditions)
- Lowers waiting times for cases in which RSTP must wait

For instance, when a link remains up, but hello BPDUs simply stop arriving regularly on a port, STP requires a switch to wait for MaxAge seconds. STP defines the MaxAge timers based on 10 times the hello timer, or 20 seconds, by default. RSTP shortens this timer, defining MaxAge as three times the hello timer.

The best way to get a sense for these mechanisms is to see how the RSTP alternate port and the backup port both work. RSTP uses the term *alternate port* to refer to a switch's other ports that could be used as root port if the root port ever fails. The *backup port* concept provides a backup port on the local switch for a designated port, but only applies to some topologies that frankly do not happen often with a modern datacenter design. However, both are instructive about how RSTP works. Table 11-9 lists these RSTP port roles.

Table 11-9   Port Roles in 802.1w RSTP

Function	Port Roles
Nonroot switch's best path to the root	Root port
Replaces the root port when the root port fails	Alternate port
Switch port designated to forward onto a collision domain	Designated port
Replaces a designated port when a designated port fails	Backup port
Port that is administratively disabled	Disabled port

RSTP and the Alternate (Root) Port

With STP, each nonroot switch places one port in the STP root port (RP) role. RSTP follows that same convention, with the same exact rules for choosing the RP. RSTP then takes another step, naming other possible RPs, identifying them as *alternate ports.*

To be an alternate port, that switch port must also be hearing a hello BPDU that declares the same switch to be the root switch. For instance, in Figure 11-10, SW1 is the root. SW3 will receive hello BPDUs on two ports: G0/1 and G0/2. Both hellos list SW1's BID as the root switch, so whichever port is not the root port meets the criteria to be an alternate port. SW3 picks G0/1 as its root port in this case, and then makes G0/2 an alternate port.

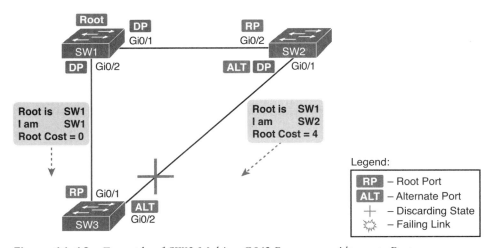

Figure 11-10   *Example of SW3 Making G0/2 Become an Alternate Port*

An alternate port basically works like the second-best option for root port. The alternate port can take over for the former root port, often very rapidly, without requiring a wait in other interim RSTP states. For instance, when the root port fails, or when hellos stop arriving on the original root port, the switch moves the original root port to a disabled role, and transitions to a discarding state (the equivalent of STP's blocking state). Without waiting on any timers, the best alternate port then becomes the new root port. That new root port also does not need to spend time in other states, like learning state, instead moving immediately to forwarding state.

Figure 11-11 shows an example of RSTP convergence in which the link between SW1 and SW3 fails. The figure begins with step 1 being the event that causes the link to fail.

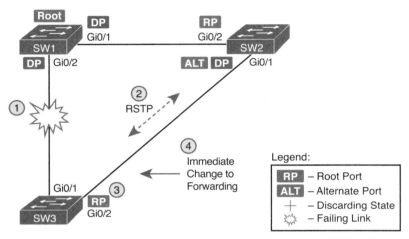

Figure 11-11 *Convergence Events with SW3 G0/1 Failure*

Following the steps in the figure:

Step 1.   The link between SW1 and SW3 fails.

Step 2.   SW3 and SW2 exchange RSTP messages to confirm that SW3 will now transition its former alternate port to be the root port. This action causes SW2 to flush the required MAC table entries.

Step 3.   SW3 transitions G0/1 to the disabled role and G0/2 to the root port role.

Step 4.   SW3 transitions G0/2 to a forwarding state immediately, without using learning state, because this is one case in which RSTP know the transition will not create a loop.

Once SW3 realizes its G0/1 interface has failed, the process shown in the figure takes very little time. None of the processes rely on timers, so as soon as the work can be done, the convergence completes. (This particular convergence example takes about one second in a lab.)

RSTP States and Processes

The depth of the example does not point out all details of RSTP, of course; however, the example does show enough details to discuss RSTP states and internal processes.

Both STP and RSTP use *port states*, but with some differences. First, RSTP keeps both the learning and forwarding states as compared with STP, for the same purposes. However,

RSTP does not even define a listening state, finding it unnecessary. Finally, RSTP renames the blocking state to the discarding state, and redefines its use slightly.

RSTP uses the discarding state for what 802.1D defines as two states: disabled state and blocking state. Blocking should be somewhat obvious by now: the interface can work physically, but STP/RSTP chooses to not forward traffic to avoid loops. STP's disabled state simply meant that the interface was administratively disabled. RSTP simply combines those into a single discarding state.

Table 11-10 shows the list of STP and RSTP states for comparison purposes.

Table 11-10   Port States Compared: 802.1D STP and 802.1w RSTP

Function	802.1D State	802.1w State
Port is administratively disabled.	Disabled	Discarding
Stable state that ignores incoming data frames and is not used to forward data frames.	Blocking	Discarding
Interim state without MAC learning and without forwarding.	Listening	Not used
Interim state with MAC learning and without forwarding.	Learning	Learning
Stable state that allows MAC learning and forwarding of data frames.	Forwarding	Forwarding

RSTP also changes its algorithm processes and message content (compared to STP) to speed convergence. STP waits for a time (forward delay) in both listening and learning states. The reason for this delay in STP is that, at the same time, the switches have all been told to time out their MAC table entries. When the topology changes, the existing MAC table entries may actually cause a loop. With STP, the switches all tell each other (with BPDU messages) that the topology has changed, and to time out any MAC table entries using the forward delay timer. This removes the entries, which is good, but it causes the need to wait in both listening and learning state for forward delay time (default 15 seconds each).

RSTP, to converge more quickly, avoids relying on timers. RSTP switches tell each other (using messages) that the topology has changed. Those messages also direct neighboring switches to flush the contents of their MAC tables in a way that removes all the potentially loop-causing entries, without a wait. As a result, RSTP creates more scenarios in which a formerly discarding port can immediately transition to a forwarding state, without waiting, and without using the learning state, as shown in the example surrounding Figure 11-11.

RSTP Backup (Designated) Ports

To complete the discussion, next consider the idea of a backup for a designated port. This concept, called a *backup port*, can be a bit confusing at first, because it only happens in designs that are a little unlikely today. The reason—a design must use hubs, which then allows the possibility that *one switch connects more than one port to the same collision domain.*

Figure 11-12 shows an example. SW3 and SW4 both connect to the same hub. SW4's port E1/1 happens to win the election as designated port (DP). The other port on SW4 that connects to the same collision domain, E1/2, acts as a backup port.

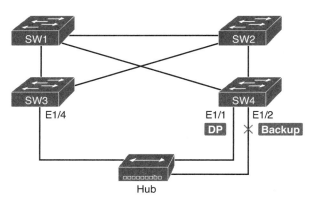

Figure 11-12 *RSTP Backup Port Example*

With a backup port, if the current designated port fails, SW4 can start using the backup port with rapid convergence. For instance, if SW4's E1/1 interface failed, SW4 could transition E1/2 to the DP role, without any delay in moving from discarding state to a forwarding state.

Exam Preparation Tasks

Review All the Key Topics

Review the most important topics from this chapter, noted with the Key Topic icon. Table 11-11 lists these key topics and where each is discussed.

Table 11-11   Key Topics for Chapter 11

Key Topic Element	Description	Page Number
Table 11-2	Lists the three main problems that occur when not using STP in a LAN with redundant links	288
Table 11-3	Lists the reasons why a switch chooses to place an interface into forwarding or blocking state	291
Table 11-4	Lists the most important fields in hello BPDU messages	291
List	Logic for the root switch election	294
Figure 11-6	Shows how switches calculate their root cost	295
List	Logic for choosing a nonroot switch's root port	296
Table 11-6	Lists the original and current default STP port costs for various interface speeds	298
Step list	A summary description of steady-state STP operations	299
Table 11-7	STP timers	299
List	Definitions of what occurs in the listening and learning states	301
Table 11-8	Summary of 802.1D states	301
Table 11-10	Comparison of port states for 802.1D STP and 802.1w RSTP	307

Complete the Tables and Lists from Memory

Print a copy of DVD Appendix I, "Memory Tables," or at least the section for this chapter, and complete the tables and lists from memory. DVD Appendix J, "Memory Tables Answer Key," includes completed tables and lists to check your work.

Definitions of Key Terms

After your first reading of the chapter, try to define these key terms, but do not be concerned about getting them all correct at that time. Chapter 23, "Final Review," directs you in how to use these terms for late-stage preparation for the exam.

blocking state, BPDU Guard, bridge ID, bridge protocol data unit (BPDU), designated port, EtherChannel, forward delay, forwarding state, hello BPDU, IEEE 802.1D, learning state, listening state, MaxAge, PortFast, root port, root switch, root cost, Spanning Tree Protocol (STP), Rapid STP (RSTP), IEEE 802.1w, alternate port, backup port, discarding state

This chapter covers the following exam topics:

2.3 Describe and Configure enhanced switching technologies

2.3b VLAN

2.3d STP

Cisco Nexus Spanning Tree Protocol Implementation

Cisco Nexus switches enable Spanning Tree Protocol (STP) by default on all interfaces in every VLAN. However, network engineers who work with medium-size to large-size data centers usually want to configure at least some STP settings, with the goal of influencing the choices made by STP. For instance, a network engineer configures so that, when all switches and links work, the engineer knows which switch is the root and which ports block. The configuration can also be set so that when links or switches fail, the engineer can predict the STP topology in those cases, as well.

This chapter discusses the configuration options for STP. The first major section weaves a story of how to change different settings, per VLAN, with the **show** commands that reveal the current STP status affected by each configuration command. The second major section of this chapter looks at how to improve STP operations, which includes a deeper examination of the STP rules discussed in Chapter 11, "Spanning Tree Protocol Concepts," plus more discussion of various switch **show** commands.

"Do I Know This Already?" Quiz

Use the "Do I Know This Already?" quiz to help decide whether you might want to skim this chapter, or a major section, moving more quickly to the "Exam Preparation Tasks" section near the end of the chapter. You can find the answers at the bottom of the page following the quiz. For thorough explanations, see Appendix A, "Answers to the 'Do I Know This Already?' Quizzes."

Table 12-1 "Do I Know This Already?" Foundation Topics Section-to-Question Mapping

Foundation Topics Section	Questions
STP Configuration and Verification	1–3
Improving STP Operations	4–6

1. On a Nexus switch, which of the following commands change the value of the bridge ID? (Choose two answers.)

   a. spanning-tree bridge-id *value*

   b. spanning-tree vlan *vlan-number* root {primary | secondary}

   c. spanning-tree vlan *vlan-number* priority *value*

   d. set spanning-tree priority *value*

2. Examine the following extract from the **show spanning-tree** command on a Cisco Nexus switch:

```
Spanning tree enabled protocol rstp
  Root ID    Priority    8193
             Address     c84c.75fa.601e
             This bridge is the root
             Hello Time  2  sec  Max Age 20 sec  Forward Delay 15 sec


  Bridge ID  Priority    8193   (priority 8192 sys-id-ext 1)
             Address     c84c.75fa.601e
             Hello Time  2  sec  Max Age 20 sec  Forward Delay 15 sec


Interface        Role Sts Cost      Prio.Nbr Type
---------------- ---- --- --------- -------- ------------------------------
Po15             Desg FWD 1         128.4110 (vPC) P2p
Po16             Desg FWD 1         128.4111 (vPC) P2p
```

Which of the following answers is true about the switch on which this command output was gathered?

a. The information is about the STP instance for VLAN 1.

b. The information is about the STP instance for VLAN 3.

c. The command output confirms that this switch cannot possibly be the root switch.

d. The command output confirms that this switch is currently the root switch.

3. A switch's Eth1/1 interface, a trunk that supports VLANs 1–10, has a speed of 10 Gbps. The switch currently has all default settings for STP. Which of the following actions results in the switch using an STP cost of 2 for that interface in VLAN 3? (Choose two answers.)

a. spanning-tree cost 2

b. spanning-tree port-cost 19

c. spanning-tree vlan 3 port-cost 19

d. Adding no configuration

4. An engineer configures a switch to put interfaces Eth1/1 and Eth1/2 into the same EtherChannel. Which of the following terms is used in the configuration commands?

a. EtherChannel

b. PortChannel

c. Ethernet-Channel

d. Channel-group

5. Switch SW3 is receiving only two hello BPDUs, both from the same root switch, received on the two interfaces listed as follows:

```
SW3# show interfaces status
Port       Name      Status       Vlan    Duplex    Speed    Type
Eth1/13              connected    1       full      10G      10Gbase-SR
Eth1/1               connected    1       full      10G      10Gbase-SR
```

SW3 has no STP-related configuration commands. The hello received on Eth1/13 lists root cost 10, and the hello received on Eth1/1 lists root cost 20. Which of the following is true about STP on SW3?

   a. SW3 will choose Eth1/13 as its root port.

   b. SW3 will choose Eth1/1 as its root port.

   c. SW3's Eth1/13 will become a designated port.

   d. SW3's Eth1/1 will become a designated port.

6. Which of the following commands lists a nonroot switch's root cost? (Choose two answers.)

   a. show spanning-tree root

   b. show spanning-tree root cost

   c. show spanning-tree bridge

   d. show spanning-tree

12

Foundation Topics

STP Configuration and Verification

By default, all Cisco Nexus switches are enabled for Rapid Per-VLAN Spanning Tree (Rapid-PVST/802.1w), which is backward compatible with Per-VLAN Spanning Tree (PVST/802.1D) for interoperability and migration purposes. You can buy some Cisco switches and connect them with Ethernet cables in a redundant topology, and STP will ensure that frames do not loop. And you never even have to think about changing any settings.

This chapter focuses on only Rapid-PVST (802.1w). As mentioned earlier Cisco Nexus switches default to using Rapid-PVST, but to set a switch to use this mode, use the **spanning-tree mode rapid-pvst** global command. Alternatively, Cisco Nexus switches allow Multiple Spanning Tree (MST) with the **spanning-tree mode mst** command. We do not cover MST because it is a more advanced concept and out of scope for DCICN.

Although Rapid-PVST works without any configuration, all data centers regardless of size benefit from some Rapid-PVST configuration. With all defaults, the switches choose the root based on the lowest burned-in MAC address on the switches because they all default to use the same STP priority. As a better option, configure the switches so that the root is predictable.

For instance, Figure 12-1 shows a typical data center design model, with two distribution/aggregation layer switches (D1 and D2). The design may have dozens of access layer switches that connect to servers; the figure shows just three access switches (A1, A2, and A3). For a variety of reasons, most network engineers make the distribution layer switches be the root. For instance, the configuration could make D1 be the root by having a lower priority, with D2 configured with the next lower priority, so it becomes root if D1 fails.

This first section of the chapter examines a variety of topics that somehow relate to STP configuration. It begins with a look at STP configuration options, as a way to link the concepts of Chapter 11 to the configuration choices in this chapter. Following that, this section introduces some **show** commands for the purpose of verifying the default STP settings before changing any configuration. At that point, this section shows examples of how to configure core STP features and some of the optional STP features.

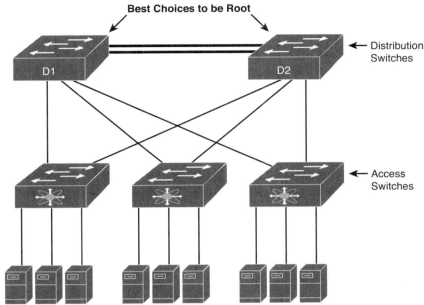

Figure 12-1   *Typical Configuration Choice: Making Distribution/Aggregation Switch Be Root*

Connecting STP Concepts to STP Configuration Options

If you think back to the details of STP operation in Chapter 11, STP uses two types of numbers for most of its decisions: the bridge ID (BID) and STP port costs. Focusing on those two types of numbers, consider this summary of what STP does behind the scenes:

- Use the BID to elect the root switch, electing the switch with the numerically lowest BID.
- Use the total STP cost in each path to the root, when each nonroot switch chooses its own root port (RP).
- Use each switch's root cost, which is in turn based on STP port costs, when switches decide which switch port becomes the designated port (DP) on each LAN segment.

Unsurprisingly, Cisco switches let you configure part of a switch's BID and the STP port cost, which in turn influences the choices each switch makes with STP.

Per-VLAN Configuration Settings

Beyond supporting the configuration of the BID and STP port costs, Cisco switches support configuring both settings per VLAN. Cisco Nexus switches implement Rapid-PVST (often abbreviated as simply RPVST today), and RPVST creates a different instance of Spanning Tree for each VLAN. The main difference between PVST+ and Rapid PVST is the convergence time when using RPVST has been greatly reduced. So, before looking at the tunable STP parameters, you need to have a basic understanding of RPVST+, because the configuration settings can differ for each instance of STP.

RPVST+ gives engineers a load-balancing tool with STP. By changing some STP configuration parameters differently for different VLANs, the engineer could cause switches to pick different RPs and DPs in different VLANs. As a result, some traffic in some VLANs can be forwarded over one trunk, and traffic for other VLANs can be forwarded over a different trunk.

Figure 12-2 shows the basic idea, with SW3 forwarding odd-numbered VLAN traffic over the left trunk (Eth1/1) and even-numbered VLANs over the right trunk (Eth1/2).

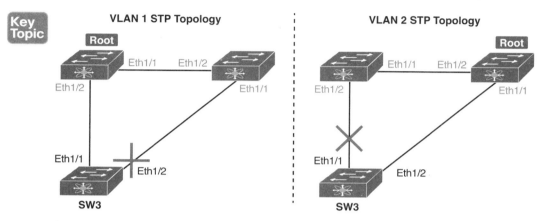

Figure 12-2   *Load Balancing with PVST+*

The next few pages look specifically at how to change the BID and STP port cost settings, per VLAN, when using the default RPVST+ mode.

The Bridge ID and System ID Extension

Originally, combining the switch's 2-byte priority and its 6-byte MAC address formed a switch's BID. Later, the IEEE changed the rules, splitting the original Priority field into two separate fields, as shown in Figure 12-3: a 4-bit Priority field and a 12-bit subfield called the *System ID Extension* (which represents the VLAN ID).

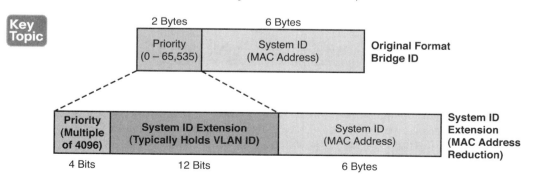

Figure 12-3   *STP System ID Extension*

Cisco switches let you configure the BID, but only the priority part. The switch fills in its universal (burned-in) MAC address as the system ID. It also plugs in the VLAN ID of a VLAN in the 12-bit System ID Extension field. The only part configurable by the network engineer is the 4-bit Priority field.

Configuring the number to put in the Priority field, however, is one of the strangest things to configure on a Cisco router or switch. As shown at the top of Figure 12-3, the Priority field was originally a 16-bit number, which represented a decimal number from 0 to 65,535. Because of that history, the current configuration command (**spanning-tree vlan** *vlan-id* **priority** *x*) requires a decimal number between 0 and 65,535. And not just any number in that range, either: It must be a multiple of 4096: 0, 4096, 8192, 12288, and so on, up through 61,440.

The switch still sets the first 4 bits of the BID based on the configured value. As it turns out, of the 16 allowed multiples of 4096, from 0 through 61,440, each has a different binary value in their first 4 bits: 0000, 0001, 0010, and so on, up through 1111. The switch sets the true 4-bit priority based on the first 4 bits of the configured value.

Although the history and configuration might make the BID priority idea seem a bit convoluted, having an extra 12-bit field in the BID works well in practice because it can be used to identify the VLAN ID. VLAN IDs range from 1 to 4094, requiring 12 bits. Cisco switches place the VLAN ID into the System ID Extension field, so each switch has a unique BID per VLAN.

For example, a switch configured with VLANs 1 through 4, with a default base priority of 32,768, has a default STP priority of 32,769 in VLAN 1, 32,770 in VLAN 2, 32,771 in VLAN 3, and so on. So, you can view the 16-bit priority as a base priority (as configured on the **spanning-tree vlan** *vlan-id* **priority** *x* command) plus the VLAN ID.

Per-VLAN Port Costs

Each switch interface defaults its per-VLAN STP cost based on the IEEE recommendations listed in Table 1-6 in Chapter 1. On interfaces that support multiple speeds, Cisco switches base the cost on the current actual speed. So, if an interface negotiates to use a lower speed, the default STP cost reflects that lower speed. If the interface negotiates to use a different speed, the switch dynamically changes the STP port cost as well.

Alternatively, you can configure a switch's STP port cost with the **spanning-tree [vlan** *vlan-id*] **cost** *cost* interface subcommand. You see this command most often on trunks because setting the cost on trunks has an impact on the switch's root cost, whereas setting STP costs on access ports does not.

For the command itself, it can include the VLAN ID, or not. The command only needs a **vlan** parameter on trunk ports to set the cost per VLAN. On a trunk, if the command omits the VLAN parameter, it sets the STP cost for all VLANs whose cost is not set by a **spanning-tree vlan** *x* **cost** command for that VLAN.

STP Configuration Option Summary

Table 12-2 summarizes the default settings for both the BID and the port costs and lists the optional configuration commands covered in this chapter.

12

Table 12-2   STP Defaults and Configuration Options

Setting	Default	Command(s) to Change Default
BID priority	Base: 32,768	**spanning-tree vlan** *vlan-id* **root** {**primary** | **secondary**}
		spanning-tree vlan *vlan-id* **priority** *priority*
Interface cost	100 for 10 Mbps	**spanning-tree vlan** *vlan-id* **cost** *cost*
	19 for 100 Mbps	
	4 for 1 Gbps	
	2 for 10 Gbps	
PortFast	Not enabled	**spanning-tree portfast**
BPDU Guard	Not enabled	**spanning-tree bpduguard enable**

Next, the configuration section shows how to examine the operation of STP in a simple network, along with how to change these optional settings.

Verifying STP Operation

Before taking a look at how to change the configuration, first consider a few STP verification commands. Looking at these commands first will help reinforce the default STP settings. In particular, the examples in this section use the network shown in Figure 12-4.

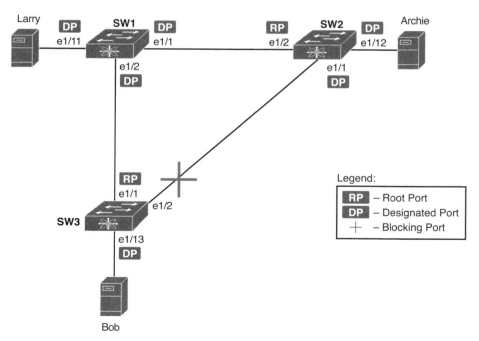

Figure 12-4 *Sample Topology for STP Configuration and Verification Examples*

Example 12-1 begins the discussion with a useful command for STP: the **show spanning-tree vlan 10** command. This command identifies the root switch and lists settings on the local switch. Example 12-1 lists the output of this command on both SW1 and SW2, as explained following the example.

Example 12-1   *STP Status with Default STP Parameters on SW1 and SW2*

```
SW1# show spanning-tree vlan 10


VLAN0010
  Spanning tree enabled protocol rstp
  Root ID    Priority    8193
             Address     c84c.75fa.6014
             This bridge is the root
             Hello Time    2 sec  Max Age 20 sec  Forward Delay 15 sec


  Bridge ID  Priority    8193    (priority 8192 sys-id-ext 1)
             Address     c84c.75fa.6014
             Hello Time    2 sec  Max Age 20 sec  Forward Delay 15 sec


Interface             Role Sts Cost      Prio.Nbr Type
------------------- ---- --- --------- -------- --------------------------------
Eth1/11               Desg FWD 4         128.11   P2p Edge
Eth1/1                Desg FWD 2         128.25   P2p
Eth1/2                Desg FWD 2         128.26   P2p
```

```
SW2# show spanning-tree vlan 10


VLAN0010
  Spanning tree enabled protocol rstp
  Root ID    Priority    32778
             Address     c84c.75fa.6014
             Cost        2
             Port        26 (Ethernet1/2)
             Hello Time    2 sec  Max Age 20 sec  Forward Delay 15 sec


  Bridge ID  Priority    32778   (priority 32768 sys-id-ext 10)
             Address     c84c.75fa.6014
             Hello Time    2 sec  Max Age 20 sec  Forward Delay 15 sec



Interface             Role Sts Cost      Prio.Nbr Type
------------------- ---- --- --------- -------- --------------------------------
Eth1/12               Desg FWD 4         128.12   P2p
Eth1/1                Desg FWD 2         128.25   P2p
Eth1/2                Root FWD 2         128.26   P2p
```

12

Example 12-1 begins with the output of the **show spanning-tree vlan 10** command on SW1. This command first lists three major groups of messages: one group of messages about the root switch, followed by another group about the local switch, and ending with interface role and status information. In this case, SW1 lists its own BID as the root, with even a specific statement that "This bridge is the root," confirming that SW1 is now the root of the VLAN 10 STP topology.

Next, compare the highlighted lines of the same command on SW2 in the lower half of the example. SW2 lists SW1's BID details as the root; in other words, SW2 agrees that SW1 has won the root election. SW2 does not list the phrase "This bridge is the root." SW1 then lists its own (different) BID details in the lines after the details about the root's BID.

The output also confirms a few default values. First, each switch lists the priority part of the BID as a separate number: 32778. This value comes from the default priority of 32768, plus VLAN 10, for a total of 32778. The output also shows the interface cost Ten Gigabit Ethernet interfaces, defaulting to 2.

Finally, the bottom of the output from the **show spanning-tree** command lists each interface in the VLAN, including trunks, with the STP port role and port state listed. For instance, on switch SW1, the output lists three interfaces, with a role of Desg for designated port (DP) and a state of FWD for forwarding. SW2 lists three interfaces, two DPs, and one root port, so all three are in an FWD or forwarding state.

Example 12-1 shows a lot of good STP information, but two other commands, shown in Example 12-2, work better for listing BID information in a shorter form. The first, **show spanning-tree root**, lists the root's BID for each VLAN. This command also lists other details, like the local switch's root cost and root port. The other command, **show spanning-tree vlan 10 bridge**, breaks out the BID into its component parts. In this example, it shows SW2's priority as the default of 32768, the VLAN ID of 10, and the MAC address.

Example 12-2 *Listing Root Switch and Local Switch BIDs on Switch SW2*

```
SW2# show spanning-tree root


                                     Root    Hello Max Fwd
Vlan                    Root ID      Cost    Time  Age Dly   Root Port
---------------- -------------------- --------- ----- --- --- ------------
VLAN0001          32769 c84c.75fa.6014    23      2    20  15   Eth1/1
VLAN0010          32778 c84c.75fa.6014     4      2    20  15   Eth1/2
VLAN0020          32788 c84c.75fa.6014     4      2    20  15   Eth1/2
VLAN0030          32798 c84c.75fa.6014     4      2    20  15   Eth1/2
VLAN0040          32808 c84c.75fa.6014     4      2    20  15   Eth1/2


SW2# show spanning-tree vlan 10 bridge


                                              Hello  Max  Fwd
Vlan                    Bridge ID             Time   Age  Dly  Protocol
---------------- ------------------------------- ----- --- --- --------
VLAN0010         32778 (32768,  10) c84c.75fa.6014   2    20   15  rstp
```

Note that both the commands in Example 12-2 have a VLAN option: **show spanning-tree** [**vlan** *x*] **root** and **show spanning-tree** [**vlan** *x*] **bridge**. Without the VLAN listed, each command lists one line per VLAN; with the VLAN, the output lists the same information, but just for that one VLAN.

Improving STP Operation

In the previous section we discussed how to configure STP on Cisco Nexus switches. To round out this chapter, we will now dig in to how to improve Spanning Tree for optimal use in data-center networks.

Configuring STP Port Costs

Changing the STP port costs requires a simple interface subcommand: **spanning-tree** [**vlan** *x*] **cost** *x*. To show how it works, consider Example 12-3, where we change the spanning-tree port cost on SW3 from Figure 12-5. We will then examine what changes in Example 12-4.

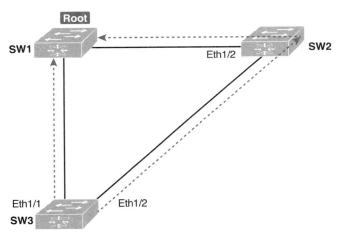

Figure 12-5   *Analysis of SW3's Current Root Cost of 4 with Defaults*

Back in Figure 12-4, with default settings, SW1 became root, and SW3 blocked on its Eth1/2 interface. A brief scan of the figure, based on the default STP cost of 2 for Ten Gigabit interfaces, shows that SW3 should have found a cost 2 path and a cost 4 path to reach the root, as shown in Figure 12-5.

To show the effects of changing the port cost, Example 12-3 shows a change to SW3's configuration, setting its Eth1/1 port cost higher so that the better path to the root goes out SW3's Eth1/2 port instead.

Example 12-3   *Manipulating STP Port Cost*

```
SW3# configure terminal
Enter configuration commands, one per line.  End with CNTL/Z.
SW3(config)# interface Ethernet1/1
SW3(config-if)# spanning-tree vlan 10 cost 30
SW3(config-if)# ^Z
```

12

This example shows the configuration to change SW3's port cost, in VLAN 10, to 30, with the **spanning-tree vlan 10 cost 30** interface subcommand. Based on the figure, the root cost through SW3's Eth1/1 will now be 30 instead of 4. As a result, SW3's best cost to reach the root is cost 4, with SW3's Eth1/2 as its root port.

Using **show** commands later can confirm the same choice by SW3, to now use its Eth1/2 port as its RP. Example 12-4 shows the new STP port cost setting on SW3, along with the new root port and root cost, using the **show spanning-tree vlan 10** command. Note that Eth1/2 is now listed as the root port. The top of the output lists SW3's root cost as 4, matching the analysis shown in Figure 12-5.

Example 12-4 *New STP Status and Settings on SW3*

```
SW3# show spanning-tree vlan 10


VLAN0010
  Spanning tree enabled protocol ieee
  Root ID     Priority    32778
              Address     1833.9d7b.0e80
              Cost        4
              Port        26 (Ethernet1/2)
              Hello Time   2 sec  Max Age 20 sec  Forward Delay 15 sec

  Bridge ID   Priority    32778  (priority 32768 sys-id-ext 10)
              Address     f47f.35cb.d780
              Hello Time   2 sec  Max Age 20 sec  Forward Delay 15 sec


Interface          Role Sts  Cost      Prio.Nbr Type
------------------ ---- ---  --------- -------- --------------------------------
Eth1/23            Desg FWD  4         128.23   P2p
Eth1/1             ·Altn BLK  30        128.25   P2p
Eth1/2             Root FWD  2         128.26   P2p
```

Configuring Priority to Influence the Root Election

The other big STP configuration option is to influence the root election by changing the priority of a switch. The priority can be set explicitly with the **spanning-tree vlan** *vlan-id* **priority** *value* global configuration command, which sets the base priority of the switch. (This is the command that requires a parameter of a multiple of 4096.)

However, Cisco gives us a better configuration option than configuring a specific priority value. In most designs, the network engineers pick two switches to be root: one to be root if all switches are up, and another to take over if the first switch fails. Switch IOS supports this idea with the **spanning-tree vlan** *vlan-id* **root primary** and **spanning-tree vlan** *vlan-id* **root secondary** commands

The **spanning-tree vlan** *vlan-id* **root primary** command tells the switch to set its priority low enough to become root right now. The switch looks at the current root in that VLAN, and at the root's priority. Then the local switch chooses a priority value that causes the local switch to take over as root.

Remembering that Cisco switches use a default base priority of 32,768, this command chooses the base priority as follows:

- If the current root has a base priority higher than 24,576, *the local switch uses a base priority of 24,576.*
- If the current root's base priority is 24,576 or lower, the local switch sets its base priority to the highest multiple of 4096 that still results in the local switch becoming root.

For the switch intended to take over as the root if the first switch fails, use the **spanning-tree vlan** *vlan-id* **root secondary** command. This command is much like the **spanning-tree vlan** *vlan-id* **root primary** command, but with a priority value worse than the primary switch but better than all the other switches. This command sets the switch's base priority to 28,672 regardless of the current root's current priority value.

For example, in Figures 12-4 and 12-5, SW1 was the root switch, and as shown in various commands, all three switches defaulted to use a base priority of 32,768. Example 12-5 shows a configuration that makes SW2 the primary root, and SW1 the secondary, just to show the role move from one to the other. These commands result in SW2 having a base priority of 24,576, and SW1 having a base priority of 28,672.

Example 12-5   *Making SW2 Become Root Primary and SW1 Root Secondary*

```
! First, on SW2:
SW2# configure terminal
Enter configuration commands, one per line.  End with CNTL/Z.
SW2(config)# spanning-tree vlan 10 root primary
SW2(config)# ^Z

! Next, SW1 is configured to back-up SW1
SW1# configure terminal
Enter configuration commands, one per line.  End with CNTL/Z.
SW1(config)# spanning-tree vlan 10 root secondary
SW1(config)# ^Z
SW1#


! The next command shows the local switch's BID (SW1)
SW1# show spanning-tree vlan 10 bridge


                                        Hello  Max  Fwd
Vlan                     Bridge ID       Time  Age  Dly  Protocol
---------------- -------------------------------- ----- --- --- --------
VLAN0010          28682 (28672,  10) 1833.9d7b.0e80   2    20   15  rstp


! The next command shows the root's BID (SW2)
SW1# show spanning-tree vlan 10 root
```

12

```
                                      Root   Hello Max Fwd
Vlan                  Root ID         Cost   Time  Age Dly Root Port
---------------- -------------------- --------- ----- --- --- ------------
VLAN0010         24586 1833.9d7b.1380       4     2  20  15  Eth1/1
```

The two **show** commands in the output clearly point out the resulting priority values on each switch. First, the **show spanning-tree bridge** command lists the local switch's BID information, while the **show spanning-tree root** command lists the root's BID, plus the local switch's root cost and root port (assuming it is not the root switch). So, SW1 lists its own BID, with priority 28,682 (base 28,672, with VLAN 10) with the **show spanning-tree bridge** command. Still on SW1, the output lists the root's priority as 24,586 in VLAN 10, implied as base 24,576 plus 10 for VLAN 10, with the **show spanning-tree root** command.

Note that alternatively you could have configured the priority settings specifically. SW1 could have used the **spanning-tree vlan 10 priority 28672** command, with SW2 using the **spanning-tree vlan 10 priority 24576** command. In this particular case, both options would result in the same STP operation.

Spanning-Tree Port Types

Cisco NX-OS provides three basic switch port types to ease in configuration. These port types bundle in extensions or features that are commonly configured on a particular type of interface:

- **Network ports:** Network ports define connections between two bridges or switches. By default, a feature called *Bridge Assurance* is enabled on these ports.

- **Normal ports:** A switchport is a normal port in respect to spanning tree and has no added configuration. These ports operate in standard bridging mode.

- **Edge ports:** Because these ports are used to connect to non-bridging Layer 2 devices, such as hosts, they transition immediately into forwarding state bypassing listening and learning states. They enable a feature known as *PortFast* to accomplish this.

NOTE   Bridge Assurance is a new feature that allows all ports to send and receive bridge protocol data units (BPDU) on all VLANs regardless of their state. This creates a bidirectional keepalive so that if a malfunctioning bridge stops sending BPDUs the ports on the BA enabled switch will be placed into inconsistent state. This helps prevent a malfunctioning bridge from creating loops. Bridge Assurance is enabled by default on all interfaces in the spanning-tree port type of network.

Configuring PortFast and BPDU Guard

In Chapter 11, you learned about the functionality and benefits of using PortFast and BPDU Guard on a host interface. Here you learn how to configure them on Nexus switches.

You can easily configure the PortFast and BPDU Guard features on any interface, but with two different configuration options. One option works best when you only want to enable these features on a few ports, and the other works best when you want to enable these features on most every access port.

First, to enable the features on just one port at a time, use the **spanning-tree port type edge** command to enable PortFast and the **spanning-tree bpduguard enable** interface subcommands. Example 12-6 shows an example of the process, with SW3's Eth1/4 interface enabling both features. (Also, note the long warning message NX-OS lists when enabling PortFast; using PortFast on a port connected to other switches can indeed cause serious problems.)

Example 12-6 *Enabling PortFast and BPDU Guard on One Interface*

```
SW3# configure terminal
Enter configuration commands, one per line.  End with CNTL/Z.
SW3(config)# interface Ethernet1/4
SW3(config-if)# spanning-tree port type edge
Warning: Edge port type (portfast) should only be enabled on ports connected to a
single host. Connecting hubs, concentrators, switches, bridges, etc... to this inter-
face when edge port type (portfast) is enabled, can cause temporary bridging loops.
 Use with CAUTION


Edge Port Type (Portfast) has been configured on Ethernet1/4 but will only
 have effect when the interface is in a non-trunking mode.
SW3(config-if)# spanning-tree bpduguard ?
  disable  Disable BPDU guard for this interface
  enable   Enable BPDU guard for this interface


SW3(config-if)# spanning-tree bpduguard enable
SW3(config-if)# ^Z
SW3#
*Mar  1 07:53:47.808: %SYS-5-CONFIG_I: Configured from console by console
SW3# show running-config interface Eth1/4
Building configuration...


Current configuration : 138 bytes
!
interface Ethernet1/4
 switchport access vlan 104
 spanning-tree port type edge
 spanning-tree bpduguard enable
end


SW3# show spanning-tree interface Ethernet1/4 edge
VLAN0104              enabled
```

12

The second half of the example confirms the configuration on the interface and the PortFast status. The **show running-config** command simply confirms that the switch recorded the two configuration commands. The **show spanning-tree interface Ethernet1/4 edge** command lists the PortFast status of the interface; note that the status only shows up as enabled if PortFast is configured and the interface is up.

The alternative configuration works better when most of a switch's ports need PortFast and BPDU Guard. By default, switches disable both features on each interface. The alternative configuration lets you reverse the default, making the default for PortFast and BPDU Guard to be enabled on each interface. Then you have the option to disable the features on a port-by-port basis.

To change the defaults, use these two global commands:

- **spanning-tree port type edge default**
- **spanning-tree port type edge bpduguard default**

Then, to override the defaults, to disable the features, use these interface subcommands:

- **no spanning-tree port type edge**
- **spanning-tree bpduguard disable**

Configuring EtherChannel

As introduced back in Chapter 1, "The TCP/IP and OSI Networking Models," two neighboring switches can treat multiple parallel links between each other as a single logical link called an *EtherChannel*. STP operates on the EtherChannel, instead of the individual physical links, so that STP either forwards or blocks on the entire logical EtherChannel for a given VLAN. As a result, a switch in a forwarding state can then load balance traffic over all the physical links in the EtherChannel. Without EtherChannel, only one of the parallel links between two switches would be allowed to forward traffic, with the rest of the links blocked by STP.

EtherChannel may be one of the most challenging switch features to make work. First, the configuration has several options, so you have to remember the details of which options work together. Second, the switches also require a variety of other interface settings to match among all the links in the channel, so you have to know those settings as well.

This section focuses on the correct EtherChannel configuration. The later section titled "Troubleshooting EtherChannel" looks at many of the potential problems with EtherChannel, including all those other configuration settings that a switch checks before allowing the EtherChannel to work.

Configuring a Manual EtherChannel

The simplest way to configure an EtherChannel is to add the correct **channel-group** configuration command to each physical interface, on each switch, all with the **on** keyword. The **on** keyword tells the switches to place a physical interface into an EtherChannel.

Before getting into the configuration and verification, however, you need to start using three terms as synonyms: *EtherChannel*, *PortChannel*, and *channel-group*. NX-OS uses the

channel-group configuration command, but then to display its status, NX-OS uses the **show port-channel summary** command.

To configure an EtherChannel manually, follow these steps:

Step 1.   Add the **channel-group** *number* **mode on** interface subcommand under each physical interface that should be in the channel.

Step 2.   Use the same number for all commands on the same switch, but the channel-group number on the neighboring switch can differ.

Example 12-7 shows a simple example, with two links between switches SW1 and SW2, as shown in Figure 12-6. The configuration shows SW1's two interfaces placed into channel-group 1, with two **show** commands to follow.

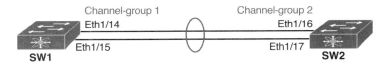

Figure 12-6   *Sample Datacenter Used in EtherChannel Example*

Example 12-7   *Configuring and Monitoring EtherChannel*

```
SW1# configure terminal
Enter configuration commands, one per line.  End with CNTL/Z.
SW1(config)# interface Eth1/14
SW1(config-if)# channel-group 1 mode on
SW1(config)# interface Eth1/15
SW1(config-if)# channel-group 1 mode on
SW1(config-if)# ^Z

SW1# show spanning-tree vlan 3

VLAN0003
  Spanning tree enabled protocol ieee
  Root ID    Priority    28675
             Address     0019.e859.5380
             Cost        4
             Port        72 (Port-channel1)
             Hello Time   2 sec  Max Age 20 sec  Forward Delay 15 sec

  Bridge ID  Priority    28675  (priority 28672 sys-id-ext 3)
             Address     0019.e86a.6f80
             Hello Time   2 sec  Max Age 20 sec  Forward Delay 15 sec
             Aging Time 300
```

12

```
Interface        Role Sts Cost      Prio.Nbr Type
---------------- ---- --- --------- -------- -------------------------------
Po1              Root FWD 12          128.64   P2p Peer(STP)


SW1# show port-channel summary
Flags:  D - Down        P - Up in port-channel (members)
        I - Individual  H - Hot-standby (LACP only)
        s - Suspended   r - Module-removed
        S - Switched    R - Routed
        U - Up (port-channel)
        M - Not in use. Min-links not met
--------------------------------------------------------------------------
Group   Port-   Type    Protocol        Member Ports
        Channel
1       Po1(SU)  Eth     NONE     Eth1/14(P)   Eth1/15(P)
```

Take a few moments to look at the output in the two **show** commands in the example, as well. First, the **show spanning-tree** command lists Po1, short for PortChannel1, as an interface. This interface exists because of the **channel-group** commands using the **1** parameter. STP no longer operates on physical interfaces Eth1/14 and Eth1/15, instead operating on the PortChannel1 interface, so only that interface is listed in the output.

Next, note the output of the **show port-channel 1 summary** command. It lists as a heading "Port-channel," with Po1 below it. It also lists both Eth1/14 and Eth1/15 in the list of ports, with a (P) beside each. Per the legend, the *P* means that the ports are bundled in the PortChannel, which is a code that means these ports have passed all the configuration checks and are valid to be included in the channel.

Configuring Dynamic EtherChannels

Cisco switches support two different protocols that allow the switches to negotiate whether a particular link becomes part of an EtherChannel. Basically, the configuration enables the protocol for a particular channel-group number. At that point, the switch can use the protocol to send messages to/from the neighboring switch and discover whether their configuration settings pass all checks. If a given physical link passes, the link is added to the EtherChannel and used; if not, it is placed in a down state, and not used, until the configuration inconsistency can be resolved.

For now, this section focuses on how to make it work, with the later "Troubleshooting EtherChannel" section focusing on these specific settings that can make it fail.

Cisco switches support the Cisco proprietary Port Aggregation Protocol (PAgP) and the IEEE standard Link Aggregation Control Protocol (LACP), based on IEEE standard 802.3ad. Although differences exist between the two, to the depth discussed here, they both accomplish the same task: negotiate so that only links that pass the configuration checks are actually used in an EtherChannel. Cisco NX-OS only supports LACP or manual configuration of channels, as shown before.

To configure LACP protocol, a switch uses the **channel-group** configuration commands on each switch, but with a keyword that either means "use this protocol and begin negotiations" or "use this protocol and wait for the other switch to begin negotiations." As shown in Figure 12-7, the **active** and **passive** keywords enable LACP. With these options, at least one side has to begin the negotiations. In other words, with LACP, at least one of the two sides must use **active**.

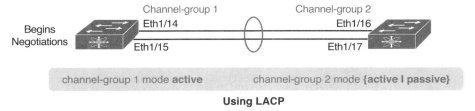

Figure 12-7   *Correct EtherChannel Configuration Combinations*

> **NOTE**   Do not use the **on** parameter on one end and either **active** or **passive** on the neighboring switch. The **on** option does not use LACP, so a configuration that uses **on**, with LACP options on the other end, would prevent the EtherChannel from working.

For instance, you could replace the configuration in Example 12-7 with **channel-group 1 mode active** for both interfaces, with SW2 using **channel-group 2 mode passive**. In NX-OS, we would need to enable the feature for LACP to work. Example 12-8 shows the enabling of LACP.

Example 12-8   *Enabling Feature Set for LACP*

```
SW1(config)# feature lacp
SW1(config)# show feature | inc lacp
lacp                  1         enabled
```

Troubleshooting EtherChannel

EtherChannels can prove particularly challenging to troubleshoot for a couple of reasons. First, you have to be careful to match the correct configuration, and there are many more incorrect configuration combinations than there are correct combinations. Second, many interface settings must match on the physical links, both on the local switch and on the neighboring switch, before a switch will add the physical link to the channel. This last topic in the chapter works through both sets of issues.

Incorrect Options on the channel-group Command

Earlier, the section titled "Configuring EtherChannel" listed the small set of working configuration options on the **channel-group** command. Those rules can be summarized as follows, for a single EtherChannel:

12

1. On the local switch, all the **channel-group** commands for all the physical interfaces must use the same channel-group number.

2. The **channel-group** number can be different on the neighboring switches.

3. If using the **on** keyword, you must use it on the corresponding interfaces of both switches.

4. If you use the **active** keyword on one switch, the switch uses LACP; the other switch must use either **active** or **passive.**

These rules summarize the correct configuration options, but the options actually leave many more incorrect choices. The following list shows some incorrect configurations that the switches allow, even though they would result in the EtherChannel not working. The list compares the configuration on one switch to another based on the physical interface configuration. Each lists the reasons why the configuration is incorrect:

■ Configuring the **on** keyword on one switch, and **active**, or **passive** on the other switch. The **on** keyword does not enable LACP, and the other options rely on LACP.

■ Configuring the **passive** keyword on both switches. Both use LACP, but both wait on the other switch to begin negotiations.

Example 12-9 shows an example that matches the last item in the list. In this case, SW1's two ports (Eth1/14 and Eth1/15) have been configured with the **passive** keyword, and SW2's matching Eth1/16 and Eth1/17 have been configured with the **passive** keyword. The example lists some telling status information about the failure, with notes following the example.

Example 12-9 *Ruling Out Switches as Root Based on Having a Root Port*

```
SW1# show port-channel summary
Flags:  D - Down         P - Up in port-channel (members)
        I - Individual   H - Hot-standby (LACP only)
        s - Suspended    r - Module-removed
        S - Switched     R - Routed
        U - Up (port-channel)
        M - Not in use. Min-links not met
--------------------------------------------------------------------------------
Group Port-        Type      Protocol  Member Ports
      Channel
--------------------------------------------------------------------------------
1     Po1(SD)      Eth       LACP      Eth1/14(I)   Eth1/15(I)


SW1# show interfaces status | include Po|14|15
Port       Name             Status        Vlan       Duplex  Speed  Type
Eth1/14                     connected     301        full    10G    10Gbase-SR
Eth1/15                     connected     301        full    10G    10Gbase-SR
Po1                         notconnect    unassigned auto    auto
```

Start at the top, in the legend of the **show port-channel summary** command. The *D* code letter means that the channel itself is down, with *S* meaning that the channel is a Layer 2

EtherChannel. Code *I* means that the physical interface is working independently from the PortChannel (described as "stand-alone"). Then, the bottom of that command's output highlights PortChannel (Po1) as Layer 2 EtherChannel in a down state (SD), with Eth1/14 and Eth1/15 as standalone interfaces (I).

Interestingly, because the problem is a configuration mistake, the two physical interfaces still operate independently, as if the PortChannel did not exist. The last command in the example shows that while the PortChannel1 interface is down, the two physical interfaces are in a connected state.

> **NOTE**   As a suggestion for attacking EtherChannel problems on the exam, rather than memorizing all the incorrect configuration options, concentrate on the list of correct configuration options. Then look for any differences between a given question's configuration as compared to the known correct configurations and work from there.

Configuration Checks Before Adding Interfaces to EtherChannels

Even when the **channel-group** commands have all been configured correctly, other configuration settings can cause problems as well. This last topic examines those configuration settings and their impact.

First, a local switch checks each new physical interface that is configured to be part of an EtherChannel, comparing each new link to the existing links. That new physical interface's settings must be the same as the existing links; otherwise, the switch does not add the new link to the list of approved and working interfaces in the channel. That is, the physical interface remains configured as part of the PortChannel, but it is not used as part of the channel, often being placed into some nonworking state.

The list of items the switch checks includes the following:

- Speed
- Duplex
- Operational access or trunking state (All must be access, or all must be trunks.)
- If an access port, the access VLAN
- If a trunk port, the allowed VLAN list (per the **switchport trunk allowed** command)
- If a trunk port, the native VLAN
- STP interface settings

In addition, switches check the settings on the neighboring switch. To do so, the switches either use LACP (if already in use), or Cisco Discovery Protocol (CDP) if using manual configuration. The neighbor must match on all parameters in this list except the STP settings.

As an example, SW1 and SW2 again use two links in one EtherChannel. Before configuring the EtherChannel, SW1's Eth1/15 was given a different STP port cost than Eth1/14. Example 12-10 picks up the story just after configuring the correct **channel-group** commands, when the switch is deciding whether to use Eth1/14 and Eth1/15 in this EtherChannel.

12

Example 12-10 *Local Interfaces Fail in EtherChannel Because of Mismatched STP Cost*

```
*Mar  1 23:18:56.132: %PM-4-ERR_DISABLE: channel-misconfig (STP) error detected on
  Po1, putting Eth1/14 in err-disable state
*Mar  1 23:18:56.132: %PM-4-ERR_DISABLE: channel-misconfig (STP) error detected on
  Po1, putting Eth1/15 in err-disable state
*Mar  1 23:18:56.132: %PM-4-ERR_DISABLE: channel-misconfig (STP) error detected on
  Po1, putting Po1 in err-disable state
*Mar  1 23:18:58.120: %LINK-3-UPDOWN: Interface Ethernet1/14, changed state to down
*Mar  1 23:18:58.137: %LINK-3-UPDOWN: Interface Port-channel1, changed state to down
*Mar  1 23:18:58.137: %LINK-3-UPDOWN: Interface Ethernet1/15, changed state to down


SW1# show port-channel summary
Flags:  D - Down        P - Up in port-channel (members)
        I - Individual  H - Hot-standby (LACP only)
        s - Suspended   r - Module-removed
        S - Switched    R - Routed
        U - Up (port-channel)
        M - Not in use. Min-links not met
--------------------------------------------------------------------------------
Group Port-       Type    Protocol  Member Ports
      Channel
--------------------------------------------------------------------------------
1     Po1(SD)     Eth     NONE      Eth1/14(D)   Eth1/15(D)
```

The messages at the top of the example specifically state what the switch does when thinking about whether the interface settings match. In this case, SW1 detects the different STP costs. SW1 does not use Eth1/14, does not use Eth1/15, and even places them into an err-disabled state. The switch also puts the PortChannel into err-disabled state. As a result, the PortChannel is not operational, and the physical interfaces are also not operational.

To solve this problem, you must reconfigure the physical interfaces to use the same STP settings. In addition, the PortChannel and physical interfaces must be **shutdown**, and then **no shutdown**, to recover from the err-disabled state. (Note that when a switch applies the **shutdown** and **no shutdown** commands to a PortChannel, it applies those same commands to the physical interfaces, as well; so, just do the **shutdown/no shutdown** on the PortChannel interface.)

Exam Preparation Tasks

Review All the Key Topics

Review the most important topics from this chapter, noted with the Key Topic icon. Table 12-3 lists these key topics and where each is discussed.

Table 12-3   Key Topics for Chapter 12

Key Topic Element	Description	Page Number
Figure 12-1	Typical design choice for which switches should be made to be root	315
Figure 12-2	Conceptual view of load-balancing benefits of PVST+	316
Figure 12-3	Shows the format of the system ID extension of the STP priority field	316
Table 12-2	Lists default settings for STP optional configuration settings and related configuration commands	318
List	Configuring priority to influence the root election	323
List	Steps to manually configure an EtherChannel	327
List	Troubleshooting EtherChannel	330
List	Interface settings that must match with other interfaces on the same switch for an interface to be included in an EtherChannel	331

Definitions of Key Terms

After your first reading of the chapter, try to define these key terms, but do not be concerned about getting them all correct at that time. Chapter 23, "Final Review," directs you in how to use these terms for late-stage preparation for the exam.

Rapid PVST+, PVST+, System ID Extension, PAgP, LACP, PortChannel, channel-group

Command Reference to Check Your Memory

Although you should not necessarily memorize the information in the tables in this section, this section does include a reference for the configuration and EXEC commands covered in this chapter. Practically speaking, you should memorize the commands as a side effect of reading the chapter and doing all the activities in this exam preparation section. To check to see how well you have memorized the commands as a side effect of your other studies, cover the left side of the table with a piece of paper, read the descriptions on the right side, and see whether you remember the command.

12

Table 12-4 Chapter 12 Configuration Command Reference

Command	Description
spanning-tree mode { rapid-pvst | mst }	Global configuration command to set the STP mode.
spanning-tree vlan *vlan-number* **root primary**	Global configuration command that changes this switch to the root switch. The switch's priority is changed to the lower of either 24,576 or 4096 less than the priority of the current root bridge when the command was issued.
spanning-tree vlan *vlan-number* **root secondary**	Global configuration command that sets this switch's STP base priority to 28,672.
spanning-tree [vlan *vlan-id*] {**priority** *priority*}	Global configuration command that changes the bridge priority of this switch for the specified VLAN.
spanning-tree [vlan *vlan-number*] **cost** *cost*	Interface subcommand that changes the STP cost to the configured value.
spanning-tree [vlan *vlan-number*] **port-priority** *priority*	Interface subcommand that changes the STP port priority in that VLAN (0 to 240, in increments of 16).
channel-group *channel-group-number* **mode { active | passive | on}**	Interface subcommand that enables EtherChannel on the interface.
spanning-tree port type edge	Interface subcommand that enables PortFast on the interface.
spanning-tree bpduguard enable	Interface subcommand to enable BPDU Guard on an interface.
spanning-tree port type edge default	Global command that changes the switch default for PortFast on access interfaces from disabled to enabled.
spanning-tree portfast bpduguard default	Global command that changes the switch default for BPDU Guard on access interfaces from disabled to enabled.
No spanning-tree port type edge	Interface subcommand that disables PortFast on the interface.
spanning-tree bpduguard disable	Interface subcommand to disable BPDU Guard on an interface

Table 12-5   Chapter 12 EXEC Command Reference

Command	Description
show spanning-tree	Lists details about the state of STP on the switch, including the state of each port
show spanning-tree *interface interface-id*	Lists STP information only for the specified port
show spanning-tree vlan *vlan-id*	Lists STP information for the specified VLAN
show spanning-tree [vlan *vlan-id*] root	Lists information about each VLAN's root or for just the specified VLAN
show spanning-tree [vlan *vlan-id*] bridge	Lists STP information about the local switch for each VLAN or for just the specified VLAN
debug spanning-tree events	Causes the switch to provide informational messages about changes in the STP topology
show spanning-tree interface *type number* portfast	Lists a one-line status message about PortFast on the listed interface
show port-channel[*channel-group-number*] {brief | detail | port | port-channel | summary}	Lists information about the state of EtherChannels on this switch

12

Part III Review

Keep track of your part review progress with the checklist shown in Table P3-1. Details on each task follow the table.

Table P3-1 Part III Review Checklist

Activity	First Date Completed	Second Date Completed
Repeat All DIKTA Questions		
Answer Part Review Questions		
Review Key Topics		
Create Command Mind Map by Category		

Repeat All DIKTA Questions

For this task, answer the "Do I Know This Already?" questions again for the chapters in this part of the book, using the PCPT software. Refer to the Introduction to this book, heading "How to View Only DIKTA Questions by Part," for help with how to make the PCPT software show you DIKTA questions for this part only.

Answer Part Review Questions

For this task, answer the Part Review questions for this part of the book, using the PCPT software. Refer to the Introduction to this book, heading "How to View Only Part Review Questions by Part," for help with how to make the PCPT software show you Part Review questions for this part only.

Review Key Topics

Browse back through the chapters and look for the Key Topic icons. If you do not remember some details, take the time to reread those topics.

Create Command Mind Map by Category

Part III of this book discusses VLANs (and related technology) and STP. The number of configuration and EXEC commands for these topics means that you can easily forget individual commands and options. This exercise is meant to help you better organize the commands in your mind.

For the exam, you do not necessarily have to memorize every command and every parameter. However, you should be able to remember all the categories of topics that can be configured for VLANs (and VLAN trunking and VTP), as well as for STP. You should also know the first word or two of most of the commands.

Create a mind map with the following categories of commands from this part of the book:

VLANs, VLAN trunks, VTP, STP

For each category, think of all configuration commands and all EXEC commands (mostly **show** commands). For each category, group the configuration commands separately from the EXEC commands. Figure P3-1 shows a sample for the switch interface branch of the commands.

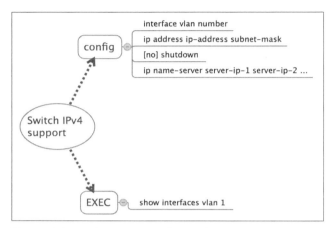

Figure P3-1   Sample *Mind Map from the Switch IPv4 Branch*

> **NOTE**   For more information on mind mapping, refer to the Introduction, in the section "About Mind Maps."

Finally, keep the following points in mind when working on this project:

- Learning happens when creating the mind map. Make an attempt; it truly does help your own brain organize the information.

- Make your first attempt without notes and without looking at the book.

- After your first attempt, then you can review notes, the book, and especially the command summary tables at the end of some chapters. Note which commands you did not remember so that you can focus on those commands when you review later.

- Do not bother to record every single parameter of every command; just write down enough of the command to remember it.

- Note which commands you feel you understand well, and which you feel less sure about.

- Repeat this exercise later when you have 10 spare minutes, as a way to find out how much you recall.

DVD Appendix K, "Mind Map Solutions," shows a sample answer, but your mind map will likely differ.

Parts II and III of this book focused on Ethernet technologies, with most of that discussion related to Layer 2 (data link) layer processing. Part IV now changes the focus of this book from Layer 2 to Layer 3 (network), setting the foundation to examine IP routing.

Part IV creates a foundation for understanding Layer 3 processing on both routers and Layer 3 switches by explaining both IP Version 4 (IPv4), IP Version 6 (IPv6), and subnetting. To deploy the Layer 3 features in a network, the network engineer must first plan some details of how IP addressing and subnetting work. Once working, all who operate the network must not only understand the generic rules for IP addressing but also the specific choices made for that network. Part IV examines those addressing concepts and rules.

Part IV

IP Addressing and Subnetting

Chapter 13: Perspectives on IPv4 Subnetting

Chapter 14: Analyzing Classful IPv4 Networks

Chapter 15: Analyzing Subnet Masks

Chapter 16: Analyzing Existing Subnets

Chapter 17: Fundamentals of IP Version 6

Part IV Review

This chapter covers the following exam topics:

1.1 Describe the purpose and functions of various network devices

1.1.a Interpret a network diagram

1.3 Use the OSI and TCP/IP models and their associated protocols to explain how data flows in a network

1.3.a IP

3.1 Describe the operation and benefits of using private and public IP addressing

3.1.a Classful IP addressing

3.1.b RFC 1918

3.2 Describe the difference between IPv4 and IPv6 addressing scheme

3.2.a Comparative address space

CHAPTER 13

Perspectives on IPv4 Subnetting

Most entry-level networking jobs require you to operate and troubleshoot a network using a preexisting IP addressing and subnetting plan. The CCNA Data Center certification requires you to be ready to analyze preexisting IP addressing and subnetting information to perform typical operations tasks, like monitoring the network, reacting to possible problems, and troubleshooting those problems.

However, some exam questions, as well as many real-life issues at work, require that you understand the design of the network so that you can better operate the network. The process of monitoring any network requires that you continually answer the question, "Is the network working as *designed*?" If a problem exists, you must consider questions such as, "What happens when the network works normally, and what is different right now?" Both questions require you to understand the intended design of the network, including details of the IP addressing and subnetting design.

This chapter provides some perspectives and answers for the bigger issues in IPv4 addressing. What addresses can be used so that they work properly? What addresses should be used? When told to use certain numbers, what does that tell you about the choices made by some other network engineer? How do these choices impact the practical job of configuring switches, routers, hosts, and operating the network on a daily basis? This chapter hopes to answer these questions while revealing details of how IPv4 addresses work.

> **NOTE** As promised in the Introduction's section "For Those Studying Routing & Switching": Readers of the *ICND1 100-101 Cert Guide* (Chapter 11 of that book) could skip most of this chapter. But do review this chapter's section titled "Subnet Rules with Layer 3 Switches," plus the text surrounding Figure 13-8.

"Do I Know This Already?" Quiz

Use the "Do I Know This Already?" quiz to help decide whether you might want to skim this chapter, or a major section, moving more quickly to the "Exam Preparation Tasks" section near the end of the chapter. You can find the answers at the bottom of the page following the quiz. For thorough explanations, see Appendix A, "Answers to the 'Do I Know This Already?' Quizzes."

Table 13-1   "Do I Know This Already?" Foundation Topics Section-to-Question Mapping

Foundation Topics Section	Questions
Analyze Requirements	1–3
Make Design Choices	4–8

1. Host A is a PC, connected to switch SW1 and assigned to VLAN 1. Which of the following are typically assigned an IP address in the same subnet as host A? (Choose two answers.)

    a. The local router's WAN interface

    b. The local router's LAN interface

    c. All other hosts attached to the same switch

    d. Other hosts attached to the same switch and also in VLAN 1

2. Why does the formula for the number of hosts per subnet ($2^H - 2$) require the subtraction of two hosts?

    a. To reserve two addresses for redundant default gateways (routers)

    b. To reserve the two addresses required for DHCP operation

    c. To reserve addresses for the subnet ID and default gateway (router)

    d. To reserve addresses for the subnet broadcast address and subnet ID

3. A Class B network needs to be subnetted such that it supports 100 subnets and 100 hosts/subnet. Which of the following answers list a workable combination for the number of network, subnet, and host bits? (Choose two answers.)

    a. Network = 16, subnet = 7, host = 7

    b. Network = 16, subnet = 8, host = 8

    c. Network = 16, subnet = 9, host = 7

    d. Network = 8, subnet = 7, host = 17

4. Which of the following are private IP networks? (Choose two answers.)

    a. 172.31.0.0

    b. 172.32.0.0

    c. 192.168.255.0

    d. 192.1.168.0

    e. 11.0.0.0

5. Which of the following are public IP networks? (Choose three answers.)

    a. 9.0.0.0

    b. 172.30.0.0

    c. 192.168.255.0

    d. 192.1.168.0

    e. 1.0.0.0

6. Before Class B network 172.16.0.0 is subnetted by a network engineer, what parts of the structure of the IP addresses in this network already exist, with a specific size? (Choose two answers.)

   a. Network

   b. Subnet

   c. Host

   d. Broadcast

7. A network engineer spends time thinking about the entire Class B network 172.16.0.0 and how to subnet that network. He then chooses how to subnet this Class B network and creates an addressing and subnetting plan, on paper, showing his choices. If you compare his thoughts about this network before subnetting the network, to his thoughts about this network after mentally subnetting the network, which of the following occurred to the parts of the structure of addresses in this network?

   a. The subnet part got smaller.

   b. The host part got smaller.

   c. The network part got smaller.

   d. The host part was removed.

   e. The network part was removed.

8. Which of the following terms are not used to reference the one number in each subnet used to uniquely identify the subnet? (Choose two answers.)

   a. Subnet ID

   b. Subnet number

   c. Subnet broadcast

   d. Subnet name

   e. Subnet address

13

Foundation Topics

Introduction to Subnetting

Suppose that you just happened to be at the sandwich shop when they were selling the world's longest sandwich. You're pretty hungry, so you go for it. Now you have one sandwich, but at more than 2 kilometers (about 1.25 miles) long, you realize it's a bit more than you need for lunch all by yourself. To make the sandwich more useful (and more portable), you chop the sandwich into meal-size pieces, and give the pieces to other folks around you, who are also ready for lunch.

Huh? Well, subnetting, at least the main concept, is similar to this sandwich story. You start with one network, but it is just one large network. As a single large entity, it might not be useful, and it is probably far too large. To make it useful, you chop it into smaller pieces, called subnets, and assign those subnets to be used in different parts of the enterprise internetwork.

This short section introduces IP subnetting. First, it shows the general ideas behind a completed subnet design that indeed chops (or subnets) one network into subnets. The rest of this section describes the many design steps that you would take to create just such a subnet design. By the end of this section, you should have the right context to then read through the subnetting design steps introduced throughout the rest of this chapter.

> **NOTE** In this book, only Chapter 17, "Fundamentals of IP Version 6," discusses IPv6 to any depth. So, in this chapter, and Chapter 14, "Analyzing Classful IP Networks," Chapter 15, "Analyzing Subnet Masks," and Chapter 16, "Analyzing Existing Subnets," all references to *IP* refer to IPv4 unless otherwise stated.

Subnetting Defined Through a Simple Example

An IP network—in other words, a Class A, B, or C network—is simply a set of consecutively numbered IP addresses that follows some preset rules. These Class A, B, and C rules, first introduced back in Chapter 4, "Fundamentals of IPv4 Addressing and Routing," in the section "Class A, B, and C IP Networks," define that for a given network, all the addresses in the network have the same value in some of the octets of the addresses. For example, Class B network 172.16.0.0 consists of all IP addresses that begin with 172.16: 172.16.0.0, 172.16.0.1, 172.16.0.2, and so on, through 172.16.255.255. Another example: Class A network 10.0.0.0 includes all addresses that begin with 10.

An IP subnet is simply a subset of a Class A, B, or C network. If fact, the word *subnet* is a shortened version of the phrase *subdivided network*. For example, one subnet of Class B network 172.16.0.0 could be the set of all IP addresses that begin with 172.16.1 and would include 172.16.1.0, 172.16.1.1, 172.16.1.2, and so on, up through 172.16.1.255. Another subnet of that same Class B network could be all addresses that begin 172.16.2.

To give you a general idea, Figure 13-1 shows some basic documentation from a completed subnet design that could be used when an engineer subnets Class B network 172.16.0.0.

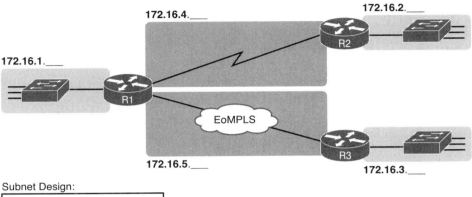

Subnet Design:

Class B   172.16.0.0
First 3 Octets are Equal

Figure 13-1   *Example Subnet Plan Document*

The design shows five subnets: one for each of the three LANs and one each for the two WAN links. The small text note shows the rationale used by the engineer for the subnets: Each subnet includes addresses that have the same value in the first three octets. For example, for the LAN on the left, the number shows 172.16.1.__, meaning "all addresses that begin with 172.16.1." Also, note that the design, as shown, does not use all the addresses in Class B network 172.16.0.0, so the engineer has left plenty of room for growth.

Operational View Versus Design View of Subnetting

Most IT jobs require you work with subnetting from an operational view. That is, someone else, before you got the job, designed how IP addressing and subnetting would work for that particular enterprise network. You need to interpret what someone else has already chosen.

To fully understand IP addressing and subnetting, you need to think about subnetting from both a design and operational perspective. For example, Figure 13-1 simply states that in all these subnets, the first three octets must be equal. Why was that convention chosen? What alternatives exist? Would those alternatives be better for your internetwork today? All these questions relate more to subnetting design rather than to operation. To help you see both perspectives, the explanations in this part of the book often point out whether you should take an operational approach to the topic, or a design approach.

The remainder of this chapter breaks the topics into three major topics, in the sequence noted in Figure 13-2.

13

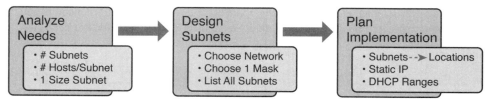

Figure 13-2 *Subnet Planning, Design, and Implementation Tasks*

Analyze Subnetting and Addressing Needs

This section discusses the meaning of four basic questions that can be used to analyze the addressing and subnetting needs for any new or changing enterprise network:

1. Which hosts should be grouped together into a subnet?
2. How many subnets does this network require?
3. How many host IP addresses does each subnet require?
4. Will we use a single subnet size for simplicity, or not?

Rules About Which Hosts Are in Which Subnet

Every device that connects to an IP internetwork needs to have an IP address. These devices include computers used by end users, servers, mobile phones, laptops, IP phones, tablets, and networking devices like routers, switches, and firewalls (in short, any device that uses IP to send and receive packets needs an IP address).

> **NOTE**   When discussing IP addressing, the term *network* has specific meaning: a Class A, B, or C IP network. To avoid confusion with that use of the term *network*, this book uses the terms *internetwork* and *enterprise network* when referring to a collection of hosts, routers, switches, and so on.

The IP addresses must be assigned according to some basic rules, and for good reasons. To make routing work efficiently, IP addressing rules group addresses into groups called subnets. The rules are as follows:

■ Addresses in the same subnet are not separated by a router.

■ Addresses in different subnets are separated by at least one router.

Figure 13-3 shows the general concept, with hosts A and B in one subnet and host C in another. In particular, note that hosts A and B are not separated from each other by any routers. However, host C, separated from A and B by at least one router, must be in a different subnet.

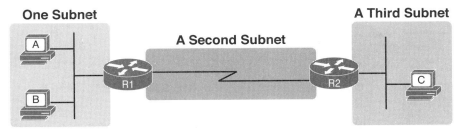

One Subnet

A Second Subnet

A Third Subnet

Figure 13-3   *PC A and B in One Subnet, and PC C in a Different Subnet*

The idea that hosts on the same link must be in the same subnet is much like the postal code concept. All mailing addresses in the same town use the same postal code (ZIP codes in the United States). Addresses in another town, whether relatively nearby or on the other side of the country, have a different postal code. The postal code gives the postal service a better ability to automatically sort the mail to deliver it to the right location. For the same general reasons, hosts on the same LAN are in the same subnet, and hosts in different LANs are in different subnets.

Note that the point-to-point WAN link in the figure also needs a subnet. Figure 13-3 shows router R1 connected to the LAN subnet on the left and to a WAN subnet on the right. Router R2 connects to that same WAN subnet. To do so, both R1 and R2 will have IP addresses on their WAN interfaces, and the addresses will be in the same subnet. (An Ethernet over Multiprotocol Label Switching [EoMPLS] WAN link has the same IP addressing needs, with each of the two routers having an IP address in the same subnet.)

The Ethernet LANs in Figure 13-3 also show a slightly different style of drawing, using simple lines with no Ethernet switch. When drawing Ethernet LANs when the details of the LAN switches do not matter, drawings simply show each device connected to the same line, as seen in Figure 13-3. (This kind of drawing mimics the original Ethernet cabling before switches and hubs existed.)

Finally, because the routers' main job is to forward packets from one subnet to another, routers typically connect to multiple subnets. For example, in this case, router R1 connects to one LAN subnet on the left and one WAN subnet on the right. To do so, R1 will be configured with two different IP addresses, one per interface. These addresses will be in different subnets because the interfaces connect the router to different subnets.

Subnet Rules with Layer 3 Switches

Thinking about subnets when using Layer 3 switches requires a little more work. When a network diagram uses router icons, there is a clear division of where the IP subnets will be needed, as demonstrated previously in Figure 13-3. By contrast, consider Figure 13-4, which shows a Nexus switch, which can be configured as a Layer 3 switch. Which of the four servers should be in the same subnet, and which should be in different subnets?

13

Figure 13-4 *The Lack of Information Makes It Unclear Which Servers Are in Which Subnets*

To know where subnets should exist when using Layer 3 switches, you must know what VLANs exist. The devices in a VLAN should be in the same IP subnet. The concept of a VLAN and an IP subnet are different. A VLAN is a Layer 2 concept, whereas a subnet is a Layer 3 concept; but they group the same devices together.

As a reminder, devices in different VLANs (and therefore different subnets) can communicate, but only if a router or Layer 3 switch is configured to forward traffic between the two subnets. For instance, Figure 13-5 repeats the same network as shown in Figure 13-4, but with VLANs and subnets shown. The figure represents the Layer 3 switching logic inside the Nexus switch with a router icon. IP packets that flow from the subnet on the left, to the subnet on the right, must be processed by the Layer 3 switching logic—routing logic if you will—inside the Nexus switch.

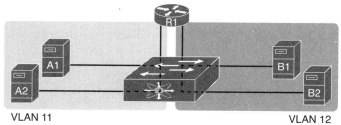

Figure 13-5 *Nexus Layer 3 Switch (Routing) Sits Between Two Subnets*

Figure 13-5 also shows enough internals of a Layer 3 switch to connect back to the subnet design rules: devices separated by a router are in different subnets. For instance, server A1 is separated from server B1 by a routing function (that is, the Layer 3 switching function configured on the Nexus switch). Therefore, A1 and B1 would be in different subnets. However, A1 and A2, not separated by a Layer 3 switching function, would be in the same subnet.

Determine the Number of Subnets

To determine the number of subnets required, the engineer must think about the internetwork as documented and apply the following rules. To do so, the engineer requires access to network diagrams, VLAN configuration details, and if you use Frame Relay WANs, details about the permanent virtual circuits (PVC). Based on this info, you should use these rules and plan for one subnet for every

- VLAN
- Point-to-point serial link
- Ethernet emulation WAN link (EoMPLS)
- Frame Relay PVC

> **NOTE**   WAN technologies like MPLS and Frame Relay allow subnetting options other than one subnet per pair of routers on the WAN, but this book only uses WAN technologies that have one subnet for each point-to-point WAN connection between two routers.

For example, imagine that the network planner has only Figure 13-6 on which to base the subnet design.

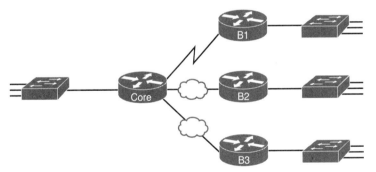

Figure 13-6   *Four-Site Internetwork with Small Central Site*

The number of subnets required cannot be fully predicted with only this figure. Certainly, three subnets will be needed for the WAN links, one per link. However, each LAN switch can be configured with a single VLAN, or with multiple VLANs. You can be certain that you need at least one subnet for the LAN at each site, but you might need more.

Next, consider the more detailed version of the same figure shown in Figure 13-7. In this case, the figure shows VLAN counts in addition to the same Layer 3 topology (the routers and the links connected to the routers). It also shows that the central site has many more switches, but the key fact on the left, regardless of how many switches exist, is that the central site has a total of 12 VLANs. Similarly, the figure lists each branch as having two VLANs. Along with the same 3 WAN subnets, this internetwork requires 21 subnets.

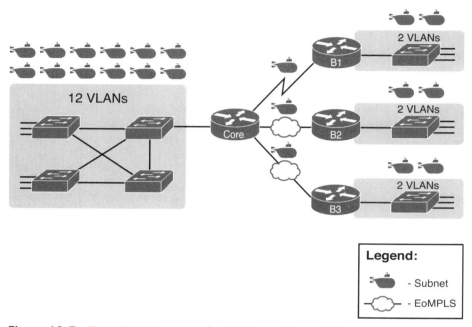

Figure 13-7   *Four-Site Internetwork with Larger Central Site*

Data centers also use subnets for EtherChannels and single Ethernet links in the Layer 3 parts of the design. The links that connect Nexus switches configured as Layer 3 switches, and that also connect the Layer 3 switches to any WAN routers, also use a subnet.

For example, consider the partial network diagram shown in Figure 13-8. The diagram shows two routers at the top, with the WAN (not shown) above the routers. Six links connect between the two WAN routers and the two End of Row (EoR) Nexus switches, which are configured to provide Layer 3 switching. The two Layer 3 switches both route packets for the ten subnets for the ten VLANs for the servers at the bottom of the figure.

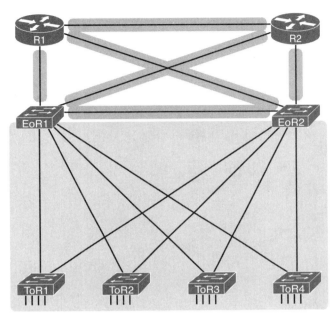

Figure 13-8   *Subnets Used for Router and Layer 3 Switch Links*

Finally, in a real job, you would consider the needs today as well as how much growth you expect in the internetwork over time. Any subnetting plan should include a reasonable estimate of the number of subnets you need to meet future needs.

Determine the Number of Hosts per Subnet

Determining the number of hosts per subnet requires knowing a few simple concepts and then doing a lot of research and questioning. Every device that connects to a subnet needs an IP address. For a totally new network, you can look at business plans—numbers of people at the site, devices on order, and so on—to get some idea of the possible devices. When expanding an existing network to add new sites, you can use existing sites as a point of comparison, and then find out which sites will get bigger or smaller. And don't forget to count the router interface IP address in each subnet and the switch IP address used to remotely manage the switch.

Instead of gathering data for each and every site, planners often just use a few typical sites for planning purposes. For example, maybe you have some large sales offices and some small sales offices. You might dig in and learn a lot about only one large sales office and only one small sales office. Add that analysis to the fact that point-to-point links need a subnet with just two addresses, plus any analysis of more one-of-a-kind subnets, and you have enough information to plan the addressing and subnetting design.

13

For example, in Figure 13-9, the engineer has built a diagram that shows the number of hosts per LAN subnet in the largest branch, B1. For the two other branches, the engineer did not bother to dig to find out the number of required hosts. As long as the number of required IP addresses at sites B2 and B3 stays below the estimate of 50, based on larger site B1, the engineer can plan for 50 hosts in each branch LAN subnet and have plenty of addresses per subnet.

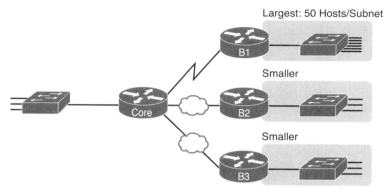

Figure 13-9   *Large Branch B1 with 50 Hosts/Subnet*

One Size Subnet Fits All (Or Not)

The final choice in the initial planning step is to decide whether you will use a simpler design by using a one-size-subnet-fits-all philosophy. A subnet's size, or length, is simply the number of usable IP addresses in the subnet. A subnetting design can either use one size subnet, or varied sizes of subnets, with pros and cons for each choice.

Defining the Size of a Subnet

Now think for a moment like the person who chooses the subnet design. To do so, the engineer assigns each subnet a *subnet mask*, and that mask, among other things, defines the size of that subnet. The mask sets aside a number of *host bits* whose purpose is to number different host IP addresses in that subnet. Because you can number 2^x things with x bits, if the mask defines H host bits, the subnet contains 2^H unique numeric values.

However, the subnet's size is not 2^H. It's $2^H - 2$, because two numbers in each subnet are reserved for other purposes. Each subnet reserves the numerically lowest value for the *subnet number* and the numerically highest value as the *subnet broadcast address*. As a result, the number of usable IP addresses per subnet is $2^H - 2$.

> **NOTE**   The terms *subnet number*, *subnet ID*, and *subnet address* all refer to the number that represents or identifies a subnet.

Figure 13-10 shows the general concept behind the three-part structure of an IP address, focusing on the host part and the resulting subnet size.

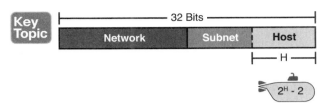

Figure 13-10 *Subnet Size Concepts*

One Size Subnet Fits All

To choose to use a single-size subnet in an enterprise network, you must use the same mask for all subnets, because the mask defines the size of the subnet. But which mask?

One requirement to consider when choosing that one mask is this: That one mask must provide enough host IP addresses to support the largest subnet. To do so, the number of host bits (H) defined by the mask must be large enough so that $2^H - 2$ is larger than (or equal to) the number of host IP addresses required in the largest subnet.

For example, consider Figure 13-11. It shows the required number of hosts per LAN subnet. (The figure ignores the subnets on the WAN links, which require only two IP addresses each.) The branch LAN subnets require only 50 host addresses, but the main site LAN subnet requires 200 host addresses. To accommodate the largest subnet, you need at least 8 host bits. Seven host bits would not be enough, because $2^7 - 2 = 126$. Eight host bits would be enough, because $2^8 - 2 = 254$, which is more than enough to support 200 hosts in a subnet.

What's the big advantage when using a single-size subnet? Operational simplicity. In other words, keeping it simple. Everyone on the IT staff who has to work with networking can get used to working with one mask—and one mask only. They will be able to answer all subnetting questions more easily, because everyone gets used to doing subnetting math with that one mask.

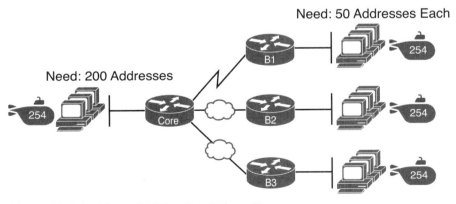

Figure 13-11 *Network Using One Subnet Size*

13

The big disadvantage for using a single-size subnet is that it wastes IP addresses. For example, in Figure 13-8, all the branch LAN subnets support 254 addresses, while the largest branch subnet needs only 50 addresses. The WAN subnets only need two IP addresses, but each supports 254 addresses, again wasting more IP addresses.

The wasted IP addresses do not actually cause a problem in most cases, however. Most organizations use private IP networks in their enterprise internetworks, and a single Class A or Class B private network can supply plenty of IP addresses, even with the waste.

Multiple Subnet Sizes (Variable-Length Subnet Masks)

To create multiple sizes of subnets in one Class A, B, or C network, the engineer must create some subnets using one mask, some with another, and so on. Different masks mean different numbers of host bits, and a different number of hosts in some subnets based on the $2^H - 2$ formula.

For example, consider the requirements listed earlier in Figure 13-11. It showed 1 LAN subnet on the left that needs 200 host addresses, 3 branch subnets that need 50 addresses, and 3 WAN links that need 2 addresses. To meet those needs, but waste fewer IP addresses, three subnet masks could be used, creating subnets of three different sizes, as shown in Figure 13-12.

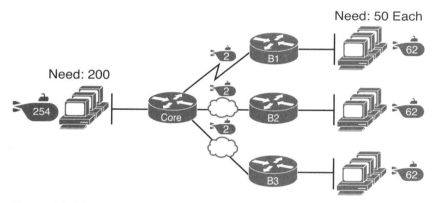

Figure 13-12   *Three Masks, Three Subnet Sizes*

The smaller subnets now waste fewer IP addresses compared to the design seen earlier in Figure 13-8. The subnets on the right that need 50 IP addresses have subnets with 6 host bits, for $2^6 - 2 = 62$ available addresses per subnet. The WAN links use masks with 2 host bits, for $2^2 - 2 = 2$ available addresses per subnet.

However, some are still wasted, because you cannot set the size of the subnet as some arbitrary size. All subnets will be a size based on the $2^H - 2$ formula, with H being the number of host bits defined by the mask for each subnet. For the most part, this book explains subnetting using designs that use a single mask, creating a single subnet size for all subnets. Why? First, it makes the process of learning subnetting easier. Second, some types of analysis that you can do about a network—specifically, calculating the number of subnets in the classful network—only make sense when a single mask is used.

Make Design Choices

Now that you know how to analyze the IP addressing and subnetting needs, the next major step examines how to apply the rules of IP addressing and subnetting to those needs and mask some choices. In other words, now that you know how many subnets you need and how many host addresses you need in the largest subnet, how do you create a useful subnetting design that meets those requirements? The short answer is that you need to do the three tasks shown on the right side of Figure 13-13.

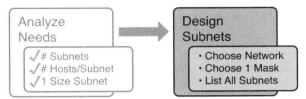

Figure 13-13 *Input to the Design Phase, and Design Questions to Answer*

Choose a Classful Network

In the original design for what we know of today as the Internet, companies used registered *public classful IP networks* when implementing TCP/IP inside the company. By the mid-1990s, an alternative became more popular: *private IP networks*. This section discusses the background behind these two choices, because it impacts the choice of what IP network a company will then subnet and implement in its enterprise internetwork.

Public IP Networks

The original design of the Internet required that any company that connected to the Internet had to use a *registered public IP network*. To do so, the company would complete some paperwork, describing the enterprise's internetwork and the number of hosts existing, plus plans for growth. After submitting the paperwork, the company would receive an assignment of either a Class A, B, or C network.

Public IP networks, and the administrative processes surrounding them, ensure that all the companies that connect to the Internet all use unique IP addresses. In particular, after a public IP network is assigned to a company, only that company should use the addresses in that network. That guarantee of uniqueness means that Internet routing can work well, because there are no duplicate public IP addresses.

For example, consider the example shown in Figure 13-14. Company 1 has been assigned public Class A network 1.0.0.0, and company 2 has been assigned public Class A network 2.0.0.0. Per the original intent for public addressing in the Internet, after these public network assignments have been made, no other companies can use addresses in Class A networks 1.0.0.0 or 2.0.0.0.

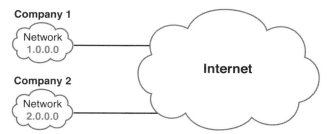

Figure 13-14 *Two Companies with Unique Public IP Networks*

This original address assignment process ensured unique IP addresses across the entire planet. The idea is much like the fact that your telephone number should be unique in the universe, your postal mailing address should also be unique, and your email address should also be unique. If someone calls you, your phone rings, but no one else's phone rings. Similarly, if Company 1 is assigned Class A network 1.0.0.0, and it assigns address 1.1.1.1 to a particular PC, that address should be unique in the universe. A packet sent through the Internet, to destination 1.1.1.1, should only arrive at this one PC inside Company 1, instead of being delivered to some other host.

Growth Exhausts the Public IP Address Space

By the early 1990s, the world was running out of public IP networks that could be assigned. During most of the 1990s, the number of hosts newly connected to the Internet was growing at a double-digit pace, *per month*. Companies kept following the rules, asking for public IP networks, and it was clear that the current address-assignment scheme could not continue without some changes. Simply put, the number of Class A, B, and C networks supported by the 32-bit address in IP Version 4 (IPv4) was not enough to support one public classful network per organization, while also providing enough IP addresses in each company.

NOTE From one perspective, the universe ran out of public IPv4 addresses in early 2011. IANA, which assigns public IPv4 address blocks to the five Internet registries around the globe, assigned the last of the IPv4 address space in early 2011.

The Internet community worked hard during the 1990s to solve this problem, coming up with several solutions, including the following:

- A new version of IP (IPv6), with much larger addresses (128 bit)
- Assigning a subset of a public IP network to each company, instead of an entire public IP network, to reduce waste
- Network Address Translation (NAT), which allows the use of private IP networks

These three solutions matter to real networks today. However, to stay focused on the topic of subnet design, this chapter focuses on the third option, and in particular, the private IP networks that can be used by an enterprise when also using NAT.

NAT allows multiple companies to use the exact same *private IP network*, using the same IP addresses as other companies, while still connecting to the Internet. For example, Figure 13-15 shows the same two companies connecting to the Internet as in Figure 13-14, but now with both using the same private Class A network 10.0.0.0.

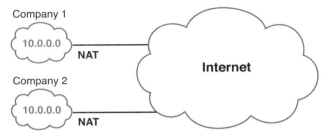

Figure 13-15   *Reusing the Same Private Network 10.0.0.0, with NAT*

Both companies use the same classful IP network (10.0.0.0). Both companies can implement their subnet design internal to their respective enterprise internetworks, without discussing their plans. The two companies can even use the exact same IP addresses inside network 10.0.0.0. And amazingly, at the same time, both companies can even communicate with each other through the Internet.

The technology called *Network Address Translation* (NAT) makes it possible for companies to reuse the same IP networks, as shown in Figure 13-15. NAT does this by translating the IP addresses inside the packets as they go from the enterprise to the Internet, using a small number of public IP addresses to support tens of thousands of private IP addresses.

NOTE   Although this book does not detail how NAT works, or how to configure NAT, if interested in more information, refer to books about the Cisco CCNA Routing and Switching certification, which does cover NAT.

Private IP Networks

RFC 1918 defines the set of private IP networks, as listed in Table 13-2. By definition, these private IP networks

- Will never be assigned to an organization as a public IP network
- Can be used by organizations that will use NAT when sending packets into the Internet
- Can also be used by organizations that never need to send packets into the Internet

So, when using NAT—and almost every organization that connects to the Internet uses NAT—the company can simply pick one or more of the private IP networks from the list of reserved private IP network numbers. RFC 1918 defines the list, which is summarized in Table 13-2.

13

Table 13-2   RFC 1918 Private Address Space

Class of Networks	Private IP Networks	Number of Networks
A	10.0.0.0	1
B	172.16.0.0 through 172.31.0.0	16
C	192.168.0.0 through 192.168.255.0	256

NOTE   According to an informal survey I ran in my blog back in late 2010, about half of the respondents said that their networks use private Class A network 10.0.0.0, as opposed to other private networks or public networks.

Choose an IP Network During the Design Phase

Today, some organizations use private IP networks along with NAT, and some use public IP networks. Most new enterprise internetworks use private IP addresses throughout the network, along with NAT, as part of the connection to the Internet. Those organizations that already have registered public IP networks—often obtained before the addresses started running short in the early 1990s—can continue to use those public addresses throughout their enterprise networks.

After the choice to use a private IP network has been made, just pick one that has enough IP addresses. You can have a small internetwork and still choose to use private Class A network 10.0.0.0. It might seem wasteful to choose a Class A network that has more than 16 million IP addresses, especially if you only need a few hundred. However, there's no penalty or problem with using a private network that is too large for your current or future needs.

For the purposes of this book, most examples use private IP network numbers. For the design step to choose a network number, just choose a private Class A, B, or C network from the list of RFC 1918 private networks.

Regardless, from a math and concept perspective, the methods to subnet a public IP network versus a private IP network are the same.

Choose the Mask

If a design engineer followed the topics in this chapter so far, in order, he would know the following:

- The number of subnets required
- The number of hosts/subnet required
- That a choice was made to use only one mask for all subnets, so that all subnets are the same size (same number of hosts/subnet)
- The classful IP network number that will be subnetted

This section completes the design process, at least the parts described in this chapter, by discussing how to choose that one mask to use for all subnets. First, this section examines default masks, used when a network is not subnetted, as a point of comparison. Next, the concept of borrowing host bits to create subnet bits is explored. Finally, this section ends with an example of how to create a subnet mask based on the analysis of the requirements.

Classful IP Networks Before Subnetting

Before an engineer subnets a classful network, the network is a single group of addresses. In other words, the engineer has not yet subdivided the network into many smaller subsets called *subnets*.

When thinking about an unsubnetted classful network, the addresses in a network have only two parts: the network part and host part. Comparing any two addresses in the classful network

- The addresses have the same value in the network part.
- The addresses have different values in the host part.

The actual sizes of the network and host part of the addresses in a network can be easily predicted, as shown in Figure 13-16.

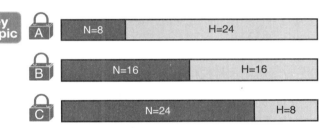

Figure 13-16 *Format of Unsubnetted Class A, B, and C Networks*

In Figure 13-16, N and H represent the number of network and host bits, respectively. Class rules define the number of network octets (1, 2, or 3) for Classes A, B, and C, respectively; the figure shows these values as a number of bits. The number of host octets is 3, 2, or 1, respectively.

Continuing the analysis of classful network before subnetting, the number of addresses in one classful IP network can be calculated with the same $2^H - 2$ formula previously discussed. In particular, the size of an unsubnetted Class A, B, or C network is as follows:

- **Class A:** $2^{24} - 2 = 16,777,214$
- **Class B:** $2^{16} - 2 = 65,534$
- **Class C:** $2^8 - 2 = 254$

Borrow Host Bits to Create Subnet Bits

To subnet a network, the designer thinks about the network and host parts, as shown in Figure 13-13, and then the engineer adds a third part in the middle: the subnet part. However,

13

the designer cannot change the size of the network part or the size of the entire address (32 bits). To create a subnet part of the address structure, the engineer borrows bits from the host part. Figure 13-17 shows the general idea.

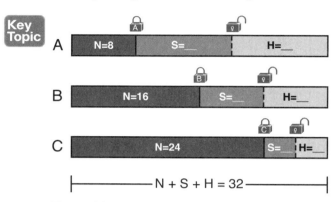

Figure 13-17   *Concept of Borrowing Host Bits*

Figure 13-17 shows a rectangle that represents the subnet mask. N, representing the number of network bits, remains locked at 8, 16, or 24, depending on the class. Conceptually, the designer moves a (dashed) dividing line into the host field, with subnet bits (S) between the network and host parts, and the remaining host bits (H) on the right. The three parts must add up to 32, because IPv4 addresses consist of 32 bits.

Choose Enough Subnet and Host Bits

The design process requires a choice of where to place the dashed line shown in Figure 13-14. But what is the right choice? How many subnet and host bits should the designer choose? The answers hinge on the requirements gathered in the early stages of the planning process:

- Number of subnets required
- Number of hosts/subnet

The bits in the subnet part create a way to uniquely number the different subnets that the design engineer wants to create. With 1 subnet bit, you can number 2^1 or 2 subnets. With 2 bits, 2^2 or four subnets, with 3 bits, 2^3 or eight subnets, and so on. The number of subnet bits must be large enough to uniquely number all the subnets, as determined during the planning process.

At the same time, the remaining number of host bits must also be large enough to number the host IP addresses in the largest subnet. Remember, in this chapter, we assume the use of a single mask for all subnets. This single mask must support both the required number of subnets and the required number of hosts in the largest subnet. Figure 13-18 shows the concept.

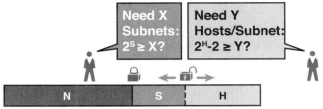

Figure 13-18   *Borrowing Enough Subnet and Host Bits*

Figure 13-18 shows the idea of the designer choosing a number of subnet (S) and host (H) bits and then checking the math. 2^S must be more than the number of required subnets, or the mask will not supply enough subnets in this IP network. Also, $2^H - 2$ must be more than the required number of hosts/subnet.

> **NOTE**   The idea of calculating the number of subnets as 2^S applies only in cases where a single mask is used for all subnets of a single classful network, as is being assumed in this chapter.

To effectively design masks, or to interpret masks that were chosen by someone else, you need a good working memory of the powers of 2. Table 13-3 lists the powers of 2 up through 2^{12}, along with a column with $2^H - 2$, for perspective when calculating the number of hosts/subnet. Appendix C, "Numeric Reference Tables," lists a table with powers of 2 up through 2^{24} for your reference.

Table 13-3   Powers of 2 Reference for Designing Masks

Number of Bits	2^X	$2^X - 2$
1	2	0
2	4	2
3	8	6
4	16	14
5	32	30
6	64	62
7	128	126
8	256	254
9	512	510
10	1024	1022
11	2048	2046
12	4096	4094

13

Example Design: 172.16.0.0, 200 Subnets, 200 Hosts

To help make sense of the theoretical discussion so far, consider an example that focuses on the design choice for the subnet mask. In this case, the planning and design choices so far tell us the following:

- Use a single mask for all subnets.
- Plan for 200 subnets.
- Plan for 200 host IP addresses per subnet.
- Use private Class B network 172.16.0.0.

To choose the mask, the designer asks this question:

How many subnet (S) bits do I need to number 200 subnets?

From Table 13-3, you can see that S = 7 is not large enough (2^7 = 128), but S = 8 is enough (2^8 = 256). So, you need *at least* 8 subnet bits.

Next, the designer asks a similar question, based on the number of hosts per subnet:

How many host (H) bits do I need to number 200 hosts per subnet?

The math is basically the same, but the formula subtracts 2 when counting the number of hosts/subnet. From Table 13-3, you can see that H = 7 is not large enough ($2^7 - 2$ = 126), but H = 8 is enough ($2^8 - 2$ = 254).

Only one possible mask meets all the requirements in this case. First, the number of network bits (N) must be 16, because the design uses a Class B network. The requirements tell us that the mask needs at least 8 subnet bits, and at least 8 host bits. The mask only has 32 bits in it; Figure 13-19 shows the resulting mask.

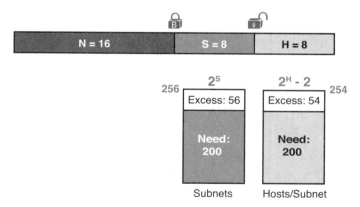

Figure 13-19 *Example Mask Choice, N = 16, S = 8, H = 8*

Masks and Mask Formats

Although engineers think about IP addresses in three parts when making design choices (network, subnet, and host), the subnet mask gives the engineer a way to communicate those design choices to all the devices in the subnet.

The subnet mask is a 32-bit binary number with a number of binary 1s on the left and with binary 0s on the right. By definition, the number of binary 0s equals the number of host bits—in fact, that is exactly how the mask communicates the idea of the size of the host part of the addresses in a subnet. The beginning bits in the mask equal binary 1, with those bit positions representing the combined network and subnet parts of the addresses in the subnet.

Because the network part always comes first, then the subnet part, and then the host part, the subnet mask, in binary form, cannot have interleaved 1s and 0s. Each subnet mask has one unbroken string of binary 1s on the left, with the rest of the bits as binary 0s.

After the engineer chooses the classful network and the number of subnet and host bits in a subnet, creating the binary subnet mask is easy. Just write down N 1s, S 1s, and then H 0s (assuming that N, S, and H represent the number of network, subnet, and host bits). Figure 13-20 shows the mask based on the previous example, which subnets a Class B network by creating 8 subnet bits, leaving 8 host bits.

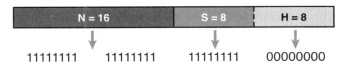

Figure 13-20   *Creating the Subnet Mask – Binary – Class B Network*

In addition to the binary mask shown in Figure 13-20, masks can also be written in two other formats: the familiar dotted-decimal notation (DDN) seen in IP addresses and an even briefer *prefix* notation. Chapter 15, "Analyzing Subnet Masks," discusses these formats and how to convert between the different formats.

Build a List of All Subnets

This final task of the subnet design step determines the actual subnets that can be used, based on all the earlier choices. The earlier design work determined the Class A, B, or C network to use, and the (one) subnet mask to use that supplies enough subnets and enough host IP addresses per subnet. But what are those subnets? How do you identify or describe a subnet? This section answers these questions.

A subnet consists of a group of consecutive numbers. Most of these numbers can be used as IP addresses by hosts. However, each subnet reserves the first and last numbers in the group, and these two numbers cannot be used as IP addresses. In particular, each subnet contains the following:

- **Subnet number:** Also called the *subnet ID* or *subnet address*, this number identifies the subnet. It is the numerically smallest number in the subnet. It cannot be used as an IP address by a host.

- **Subnet broadcast:** Also called the *subnet broadcast address* or *directed broadcast address*, this is the last (numerically highest) number in the subnet. It also cannot be used as an IP address by a host.

- **IP addresses:** All the numbers between the subnet ID and the subnet broadcast address can be used as a host IP address.

13

For example, consider the earlier case in which the design results were as follows:

Network: 172.16.0.0 (Class B)

Mask: 255.255.255.0 (for all subnets)

With some math, the facts about each subnet that exists in this Class B network can be calculated. In this case, Table 13-4 shows the first ten such subnets. It then skips many subnets and shows the last two (numerically largest) subnets.

Table 13-4   First Ten Subnets, Plus the Last Few, from 172.16.0.0, 255.255.255.0

Subnet Number	IP Addresses	Broadcast Address
172.16.0.0	172.16.0.1 – 172.16.0.254	172.16.0.255
172.16.1.0	172.16.1.1 – 172.16.1.254	172.16.1.255
172.16.2.0	172.16.2.1 – 172.16.2.254	172.16.2.255
172.16.3.0	172.16.3.1 – 172.16.3.254	172.16.3.255
172.16.4.0	172.16.4.1 – 172.16.4.254	172.16.4.255
172.16.5.0	172.16.5.1 – 172.16.5.254	172.16.5.255
172.16.6.0	172.16.6.1 – 172.16.6.254	172.16.6.255
172.16.7.0	172.16.7.1 – 172.16.7.254	172.16.7.255
172.16.8.0	172.16.8.1 – 172.16.8.254	172.16.8.255
172.16.9.0	172.16.9.1 – 172.16.9.254	172.16.9.255
Skipping many…		
172.16.254.0	172.16.254.1 – 172.16.254.254	172.16.254.255
172.16.255.0	172.16.255.1 – 172.16.255.254	172.16.255.255

Plan the Implementation

The next step, planning the implementation, is the last step before actually configuring the devices to create a subnet. The engineer first needs to choose where to use each subnet. For example, at a branch office in a particular city, which subnet from the subnet planning chart (Table 13-4) should be used for each VLAN at that site? Also, for any interfaces that require static IP addresses, which addresses should be used in each case? Finally, what range of IP addresses from inside each subnet should be configured in the DHCP server, to be dynamically leased to hosts for use as their IP address? Figure 13-21 summarizes the list of implementation planning tasks.

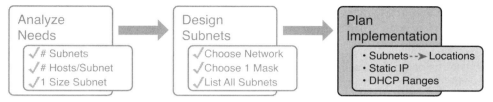

Figure 13-21 *Facts Supplied to the Plan Implementation Step*

Assign Subnets to Different Locations

The job is simple: Look at your network diagram, identify each location that needs a subnet, and pick one from the table you made of all the possible subnets. Then, track it so that you know which ones you use where, using a spreadsheet or some other purpose-built subnet-planning tool. That's it! Figure 13-22 shows a completed design example using Table 13-4, which happens to match the initial design example shown way back in Figure 13-1.

Although this design could have used any five subnets from Table 13-4, in real networks, engineers usually give more thought to some strategy for assigning subnets. For example, you might assign all LAN subnets lower numbers and WAN subnets higher numbers. Or you might slice off large ranges of subnets for different divisions of the company. Or you might follow that same strategy, but ignore organizational divisions in the company, paying more attention to geographies.

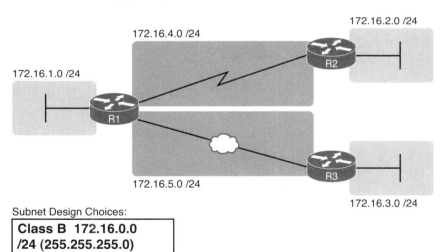

Figure 13-22 *Example of Subnets Assigned to Different Locations*

Choose Static and Dynamic Ranges per Subnet

Devices receive their IP address and mask assignment in one of two ways: dynamically by using Dynamic Host Control Protocol (DHCP) or statically through configuration. For DHCP to work, the network engineer must tell the DHCP server the subnets for which it must assign IP addresses. In addition, that configuration limits the DHCP server to only a

13

subset of the addresses in the subnet. For static addresses, you simply configure the device to tell it what IP address and mask to use.

To keep things as simple as possible, most shops use a strategy to separate the static IP addresses on one end of each subnet, and the DHCP-assigned dynamic addresses on the other. It does not really matter whether the static addresses sit on the low end of the range of addresses or the high end.

For example, imagine that the engineer decides that, for the LAN subnets in Figure 13-22, the DHCP pool comes from the high end of the range—namely, addresses that end in .101 through .254. (The address that ends in .255 is, of course, reserved.) The engineer also assigns static addresses from the lower end, with addresses ending in .1 through .100. Figure 13-23 shows the idea.

Figure 13-23 shows all three routers with statically assigned IP addresses that end in .1. The only other static IP address in the figure is assigned to the server on the left, with address 172.16.1.11 (abbreviated simply as .11 in the figure).

On the right, each LAN has two PCs that use DHCP to dynamically lease their IP addresses. DHCP servers often begin by leasing the addresses at the bottom of the range of addresses, so in each LAN, the hosts have leased addresses that end in .101 and .102, which are at the low end of the range chosen by design.

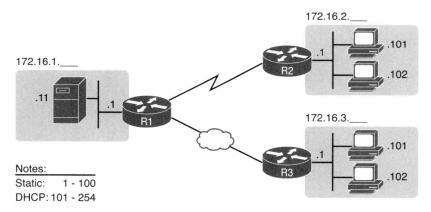

Figure 13-23   *Static from the Low End and DHCP from the High End*

Foundation Topics

Review All the Key Topics

Review the most important topics from this chapter, noted with the Key Topic icon. Table 13-5 lists these key topics and where each is discussed.

Table 13-5   Key Topics for Chapter 13

Key Topic Element	Description	Page Number
List	Key facts about subnets	348
Figure 13-5	Conceptual figure of subnets with a Layer 3 switch	350
List	Rules about what places in a network topology need a subnet	351
Figure 13-10	Locations of the network, subnet, and host parts of an IPv4 address	355
List	Features that extended the life of IPv4	358
Figure 13-16	Formats of Class A, B, and C addresses when not subnetted	361
Figure 13-17	Formats of Class A, B, and C addresses when subnetted	362
Figure 13-18	General logic when choosing the size of the subnet and host parts of addresses in a subnet	363
List	Items that together define a subnet	365

Complete the Tables and Lists from Memory

Print a copy of DVD Appendix I, "Memory Tables," or at least the section for this chapter, and complete the tables and lists from memory. DVD Appendix J, "Memory Tables Answer Key," includes completed tables and lists for you to check your work.

Definitions of Key Terms

After your first reading of the chapter, try to define these key terms, but do not be concerned about getting them all correct at that time. Chapter 23, "Final Review," directs you in how to use these terms for late-stage preparation for the exam.

subnet, network, classful network, network part, subnet part, host part, public IP network, private IP network, subnet mask

13

This chapter covers the following exam topics:

1.3 Use the OSI and TCP/IP models and their associated protocols to explain how data flows in a network

1.3.a IP

3.1 Describe the operation and benefits of using private and public IP addressing

3.1.a Classfull IP addressing

3.1.b RFC 1918

3.2 Describe the difference between IPv4 and IPv6 addressing scheme

3.2.a Comparative address space

CHAPTER 14

Analyzing Classful IPv4 Networks

When operating a network, you often start investigating a problem based on an IP address and mask. Based on the IP address alone, you should be able to determine several facts about the Class A, B, or C network in which the IP address resides. These facts can be useful when troubleshooting some networking problems.

This chapter lists the key facts about classful IP networks and explains how to discover these facts. Following that, this chapter lists some practice problems. Before moving to the next chapter, you should practice until you can consistently determine all these facts, quickly and confidently, based on an IP address.

Note As promised in the Introduction's section, "For Those Studying Routing & Switching": This chapter covers the same content as the *ICND1 100-101 Official Cert Guide*'s Chapter 12. Feel free to skim or skip this chapter if you have already read that chapter in the other book.

"Do I Know This Already?" Quiz

Use the "Do I Know This Already?" quiz to help decide whether you might want to skim this chapter, or a major section, moving more quickly to the "Exam Preparation Tasks" section near the end of the chapter. You can find the answers at the bottom of the page following the quiz. For thorough explanations, see Appendix A, "Answers to the 'Do I Know This Already?' Quizzes."

Table 14-1 "Do I Know This Already?" Foundation Topics Section-to-Question Mapping

Foundation Topics Section	Questions
Classful Network Concepts	1–6

1. Which of the following are not valid Class A network IDs? (Choose two answers.)

   a. 1.0.0.0

   b. 130.0.0.0

   c. 127.0.0.0

   d. 9.0.0.0

2. Which of the following are not valid Class B network IDs?

   a. 130.0.0.0

   b. 191.255.0.0

   c. 128.0.0.0

   d. 150.255.0.0

   e. All are valid Class B network IDs

3. Which of the following are true about IP address 172.16.99.45's IP network? (Select two answers.)

   a. The network ID is 172.0.0.0.

   b. The network is a Class B network.

   c. The default mask for the network is 255.255.255.0.

   d. The number of host bits in the unsubnetted network is 16.

4. Which of the following are true about IP address 192.168.6.7's IP network? (Select two answers.)

   a. The network ID is 192.168.6.0.

   b. The network is a Class B network.

   c. The default mask for the network is 255.255.255.0.

   d. The number of host bits in the unsubnetted network is 16.

5. Which of the following is a network broadcast address?

    a.   10.1.255.255

    b.   192.168.255.1

    c.   224.1.1.255

    d.   172.30.255.255

6. Which of the following is a Class A, B, or C network ID?

    a.   10.1.0.0

    b.   192.168.1.0

    c.   127.0.0.0

    d.   172.20.0.1

14

Foundation Topics

Classful Network Concepts

Imagine that you have a job interview for your first IT job. As part of the interview, you're given an IPv4 address and mask: 10.4.5.99, 255.255.255.0. What can you tell the interviewer about the classful network (in this case, the Class A network) in which the IP address resides?

This section, the first of two major sections in this chapter, reviews the concepts of *classful IP networks* (in other words, Class A, B, and C networks). In particular, this chapter examines how to begin with a single IP address and then determine the following facts:

- Class (A, B, or C)
- Default mask
- Number of network octets/bits
- Number of host octets/bits
- Number of host addresses in the network
- Network ID
- Network broadcast address
- First and last usable address in the network

IPv4 Network Classes and Related Facts

IP version 4 (IPv4) defines five address classes. Three of the classes, Classes A, B, and C, consist of unicast IP addresses. Unicast addresses identify a single host or interface so that the address uniquely identifies the device. Class D addresses serve as multicast addresses, so that one packet sent to a Class D multicast IPv4 address can actually be delivered to multiple hosts. Finally, Class E addresses are experimental.

The class can be identified based on the value of the first octet of the address, as shown in Table 14-2.

Table 14-2   IPv4 Address Classes Based on First Octet Values

Class	First Octet Values	Purpose
A	1–126	Unicast (large networks)
B	128–191	Unicast (medium-sized networks)
C	192–223	Unicast (small networks)
D	224–239	Multicast
E	240–255	Experimental

The exam focuses on the unicast classes (A, B, and C) rather than Classes D and E. After you identify the class as either A, B, or C, many other related facts can be derived just through memorization. Table 14-3 lists that information for reference and later study; each of these concepts is described in this chapter.

Table 14-3   Key Facts for Classes A, B, and C

	Class A	Class B	Class C
First octet range	1 – 126	128 – 191	192 – 223
Valid network numbers	1.0.0.0 – 126.0.0.0	128.0.0.0 – 191.255.0.0	192.0.0.0 – 223.255.255.0
Total networks	$2^7 - 2 = 126$	$2^{14} = 16,384$	$2^{21} = 2,097,152$
Hosts per network	$2^{24} - 2$	$2^{16} - 2$	$2^8 - 2$
Octets (bits) in network part	1 (8)	2 (16)	3 (24)
Octets (bits) in host part	3 (24)	2 (16)	1 (8)
Default mask	255.0.0.0	255.255.0.0	255.255.255.0

Actual Class A, B, and C Networks

Table 14-3 lists the range of Class A, B, and C network numbers. However, some key points can be lost just referencing a table of information. This section examines the Class A, B, and C network numbers, focusing on the more important points and the exceptions and unusual cases.

First, the number of networks from each class significantly differs. Only 126 Class A networks exist: network 1.0.0.0, 2.0.0.0, 3.0.0.0, and so on, up through network 126.0.0.0. However, 16,384 Class B networks exist, with over 2 million Class C networks.

Next, note that the size of networks from each class also significantly differs. Each Class A network is relatively large—over 16 million host IP addresses per network—so they were originally intended to be used by the largest companies and organizations. Class B networks are smaller, with over 65,000 hosts per network. Finally, Class C networks, intended for small organizations, have 254 hosts in each network. Figure 14-1 summarizes those facts.

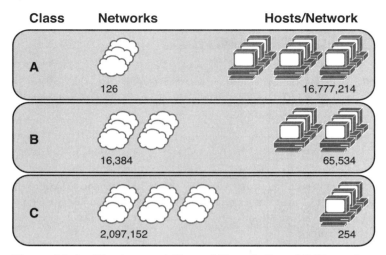

Figure 14-1 *Numbers and Sizes of Class A, B, and C Networks*

Address Formats

In some cases, an engineer might need to think about a Class A, B, or C network as if the network has not been subdivided through the subnetting process. In such a case, the addresses in the classful network have a structure with two parts: the *network part* (sometimes called the *prefix*) and the *host part*. Then, comparing any two IP addresses in one network, the following observations can be made:

The addresses in the same network have the same values in the network part.

The addresses in the same network have different values in the host part.

For example, in Class A network 10.0.0.0, by definition, the network part consists of the first octet. As a result, all addresses have an equal value in the network part, namely a 10 in the first octet. If you then compare any two addresses in the network, the addresses have a different value in the last three octets (the host octets). For example, IP addresses 10.1.1.1 and 10.1.1.2 have the same value (10) in the network part, but different values in the host part.

Figure 14-2 shows the format and sizes (in number of bits) of the network and host parts of IP addresses in Class A, B, and C networks, before any subnetting has been applied.

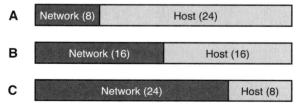

Figure 14-2 *Sizes (Bits) of the Network and Host Parts of Unsubnetted Classful Networks*

14

Default Masks

Although we humans can easily understand the concepts behind Figure 14-2, computers prefer numbers. To communicate those same ideas to computers, each network class has an associated *default mask* that defines the size of the network and host parts of an unsubnetted Class A, B, and C network. To do so, the mask lists binary 1s for the bits considered to be in the network part and binary 0s for the bits considered to be in the host part.

For example, Class A network 10.0.0.0 has a network part of the first single octet (8 bits) and a host part of last three octets (24 bits). As a result, the Class A default mask is 255.0.0.0, which in binary is

11111111 00000000 00000000 00000000

Figure 14-3 shows default masks for each network class, both in binary and dotted-decimal format.

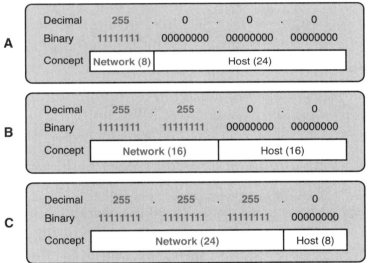

Figure 14-3 *Default Masks for Classes A, B, and C*

NOTE Decimal 255 converts to the binary value 11111111. Decimal 0, converted to 8-bit binary, is 00000000. See Appendix C, "Numeric Reference Tables," for a conversion table.

Number of Hosts per Network

Calculating the number of hosts per network requires some basic binary math. First, consider a case where you have a single binary digit. How many unique values are there? There are, of course, two values: 0 and 1. With 2 bits, you can make four combinations: 00, 01, 10, and 11. As it turns out, the total combination of unique values you can make with N bits is 2^N.

Host addresses—the IP addresses assigned to hosts—must be unique. The host bits exist for the purpose of giving each host a unique IP address by virtue of having a different value in the host part of the addresses. So, with H host bits, 2^H unique combinations exist.

However, the number of hosts in a network is not 2^H; instead, it is $2^H - 2$. Each network reserves two numbers that would have otherwise been useful as host addresses, but have instead been reserved for special use: one for the network ID and one for the network broadcast address. As a result, the formula to calculate the number of host addresses per Class A, B, or C network is

$$2^H - 2$$

where H is the number of host bits.

Deriving the Network ID and Related Numbers

Each classful network has four key numbers that describe the network. You can derive these four numbers if you start with just one IP address in the network. The numbers are as follows:

- Network number
- First (numerically lowest) usable address
- Last (numerically highest) usable address
- Network broadcast address

First, consider both the network number and first usable IP address. The *network number*, also called the *network ID* or *network address*, identifies the network. By definition, the network number is the numerically lowest number in the network. However, to prevent any ambiguity, the people that made up IP addressing added the restriction that the network number cannot be assigned as an IP address. So, the lowest number in the network is the network ID. Then, the first (numerically lowest) host IP address is *one larger than* the network number.

Next, consider the network broadcast address along with the last (numerically highest) usable IP address. The TCP/IP RFCs define a network broadcast address as a special address in each network. This broadcast address could be used as the destination address in a packet, and the routers would forward a copy of that one packet to all hosts in that classful network. Numerically, a network broadcast address is always the highest (last) number in the network. As a result, the highest (last) number usable as an IP address is the address that is simply *one less than* the network broadcast address.

Simply put, if you can find the network number and network broadcast address, finding the first and last usable IP addresses in the network is easy. For the exam, you should be able to find all four values with ease; the process is as follows:

Step 1.   Determine the class (A, B, or C) based on the first octet.

Step 2.   Mentally divide the network and host octets based on the class.

Step 3.   To find the network number, change the IP address's host octets to 0.

Step 4.   To find the first address, add 1 to the fourth octet of the network ID.

Step 5.   To find the broadcast address, change the network ID's host octets to 255.

Step 6.   To find the last address, subtract 1 from the fourth octet of the network broadcast address.

The written process actually looks harder than it is. Figure 14-4 shows an example of the process, using Class A IP address 10.17.18.21, with the circled numbers matching the process.

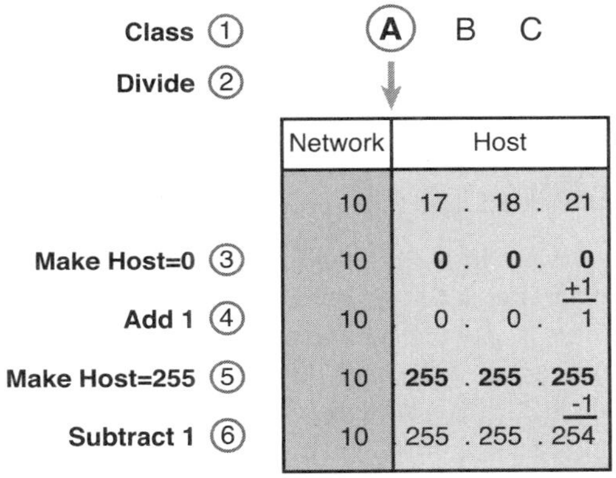

Figure 14-4   *Example of Deriving the Network ID and Other Values from 10.17.18.21*

Figure 14-4 shows the identification of the class as Class A (Step 1) and the number of network/host octets as 1 and 3, respectively. So, to find the network ID at Step 3, the figure copies only the first octet, setting the last three (host) octets to 0. At Step 4, just copy the network ID and add 1 to the fourth octet. Similarly, to find the broadcast address at Step 5, copy the network octets, but set the host octets to 255. Then, at Step 6, subtract 1 from the fourth octet to find the last (numerically highest) usable IP address.

Just to show an alternative example, consider IP address 172.16.8.9. Figure 14-5 shows the process applied to this IP address.

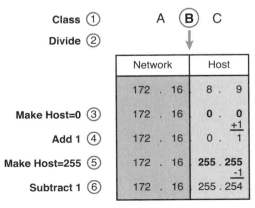

Figure 14-5   *Example Deriving the Network ID and Other Values from 172.16.8.9*

Figure 14-5 shows the identification of the class as Class B (Step 1) and the number of network/host octets as 2 and 2, respectively. So, to find the network ID at Step 3, the figure copies only the first two octets, setting the last two (host) octets to 0. Similarly, Step 5 shows the same action, but with the last two (host) octets being set to 255.

Unusual Network IDs and Network Broadcast Addresses

Some of the more unusual numbers in and around the range of Class A, B, and C network numbers can cause some confusion. This section lists some examples of numbers that make many people make the wrong assumptions about the meaning of the number.

For Class A, the first odd fact is that the range of values in the first octet omits the numbers 0 and 127. As it turns out, what would be Class A network 0.0.0.0 was originally reserved for some broadcasting requirements, so all addresses that begin with 0 in the first octet are reserved. What would be Class A network 127.0.0.0 is still reserved because of a special address used in software testing, called the loopback address (127.0.0.1).

For Class B (and C), some of the network numbers can look odd, particularly if you fall into a habit of thinking that 0s at the end means the number is a network ID, and 255s at the end means it's a network broadcast address. First, Class B network numbers range from 128.0.0.0 to 191.255.0.0, for a total of 2^{14} networks. However, even the very first (lowest number) Class B network number (128.0.0.0) looks a little like a Class A network number, because it ends with three 0s. However, the first octet is 128, making it a Class B network with a two-octet network part (128.0).

For another Class B example, the high end of the Class B range also might look strange at first glance (191.255.0.0), but this is indeed the numerically highest of the valid Class B network numbers. This network's broadcast address, 191.255.255.255, might look a little like a Class A broadcast address because of the three 255s at the end, but it is indeed the broadcast address of a Class B network.

Other valid Class B network IDs that look unusual include 130.0.0.0, 150.0.0.0, 155.255.0.0, and 190.0.0.0. All of these follow the convention of a value from 128 to 191 in the first octet, a value from 0 to 255 in the second octet, and two more 0s, so they are indeed valid Class B network IDs.

Class C networks follow the same general rules as Class B, but with the first three octets defining the network. The network numbers range from 192.0.0.0 to 223.255.255.0, with all addresses in a single network sharing the same value in the first three octets.

Similar to Class B networks, some of the valid Class C network numbers do look strange. For example, Class C network 192.0.0.0 looks a little like a Class A network because of the last three octets being 0, but because it is a Class C network, it consists of all addresses that begin with three octets equal to 192.0.0. Similarly, Class C network 223.255.255.0, another valid Class C network, consists of all addresses that begin with 223.255.255.

Other valid Class C network IDs that look unusual include 200.0.0.0, 220.0.0.0, 205.255.255.0, and 199.255.255.0. All of these follow the convention of a value from 192 to 223 in the first octet, a value from 0 to 255 in both the second and third octets, and a 0 in the fourth octet.

Practice with Classful Networks

As with all areas of IP addressing and subnetting, you need to practice to be ready for the exams. Before the exam, you should master the concepts and processes in this chapter and be able to get the right answer every time—with speed. I cannot overemphasize the importance of mastering IP addressing and subnetting for the exams: Know the topics, and know them well.

However, you do not need to completely master everything in this chapter right now. You should practice some now to make sure that you understand the processes, but you can use your notes, use this book, or whatever. After you practice enough to confirm you can get the right answers using any help available, you understand the topics in this chapter well enough to move to the next chapter.

Then, before the exam, practice until you master the topics in this chapter and can move pretty fast. Table 14-4 summarizes the key concepts and suggestions for this two-phase approach.

Table 14-4   Keep-Reading and Take-Exam Goals for This Chapter's Topics

Time Frame	After Reading This Chapter	Before Taking the Exam
Focus On...	Learning how	Being correct and fast
Tools Allowed	All	Your brain and a notepad
Goal: Accuracy	90% correct	100% correct
Goal: Speed	Any speed	10 seconds

Practice Deriving Key Facts Based on an IP Address

Practice finding the various facts that can be derived from an IP address, as discussed throughout this chapter. To do so, complete Table 14-5.

Table 14-5 Practice Problems: Find the Network ID and Network Broadcast

	IP Address	Class	Number of Network Octets	Number of Host Octets	Network ID	Network Broadcast Address
1	1.1.1.1					
2	128.1.6.5					
3	200.1.2.3					
4	192.192.1.1					
5	126.5.4.3					
6	200.1.9.8					
7	192.0.0.1					
8	191.255.1.47					
9	223.223.0.1					

The answers are listed in the section "Answers to Earlier Practice Problems," later in this chapter.

Practice Remembering the Details of Address Classes

Tables 14-2 and 14-3, shown earlier in this chapter, summarized some key information about IPv4 address classes. Tables 14-6 and 14-7 show sparse versions of these same tables. To practice recalling those key facts, particularly the range of values in the first octet that identifies the address class, complete these tables. Then, refer to Tables 14-2 and 14-3 to check your answers. Repeat this process until you can recall all the information in the tables.

Table 14-6 Sparse Study Table Version of Table 14-2

Class	First Octet Values	Purpose
A		
B		
C		
D		
E		

Table 14-7   Sparse Study Table Version of Table 14-3

	Class A	Class B	Class C
First octet range			
Valid network numbers			
Total networks			
Hosts per network			
Octets (bits) in network part			
Octets (bits) in host part			
Default mask			

Additional Practice

For additional practice with classful networks, consider the following:

- DVD Appendix E, "Practice for Chapter 14: Analyzing Classful IPv4 Networks," has additional practice problems. This appendix also includes explanations about how to find the answer of each problem.

- Create your own problems. You can randomly choose any IP address and try to find the same information asked for by the practice problems in this section. Then, to check your work, use any subnet calculator. Most subnet calculators list the class and network ID.

Exam Preparation Tasks

Review All the Key Topics

Review the most important topics from this chapter, noted with the Key Topic icon. Table 14-8 lists these key topics and where each is discussed.

Table 14-8   Key Topics for Chapter 14

Key Topic Elements	Description	Page Number
Table 14-2	Address classes	375
Table 14-3	Key facts about Class A, B, and C networks	375
List	Comparisons of network and host parts of addresses in the same classful network	376
Figure 14-3	Default masks	377
Paragraph	Function to calculate the number of hosts per network	378
List	Steps to find information about a classful network	378

Complete the Tables and Lists from Memory

Print a copy of DVD Appendix I, "Memory Tables," or at least the section for this chapter, and complete the tables and lists from memory. DVD Appendix J, "Memory Tables Answer Key," includes completed tables and lists for you to check your work.

Definitions of Key Terms

After your first reading of the chapter, try to define these key terms, but do not be concerned about getting them all correct at that time. Chapter 23 directs you in how to use these terms for late-stage preparation for the exam.

network, classful network, network number, network ID, network address, network broadcast address, first address, last address, network part, host part, default mask

Practice

If you have not done so already, practice discovering the details of a classful network as discussed in this chapter. Refer to the earlier section "Practice with Classful Networks" for suggestions.

Answers to Earlier Practice Problems

Table 14-5, shown earlier, listed several practice problems. Table 14-9 lists the answers.

Table 14-9   Practice Problems: Find the Network ID and Network Broadcast

	IP Address	Class	Number of Network Octets	Number of Host Octets	Network ID	Network Broadcast
1	1.1.1.1	A	1	3	1.0.0.0	1.255.255.255
2	128.1.6.5	B	2	2	128.1.0.0	128.1.255.255
3	200.1.2.3	C	3	1	200.1.2.0	200.1.2.255
4	192.192.1.1	C	3	1	192.192.1.0	192.192.1.255
5	126.5.4.3	A	1	3	126.0.0.0	126.255.255.255
6	200.1.9.8	C	3	1	200.1.9.0	200.1.9.255
7	192.0.0.1	C	3	1	192.0.0.0	192.0.0.255
8	191.255.1.47	B	2	2	191.255.0.0	191.255.255.255
9	223.223.0.1	C	3	1	223.223.0.0	223.223.0.255

The class, number of network octets, and number of host octets, all require you to look at the first octet of the IP address to determine the class. If a value is between 1 and 126, inclusive, the address is a Class A address, with one network and three host octets. If a value is between 128 and 191 inclusive, the address is a Class B address, with two network and two host octets. If a value is between 192 and 223, inclusive, it is a Class C address, with three network and one host octet.

The last two columns can be found based on Table 14-3, specifically the number of network and host octets along with the IP address. To find the network ID, copy the IP address, but change the host octets to 0. Similarly, to find the network broadcast address, copy the IP address, but change the host octets to 255.

The last three problems can be confusing, and were included on purpose so that you could see an example of these unusual cases, as follows.

Answers to Practice Problem 7 (From Table 14-5)

Consider IP address 192.0.0.1. First, 192 is on the lower edge of the first octet range for Class C; as such, this address has three network and one host octet. To find the network ID, copy the address, but change the single host octet (the fourth octet) to 0, for a network ID of 192.0.0.0. It looks strange, but it is indeed the network ID.

The network broadcast address choice for problem 7 can also look strange. To find the broadcast address, copy the IP address (192.0.0.1), but change the last octet (the only host octet) to 255, for a broadcast address of 192.0.0.255. In particular, if you decide that the broadcast should be 192.255.255.255, you might have fallen into the trap of logic, like

"Change all 0s in the network ID to 255s," which is not the correct logic. Instead, change all host octets in the IP address (or network ID) to 255s.

Answers to Practice Problem 8 (From Table 14-5)

The first octet of problem 8 (191.255.1.47) sits on the upper edge of the Class B range for the first octet (128–191). As such, to find the network ID, change the last two octets (host octets) to 0, for a network ID of 191.255.0.0. This value sometimes gives people problems, because they are used to thinking that 255 somehow means the number is a broadcast address.

The broadcast address, found by changing the two host octets to 255, means that the broadcast address is 191.255.255.255. It looks more like a broadcast address for a Class A network, but it is actually the broadcast address for Class B network 191.255.0.0.

Answers to Practice Problem 9 (From Table 14-5)

The last problem with IP address 223.223.0.1 is that it's near the high end of the Class C range. As a result, only the last (host) octet is changed to 0 to form the network ID 223.223.0.0. It looks a little like a Class B network number at first glance, because it ends in two octets of 0. However, it is indeed a Class C network ID (based on the value in the first octet).

This chapter covers the following exam topics:

1.3 Use the OSI and TCP/IP models and their associated protocols to explain how data flows in a network

   1.3.a IP

3.1 Describe the operation and benefits of using private and public IP addressing

   3.1.a Classfull IP addressing

3.2 Describe the difference between IPv4 and IPv6 addressing scheme

   3.2.a Comparative address space

CHAPTER 15

Analyzing Subnet Masks

The subnet mask used in one or many subnets in an IP internetwork says a lot about the intent of the subnet design. First, the mask divides addresses into two parts: *prefix* and *host*, with the host part defining the size of the subnet. Then, the class (A, B, or C) further divides the structure of addresses in a subnet, breaking the prefix part into the *network* and *subnet* parts. The subnet part defines the number of subnets that could exist inside one classful IP network, assuming that one mask is used throughout the classful network.

The subnet mask holds the key to understanding several important subnetting design points. However, to analyze a subnet mask, you first need some basic math skills with masks. The math converts masks between the three different formats used to represent a mask:

Binary

Dotted-decimal notation (DDN)

Prefix (also called CIDR)

This chapter has two major sections. The first focuses totally on the mask formats and the math used to convert between the three formats. The second section explains how to take an IP address and its subnet mask and analyze those values. In particular, it shows how to determine the three-part format of the IPv4 address and describes the facts about the subnetting design that are implied by the mask.

> **NOTE** As promised in the Introduction's section, "For Those Studying Routing & Switching": This chapter covers the same content as the *ICND1 100-101 Official Cert Guide*'s Chapter 13. Feel free to skim or skip this chapter if you have already read that chapter in the other book.

"Do I Know This Already?" Quiz

Use the "Do I Know This Already?" quiz to help decide whether you might want to skim this chapter, or a major section, moving more quickly to the "Exam Preparation Tasks" section near the end of the chapter. You can find the answers at the bottom of the page following the quiz. For thorough explanations, see Appendix A, "Answers to the 'Do I Know This Already?' Quizzes."

Table 15-1 "Do I Know This Already?" Foundation Topics Section-to-Question Mapping

Foundation Topics Section	Questions
Subnet Mask Conversion	1–4
Defining the Format of IPv4 Addresses	5–9

1. Which of the following answers lists the prefix (CIDR) format equivalent of 255.255.254.0?

   a. /19

   b. /20

   c. /23

   d. /24

   e. /25

2. Which of the following answers lists the prefix (CIDR) format equivalent of 255.255.255.240?

   a. /26

   b. /28

   c. /27

   d. /30

   e. /29

3. Which of the following answers lists the dotted-decimal notation (DDN) equivalent of /24?

   a. 255.255.240.0

   b. 255.255.252.0

   c. 255.255.255.0

   d. 255.255.255.192

   e. 255.255.255.240

4. Which of the following answers lists the dotted-decimal notation (DDN) equivalent of /30?

   a. 255.255.255.192

   b. 255.255.255.252

   c. 255.255.255.240

   d. 255.255.254.0

   e. 255.255.255.0

5. Working at the help desk, you receive a call and learn a user's PC IP address and mask (10.55.66.77, mask 255.255.255.0). When thinking about this using classful logic, you determine the number of network (N), subnet (S), and host (H) bits. Which of the following is true in this case?

   a. N=12

   b. S=12

   c. H=8

   d. S=8

   e. N=24

6. Working at the help desk, you receive a call and learn a user's PC IP address and mask (192.168.9.1/27). When thinking about this using classful logic, you determine the number of network (N), subnet (S), and host (H) bits. Which of the following is true in this case?

    a. N=24

    b. S=24

    c. H=8

    d. H=7

7. An engineer is thinking about the following IP address and mask using classless IP addressing logic: 10.55.66.77, 255.255.255.0. Which of the following statements are true when using classless addressing logic? (Choose two.)

    a. The network part's size is 8 bits.

    b. The prefix length is 24 bits.

    c. The prefix length is 16 bits.

    d. The host part's size is 8 bits.

8. Which of the following statements is true about classless IP addressing concepts?

    a. Uses a 128-bit IP address

    b. Applies only for Class A and B networks

    c. Separates IP addresses into network, subnet, and host parts

    d. Ignores Class A, B, and C network rules

9. Which of the following masks, when used as the only mask within a Class B network, would supply enough subnet bits to support 100 subnets? (Choose two.)

    a. /24

    b. 255.255.255.252

    c. /20

    d. 255.255.252.0

Foundation Topics

Subnet Mask Conversion

This section describes how to convert between different formats for the subnet mask. You can then use these processes when you practice. If you already know how to convert from one format to the other, go ahead and move to the section "Practice Converting Subnet Masks," later in this chapter.

Three Mask Formats

Subnet masks can be written as 32-bit binary numbers, but not just any binary number. In particular, the binary subnet mask must follow these rules:

- The value must not interleave 1s and 0s.
- If 1s exist, they are on the left.
- If 0s exist, they are on the right.

For example, the following values would be illegal. The first is illegal because the value interleaves 0s and 1s, and the second is illegal because it lists 0s on the left and 1s on the right:

    10101010 01010101 11110000 00001111
    00000000 00000000 00000000 11111111

The following two binary values meet the requirements, in that they have all 1s on the left, followed by all 0s, with no interleaving of 1s and 0s:

    11111111 00000000 00000000 00000000
    11111111 11111111 11111111 00000000

Two alternate subnet mask formats exist so that we humans do not have to work with 32-bit binary numbers. One format, *dotted-decimal notation (DDN)*, converts each set of 8 bits into the decimal equivalent. For example, the two previous binary masks would convert to the following DDN subnet masks, because binary 11111111 converts to decimal 255, and binary 00000000 converts to decimal 0:

    255.0.0.0
    255.255.255.0

Although the DDN format has been around since the beginning of IPv4 addressing, the third mask format was added later, in the early 1990s: the *prefix* format. This format takes advantage of the rule that the subnet mask starts with some number of 1s, and then the rest of the digits are 0s. Prefix format lists a slash (/) followed by the number of binary 1s in the binary mask. Using the same two examples as earlier in this section, the prefix format equivalent masks are as follows:

/8

/24

Note that although the terms *prefix* or *prefix mask* can be used, the terms *CIDR mask* or *slash mask* can also be used. This newer prefix style mask was created around the same time as the *classless interdomain routing (CIDR)* specification back in the early 1990s, and the acronym CIDR grew to be used for anything related to CIDR, including prefix-style masks. Additionally, the term *slash mask* is sometimes used because the value includes a slash mark (/).

You need to be able to think about masks in different formats. The rest of this section examines how to convert between the three formats.

Converting Between Binary and Prefix Masks

Converting between binary and prefix masks should be relatively intuitive after you know that the prefix value is simply the number of binary 1s in the binary mask. For the sake of completeness, the processes to convert in each direction are

Binary to prefix: Count the number of binary 1s in the binary mask, and write the total, in decimal, after a /.

Prefix to binary: Write P binary 1s, where P is the prefix value, followed by as many binary 0s as required to create a 32-bit number.

Tables 15-2 and 15-3 show some examples.

Table 15-2   Example Conversions: Binary to Prefix

Binary Mask	Logic	Prefix Mask
11111111 11111111 11000000 00000000	Count 8 + 8 + 2 = 18 binary 1s	/18
11111111 11111111 11111111 11110000	Count 8 + 8 + 8 + 4 = 28 binary 1s	/28
11111111 11111000 00000000 00000000	Count 8 + 5 = 13 binary 1s	/13

Table 15-3   Example Conversions: Prefix to Binary

Prefix Mask	Logic	Binary Mask
/18	Write 18 1s, then 14 0s, total 32	11111111 11111111 11000000 00000000
/28	Write 28 1s, then 4 0s, total 32	11111111 11111111 11111111 11110000
/13	Write 13 1s, then 19 0s, total 32	11111111 11111000 00000000 00000000

Converting Between Binary and DDN Masks

By definition, a *dotted-decimal number (DDN)* used with IPv4 addressing contains four decimal numbers, separated by dots. Each decimal number represents 8 bits. So, a single DDN shows four decimal numbers that together represent some 32-bit binary number.

Conversion from a DDN mask to the binary equivalent is relatively simple to describe, but can be laborious to perform. First, to do the conversion, the process is as follows:

   For each octet, perform a decimal-to-binary conversion.

However, depending on your comfort level with doing decimal-to-binary conversions, that process can be difficult or time-consuming. If you want to think about masks in binary for the exam, consider picking one of the following methods to do the conversion and practicing until you can do it quickly and accurately:

■ Do the decimal-binary conversions, but practice your decimal-binary conversions to get fast. If you choose this path, consider the Cisco Binary Game, which you can find by searching its name at the Cisco Learning Network (CLN) (http://learningnetwork.cisco.com).

■ Although this chapter teaches you how to convert the masks quickly, if you are weak at basic numeric conversions, take the time to practice converting binary-hex and binary-decimal conversions as an end to itself.

■ Use the decimal-binary conversion chart in Appendix C, "Numeric Reference Tables." This lets you find the answer more quickly now, but you cannot use the chart on exam day.

■ Memorize the nine possible decimal values that can be in a decimal mask, and practice using a reference table with those values.

The third method, which is the method recommended in this book, takes advantage of the fact that any and every DDN mask octet must be one of only nine values. Why? Well, remember how a binary mask cannot interleave 1s and 0s, and the 0s must be on the right? It turns out that only nine different 8-bit binary numbers conform to these rules. Table 15-4 lists the values, along with other relevant information.

Table 15-4   Nine Possible Values in One Octet of a Subnet Mask

Binary Mask Octet	Decimal Equivalent	Number of Binary 1s
00000000	0	0
10000000	128	1
11000000	192	2
11100000	224	3
11110000	240	4
11111000	248	5
11111100	252	6
11111110	254	7
11111111	255	8

Many subnetting processes can be done with or without binary math. Some of those processes—mask conversion included—use the information in Table 15-4. You should plan to memorize the information in the table. I recommend making a copy of the table to keep handy while you practice. (You will likely memorize the contents of this table simply by practicing the conversion process enough to get both good and fast at the conversion.)

Using the table, the conversion processes in each direction with binary and decimal masks are as follows:

Binary to decimal: Organize the bits into four sets of eight. For each octet, find the binary value in the table and write down the corresponding decimal value.

Decimal to binary: For each octet, find the decimal value in the table and write down the corresponding 8-bit binary value.

Tables 15-5 and 15-6 show some examples.

Table 15-5   Example Conversions: Binary to Decimal

Binary Mask	Logic	Decimal Mask
11111111 11111111 11000000 00000000	11111111 maps to 255 11000000 maps to 192 00000000 maps to 0	255.255.192.0
11111111 11111111 11111111 11110000	11111111 maps to 255 11110000 maps to 240	255.255.255.240
11111111 11111000 00000000 00000000	11111111 maps to 255 11111000 maps to 248 00000000 maps to 0	255.248.0.0

Table 15-6   Example Conversions: Decimal to Binary

Decimal Mask	Logic	Binary Mask
255.255.192.0	255 maps to 11111111 192 maps to 11000000 0 maps to 00000000	11111111 11111111 11000000 00000000
255.255.255.240	255 maps to 11111111 240 maps to 11110000	11111111 11111111 11111111 11110000
255.248.0.0	255 maps to 11111111 248 maps to 11111000 0 maps to 00000000	11111111 11111000 00000000 00000000

Converting Between Prefix and DDN Masks

When learning, the best way to convert between the prefix and decimal formats is to first convert to binary. For example, to move from decimal to prefix, first convert decimal to binary and then from binary to prefix.

For the exams, set a goal to master these conversions doing the math in your head. While learning, you will likely want to use paper. To train yourself to do all this without writing it down, instead of writing each octet of binary, just write the number of binary 1s in that octet.

Figure 15-1 shows an example with a prefix-to-decimal conversion. The left side shows the conversion to binary as an interim step. For comparison, the right side shows the binary interim step in shorthand that just lists the number of binary 1s in each octet of the binary mask.

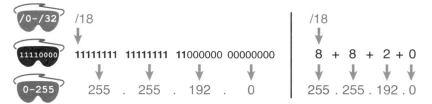

Figure 15-1   *Conversion from Prefix to Decimal: Full Binary Versus Shorthand*

Similarly, when converting from decimal to prefix, mentally convert to binary along the way, and as you improve, just think of the binary as the number of 1s in each octet. Figure 15-2 shows an example of such a conversion.

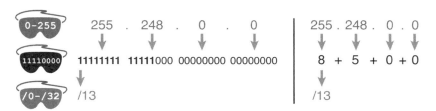

Figure 15-2   *Conversion from Decimal to Prefix: Full Binary Versus Shorthand*

Note that Appendix C has a table that lists all 33 legal subnet masks, with all three formats shown.

Practice Converting Subnet Masks

Before moving to the second half of this chapter, and thinking about what these subnet masks mean, first do some practice. Practice the processes discussed in this chapter until you get the right answer most of the time. Use any tools you want, and take all the time you need, until you meet the goal in Table 15-7 for being ready to move on to the next section. Later, before taking the exam, practice more until you master the topics in this chapter and can move pretty fast, as outlined in the right column of Table 15-7.

Table 15-7 Keep-Reading and Take-Exam Goals for This Chapter's Topics

Time Frame	Before Moving to the Next Section	Before Taking the Exam
Focus On...	Learning how	Being correct and fast
Tools Allowed	All	Your brain and a notepad
Goal: Accuracy	90% correct	100% correct
Goal: Speed	Any speed	10 seconds

Table 15-8 lists eight practice problems. The table has three columns, one for each mask format. Each row lists one mask, in one format. Your job is to find the mask's value in the other two formats for each row. Table 15-11, located in the section "Answers to Earlier Practice Problems," later in this chapter, lists the answers.

Table 15-8 Practice Problems: Find the Mask Values in the Other Two Formats

Prefix	Binary Mask	Decimal
	11111111 11111111 11000000 00000000	
		255.255.255.252
/25		
/16		
		255.0.0.0
	11111111 11111111 11111100 00000000	
		255.254.0.0
/27		

For additional practice converting subnet masks, consider the following:

■ DVD Appendix F, "Practice for Chapter 15: Analyzing Subnet Masks," has some additional practice problems listed. This section also includes explanations as to how to find the answer of each problem.

- Create your own problems. Only 33 legal subnet masks exist, so pick one, and convert that mask to the other two formats. Then check your work based on Appendix C, which lists all mask values in all three formats. (Recommendation: Think of a prefix and convert it to binary and then decimal. Then, think of a DDN mask and convert it to binary and to prefix format.)

Note that many other subnetting problems will require you to do these conversions, so you will get extra practice as well.

Identifying Subnet Design Choices Using Masks

Subnet masks have many purposes. In fact, if ten experienced network engineers were independently asked, "What is the purpose of a subnet mask?" the engineers would likely give a variety of true answers. The subnet mask plays several roles.

This chapter focuses on one particular use of a subnet mask: defining the prefix part of the IP addresses in a subnet. The prefix part must be the same value for all addresses in a subnet. In fact, a single subnet can be defined as all IPv4 addresses that have the same value in the prefix part of their IPv4 addresses.

While the previous paragraph might sound a bit formal, the idea is relatively basic, as shown in Figure 15-3. The figure shows a network diagram, focusing on two subnets: a subnet of all addresses that begin with 172.16.2 and another subnet made of all addresses that begin with 172.16.3. In this example, the prefix—the part that has the same value in all the addresses in the subnet—is the first three octets.

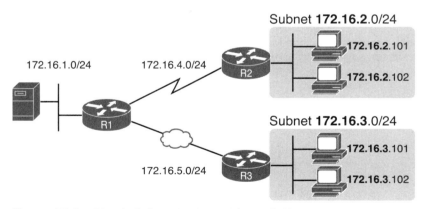

Figure 15-3 *Simple Subnet Design, with Mask /24*

While people can sit around a conference table and talk about how a prefix is three octets long, computers communicate that same concept using a subnet mask. In this case, the subnets use a subnet mask of /24, which means that the prefix part of the addresses is 24 bits (3 octets) long.

This section explains more about how to use a subnet mask to understand this concept of a prefix part of an IPv4 address, along with these other uses for a subnet mask. Note that this section discusses the first five items in the list.

- Defines the size of the prefix (combined network and subnet) part of the addresses in a subnet
- Defines the size of the host part of the addresses in the subnet
- Can be used to calculate the number of hosts in the subnet
- Provides a means for the network designer to communicate the design details—the number of subnet and host bits—to the devices in the network
- Under certain assumptions, can be used to calculate the number of subnets in the entire classful network
- Can be used in binary calculations of both the subnet ID and the subnet broadcast address

Masks Divide the Subnet's Addresses into Two Parts

The subnet mask subdivides the IP addresses in a subnet into two parts: the *prefix*, or *subnet part*, and the *host part*.

The prefix part identifies the addresses that reside in the same subnet, because all IP addresses in the same subnet have the same value in the prefix part of their addresses. The idea is much like the postal code (ZIP codes in the United States) in mailing addresses. All mailing addresses in the same town have the same postal code. Likewise, all IP addresses in the same subnet have identical values in the prefix part of their addresses.

The host part of an address identifies the host uniquely inside the subnet. If you compare any two IP addresses in the same subnet, their host parts will differ, even though the prefix parts of their addresses have the same value. To summarize these key comparisons:

Prefix (subnet) part: Equal in all addresses in the same subnet.

Host part: Different in all addresses in the same subnet.

For example, imagine a subnet that, in concept, includes all addresses whose first three octets are 10.1.1. So, the following list shows several addresses in this subnet:

10.1.1.**1**

10.1.1.**2**

10.1.1.**3**

In this list, the prefix or subnet part (the first three octets of 10.1.1) are equal. The host part (the last octet [in bold]) are different. So, the prefix or subnet part of the address identifies the group, and the host part identifies the specific member of the group.

The subnet mask defines the dividing line between the prefix and the host part. To do so, the mask creates a conceptual line between the binary 1s in the binary mask and the binary 0s in the mask. In short, if a mask has P binary 1s, the prefix part is P bits long and the rest of the bits are host bits. Figure 15-4 shows the general concept.

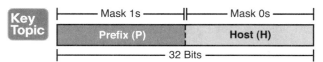

Figure 15-4   *Prefix (Subnet) and Host Parts Defined by Masks 1s and 0s*

The next figure, Figure 15-5, shows a specific example using mask 255.255.255.0. Mask 255.255.255.0 (/24) has 24 binary 1s, for a prefix length of 24 bits.

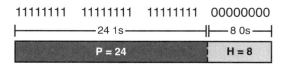

Figure 15-5   *Mask 255.255.255.0: P=24, H=8*

Masks and Class Divide Addresses into Three Parts

In addition to the two-part view of IPv4 addresses, you can also think about IPv4 addresses as having three parts. To do so, just apply Class A, B, and C rules to the address format to define the network part at the beginning of the address. This added logic divides the prefix into two parts: the *network* part and the *subnet* part. The class defines the length of the network part, with the subnet part simply being the rest of the prefix. Figure 15-6 shows the idea.

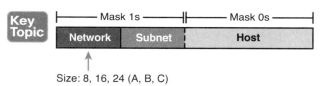

Figure 15-6   *Class Concepts Applied to Create Three Parts*

The combined network and subnet parts act like the prefix because all addresses in the same subnet must have identical values in the network and subnet parts. The size of the host part remains unchanged, whether viewing the addresses as having two parts or three parts.

To be complete, Figure 15-7 shows the same example as in the previous section, with the subnet of "all addresses that begin with 10.1.1." In that example, the subnet uses mask 255.255.255.0, and the addresses are all in Class A network 10.0.0.0. The class defines 8 network bits, and the mask defines 24 prefix bits, meaning that 24 – 8 = 16 subnet bits exist. The host part remains as 8 bits per the mask.

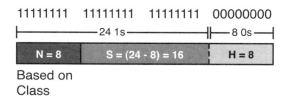

Figure 15-7   *Subnet 10.1.1.0, Mask 255.255.255.0: N=8, S=16, H=8*

Classless and Classful Addressing

The terms *classless addressing* and *classful addressing* refer to the two different ways to think about IPv4 addresses as described so far in this chapter. Classful addressing means that you think about Class A, B, and C rules, so the prefix is separated into the network and subnet parts, as shown in Figures 15-6 and 15-7. Classless addressing means that you ignore the Class A, B, and C rules and treat the prefix part as one part, as shown in Figures 15-4 and 15-5. The following more formal definitions are listed for reference and study:

Classless addressing: The concept that an IPv4 address has two parts—the prefix part plus the host part—as defined by the mask, with *no consideration of the class* (A, B, or C).

Classful addressing: The concept that an IPv4 address has three parts—network, subnet, and host—as defined by the mask *and Class A, B, and C rules*.

> **NOTE**   Networking includes two other related topics that are (unfortunately) also referenced as *classless* and *classful*. In addition to the classless and classful addressing described here, each routing protocol can be categorized as either a *classless routing protocol* or a *classful routing protocol*. Additionally, the terms *classless routing* and *classful routing* refer to some details of how Cisco routers forward (route) packets using the default route in some cases (which do not happen to be within the scope of this book). As a result, these terms can be easily confused and misused. So, when you see the words *classless* and *classful*, be careful to note the context: addressing, routing, or routing protocols.

Calculations Based on the IPv4 Address Format

After you know how to break an address down using both classless and classful addressing rules, you can easily calculate a couple of important facts using some basic math formulas.

First, for any subnet, after you know the number of host bits, you can calculate the number of host IP addresses in the subnet. Next, if you know the number of subnet bits (using classful addressing concepts) and you know that only one subnet mask is used throughout the network, you can also calculate the number of subnets in the network. The formulas just require that you know the powers of 2:

Hosts in the subnet: $2^H - 2$, where H is the number of host bits.

Subnets in the network: 2^S, where S is the number of subnet bits. Only use this formula if only one mask is used throughout the network.

> **NOTE**   Chapter 11's section "Choose the Mask" details many concepts related to masks, including comments about this assumption of one mask throughout a single Class A, B, or C network.

The sizes of the parts of IPv4 addresses can also be calculated. The math is basic, but the concepts are important. Keeping in mind that IPv4 addresses are 32 bits long, the two parts with classless addressing must add up to 32 (P + H = 32), and with classful addressing, the three parts must add up to 32 (N + S + H = 32). Figure 15-8 shows the relationships.

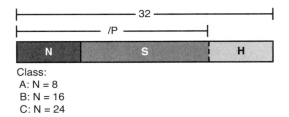

Class:
A: N = 8
B: N = 16
C: N = 24

Figure 15-8 *Relationship Between /P, N, S, and H*

You often begin with an IP address and mask. Based on the information in this chapter and earlier chapters, you should be able to find all the information in Figure 15-8 and then calculate the number of hosts/subnet and the number of subnets in the network. For reference, the following process spells out the steps:

Step 1. Convert the mask to prefix format (/P) as needed. (See the earlier section "Practice Converting Subnet Masks" for review.)

Step 2. Determine N based on the class. (See Chapter 14, "Analyzing Classful IPv4 Networks," for review.)

Step 3. Calculate S = P − N.

Step 4. Calculate H = 32 − P.

Step 5. Calculate hosts/subnet: $2^H - 2$.

Step 6. Calculate number of subnet: 2^S.

For example, consider the case of IP address 8.1.4.5 with mask 255.255.0.0. Following the process:

Step 1. 255.255.0.0 = /16, so P=16.

Step 2. 8.1.4.5 is in the range 1–126 in the first octet, so it is Class A; so N=8.

Step 3. S = P − N = 16 − 8 = 8.

Step 4. H = 32 − P = 32 − 16 = 16.

Step 5. $2^{16} - 2 = 65{,}534$ hosts/subnet.

Step 6. $2^8 = 256$ subnets.

Figure 15-9 shows a visual analysis of the same problem.

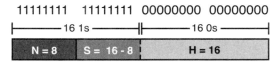

Figure 15-9 *Visual Representation of Problem: 8.1.4.5, 255.255.0.0*

For another example, consider address 200.1.1.1, mask 255.255.255.252. Following the process:

Step 1.   255.255.255.252 = /30, so P=30.

Step 2.   200.1.1.1 is in the range 192–223 in the first octet, so it is Class C; so N=24.

Step 3.   S = P − N = 30 − 24 = 6.

Step 4.   H = 32 − P = 32 − 30 = 2.

Step 5. $2^2 − 2 = 2$ hosts/subnet

Step 6. $2^6 = 64$ subnets.

This example uses a popular mask for serial links, because serial links only require two host addresses, and the mask supports only two host addresses.

Practice Analyzing Subnet Masks

Before moving to the next chapter, practice until you get the right answer most of the time, but use any tools you want and take all the time you need. Then, you can move on with your reading.

However, before taking the exam, practice until you master the topics in this chapter and can move pretty fast. As for time, you should be able to find the entire answer—the size of the three parts, plus the formulas to calculate the number of subnets and hosts—in around 15 seconds. Table 15-9 summarizes the key concepts and suggestions for this two-phase approach.

Table 15-9 Goals: To Keep Reading and to Take the Exam

Time Frame	Before Moving to the Next Chapter	Before Taking the Exam
Focus On...	Learning how	Being correct and fast
Tools Allowed	All	Your brain and a notepad
Goal: Accuracy	90% correct	100% correct
Goal: Speed	Any speed	15 seconds

On a piece of scratch paper, answer the following questions. In each case:

- Determine the structure of the addresses in each subnet based on the class and mask, using classful IP addressing concepts. In other words, find the size of the network, subnet, and host parts of the addresses.

- Calculate the number of hosts in the subnet.

- Calculate the number of subnets in the network, assuming that the same mask is used throughout.

  1. 8.1.4.5, 255.255.254.0
  2. 130.4.102.1, 255.255.255.0
  3. 199.1.1.100, 255.255.255.0
  4. 130.4.102.1, 255.255.252.0
  5. 199.1.1.100, 255.255.255.224

The answers are listed in the section "Answers to Earlier Practice Problems," later in this chapter.

For additional practice analyzing subnet masks, consider the following:

- DVD Appendix F, "Practice for Chapter 15: Analyzing Subnet Masks," has some additional practice problems listed. This section also includes explanations as to how to find the answer to each problem.

- DVD Appendix G, "Practice for Chapter 16: Analyzing Existing Subnets," has another 25 practice problems related to this chapter. Although Appendix F focuses on the topics in this chapter, the problems in Appendix F and Appendix G both begin with an IP address and mask. So, Appendix G also includes commentary and answers for items such as the number of network, subnet, and host bits, and other topics related to this chapter.

- Create your own problems. Many subnet calculators show the number of network, subnet, and host bits when you type in an IP address and mask, so make up an IP address and mask on paper, and then find N, S, and H. Then, to check your work, use any subnet calculator. Most subnet calculators list the class and network ID.

Exam Preparation Tasks

Review All the Key Topics

Review the most important topics from this chapter, noted with the Key Topic icon. Table 15-10 lists these key topics and where each is discussed.

Table 15-10   Key Topics for Chapter 15

Key Topic Element	Description	Page Number
List	Rules for binary subnet mask values	392
List	Rules to convert between binary and prefix masks	393
Table 15-4	Nine possible values in a decimal subnet mask	395
List	Rules to convert between binary and DDN masks	395
List	Some functions of a subnet mask	399
List	Comparisons of IP addresses in the same subnet	399
Figure 15-4	Two-part classless view of an IP address	400
Figure 15-6	Three-part classful view of an IP address	400
List	Definitions of classful addressing and classless addressing	401
List	Formal steps to analyze masks and calculate values	402

Complete the Tables and Lists from Memory

Print a copy of DVD Appendix I, "Memory Tables," or at least the section for this chapter, and complete the tables and lists from memory. DVD Appendix J, "Memory Tables Answer Key," includes completed tables and lists for you to check your work.

Definitions of Key Terms

After your first reading of the chapter, try to define these key terms, but do not be concerned about getting them all correct at that time. Chapter 23 directs you in how to use these terms for late-stage preparation for the exam.

binary mask, dotted-decimal notation (DDN), decimal mask, prefix mask, slash mask, CIDR mask, classful addressing, classless addressing

Practice

If you have not done so already, practice converting and analyzing subnet masks as discussed in this chapter. Refer to the earlier sections "Practice Converting Subnet Masks" and "Practice Analyzing Subnet Masks" for suggestions.

Answers to Earlier Practice Problems

Table 15-8, shown earlier, listed several practice problems for converting subnet masks; Table 15-11 lists the answers.

Table 15-11   Answers to Problems in Table 15-8

Prefix	Binary Mask	Decimal
/18	11111111 11111111 11000000 00000000	255.255.192.0
/30	11111111 11111111 11111111 11111100	255.255.255.252
/25	11111111 11111111 11111111 10000000	255.255.255.128
/16	11111111 11111111 00000000 00000000	255.255.0.0
/8	11111111 00000000 00000000 00000000	255.0.0.0
/22	11111111 11111111 11111100 00000000	255.255.252.0
/15	11111111 11111110 00000000 00000000	255.254.0.0
/27	11111111 11111111 11111111 11100000	255.255.255.224

Table 15-12 lists the answers to the practice problems from the earlier section "Practice Analyzing Subnet Masks."

Table 15-12   Answers to Problems from Earlier in the Chapter

	Problem	/P	Class	N	S	H	2^S	$2^H - 2$
1	8.1.4.5 255.255.254.0	23	A	8	15	9	32,768	510
2	130.4.102.1 255.255.255.0	24	B	16	8	8	256	254
3	199.1.1.100 255.255.255.0	24	C	24	0	8	N/A	254
4	130.4.102.1 255.255.252.0	22	B	16	6	10	64	1022
5	199.1.1.100 255.255.255.224	27	C	24	3	5	8	30

The following list reviews the problems:

1. For 8.1.4.5, the first octet (8) is in the 1–126 range, so it is a Class A address, with 8 network bits. Mask 255.255.254.0 converts to /23, so P − N = 15, for 15 subnet bits. H can be found by subtracting /P (23) from 32, for 9 host bits.

2. 130.4.102.1 is in the 128–191 range in the first octet, making it a Class B address, with N = 16 bits. 255.255.255.0 converts to /24, so the number of subnet bits is 24 − 16 = 8. With 24 prefix bits, the number of host bits is 32 − 24 = 8.

3. The third problem purposely shows a case where the mask does not create a subnet part of the address. The address, 199.1.1.100, has a first octet between 192 and 223, making it a Class C address with 24 network bits. The prefix version of the mask is /24, so the number of subnet bits is 24 – 24 = 0. The number of host bits is 32 minus the prefix length (24), for a total of 8 host bits. So in this case, the mask shows that the network engineer is using the default mask, which creates no subnet bits and no subnets.

4. With the same address as the second problem, 130.4.102.1 is a Class B address with N = 16 bits. This problem uses a different mask, 255.255.252.0, which converts to /22. This makes the number of subnet bits 22 – 16 = 6. With 22 prefix bits, the number of host bits is 32 – 22 = 10.

5. With the same address as the third problem, 199.1.1.100 is a Class C address with N = 24 bits. This problem uses a different mask, 255.255.255.224, which converts to /27. This makes the number of subnet bits 27 – 24 = 3. With 27 prefix bits, the number of host bits is 32 – 27 = 5.

15

This chapter covers the following exam topics:

1.3 Use the OSI and TCP/IP models and their associated protocols to explain how data flows in a network

    1.3.a IP

3.1 Describe the operation and benefits of using private and public IP addressing

    3.1.a Classfull IP addressing

    3.1.b RFC 1918

3.2 Describe the difference between IPv4 and IPv6 addressing scheme

    3.2.a Comparative address space

CHAPTER 16

Analyzing Existing Subnets

Often, a networking task begins with the discovery of the IP address and mask used by some host. Then, to understand how the internetwork routes packets to that host, you must find key pieces of information about the subnet, specifically:

■ Subnet ID

■ Subnet broadcast address

■ Subnet's range of usable unicast IP addresses

This chapter discusses the concepts and math to take a known IP address and mask, and then fully describe a subnet by finding the values in this list. These specific tasks might well be the most important IP skills in the entire IP addressing and subnetting topics in this book, because these tasks might be the most commonly used tasks when operating and troubleshooting real networks.

> **NOTE** As promised in the Introvduction's section, "For Those Studying Routing & Switching": This chapter covers the same content as the *ICND1 100-101 Official Cert Guide*'s Chapter 14. Feel free to skim or skip this chapter if you have already read that chapter in the other book.

"Do I Know This Already?" Quiz

Use the "Do I Know This Already?" quiz to help decide whether you might want to skim this chapter, or a major section, moving more quickly to the "Exam Preparation Tasks" section near the end of the chapter. You can find the answers at the bottom of the page following the quiz. For thorough explanations, see Appendix A, "Answers to the 'Do I Know This Already?' Quizzes."

Table 16-1 "Do I Know This Already?" Foundation Topics Section-to-Question Mapping

Foundation Topics Section	Questions
Defining a Subnet	1
Analyzing Existing Subnets: Binary	2
Analyzing Existing Subnets: Decimal	3–7

1. When thinking about an IP address using classful addressing rules, an address can have three parts: network, subnet, and host. If you examined all the addresses in one subnet, in binary, which of the following answers correctly states which of the three parts of the addresses will be equal among all addresses? Pick the best answer.

   a. Network part only

   b. Subnet part only

   c. Host part only

   d. Network and subnet parts

   e. Subnet and host parts

2. Which of the following statements are true regarding the binary subnet ID, subnet broadcast address, and host IP address values in any single subnet? (Choose two.)

   a. The host part of the broadcast address is all binary 0s.

   b. The host part of the subnet ID is all binary 0s.

   c. The host part of a usable IP address can have all binary 1s.

   d. The host part of any usable IP address must not be all binary 0s.

3. Which of the following is the resident subnet ID for IP address 10.7.99.133/24?

   a. 10.0.0.0

   b. 10.7.0.0

   c. 10.7.99.0

   d. 10.7.99.128

4. Which of the following is the resident subnet for IP address 192.168.44.97/30?

   a. 192.168.44.0

   b. 192.168.44.64

   c. 192.168.44.96

   d. 192.168.44.128

5. Which of the following is the subnet broadcast address for the subnet in which IP address 172.31.77.201/27 resides?

   a.   172.31.201.255

   b.   172.31.255.255

   c.   172.31.77.223

   d.   172.31.77.207

6. A fellow engineer tells you to configure the DHCP server to lease the last 100 usable IP addresses in subnet 10.1.4.0/23. Which of the following IP addresses could be leased as a result of your new configuration?

   a.   10.1.4.156

   b.   10.1.4.254

   c.   10.1.5.200

   d.   10.1.7.200

   e.   10.1.255.200

7. A fellow engineer tells you to configure the DHCP server to lease the first 20 usable IP addresses in subnet 192.168.9.96/27. Which of the following IP addresses could be leased as a result of your new configuration?

   a.   192.168.9.126

   b.   192.168.9.110

   c.   192.168.9.1

   d.   192.168.9.119

16

Foundation Topics

Defining a Subnet

An IP subnet is a subset of a classful network, created by choice of some network engineer. However, that engineer cannot pick just any arbitrary subset of addresses; instead, the engineer must follow certain rules, such as the following:

- The subnet contains a set of consecutive numbers.
- The subnet holds 2^H numbers, where H is the number of host bits defined by the subnet mask.
- Two special numbers in the range cannot be used as IP addresses:
  - The first (lowest) number acts as an identifier for the subnet (*subnet ID*).
  - The last (highest) number acts as a *subnet broadcast address*.
- The remaining addresses, whose values sit between the subnet ID and subnet broadcast address, are used as *unicast IP addresses*.

This section reviews and expands the basic concepts of the subnet ID, subnet broadcast address, and range of addresses in a subnet.

An Example with Network 172.16.0.0 and Four Subnets

Imagine that you work at the customer support center, where you receive all initial calls from users who have problems with their computer. You coach the user through finding her IP address and mask: 172.16.150.41, mask 255.255.192.0. One of the first and most common tasks you will do based on that information is to find the subnet ID of the subnet in which that address resides. (In fact, this subnet ID is sometimes called the *resident subnet*, because the IP address exists in or resides in that subnet.)

Before getting into the math, examine the mask (255.255.192.0) and classful network (172.16.0.0) for a moment. From the mask, based on what you learned in Chapter 15, "Analyzing Subnet Masks," you can find the structure of the addresses in the subnet, including the number of host and subnet bits. That analysis tells you that 2 subnet bits exist, meaning that there should be four (2^2) subnets. (If these concepts are not yet clear, review Chapter 15's section "How Masks Define the Format of Addresses.") Figure 16-1 shows the idea.

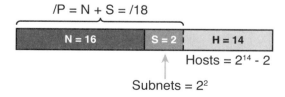

Figure 16-1 *Address Structure: Class B Network, /18 Mask*

NOTE This chapter, like the others in this part of the book, assumes that one mask is used throughout an entire classful network.

Because each subnet uses a single mask, all subnets of this single IP network must be the same size, because all subnets have the same structure. In this example, all four subnets will have the structure shown in the figure, so all four subnets will have $2^{14} - 2$ host addresses.

Next, consider the big picture of what happens with this example subnet design: The one Class B network now has four subnets of equal size. Conceptually, if you represent the entire Class B network as a number line, each subnet consumes one-fourth of the number line, as shown in Figure 16-2. Each subnet has a subnet ID—the numerically lowest number in the subnet—so it sits on the left of the subnet. And each subnet has a subnet broadcast address—the numerically highest number in the subnet—so it sits on the right side of the subnet.

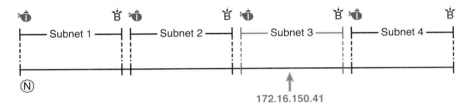

Legend:

Ⓝ	Network ID
🔸	Subnet ID
🔻	Subnet Broadcast Address

Figure 16-2 *Network 172.16.0.0, Divided into Four Equal Subnets*

The rest of this chapter focuses on how to take one IP address and mask and discover the details about that one subnet in which the address resides. In other words, you see how to find the resident subnet of an IP address. Again, using IP address 172.16.150.41 and mask 255.255.192.0 as an example, Figure 16-3 shows the resident subnet, along with the subnet ID and subnet broadcast address that bracket the subnet.

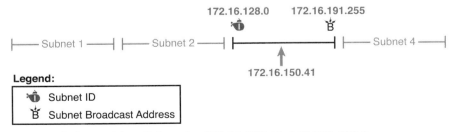

Legend:

🔸	Subnet ID
🔻	Subnet Broadcast Address

Figure 16-3 *Resident Subnet for 172.16.150.41, 255.255.192.0*

Subnet ID Concepts

A subnet ID is simply a number used to succinctly represent a subnet. When listed along with its matching subnet mask, the subnet ID identifies the subnet and can be used to derive the subnet broadcast address and range of addresses in the subnet. Rather than having to write down all these details about a subnet, you simply need to write down the subnet ID and mask, and you have enough information to fully describe the subnet.

The subnet ID appears in many places, but it is seen most often in IP routing tables. For example, when an engineer configures a router with its IP address and mask, the router calculates the subnet ID and puts a route into its routing table for that subnet. The router typically then advertises the subnet ID/mask combination to neighboring routers with some IP routing protocol. Eventually, all the routers in an enterprise learn about the subnet—again using the subnet ID and subnet mask combination—and display it in their routing tables. (You can display the contents of a router's IP routing table using the **show ip route** command.)

Unfortunately, the terminology related to subnets can sometimes cause problems. First, the terms *subnet ID*, *subnet number*, and *subnet address* are synonyms. Additionally, people sometimes simply say *subnet* when referring to both the idea of a subnet and the number that is used as the subnet ID. When talking about routing, people sometimes use the term *prefix* instead of *subnet*. The term *prefix* refers to the same idea as *subnet*; it just uses terminology from the classless addressing way to describe IP addresses, as discussed in Chapter 15's section "Classless and Classful Addressing."

The biggest terminology confusion arises between the terms *network* and *subnet*. In the real world, people often use these terms synonymously, and that is perfectly reasonable in some cases. In other cases, the specific meaning of these terms, and their differences, matter to what is being discussed.

For example, people often might say, "What is the network ID?" when they really want to know the subnet ID. In another case, they might want to know the Class A, B, or C network ID. So, when one engineer asks something like, "What's the net ID for 172.16.150.41 slash 18?" use the context to figure out whether he wants the literal classful network ID (172.16.0.0, in this case) or the literal subnet ID (172.16.128.0, in this case).

For the exams, be ready to notice when the terms *subnet* and *network* are used, and then use the context to figure out the specific meaning of the term in that case.

Table 16-2 summarizes the key facts about the subnet ID, along with the possible synonyms, for easier review and study.

Table 16-2   Summary of Subnet ID Key Facts

Definition	Number that represents the subnet
Numeric Value	First (smallest) number in the subnet
Literal Synonyms	Subnet number, subnet address, prefix, resident subnet
Common-Use Synonyms	Network, network ID, network number, network address
Typically Seen In...	Routing tables, documentation

Subnet Broadcast Address

The subnet broadcast address has two main roles: to be used as a destination IP address for the purpose of sending packets to all hosts in the subnet, and as a means to find the high end of the range of addresses in a subnet.

The original purpose for the subnet broadcast address was to give hosts a way to send one packet to all hosts in a subnet, and to do so efficiently. For example, a host in subnet A could send a packet with a destination address of subnet B's subnet broadcast address. The routers would forward this one packet just like a packet sent to a host in subnet B. After the packet arrives at the router connected to subnet B, that last router would then forward the packet to all hosts in subnet B, typically by encapsulating the packet in a data link layer broadcast frame. As a result, all hosts in host B's subnet would receive a copy of the packet.

The subnet broadcast address also helps you find the range of addresses in a subnet, because the broadcast address is the last (highest) number in a subnet's range of addresses. To find the low end of the range, calculate the subnet ID; to find the high end of the range, calculate the subnet broadcast address.

Table 16-3 summarizes the key facts about the subnet broadcast address, along with the possible synonyms, for easier review and study.

Table 16-3   Summary of Subnet Broadcast Address Key Facts

Definition	A reserved number in each subnet that, when used as the destination address of a packet, causes the routers to forward the packet to all hosts in that subnet
Numeric Value	Last (highest) number in the subnet
Literal Synonyms	Directed broadcast address
Broader-Use Synonyms	Network broadcast
Typically Seen In...	In calculations of the range of addresses in a subnet

Range of Usable Addresses

The engineers implementing an IP internetwork need to know the range of unicast IP addresses in each subnet. Before you can plan which addresses to use as statically assigned IP addresses, which to configure to be leased by the DHCP server, and which to reserve for later use, you need to know the range of usable addresses.

To find the range of usable IP addresses in a subnet, first find the subnet ID and the subnet broadcast address. Then, just add 1 to the fourth octet of the subnet ID to get the first (lowest) usable address, and subtract 1 from the fourth octet of the subnet broadcast address to get the last (highest) usable address in the subnet.

For example, Figure 16-3 showed subnet ID 172.16.128.0, mask /18. The first usable address is simply 1 more than the subnet ID (in this case, 172.16.128.1). That same figure showed a subnet broadcast address of 172.16.191.255, so the last usable address is 1 less, or 172.16.191.254.

Now that this section has described the concepts behind the numbers that collectively define a subnet, the rest of this chapter focuses on the math used to find these values.

Analyzing Existing Subnets: Binary

What does it mean to "analyze a subnet"? For this book, it means that you should be able to start with an IP address and mask and then define key facts about the subnet in which that address resides. Specifically, that means discovering the subnet ID, subnet broadcast address, and range of addresses. The analysis can also include the calculation of the number of addresses in the subnet as discussed in Chapter 15, but this chapter does not review those concepts.

Many methods exist to calculate the details about a subnet based on the address/mask. This section begins by discussing some calculations that use binary math, with the next section showing alternatives that use only decimal math. Although many people prefer the decimal method for going fast on the exams, the binary calculations ultimately give you a better understanding of IPv4 addressing. In particular, if you plan to move on to attain Cisco routing and switching certifications, you should take the time to understand the binary methods discussed in this section, even if you use the decimal methods for the exams.

Finding the Subnet ID: Binary

To start this section that uses binary, first consider a simple decimal math problem. The problem: Find the smallest three-digit decimal number that begins with 4. The answer, of course, is 400. And although most people would not have to break down the logic into steps, you know that 0 is the lowest-value digit you can use for any digit in a decimal number. You know that the first digit must be a 4, and the number is a three-digit number, so you just use the lowest value (0) for the last two digits, and find the answer: 400.

This same concept, applied to binary IP addresses, gives you the subnet ID. You have seen all the related concepts in other chapters, so if you already intuitively know how to find the subnet ID in binary, great! If not, the following key facts should help you see the logic:

All numbers in the subnet (subnet ID, subnet broadcast address, and all usable IP addresses) have the same value in the prefix part of the numbers.

The subnet ID is the lowest numeric value in the subnet, so its host part, in binary, is all 0s.

To find the subnet ID in binary, you take the IP address in binary and change all host bits to binary 0. To do so, you need to convert the IP address to binary. You also need to identify the prefix and host bits, which can be easily done by converting the mask (as needed) to prefix format. (Note that Appendix C, "Numeric Reference Tables," includes a decimal-binary conversion table.) Figure 16-4 shows the idea, using the same address/mask as in the earlier examples in this chapter: 172.16.150.41, mask /18.

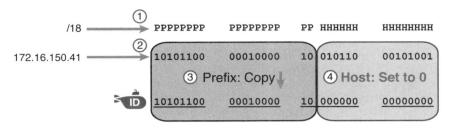

Legend:

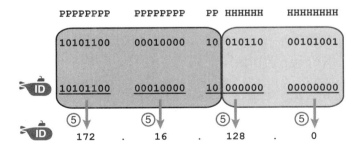 Subnet ID

Figure 16-4 *Binary Concept: Convert the IP Address to the Subnet ID*

Starting at the top of Figure 16-4, the format of the IP address is represented with 18 prefix (P) and 14 host (H) bits in the mask (Step 1). The second row (Step 2) shows the binary version of the IP address, converted from the dotted-decimal notation (DDN) value 172.16.150.41. (If you have not used the conversion table in Appendix C yet, it might be useful to double-check the conversion of all four octets based on the table.)

The next two steps show the action to copy the IP address's prefix bits (Step 3) and give the host bits a value of binary 0 (Step 4). This resulting number is the subnet ID (in binary).

The last step, not shown in Figure 16-4, is to convert the subnet ID from binary to decimal. This book shows that conversion as a separate step, in Figure 16-5, mainly because many people make a mistake at this step in the process. When converting a 32-bit number (like an IP address or IP subnet ID) back to an IPv4 DDN, you must follow this rule:

Convert 8 bits at a time from binary to decimal, regardless of the line between the prefix and host parts of the number.

Figure 16-5 *Converting the Subnet ID from Binary to DDN*

Figure 16-5 shows this final step. Note that the third octet (the third set of 8 bits) has 2 bits in the prefix and 6 bits in the host part of the number, but the conversion occurs for all 8 bits.

> **NOTE**   You can do the numeric conversions in Figures 16-4 and 16-5 by relying on the conversion table in Appendix C. To convert from DDN to binary, for each octet, find the decimal value in the table and then write down the 8-bit binary equivalent. To convert from binary back to DDN, for each octet of 8 bits, find the matching binary entry in the table and write down the corresponding decimal value. For example, 172 converts to binary 10101100, and 00010000 converts to decimal 16.

Finding the Subnet Broadcast Address: Binary

Finding the subnet broadcast address uses a similar process. To find the subnet broadcast address, use the same binary process used to find the subnet ID, but instead of setting all the host bits to the lowest value (all binary 0s), set the host part to the highest value (all binary 1s). Figure 16-6 shows the concept.

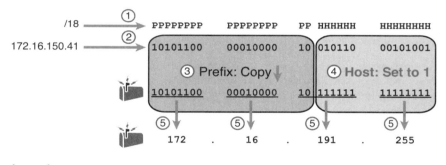

Legend:

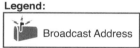
Broadcast Address

Figure 16-6   *Finding a Subnet Broadcast Address: Binary*

The process in Figure 16-6 demonstrates the same first three steps shown in Figure 16-4. Specifically, it shows the identification of the prefix and host bits (Step 1), the results of converting the IP address 172.16.150.41 to binary (Step 2), and the copying of the prefix bits (first 18 bits, in this case). The difference occurs in the host bits on the right, changing all host bits (the last 14, in this case) to the largest possible value (all binary 1s). The final step converts the 32-bit subnet broadcast address to DDN format. Also, remember that with any conversion from DDN to binary or vice versa, the process always converts using 8 bits at a time. In particular, in this case, the entire third octet of binary 10111111 is converted back to decimal 191.

Binary Practice Problems

Figures 16-4 and 16-5 demonstrate a process to find the subnet ID using binary math. The following process summarizes those steps in written form for easier reference and practice:

Step 1.   Convert the mask to prefix format to find the length of the prefix (/P) and the length of the host part (32 – P).

Step 2.   Convert the IP address to its 32-bit binary equivalent.

Step 3.   Copy the prefix bits of the IP address.

Step 4.   Write down 0s for the host bits.

Step 5.   Convert the resulting 32-bit number, 8 bits at a time, back to decimal.

The process to find the subnet broadcast address is exactly the same, except in Step 4, you set the bits to 1s, as seen in Figure 16-6.

Take a few moments and run through the following five practice problems on scratch paper. In each case, find both the subnet ID and subnet broadcast address. Also, record the prefix style mask:

1. 8.1.4.5, 255.255.0.0
2. 130.4.102.1, 255.255.255.0
3. 199.1.1.100, 255.255.255.0
4. 130.4.102.1, 255.255.252.0
5. 199.1.1.100, 255.255.255.224

Tables 16-4 through 16-8 show the results for the five different examples. The tables show the host bits in bold, and they include the binary version of the address and mask and the binary version of the subnet ID and subnet broadcast address.

Table 16-4   Subnet Analysis for Subnet with Address 8.1.4.5, Mask 255.255.0.0

Prefix Length	/16	11111111 11111111 **00000000 00000000**
Address	8.1.4.5	00001000 00000001 **00000100 00000101**
Subnet ID	8.1.0.0	00001000 00000001 **00000000 00000000**
Broadcast Address	8.1.255.255	00001000 00000001 **11111111 11111111**

Table 16-5   Subnet Analysis for Subnet with Address 130.4.102.1, Mask 255.255.255.0

Prefix Length	/24	11111111 11111111 11111111 **00000000**
Address	130.4.102.1	10000010 00000100 01100110 **00000001**
Subnet ID	130.4.102.0	10000010 00000100 01100110 **00000000**
Broadcast Address	130.4.102.255	10000010 00000100 01100110 **11111111**

Table 16-6   Subnet Analysis for Subnet with Address 199.1.1.100, Mask 255.255.255.0

Prefix Length	/24	11111111 11111111 11111111 **00000000**
Address	199.1.1.100	11000111 00000001 00000001 **01100100**
Subnet ID	199.1.1.0	11000111 00000001 00000001 **00000000**
Broadcast Address	199.1.1.255	11000111 00000001 00000001 **11111111**

Table 16-7   Subnet Analysis for Subnet with Address 130.4.102.1, Mask 255.255.252.0

Prefix Length	/22	11111111 11111111 111111**00 00000000**
Address	130.4.102.1	10000010 00000100 011001**10 00000001**
Subnet ID	130.4.100.0	10000010 00000100 011001**00 00000000**
Broadcast Address	130.4.103.255	10000010 00000100 011001**11 11111111**

Table 16-8   Subnet Analysis for Subnet with Address 199.1.1.100, Mask 255.255.255.224

Prefix Length	/27	11111111 11111111 11111111 111**00000**
Address	199.1.1.100	11000111 00000001 00000001 011**00100**
Subnet ID	199.1.1.96	11000111 00000001 00000001 011**00000**
Broadcast Address	199.1.1.127	11000111 00000001 00000001 011**11111**

Shortcut for the Binary Process

The binary process described in this section so far requires that all four octets be converted to binary and then back to decimal. However, you can easily predict the results in at least three of the four octets, based on the DDN mask. You can then avoid the binary math in all but one octet and reduce the number of binary conversions you need to do.

First, consider an octet, and that octet only, whose DDN mask value is 255. The mask value of 255 converts to binary 11111111, which means that all 8 bits are prefix bits. Thinking through the steps in the process, at Step 2, you convert the address to some number. At Step 3, you copy the number. At Step 4, you convert the same 8-bit number back to decimal. All you did in those three steps, in this one octet, is convert from decimal to binary and convert the same number back to the same decimal value!

In short, the subnet ID (and subnet broadcast address) are equal to the IP address in octets for which the mask is 255.

For example, the resident subnet ID for 172.16.150.41, mask 255.255.192.0 is 172.16.128.0. The first two mask octets are 255. Rather than think about the binary math, you could just start by copying the address's value in those two octets: 172.16.

Another shortcut exists for octets whose DDN mask value is decimal 0, or binary 00000000. With a decimal mask value of 0, the math always results in a decimal 0 for the subnet ID, no matter the beginning value in the IP address. Specifically, just look at Steps 4 and 5 in this case: At Step 4, you would write down 8 binary 0s, and at Step 5, convert 00000000 back to decimal 0.

The following revised process steps take these two shortcuts into account. However, when the mask is neither 0 nor 255, the process requires the same conversions. At most, you have to do only one octet of the conversions. To find the subnet ID, apply the logic in these steps for each of the four octets:

Step 1.   If the mask = 255, copy the decimal IP address for that octet.

Step 2.   If the mask = 0, write down a decimal 0 for that octet.

Step 3.   If the mask is neither 0 nor 255 in this octet, use the same binary logic as shown in the section "Finding the Subnet ID: Binary," earlier in this chapter.

Figure 16-7 shows an example of this process, again using 172.16.150.41, 255.255.192.0.

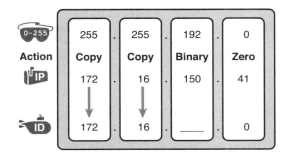

Legend:

Figure 16-7   *Binary Shortcut Example*

A similar shortcut exists when finding the subnet broadcast address. For DDN mask octets equal to decimal 0, set the decimal subnet broadcast address value to 255 instead of 0, as noted in the following list:

Step 1.   If the mask = 255, copy the decimal IP address for that octet.

Step 2.   If the mask = 0, write down a decimal 255 for that octet.

Step 3.   If the mask is neither 0 nor 255 in this octet, use the same binary logic as shown in the section "Finding the Subnet Broadcast Address: Binary," earlier in this chapter.

Brief Note About Boolean Math

So far, this chapter has described how humans can use binary math to find the subnet ID and subnet broadcast address. However, computers typically use an entirely different binary process to find the same values, using a branch of mathematics called *Boolean Algebra*. Computers already store the IP address and mask in binary form, so they do not have to do any conversions to and from decimal. Then, certain Boolean operations allow the computers to calculate the subnet ID and subnet broadcast address with just a few CPU instructions.

You do not need to know Boolean math to have a good understanding of IP subnetting. However, in case you are interested, computers use the following Boolean logic to find the subnet ID and subnet broadcast address, respectively:

Perform a *Boolean AND* of the IP address and mask. This process converts all host bits to binary 0.

Invert the mask, and then perform a *Boolean OR* of the IP address and inverted subnet mask. This process converts all host bits to binary 1s.

Finding the Range of Addresses

Finding the range of usable addresses in a subnet, after you know the subnet ID and subnet broadcast address, requires only simple addition and subtraction. To find the first (lowest) usable IP address in the subnet, simply add 1 to the fourth octet of the subnet ID. To find the last (highest) usable IP address, simply subtract 1 from the fourth octet of the subnet broadcast address.

Analyzing Existing Subnets: Decimal

Analyzing existing subnets using the binary process works well. However, some of the math takes time for most people, particularly the decimal-binary conversions. And you need to do the math quickly for the exam. When using binary methods, most people require a lot of practice to be able to find these answers, even when using the abbreviated binary process.

This section discusses how to find the subnet ID and subnet broadcast address using only decimal math. Most people can find the answers more quickly using this process, at least after a little practice, as compared with the binary process. However, the decimal process does not tell you anything about the meaning behind the math. So, if you have not read the earlier section "Analyzing Existing Subnets: Binary," it is worthwhile to read it for the sake of understanding subnetting. This section focuses on getting the right answer using a method that, after you have practiced, should be faster.

Analysis with Easy Masks

With three easy subnet masks in particular, finding the subnet ID and subnet broadcast address requires only easy logic and literally no math. Three easy masks exist:

255.0.0.0

255.255.0.0

255.255.255.0

These easy masks have only 255 and 0 in decimal. In comparison, difficult masks have one octet that has neither a 255 nor a 0 in the mask, which makes the logic more challenging.

> **NOTE**   The terms *easy mask* and *difficult mask* are terms created for use in this book to describe the masks and the level of difficulty when working with each.

When the problem uses an easy mask, you can quickly find the subnet ID based on the IP address and mask in DDN format. Just use the following process for each of the four octets to find the subnet ID:

Step 1.   If the mask octet = 255, copy the decimal IP address.

Step 2.   If the mask octet = 0, write a decimal 0.

A similar simple process exists to find the subnet broadcast address, as follows:

Step 1.   If the mask octet = 255, copy the decimal IP address.

Step 2.   If the mask octet = 0, write a decimal 255.

Before moving to the next section, take some time to fill in the blanks in Table 16-9. Check your answers against Table 16-14 in the section "Answers to Earlier Practice Problems," later in this chapter. Complete the table by listing the subnet ID and subnet broadcast address.

Table 16-9   Practice Problems: Find Subnet ID and Broadcast, Easy Masks

	IP Address	Mask	Subnet ID	Broadcast Address
1	10.77.55.3	255.255.255.0		
2	172.30.99.4	255.255.255.0		
3	192.168.6.54	255.255.255.0		
4	10.77.3.14	255.255.0.0		
5	172.22.55.77	255.255.0.0		
6	1.99.53.76	255.0.0.0		

Predictability in the Interesting Octet

Although three masks are easier to work with (255.0.0.0, 255.255.0.0, and 255.255.255.0), the rest make the decimal math a little more difficult, so we call these masks difficult masks. With difficult masks, one octet is neither a 0 nor a 255. The math in the other three octets is easy and boring, so this book calls the one octet with the more difficult math the *interesting octet*.

If you take some time to think about different problems and focus on the interesting octet, you will begin to see a pattern. This section takes you through that examination so that you can learn how to predict the pattern, in decimal, and find the subnet ID.

First, the subnet ID value has a predictable decimal value because of the assumption that a single subnet mask is used for all subnets of a single classful network. The chapters in this part of the book assume that, for a given classful network, the design engineer chooses to use a single subnet mask for all subnets.

To see that predictability, consider some planning information written down by a network engineer, as shown in Figure 16-8. The figure shows four different masks the engineer is considering using in an IPv4 network, along with Class B network 172.16.0.0. The figure shows the third-octet values for the subnet IDs that would be created when using mask 255.255.128.0, 255.255.192.0, 255.255.224.0, and 255.255.240.0, from top to bottom in the figure.

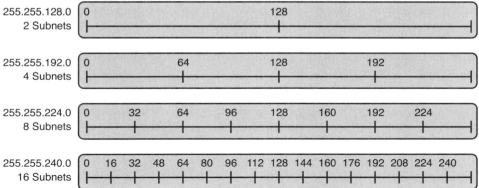

Figure 16-8 *Numeric Patterns in the Interesting Octet*

First, to explain the figure further, look at the top row of the figure. If the engineer uses 255.255.128.0 as the mask, the mask creates two subnets, with subnet IDs 172.16.0.0 and 172.16.128.0. If the engineer uses mask 255.255.192.0, the mask creates four subnets, with subnet IDs 172.16.0.0, 172.16.64.0, 172.16.128.0, and 172.16.192.0.

If you take the time to look at the figure, the patterns become obvious. In this case:

> Mask: 255.255.128.0   Pattern: Multiples of 128
>
> Mask: 255.255.192.0   Pattern: Multiples of 64
>
> Mask: 255.255.224.0   Pattern: Multiples of 32
>
> Mask: 255.255.240.0   Pattern: Multiples of 16

To find the subnet ID, you just need a way to figure out what the pattern is. If you start with an IP address and mask, just find the subnet ID closest to the IP address, without going over, as discussed in the next section.

Finding the Subnet ID: Difficult Masks

The following written process lists all the steps for find the subnet ID, using only decimal math. This process adds to the earlier process used with easy masks. For each octet:

Step 1.   If the mask octet = 255, copy the decimal IP address.

Step 2.   If the mask octet = 0, write a decimal 0.

Step 3.   If the mask is neither, refer to this octet as the *interesting octet*:

    A.   Calculate the *magic number* as 256 – mask.

    B.   Set the subnet ID's value to the multiple of the magic number that is closest to the IP address without going over.

The process uses two new terms created for this book: *magic number* and *interesting octet*. The term *interesting octet* refers to the octet identified at Step 3 in the process; in other words, it is the octet with the mask that is neither 255 nor 0. Step 3A then uses the term *magic number*, which is derived from the DDN mask. Conceptually, the magic number is the number you add to one subnet ID to get the next subnet ID in order, as shown in Figure 16-8. Numerically, it can be found by subtracting the DDN mask's value, in the interesting octet, from 256, as mentioned in Step 3A.

The best way to learn this process is to see it happen. In fact, if you can, stop reading now, use the DVD accompanying this book, and watch the videos about finding the subnet ID with a difficult mask. These videos demonstrate this process. You can also use the examples on the next few pages that show the process being used on paper. Then, follow the practice opportunities outlined in the section "Practice Analyzing Existing Subnets," later in this chapter.

Resident Subnet Example 1

For example, consider the requirement to find the resident subnet for IP address 130.4.102.1, mask 255.255.240.0. The process does not require you to think about prefix bits versus host bits, convert the mask, think about the mask in binary, or convert the IP address to and from binary. Instead, for each of the four octets, choose an action based on the value in the mask. Figure 16-9 shows the results; the circled numbers in the figure refer to the step numbers in the written process to find the subnet ID, as listed in the previous few pages.

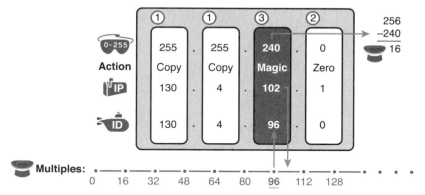

Figure 16-9 *Find the Subnet ID: 130.4.102.1, 255.255.240.0*

First, examine the three uninteresting octets (1, 2, and 4, in this example). The process keys on the mask, and the first two octets have a mask value of 255, so simply copy the IP address to the place where you intend to write down the subnet ID. The fourth octet has a mask value of 0, so write down a 0 for the fourth octet of the subnet ID.

The most challenging logic occurs in the interesting octet, which is the third octet in this example, because of the mask value 240 in that octet. For this octet, Step 3A asks you to calculate the magic number as 256 – mask. That means you take the mask's value in the interesting octet (240, in this case) and subtract it from 256: 256 – 240 = 16. The subnet ID's value in this octet must be a multiple of decimal 16, in this case.

Step 3B then asks you to find the multiples of the magic number (16, in this case) and choose the one closest to the IP address without going over. Specifically, that means that you should mentally calculate the multiples of the magic number, starting at 0. (Do not forget to start at 0!) Counting, starting at 0: 0, 16, 32, 48, 64, 80, 96, 112, and so on. Then, find the multiple closest to the IP address value in this octet (102, in this case), without going over 102. So, as shown in Figure 16-9, you make the third octet's value 96 to complete the subnet ID of 130.4.96.0.

Resident Subnet Example 2

Consider another example: 192.168.5.77, mask 255.255.255.224. Figure 16-10 shows the results.

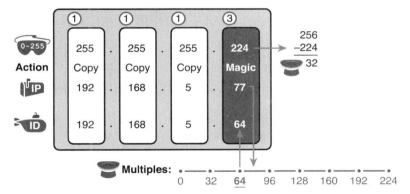

Figure 16-10   *Resident Subnet for 192.168.5.77, 255.255.255.224*

The three uninteresting octets (1, 2, and 3, in this case) require only a little thought. For each octet, each with a mask value of 255, just copy the IP address.

For the interesting octet, at Step 3A, the magic number is 256 – 224 = 32. The multiples of the magic number are 0, 32, 64, 96, and so on. Because the IP address value in the fourth octet is 77, in this case, the multiple must be the number closest to 77 without going over; therefore, the subnet ID ends with 64, for a value of 192.168.5.64.

Resident Subnet Practice Problems

Before moving to the next section, take some time to fill in the blanks in Table 16-10. Check your answers against Table 16-15 in the section "Answers to Earlier Practice Problems," later in this chapter. Complete the table by listing the subnet ID in each case. The text following Table 16-15 also lists explanations for each problem.

Table 16-10 Practice Problems: Find Subnet ID, Difficult Masks

Problem	IP Address	Mask	Subnet ID
1	10.77.55.3	255.248.0.0	
2	172.30.99.4	255.255.192.0	
3	192.168.6.54	255.255.255.252	
4	10.77.3.14	255.255.128.0	
5	172.22.55.77	255.255.254.0	
6	1.99.53.76	255.255.255.248	

Finding the Subnet Broadcast Address: Difficult Masks

To find a subnet's broadcast address, a similar process can be used. For simplicity, this process begins with the subnet ID, rather than the IP address. If you happen to start with an IP address instead, use the processes in this chapter to first find the subnet ID, and then use the following process to find the subnet broadcast address for that same subnet. For each octet:

Step 1.   If the mask octet = 255, copy the subnet ID.

Step 2.   If the mask octet = 0, write a 255.

Step 3.   If the mask is neither, identify this octet as the *interesting octet*:

    A.   Calculate the *magic number* as 256 – mask.

    B.   Take the subnet ID's value, add the magic number, and subtract 1 (ID + magic – 1).

As with the similar process used to find the subnet ID, you have several options for how to best learn and internalize the process. If you can, stop reading now, use the DVD accompanying this book, and watch the videos about finding the subnet broadcast address with a difficult mask. Also, look at the examples in this section, which show the process being used on paper. Then, follow the practice opportunities outlined in the section "Additional Practice."

Subnet Broadcast Example 1

The first example continues the first example from the section "Finding the Subnet ID: Difficult Masks," earlier in this chapter, as demonstrated in Figure 16-9. That example started with the IP address/mask of 130.4.102.1, 255.255.240.0, and showed how to find subnet ID 130.4.96.0. Figure 16-11 now begins with that subnet ID and the same mask.

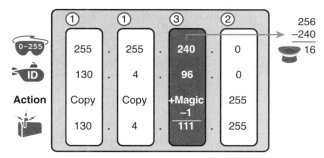

Figure 16-11   *Find the Subnet Broadcast: 130.4.96.0, 255.255.240.0*

First, examine the three uninteresting octets (1, 2, and 4). The process keys on the mask, and the first two octets have a mask value of 255, so simply copy the subnet ID to the place where you intend to write down the subnet broadcast address. The fourth octet has a mask value of 0, so write down a 255 for the fourth octet.

The logic related to the interesting octet occurs in the third octet in this example, because of the mask value 240. First, Step 3A asks you to calculate the magic number, as 256 − mask. (If you had already calculated the subnet ID using the decimal process in this book, you should already know the magic number.) At Step 3B, you take the subnet ID's value (96), add magic (16), and subtract 1, for a total of 111. That makes the subnet broadcast address 130.4.111.255.

Subnet Broadcast Example 2

Again, this example continues an earlier example, from the section "Resident Subnet Example 2," as demonstrated in Figure 16-10. That example started with the IP address/mask of 192.168.5.77, mask 255.255.255.224 and showed how to find subnet ID 192.168.5.64. Figure 16-12 now begins with that subnet ID and the same mask.

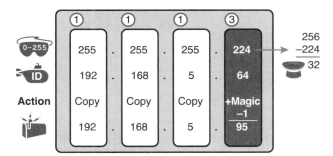

Figure 16-12   *Find the Subnet Broadcast: 192.168.5.64, 255.255.255.224*

First, examine the three uninteresting octets (1, 2, and 3). The process keys on the mask, and the first three octets have a mask value of 255, so simply copy the subnet ID to the place where you intend to write down the subnet broadcast address.

The interesting logic occurs in the interesting octet, the fourth octet in this example, because of the mask value 224. First, Step 3A asks you to calculate the magic number, as 256 – mask. (If you had already calculated the subnet ID, it is the same magic number, because the same mask is used.) At Step 3B, you take the subnet ID's value (64), add magic (32), and subtract 1, for a total of 95. That makes the subnet broadcast address 192.168.5.95.

Subnet Broadcast Address Practice Problems

Before moving to the next section, take some time to do several practice problems on a scratch piece of paper. Go back to Table 16-10, which lists IP addresses and masks, and practice by finding the subnet broadcast address for all the problems in that table. Then check your answers against Table 16-16 in the section "Answers to Earlier Practice Problems," later in this chapter.

Practice Analyzing Existing Subnets

Before moving to the next chapter, practice until you get the right answer most of the time—but use any tools you want and take all the time you need. Then, you can move on with your reading.

However, before taking the exam, practice until you master the topics in this chapter and can move pretty fast. As for time, you should be able to find the subnet ID, based on an IP address and mask, in around 15 seconds. You should also strive to start with a subnet ID/mask, and find the broadcast address and range of addresses, in another 15 seconds. Table 16-11 summarizes the key concepts and suggestions for this two-phase approach.

Table 16-11   Keep-Reading and Take-Exam Goals for This Chapter's Topics

Time Frame	Before Moving to the Next Chapter	Before Taking the Exam
Focus On...	Learning how	Being correct and fast
Tools Allowed	All	Your brain and a notepad
Goal: Accuracy	90% correct	100% correct
Goal: Speed	Any speed	30 seconds

A Choice: Memorize or Calculate

As described in this chapter, the decimal processes to find the subnet ID and subnet broadcast address do require some calculation, including the calculation of the magic number (256 – mask). The processes also use a DDN mask, so if an exam question gives you a prefix-style mask, you need to convert to DDN format before using the process in this book.

Over the years, some people have told me they prefer to memorize a table to find the magic number. These tables could list the magic number for different DDN masks and prefix masks, so you avoid converting from the prefix mask to DDN. Table 16-12 shows an example of such a table. Feel free to ignore this table, use it, or make your own.

Table 16-12 Reference Table: DDN Mask Values, Binary Equivalent, Magic Numbers, and Prefixes

Prefix, interesting octet 2	/9	/10	/11	/12	/13	/14	/15	/16
Prefix, interesting octet 3	/17	/18	/19	/20	/21	/22	/23	/24
Prefix, interesting octet 4	/25	/26	/27	/28	/29	/30		
Magic number	128	64	32	16	8	4	2	1
DDN mask in the interesting octet	128	192	224	240	248	252	254	255

16

Additional Practice

This section lists several options for additional practice:

■ DVD Appendix G, "Practice for Chapter 16: Analyzing Existing Subnets," has some additional practice problems. This appendix also includes explanations about how to find the answer of each problem.

■ Create your own problems. Many subnet calculators list the number of network, subnet, and host bits when you type in an IP address and mask, so make up an IP address and mask on paper, and find the subnet ID and range of addresses. Then, to check your work, use any subnet calculator. (Check the author's web pages for this book, as listed in the Introduction, for some suggested calculators.)

Exam Preparation Tasks

Review All the Key Topics

Review the most important topics from this chapter, noted with the Key Topic icon. Table 16-13 lists these key topics and where each is discussed.

Table 16-13   Key Topics for Chapter 16

Key Topic Element	Description	Page Number
List	Definition of a subnet's key numbers	412
Table 16-2	Key facts about the subnet ID	414
Table 16-3	Key facts about the subnet broadcast address	415
List	Steps to use binary math to find the subnet ID	419
List	General steps to use binary and decimal math to find the subnet ID	421
List	Steps to use decimal and binary math to find the subnet broadcast address	422
List	Steps to use only decimal math to find the subnet ID	425
List	Steps to use only decimal math to find the subnet broadcast address	428

Complete the Tables and Lists from Memory

Print a copy of DVD Appendix I, "Memory Tables," or at least the section for this chapter, and complete the tables and lists from memory. DVD Appendix J, "Memory Tables Answer Key," includes completed tables and lists for you to check your work.

Definitions of Key Terms

After your first reading of the chapter, try to define these key terms, but do not be concerned about getting them all correct at that time. Chapter 23 directs you in how to use these terms for late-stage preparation for the exam.

resident subnet, subnet ID, subnet number, subnet address, subnet broadcast address

Practice

If you have not done so already, practice finding the subnet ID, range of addresses, and subnet broadcast address associated with an IP address and mask. Refer to the earlier section "Practice Analyzing Existing Subnets" for suggestions.

Answers to Earlier Practice Problems

This chapter includes practice problems spread around different locations in the chapter. The answers are located in Tables 16-14, 16-15, and 16-16.

Table 16-14   Answers to Problems in Table 16-9

	IP Address	Mask	Subnet ID	Broadcast Address
1	10.77.55.3	255.255.255.0	10.77.55.0	10.77.55.255
2	172.30.99.4	255.255.255.0	172.30.99.0	172.30.99.255
3	192.168.6.54	255.255.255.0	192.168.6.0	192.168.6.255
4	10.77.3.14	255.255.0.0	10.77.0.0	10.77.255.255
5	172.22.55.77	255.255.0.0	172.22.0.0	172.22.255.255
6	1.99.53.76	255.0.0.0	1.0.0.0	1.255.255.255

Table 16-15   Answers to Problems in Table 16-10

	IP Address	Mask	Subnet ID
1	10.77.55.3	255.248.0.0	10.72.0.0
2	172.30.99.4	255.255.192.0	172.30.64.0
3	192.168.6.54	255.255.255.252	192.168.6.52
4	10.77.3.14	255.255.128.0	10.77.0.0
5	172.22.55.77	255.255.254.0	172.22.54.0
6	1.99.53.76	255.255.255.248	1.99.53.72

The following list explains the answers for Table 16-15:

1. The second octet is the interesting octet, with magic number 256 − 248 = 8. The multiples of 8 include 0, 8, 16, 24, ..., 64, 72, and 80. 72 is closest to the IP address value in that same octet (77) without going over, making the subnet ID 10.72.0.0.

2. The third octet is the interesting octet, with magic number 256 − 192 = 64. The multiples of 64 include 0, 64, 128, and 192. 64 is closest to the IP address value in that same octet (99) without going over, making the subnet ID 172.30.64.0.

3. The fourth octet is the interesting octet, with magic number 256 − 252 = 4. The multiples of 4 include 0, 4, 8, 12, 16, ..., 48, and 52, 56. 52 is the closest to the IP address value in that same octet (54) without going over, making the subnet ID 192.168.6.52.

4. The third octet is the interesting octet, with magic number 256 − 128 = 128. Only two multiples exist that matter: 0 and 128. 0 is the closest to the IP address value in that same octet (3) without going over, making the subnet ID 10.77.0.0.

5. The third octet is the interesting octet, with magic number 256 – 254 = 2. The multiples of 2 include 0, 2, 4, 6, 8, and so on—essentially all even numbers. 54 is closest to the IP address value in that same octet (55) without going over, making the subnet ID 172.22.54.0.

6. The fourth octet is the interesting octet, with magic number 256 – 248 = 8. The multiples of 8 include 0, 8, 16, 24, ..., 64, 72, and 80. 72 is closest to the IP address value in that same octet (76) without going over, making the subnet ID 1.99.53.72.

Table 16-16 Answers to Problems in the Section "Subnet Broadcast Address Practice Problems"

	Subnet ID	Mask	Broadcast Address
1	10.72.0.0	255.248.0.0	10.79.255.255
2	172.30.64.0	255.255.192.0	172.30.127.255
3	192.168.6.52	255.255.255.252	192.168.6.55
4	10.77.0.0	255.255.128.0	10.77.127.255
5	172.22.54.0	255.255.254.0	172.22.55.255
6	1.99.53.72	255.255.255.248	1.99.53.79

The following list explains the answers for Table 16-16:

1. The second octet is the interesting octet. Completing the three easy octets means that the broadcast address in the interesting octet will be 10.___.255.255. With a magic number 256 – 248 = 8, the second octet will be 72 (from the subnet ID), plus 8, minus 1, or 79.

2. The third octet is the interesting octet. Completing the three easy octets means that the broadcast address in the interesting octet will be 172.30.___.255. With magic number 256 – 192 = 64, the interesting octet will be 64 (from the subnet ID), plus 64 (the magic number), minus 1, for 127.

3. The fourth octet is the interesting octet. Completing the three easy octets means that the broadcast address in the interesting octet will be 192.168.6.___. With magic number 256 – 252 = 4, the interesting octet will be 52 (the subnet ID value), plus 4 (the magic number), minus 1, or 55.

4. The third octet is the interesting octet. Completing the three easy octets means that the broadcast address will be 10.77.___.255. With magic number 256 – 128 = 128, the interesting octet will be 0 (the subnet ID value), plus 128 (the magic number), minus 1, or 127.

5. The third octet is the interesting octet. Completing the three easy octets means that the broadcast address will be 172.22.___.255. With magic number 256 − 254 = 2, the broadcast address in the interesting octet will be 54 (the subnet ID value), plus 2 (the magic number), minus 1, or 55.

6. The fourth octet is the interesting octet. Completing the three easy octets means that the broadcast address will be 1.99.53.___. With magic number 256 − 248 = 8, the broadcast address in the interesting octet will be 72 (the subnet ID value), plus 8 (the magic number), minus 1, or 79.

16

This chapter covers the following exam topics:

1.3 Use the OSI and TCP/IP models and their associated protocols to explain how data flows in a network

1.3.a IP

3.1 Describe the operation and benefits of using private and public IP addressing

3.1.c RFC 4193

3.2 Describe the difference between IPv4 and IPv6 addressing scheme

3.2.b Host addressing

CHAPTER 17

Fundamentals of IP Version 6

Much of the work to standardize IP Version 4 (IPv4) occurred in the 1970s—an era when most families did not own a computer and when a home computer with 16 kilobytes of RAM was considered a lot of RAM. At the time, a 32-bit IPv4 address, which could number more than 4 billion hosts, seemed ridiculously large. However, by the early 1990s, the IPv4-based Internet not only showed signs of running out of addresses, but it also risked running out of addresses very soon—endangering the emergence of the global Internet as a world-wide network available to all.

The Internet community came together to create both short-term and long-term solutions. The biggest short-term solution, Network Address Translation (NAT), reduced the number of unique IPv4 addresses needed by each company, putting off the day when the world would run out of IPv4 addresses. The long-term solution required a new version of IP, called IP Version 6 (IPv6).

IPv6 solves the long-term addressing problem with a mind-staggering 128-bit address, providing a little more than 3.4×10^{38} IPv6 addresses. For perspective, that number is far larger than most estimates for the number of grains of sand on Earth, and for the number of stars in the entire universe.

This chapter introduces IPv6, with comparisons to IPv4.

"Do I Know This Already?" Quiz

Use the "Do I Know This Already?" quiz to help decide whether you might want to skim this chapter, or a major section, moving more quickly to the "Exam Preparation Tasks" section near the end of the chapter. You can find the answers at the bottom of the page following the quiz. For thorough explanations, see Appendix A, "Answers to the 'Do I Know This Already?' Quizzes."

Table 17-1 "Do I Know This Already?" Foundation Topics Section-to-Question Mapping

Foundation Topics Section	Questions
Introduction to IP Version 6	1–4
IPv6 Addressing and Subnetting	5–7
Implementing IPv6	8

1. Of the following list of motivations for the Internet community to create IPv6 to replace IPv4, which was the most important reason?

   a. To remove the requirement to use NAT when connecting to the Internet

   b. To simplify the IP header to simplify router forwarding CPU time

   c. To improve support to allow mobile devices to move in a network

   d. To provide more addresses to relieve the address exhaustion problem

2. Which of the following is the shortest valid abbreviation for FE80:0000:0000:0100:0000:0000:0000:0123?

   a. FE80::100::123

   b. FE8::1::123

   c. FE80::100:0:0:0:123:4567

   d. FE80:0:0:100::123

3. Which of the following is the shortest valid abbreviation for 2000:0300:0040:0005:6000:0700:0080:0009?

   a. 2:3:4:5:6:7:8:9

   b. 2000:300:40:5:6000:700:80:9

   c. 2000:300:4:5:6000:700:8:9

   d. 2000:3:4:5:6:7:8:9

4. Which of the following is the prefix for address 2000:0000:0000:0005:6000:0700:0080:0009, assuming a mask of /64?

   a. 2000::5::/64

   b. 2000::5:0:0:0:0/64

   c. 2000:0:0:5::/64

   d. 2000:0:0:5:0:0:0:0/64

5. Which of the following IPv6 addresses appears to be a global unicast address, based on its first few hex digits?

   a. 3123:1:3:5::1

   b. FE80::1234:56FF:FE78:9ABC

   c. FDAD::1

   d. FF00::5

6. When subnetting an IPv6 address block, an engineer shows a drawing that breaks the address structure into three pieces. Comparing this concept to a three-part IPv4 address structure, which part of the IPv6 address structure is most like the IPv4 network part of the address?

    a. subnet

    b. interface ID

    c. network

    d. global routing prefix

    e. subnet router anycast

7. When subnetting an IPv6 address block, an engineer shows a drawing that breaks the address structure into three pieces. Assuming that all subnets use the same prefix length, which of the following answers lists the name of the field on the far right side of the address?

    a. Subnet

    b. Interface ID

    c. Network

    d. Global routing prefix

    e. Subnet router anycast

8. Host PC1 dynamically learns its IPv6 settings using stateless address autoconfiguration (SLAAC). Think about the host's unicast address as two parts: the prefix and the interface ID. Which of the answers lists a way that SLAAC learns or builds the value of the interface ID portion of the host's address? (Choose two answers.)

    a. Learned from a DHCPv6 server

    b. Built by the host using EUI-64 rules

    c. Learned from a router using NDP RS/RA messages

    d. Built by the host using a random value

17

Foundation Topics

Introduction to IP Version 6

IP Version 6 (IPv6) serves as the replacement protocol for IP Version 4 (IPv4). And although IPv6 has many benefits compared to IPv4, the overwhelming motivation to create IPv6 was to solve the shortage of IPv4 addresses by creating a new IP protocol with many more addresses.

This introductory section of the chapter begins by discussing the motivations and effects of the world's migration from IPv4 to IPv6. The rest of the introduction then examines the IPv6 addresses and prefixes that solve the primary issue of not having enough IPv4 addresses.

The Need and Effect of a New Internet Protocol

In the past 40 years, the Internet has gone from its infancy to being a huge influence in the world. It first grew through research at universities, from the ARPANET beginnings of the Internet in the late 1960s into the 1970s. The Internet kept growing fast in the 1980s, with the Internet's fast growth still primarily driven by research and the universities that joined in that research. By the early 1990s, the Internet began to transform to allow commerce, allowing people to sell services and products over the Internet, which drove yet another steep spike upward in the growth of the Internet. Figure 17-1 shows some of these major milestones.

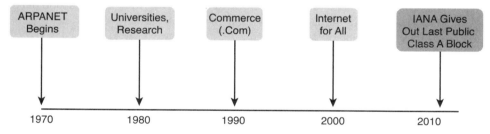

Figure 17-1 *Some Major Events in the Growth of the Internet*

Note that the figure ends the timeline with an event in which IANA/ICANN, the groups that assign public IPv4 addresses, gave out the last public IPv4 address blocks. IANA/ICANN assigned the final class A networks to each the Regional Internet Registries (RIRs) in February 2011. This event was an important event for the Internet, bringing us closer to the day when a company simply cannot get new IPv4 public address blocks.

In other words, one day, a company could be rejected when they attempt to connect to the Internet, all because no more public IPv4 addresses exist.

Even though the press made a big deal about running out of IPv4 addresses in 2011, those who care about the Internet knew about this potential problem since the late 1980s. The problem, generally called the *IPv4 address-exhaustion* problem, could literally have caused the huge growth of the Internet in the 1990s to have come to a screeching halt! Something had to be done.

The IETF came up with several short-term solutions to make IPv4 last longer, hoping to put off the day when the world ran out of public IPv4 addresses. The two primary short-term solutions were Network Address Translation/Port Address Translation (NAT/PAT) and classless interdomain routing (CIDR). Both worked wonderfully. At the time, the Internet community hoped to extend the life of IPv4 for a few more years. In practice, these tools help extend IPv4's life another couple of decades, as shown in the timeline of Figure 17-2.

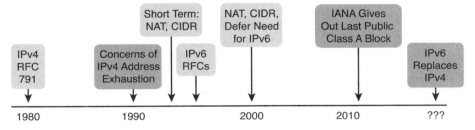

Figure 17-2   *Timeline for IPv4 Address Exhaustion and Short/Long-Term Solutions*

> **NOTE**   The website www.potaroo.net, by Geoff Huston, shows many interesting statistics about the growth of the Internet, including IPv4 address exhaustion.

While the short-term solutions to IPv4 address exhaustion problem gave us all a few more decades to use IPv4, IPv6 gives the world a long-term solution to the problem. IPv6 replaces IPv4 as the core Layer 3 protocol, with a new IPv6 header and new IPv6 addresses. These addresses support a huge number of addresses, solving the address shortage problem for generations (we hope).

> **NOTE**   You may wonder why the next version of IP is not called IP Version 5. There was an earlier effort to create a new version of IP, and it was numbered version 5. IPv5 did not progress to the standards stage. However, to prevent any issues, because version 5 had been used in some documents, the next effort to update IP was numbered as version 6.

Additional Motivations for IPv6

While the need for more addresses drove the need for a new standard, IPv6 provides other benefits as well. For example, the designers of IPv6 acted on the decades of experience with IPv4 to make other improvements. The IPv6 header is actually simpler than the IPv4 header, streamlining the work routers do when forwarding packets. IPv6 supports some security and device mobility processes much more naturally than IPv4 as well.

Another big advantage for IPv6 is that enterprises no longer have to use NAT at the point of the enterprise's connection to the Internet. Today, most every company must use NAT, because without it, the Internet would have run out of IPv4 addresses a long time ago.

Unfortunately, NAT happens to cause problems for some applications. IPv6 removes the requirement for NAT, solving a variety of problems with different applications.

A variety of other small motivations existed as well. IPv6 improved security, added new address autoconfiguration options, improvements to support device mobility more easily, and several others.

Many Protocols Updated

The upgrade to IPv6 begins with a new protocol called IP Version 6, but it includes many more new standards as well.

First, IPv6 does have a new protocol definition, as defined in RFC 2460. This RFC defines familiar concepts: a packet concept, addresses for those packets, and the role of hosts and routers. These rules allow the devices to forward IPv6 packets, sourced by IPv6 hosts, through multiple IPv6 routers, so that they arrive at the correct destination IPv6 host. (IPv4 defines those same concepts for IPv4 back in RFC 791.)

As you might imagine, IPv4 touches many other protocols as well, so an upgrade of IP from IPv4 to IPv6 required many other protocols to be upgraded as well. Some other RFCs define how to migrate from IPv4 to IPv6. Others define new versions of familiar protocols, or replace old protocols with new ones. For instance:

- **Older OSPF Version 2 Upgraded to OSPF Version 3:** The older OSPF Version 2 works for IPv4, but not for IPv6, so a newer version, OSPF Version 3, was created to support IPv6.

- **ICMP Upgraded to ICMP Version 6:** ICMP worked well with IPv4, but needed to be changed to support IPv6. The new name is ICMPv6.

- **ARP Replaced by Neighbor Discovery Protocol:** For IPv4, ARP discovers the MAC address used by neighbors. IPv6 replaces ARP with a more general Neighbor Discovery Protocol (NDP).

NOTE   But if you go to any website that lists the RFCs, like www.rfc-editor.org, you can find almost 300 RFCs that have IPv6 in the title.

Introduction to IPv6 Addresses and Prefixes

The other chapters in Part IV of this book have explained many details of how IPv4 addressing and subnetting work. For instance, with IPv4, you need to be able to interpret IPv4 addresses, like 172.21.73.14. You need to be able to work with prefix-style masks, like /25, and interpret what that means when used with a particular IPv4 address. And you need to be able to take an address and mask, like 172.21.73.14/25, and find the subnet ID.

The next few pages introduce the equivalent work with IPv6. Thankfully, even though the IPv6 addresses are much longer, the math is typically much more obvious and easier to do. In particular, this section looks at the following:

- How to write and interpret unabbreviated IPv6 addresses (32 hex digits in length)
- How to abbreviate IPv6 addresses, and how to interpret abbreviated addresses
- How to interpret the IPv6 prefix length mask
- How to find the IPv6 prefix (subnet ID), based on an address and prefix length mask

The biggest challenge with these tasks lies in the sheer size of the numbers. Thankfully, the math to find the subnet ID—often a challenge for IPv4—is easier for IPv6, at least to the depth discussed in this book.

17

Representing Full (Unabbreviated) IPv6 Addresses

IPv6 uses a convenient hexadecimal (hex) format for addresses. To make it more readable, IPv6 uses a format with eight sets of four hex digits, with each set of four digits separated by a colon. For example:

2340:1111:AAAA:0001:1234:5678:9ABC:1234

NOTE For convenience, the author uses the term *quartet* for one set of four hex digits, with eight quartets in each IPv6 address. Note that the IPv6 RFCs do not use the term quartet.

NOTE The IPv6 address format shown here may be referred to as *delimited hexadecimal*.

IPv6 addresses also have a binary format as well, but thankfully, most of the time you do not need to look at the binary version of the addresses. However, in those cases, converting from hex to binary is relatively easy. Just change each hex digit to the equivalent 4-bit value as listed in the hexadecimal-binary conversion table in Appendix C, "Numeric Reference Tables."

Abbreviating IPv6 Addresses

IPv6 also defines ways to abbreviate or shorten how you write or type an IPv6 address. Why? Although using a 32-digit hex number works much better than working with a 128-bit binary number, 32 hex digits is still a lot of digits to remember, recognize in command output, and type on a command line. The IPv6 address abbreviation rules let you shorten these numbers.

NOTE Computers and routers typically use the shortest abbreviation, even if you type all 32 hex digits of the address. So, even if you would prefer to use the longer unabbreviated version of the IPv6 address, you need to be ready to interpret the meaning of an abbreviated IPv6 address as listed by a router or host.

To be ready for the exam, you should be ready to abbreviate a full 32-digit IPv6 address, and to do the reverse: expand an abbreviated address back to its full 32-digits. Two basic rules let you, or any computer, shorten or abbreviate an IPv6 address:

1. Inside each quartet of four hex digits, remove the leading 0s (0s on the left side of the quartet) in the three positions on the left. (Note that at this step, a quartet of 0000 will leave a single 0.)

2. Find any string of two or more consecutive quartets of all hex 0s, and replace that set of quartets with double colon (::). The :: means "two or more quartets of all 0s." However, you can only use :: once in a single address, because otherwise the exact IPv6 address might not be clear.

For example, consider the following IPv6 address. The bold digits represent digits in which the address could be abbreviated.

FE00:**0000:0000:0001:0000:0000:0000:00**56

Applying the first rule, you would look at all eight quartets independently. In each, remove all the leading 0s. Note that five of the quartets have four 0s, so for these, only remove three 0s, leaving the following value:

FE00:**0:0:1:0:0:0**:56

This abbreviation is valid, but the address can be abbreviated more, using the second rule. In this case, two instances exist where more than one quartet in a row has only a 0. Pick the longest such sequence, and replace it with ::, giving you the shortest legal abbreviation:

FE00:0:0:1::56

FE00:0:0:1::56 is indeed the shortest abbreviation, but this example happens to make it easier to see the two most common mistakes when abbreviating IPv6 addresses. First, never remove trailing 0s in a quartet (0s on the right side of the quartet). In this case, the first quartet of FE00 cannot be shortened at all, because the two 0s trail. So, the following address, which begins now with only FE in the first quartet, is not a correct abbreviation of the original IPv6 address:

FE:0:0:1::56

The second common mistake is to replace all series of all 0 quartets with a double colon. For instance, the following abbreviation would be incorrect for the original IPv6 address listed in this topic:

FE00::1::56

The reason this abbreviation is incorrect is because now you do not know how many quartets of all 0s to substitute into each :: to find the original unabbreviated address.

Expanding IPv6 Addresses

To expand an IPv6 address back into its full unabbreviated 32-digit number, use two similar rules. The rules basically reverse the logic of the previous two rules.

1. In each quartet, add leading 0s as needed until the quartet has four hex digits

2. If a double colon (::) exists, count the quartets currently shown; the total should be less than eight. Replace the :: with multiple quartets of 0000 so that eight total quartets exist.

The best way to get comfortable with these addresses and abbreviations is to do some yourself. Table 17-2 lists some practice problems, with the full 32-digit IPv6 address on the left, and the best abbreviation on the right. The table gives you either the expanded or abbreviated address, and you need to supply the opposite value. You can find the answers at the end of the chapter, under the heading "Answers to Earlier Practice Problems."

Table 17-2 IPv6 Address Abbreviation and Expansion Practice

Full	Abbreviation
2340:0000:0010:0100:1000:ABCD:0101:1010	
	30A0:ABCD:EF12:3456:ABC:B0B0:9999:9009
2222:3333:4444:5555:0000:0000:6060:0707	
	3210::
210F:0000:0000:0000:CCCC:0000:0000:000D	
	34BA:B:B::20
FE80:0000:0000:0000:DEAD:BEFF:FEEF:CAFE	
	FE80::FACE:BAFF:FEBE:CAFE
FE80:000F:00E0:0D00:FACE:BAFF:FE00:0000	
	FE80:800:0:40:CAFE:FF:FE00:1

17

You will become more comfortable with these abbreviations as you get more experience. The "Exam Preparation Tasks" section at the end of this chapter lists several suggestions for getting more practice.

Representing the Prefix Length of an Address

IPv6 uses a mask concept, called *the prefix length*, similar to IPv4 subnet masks. Similar to the IPv4 prefix-style mask, the IPv6 prefix length is written as a /, followed by a decimal number. The prefix length defines how many bits of the IPv6 address defines the IPv6 prefix, which is basically the same concept as the IPv4 subnet ID.

When writing IPv6 addresses, if the prefix length matters, the prefix length follows the IPv6 address. For example, use either of these for an address with a 64-bit prefix length:

2222:1111:0:1:A:B:C:D/64

2222:1111:0:1:A:B:C:D /64

Finally, note that the prefix length is a number of bits, so with IPv6, the legal value range is from 0 through 128, inclusive.

Calculating the IPv6 Prefix (Subnet ID)

With IPv4, you can take an IP address and the associated subnet mask, and calculate the subnet ID. With IPv6 subnetting, you can take an IPv6 address and the associated prefix length, and calculate the IPv6 equivalent of the subnet ID: an *IPv6 prefix*.

Each IPv6 prefix, or *subnet* if you prefer, has a number that represents the group. Per the IPv6 RFCs, the number itself is also called the *prefix*, but many people just call it a subnet number or subnet ID, using the same terms as IPv4.

Like with different IPv4 subnet masks, some IPv6 prefix lengths make for an easy math problem to find the IPv6 prefix, while some prefix lengths make the math more difficult. For many good reasons, almost every subnet uses a prefix length of /64. And even better, a /64 prefix length makes the math to find the IPv6 prefix incredibly simple.

More generally, for any prefix length, you follow some basic rules to find the IPv6 subnet based on the IPv6 address and prefix length. If the prefix length is /P, use these rules:

1. Copy the first P bits.
2. Change the rest of the bits to 0.

However, because this book assumes that only /64 is used, the process can be even further simplified. Simply put, copy the first half of the address, and change the second half to all hexadecimal 0. Figure 17-3 shows an example.

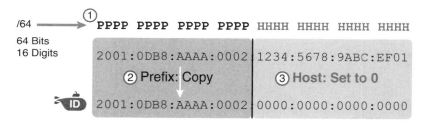

Figure 17-3   *Creating the IPv6 Prefix from an Address/Length*

After you find the IPv6 prefix, you should also be ready to abbreviate the IPv6 prefix using the same rules you use to abbreviate IPv6 addresses. However, pay extra attention to the end of the prefix, because it often has several octets of all 0 values. As a result, the abbreviation typically ends with two colons (::).

For example, consider the following IPv6 address that is assigned to a host on a LAN:

  2000:1234:5678:9ABC:1234:5678:9ABC:1111/64

This example shows an IPv6 address that itself cannot be abbreviated. After you calculate the prefix for the subnet in which the address resides, by zeroing out the last 64 bits (16 digits) of the address, you find the following prefix value:

  2000:1234:5678:9ABC:**0000:0000:0000:0000**/64

This value can be abbreviated, with four quartets of all 0s at the end, as follows:

  2000:1234:5678:9ABC::/64

To get better at the math, take some time to work through finding the prefix for several practice problems, as listed in Table 17-3. You can find the answers at the end of the chapter, under the heading "Answers to Earlier Practice Problems."

Table 17-3   Finding the IPv6 Prefix from an Address/Length Value

Address/Length	Prefix
2340:0:10:100:1000:ABCD:101:1010/64	
30A0:ABCD:EF12:3456:ABC:B0B0:9999:9009/64	
2222:3333:4444:5555::6060:707/64	
3210::ABCD:101:1010/64	
210F::CCCC:B0B0:9999:9009/64	
34BA:B:B:0:5555:0:6060:707/64	
3124::DEAD:CAFE:FF:FE00:1/64	
2BCD::FACE:BEFF:FEBE:CAFE/64	
3FED:F:E0:D00:FACE:BAFF:FE00:0/64	
3BED:800:0:40:FACE:BAFF:FE00:0/64	

Assigning Unique IPv6 Prefixes Across the Globe

IPv6 global unicast addresses allow IPv6 to work more like the original design of the IPv4 Internet. In other words, each organization asks for a block of IPv6 addresses that no one else can use. That organization further subdivides the address block into smaller chunks, called *subnets*. Finally, to choose what IPv6 address to use for any host, the engineer chooses an address from the right subnet.

That reserved block of IPv6 addresses—a set of unique addresses that only one company can use—is called a *global routing prefix*. Each organization that wants to connect to the Internet, and use IPv6 global unicast addresses, should ask for and receive a global routing prefix. Very generally, you can think of the global routing prefix like an IPv4 Class A, B, or C network number from the range of public IPv4 addresses.

The term *global routing prefix* might not make you think of a block of IPv6 addresses at first. The term actually refers to the idea that Internet routers can have one route that refers to all the addresses inside the address block, without a need to have routes for smaller parts of that block. For instance, Figure 17-4 shows three companies, with three different IPv6 global routing prefixes; the router on the right (R4) has one IPv6 route for each global routing prefix.

The global routing prefix sets those IPv6 addresses apart for use by that one company, just like a public IPv4 network or CIDR address block does in IPv4. All IPv6 addresses inside that company should begin with that global routing prefix, to avoid using other companies' IPv6 addresses. No other companies should use IPv6 addresses with that same prefix. And thankfully, IPv6 has plenty of space to allow all companies to have a global routing prefix, with plenty of addresses.

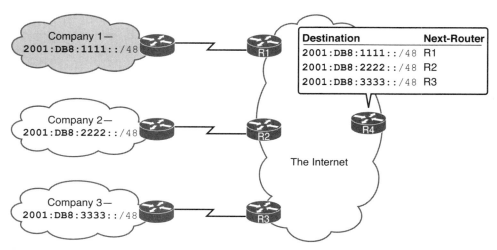

Figure 17-4 *Three Global Routing Prefixes, with One Route per Prefix*

Both the IPv6 and IPv4 address assignment process rely on the same organizations: IANA (along with ICANN), the RIRs, and ISPs. For example, an imaginary company, Company 1, received the assignment of a global routing prefix. The prefix means "All addresses whose first 12 hex digits are 2001:0DB8:1111," as represented by prefix 2001:0DB8:1111::/48. To receive that assignment, the process shown in Figure 17-5 happened.

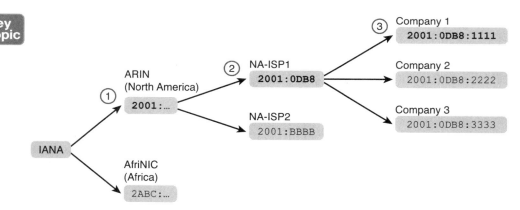

Figure 17-5 *Prefix Assignment with IANA, RIRs, and ISPs*

The event timeline in the figure uses a left-to-right flow; in other words, the event on the far left must happen first. Following the flow left-to-right in the figure:

1. **IANA gives ARIN prefix 2001::/16:** ARIN (the RIR for North America) asks IANA for the assignment of a large block of addresses. In this imaginary example, IANA gives ARIN a prefix of "all addresses that begin 2001," or 2001::/16.

2. **ARIN gives NA-ISP1 prefix 2001:0DB8::/32:** NA-ISP1, an imaginary ISP based in North America, asks ARIN for a new IPv6 prefix. ARIN takes a subset of its 2001::/16 prefix, specifically all addresses that begin with the 32 bits (8 hex digits) 2001:0DB8, and gives it to the ISP.

3. **NA-ISP1 gives Company 1 2002:0DB8:1111::/48:** Company 1 decides to start supporting IPv6, so they go to their ISP, NA-ISP1, to ask for a block of global unicast addresses. NA-ISP1 gives Company 1 a "small" piece of NA-ISP1's address block, in this case the addresses that begin with the 48 bits (12 hex digits) of 2001:0DB8:1111 (2001:0DB8:1111::/48).

Once a company has its IPv6 global routing prefix, the network engineers in that company can begin to subnet that block of addresses into subnets usable inside the company, as described later in this chapter in the section titled "IPv6 Subnetting Using Global Unicast Addressing."

Now that you know a few of the basics of IPv6, the next section dives into more detail about IPv6 addressing.

IPv6 Addressing and Subnetting

IPv6 defines many types of addresses. For instance, all the earlier examples in this chapter use *global unicast* addresses. The word *unicast* refers to the fact that each address represents a single host interface. The word *global* refers to the fact that with proper address assignment, the addresses should be unique across the globe. In other words, IPv6 global unicast addresses basically act like the equivalent of public IPv4 addresses.

This second of three major sections of this chapter examines several types of addresses. In particular, this section looks at the two major types of unicast addresses—global unicast addresses and unique local addresses—plus several types of specialized IPv6 addresses as well. Note that each type of address can be identified by the first few hex digits of the address, as noted in Table 17-4.

Table 17-4   Some Types of IPv6 Addresses and Their First Hex Digit(s)

Address Type	First Hex Digits
Global Unicast	2 or 3 (originally); today, all addresses not otherwise reserved
Unique Local	FD
Multicast	FF
Link Local	FE80

Note that this section also discusses IPv6 subnetting, in the same section that explains global unicast addressing.

Global Unicast Addresses and IPv6 Subnetting

Global unicast addresses give the world a way to give each and every IPv6 host a unique IPv6 address, without having to reuse the same addresses inside each company with something like IPv4 private addresses.

The process to give each host a global unicast address that is unique in the universe is relatively basic. As discussed earlier in the section titled "Assigning Unique IPv6 Prefixes Across the Globe," each company can apply for and receive a unique IPv6 prefix. (This prefix comes from the range of global unicast addresses, by the way.) The prefix gives the company a block of addresses—that is, all the addresses that begin with that prefix. Then, the engineers at the company further subdivide the address block into IPv6 subnets. Finally, each host can be assigned a unique address from the correct IPv6 subnet. Following this process gives each host a unique address.

The next few pages walk through the process described in the previous paragraph.

NOTE If the IPv4 subnetting concepts are a little vague, you might want to reread this book's Chapter 13, "Perspectives on IPv4 Subnetting," which discusses the subnetting concepts for IPv4.

IPv6 Subnetting Concepts

First, IPv6 and IPv4 both use the same concepts about where a subnet is needed: one for each VLAN, one for each point-to-point WAN connection (serial and Ethernet over Multiprotocol Label Switching [EoMPLS]), and so on. Figure 17-6 shows an example of the idea, using the small enterprise internetwork of Company 1. Company 1 needs one subnet for the branch office LAN on the left, one subnet for the point-to-point serial link connecting the sites, and two subnets for the two server VLANs at the central site on the right.

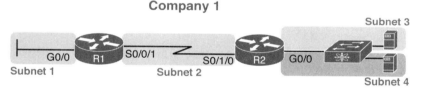

Figure 17-6 *Locations for IPv6 Subnets*

Next, think like the network engineer at Company 1, just after receiving the assignment of a global routing prefix from some ISP. The global routing prefix is a prefix, but it also represents a block of global unicast addresses. For instance:

2001:0DB8:1111 means: The block of addresses that begins 2001:0DB8:1111

With IPv4, to create subnets of a network, you add a subnet field just after the network field in the IPv4 address structure. That subnet field can be used to number and identify different subnets. With IPv6, you do the same thing, adding a subnet field after the global routing prefix, as shown in Figure 17-7.

Just think about the general idea in Figure 17-7, compared with IPv4 subnetting with the network, subnet, and host parts of an IPv4 address. The IPv6 global routing prefix acts like the IPv4 network part of the address structure. The IPv6 subnet part acts like the IPv4 subnet part. And the right side of the IPv6, formally called the *interface ID* (short for interface identifier), acts like the IPv4 host field.

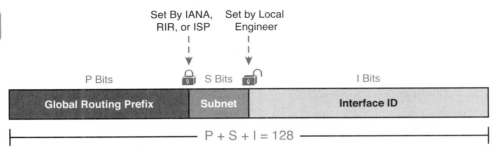

Figure 17-7 *Structure of Subnetted IPv6 Global Unicast Addresses*

The size of the fields will vary from company to company; however, most every company chooses to use a 64-bit interface ID field. As you will learn later in this chapter, a 64-bit interface ID field fits nicely with some of the other IPv6 protocols. Because most installations use a 64-bit interface ID, this book shows all the global unicast addresses with a 64-bit interface ID.

The length of the global routing prefix will also vary from company to company, as set by the company that assigns the prefix to the company. For instance, one company might receive a global routing prefix from an ISP, with prefix length /40; another company might receive a slightly smaller block with a /48 prefix length.

Finally, the subnet field would sit in the bits between the global routing prefix and the interface ID. For instance, bringing the general concepts into an example, consider the structure of a specific global unicast IPv6 address, 2001:0DB8:1111:0001:0000:0000:0000:0001, as shown in Figure 17-8. In this case

- The company was assigned prefix 2001:0DB8:1111, with prefix length /48.
- The company uses the usual 64-bit interface ID.
- The company has a subnet field of 16 bits, allowing for 2^{16} IPv6 subnets.

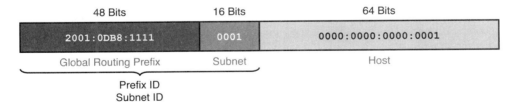

Figure 17-8 *Address Structure for Company 1 Example*

The example in Figure 17-8, along with a little math, shows one reason why so many companies use a /64 prefix length for all subnets. With this structure, Company 1 can support 2^{16} possible subnets (65,536). Very few companies need that many subnets. Then, each subnet supports over 10^{18} addresses per subnet (2^{64}, minus some reserved values). So, for both subnets and hosts, the address structure supports far more than are needed. Plus, the /64 prefix length for all subnets makes the math simple, because it cuts the 128-bit IPv6 address in half, so that the IPv6 subnet ID in this case would be as follows:

2001:DB8:1111:1::/64

> **NOTE**   The IPv6 subnet ID, more formally called the *subnet router anycast address*, is reserved, and should not be used as an IPv6 address for any host.

Assign Subnets and Addresses

The network engineer can determine all the IPv6 subnet IDs and then plan which subnet ID to use on each link that needs an IPv6 subnet. Just like with IPv4, each VLAN, each serial link, each EoMPLS link, and many other data-link instances need an IPv6 subnet. Figure 17-9 shows just such an example, with the same Company 1 network shown earlier in Figure 17-6. The figure shows four subnet IDs.

Company 1

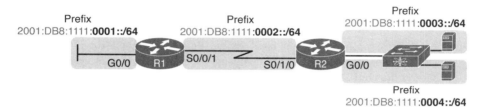

Figure 17-9   *Subnets in Company 1, with Global Routing Prefix of 2001:0DB8:1111::/48*

> **NOTE**   In IPv6, you can use two terms to refer to the groups of addresses as shown in Figure 17-9: prefix and subnet. Similarly, the last field in the structure of the address can be called either the *interface ID* or *host*. The pairs of terms include the traditional IPv4 terms as well as the newer terms specific to IPv6.

Now that the engineer has planned which IPv6 subnet will be used in each location, the individual IPv6 addressing can be planned and implemented. Each address must be unique, in that no other host interface uses the same IPv6 address. Also, the hosts cannot use the subnet ID itself.

Engineers can simply statically assign the addresses, as shown in Figure 17-10. Static assignment is common for devices in the control of IT, like routers, switches, and servers. Addresses can be configured statically, along with the prefix length, default router, and DNS servers' IPv6 addresses. Figure 17-10 shows the interfaces that will be assigned different addresses for three of the IPv6 subnets; note that the addresses in the same subnet (per Figure 17-9) have the same 64-bit prefix values, which puts them in the same subnet.

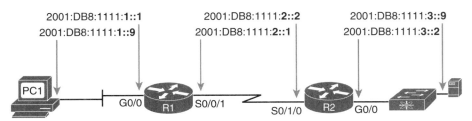

Figure 17-10 *Example of Static IPv6 Addresses Based on the Subnet Design of Figure 17-9*

The Actual Global Unicast Addresses

IANA reserves certain parts of the entire range of IPv6 addresses for different types of addresses. IANA originally reserved a large part of the entire IPv6 address space—all addresses that begin with hex 2 or hex 3—for global unicast addresses. IANA later expanded that range even further, stating that addresses not otherwise reserved for some other purpose were included in the range of global addresses.

> **NOTE** You may see the idea "all addresses that begin with hex 2 or 3" written as a prefix of 2000::/3. This prefix means "all addresses whose first three bits match hex 2000." If you look at the value in binary, you would see that the values include all hex IPv6 addresses that begin with a 2 or 3.

Unique Local Unicast Addresses

When a company decides to implement IPv6, they can choose to use global unicast addresses. To do so, they obtain a prefix from an ISP, do some subnet planning as just discussed in this chapter, and start using the addresses.

Alternately, a company can choose to not use global unicast addresses, but instead use *unique local* unicast addresses. These unique local addresses act somewhat like private IPv4 addresses, in that the company's network engineer can pick some values to use without registering any public addresses with an ISP or other organization. So, although not the literal equivalent of private IPv4 addresses, they can serve the same overall purpose.

Although the network engineer creates unique local addresses without any registration or assignment process, the addresses still need to follow some rules, as follows:

■ Use FD as the first two hex digits (as required by IANA).

■ Choose a unique 40-bit global ID.

■ Append the 40-bit global ID behind the FD to create a 48-bit prefix, used as the prefix for all that company's addresses.

■ Use the next 16 bits as a subnet field.

■ Note that the structure leaves a convenient 64-bit interface ID field

Figure 17-11 shows the format of these unique local unicast addresses.

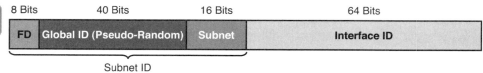

Figure 17-11   *IPv6 Unique Local Unicast Address Format*

> **NOTE**   Just to be completely exact, IANA actually reserves prefix FC00::/7, and not FD00::/8, for these addresses. FC00::/7 includes all addresses that begin with hex FC and FD. However, an RFC (4193) requires that the eighth bit of these addresses to be set to 1, making the first two hex digits FD; so in practice today, the unique local addresses all begin with their first two digits as FD.

After the engineer has determined the 48-bit prefix to use inside the company, the rest of the subnetting and address assignment concepts work exactly like they do with global unicast addresses.

Link Local Addresses

IPv6 uses both global unicast and unique local addresses for the same purposes as IPv4 addresses. Hosts use one of these types of IPv6 addresses for their interfaces, routers use one per interface, and packets use these addresses as the source and destination of IPv6 packets that flow from end to end through the network.

IPv6 also defines *link local* addresses: a completely new type of unicast address that is not used for normal user traffic, but is instead used for some special types of IPv6 packets. As the name implies, packets that use a link local address stay on the local link and are not routed by a router to the next subnet. Instead, IPv6 uses link local addresses for some overhead protocols and for routing, with some examples over the next few pages.

For instance, routers use link local addresses as the next-hop IP addresses in IPv6 routes, as shown in Figure 17-12. IPv6 hosts also use a default router (default gateway) concept, like IPv4, but instead of the default router address being in the same subnet, hosts refer to the router's link local address. The next-hop address in IPv6 routing tables also lists the neighboring router's link local address.

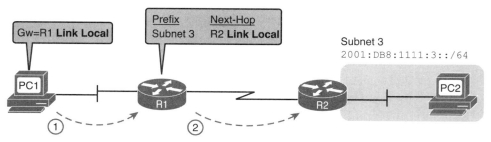

Figure 17-12   *IPv6 Using Link Local Addresses as the Next-Hop Address*

Link local addresses also solve some initialization issues. Hosts can calculate a complete link local address to use even before they dynamically learn their other (global unicast or unique local) address that they use for user traffic. Having an IPv6 address that can be used when sending packets on the local link helps the operation of several overhead protocols.

The following list summarizes the key facts about link local addresses:

Unicast (not multicast): Link local addresses represent a single host (in other words, it is a unicast address), and packets sent to a link local address should be processed by only that one IPv6 host.

Forwarding scope is the local link only: Packets flow on-link only, because routers do not forward packets with link local destination addresses

Automatically generated: Every IPv6 host interface (and router interface) can create their own link local address automatically, solving some initialization problems for hosts before they learn a dynamically learned global unicast address

Common Uses: Used for some overhead protocols that stay local to one subnet, and as the next-hop address for IPv6 routes.

IPv6 hosts and routers can calculate their own link local address, for each interface, using some basic rules. First, all link local addresses start with the same prefix, as shown on the left side of Figure 17-13. By definition, the first 10 bits must match prefix FE80::/10, meaning that the first three hex digits will be either FE8, FE9, FEA, or FEB. However, when following the RFC, the next 54 bits should be binary 0, so the link local address should always start with FE80:0000:0000:0000 as the first four unabbreviated quartets.

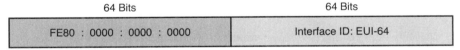

Figure 17-13 *Link Local Address Format*

The second half of the link local address, in practice, can be formed with different rules. It can be randomly generated, statically configured, or set based on the interface MAC address using EUI-64 rules. The upcoming section "Dynamic Assignment of the Interface ID Using EUI-64 Rules" discusses the automatic process based on the EUI-64 rules.

IPv6 Multicast Addresses

IPv6 does not define or use the concept of a broadcast IPv6 address, but it does define and use many types of IPv6 multicast addresses. Multicast addresses have an advantage for the network because only a subset of the hosts in the network will receive and process a packet sent to a multicast address, whereas packets sent to an IPv4 broadcast address arrive at all hosts.

IPv6 defines different types of multicast addresses based on the scope of where the packets should flow. In some cases, multicast messages need to stay within one subnet, but in other cases, they need to be able to flow to many subnets. To aid that logic, IPv6 defines some ranges of multicast addresses so that a packet sent to that address should stay on the link; these addresses have a *link local* scope. Multicast addresses that allow the packets to be routed to other subnets inside the enterprise have an *organization local* scope.

Table 17-5 shows a sampling of some link-local scope multicast addresses. IANA defines all multicast addresses from within the range of addresses that begin with FF, or more formally, prefix FF00::/8. IANA reserves the more specific range of addresses that begin with FF02 (formally, FF02::/16) for link local scope multicast addresses.

Table 17-5   Key IPv6 Local Scope Multicast Addresses

Short Name	Multicast Address	Meaning	IPv4 Equivalent
All-nodes	FF02::1	All nodes (all interfaces that use IPv6 that are on the link)	A subnet broadcast address
All-routers	FF02::2	All routers (all IPv6 router interfaces on the link)	None
RIPng routers	FF02::9	All RIPng routers	224.0.0.9
All-OSPF, All-OSPF-DR	FF02::5, FF02::6	All OSPF routers and all OSPF designated routers, respectively	224.0.0.5, 224.0.0.6
EIGRPv6 routers	FF02::A	All routers using EIGRP for IPv6 (EIGRPv6)	224.0.0.10

The table mentions a few routing protocols with familiar-looking names. RIP, OSPF, and EIGRP all have IPv6-compatible versions. RIP for IPv6 goes by the name RIPng, for RIP next generation. OSPF Version 3 (OSPFv3) is simply the next version of OSPF, with the normal OSPF version used with IPv4 happening to be OSPF Version 2. EIGRP for IPv6 may be called EIGRPv6 in reference to IPv6, although there is no published EIGRP version number.

Miscellaneous IPv6 Addresses

To round out the discussion, two other special IPv6 addresses exist that can be commonly seen even with basic implementations of IPv6:

■ The unknown (unspecified) IPv6 address, ::, or all 0s

■ The loopback IPv6 address, ::1, or 127 binary 0s with a single 1

The unknown address (::) can be used by a host when its own IPv6 address is not yet known or when the host wonders if its own IPv6 address may have problems. For instance, hosts use the unknown address during the early stages of dynamically discovering their IPv6 address. When a host does not yet know what IPv6 address to use, it can use the :: address as its source IPv6 address.

The IPv6 loopback address gives each IPv6 host a way to test its own protocol stack. Just like the IPv4 127.0.0.1 loopback address, packets sent to ::1 do not leave the host, but are instead simply delivered down the stack to IPv6 and back up the stack to the application on the local host.

Implementing IPv6

IPv6 implementation often begins with the simple act of enabling IPv6 on an interface by giving it an IPv6 address. This final of three major sections of the chapter introduces the available options for giving IPv6 addresses to hosts, ranging from fully automated processes to simply typing the address into the configuration of the device.

This section closes with a brief introduction to one of the big questions each installation must ask when implementing IPv6: how do you migrate from IPv4 and have IPv6 coexist with IPv4 while the migration takes place?

IPv6 Address Assignment

To implement IPv6, routers, user devices, servers, switches, and other devices need IPv6 addresses. For instance, the entire IPv6 address and prefix length can simply be configured. The process works much like it does for IPv4, from a graphical interface on most user operating systems, to the **ipv6 address** command on most Cisco platforms. The next few pages review the methods of assigning IPv6 addresses that require more than simply typing the information, emphasizing the differences between IPv4 and IPv6.

Dynamic Assignment of the Interface ID with EUI-64

Stop for a moment and think about the subnet planning process, versus the process of choosing the specific IPv6 address for each host and router interface. Some network engineer must plan which subnet ID to use for each location in the network. Once chosen, the IPv6 addresses inside a given subnet must have the same prefix value, and a unique value in the interface ID (host) part of the address.

In fact, most engineers do not care what specific interface ID each host in a subnet uses, as long as it is unique among all hosts in the same subnet.

The EUI-64 option gives devices a way to automatically generate a unique interface ID. Someone statically configures the prefix, lets the device create a unique interface ID, and the process is complete.

The process to create the interface ID uses another unique number: the interface's MAC address. The process works as follows:

1. Split the 6-byte (12 hex digit) MAC address in two halves (6 hex digits each).
2. Insert FFFE in between the two, making the interface ID now have a total of 16 hex digits (64 bits).
3. Invert the seventh bit of the interface ID.

Figure 17-14 shows the major pieces of how the address is formed.

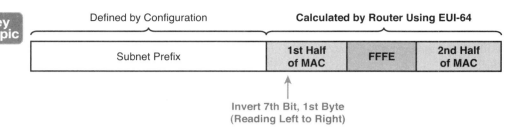

Figure 17-14 *IPv6 Address Format with Interface ID and EUI-64*

Although it might seem a bit convoluted, it works. Also, with a little practice, you can look at an IPv6 address and quickly notice the FFFE in the middle of the interface ID, and then easily find the two halves of the corresponding interface's MAC address. But you need to be ready to do the same math, in this case to predict the EUI-64 formatted IPv6 address on an interface.

For example, if you ignore the final step of inverting the seventh bit, the rest of the steps just require that you move the pieces around. Figure 17-15 shows two examples, just so you see the process.

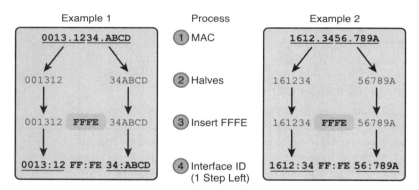

Figure 17-15 *Two Examples of Most of the EUI-64 Interface ID Process*

Both examples follow the same process. Each starts with the MAC address, breaking it into two halves (Step 2). The third step inserts FFFE in the middle, and the fourth step inserts a colon every four hex digits, keeping with IPv6 conventions.

The examples in Figure 17-15 show most of the steps, but they omit the final step of inverting the seventh bit. Figure 17-16 completes the work, showing the conversion of the first byte (first two hex digits) to binary, flipping the bit, and converting back to hexadecimal.

NOTE If you do not have those handy in your memory, take a few moments to look at Table C-2 in Appendix C, "Numeric Reference Tables."

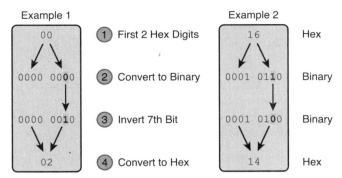

Figure 17-16 *Inverting the Seventh Bit of an EUI-64 Interface ID Field*

To summarize, these two examples translate the MAC addresses into the 64-bit (16 hex digit) interface ID values as follows:

MAC 0013.1234.ABCD results in interface ID 0213:12FF:FE34:ABCD.

MAC 1612.3456.789A results in interface ID 1412:34FF:FE56:789A.

Discovering the IPv6 Prefix with SLAAC

In some cases, the network engineer may want to configure the prefix and let the device create its own unique interface ID value, as just shown. However, in other cases, the engineer may want the device to create its entire IPv6 address automatically. IPv4 lets hosts lease an IPv4 address from a DHCP server, and IPv6 supports an equivalent process also using Dynamic Host Control Protocol (DHCP). However, IPv6 supports another automatic process, called *stateless address autoconfiguration*, or *SLAAC*.

A host using SLAAC relies on two key processes. First, the host learns the subnet prefix from a router that sits on the same subnet, using the IPv6 Neighbor Discovery Protocol (NDP). The second process is familiar: The host calculates the interface ID using EUI-64 rules.

NDP defines several features, including a process to discover the existence of IPv6 routers and to discover some basic information from the router. The NDP Router Solicitation (RS) message generally means something like this: "IPv6 routers, tell me information that you know!" The Router Advertisement (RA) message gives IPv6 routers a means to distribute the information: "Here is the information that I know!" Figure 17-17 shows one fact learned through the RS and RA messages, namely the IPv6 address of the IPv6 router.

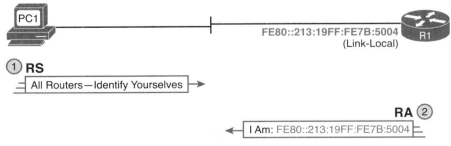

Figure 17-17 *Using NDP RS/RA to Discover the Prefix/Length on the LAN*

> **NOTE**   IPv6 allows multiple prefixes and multiple default routers to be listed in the RA message; the figure just shows one of each for simplicity's sake.

Pulling these ideas together, when using SLAAC, a host does not lease its IPv6 address, or even learn its IPv6 address from some other device. Instead, the host learns part of the address—the prefix—and then makes up the rest of its own IPv6 address. Specifically, a host using SLAAC to choose its own IPv6 address uses the following steps:

1. Learn the IPv6 prefix used on the link, from any router, using NDP RS/RA messages.
2. Choose a unique interface ID, either randomly, or using EUI-64 rules.

Before leaving SLAAC, take a moment to stop and think about the bigger picture of IPv6 implementation on all devices. With SLAAC, routers supplied the prefix information, so the routers have to have some way to first know the prefixes. To make that happen, most routers and Layer 3 switches are configured with either static IPv6 addresses, or statically configured with the prefix while using EUI-64 to derive the router's interface ID. In other words, the router knows the prefix because the network engineer typed that information into the configuration. SLAAC makes more sense as a tool for end-user devices, with the SLAAC process relying on the prefix information known by the routers and Layer 3 switches.

Dynamic Configuration Using Stateful DHCP

DHCP for IPv6 (DHCPv6) gives an IPv6 host a way to learn host IPv6 configuration settings, using the same general concepts as DHCP for IPv4. The host exchanges messages with a DHCP server, and the server supplies the host with configuration information, including a lease of an IPv6 address, along with prefix length and DNS server address information.

> **NOTE**   The DHCP version is not actually version 6; the name just ends in v6 in reference to the support for IPv6.

More specifically, stateful DHCPv6 works like the more familiar DHCP for IPv4 in many other general ways, as follows:

- DHCP clients on a LAN send messages that flow only on the local LAN, hoping to find a DHCP server.
- If the DHCP server sits on the same LAN as the client, the client and server can exchange DHCP messages directly, without needing help from a router.
- If the DHCP server sits on another link as compared to the client, the client and server rely on a router to forward the DHCP messages.
- The router that forwards messages from one link, to a server in a remote subnet, must be configured as a DHCP relay agent, with knowledge of the DHCP server's IPv6 address.
- Servers have configuration that lists pools of addresses for each subnet from which the server allocates addresses.

- Servers offer a lease of an IP address to a client, from the pool of addresses for the client's subnet; the lease lasts a set time period (usually days or weeks).

- The server tracks state information, specifically a client identifier (often based on the MAC address), along with the address that is currently leased to that client.

DHCPv6 also updates the protocol messages to use IPv6 packets instead of IPv4 packets, with new messages and fields as well. For instance, Figure 17-18 shows the names of the DHCPv6 messages, which replace the DHCPv4 Discover, Offer, Request, and Acknowledgment (DORA) messages. Instead, DHCPv6 uses the Solicit, Advertise, Request, and Reply messages.

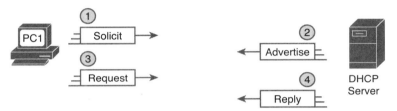

Figure 17-18 *Four Stateful DHCPv6 Messages Between Client and Server*

The four DHCPv6 messages work in two matched pairs with the same general flow as the similar DHCPv4 messages. The Solicit and Advertise messages complete the process of the client searching for the IPv6 address of a DHCPv6 server (the Solicit message), and the server advertising an address (and other configuration settings) for the client to possibly use (the Advertise message). The Request and Reply message let the client ask to lease the address, with the server confirming the lease in the Reply message.

NOTE This section describes the operation of DHCPv6 called stateful DHCP. DHCPv6 can also operate as stateless DHCP, which is a useful function when also using SLAAC. Stateless DHCP is not discussed in this book.

IPv6 Transition and Coexistence

IPv4 exists on most every electronic device on the planet. Most every PC, tablet, phone, and server use IPv4. Most consumer electronics have support for IPv4 as well, with IPv4 commonly used in game systems and televisions. And with the emergence of the concept called the Internet of Things, in which a large number of physical devices connect to the Internet, the need for addresses will grow even more.

Transitioning a world that uses IPv4 on most every existing network-connected device cannot happen overnight, or even in a single year. In fact, such a transition cannot happen quickly even inside a single company. To deal with the challenges of migration, IPv6 defines several transition and coexistence strategies that allow the Internet and enterprises to add IPv6 support, operate a network with some IPv4 and some IPv6, and eventually, one day, complete a migration to use only IPv6.

Dual Stack

One way to begin the migration to IPv6 requires the addition of IPv6 to all layer three devices (routers and Layer 3 switches). The routers and Layer 3 switches continue to support IPv4 as always, with IPv6 configuration added. For each interface on which a router formerly supported IPv4, the router now supports both IPv4 and IPv6. This transition method is called *dual stack*.

Once the routers can route both IPv4 packets and IPv6 packets, then the end-user devices, servers, and other devices can migrate to IPv6. Those devices can also add support for IPv6, keeping the old support for IPv4. Eventually, over time, all devices can migrate to IPv6, so at some point, IPv4 support can finally be disabled.

The process of running both IPv4 and IPv6 is called dual stack. Figure 17-19 reinforces the idea. The PCs and the routers all support both IPv4 and IPv6. On the top, PC1 has sent an IPv4 packet to Server 1's IPv4 address, with router R1 forwarding the packet to the next router. PC2 then sends an IPv6 packet to that same server. R1 and the other routers, running IPv6, support the ability to route the IPv6 packet through the network to reach the server.

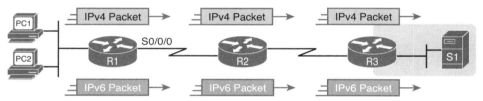

Figure 17-19   *Dual Stack Implemented on Three Routers*

Tunneling IPv6 Inside IPv4

IPv6 also provides several different coexistence tools in which the IPv6 packets tunnel through the IPv4 network. The general idea works like this:

1.   The user devices and servers at some locations can begin to support IPv6.

2.   The router directly connected to each user or server subnet runs dual stack, but the routers in between do not.

3.   The routers directly connected to the user or server subnets create tunnels between each other.

4.   The routers forward IPv6 packets by encapsulating them in an IPv4 packet, forwarding the IPv4 packet to another dual-stack router, which removes the original IPv6 packet.

An example surely helps in this case. Figure 17-20 shows just such an example, in which PC1 and server S1 both now support IPv6. Routers R1 and R3 also now support IPv6, and they create a tunnel through the IPv4 network. Note that all other routers between R1 and R3, like router R2 in the figure, can still use only IPv4, and have no knowledge of IPv6.

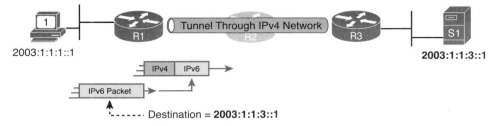

Figure 17-20   *Tunneling IPv6 in IPv4 as a Coexistence Method*

Reading the figure from left to right, PC1 sends an IPv6 packet to the server. When the IPv6 packet arrives at router R1, R1 encapsulates the IPv6 packet behind an IPv4 header. R1 and R2 forward this IPv4 packet to R3, as an IPv4 packet, so that R3 can remove the original IPv6 packet and forward it to server S1.

IPv6 supports several different tunneling methods to meet different transition needs.

17

Exam Preparation Tasks

Review All the Key Topics

Review the most important topics from this chapter, noted with the Key Topic icon. Table 17-6 lists these key topics and where each is discussed.

Table 17-6   Key Topics for Chapter 17

Key Topic Element	Description	Page Number
List	Rules to abbreviate IPv6 addresses	444
List	Rules to expand an abbreviated IPv6 address	444
Figure 17-5	Description of the IPv6 prefix (address block) assignment process	448
Table 17-4	List of address types and their initial digits	449
Figure 17-7	Structure of a subnetted global unicast address	451
Figure 17-11	Structure of a unique local address	454
List	Uses for link local addresses	455
Figure 17-14	Summary of EUI-64 structure and logic	458
List	Summary of SLAAC rules	460
List	Comparison points for DHCPv4 versus DHCPv6	460

Complete the Tables and Lists from Memory

Print a copy of DVD Appendix I, "Memory Tables," or at least the section for this chapter, and complete the tables and lists from memory. DVD Appendix J, "Memory Tables Answer Key," includes completed tables and lists for you to check your work.

Definitions of Key Terms

After your first reading of the chapter, try to define these key terms, but do not be concerned about getting them all correct at that time. Chapter 23, "Final Review," directs you in how to use these terms for late-stage preparation for the exam.

IP version 6, network address translation, IPv4 address exhaustion, global unicast address, unique local address, global routing prefix, link local address, EUI-64, stateless address autoconfiguration (SLAAC), DHCP, dual stack, tunneling, OSPF Version 3 (OSPFv3), EIGRP Version 6 (EIGRPv6), prefix, prefix length, quartet

Answers to Earlier Practice Problems

This chapter includes practice problems spread around different locations in the chapter. The answers are located in Tables 17-7 and 17-8.

Table 17-7   Answers to Questions in Earlier Table 17-2

Full	Abbreviation
2340:0000:0010:0100:1000:ABCD:0101:1010	2340:0:10:100:1000:ABCD:101:1010
30A0:ABCD:EF12:3456:0ABC:B0B0:9999:9009	30A0:ABCD:EF12:3456:ABC:B0B0:9999:9009
2222:3333:4444:5555:0000:0000:6060:0707	2222:3333:4444:5555::6060:707
3210:0000:0000:0000:0000:0000:0000:0000	3210::
210F:0000:0000:0000:CCCC:0000:0000:000D	210F::CCCC:0:0:D
34BA:000B:000B:0000:0000:0000:0000:0020	34BA:B:B::20
FE80:0000:0000:0000:DEAD:BEFF:FEEF:CAFE	FE80::DEAD:BEFF:FEEF:CAFE
FE80:0000:0000:0000:FACE:BAFF:FEBE:CAFE	FE80::FACE:BAFF:FEBE:CAFE
FE80:000F:00E0:0D00:FACE:BAFF:FE00:0000	FE80:F:E0:D00:FACE:BAFF:FE00:0
FE80:0800:0000:0040:CAFE:00FF:FE00:0001	FE80:800:0:40:CAFE:FF:FE00:1

Table 17-8   Answers to Questions in Earlier Table 17-3

Address/Length	Prefix
2340:0:10:100:1000:ABCD:101:1010/64	2340:0:10:100::/64
30A0:ABCD:EF12:3456:ABC:B0B0:9999:9009/64	30A0:ABCD:EF12:3456::/64
2222:3333:4444:5555::6060:707/64	2222:3333:4444:5555::/64
3210::ABCD:101:1010/64	3210::/64
210F::CCCC:B0B0:9999:9009/64	210F::/64
34BA:B:B:0:5555:0:6060:707/64	34BA:B:B::/64
3124::DEAD:CAFE:FF:FE00:1/64	3124:0:0:DEAD::/64
2BCD::FEED:FACE:BEEF:FEBE:CAFE/64	2BCD:0:0:FEED::/64
3FED:F:E0:D00:FACE:BAFF:FE00:0/64	3FED:F:E0:D00::/64
3BED:800:0:40:FACE:BAFF:FE00:0/64	3BED:800:0:40::/64

Part IV Review

Keep track of your part review progress with the checklist shown in Table P4-1. Details on each task follow the table.

Table P4-1 Part IV Review Checklist

Activity	First Date Completed	Second Date Completed
Repeat All DIKTA Questions		
Answer Part Review Questions		
Review Key Topics		
Create Subnet Terms Mind Map A		
Create Subnet Math Mind Map B		
Create IPv6 Addressing Mind Map C		

Repeat All DIKTA Questions

For this task, answer the "Do I Know This Already?" questions again for the chapters in this part of the book, using the PCPT software. Refer to the Introduction to this book, heading "How to View Only DIKTA Questions by Part," for help with how to make the PCPT software show you DIKTA questions for this part only.

Answer Part Review Questions

For this task, answer the Part Review questions for this part of the book, using the PCPT software. Refer to the Introduction to this book, heading "How to View Only Part Review Questions by Part," for help with how to make the PCPT software show you Part Review questions for this part only.

Review Key Topics

Browse back through the chapters and look for the Key Topic icons. If you do not remember some details, take the time to reread those topics.

Create Mind Map A: Subnetting Terms

The topic of IPv4 addressing and subnetting happens to have many terms that are literal synonyms, many terms with similar meanings, along with terms that describe something about another term. This first Part Review mind map (Part IV, Mind Map A) asks you to organize all IP addressing and subnetting terms you remember into four topic areas, but inside each area, subdivide terms as to whether they are either a synonym, a similar term, or a description.

Figure P4-1 shows the beginnings of one branch of the mind map to give you the general idea. For this branch, you would just remember any terms related to *IP address* and place them into one of these three categories. Your map can, of course, look different. As usual, first do this exercise without the book or your notes. Later, when you do look at the book again, make sure that you have at least included all the key terms from the ends of the chapters.

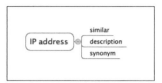

Figure P4-2   *Sample Beginning Point for Part IV Mind Map A*

> **NOTE**   For more information on mind mapping, refer to the Introduction, in the section "About Mind Maps."

Create Mind Map B: Subnet Math

This book part explains several types of subnetting problems that you can analyze and solve. The next mind map exercise helps to review the big ideas of what each type of problem does. This review does not focus on the details of how to find the answer to any one problem, leaving that for all the other practice suggestions included near the end of Chapters 12, 13, and 14. Those chapters discussed four major types of problems that can be solved with some arithmetic:

- **Classful facts:** Based on an IP address, find many facts about the associated classful IP network.

- **Mask conversion:** Given a subnet mask, find the equivalent mask in the other two mask formats.

- **Mask analysis:** Given a subnet mask, address, and an assumption, find the number of hosts per subnet and the number of subnets.

- **Subnet analysis:** Given a subnet mask and address, find the numbers that define the resident subnet (the subnet ID, subnet broadcast address, and range of usable IP addresses).

Create a mind map with four branches, one for each topic in the list. For each branch, begin with the core concept, and then branch into three subtopics:

- **Given:** The information you have and the assumptions you make to start the problem.

- **Process:** The information or terms used during the process. Do not write the specific steps of the process; the goal here is just to make memory connections so that you know it is this process, and not some other process.

- **Result:** The facts you determine by doing the problem.

Figure P4-2 shows a sample (incomplete) map for the classful facts problem, just to show the basic idea.

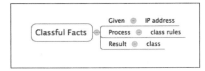

Figure P4-2   *Sample Mind Map for Part IV Mind Map B*

Create Mind Map C: IPv6 Addressing

Addressing is the biggest difference between IPv4 and IPv6. Think about IPv6 addresses for a few moments (the terms, the structure, the types, and anything related to addressing). Then make a mind map that collects all the addressing concepts and terms into one mind map.

When thinking about addressing, try to organize the information to your liking. There is no one right answer. However, if you want some guidance on how to organize the information, some of the concepts and terms can be organized by type of address. For instance, link-local addresses would be one type. In that part of the mind map, you could list all terms and facts about link-local addresses, as shown in Figure P4-3.

Figure P4-3   *Sample Mind Map for the Link-Local Branch*

Try to fit all the addressing terms from the Key Terms heading near the end of Chapter 17, along with all of the IPv6 addressing concepts and the values that identify an address as being a particular type of IPv6 address.

Tracking Your Mind Maps

If you do choose to use mind map software, rather than paper, you might want to remember where you stored your mind map files. Table P4-2 lists the mind maps for this part review and a place to record those filenames.

Table P4-2   Configuration Mind Maps for Part IV Review

Map	Description	Where You Saved It
1	Mind Map A: Subnetting Terms	
2	Mind Map B: Subnetting Math	
3	Mind Map C: IPv6 Addressing	

DVD Appendix K, "Mind Map Solutions," shows a sample answer, but your mind map will likely differ.

Data center networks use Ethernet technology, a technology that implements Layers 1 and 2 of the OSI model. Data center designers also need to use routing technology as well, to forward IP packets from the IP subnet on each virtual local-area network (VLAN) to the IP subnets on the other VLANs. In other words, to allow communications between VLANs, data centers use routing.

Cisco Nexus data center switches implement routing concepts by acting as a multilayer switch (also called a Layer 3 switch). Basically, the switch can be configured to also perform IP routing. As for terminology, because the device is called a "switch," the industry refers to this IP routing in a switch with other terms, for instance, "Layer 3 switching," to emphasize the Layer 3 nature of IP routing, while referring to the type of device (a switch).

Part V of this book completes the book with five chapters of concepts and configuration related to the Layer 3 features of Nexus switches. Chapters 18 and 19 focus on the IP routing process itself, with Chapter 18 discussing the concepts, and Chapter 19 looking at Nexus configuration. To route IP packets, the Nexus switch often uses a routing protocol with which to learn IP routes; Chapters 20 and 21 examine the concepts and configuration (respectively) of routing protocols.

Part V ends with a single chapter about IP access control lists (ACLs). ACLs give Cisco networking devices the ability to examine frames and packets as they pass through the device, choosing whether to discard the message or not. Chapter 22 discusses the concepts and configuration of Layer 3 ACLs on Nexus switches.

Part V

IPv4 Routing

Chapter 18: IPv4 Routing Concepts

Chapter 19: Cisco Nexus IPv4 Routing Configuration

Chapter 20: IPv4 Routing Protocol Concepts

Chapter 21: Nexus Routing Protocol Configuration

Chapter 22: IPv4 Access Control Lists on Cisco Nexus Switches

Part V Review

This chapter covers the following exam topics:

4.1 Describe and Configure basic routing concepts

4.1.a Packet forwarding

4.1.b Router look-up process (exec mode, exec commands, configuration mode)

4.2 Describe the operation of Cisco routers

4.2.a Router boot-up process

4.2.b POST

4.3.c Router components

CHAPTER 18

IPv4 Routing Concepts

Routers route IPv4 packets. That simple statement actually carries a lot of hidden meaning. For routers to route packets, routers follow a routing process. That routing process relies on information called *IP routes*. Each IP route lists a destination—an IP network, IP subnet, or some other group of IP addresses. Each route also lists instructions that tell the router where to forward packets sent to addresses in that IP network or subnet. For routers to do a good job of routing packets, routers need to have a detailed, accurate list of IP routes.

Routers use three methods to add IPv4 routes to their IPv4 routing tables. Routers first learn *connected routes*, which are routes for subnets attached to a router interface. Routers can also use *static routes*, which are routes created through a configuration command (**ip route**) that tells the router what route to put in the IPv4 routing table. And routers can use a routing protocol, in which routers tell each other about all their known routes, so that all routers can learn and build routes to all networks and subnets.

This chapter begins by reintroducing the IP routing process that relies on these routes. This IP routing discussion both reviews the concepts from Chapter 4, "Fundamentals of IPv4 Addressing and Routing," plus takes the concepts deeper, including showing information needed in a single IP route. Then, the second major heading in this chapter discusses connected routes, including variations of connected routes to VLANs connected to a router's VLAN trunk, and for connected routes on Layer 3 switches.

NOTE As promised in the Introduction's section, "For Those Studying Routing & Switching": You have already read about the concepts in the first major heading of this chapter, which comprises most of the chapter. Feel free to skip ahead to the section titled "Layer 3 Switch Operations with Routing," later in this chapter. The first major heading covers generic routing and the second will get into Cisco Nexus specifics.

"Do I Know This Already?" Quiz

Use the "Do I Know This Already?" quiz to help decide whether you might want to skim this chapter, or a major section, moving more quickly to the "Exam Preparation Tasks" section near the end of the chapter. You can find the answers at the bottom of the page following the quiz. For thorough explanations, see Appendix A, "Answers to the 'Do I Know This Already?' Quizzes."

Table 18-1 "Do I Know This Already?" Foundation Topics Section-to-Question Mapping

Foundation Topics Section	Questions
IP Routing	1–2
Cisco Nexus Switch Operation with Routing	3–5

1. A PC opens a command prompt and uses the **ipconfig** command to see that the PC's IP address and mask are 192.168.4.77 and 255.255.255.224. The user then runs a test using the **ping 192.168.4.117** command. Which of the following answers is the most likely to happen?

   a. The PC sends packets directly to the host with address 192.168.4.117.

   b. The PC sends packets to its default gateway.

   c. The PC sends a DNS query for 192.168.4.117.

   d. The PC sends an ARP looking for the MAC address of the DHCP server.

2. Router R1 lists a route in its routing table. Which of the following answers list a fact from a route, that the router then compares to the packet's destination address? (Choose two answers.)

   a. Mask

   b. Next-hop router

   c. Subnet ID

   d. Outgoing interface

3. Which implementation on a Cisco Nexus switch turns off all Layer 2 protocol functions on an interface?

   a. Routed interface

   b. Switched virtual interface (SVI)

   c. Switchport access interface

   d. Switchport trunk interface

4. Which interface is preferred if you what to support both Layer 2 and Layer 3 for a VLAN on a Cisco Nexus switch?

   a. Trunk

   b. Access

   c. Switched virtual interface (SVI)

   d. Switchport

5. Which interface implementation on a Cisco Nexus switch allows for the faster interface or link down detection when router peering?

   a. Switched virtual interface (SVI)

   b. Routed interface

   c. Trunk

   d. ISL

Foundation Topics

IP Routing

IP routing—the process of forwarding IP packets—delivers packets across entire TCP/IP networks, from the device that originally builds the IP packet to the device that is supposed to receive the packet. In other words, IP routing delivers IP packets from the sending host to the destination host.

The complete end-to-end routing process relies on network layer logic on hosts and on routers. The sending host uses Layer 3 concepts to create an IP packet, forwarding the IP packet to the host's default gateway (default router). The process requires Layer 3 logic on the routers as well, by which the routers compare the destination address in the packet to their routing tables, to decide where to forward the IP packet next.

The routing process also relies on the data link and physical details at each link. IP routing relies on serial links, Ethernet LANs, wireless LANs, and many other networks that implement data link and physical layer standards. These lower-layer devices and protocols move the IP packets around the TCP/IP network by encapsulating and transmitting the packets inside data link layer frames.

Those previous two paragraphs summarize the key concepts about IP routing as introduced back in Chapter 4. Next, this section reviews IP routing, while taking the discussion another step or two deeper, taking advantage of the additional depth of knowledge discussed in Parts II and III of this book.

18

> **NOTE** Some references also incorrectly claim that the term *IP routing* includes the function of dynamically learning routes with IP routing protocols. Although IP routing protocols play an important role, the term *IP routing* refers to the packet-forwarding process only.

IPv4 Routing Process Reference

Because you have already seen the basics back in Chapter 4, this section collects the routing process into steps for reference. The steps use many specific terms discussed in Parts II and III of this book. The upcoming descriptions and example then discuss these summaries of routing logic to make sure that each step is clear.

The routing process starts with the host that creates the IP packet. First, the host asks the question: Is the destination IP address of this new packet in my local subnet? The host uses its own IP address/mask to determine the range of addresses in the local subnet. Based on its own opinion of the range of addresses in the local subnet, a LAN-based host acts as follows:

Step 1.   If the destination is local, send directly:

      A.   Find the destination host's MAC address. Use the already known Address Resolution Protocol (ARP) table entry, or use ARP messages to learn the information.

B. Encapsulate the IP packet in a data-link frame, with the destination data-link address of the *destination host*.

Step 2. If the destination is not local, send to the default gateway:

A. Find the default gateway's MAC address. Use the already known ARP table entry, or use ARP messages to learn the information.

B. Encapsulate the IP packet in a data-link frame, with the destination data-link address of the *default gateway*.

Figure 18-1 summarizes these same concepts. In the figure, host A sends a local packet directly to host D. However, for packets to host B, on the other side of a router and therefore in a different subnet, host A sends the packet to its default router (R1). (As a reminder, the terms *default gateway* and *default router* are synonyms.)

Local Subnet

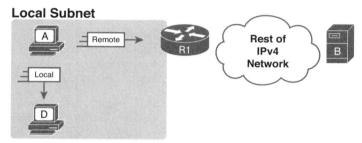

Figure 18-1 *Host Routing Logic Summary*

Routers have a little more routing work to do as compared with hosts. While the host logic began with an IP packet sitting in memory, a router has some work to do before getting to that point. With the following five-step summary of a router's routing logic, the router takes the first two steps just to receive the frame and extract the IP packet, before thinking about the packet's destination address at Step 3. The steps are as follows:

1. For each received data-link frame, choose whether or not to process the frame. Process it if

   A. The frame has no errors (per the data-link trailer Frame Check Sequence, or FCS, field)

   B. The frame's destination data-link address is the router's address (or an appropriate multicast or broadcast address).

2. If choosing to process the frame at Step 1, de-encapsulate the packet from inside the data-link frame.

3. Make a routing decision. To do so, compare the packet's destination IP address to the routing table and find the route that matches the destination address. This route identifies the outgoing interface of the router and possibly the next-hop router.

4. Encapsulate the packet into a data-link frame appropriate for the outgoing interface. When forwarding out LAN interfaces, use ARP as needed to find the next device's MAC address.

5. Transmit the frame out the outgoing interface, as listed in the matched IP route.

NOTE   The fact that this list has five steps, instead of breaking the logic into some other number of steps, does not matter. The concepts inside each step matter a lot—know them— but for the exams, there is no need to memorize which piece of logic goes with a particular step number.

This routing process summary lists many details, but sometimes you can think about the routing process in simpler terms. For example, leaving out some details, this paraphrase of the step list details the same big concepts:

> The router receives a frame, removes the packet from inside the frame, decides where to forward the packet, puts the packet into another frame, and sends the frame.

To give you a little more perspective on these steps, Figure 18-2 breaks down the same five-step routing process as a diagram. The figure shows a packet arriving from the left, entering a router Ethernet interface, with an IP destination of host C. The figure shows the packet arriving, encapsulated inside an Ethernet frame (both header and trailer).

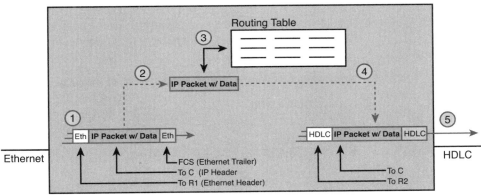

Router R1

Figure 18-2   *Router Routing Logic Summary*

Router R1 processes the frame and packet as shown with the numbers in the figure, matching the same five-step process described just before the figure, as follows:

1. Router R1 notes that the received Ethernet frame passes the FCS check, and that the destination Ethernet MAC address is R1's MAC address, so R1 processes the frame.

2. R1 deencapsulates the IP packet from inside the Ethernet frame's header and trailer.

3. R1 compares the IP packet's destination IP address to R1's IP routing table.

4. R1 encapsulates the IP packet inside a new data-link frame, in this case, inside a High-Level Data Link Control (HDLC) header and trailer.

5. R1 transmits the IP packet, inside the new HDLC frame, out the serial link on the right.

> **NOTE**   This chapter uses several figures that show an IP packet encapsulated inside a data link layer frame. These figures often show both the data-link header as well as the data-link trailer, with the IP packet in the middle. The IP packets all include the IP header, plus any encapsulated data.

An Example of IP Routing

The next several pages walk you through an example that discusses each routing step, in order, through multiple devices. That example uses a case in which host A (172.16.1.9) sends a packet to host B (172.16.2.9), with host routing logic and the five steps showing how R1 forwards the packet.

Figure 18-3 shows a typical IP addressing diagram for an IPv4 network with typical address abbreviations. The diagram can get a little too messy if it lists the full IP address for every router interface. When possible, these diagrams usually list the subnet, and then the last octet or two of the individual IP addresses—just enough so that you know the IP address, but with less clutter. For example, host A uses IP address 172.16.1.9, taking from subnet 172.16.1.0/24 (in which all addresses begin 172.16.1), and the ".9" beside the host A icon. As another example, R1 uses address 172.16.1.1 on its LAN interface, 172.16.4.1 on one serial interface, and 172.16.5.1 on the other serial interface.

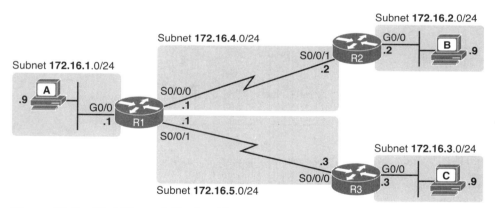

Figure 18-3   *IPv4 Network Used to Show Five-Step Routing Example*

Now on to the example, with host A (172.16.1.9) sending a packet to host B (172.16.2.9).

Host Forwards the IP Packet to the Default Router (Gateway)

In this example, host A uses some application that sends data to host B (172.16.2.9). After host A has the IP packet sitting in memory, host A's logic reduces to the following:

■ My IP address/mask is 172.16.1.9/24, so my local subnet contains numbers 172.16.1.0–172.16.1.255 (including the subnet ID and subnet broadcast address).

■ The destination address is 172.16.2.9, which is clearly not in my local subnet.

■ Send the packet to my default gateway, which is set to 172.16.1.1.

■ To send the packet, encapsulate it in an Ethernet frame. Make the destination MAC address be R1's G0/0 MAC address (host A's default gateway).

Figure 18-4 pulls these concepts together, showing the destination IP address and destination MAC address in the frame and packet sent by host A in this case.

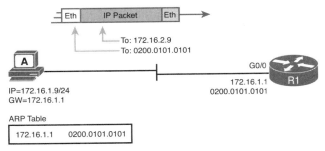

Figure 18-4 *Host A Sends Packet to Host B*

Note that the figure shows the Ethernet LAN as simple lines, but the LAN can include any of the devices discussed in Part II of this book. The LAN could be a single cable between host A and R1, or it could be 100 LAN switches connected across a huge campus of buildings. Regardless, host A and R1 sit in the same VLAN, and the Ethernet LAN then delivers the Ethernet frame to R1's G0/0 interface.

Routing Step 1: Decide Whether to Process the Incoming Frame

Routers receive many frames in an interface, particularly LAN interfaces. However, a router can and should ignore some of those frames. So, the first step in the routing process begins with a decision of whether a router should process the frame or silently discard (ignore) the frame.

First, the router does a simple but important check (Step 1A in the process summary) so that the router ignores all frames that had bit errors during transmission. The router uses the data-link header's Frame Check Sequence (FCS) field to check the frame, and if errors occurred in transmission, the router discards the frame. (The router makes no attempt at error recovery; that is, the router does not ask the sender to retransmit the data.)

The router also checks the destination data-link address (Step 1B in the summary) to decide whether the frame is intended for the router. For example, frames sent to the router's unicast MAC address for that interface are clearly sent to that router. However, a router can actually receive a frame sent to some other unicast MAC address, and routers should ignore these frames.

For example, routers will receive some unicast frames sent to other devices in the VLAN just because of how LAN switches work. Think back to how LAN switches forward unknown unicast frames: frames for which the switch does not list the destination MAC address in the MAC address table. The LAN switch floods those frames. The result? Routers sometimes receive frames destined for some other device, with some other device's MAC address listed as the destination MAC address. Routers should ignore those frames.

In this example, host A sends a frame destined for R1's MAC address. So, after the frame is received, and after R1 confirms with the FCS that no errors occurred, R1 confirms that the frame is destined for R1's MAC address (0200.0101.0101 in this case). All checks have been passed, so R1 will process the frame, as shown in Figure 18-5. (Note that the large rectangle in the figure represents the internals of router R1.)

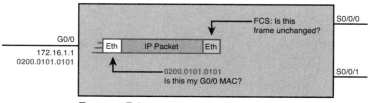

Router R1

Figure 18-5 *Routing Step 1, on Router R1: Checking FCS and Destination MAC*

Routing Step 2: Deencapsulation of the IP Packet

After the router knows that it ought to process the received frame (per Step 1), the next step is a relatively simple step: deencapsulating the packet. In router memory, the router no longer needs the original frame's data-link header and trailer, so the router removes and discards them, leaving the IP packet, as shown in Figure 18-6. Note that the destination IP address remains unchanged (172.16.2.9).

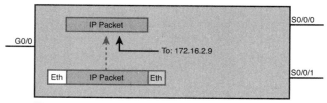

Router R1

Figure 18-6 *Routing Step 2 on Router R1: Deencapsulating the Packet*

Routing Step 3: Choosing Where to Forward the Packet

Routing Step 2 required little thought, but Step 3 requires the most thought of all the steps. At this point, the router needs to make a choice about where to forward the packet next. That process uses the router's IP routing table, with some matching logic to compare the packet's destination address with the table.

First, an IP routing table lists multiple routes. Each individual route contains several facts, which in turn can be grouped as shown in Figure 18-7. Part of each route is used to match the destination address of the packet, while the rest of the route lists forwarding instructions: where to send the packet next.

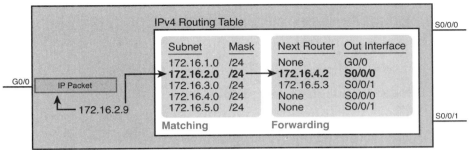

Router R1

Figure 18-7   *Routing Step 3 on Router R1: Matching the Routing Table*

Focus on the entire routing table for a moment, and notice the fact that it lists five routes. Earlier, Figure 18-3 showed the entire example network, with five subnets, so R1 has a route for each of the five subnets.

Next, look at the part of the five routes that router R1 will use to match packets. To fully define each subnet, each route lists both the subnet ID and the subnet mask. When matching the IP packet's destination with the routing table, the router looks at the packet's destination IP address (172.16.2.9) and compares it to the range of addresses defined by each subnet. Specifically, the router looks at the subnet and mask information, which with a little math, the router can figure out in which of those subnets 172.16.2.9 resides (the route for subnet 172.16.2.0/24).

Finally, look to the right side of the figure, to the forwarding instructions for these five routes. After the router matches a specific route, the router uses the forwarding information in the route to tell the router where to send the packet next. In this case, the router matched the route for subnet 172.16.2.0/24, so R1 will forward the packet out its own interface S0/0/0, to router R2 next, listed with its next-hop router IP address of 172.16.4.2.

NOTE   Routes for remote subnets typically list both an outgoing interface and next-hop router IP address. Routes for subnets that connect directly to the router list only the outgoing interface, because packets to these destinations do not need to be sent to another router.

Routing Step 4: Encapsulating the Packet in a New Frame

At this point, the router knows how it will forward the packet. However, routers cannot forward a packet without first wrapping a data-link header and trailer around it (encapsulation).

Encapsulating packets for serial links does not require a lot of thought, because of the simplicity of the HDLC and PPP protocols. As discussed back in Chapter 3, "Fundamentals of WANs," because serial links have only two devices on the link—the sender and the then-obvious receiver—the data-link addressing does not matter. In this example, R1 forwards the packet out S0/0/0, after encapsulating the packet inside an HDLC frame, as shown in Figure 18-8.

18

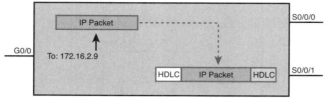

Router R1

Figure 18-8 *Routing Step 4 on Router R1: Encapsulating the Packet*

Note that with some other types of data links, the router has a little more work to do at this routing step. For example, sometimes a router forwards packets out an Ethernet interface. To encapsulate the IP packet, the router would need to build an Ethernet header, and that Ethernet header's destination MAC address would need to list the correct value.

For example, consider this different sample network, with an Ethernet WAN link between routers R1 and R2. R1 matches a route that tells R1 to forward the packet out R1's G0/1 Ethernet interface to 172.16.6.2 (R2) next. R1 needs to put R2's MAC address in the header, and to do that, R1 uses its IP ARP table information, as shown in Figure 18-9. If R1 did not have an ARP table entry for 172.16.6.2, R1 would first have to use ARP to learn the matching MAC address.

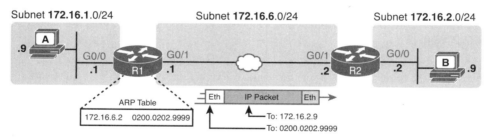

Figure 18-9 *Routing Step 4 on Router R1 with a LAN Outgoing Interface*

Routing Step 5: Transmitting the Frame

After the frame has been prepared, the router simply needs to transmit the frame. The router might have to wait, particularly if other frames are already waiting their turn to exit the interface.

Internal Processing on Cisco Routers

The discussion so far in this chapter explains one way to think about how a host and a router do their work internally. However, for Cisco to compete well in the router marketplace, it must be ready to make its routers perform that routing process well, and quickly, in all kinds of environments. If not, Cisco competitors could argue that their routers performed better, could route more packets per second (pps), and could win business away from Cisco.

This next topic looks a little deeper at how Cisco actually implements IP routing internal to a router. The discussion so far in this chapter was fairly generic, but it matches an early type of internal processing on Cisco routers called *process switching*. This section discusses the issues that drove Cisco to improve the internal routing process, while having the same result: A packet arrives inside one frame, a choice is made, and it exits the router inside another frame.

Potential Routing Performance Issues

When learning about IP routing, it helps to think through all the particulars of the routing process, as discussed over the last five or so pages. However, routers barely spend any processing time to route a single IP packet. In fact, even slower routers need to forward tens of thousands of packets per second; to do that, the routers cannot spend a lot of effort processing each packet.

The process of matching a packet's destination address with the IP routing table can actually take a lot of CPU time. The example in this chapter (Figure 18-7) listed only five routes, but enterprise networks routinely have thousands of IP routes, and routers in the core of the Internet have hundreds of thousands of routes. Now think about a router CPU that needs to search a list 100,000 entries long, for every packet, for a router that needed to forward hundreds of thousands of packets per second! And what if the router had to do subnetting math each time, calculating the range of addresses in each subnet for each route? Those actions would take too many CPU cycles.

Over the years, Cisco has created several ways to optimize the internal process of how routers forward packets. Some methods tie to a specific model series of router. Layer 3 switches do the forwarding in application-specific integrated circuits (ASIC), which are computer chips built for the purpose of forwarding frames or packets. All these optimizations take the basic logic from the five-step list here in the book, but work differently inside the router hardware and software, in an effort to use fewer CPU cycles and reduce the overhead of forwarding IP packets.

Cisco Router Fast Switching and CEF

Historically, Cisco has had three major variations of internal routing logic that apply across the entire router product family. First, Cisco routers used internal logic called *process switching* in the early days of Cisco routers, dating back to the late 1980s and early 1990s. Process switching works basically like the routing process detailed so far in this chapter, without any of the extra optimizations.

Next, in the early 1990s, Cisco introduced alternate internal routing logic called *fast switching*. Fast switching made a couple of optimizations compared to the older process-switching logic. First, it kept another list in addition to the routing table, listing specific IP addresses for recently forwarded packets. This fast-switching cache also kept a copy of the new data-link headers used when forwarding packets to each destination, so rather than build a new data-link header for each packet destined for a particular IP address, the router saved a little effort by copying the old data-link header.

Cisco improved over fast switching with the introduction of Cisco Express Forwarding (CEF) later in the 1990s. Like fast switching, CEF uses additional tables for faster searches, and it saves outgoing data-link headers. However, CEF organizes its tables for all routing table destinations, ahead of time, not just for some of the specific destination IP addresses. CEF also uses much more sophisticated search algorithms and binary tree structures as compared to fast switching. As a result, the CEF table lookups that replace the routing table matches take even less time than with fast switching. And it caches the data-link headers as well.

Today, current models of Cisco routers, and current IOS versions, use CEF by default. Table 18-2 lists a summary of the key comparison points between process switching, fast switching, and CEF.

Table 18-2   Comparisons of Packet Switching, Fast Switching, and CEF

Improves Routing Efficiency By...	Process Switching	Fast Switching	CEF
...saving data-link headers used for encapsulating packets	No	Yes	Yes
...using other tables, with faster lookup time, before looking at the routing table	No	Yes	Yes
...organizing the tables using tree structures for very fast searches and less time to route packets	No	No	Yes

Cisco Nexus Switch Operations with Routing

A multilayer switch is essentially a switch at Layer 2 that has routing functionality. Multilayer switches traditionally have been built to give you the ability to have multiple VLANs on a given switch and route between them if needed without the need for an external dedicated router. Also, multilayer switches are primarily created in the same manner as traditional Layer 2 switches, where they only have Ethernet interfaces ranging from 10 Mb to 100 Gigabit Ethernet based on the switch chosen. Switches use ASICs to provide forwarding in hardware to accelerate the process of packet switching and routing, in comparison to the original routers, which did this primarily in software.

The second major difference between multilayer and Layer 2 switches is based on how routing is implemented or configured on them. On a Layer 3 switch, you can implement a switched virtual interface (SVI) or a Layer 3 routed interface (sometimes referred to as a *router port*). Let's explore each one a little deeper to understand the difference.

NOTE   Cisco Nexus switches have both Layer 2 and Layer 3 functionality and are considered to be multilayer switches. Through the rest of this section, we refer to them as Cisco Nexus switches.

The first thing to understand is how a Cisco Nexus switch implements the logical routed interface known as an SVI and when you would want to use it in you data center. Figure 18-10 shows what an SVI looks like logically in a Nexus switch.

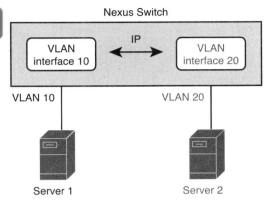

Figure 18-10 *SVI Logically Represented on a Nexus Switch*

As you can see, the Nexus switch in Figure 18-10 creates a VLAN for both hosts to communicate then enables an interface for VLAN 10 and 20 that has IP connectivity enabled. The top layer of this figure is representative of a logical router that is created for each VLAN (10 and 20, respectively) and assigned an IP address. This allows for many Layer 2 interfaces to be part of either of these networks and also enables the Cisco Nexus switch to route between them if communication is needed using the SVI interfaces. In the past, when there were no multilayer switches like a Cisco Nexus switch, you had to attach separate physical routers to your switched network and send packets up to them to route between different networks, as shown in Figure 18-11.

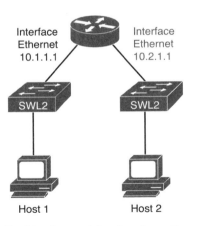
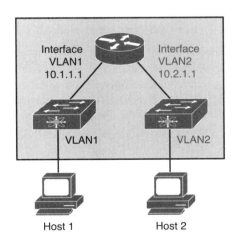
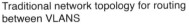

Figure 18-11 *SVI Replacing Dedicated Routers for Inter-VLAN Communication*

Now with Cisco Nexus switches being able to perform both routing and switching simultaneously, you can enable SVIs or logical routers on them and allow for inter-VLAN routing without having to go to another external device. The typical use case for this in the data center is at the distribution or access layer, where you need to do inter-VLAN routing and support many downstream Layer 2 networks at the same time, as shown in Figure 18-12.

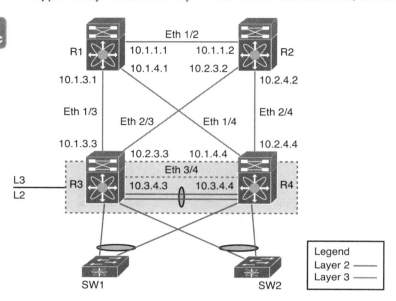

Figure 18-12 *Typical Layer 3 and Layer 2 Placement in Data Center*

In Figure 18-12, we would enable SVIs on R3 and R4 for any Layer 2 networks below them or off of SW1 and SW2. This allows for multiple devices to join these networks by being assigned to a VLAN and for inter-VLAN communication to happen at R3 and R4.

The second way to implement routing on a Cisco Nexus switch is by using a routed interface—which is implemented when you configure an interface on a Layer 3 switch to not have any switching functionality. Figure 18-12 shows these between R1, R2, R3, and R4. As mentioned previously, a routed interface does not have any Layer 2 functionality enabled on it and is typically used for Cisco Nexus to Nexus connections as peering points for routing or when directly connecting to a separate physical router over a strictly Layer 3 interconnect.

The question that now usually gets asked is this: "When do I use an SVI versus a routed interface?" We have answered this question already, but let's now review when it might be good to use them and look at a few considerations when using an SVI or a routed interface.

The SVI is most useful when we need to support Layer 2 and Layer 3 simultaneously for a given subnet. You're probably wondering what that means. If you refer to Figure 18-12, in a typical data center design we have an aggregation layer where all the Layer 2 connected devices live, but we need to provide default gateways for them as dedicated routers normally would if connected to a switched network in the past. Using an SVI here lets us run Layer 2 protocols such as Spanning Tree Protocol (STP) and run a logical router that acts as the default gateway for a VLAN or many VLANs. (Each VLAN has its own logical router or SVI interface.) This enables us to add devices to this Layer 2 network and point them to their gateway (SVI or logical router) to talk to other networks.

So, when should you use a routed interface? A routed interface is useful when you don't need any Layer 2 devices on a routed segment, such as when you want to peer from a routing perspective with another router or multilayer switch. In this case, you create a small subnet (usually a /30) between the devices and dedicate an interface for peering, because no other devices will live on this segment except the peering routers, which do not need to support Layer 2 because we use routed interfaces for this connection.

NOTE   One benefit from using routed interfaces when dedicating them for router peering is that they provide faster downtime detection of a failed interface or link. If you are using SVI peering, it takes longer from the time the interface or link fails for the router to, in turn, shut down the SVI than it would if it were a routed interface.

18

Exam Preparation Tasks

Review All the Key Topics

Review the most important topics from this chapter, noted with the Key Topic icon. Table 18-3 lists these key topics and where each is discussed.

Table 18-3   Key Topics for Chapter 18

Key Topic Element	Description	Page Number
List	Steps taken by a host when forwarding IP packets	475
List	Steps taken by a router when forwarding IP packets	476
Figure 18-2	Diagram of five routing steps taken by a router	477
Figure 18-7	Breakdown of IP routing table with matching and forwarding details	481
Figure 18-10	SVI logically represented on a Nexus switch	485
Figure 18-12	Typical Layer 3 and Layer 2 placement in the data center	486
Paragraph	SVI versus routed interface discussion	486

Complete the Tables and Lists from Memory

Print a copy of DVD Appendix I, "Memory Tables," or at least the section for this chapter, and complete the tables and lists from memory. DVD Appendix J, "Memory Tables Answer Key," includes completed tables and lists for you to check your work.

Definitions of Key Terms

After your first reading of the chapter, try to define these key terms, but do not be concerned about getting them all correct at that time. Chapter 23, "Final Review," directs you in how to use these terms for late-stage preparation for the exam.

default gateway/router, ARP table, routing table, next-hop router, outgoing interface, subinterface, VLAN interface, multilayer switch, Cisco Express Forwarding (CEF), connected route, static route, default route, zero subnet, switched virtual interface (SVI), routed interface, Inter-VLAN routing

This chapter covers the following exam topics:

4.1 Describe and configure basic routing concepts

4.1.a Packet forwarding

4.1.b Router look-up process (exec mode, exec commands, configuration mode)

CHAPTER 19

Cisco Nexus IPv4 Routing Configuration

This chapter focuses on how to implement or configure IPv4 routing on a Cisco Nexus switch. The chapter begins by exploring two forms of connected routes you often see on a Nexus switch. The two common types of connected routes are direct and local.

The final major section then looks at static routes, which let the engineer tell the router what route(s) to add to the router's IP routing table. The static route section also shows how to configure a static default route that is used when no other route matches an IP packet. Dynamic routing, using the Open Shortest Path First (OSPF) routing protocol, awaits in Chapter 21, "Nexus Routing Protocol Configuration."

> **NOTE** As promised in the Introduction's section "For Those Studying Routing & Switching": Read this whole chapter. While many of the commands in this chapter mirror the same function in IOS, small differences exist, especially in **show** command output and in Layer 3 switching configuration, so take the time to read the entire chapter.

"Do I Know This Already?" Quiz

Use the "Do I Know This Already?" quiz to help decide whether you might want to skim this chapter, or a major section, moving more quickly to the "Exam Preparation Tasks" section near the end of the chapter. You can find the answers at the bottom of the page following the quiz. For thorough explanations, see Appendix A, "Answers to the 'Do I Know This Already?' Quizzes."

Table 19-1 "Do I Know This Already?" Foundation Topics Section-to-Question Mapping

Foundation Topics Section	Questions
IP Routing	1–3
Configuring Connected Routes	4
Configuring Static Routes	5–6

1. Which implementation on a Cisco Nexus switch turns off all Layer 2 protocol functions on an interface?

   a. **no switchport** under the interface configuration mode

   b. **interface vlan 1** under the interface configuration mode

   c. **ip address** under the interface configuration mode

   d. **router ospf** under the routing process

2. Which command under an interface on a Layer 3 switch enables a VLAN 10 to be assigned to it?

   a. **no switchport vlan 10**

   b. **switchport trunk allowed vlan 10**

   c. **switchport access vlan 10**

   d. **vlan 10 switchport**

3. Which implementation on a Cisco Nexus switch allows for an IP address to be assigned to a switched virtual interface (SVI) for VLAN 10 if the **feature interface-vlan** command has already been enabled?

   a. **ip address** command under a physical interface assigned to a VLAN 10

   b. **ip address** command under the **interface vlan 10** configuration mode

   c. **ip address** command under the **interface** configuration mode

   d. **ip address** command assigned to VLAN 10 under the **vlan** configuration mode

4. A Layer 3 switch has been configured to route IP packets between VLANs 1, 2, and 3, which connect to subnets 172.20.1.0/25, 172.20.2.0/25, and 172.20.3.0/25, respectively. The engineer issues a **show ip route** command on the Layer 3 switch, listing the connected routes. Which of the following answers lists a piece of information that should be in at least one of the routes?

   a. Interface Ethernet 1/1

   b. Next-hop router 172.20.4.1

   c. Interface VLAN 2

   d. Mask 255.255.255.0

5. An engineer configures a static IPv4 route on router R1. Which of the following pieces of information should not be listed as a parameter in the configuration command that creates this static IPv4 route?

   a. The destination subnet's subnet ID

   b. The next-hop router's IP address

   c. The next-hop router's neighboring interface

   d. The subnet mask

6. Which of the following commands correctly configures a static route?

    a. ip route 10.1.3.0 255.255.255.0

    b. ip route 10.1.3.0 Ethernet 1/1

    c. ip route 10.1.3.0 0.0.0.255

    d. ip route 10.1.3.0 /24 Ethernet 1/2

19

Foundation Topics

Configuring Connected Routes on Cisco Nexus Switches

When routers and Layer 3 switches configure IP addresses on their interfaces, the device knows about the subnets connected, based on what has been configured. The devices then use these subnets to build a routing table for any subnet that is directly connected to one of its interfaces. Although Cisco Nexus switches enable IPv4 routing globally, you must enable particular routing features in Nexus L3-enabled products to enable the appropriate feature. Table 19-2 shows the feature commands for basic routing and the associated functionality that they enable.

Table 19-2   Basic Routing Feature Commands for Cisco Nexus

Feature Command	Description
(no) feature interface-vlan	Enables/disables the ability to configure SVIs using **interface vlan** *x* command
(no) ip address	Enables IP address on an interface or SVI
ip route	Enables a static route with a destination network and next-hop router address or outgoing interface

To make the router be ready to route packets on a particular interface, the router must be configured with an IP address, and the interface must be configured such that it comes up, reaching a "line status up, line protocol up" state. Only at that point can routers route IP packets in and out a particular interface.

After a router can route IP packets out one or more interfaces, the router needs some routes. Routers can add routes to their routing tables through three methods:

- **Connected routes:** Added because of the configuration of the **ip address** interface sub-command on the local router
- **Static routes:** Added because of the configuration of the **ip route** global command on the local router
- **Routing protocols:** Added as a function by configuration on all routers, resulting in a process by which routers dynamically tell each other about the network so that they all learn routes

This chapter discusses how to use connected and static routes. Chapter 21 then covers how you can configure routing protocols for use with Cisco Nexus switches.

Direct and Local Routes and the ip address Command

A Cisco Nexus L3 switch automatically adds two routes to its routing table based on the IPv4 address configured for an interface, assuming that the following two facts are true:

- The interface is in a working state—in other words, the interface status in the **show interfaces** command lists a line status of up and a protocol status of up.
- The interface has an IP address assigned through the **ip address** interface subcommand.

The two routes, called a *direct* and a *local route*, route packets to the subnet directly connected to that interface. The router, of course, needs to know the subnet number used on the physical network connected to each of its interfaces, so the router can route packets to that subnet. The router can simply do the math, taking the interface IP address and mask, and calculate the subnet ID. However, the router needs that route only when the interface is up and working, so the router includes a directly connected route in the routing table only when the interface is working.

Example 19-1 shows the direct and local routes on router R1 in Figure 19-1. The first part of the example shows the configuration of IP addresses on all three of R1's interfaces. The end of the example lists the output from the **show ip route** command, which lists these routes with direct or local as the route code, meaning *connected*.

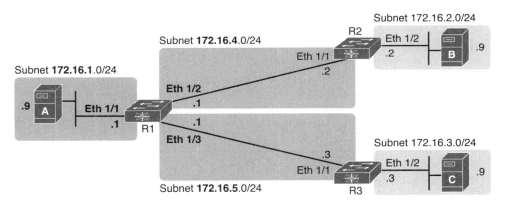

Figure 19-1 *Sample Network to Show Connected Routes*

Example 19-1 *Connected and Local Routes on R1*

```
! Excerpt from show running-config follows...
!
interface Ethernet1/1
 no switchport
 ip address 172.16.1.1/24
 no shutdown

!
interface Ethernet 1/2
 no switchport
 no shutdown
 ip address 172.16.4.1/24

!
```

```
interface Ethernet 1/3
 no switchport
 no shutdown
 ip address 172.16.5.1/24


R1# show ip route
IP Route Table for VRF "default"
'*' denotes best ucast next-hop
'**' denotes best mcast next-hop
'[x/y]' denotes [preference/metric]
'%<string>' in via output denotes VRF <string>


172.16.1.0/24, ubest/mbest: 1/0, attached
    *via 172.16.1.1, Eth1/1, [0/0], 2w0d, direct
172.16.1.1/32, ubest/mbest: 1/0, attached
    *via 172.16.1.1, Eth1/1, [0/0], 2w0d, local
172.16.4.0/24, ubest/mbest: 1/0, attached
    *via 172.16.4.1, Eth1/1, [0/0], 2w0d, direct
172.16.4.1/32, ubest/mbest: 1/0, attached
    *via 172.16.4.1, Eth1/1, [0/0], 2w0d, local
172.16.5.0/24, ubest/mbest: 1/0, attached
    *via 172.16.5.1, Eth1/1, [0/0], 2w0d, direct
172.16.5.1/32, ubest/mbest: 1/0, attached
    *via 172.16.5.1, Eth1/1, [0/0], 2w0d, local
```

Focus on the lists with highlights, which focus on the direct and local routes related to R1's E1/1 interface. First, the output shows a route to subnet 172.16.1.0/24—the subnet off R1's E1/1 interface—with an ending word of *direct*. This route represents the entire directly connected subnet. R1 will use this route when forwarding packets to other hosts in subnet 172.16.1.0/24.

The second highlighted route, the local route, lists 172.16.1.1/32. Look back to the top of the example, to R1's configuration on interface E1/1. Because the configuration shows 172.16.1.1 as the exact IP address on that interface, R1 adds a route with a /32 prefix length for that address, with outgoing interface E1/1. This route matches packets sent to 172.16.1.1 only. R1 then lists this route as a local route, as noted at the end of the second line for that route.

In the configuration in Example 19-1, notice the **no switchport** command, which is highlighted under each Ethernet interface. You learned in Chapter 18, "IPv4 Routing Concepts," that there are two ways to configure routing on a Cisco Nexus switch:

■ A routed interface, which is enabled by using the **no switchport** command. Remember that when using this command, we are disabling any Layer 2 functionality on an interface.

■ Switched virtual interface (SVI), which you use when you route between VLANs and support Layer 2 with Layer 3 simultaneously.

Routing Between Subnets on VLANs

Almost all enterprise networks use VLANs. To route IP packets in and out of those VLANs—or more accurately, the subnets that sit on each of those VLANs—some router needs to have an IP address in each subnet and have a connected route to each of those subnets. Then the hosts in each subnet can use the router IP addresses as their default gateways, respectively.

Three options exist for connecting a router to each subnet on a VLAN. However, the first option requires too many interfaces and links, and is mentioned only to make the list complete:

- Use a router, with one router LAN interface and cable connected to the switch for each and every VLAN (typically not used).
- Use a router, with a VLAN trunk connecting to a LAN switch.
- Use a Layer 3 switch.

Configuring Routing to VLANs Using a Layer 3 Switch

The other option for routing traffic to VLANs uses a device called a *Layer 3 switch* or *multilayer switch*. As introduced back in Chapter 9, "VLAN and Trunking Concepts," a Layer 3 switch is one device that does two primary functions: Layer 2 LAN switching and Layer 3 IP routing. The Layer 2 switch function forwards frames inside each VLAN, but it will not forward frames between VLANs. The Layer 3 forwarding logic—routing—forwards IP packets between VLANs.

The configuration of a Layer 3 switch mostly looks like the Layer 2 switching configuration, with a small bit of configuration added for the Layer 3 functions. The Layer 3 switching function needs a virtual interface connected to each VLAN internal to the switch. These VLAN interfaces act like router interfaces, with an IP address and mask. The Layer 3 switch has an IP routing table, with connected routes off each of these VLAN interfaces. (These interfaces are also referred to as SVIs.)

Figure 19-2 shows the Layer 3 switch function with a router icon inside the switch, to emphasize that the switch routes the packets. The datacenter has three server VLANs, so the Layer 3 switch needs one VLAN interface for each VLAN.

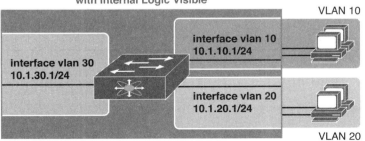

Figure 19-2 *Routing on VLAN Interfaces in a Layer 3 Switch*

The following steps show how to configure Cisco Nexus Layer 3 switching. Note that on some switches (such as the 5500 switches used for the examples in this book), the ability to route IPv4 packets requires the addition of a Layer 3 module with associated licensing, with a **reload** of the switch required to enable the feature. The rest of the steps after Step 1 would apply to all models of Cisco switches that are capable of doing Layer 3 switching.

Step 1.   Enable Feature for configuring interface VLANs (**feature interface-vlan**).

Step 2.   Create VLAN interfaces for each VLAN for which the Layer 3 switch is routing packets (**interface vlan** *vlan_id*).

Step 3.   Configure an IP address and mask on the VLAN interface (in interface configuration mode for that interface), enabling IPv4 on that VLAN interface (**ip address** *address mask*).

Step 4.   If the switch defaults to place the VLAN interface in a disabled (shutdown) state, enable the interface (**no shutdown**).

Example 19-2 shows the configuration to match Figure 19-2. In this case, the switch is a Cisco Nexus switch. The example shows the related configuration on all three VLAN interfaces.

Example 19-2   *VLAN Interface Configuration for Layer 3 Switching*

```
feature Interface-vlan
!
interface vlan 10
 ip address 10.1.10.1/24
!
interface vlan 20
 ip address 10.1.20.1/24
!
interface vlan 30
 ip address 10.1.30.1/24
```

With the VLAN configuration shown here, the switch is ready to route packets between the VLANs, as shown in Figure 19-2. To support the routing of packets, the switch adds connected IP routes, as shown in Example 19-3. Note that each route is listed as being direct to a different VLAN interface.

Example 19-3   *Connected Routes on a Layer 3 Switch*

```
SW1# show ip route
! legend omitted for brevity

10.1.10.0/24, ubest/mbest: 1/0, attached
    *via 10.1.10.1, Vlan 0010, [0/0], 2w0d, direct
10.1.10.1/32, ubest/mbest: 1/0, attached
    *via 10.1.10.1, Vlan 0010, [0/0], 2w0d, local
```

```
10.1.20.0/24, ubest/mbest: 1/0, attached
    *via 10.1.20.1, Vlan0020, [0/0], 1w6d, direct
10.1.20.1/32, ubest/mbest: 1/0, attached
    *via 10.1.20.1, Vlan0020, [0/0], 1w6d, local
10.1.30.0/24, ubest/mbest: 1/0, attached
    *via 10.1.30.1, Vlan0020, [0/0], 1w6d, direct
10.1.30.1/32, ubest/mbest: 1/0, attached
    *via 10.1.30.1, Vlan0020, [0/0], 1w6d, local
```

The switch also needs additional routes to the rest of the network shown in Figure 19-2, possibly using static routes, as discussed in the final major section of this chapter.

Configuring Static Routes

All routers add connected routes, as discussed in the previous section. Then, most networks use dynamic routing protocols to cause each router to learn the rest of the routes in an internetwork. Networks use static routes—routes added to a routing table through direct configuration—much less often than dynamic routing. However, static routes can be useful at times, and they happen to be useful learning tools as well. This last of three major sections in the chapter discusses static routes.

Static Route Configuration

NX-OS allows the definition of individual static routes using the **ip route** global configuration command. Every **ip route** command defines a destination that can be matched, usually with a subnet ID and mask. The command also lists the forwarding instructions, typically listing either the outgoing interface or the next-hop router's IP address. NX-OS then takes that information and adds that route to the IP routing table.

As an example, Figure 19-3 shows a small IP network.. The figure shows only the details related to a static route on R1, for subnet 172.16.2.0/24, which sits on the far right. To create that static route on R1, R1 will configure the subnet ID and mask, and either R1's outgoing interface (Ethernet 1/1), or R2 as the next-hop router IP address (172.16.4.2).

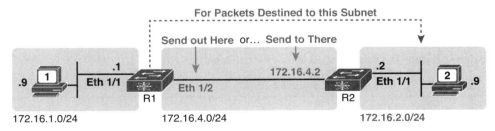

Figure 19-3 *Static Route Configuration Concept*

Example 19-4 shows the configuration of a couple of sample static routes. In particular, it shows routes on R1 in Figure 19-4, for the two subnets on the right side of the figure.

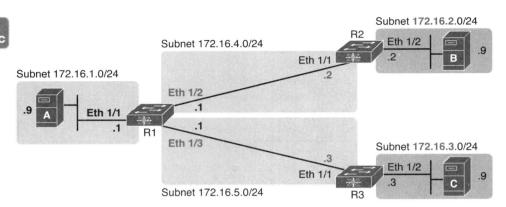

Figure 19-4 *Sample Network Used in Static Route Configuration Examples*

Example 19-4 *Static Routes Added to R1*

```
ip route 172.16.2.0 255.255.255.0 172.16.4.2
ip route 172.16.3.0 255.255.255.0 Ethernet 1/1
```

The two example **ip route** commands show the two different styles. The first command shows subnet 172.16.2.0, mask 255.255.255.0, which sits in the datacenter near Nexus R2. That same first command lists 172.16.4.2, R2's IP address, as the next-hop router. This route basically says this: To send packets to the subnet off Nexus R2, send them to R2.

The second route has the same kind of logic, but instead of identifying the next router by IP address, it lists the local router's outgoing interface. This route basically states: To send packets to the subnet off router R3, send them out my own local Ethernet 1/1 interface (which happens to connect to R3).

The routes created by these two **ip route** commands actually look a little different in the IP routing table. Both are static routes. However, the route that used the outgoing interface configuration is also noted as a connected route; this is just a quirk of the output of the **show ip route** command.

Example 19-4 lists these two routes using the **show ip route static** command. This command lists the details of static routes only, but it also lists a few statistics about all IPv4 routes. For example, the example shows two lines, for the two static routes configured in Example 19-5, but statistics state that this route has routes for ten subnets.

Example 19-5 *Static Routes Added to R1*

```
R1# show ip route static
IP Route Table for VRF "default"
'*' denotes best ucast next-hop
'**' denotes best mcast next-hop
'[x/y]' denotes [preference/metric]
'%<string>' in via output denotes VRF <string>
```

```
172.16.2.0//24, ubest/mbest: 1/0
    *via 172.16.4.2 [1/0], 00:00:05, static
172.16.3.0/24, ubest/mbest: 1/0, attached
    *via Ethernet1/1, [1/0], 00:00:05, static
```

NX-OS adds and removes these static routes dynamically over time, based on whether the outgoing interface is working. For example, in this case, if R1's Ethernet 1/1 interface fails, R1 removes the static route to 172.16.3.0/24 from the IPv4 routing table. Later, when the interface comes up again, NX-OS adds the route back to the routing table.

Finally, if using static routes, and not using any dynamic routing protocols at all, all routers would need to have some static routes configured. For example, at this point, in the network in Figure 19-4, PC A would not be able to receive packets back from PC B because router R2 does not have a route for PC A's subnet. R2 would need static routes for other subnets, as would R3.

Static Default Routes

When a router tries to route a packet, the router might not match the packet's destination IP address with any route. When that happens, the router normally just discards the packet.

Routers can be configured so that they use either a statically configured or dynamically learned default route. The default route matches all packets, so that if a packet does not match any other more specific route in the routing table, the router can at least forward the packet based on the default route.

NX-OS allows the configuration of a static default route by using special values for the subnet and mask fields in the **ip route** command: 0.0.0.0 and 0.0.0.0. For example, the command **ip route 0.0.0.0 0.0.0.0 vlan 16** creates a static default route on Cisco Nexus switch—a route that matches all IP packets—and sends those packets out SVI VLAN 16.

Example 19-6 shows a static default route using a Cisco Nexus switch.

Example 19-6 *Adding a Static Default Route on Cisco Nexus Switch*

```
SW1# configure terminal
Enter configuration commands, one per line.  End with CNTL/Z.
R2(config)# ip route 0.0.0.0 0.0.0.0 Vlan 16
R2(config)# ^Z
SW1# sh ip route
IP Route Table for VRF "default"
'*' denotes best ucast next-hop
'**' denotes best mcast next-hop
'[x/y]' denotes [preference/metric]
'%<string>' in via output denotes VRF <string>


0.0.0.0/0, ubest/mbest: 1/0, attached
    *via Vlan16, [1/0], 00:00:04, static
```

Exam Preparation Tasks

Review All the Key Topics

Review the most important topics from this chapter, noted with the Key Topic icon. Table 19-3 lists these key topics and where each is discussed.

Table 19-3   Key Topics for Chapter 19

Key Topic Element	Description	Page Number
Table 19-2	Basic routing feature commands for Cisco Nexus switches	494
Figure 19-2	Layer 3 switching concept and configuration	497
List	Layer 3 switching configuration	498
Example 19-3	Connected routes on a Layer 3 switch	498
Figure 19-4	Static route configuration concept	500

Complete the Tables and Lists from Memory

Print a copy of DVD Appendix I, "Memory Tables," or at least the section for this chapter, and complete the tables and lists from memory. DVD Appendix J, "Memory Tables Answer Key," includes completed tables and lists for you to check your work.

Definitions of Key Terms

After your first reading of the chapter, try to define these key terms, but do not be concerned about getting them all correct at that time. Chapter 23, "Final Review," directs you in how to use these terms for late-stage preparation for the exam.

VLAN interface, Layer 3 switch, connected route, static route, default route, local route, direct route, **feature interface-vlan, show ip route**

Command Reference to Check Your Memory

Although you should not necessarily memorize the information in the tables in this section, this section does include a reference for the configuration and EXEC commands covered in this chapter. Practically speaking, you should memorize the commands as a side effect of reading the chapter and doing all the activities in this exam preparation section. To check to see how well you have memorized the commands as a side effect of your other studies, cover the left side of the table with a piece of paper, read the descriptions on the right side, and see whether you remember the command.

Table 19-4   Chapter 19 Configuration Command Reference

Command	Description
ip address *ip-address mask* [**secondary**]	Interface subcommand that assigns the interface's IP address and optionally makes the address a secondary address
(**no**) **feature interface-vlan**	Global command that enables (**ip routing**) or disables (**no ip routing**) the routing of IPv4 packets on a Nexus Layer 3 switch
interface vlan *vlan_id*	Global command on a Layer 3 switch to create a VLAN interface and to enter configuration mode for that VLAN interface
ip route *prefix mask* {*ip-address* | *interface-type interface-number*} [*distance*] [**permanent**]	Global configuration command that creates a static route

Table 19-5   Chapter 19 EXEC Command Reference

Command	Description
show ip route	Lists the router's entire routing table
show ip route [**connected** | **static** | **ospf**]	Lists a subnet of the IP routing table
show ip route *ip-address*	Lists detailed information about the route that a router matches for the listed IP address
show vlans	Lists VLAN configuration and statistics for VLAN trunks configured on routers

19

This chapter covers the following exam topics:

4.1 Describe and configure basic routing concepts

4.1.a Packet forwarding

4.2 Describe the operation of Cisco routers

4.2.c Router components

CHAPTER 20

IPv4 Routing Protocol Concepts

Routers and Layer 3 switches add IP routes to their routing tables using three methods: connected routes, static routes, and routes learned by using *dynamic routing protocols*. The routing process forwards IP packets, but if a router does not have any routes in its IP routing table that match a packet's destination address, the router discards the packet. Routers need routing protocols so that the routers can learn all the possible routes and add them to the routing table, so that the routing process can forward (route) routable protocols such as IP.

IPv4 supports several different routing protocols, some of which are primarily used inside one company, while one is meant primarily for use between companies to create the Internet. This chapter introduces the concepts behind Interior Gateway Protocols (IGPs), typically used inside one company. In particular, this chapter discusses the theory behind types of routing protocols, including distance vector and link-state logic. The chapter also introduces the Routing Information Protocol (RIP), Enhanced Interior Gateway Routing Protocol (EIGRP), and Open Shortest Path First (OSPF) routing protocol.

> **NOTE** As promised in the Introduction's section "For Those Studying Routing & Switching": Read this chapter. It contains a variety of topics not found in the ICND1 book.

"Do I Know This Already?" Quiz

Use the "Do I Know This Already?" quiz to help decide whether you might want to skim this chapter, or a major section, moving more quickly to the "Exam Preparation Tasks" section near the end of the chapter. You can find the answers at the bottom of the page following the quiz. For thorough explanations, see Appendix A, "Answers to the 'Do I Know This Already?' Quizzes."

Table 20-1 "Do I Know This Already?" Foundation Topics Section-to-Question Mapping

Foundation Topics Section	Questions
Distance Vector Routing Protocol Features	1–2
RIP Concepts and Operation	3–4
EIGRP Concepts and Operation	5–6
OSPF Concepts and Operation	7–8

1. Which of the following distance vector features prevents routing loops by causing the routing protocol to advertise only a subset of known routes, as opposed to the full routing table, under normal stable conditions?

   a. Route poisoning

   b. Dijkstra SPF

   c. Hello

   d. Split horizon

2. Which of the following distance vector features prevents routing loops by advertising an infinite metric route when a route fails?

   a. Dijkstra SPF

   b. Hello

   c. Split horizon

   d. Route poisoning

3. Which of the following is true about both RIPv1 and RIPv2? (Choose two answers.)

   a. Uses a hop-count metric

   b. Sends update messages to multicast address 224.0.0.9

   c. Supports authentication

   d. Uses split horizon

4. Router R1 uses RIPv1, and learns one possible route to reach subnet 10.1.1.0/24. That route would have a metric of 15 from R1's perspective. Which of the following is true?

   a. R1 cannot use the route, because metric 15 is considered to be infinity.

   b. R1 will add the route to its routing table.

   c. The cumulative bandwidth between R1 and subnet 10.1.1.0/24 is 15 Mbps.

   d. The slowest bandwidth of the links between R1 and subnet 10.1.1.0/24 is 15 Kbps.

5. Routers A and B use EIGRP. How does router A watch for the status of router B so that router A can react if router B fails?

   a. By using EIGRP hello messages, with A needing to receive periodic hello messages to believe B is still working

   b. By using EIGRP update messages, with A needing to receive periodic update messages to believe B is still working

   c. Using a periodic ping of B's IP address based on the EIGRP neighbor timer

   d. None of the other answers are correct.

6. Which of the following affect the calculation of EIGRP metrics when all possible default values are used? (Choose two answers.)

   a. Bandwidth

   b. Delay

   c. Load

   d. Reliability

   e. Hop count

7. Which of the following routing protocols are considered to use link-state logic?

   a. RIPv1

   b. RIPv2

   c. EIGRP

   d. OSPF

8. Which of the following is true about how a router using a link-state routing protocol chooses the best route to reach a subnet?

   a. The router finds the best route in the link-state database.

   b. The router calculates the best route by running the SPF algorithm against the information in the link-state database.

   c. The router compares the metrics listed for that subnet in the updates received from each neighbor and picks the best (lowest) metric route.

   d. The router uses the path that has the lowest hop count.

20

Foundation Topics

Introduction to Routing Protocols

Many IP routing protocols exist, in part due to the long history of IP; however, if you compare all the IP routing protocols, they all have some core features in common. Each routing protocol causes routers (and Layer 3 switches) to

1. Learn routing information about IP subnets from other neighboring routers

2. Advertise routing information about IP subnets to other neighboring routers

3. Choose the best route among multiple possible routes to reach one subnet, based on that routing protocol's concept of a metric

4. React and converge to use a new choice of best route for each destination subnet when the network topology changes—for example, when a link fails

All the routing protocols discussed in this chapter do these same four functions, but the protocols differ in other ways. The rest of this chapter works through enough of the logic and features of each routing protocol so that you can see the differences, while understanding the basics of how each routing protocol learns routes, advertises routes, picks the best route, and converges when the network changes.

History of Interior Gateway Protocols

Historically speaking, RIP Version 1 (RIPv1) was the first popularly used IP routing protocol, with the Cisco-proprietary Interior Gateway Routing Protocol (IGRP) being introduced a little later, as shown in Figure 20-1.

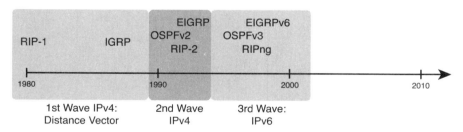

Figure 20-1 *Timeline for IP IGPs*

By the early 1990s, business and technical factors pushed the IPv4 world toward a second wave of better routing protocols. RIPv1 and IGRP had some technical limitations, even though they were great options for the technology levels of the 1980s. The huge movement toward TCP/IP in the 1990s drove the need for better IPv4 routing protocols. In the 1990s, many enterprises migrated from older vendor-proprietary networks to networks built with routers, LANs, and TCP/IP. These businesses needed better performance from their routing protocols, including better metrics and better convergence. All these factors led to the introduction of a new wave of IPv4 Interior routing protocols: RIP Version 2 (RIPv2), OSPF Version 2 (OSPFv2), and EIGRP.

NOTE   As an aside, many documents refer to EIGRP's support for learning IPv4 routes simply as EIGRP, and EIGRP support for IPv6 as EIGRPv6. This book follows that same convention. OSPF RFCs define specific versions, OSPF Version 2 (OSPFv2) learning IPv4 routes, and OSPF Version 3 (OSPFv3) learning IPv6 routes.

Comparing IGPs

What is an IGP in the first place? All the routing protocols mentioned so far in this chapter happen to be categorized as Interior Gateway Protocols (IGPs) rather than as Exterior Gateway Protocols (EGPs). First, the term *gateway* was used instead of *router* in the early days of IP routing, so the terms IGP and EGP really do refer to routing protocols. The designers of some routing protocols intended the routing protocol for use inside one company or organization (IGP), with other routing protocols intended for use between companies and between Internet service providers (ISPs) in the Internet (EGPs).

This chapter falls back to using the term IGP when talking about all the routing protocols mentioned in this chapter.

When deploying a new network, the network engineer can choose between a variety of IGPs. Today, most enterprises use EIGRP and OSPFv2. RIPv2 has fallen away as a serious competitor, in part due to its less robust hop-count metric, and in part due to its slower (worse) convergence time. This chapter discusses enough of the basics of all of these IGPs so that you get a sense of some of the basic trade-offs when comparing these routing protocols. A few key comparison points are as follows:

- **The underlying routing protocol algorithm:** Specifically, whether the routing protocol used logic referenced as distance vector (DV) or link state (LS).

- **The usefulness of the metric:** The routing protocol chooses which route is best based on its metric; so the better the metric, the better the choices made by that routing protocol.

- **The speed of convergence:** How long does it take all the routers to learn about a change in the network and update their IPv4 routing tables? That concept, called *convergence time*, varies depending on the routing protocol.

- **Whether the protocol is a public standard or a vendor-proprietary function:** RIP and OSPF happen to be standards, defined by RFCs. EIGRP happens to be defined by Cisco, and until 2013, was kept private.

For example, RIP uses a basic metric of hop count. Hop count treats each router as a hop, so the hop count is the number of other routers between a router and some remote subnet. RIP's hop-count metric means that RIP picks the route with the smallest number of links and routers. However, that shortest route may have the slowest links; a routing protocol that uses a metric based in part on link speed (called *bandwidth*) might make a better choice. In contrast, EIGRP's metric calculation uses a math formula that gives routes with slow links a worse metric, and routes with fast links a lower metric, so EIGRP prefers faster routes.

For example, Figure 20-2 shows two copies of the same topology. The topology shows three Nexus switches configured to act as Layer 3 switches. The figure focuses on router B's route to a subnet off router A. As you can see on the left in the figure, RIP on router B chooses the shorter hop route over the top of the network, over the single link, even though that link runs at 1 Gbps. EIGRP, on the right side of the figure, chooses the route that happens to have more links through the network, but both links have a faster bandwidth of 10 Gbps.

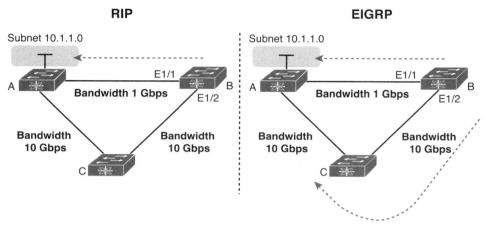

Figure 20-2   *EIGRP Choosing the Longer but Better Route to Subnet 10.1.1.0*

On another comparison point, the biggest negative about EIGRP has traditionally been that it required Cisco routers. That is, using EIGRP locked you into using Cisco products, because Cisco kept EIGRP as a Cisco proprietary protocol. In an interesting change, Cisco published EIGRP as an informational RFC in 2013, meaning that now other vendors can choose to implement EIGRP as well. In the past, many companies chose to use OSPF rather than EIGRP to give themselves options for what router vendor to use for future router hardware purchases. In the future, it might be that you can buy some routers from Cisco, some from other vendors, and still run EIGRP on all routers.

For reference and study, Table 20-2 lists several features of OSPFv2 and EIGRP, as well as RIPv2. Note that the table includes a few features that have not yet been introduced (but will be introduced before the end of the chapter).

Table 20-2   Interior IP Routing Protocols Compared

Feature	RIPv1	RIPv2	EIGRP	OSPF
Distance vector (DV) or link state (LS)	DV	DV	DV[1]	LS
Default metrics based on link bandwidth	No	No	Yes	Yes
Convergence time	Slow	Slow	Fast	Fast
Originally Cisco proprietary	No	No	Yes	No
Uses areas for design	No	No	No	Yes
Routing updates are sent to a multicast IP address	No	Yes	Yes	Yes
Classless/supports VLSM	No	Yes	Yes	Yes

1 EIGRP is often described as a balanced hybrid routing protocol, instead of LS or DV. Some documents refer to EIGRP as an advanced distance vector protocol.

Distance Vector Basics

Each IGP can be categorized based on its internal logic, either DV or LS. As a starting point to better understand IGPs, the next few pages explain more about how a DV protocol actually exchanges routing information. These pages use RIP as an example, showing RIP's simple hop-count metric, which, although a poor option in real networks today, is a much simpler option for learning.

The Concept of a Distance and a Vector

The term *distance vector* describes what a router knows about each route. At the end of the process, when a router learns about a route to a subnet, all the router knows is some measurement of distance (the metric) and the next-hop router and outgoing interface to use for that route (a vector, or direction).

Figure 20-3 shows a view of both the vector and the distance as learned with RIP. The figure shows the flow of RIP messages that cause R1 to learn some IPv4 routes, specifically three routes to reach subnet X:

- The four-hop route through R2
- The three-hop route through R5
- The two-hop route through R7

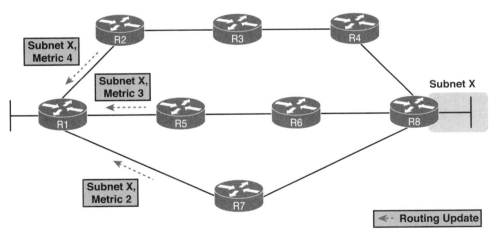

Figure 20-3 *Information Learned Using DV Protocols*

DV protocols learn two pieces of information about a possible route to reach a subnet:

- The distance (metric)
- The vector (the next-hop router)

In Figure 20-3, R1 learns three routes to reach subnet X, through three different neighboring routers. If R1 had learned only one route to subnet X, R1 would use that route. However, having learned three routes to subnet X, R1 picks the two-hop route through next-hop router R7 because that route has the lowest RIP metric.

While Figure 20-3 shows how R1 learns the routes with RIP updates, Figure 20-4 gives a better view into R1's DV logic. The figure shows R1's three competing routes to subnet X as vectors, with longer vectors for routes with larger metrics. R1 knows three routes, each with

Distance: The metric for a possible route

Vector: The direction, based on the next-hop router for a possible route

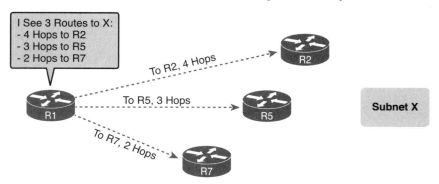

Figure 20-4 *Graphical Representation of the DV Concept*

Full Update Messages and Split Horizon

Some DV protocols, such as RIP (both RIPv1 and RIPv2), send periodic full routing updates based on a relatively short timer. Specifically, *full update* means that a router advertises all its routes, using one or more RIP update messages, no matter whether the route has changed or not. So, if a route does not change for months, the router keeps advertising that same route over and over.

Figure 20-5 illustrates this concept in an internetwork with two Nexus switches configured as Layer 3 switches, with four total subnets. The figure shows both routers' full routing tables, and lists the periodic full updates sent by each router.

This figure shows a lot of information, so take the time to work through the details. For example, consider what switch S1 learns for subnet 172.30.22.0/24, which is the subnet connected to S2's E1/4 interface:

1. S2 interface E1/4 has an IP address, and is in an up/up state.

2. S2 adds a connected route for 172.30.22.0/24, off interface E1/4, to R2's routing table.

3. S2 advertises its route for 172.30.22.0/24 to S1, with metric 1, meaning that S1's metric to reach this subnet will be metric 1 (hop count 1).

4. S1 adds a route for subnet 172.30.22.0/24, listing it as a RIP learned route with metric 1.

Also, take a moment to focus more on the route learned at Step 4: The bold route in S1's routing table. This route is for 172.30.22.0/24, as learned from S2. It lists S1's local E1/2 interface as the outgoing interface because S1 receives the update on that interface. It also lists S2's IP address of 172.30.1.2 as next-hop router because that's the IP address from which S1 learned the route.

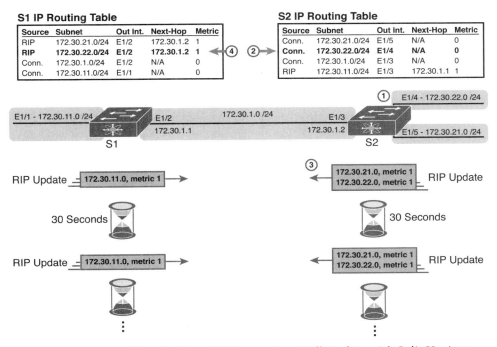

S1 IP Routing Table

Source	Subnet	Out Int.	Next-Hop	Metric
RIP	172.30.21.0/24	E1/2	172.30.1.2	1
RIP	**172.30.22.0/24**	**E1/2**	**172.30.1.2**	**1**
Conn.	172.30.1.0/24	E1/2	N/A	0
Conn.	172.30.11.0/24	E1/1	N/A	0

S2 IP Routing Table

Source	Subnet	Out Int.	Next-Hop	Metric
Conn.	172.30.21.0/24	E1/5	N/A	0
Conn.	**172.30.22.0/24**	**E1/4**	**N/A**	**0**
Conn.	172.30.1.0/24	E1/3	N/A	0
RIP	172.30.11.0/24	E1/3	172.30.1.1	1

Figure 20-5 *Normal Steady-State RIP Operations: Full Update with Split Horizon*

Monitoring Neighbor State with Periodic RIP Updates

RIPv1 and RIPv2 also send *periodic updates*, as shown in the bottom of Figure 20-5. That means that each router sends a new update (a full update) on a relatively short time period (30 seconds with RIP).

Many of the early DV protocols used this short periodic timer, repeating their full updates, as a way to let each router know whether a neighbor had failed. Routers need to react when a neighboring router fails or if the link between two routers fails. If both routers on a link must send updates every 30 seconds, when a local router no longer receives those updates, it knows that a problem has occurred, and it can react to converge to use alternate routes.

Note that newer DV protocols, such as EIGRP, do not require routers to keep sending updates for the purpose of tracking the state of the neighbor. Instead, they both define a simple hello protocol that allows the routers to send short messages to each other, instead of the long full routing updates, for the purpose of knowing when a neighbor fails.

Split Horizon

Figure 20-5 also shows a common DV feature called *split horizon*. Note that both routers list all four subnets in their IP routing tables. However, the RIP update messages do not list four subnets. The reason? Split horizon.

Split horizon is a DV feature that tells a router to omit some routes from an update sent out an interface. Which routes are omitted from an update sent out interface X? The routes that would like interface X as the outgoing interface. Those routes that are not advertised on an interface usually include the routes learned in routing updates received on that interface.

Split horizon is difficult to learn by reading words, and much easier to learn by seeing an example. Figure 20-6 continues the same example as Figure 20-5, but focusing on S1's RIP update sent out S1's E1/2 interface to S2. Figure 20-6 shows S1's routing table with three light-colored routes, all of which list E1/2 as the outgoing interface. When building the RIP update to send out E1/2, split-horizon rules tell S1 to ignore those light-colored routes. Only the bold route, which does not list E1/2 as an outgoing interface, can be included in the RIP update sent out E1/2.

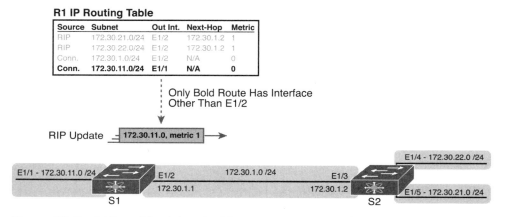

Figure 20-6 *R1 Does Not Advertise Three Routes Due to Split Horizon*

Route Poisoning

DV protocols help prevent routing loops by ensuring that every router learns that the route has failed, through every means possible, as quickly as possible. One of these features, *route poisoning*, helps all routers know for sure that a route has failed.

Route poisoning refers to the practice of advertising a failed route, but with a special metric value called *infinity*. Routers consider routes advertised with an infinite metric to have failed.

Figure 20-7 shows an example of route poisoning with RIP, with S2's E1/4 interface failing, meaning that S2's route for 172.30.22.0/24 has failed. RIP defines infinity as 16.

Figure 20-7 shows the following process:

1. S2's E1/4 interface fails.

2. S2 removes its connected route for 172.30.22.0/24 from its routing table.

3. S2 advertises 172.30.22.0 with an infinite metric (which for RIP is 16).

4. Depending on other conditions, S1 either immediately removes the route to 172.30.22.0 from its routing table, or marks the route as unusable (with an infinite metric) for a few minutes before removing the route.

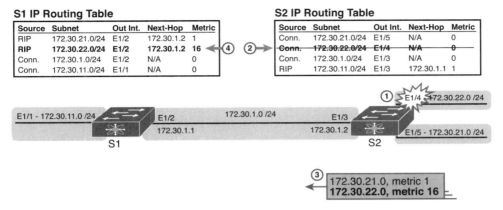

Figure 20-7 *Route Poisoning*

By the end of this process, router S1 knows for sure that its old route for subnet 172.30.22.0/24 has failed, which helps S1 avoid introducing looping IP routes.

Each routing protocol has its own definition of an infinite metric. RIP uses 16, as shown in the figure, with 15 being a valid metric for a usable route. EIGRP has long used $2^{32} - 1$ as infinity (a little more than 4 billion), with some Cisco products bumping that value to $2^{56} - 1$ (more than 10^{16}). OSPFv2 uses $2^{24} - 1$ as infinity.

The previous few pages focused on DV concepts, using RIP as an example. This chapter next turns the focus to the particulars of both RIPv1 and RIPv2.

RIP Concepts and Operation

The Routing Information Protocol (RIP) was the first commonly used IGP in the history of TCP/IP. Organizations used RIP inside their networks commonly in the 1980s, and into the 1990s. RIPv2, created in the mid-1990s, improved RIPv2, giving engineers an option for easy migration and co-existence to move from RIPv1 to the better RIPv2.

This second of four major sections of the chapter compares RIPv1 and RIPv2, while discussing a few of the core features that apply to both.

Features of Both RIPv1 and RIPv2

Like all IGPs, both RIPv1 and RIPv2 perform the same core features. That is, when using either RIPv1 or RIPv2, a router advertises information to help other routers learn routes; a router learns routes by listening to messages from other routers; a router chooses the best route to each subnet by looking at the metric of the competing routes; and the routing protocol converges to use new routes when something changes about the network.

RIPv1 and RIPv2 use the same logic to achieve most of those core functions. The similarities include the following:

- Both send regular full periodic routing updates on a 30-second timer, with *full* meaning that the update messages include all known routes.
- Both use split-horizon rules, as shown in Figure 20-6.

- Both use hop count as the metric.

- Both allow a maximum hop count of 15.

- Both use route poisoning as a loop-prevention mechanism (see Figure 20-7), with hop count 16 used to imply an unusable route with an infinite metric.

Although you might be puzzled why the creators of RIPv2 made it so much like RIPv1, the goal was simple: interoperability. A network that used RIPv1 could slowly migrate to RIPv2, enabling RIPv2 on some routers on one weekend, some more on the next, and so on. Done correctly, the network could migrate over time. The fact that both RIPv1 and RIPv2 used the same metric, and same loop-prevention mechanisms, allowed for a smooth migration.

Differences Between RIPv1 and RIPv2

Of course, RIPv2 needed to be better than RIPv1 in some ways, otherwise, what is the point of having a new version of RIP? RIPv2 made many changes to RIPv1: solutions to known problems, improved security, and new features as well. However, while RIPv2 improved RIP beyond RIPv1, it did not compete well with OSPF and EIGRP, particularly due to somewhat slow convergence compared to OSPF and EIGRP. However, for the sake of completeness, the next few pages walk through a few of the differences.

First, RIPv1 had one protocol feature that prevented it from using variable-length subnet masks (VLSMs). To review, VLSM means that inside one classful network (one Class A, B, or C network), that more than one subnet mask is used. For instance, in Figure 20-8, all the subnets are from Class A network 10.0.0.0, but some subnets use a /24 mask, whereas others use a /30 mask.

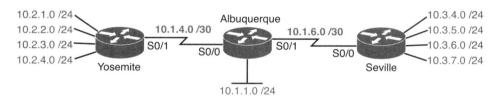

Figure 20-8   *An Example of VLSM*

RIPv1 could not support a network that uses VLSM because RIPv1 did not send mask information in the RIPv1 update message. Basically, RIPv1 routers had to guess what mask applied to each advertised subnet, and a design with VLSM made routers guess wrong. RIPv2 solved that problem by using an improved update message, which includes the subnet mask with each route, removing any need to guess what mask to use, so RIPv2 correctly supports VLSM.

RIPv2 fixed a couple of other perceived RIPv1 shortcomings as well. RIPv2 added authentication (RIPv1 had none), which can avoid cases in which an attacker introduces incorrect routes into a router's routing table. RIPv2 changed from using IP broadcasts sent to the 255.255.255.255 broadcast address (as in RIPv1) by instead sending updates to the 224.0.0.9 IPv4 multicast address. Using multicasts means that RIP messages can be more easily ignored by other devices, wasting less CPU on those devices.

Table 20-3 summarizes some of the key features of RIPv1 and RIPv2.

Table 20-3   Key Features of RIPv1 and RIPv2

Feature	RIPv1	RIPv2
Hop-count metric	Yes	Yes
Sets 15 as the largest metric for a working route	Yes	Yes
Sends full routing updates	Yes	Yes
Uses split horizon	Yes	Yes
Uses route poisoning, with metric 16	Yes	Yes
Sends mask in routing update	No	Yes
Supports discontiguous classful networks	No	Yes
Sends updates to 224.0.0.9 multicast address	No	Yes
Supports authentication	No	Yes

EIGRP Concepts and Operation

Enhanced Interior Gateway Routing Protocol (EIGRP) went through a similar creation process as compared to RIP, but with the work happening inside Cisco. Cisco has already created the Interior Gateway Routing Protocol (IGRP) in the 1980s, and the same needs that drove people to create RIPv2 and OSPF drove Cisco to improve IGRP as well. Instead of naming the original IGRP Version 1, and the new one IGRP Version 2, Cisco named the new version Enhanced IGRP (EIGRP).

EIGRP acts a little like a DV protocol, and a little like no other routing protocol. Frankly, over the years, different Cisco documents and different books (mine included) have characterized EIGRP as either its own category, called a *balanced hybrid routing protocol*, or as some kind of advanced DV protocol.

Regardless of what label you put on EIGRP, the protocol uses several features that work either like basic DV protocols such as RIP, or they work similarly enough. Routers that use EIGRP send messages so that other routers learn routes, they listen for messages to learn routes, they choose the best route among multiple routes to the same subnet based on a metric, and they react and converge when the network topology changes.

Of course, EIGRP works differently in several ways as compared to RIPv2. This third of four sections of the chapter discusses some of those similarities and differences, so you get a sense of how EIGRP works. Note that this section does not attempt to mention all the features of EIGRP, but instead to give some highlights that point out some of EIGRP's unique features compared to other IGPs. Regardless, at the end of the day, once you enable EIGRP on all your routers and Layer 3 switches, the devices will learn good routes for all the subnets in the network.

20

EIGRP Maintains Neighbor Status Using Hello

Unlike RIP, EIGRP does not send full or partial update messages based on a periodic timer. When a router first comes up, it advertises known routing information. Then, over time, as facts change, the router simply reacts, sending partial updates with the new information.

The fact that EIGRP does not send routing information on a short periodic timed basis greatly reduces EIGRP overhead traffic, but it also means that EIGRP cannot rely on these updates to monitor the state of neighboring routers. Instead, EIGRP defines the concept of a neighbor relationship, using EIGRP hello messages to monitor that relationship. The EIGRP hello message and protocol defines that each router should send a periodic hello message on each interface, so that all EIGRP routers know that the router is still working. Figure 20-9 shows the idea.

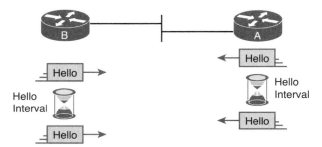

Figure 20-9   *EIGRP Hello Packets*

The routers use their own independent hello interval, which defines the time period between each EIGRP hello. For instance, routers R1 and R2 do not have to send their hellos at the same time. Routers also must receive a hello from a neighbor with a time called the *hold interval*, with a default setting of three times the hello interval.

For instance, imagine both R1 and R2 use default settings of 5 and 15 for their hello and hold intervals. Under normal conditions, R1 receives hellos from R2 every 5 seconds, well within R1's hold interval (15 seconds) before R1 would consider R2 to have failed. If R2 does fail, R2 no longer sends hello messages. R1 notices that 15 seconds pass without receiving a hello from R2, so then R1 can choose new routes that do not use R2 as a next-hop router.

EIGRP Topology and the Metric Calculation

One of the most compelling reasons to consider using EIGRP instead of other IGPs is the strength of the EIGRP metric. EIGRP uses a math function to calculate the metric. More importantly, that function uses two input variables by default:

- The slowest link in the end-to-end route
- The cumulative delay for all links in the route

As a result, EIGRP defines the concept of the best route based on the constraining bandwidth (speed) of the links in the route, plus the total delay in the route.

The words *bandwidth* and *delay* have specific meaning with EIGRP. *Bandwidth* refers to the perceived speed of each link. *Delay* refers to the router's perception of the time it takes to send a frame over the link. Both bandwidth and delay are settings on router interfaces; although routers do have default values for both bandwidth and delay on each interface, the settings can be configured as well.

EIGRP calls the calculated metric value the *composite metric*, with the individual inputs into the formula being the metric components. The formula itself is not as important as the effect of the metric components on the calculation:

- A smaller bandwidth yields a larger composite metric because less bandwidth is worse than more bandwidth.

- A smaller delay yields a smaller composite metric because less delay is better than more delay.

Using these two inputs gives EIGRP a much better metric than RIP. Basically, EIGRP prefers routes with faster links, avoiding routes with slower links. Slow links, besides the obvious negative of being slow, also may experience more congestion, with packets waiting longer to get a turn to cross the link. For example, EIGRP could prefer a route with multiple 10-Gbps links rather than a single-hop route over a 1-Gbps or 100-Mbps link.

EIGRP Convergence

Another compelling reason to choose EIGRP as an IGP has to do with EIGRP's much better convergence time as compared with RIP. EIGRP converges more quickly than RIP in all cases, and in some cases, EIGRP converges much more quickly.

For perspective, with RIPv2 in normal operation, convergence could take several minutes. During those minutes, some user traffic was not delivered to the correct destination, even though a physical path existed. With EIGRP, those same worst cases typically experience convergence of less than a minute, often less than 20 seconds, with some cases taking a second or two.

EIGRP does loop avoidance completely differently than RIP by keeping some basic topological information. The EIGRP topology database on each router holds some information about the local router, plus some information about the next-hop router in each possible route for each known subnet. That extra topology information lets EIGRP on each router take the following approach for all the possible routes to reach one subnet:

- Similar to how other routing protocols work, a local router calculates the metric for each possible route to reach a subnet, and chooses the best route based on the best metric.

- Unlike other routing protocols, the local router uses that extra topology information to look at the routes that were not chosen as the best route, to *find all alternate routes that, if the best route fails, could be immediately used without causing a loop.*

That second bullet reveals the key to understanding how EIGRP converges very quickly. Without getting into all the details, a simple example of the power of this fast EIGRP convergence can help. To begin, consider Figure 20-10, which focuses on router E's three possible routes to reach subnet 1 on the right.

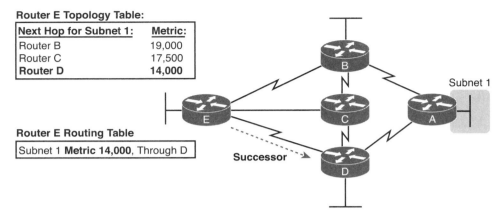

Figure 20-10 *Route Through Router D Is the Successor Route to Subnet 1*

The upper left shows router E's topology table information about the three competing routes to reach subnet 1: a route through router B, another through router C, and another through router D. The metrics in the upper left show the metrics from router E's perspective, so router E chooses the route with the smallest metric: the route through next-hop router D. EIGRP on router E places that route, with next-hop router D, into its IP routing table, represented on the lower left of the figure.

> **NOTE** EIGRP calls the best route to reach a subnet the successor route.

At the same time, EIGRP on router E uses additional topology information to decide whether either of the other routes—the routes through B and C—could be used if the route through router D fails, without causing a loop. Ignoring the details of how router E decides, imagine that router E does that analysis, and decides that E's route for subnet 1 through router B could be used without causing a loop, but the route through router C could not. Router E would call that route through router B a *feasible successor* route, as noted in Figure 20-11.

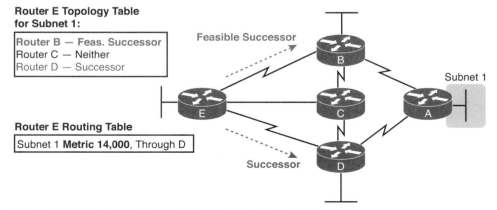

Figure 20-11 *Route Through Router B Is a Feasible Successor*

As long as the network stays stable, router E has chosen the best route, and is ready to act, as follows:

■ Router E uses the successor route as its only route to subnet 1, as listed in the IPv4 routing table.

■ Router E lists the route to subnet 1, through router B, as a feasible successor, as noted in the EIGRP topology table.

Later, when convergence to a new route to subnet 1 needs to occur—days later, weeks later, whenever—the convergence is almost instant. As soon as router E realizes that the current route through router D has failed, router E can immediately remove the old route from its IPv4 routing table, and add a route to subnet 1 listing router B as the next-hop router.

EIGRP Summary

As you can see, EIGRP provides many advantages over both RIPv1 and RIPv2. Most significantly, it uses a much better metric, and it converges much more quickly than does RIP.

The biggest downside to EIGRP has traditionally been that EIGRP was a Cisco proprietary protocol. That is, to run EIGRP, you had to use Cisco products only. Interestingly, Cisco has published EIGRP as an informational RFC in 2013, so now other vendors could choose to add EIGRP support to their products. Over time, maybe this one negative about EIGRP will fade away.

The next topic introduces the final routing protocol for this chapter, OSPF, which has always been a public standard.

20

Understanding the OSPF Link-State Routing Protocol

To complete this chapter, this final major section examines one more routing protocol: Open Shortest Path First (OSPF) Protocol. Like EIGRP, OSPF converges quickly. Like EIGRP, OSPF bases its metric by default on link bandwidth, so that OSPF makes a better choice than simply relying on the router hop-count metric used by RIP. But OSPF uses much different internal logic, being a link-state routing protocol rather than a distance vector protocol.

This section introduces OSPF, first by listing some of the more obvious similarities and differences between OSPF and EIGRP. The rest of this section then explains a few of the internals of OSPF, again not a comprehensive look at OSPF internals, instead giving you some insights into a few key differences between OSPF and other IGPs.

OSPF Comparisons with EIGRP

Like all the IGPs discussed in this chapter, OSPF causes routers to learn routes, choose the best route to each subnet based on a metric, and to converge to choose new best routes when the network changes.

Although EIGRP uses DV logic, and OSPF uses LS logic, OSPF and EIGRP have three major activities that, from a general perspective, appear to be the same:

1. Both OSPF and EIGRP use a hello protocol to find neighboring routers, maintain a list of working neighbors, monitor ongoing hello messages to make sure the neighbor is still reachable, and to notice when the path to a neighbor has failed.

2. Both OSPF and EIGRP exchange topology data, which each router stores locally in a topology database. The topology database describes facts about the network, but is a different entity than the router's IPv4 routing table.

3. Both OSPF and EIGRP cause each router to process its topology database, from which the router can choose the currently best route (lowest metric route) to reach each subnet, adding those best routes to the IPv4 routing table.

For instance, in a network that uses Nexus Layer 3 switches, you could use OSPF or EIGRP. If using OSPF, you could display a Layer 3 switch's OSPF neighbors (**show ip ospf neighbor**), the OSPF database (**show ip ospf database**), and the IPv4 routing table (**show ip route**). Alternatively, if you instead used EIGRP, you could display the equivalent in EIGRP: EIGRP neighbors (**show ip eigrp neighbor**), the EIGRP topology database (**show ip eigrp topology**), and the IPv4 routing table (**show ip route**).

However, if you dig a little deeper, OSPF and EIGRP clearly use different conventions and logic. The protocols, of course, are different, with EIGRP being created inside Cisco and OSPF developed as an RFC. The topology databases differ significantly, with OSPF collecting much more detail about the topology, and with EIGRP collecting just enough to make choices about successor and feasible successor routes. The method of processing the database, which then determines the best route for each subnet, differs significantly as well.

Most of the similarities end here, with OSPF, as an LS protocol, simply using an entirely different approach to choosing the currently best route for each subnet. The rest of this section describes LS behavior, using OSPF as the example.

Building the OSPF LSDB and Creating IP Routes

Link-state protocols build IP routes with a couple of major steps. First, the routers build a detailed database of information about the network and flood that so that all routers have a copy of the same information. (The information is much more detailed than the topology data collected by EIGRP.) That database, called the *link-state database* (LSDB), gives each router the equivalent of a roadmap for the network, showing all routers, all router interfaces, all links between routers, and all subnets connected to routers. Second, each router runs a complex mathematical formula (the details of which we can all ignore) to calculate the best route to reach each subnet.

The next few pages walk through both parts of the process: building the LSDB, and then processing the LSDB to choose the best routes.

Topology Information and LSAs

Routers using LS routing protocols need to collectively advertise practically every detail about the internetwork to all the other routers. At the end of the process of *flooding* the information to all routers, every router in the internetwork has the exact same information about the internetwork. Flooding a lot of detailed information to every router sounds like a lot of work, and relative to DV routing protocols, it is.

OSPF, the most popular LS IP routing protocol, organizes topology information using link-state advertisements (LSAs) and the link-state database (LSDB). Figure 20-12 represents the ideas. Each LSA is a data structure with some specific information about the network topology—for instance, each router must be described by a separate LSA. The LSDB holds the collection of all the LSAs known to a router. Think of the LSDB as having one LSA for every router, one for every link, with several other types as well.

Link State Database (LSDB)

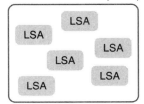

Figure 20-12 *LSA and LSDB Relationship*

LS protocols rely on having all routers knowing the same view of the network topology and link status (link state) by all having a copy of the LSDB. The idea is like giving all routers a copy of the same updated road map. If all routers have the exact same road map, and they base their choices of best routes on that same road map, then the routers, using the same algorithm, will never create any routing loops.

To create the LSDB, each router will create some of the LSAs needed. Each router floods both the LSAs it creates, plus others learned from neighboring routers, so that all the routers have a copy of each LSA. Figure 20-13 shows the general idea of the flooding process, with R8 creating and flooding an LSA that describes itself (called a *router LSA*). The router LSA for router R8 describes the router itself, including the existence of subnet 172.16.3.0/24, as shown on the right side of the figure. (Note that Figure 20-13 actually shows only a subset of the information in R8's router LSA.)

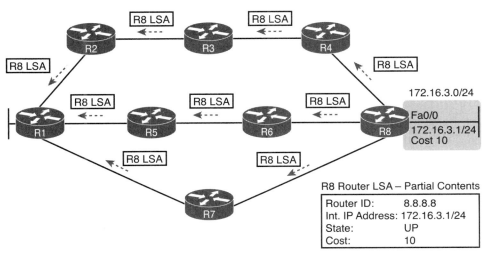

Figure 20-13 *Flooding LSAs Using an LS Routing Protocol*

Figure 20-13 shows the rather basic flooding process, with R8 sending the original LSA for itself and with the other routers flooding the LSA by forwarding it until every router has a copy. The flooding process has a way to prevent loops so that the LSAs do not get flooded around in circles. Basically, before sending an LSA to yet another neighbor, routers communicate and ask "do you already have this LSA?" Then they avoid flooding the LSA to neighbors that already have it.

Applying Dijkstra SPF Math and OSPF Metrics to Find the Best Routes

Although incredibly detailed and useful, the LSDB does not explicitly state each router's best route to reach a destination. Instead, it lists the data from which a router can derive its currently best route to reach each subnet, by doing some math.

All LS protocols use a type of math algorithm called the Dijkstra shortest path first (SPF) algorithm to process the LSDB. That algorithm analyzes (with math) the LSDB, and builds the routes that the local router should add to the IP routing table—routes that list a subnet number and mask, an outgoing interface, and a next-hop router IP address.

Although engineers do not need to know the details of how SPF does the math, you can easily predict what SPF will choose, given some basic information about the network. The key is that once SPF has identified a route, it calculates the metric for a route as follows:

   The sum of the OSPF interface costs for all outgoing interfaces in the route

The OSPF metric for a route is the sum of the interface costs for all outgoing interfaces in the route. By default, a router's OSPF interface cost is actually derived from the interface bandwidth: The faster the bandwidth, the lower the cost. So, a lower OSPF cost means that the interface is better than an interface with a higher OSPF cost.

Armed with the facts in the previous few paragraphs, you can look at the example in Figure 20-14 and predict how the OSPF SPF algorithm will analyze the available routes and choose a best route. This figure features the logic on router R1, with its three competing routes to subnet X (172.16.3.0/24) at the bottom of the figure.

> **NOTE**   OSPF considers the costs of the outgoing interfaces (only) in each route. It does not add the cost for incoming interfaces in the route.

Table 20-4 lists the three routes shown in Figure 20-14, with their cumulative costs, showing that R1's best route to 172.16.3.0/24 starts by going through R5.

Table 20-4   Comparing R1's Three Alternatives for the Route to 172.16.3.0/24

Route	Location in Figure 20-14	Cumulative OSPF Cost
R1–R7–R8	Left	10 + 180 + 10 = 200
R1–R5–R6–R8	Middle	20 + 30 + 40 + 10 = 100
R1–R2–R3–R4–R8	Right	30 + 60 + 20 + 5 + 10 = 125

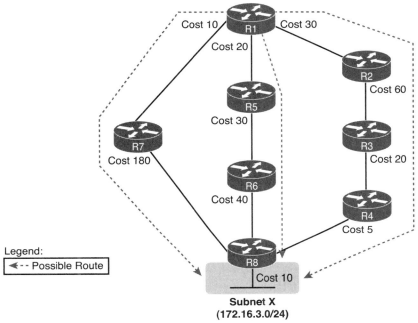

Figure 20-14 *SPF Tree to Find R1's Route to 172.16.3.0/24*

20

As a result of the SPF algorithm's analysis of the LSDB, R1 adds a route to subnet 172.16.3.0/24 to its routing table, with the next-hop router of R5.

NOTE OSPF calculates costs using different processes depending on the area design. The example surrounding Figure 20-14 best matches OSPF's logic when using a single area design.

Scaling OSPF Through Hierarchical Design

OSPF can be used in some networks with very little thought about design issues. You just turn on OSPF in all the routers, and it works! However, in large networks, engineers need to think about and plan how to use several OSPF features that allow OSPF to scale well. For instance, the OSPF design in Figure 20-15 uses a single OSPF area, because this small inter-network does not need the scalability benefits of OSPF areas.

Using a single OSPF area for smaller internetworks, as in Figure 20-15, works well. The con-figuration is simple, and some of the hidden details in how OSPF works remain simple. In fact, with a small OSPF internetwork, you can just enable OSPF, with all interfaces in the same area, and mostly ignore the idea of an OSPF area.

Area 0 (Backbone)

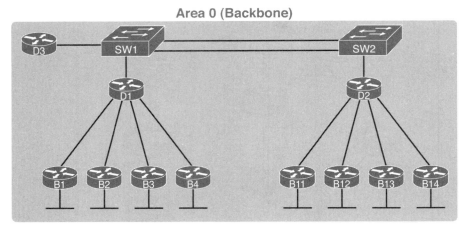

Figure 20-15   *Single-Area OSPF*

Now imagine a network with 900 routers, instead of only 11, and several thousand subnets. In that size of network, the sheer amount of processing required to run the complex SPF algorithm might cause convergence time to be slow just because of the time it takes each router to process all the math. Also, the routers might experience memory shortages. The problems can be summarized as follows:

- A larger topology database requires more memory on each router.

- The router CPU time required to run the SPF algorithm grows exponentially with the size of the LSDB.

- With a single area, a single interface status change (up to down, or down to up) forces every router to run SPF again!

OSPF provides a way to manage the size of the LSDB by breaking up a larger network into smaller pieces using a concept called OSPF *areas*. The engineer places some links in one area, some in another, others in yet a third area, and so on. OSPF then creates a separate and smaller LSDB per area, rather than one huge LSDB for all links and routers in the internetwork. With smaller topology databases, routers consume less memory and take less processing time to run SPF.

OSPF multi-area design puts all ends of a link—a serial link, and VLAN, and so on—inside an area. To make that work, some routers (Area Border Routers, or ABRs) sit at the border between multiple areas. Routers D1 and D2 serve as ABRs in the area design shown in Figure 20-16, which shows the same network as Figure 20-15, but with three OSPF areas (0, 1, and 2).

Figure 20-16 shows a sample area design and some terminology related to areas, but it does not show the power and benefit of the areas. By using areas, the OSPF SPF algorithm ignores the details of the topology in the other areas. For example, OSPF on router B1 (area 1), when doing the complex SPF math processing, ignores the topology information about area 0 and area 2. Each router has much less SPF work to do, so each router more quickly finishes its SPF work, finding the currently best OSPF routes.

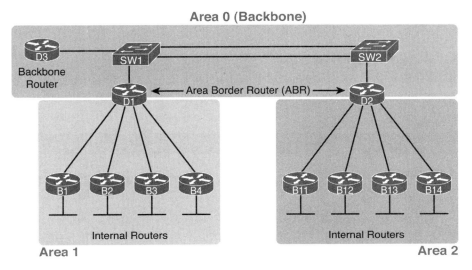

Figure 20-16   *Three-Area OSPF*

Exam Preparation Tasks

Review All the Key Topics

Review the most important topics from this chapter, noted with the Key Topic icon. Table 20-5 lists these key topics and where each is discussed.

Table 20-5   Key Topics for Chapter 20

Key Topic Element	Description	Page Number
Table 20-3	Key features of RIPv1 and RIPv2	517
Paragraph	How SPF calculates the metric for a route	524
Figure 20-14	How OSPF's SPF algorithm analyzes and selects the best route	525

Definitions of Key Terms

After your first reading of the chapter, try to define these key terms, but do not be concerned about getting them all correct at that time. Chapter 23, "Final Review," directs you in how to use these terms for late-stage preparation for the exam.

convergence, distance vector, Interior Gateway Protocol (IGP), partial update, poisoned route, split horizon, feasible successor, successor, shortest path first (SPF) algorithm, link state, link-state advertisement (LSA), link-state database (LSDB)

This chapter covers the following exam topics:

4.1 Describe and configure basic routing concepts

4.1a Packet forwarding

4.2 Describe the operation of Cisco routers

4.2c Route components

CHAPTER 21

Nexus Routing Protocol Configuration

As you learned in Chapter 20, "IPv4 Routing Protocol Concepts," there are three main types of routing protocols for IPv4:

■ Distance vector, such as RIPv2

■ Link state, as in the case of OSPF

■ A hybrid of the two with EIGRP

This chapter shows you how each of these three routing protocols are configured in NX-OS on Cisco Nexus switches that have Layer 3 capabilities. To do this, the chapter provides examples of how to configure each one of the routing protocols and verify their operation, and it covers the troubleshooting basics. The chapter starts with Routing Information Protocol Version 2 (RIPv2), then Enhanced Interior Gateway Routing Protocol (EIGRP), and finishes up with Open Shortest Path First (OSPF) Protocol in a single area. Each routing protocol is applied to a single network topology with two configuration examples.

"Do I Know This Already?" Quiz

Use the "Do I Know This Already?" quiz to help decide whether you might want to skim this chapter, or a major section, moving more quickly to the "Exam Preparation Tasks" section near the end of the chapter. You can find the answers at the bottom of the page following the quiz. For thorough explanations, see Appendix A, "Answers to the 'Do I Know This Already?' Quizzes."

Table 21-1 "Do I Know This Already?" Foundation Topics Section-to-Question Mapping

Foundation Topics Section	Questions
RIP Version 2 Configuration on NX-OS	1–2
OSPF Configuration on NX-OS	3
EIGRP Configuration on NX-OS	4–5

1. RIP is what type of routing protocol?

   a. Link state

   b. Hybrid

   c. Distance vector

   d. Single hop

2. Which command shows you all of your RIP-specific configuration on a Cisco Nexus Layer 3 switch?

   a.   show interface status

   b.   show running-config rip

   c.   show ip route

   d.   show routing process rip

3. What is the default interface type for OSPF on an Ethernet interface?

   a.   Point to point

   b.   Nonbroadcast multiaccess

   c.   Broadcast

   d.   Point to multipoint

4. Which two K values does EIGRP enable by default?

   a.   K1 bandwidth

   b.   K5 MTU

   c.   K3 delay

   d.   K12 pipe density

5. Which command under an EIGRP routing process enables you to manually set the identity of the router 2 across the network?

   a.   routing process identifier 2

   b.   router 2

   c.   router-id 2.2.2.2

   d.   routing-id 2.2.2.2

Foundation Topics

The Cisco Nexus switches have the capability to be enabled for IP Version 4 and 6 routing protocols; this chapter focuses on IPv4 routing protocol configurations. When implementing these protocols on a Cisco Nexus switch, it is important to understand the fundamentals of routing on any Cisco Layer 3 switch. First, two different types of interfaces can participate in Layer 3 operations. One is referred to as a *routed interface*, where you disable switching on this interface using the **no switchport** command and dedicate it for Layer 3 operations. Example 21-1 shows how you would configure a routed interface on a Cisco Nexus Layer 3 switch.

Example 21-1   *"Routed" Interface Configuration*

```
R2# configure terminal
Enter configuration commands, one per line. End with CNTL/Z.
 R2# configure terminal
 R2(config)# interface Ethernet1/1
 R2(config-if)# no switchport
 R2(config-if)# ip address 10.1.1.1/24
 R2(config-if)# no shutdown
```

The second interface that can participate in Layer 3 operations is a switched virtual interface (SVI), which was discussed in Chapters 18, "IPv4 Routing Concepts," and 19, "Cisco Nexus IPv4 Routing Configuration," where a group of Layer 2 interfaces are associated with a VLAN, and then a Layer 3 SVI is configured for routing over this VLAN. Example 21-2 shows the enabling of an SVI on a Cisco Nexus Layer 3 switch. After configuring these two options, you then enable IPv4 routing protocols to enable participation with the routing protocol of your choice.

Example 21-2   *"SVI" Interface Configuration*

```
R2# configure terminal
R2(config)# interface Ethernet 1/3
R2(config-if)# switchport
R2(config-if)# switchport access vlan 88
R2(config-if)# exit
R2(config)# interface Vlan 88
R2(config-if)# ip address 10.8.1.1/24
R2(config-if)# no shutdown
```

Another fundamental to note in NX-OS, which is different from previous Cisco operating systems, is that you enable the routing instance on each interface or SVI that you would like to have participating in the routing process. This is important to note for two reasons:

- In older versions of IOS, when enabling IPv4 routing protocols, you would specify the networks under the **router** *protocol tag*, which in some cases enabled routing process for multiple interfaces, especially on Layer 3 switches that had an IP address in that subnet range. Why this is important is that in Layer 3 routing protocols, you want to minimize

21

the amount of adjacencies per routing protocol to aid in the stability, recovery, and convergence of the network. By enabling under the interface, you can be more granular on which interface/subnets will participate or be advertised to neighbors.

■ The second benefit is that in earlier IOS versions, when you enabled a **network** statement under the routing process that covered multiple interface addresses, the router would also start sending hello messages out of those interfaces. To limit the number of neighbor adjacencies, you would use the **passive** *interface* command to limit which interfaces would send hellos. NX-OS simplifies this because you enable the routing process only under the interfaces with their associated subnets; in turn, you only have to add the **passive** *interface* command under the interfaces you don't want to form neighbor adjacencies on but would like their subnets advertised to neighbors.

Example 21-3 shows IOS-based configuration versus NX-OS configuration of the EIGRP routing process.

Example 21-3   *Routing Process Enablement IOS and NX-OS with Passive Interface*

```
IOS
R1# configure terminal
R1(config)# ip routing
R1(config)# router eigrp 1
R1(config-router)# network 10.0.0.0
R1(config-router)# passive-interface vlan 13
R1(config-router)# passive-interface vlan 14
R1(config)# interface vlan 12
R1(config-if)# ip address 10.1.1.1/24
R1(config-if)# no shutdown
R1(config)# interface vlan 13
R1(config-if)# ip address 10.1.3.1/24
R1(config-if)# no shutdown
R1(config)# interface vlan 14
R1(config-if)# ip address 10.1.4.1/24
R1(config-if)# no shutdown
```

```
NX-OS
R1# Configure terminal
R1(config)# feature eigrp
R1(config)# feature interface-vlan
R1(config)# router eigrp 1
R1(config)# interface vlan 12
R1(config-if)# ip address 10.1.1.1/24
R1(config-if)# no shutdown
R1(config-if)# ip router eigrp 1
R1(config)# interface vlan 13
R1(config-if)# ip address 10.1.3.1/24
R1(config-if)# no shutdown
R1(config-if)# ip router eigrp 1
R1(config-if)# ip passive-interface eigrp 1
```

```
R1(config)# interface vlan 14
R1(config-if)# ip address 10.1.4.1/24
R1(config-if)# no shutdown
R1(config-if)# ip router eigrp 1
R1(config-if)# ip passive-interface eigrp 1
```

Before we get into our three different routing protocol configurations, we need to explore a common tool you will use to troubleshoot and verify routing in your network no matter what routing protocol you use, and this is the routing table. You have learned about this in previous chapters, but let's spend some time looking at the routing table and what we need to look at to verify your networks are working the way you expect them to. Example 21-4 shows a sample routing table on a Nexus switch.

Example 21-4   *Sample Routing Table*

```
SW1# show ip route

IP Route Table for VRF "default"
'*' denotes best ucast next-hop
'**' denotes best mcast next-hop
'[x/y]' denotes [preference/metric]
'%<string>' in via output denotes VRF <string>

0.0.0.0/0, ubest/mbest: 1/0
    *via 172.16.31.6, Eth1/8, [170/3328], 1d01h, eigrp-1, external
10.0.0.0/24, ubest/mbest: 1/0, attached
    *via 10.0.0.252, Vlan500, [0/0], 1d01h, direct
10.0.0.252/32, ubest/mbest: 1/0, attached
    *via 10.0.0.252, Vlan500, [0/0], 1d01h, local
10.0.0.254/32, ubest/mbest: 1/0
    *via 10.0.0.254, Vlan500, [0/0], 1d01h, hsrp
10.0.2.0/24, ubest/mbest: 1/0, attached
    *via 10.0.2.154, Vlan502, [0/0], 1d01h, direct
10.0.2.154/32, ubest/mbest: 1/0, attached
    *via 10.0.2.154, Vlan502, [0/0], 1d01h, local
10.0.2.254/32, ubest/mbest: 1/0
    *via 10.0.2.254, Vlan502, [0/0], 1d01h, hsrp
10.0.3.0/24, ubest/mbest: 1/0, attached
    *via 10.0.3.154, Vlan503, [0/0], 1d01h, direct
10.0.3.154/32, ubest/mbest: 1/0, attached
    *via 10.0.3.154, Vlan503, [0/0], 1d01h, local
10.0.3.254/32, ubest/mbest: 1/0
    *via 10.0.3.254, Vlan503, [0/0], 1d01h, hsrp
10.0.128.103/32, ubest/mbest: 3/0
    *via 10.0.0.253, Vlan500, [90/130816], 1d01h, eigrp-1, internal
    *via 10.0.2.54, Vlan502, [90/130816], 1d01h, eigrp-1, internal
    *via 10.0.3.54, Vlan503, [90/130816], 1d01h, eigrp-1, internal
```

21

In the output, you see a couple of highlighted areas that are important to look at when you verify your networking by looking at the routing table. First, you can see the route highlighted in the top left (10.0.0.0/24), which is a destination you have the capability to route to. Just below, as part of the routing table output, you see that you can reach this network via 10.0.0.252 and that it is a direct route. A *direct* route means that you have an interface directly connected on this device that lives in that network. To see a network to which you have access that is not directly connected to this Cisco Nexus switch (see the route for 10.0.128.103/32 highlighted), this route actually can be reached through three different paths, and you see that the admin cost of 90 is associated, letting you know it is an EIGRP route. You also see that it is an EIGRP route by the end of the same line. Whichever routing protocol you use, viewing the **show ip route** command output can provide a great amount of detail of how your network and routers see the network, which can assist in verification and troubleshooting. If you want to look just at routes learned from a particular routing protocol, you can also use a more specific **show ip route** command by adding the routing protocol name at the end of the command; for example, **show ip route** (**rip/eigrp/ospf**).

RIP Version 2 Configuration on NX-OS

As you learned in Chapter 20, RIP is a distance vector routing protocol. This section describes how to enable RIPv2 (the default version on Cisco Nexus switches), validate configuration, and perform basic troubleshooting. Figure 21-1 shows routing between four Nexus switches—a topology common in today's data centers. You will use this topology to configure RIPv2 in two ways:

- RIPv2 enabled via routed interfaces
- Based on SVI being enabled as the Layer 3 interface for routing protocol participation.

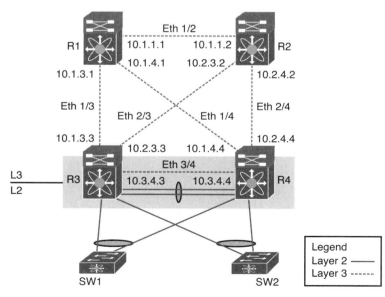

Figure 21-1   *Network Topology for RIPv2 Configuration Using Routed Interfaces*

Example 21-5 shows the configuration steps to enable RIPv2 on R1 and R2 of the Nexus switches connected via Layer 3 interfaces at the top of the topology.

Example 21-5   *RIPv2 Configuration on R1 and R2 Using Routed Interface*

```
R1 Configuration
 R1# configure terminal
 R1(config)# feature rip
 R1(config)# interface Ethernet1/2
 R1(config-if)# no switchport
 R1(config-if)# ip address 10.1.1.1/24
 R1(config-if)# no shutdown
 R1(config-if)# ip router rip enterprise
 R1(config)# interface Ethernet1/3
 R1(config-if)# no switchport
 R1(config-if)# ip address 10.1.3.1/24
 R1(config-if)# no shutdown
 R1(config-if)# ip router rip enterprise
R1(config)# interface Ethernet1/4
 R1(config-if)# no switchport
 R1(config-if)# ip address 10.1.4.1/24
 R1(config-if)# no shutdown
 R1(config-if)# ip router rip enterprise
 R1(config)# router rip enterprise
```

```
R2 Configuration
 R2# Configure terminal
 R2(config)# feature rip
 R2(config)# interface Ethernet1/2
 R2(config-if)# no switchport
 R2(config-if)# ip address 10.1.1.2/24
 R2(config-if)# no shutdown
 R2(config-if)# ip router rip enterprise
 R2(config)# interface Ethernet2/3
 R2(config-if)# no switchport
 R2(config-if)# ip address 10.2.3.2/24
 R2(config-if)# no shutdown
 R2(config-if)# ip router rip enterprise
 R2(config)# interface Ethernet2/4
 R2(config-if)# no switchport
 R2(config-if)# ip address 10.2.4.2/24
 R2(config-if)# no shutdown
 R2(config-if)# ip router rip enterprise
 R2(config)# router rip enterprise
```

21

As shown in the configurations in Example 21-5, each Nexus, R1 through R4, would have similar configurations for **feature rip** being enabled globally, with **no switchport** under the physical interface to put the interfaces into a strict L3-only mode (no switching). From there, you enable the routing process for RIP using the **ip router rip enterprise** command. Also, you would need to enable the **router rip** *instance-tag*; this example uses **enterprise** as the instance tag to identify the routing process to be enabled on the interfaces.

NOTE   Nexus 7000 series switches by default have all physical interfaces in no switchport or Layer 3 mode, while Nexus 5000 series switches have switchport enabled on each physical interface by default.

So far, you have learned how to configure RIPv2 on a Nexus Layer 3 routed interface. The next task is to learn how to do this using interface VLAN or switched virtual interface (SVI) at Layer 3. Figure 21-2 uses the same basic topology as Figure 21-1, but peers R1 and R2 over a VLAN using RIPv2.

NOTE   Nexus 5ks have all of the interface enabled or in a no shutdown state, while Nexus 7ks by default have them disabled or in a shutdown state. It is important to check this while configuring your 7k or 5k.

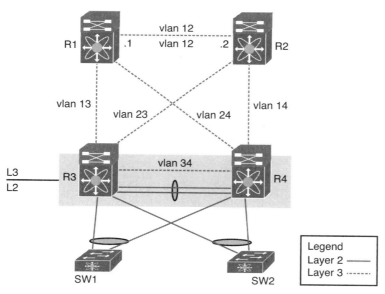

Figure 21-2   *Network Topology for RIPv2 Configuration Using SVIs*

Example 21-6 shows the configuration for SVI configuration and enabling RIPv2.

Example 21-6 *RIPv2 Configuration on R1 and R2 Using SVI*

```
R1 Configuration
R1# configure terminal
R1(config)# feature rip
R1(config)# router rip enterprise
R1(config)# feature interface-vlan
R1(config)# interface vlan 12
R1(config-if)# ip address 10.1.1.1/24
R1(config-if)# no shutdown
R1(config-if)# ip router rip enterprise
R1(config)# interface vlan 13
R1(config-if)# ip address 10.1.3.1/24
R1(config-if)# no shutdown
R1(config-if)# ip router rip enterprise
R1(config)# interface vlan 14
R1(config-if)# ip address 10.1.4.1/24
R1(config-if)# no shutdown
R1(config-if)# ip router rip enterprise
```

```
R2 Configuration
R2# configure terminal
R2(config)# feature rip
R2(config)# router rip enterprise
R2(config)# feature interface-vlan
R2(config)# interface vlan 12
R2(config-if)# ip address 10.1.1.2/24
R2(config-if)# no shutdown
R2(config-if)# ip router rip enterprise
R2(config)# interface vlan 23
R2(config-if)# ip address 10.2.3.2/24
R2(config-if)# no shutdown
R2(config-if)# ip router rip enterprise
R2(config)# interface vlan 24
R2(config-if)# ip address 10.2.4.2/24
R2(config-if)# no shutdown
R2(config-if)# ip router rip enterprise
```

21

Finally, you need to verify that your RIP configuration is correct, followed by some basic troubleshooting for RIPv2 2 on Cisco Nexus switches. Example 21-7 uses **show** commands to validate that the neighboring Layer 3 Nexus switches are communicating with each other and learning routing via the RIPv2 routing protocol.

Example 21-7   *RIPv2 Verification on R1*

```
R1# show ip rip
Process Name "rip-enterprise" VRF "default"
RIP port 520, multicast-group 224.0.0.9
Admin-distance: 120
Updates every 30 sec, expire in 180 sec
Collect garbage in 120 sec
Default-metric: 1
Max-paths: 8
Process is up and running
  Interfaces supported by ipv4 RIP :
    Vlan 12
    Vlan 13
    Vlan 14
R1# show running-config rip
    feature rip

router rip enterprise

interface Vlan12
  ip router rip enterprise
interface Vlan13
  ip router rip enterprise
interface Vlan14
  ip router rip enterprise

R1# show ip rip neighbor
Process Name "rip-enterprise" VRF "default"
RIP Neighbor Information (number of neighbors = 3)
('dead' means more than 300 seconds ago)

10.1.1.2, Vlan12
    Last Response sent/received: 00:00:20/00:00:08
    Last Request  sent/received: 00:04:58/never
    Bad Pkts Received: 0
    Bad Routes Received: 0
10.1.3.3, Vlan13
    Last Response sent/received: 00:00:22/00:00:10
    Last Request  sent/received: 00:04:58/never
    Bad Pkts Received: 0
    Bad Routes Received: 0
10.1.4.4, Vlan14
    Last Response sent/received: 00:00:28/00:00:16
    Last Request  sent/received: 00:04:59/never
    Bad Pkts Received: 0
    Bad Routes Received: 0
```

Example 21-6 highlights a few lines from each **show** command to enable you to understand the values and how they can validate or troubleshoot what you have configured on R1. These same commands would validate both of the configuration examples, whether it is for routed interface or SVI.

From the **show ip rip** command output, you can validate on the local Layer 3 switch which interfaces are enabled for IPv4 RIP, whether the process is enabled on the Layer 3 switch, as well as confirm the configured process name. From the **show running-config rip** command output, the highlighted items isolate what interfaces have been configured for the RIP process. **show running-config rip** is an important command for ensuring that you configured the instance-tag correct globally and on the interfaces you want enabled for RIP. The final **show** command in Example 21-6 is **show ip rip neighbor**, which enables you to see that the neighbors have come up, the IP addresses with which you are peering, and how many you have. If you see that you do not have the number of neighbors in comparison to the interfaces/SVI with which you have enabled RIP, this provides a good indication of which interfaces on R1 and the adjacent Layer 3 switch for which you need to validate the configuration.

As you can see, using these three **show** commands individually and together, you can validate and troubleshoot your configurations of RIP on the Cisco Nexus switches.

EIGRP Configuration on NX-OS

Enhanced Interior Gateway Routing Protocol (EIGRP) is as the name says—an enhanced version of the original IGRP. EIGRP is sometimes referred to as an *advanced* version of a distance vector routing protocol because it brings some of the benefits of a link-state routing protocol but also has some characteristics of a standard distance vector routing protocol. This section of the chapter demonstrates the ways to configure EIGRP on SVIs and routed interfaces as well as how to verify/troubleshoot the configuration of EIGRP. Through this verification and configuration, you will be able to see why EIGRP is seen as an advanced distance vector routing protocol.

Refer to Figure 21-1 for the routed interface example and Figure 21-2 for the SVI example. Example 21-8 shows the configuration of EIGRP on NX-OS using the routed interface example based on Figure 21-1. Example 21-9 shows configuration of EIGRP on NX-OS using SVIs based on Figure 21-2.

Example 21-8 *EIGRP Configuration: Routed Interface (R1 and R2)*

```
R1 Configuration
R1# configure terminal
R1(config)# feature eigrp
R1(config)# router eigrp 1
R1(config-router)# router-id 1.1.1.1
R1(config)# interface Ethernet1/2
R1(config-if)# no switchport
R1(config-if)# ip address 10.1.1.1/24
R1(config-if)# no shutdown
R1(config-if)# ip router eigrp 1
R1(config)# interface Ethernet1/3
```

```
R1(config-if)# no switchport
R1(config-if)# ip address 10.1.3.1/24
R1(config-if)# no shutdown
R1(config-if)# ip router eigrp 1
R1(config)# interface Ethernet1/4
R1(config-if)# no switchport
R1(config-if)# ip address 10.1.4.1/24
R1(config-if)# no shutdown
R1(config-if)# ip router eigrp 1
R2 Configuration
R2# configure terminal
R2(config)# feature eigrp
R2(config)# router eigrp 1
R2(config-router)# router-id 2.2.2.2
R2(config)# interface Ethernet1/2
R2(config-if)# no switchport
R2(config-if)# ip address 10.1.1.2/24
R2(config-if)# no shutdown
R2(config-if)# ip router eigrp 1
R2(config)# interface Ethernet2/3
R2(config-if)# no switchport
R2(config-if)# ip address 10.2.3.2/24
R2(config-if)# no shutdown
R2(config-if)# ip router eigrp 1
R2(config)# interface Ethernet2/4
R2(config-if)# no switchport
R2(config-if)# ip address 10.2.4.2/24
R2(config-if)# no shutdown
R2(config-if)# ip router eigrp 1
```

Example 21-9   *EIGRP Configuration: SVI (R1 and R2)*

```
R1 Configuration
R1# configure terminal
R1(config)# feature eigrp
R1(config)# feature interface-vlan
R1(config)# router eigrp 1
R1(config-router)# router-id 1.1.1.1
R1(config)# interface vlan 12
R1(config-if)# ip address 10.1.1.1/24
R1(config-if)# no shutdown
R1(config-if)# ip router eigrp 1
R1(config)# interface vlan 13
R1(config-if)# ip address 10.1.3.1/24
R1(config-if)# no shutdown
R1(config-if)# ip router eigrp 1
```

```
R1(config)# interface vlan 14
R1(config-if)# ip address 10.1.4.1/24
R1(config-if)# no shutdown
R1(config-if)# ip router eigrp 1
R2 Configuration
R2# configure terminal
R2(config)# feature eigrp
R2(config)# feature interface-vlan
R2(config)# router eigrp 1
R2(config-router)# router-id 2.2.2.2
R2(config)# interface vlan 12
R2(config-if)# ip address 10.1.1.2/24
R2(config-if)# no shutdown
R2(config-if)# ip router eigrp 1
R2(config)# interface vlan 23
R2(config-if)# ip address 10.2.3.2/24
R2(config-if)# no shutdown
R2(config-if)# ip router eigrp 1
R2(config)# interface vlan 24
R2(config-if)# ip address 10.2.4.2/24
R2(config-if)# no shutdown
R2(config-if)# ip router eigrp 1
```

As you can see, these configurations are very similar to how RIP was configured in the previous section. Because EIGRP is still a distance vector routing protocol, its implementation is almost exactly the same as other distance vector routing protocols. One new command that differs in the configurations for EIGRP is the use of the **router-id** *x.x.x.x* under the **router eigrp 1** process. Router IDs are important for identifying the router with a unique identifier in the routing protocol; each router will have a unique router ID that can be manually configured or dynamically assigned based on a selection process. In NX-OS, the process for selecting the router ID is as follows:

1. A router ID has been manually configured under the routing process (preferred).
2. The highest local IP address is selected, and loopback interfaces are preferred.
3. If no loopback interfaces are configured, use the highest IP address of a local interface.

Example 21-10 showcases some **show** commands used to validate and troubleshoot the EIGRP configurations from Examples 21-8 and 21-9. As mentioned earlier in the RIP section, the validation is the same whether you use SVI or routed interface configurations. Example 21-10 shows three different **show** commands and their output for validating and troubleshooting.

21

Example 21-10   *EIGRP Configuration on NX-OS: Validation and Troubleshooting*

```
R1# show running-config eigrp

feature eigrp

router eigrp 1
  autonomous-system 1
  router-id 1.1.1.1

interface Vlan12
  ip router eigrp 1
interface Vlan13
  ip router eigrp 1
interface Vlan14
  ip router eigrp 1


  R1#show ip eigrp

IP-EIGRP AS 1 ID 1.1.1.1 VRF default
  Process-tag: 1
  Instance Number: 1
  Status: running
  Authentication mode: none
  Authentication key-chain: none
  Metric weights: K1=1 K2=0 K3=1 K4=0 K5=0
  IP proto: 88 Multicast group: 224.0.0.10
  Int distance: 90 Ext distance: 170
  Max paths: 8
  Number of EIGRP interfaces: 3 (0 loopbacks)
  Number of EIGRP passive interfaces: 0
  Number of EIGRP peers: 3
  Graceful-Restart: Enabled
  Stub-Routing: Disabled
  NSF converge time limit/expiries: 120/0
  NSF route-hold time limit/expiries: 240/1
  NSF signal time limit/expiries: 20/0
  Redistributed max-prefix: Disabled



R1#sh ip eigrp neighbors 10.1.1.2
IP-EIGRP neighbors for process 1 VRF default
H   Address               Interface       Hold  Uptime  SRTT   RTO  Q   Seq
                                          (sec)         (ms)        Cnt Num

0   10.1.1.2              Vlan12      11   4d02h    1     50   0   14
```

In the output for the SVI configuration in Example 21-9, you see three different **show** command outputs from R1, each of which needs to be looked at individually and together to help you make sure that you have configured the routing protocol correctly. Start by taking a look at the first **show** command and identify the key parts of the output that can help validate or troubleshoot your configurations. From the **show running-config eigrp** command, you see the configuration output of what you have configured in particular to EIGRP on this Nexus device. Notice that the EIGRP autonomous system ID of 1 is the same for the **router eigrp 1** command as it is for the **ip router eigrp 1** subinterface command. This tells you that you have configured the correct EIGRP process on each interface for the global routing process, which is key to validating that your configuration is correct. You can execute these same commands on each Layer 3 switch to confirm correct configurations are in place.

NOTE   EIGRP uses what is known as an *autonomous system ID*. This number must match for the routers to form as neighbors. In our example, number 1 is the autonomous system number (between 1 and 65,535), which must be the same on all EIGRP-speaking routers in the network that would like to communicate and share routing information.

The last two **show** commands, **show ip eigrp** and **show ip eigrp neighbors**, enable you to validate or troubleshoot that you have formed neighbor relationships with other Layer 3 switches and that they are communicating/sharing information. The highlighted output from **show ip eigrp** focuses on some key information. First, you can again validate that the process ID is configured correctly (also referred to as autonomous system ID if a number is used), and you can also see the status as running. The next piece of key information is based on information you learned in Chapter 20. The K values in EIGRP are referring to what makes up the composite metric. By default, EIGRP uses bandwidth and delay with K value modifiers to calculate this metric to choose the best route to install in the routing table (successor) for any given destination. We do not go deep into this calculation here, but it is important to note that K1 is the bandwidth modifier for calculation and K3 is the delay modifier for calculation, so by default in your output, you should see K1 and K3 set to 1 and all other K values set to 0.

Finally, you see the number of neighbors (peers) and interfaces participating. Though these numbers for peers and interfaces do not always match, as in the case of peering with multiple neighbors on a local-area network over one interface, it can help you understand the peering and interface configurations. In the final output from **show ip eigrp neighbors 10.1.1.2**, you can validate that the neighbors are up, how long they have been up, their IP address, and the interface in which the peering happened. Note one final thing about EIGRP (which you can see in the outputs) that differentiates it from other distance vector routing protocols: its hello and update methodology. As explained in Chapter 20, and as the examples show, EIGRP does certainly qualify as more of an advanced distance vector routing protocol.

21

OSPF Configuration on NX-OS

The Open Shortest Path First (OSPF) Protocol is the final routing protocol to look at from a configuration perspective. In comparison to RIP and EIGRP, OSPF is considered a link-state routing protocol, and the following examples point out the differences in configuration, validation, and troubleshooting of this routing protocol from RIPv2 and EIGRP.

Again, refer to Figures 21-1 and 21-2 for the coverage of how to implement OSPF on NX-OS. Example 21-11 shows the configuration of a single area (0) with routed interfaces, and Example 21-12 explores configuring OSPF using SVIs for a single area (0).

Example 21-11 *OSPF Configuration on NX-OS with Routed Interfaces in a Single Area (0)*

```
R1 Configuration
R1# configure terminal
R1(config)# feature ospf
R1(config)# router ospf 1
R1(config-router)# router-id 1.1.1.1
R1(config)# interface Ethernet1/2
R1(config-if)# no switchport
R1(config-if)# ip address 10.1.1.1/24
R1(config-if)# no shutdown
R1(config-if)# ip router ospf 1 area 0
R1(config)# interface Ethernet1/3
R1(config-if)# no switchport
R1(config-if)# ip address 10.1.3.1/24
R1(config-if)# no shutdown
R1(config-if)# ip router ospf 1 area 0
R1(config)# interface Ethernet1/4
R1(config-if)# no switchport
R1(config-if)# ip address 10.1.4.1/24
R1(config-if)# no shutdown
R1(config-if)# ip router ospf 1 area 0
```

```
R2 Configuration
R2# configure terminal
R2(config)# feature ospf
R2(config)# router ospf 1
R2(config-router)# router-id 2.2.2.2
R2(config)# interface Ethernet1/2
R2(config-if)# no switchport
R2(config-if)# ip address 10.1.1.2/24
R2(config-if)# no shutdown
R2(config-if)# ip router ospf 1 area 0
R2(config)# interface Ethernet2/3
R2(config-if)# no switchport
R2(config-if)# ip address 10.2.3.2/24
R2(config-if)# no shutdown
```

```
R2(config-if)# ip router ospf 1 area 0
R2(config)# interface Ethernet2/4
R2(config-if)# no switchport
R2(config-if)# ip address 10.2.4.2/24
R2(config-if)# no shutdown
R2(config-if)# ip router ospf 1 area 0
```

Example 21-12   *OSPF Configuration on NX-OS with SVIs in a Single Area (0)*

```
R1 Configuration
R1# Configure terminal
R1(config)# feature ospf
R1(config)# router ospf 1
R1(config-router)# router-id 1.1.1.1
R1(config)# feature interface-vlan
R1(config)# interface vlan 12
R1(config-if)# ip address 10.1.1.1/24
R1(config-if)# no shutdown
R1(config-if)# ip router ospf 1 area 0
R1(config)# interface vlan 13
R1(config-if)# ip address 10.1.3.1/24
R1(config-if)# no shutdown
R1(config-if)# ip router ospf 1 area 0
R1(config)# interface vlan 14
R1(config-if)# ip address 10.1.4.1/24
R1(config-if)# no shutdown
R1(config-if)# ip router ospf 1 area 0
```

```
R2 Configuration
R2# Configure terminal
R2(config)# feature ospf
R2(config)# router ospf 1
R2(config-router)# router-id 2.2.2.2
R2(config)# feature interface-vlan
R2(config)# interface vlan 12
R2(config-if)# ip address 10.1.1.2/24
R2(config-if)# no shutdown
R2(config-if)# ip router ospf 1 area 0
R2(config)# interface vlan 23
R2(config-if)# ip address 10.2.3.2/24
R2(config-if)# no shutdown
R2(config-if)# ip router ospf 1 area 0
R2(config)# interface vlan 24
R2(config-if)# ip address 10.2.4.2/24
R2(config-if)# no shutdown
R2(config-if)# ip router ospf 1 area 0
```

21

Both of these examples show one difference from the RIP and EIGRP examples: the **area** tag at the end of the **ip router ospf 1 area 0** command. As mentioned in depth in Chapter 20, OSPF uses the concept of *areas* to segment and build hierarchy with the routed environment. This is a key attribute to scaling OSPF implementations, so it is important to note that each interface on a router or Layer 3 switch can belong to the same or different areas based on the network design you are using.

> **NOTE**   OSPF uses what is known as a *process ID*. This number does not have to match for the routers to form as neighbors. Unlike EIGRP, which uses this as an autonomous system number, the process ID for OSPF is locally significant.

Next, look at the output of **show** commands to again validate and troubleshoot the configurations in Examples 21-11 and 21-12. Example 21-13 focuses on three **show** commands commonly used for troubleshooting and validating OSPF configuration on NX-OS.

Example 21-13   *OSPF Configuration Troubleshooting and Validation on NX-OS*

```
R1# show running-config ospf

feature ospf

router ospf 1
  router-id 1.1.1.1

interface Vlan12
  ip router ospf 1 area 0
interface Vlan13
  ip router ospf 1 area 0
interface Vlan14
  ip router ospf 1 area 0


R1# sh ip ospf 1
    Routing Process 1 with ID 1.1.1.1 VRF default
 Routing Process Instance Number 1
 Stateful High Availability enabled
 Graceful-restart is configured
   Grace period: 60 state: Inactive
   Last graceful restart exit status: None
 Supports only single TOS(TOS0) routes
 Supports opaque LSA
 Administrative distance 110
 Reference Bandwidth is 40000 Mbps
 SPF throttling delay time of 200.000 msecs,
   SPF throttling hold time of 1000.000 msecs,
   SPF throttling maximum wait time of 5000.000 msecs
```

```
LSA throttling start time of 0.000 msecs,
   LSA throttling hold interval of 5000.000 msecs,
   LSA throttling maximum wait time of 5000.000 msecs
Minimum LSA arrival 1000.000 msec
LSA group pacing timer 10 secs
Maximum paths to destination 8
Number of external LSAs 0, checksum sum 0
Number of opaque AS LSAs 0, checksum sum 0
Number of areas is 1, 1 normal, 0 stub, 0 nssa
Number of active areas is 1, 1 normal, 0 stub, 0 nssa
Install discard route for summarized external routes.
Install discard route for summarized internal routes.
    Area BACKBONE(0.0.0.0) (Active)
         Area has existed for 03:49:02
            Interfaces in this area: 3 Active interfaces: 3
            Passive interfaces: 0  Loopback interfaces: 0
            No authentication available
            SPF calculation has run 2 times
             Last SPF ran for 0.000256s
            Area ranges are
            Number of LSAs: 1, checksum sum 0xba7e
R1# sh ip ospf interface vlan 12
    Vlan12 is up, line protocol is up
      IP address 10.1.1.1/24, Process ID 1 VRF default, area 0.0.0.0
      Enabled by interface configuration
      State DR, Network type BROADCAST, cost 40
      Index 3, Transmit delay 1 sec, Router Priority 1
      Designated Router ID: 1.1.1.1, address: 10.1.1.1
      No backup designated router on this network
      Timer intervals: Hello 10, Dead 40, Wait 40, Retransmit 5
        Hello timer due in 00:00:03
      No authentication
      Number of opaque link LSAs: 0, checksum sum 0
R1# sh ip ospf neighbor vlan 12
Neighbor ID     Pri    State      Dead Time   Address        Interface
2.2.2.2          1     FULL/BDR   00:00:34    10.1.1.2       vlan 12
```

The **show running-config ospf** command is the same command used with the other routing protocols, the difference being **ospf** at the end. This **show** command is your first step in verifying that the configuration you think you have implemented is as you think it should be. The highlighted parts of this first **show** command emphasize what you want to focus on—that your process ID for the **router ospf command** of 1 is the same implemented on each interface. In addition, you want to make sure that you have enabled the interfaces in the correct area (in this case, area 0, which you can confirm by finding **ip router ospf 1 area 0** under the interfaces or SVIs).

21

The **show ip ospf 1** command is one of the more powerful commands as far as what it helps you to understand is happening on R1 with the OSPF configuration you have applied. The highlighted parts of this output show the router ID. If the router ID was not manually configured, it shows what was given through the selection process. Further down in the output, you see how many areas this router or Layer 3 switch is participating in. You also see how many associated interfaces are with a given area, which is important information to validate that you have configured the device correctly. The last **show** command, **sh ip ospf interface vlan 12**, is valuable to show how OSPF is running on each interface or SVI. The highlighted parts of this **show** command reveal whether the interface or SVI is physically up and also up from a line protocol perspective. In addition, it shows what has been chosen by default as an interface type by OSPF. In this case, it is broadcast interface, which you normally see on LANs or Layer 3 switch implementations. Because of the interface being broadcast, as you learned in Chapter 20, a designated router is needed in this OSPF area. As you can see, the last highlighted line of output shows the router ID of this designated router. The last output shows the neighbors what state they are in and their IP address.

Exam Preparation Tasks

Review All the Key Topics

Review the most important topics from this chapter, noted with the Key Topic icon. Table 21-2 lists these key topics and where each is discussed.

Table 21-2   Key Topics for Chapter 21

Key Topic Element	Description	Page Number
Example 21-1	Routed interface configuration	533
Example 21-2	SVI interface configuration	533
Example 21-3	Routing process enablement IOS and NX-OS with passive interface	534
Example 21-4	Routing table example	535
Example 21-5	RIPv2 configuration on R1 and R2 using a routed interface	537
Example 21-6	RIPv2 configuration on R1 and R2 using an SVI interface	539
Example 21-8	EIGRP configuration: routed interface (R1 and R2)	541
Example 21-9	EIGRP configuration: SVI (R1 and R2)	542
List	Router ID selection process for EIGRP	543
Example 21-10	EIGRP configuration on NX-OS: validation and troubleshooting	544
Example 21-11	OSPF configuration on NX-OS with routed interfaces in a single area (0)	546
Example 21-13	OSPF configuration troubleshooting and validation on NX-OS	548

Definitions of Key Terms

After your first reading of the chapter, try to define these key terms, but do not be concerned about getting them all correct at that time. Chapter 23, "Final Review," directs you in how to use these terms for late-stage preparation for the exam.

distance vector, autonomous system ID, link state, process ID, instance tag, cost, K values

Command Reference to Check Your Memory

Although you should not necessarily memorize the information in the tables in this section, this section does include a reference for the configuration and EXEC commands covered in this chapter. Practically speaking, you should memorize the commands as a side effect of reading the chapter and doing all the activities in this exam preparation section. To check to see how well you have memorized the commands as a side effect of your other studies, cover the left side of the table with a piece of paper, read the descriptions on the right side, and see whether you remember the command.

Table 21-3   Chapter 21 Configuration Command Reference

Command	Description
feature interface-vlan	Enables you to configure SVIs on a Nexus switch

Table 21-4   Chapter 21 EXEC Command Reference

Command	Description
feature rip	Enables RIPv2 process on a Cisco Nexus switch
feature eigrp	Enables EIGRP process on a Cisco Nexus switch
feature ospf	Enables OSPFv2 process on a Cisco Nexus switch
no switchport	Disables Layer 2 functionality on a physical interface
show running-config rip	Show only the RIP configuration in the running configuration
show running-config eigrp	Show only the EIGRP configuration in the running configuration
show running-config ospf	Show only the OSPF configuration in the running configuration
sh ip eigrp neighbors	Displays the active EIGRP neighbors
sh ip ospf neighbors	Displays the active OSPF neighbors
show ip rip	Displays the local router's RIP process information
sh ip ospf 1	Displays the local router's OSPF process information

This chapter covers the following exam topics:

4.1 Describe and configure basic routing concepts

4.1a Packet forwarding

IPv4 Access Control Lists on Cisco Nexus Switches

Most every other topic in the scope of CCNA-DC focuses on achieving a core goal of any TCP/IP network: delivering IPv4 packets from the source host to the destination host. This chapter focuses instead on preventing a subset of those packets from being allowed to reach their destinations, by using IPv4 access control lists (ACL).

IPv4 ACLs have many uses, but the CCNA-DC exam focuses on their most commonly known use: as packet filters. You want hosts in one subnet to be able to communicate throughout your corporate network, but perhaps there is a pocket of servers with sensitive data that must be protected. Maybe government privacy rules require you to further secure and protect access, not just with usernames and login, but even to protect the ability to deliver a packet to the protected host or server. IP ACLs provide a useful solution to achieve those goals.

This chapter discusses the basics of IPv4 ACLs on Nexus switches. This chapter starts by covering the basics and types of ACLs supported by Cisco Nexus switches. The second part of the chapter completes the discussion by describing IPv4 ACLs basics and configurations.

NOTE IPv6 ACLs exist as well, but they are not included in this book.

"Do I Know This Already?" Quiz

Use the "Do I Know This Already?" quiz to help decide whether you might want to skim this chapter, or a major section, moving more quickly to the "Exam Preparation Tasks" section near the end of the chapter. You can find the answers at the bottom of the page following the quiz. For thorough explanations, see Appendix A, "Answers to the 'Do I Know This Already?' Quizzes."

Table 22-1 "Do I Know This Already?" Foundation Topics Section-to-Question Mapping

Foundation Topics Section	Questions
IPv4 Access Control List Basics	1–4
Practice Cisco Nexus IPv4 ACLs	5

1. Barney is a host with IP address 10.1.1.1 in subnet 10.1.1.0/24. Which of the following are things that a standard IP ACL could be configured to do? (Choose two answers.)

    a. Match the exact source IP address

    b. Match IP addresses 10.1.1.1 through 10.1.1.4 with one **access-list** command without matching other IP addresses

    c. Match all IP addresses in Barney's subnet with one **access-list** command without matching other IP addresses

    d. Match only the packet's destination IP address

2. Which of the following wildcard masks is most useful for matching all IP packets in subnet 10.1.128.0, mask 255.255.255.0?

    a. 0.0.0.0

    b. 0.0.0.31

    c. 0.0.0.240

    d. 0.0.0.255

    e. 0.0.15.0

    f. 0.0.248.255

3. Which of the following masks is most useful for matching all IP packets in subnet 10.1.128.0, mask 255.255.240.0?

    a. 0.0.0.0

    b. 0.0.0.31

    c. 0.0.0.240

    d. 0.0.0.255

    e. 0.0.15.255

    f. 0.0.248.255

4. ACL 1 has three statements, in the following order, with address and mask values as follows: 1.0.0.0/8, 1.1.0.0/16, and 1.1.1.0/24. If a router tried to match a packet sourced from IP address 1.1.1.1 using this ACL, which ACL statement does a router consider the packet to have matched?

    a. First

    b. Second

    c. Third

    d. Implied deny at the end of the ACL

5. On a Cisco nexus switch, what command will allow only host 10.1.1.1 to talk with host 192.168.1.3 for web traffic that is unencrypted for ACL web subcommands?

    a. **permit tcp host 10.1.1.1 host 192.168.1.3 eq 80**

    b. **permit ip 10.1.1.0/24 host 192.168.1.3**

    c. **permit tcp 10.1.1.0/24 192.168.1.0/24 eq 80**

    d. **permit ip any any**

Foundation Topics

IPv4 Access Control List Basics

IPv4 access control lists (IP ACLs) give network engineers a way to identify different types of packets. To do so, the ACL configuration lists values that the routed interfaces can see in the IP, TCP, UDP, and other headers. For example, an ACL can match packets whose source IP address is 1.1.1.1, or packets whose destination IP address is some address in subnet 10.1.1.0/24, or packets with a destination port of TCP port 23 (Telnet).

IPv4 ACLs perform many functions in Cisco routers, with the most common use as a packet filter. Engineers can enable ACLs on a router so that the ACL sits in the forwarding path of packets as they pass through the router. After it is enabled, the router considers whether each IP packet will either be discarded or allowed to continue as if the ACL did not exist.

However, ACLs can be used for many other IOS features as well. For example, ACLs can be used to match packets for applying quality of service (QoS) features. QoS allows a router to give some packets better service and other packets worse service. For example, packets that hold digitized voice need to have very low delay, so ACLs can match voice packets with QoS logic, in turn forwarding voice packets more quickly than forwarding data packets.

This first section introduces IP ACLs as used for packet filtering, focusing on these aspects of ACLs: the locations and direction in which to enable ACLs, matching packets by examining headers, and taking action after a packet has been matched.

ACL Location and Direction

Cisco Nexus can apply ACL logic to packets at the point at which the IP packets enter an interface or the point at which they exit an interface. In other words, the ACL becomes associated with an interface and for a direction of packet flow (either in or out). That is, the ACL can be applied inbound to the router, before the router makes its forwarding (routing) decision, or outbound, after the router makes its forwarding decision and has determined the exit interface to use.

The arrows in Figure 22-1 show the locations at which you could filter packets, flowing left to right in the topology. Suppose, for instance, that you want to allow packets sent by host A to server S1, but to discard packets sent by host B to server S1. Each arrowed line represents a location and direction at which a router could apply an ACL, filtering the packets sent by host B.

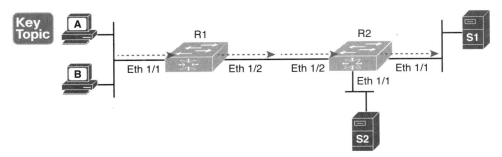

Figure 22-1 *Locations to Filter Packets from Hosts A and B Going Toward Server S1*

The four arrowed lines in the figure point out the location and direction for the routed interfaces used to forward the packet from host B to server S1. In this particular example, those interfaces and directions are as follows:

- Inbound on R1's Eth1/1 interface
- Outbound on R1's Eth1/2 interface
- Inbound on R2's Eth1/2 interface
- Outbound on R2's Eth1/1 interface

If, for example, you were to enable an ACL on R2's Eth1/1 interface, in either direction, that ACL could not possibly filter the packet sent from host B to server S1, because R2's Eth1/1 interface is not part of the route from B to S1.

In short, to filter a packet, you must enable an ACL on an interface that processes the packet, in the same direction the packet flows through that interface.

When enabled, the router then processes every inbound or outbound IP packet using that ACL. For example, if enabled on R1 for packets inbound on interface Eth1/1, R1 would compare every inbound IP packet on Eth1/1 to the ACL to decide that packet's fate: to continue unchanged or to be discarded.

Matching Packets

When you think about the location and direction for an ACL, you must already be thinking about what packets you plan to filter (discard) and which ones you want to allow through. To tell the router those same ideas, you must configure the router with an IP ACL that matches packets. Matching packets refers to how to configure the ACL commands to look at each packet, listing how to identify which packets should be discarded and which should be allowed through.

Each IP ACL consists of one or more configuration commands, with each command listing details about values to look for inside a packet's headers. Generally, an ACL command uses logic like "look for these values in the packet header, and if found, discard the packet." (The action could instead be to allow the packet, rather than discard.) Specifically, the ACL looks for header fields you should already know well, including the source and destination IP addresses, plus TCP and UDP port numbers.

For instance, consider an example with Figure 22-2, in which you want to allow packets from host A to server S1, but to discard packets from host B going to that same server. The hosts all now have IP addresses, and the figure shows pseudocode for an ACL on R2. Figure 22-2 also shows the chosen location to enable the ACL: inbound on R2's Eth1/2 interface.

Figure 22-2 shows a two-line ACL in a rectangle at the bottom, with simple matching logic: Both statements just look to match the source IP address in the packet. When enabled, R2 looks at every inbound IP packet on that interface and compares each packet to those two ACL commands. Packets sent by host A (source IP address 10.1.1.1) are allowed through, and those sent by host B (source IP address 10.1.1.2) are discarded.

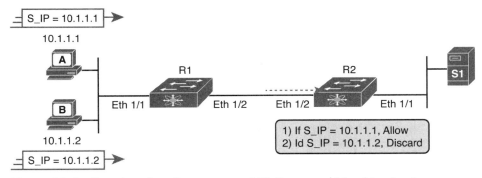

Figure 22-2 *Pseudocode to Demonstrate ACL Command-Matching Logic*

Taking Action When a Match Occurs

When using IP ACLs to filter packets, only one of two actions can be chosen. The configuration commands use keywords **deny** and **permit**, and they mean (respectively) to discard the packet or to allow it to keep going as if the ACL did not exist.

This book focuses on using ACLs to filter packets, but NX-OS uses ACLs for many more features. Those features typically use the same matching logic. However, in other cases, the **deny** or **permit** keywords imply some other action.

Types of IP ACLs

Cisco IOS has supported IP ACLs since the early days of Cisco routers. Beginning with the original standard numbered IP ACLs in the early days of IOS, which could enable the logic shown earlier around Figure 22-2, Cisco has added many ACL features, including the following:

- Standard numbered ACLs (1–99)
- Extended numbered ACLs (100–199)
- Additional ACL numbers (1300–1999 standard, 2000–2699 extended)
- Named ACLs
- Improved editing with sequence numbers

This chapter focuses solely on the Cisco Nexus implementation of IPv4 ACLs, which are extended named ACLs. Briefly, IP ACLs will be either numbered or named, in that the configuration identifies the ACL either using a number or a name. ACLs will also be either standard or extended, with extended ACLs having much more robust abilities in matching packets. Figure 22-3 summarizes the big ideas related to categories of IP ACLs when they were used in IOS.

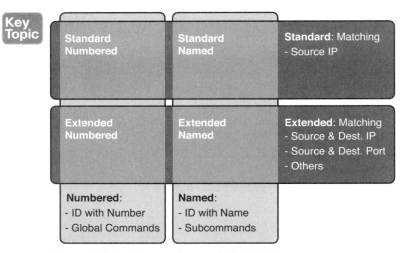

Figure 22-3 *Comparisons of IP ACL Types*

List Logic with IP ACLs

A single ACL is both a single entity and, at the same time, a list of one or more configuration commands. As a single entity, the configuration enables the entire ACL on an interface, in a specific direction, as shown earlier around Figure 22-1. As a list of commands, each command has different matching logic that the router must apply to each packet when filtering using that ACL.

When doing ACL processing, the router processes the packet, compared to the ACL, as follows:

ACLs use first-match logic. Once a packet matches one line in the ACL, the router takes the action listed in that line of the ACL, and stops looking further in the ACL.

To see exactly what that means, consider the example built around Figure 22-4. The figure shows an example ACL 1 with three lines of pseudocode. This example applies ACL 1 on R2's Eth1/2 interface, inbound (the same location as in earlier Figure 22-2).

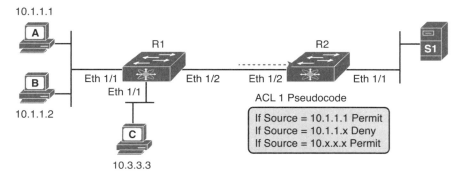

Figure 22-4 *Backdrop for Discussion of List Process with IP ACLs*

Consider the first-match ACL logic for a packet sent by host A to server S1. The source IP address will be 10.1.1.1, and it will be routed so that it enters R2's Eth 1/2 interface, driving R2's ACL 1 logic. R2 compares this packet to the ACL, matching the first item in the list with a permit action. So, this packet should be allowed through, as shown in Figure 22-5, on the left.

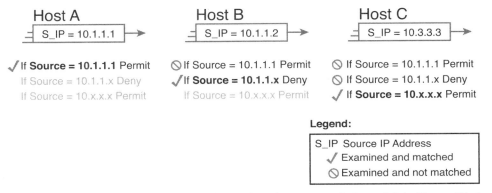

Figure 22-5   *ACL Items Compared for Packets from Hosts A, B, and C in Figure 22-4*

Next, consider a packet sent by host B, source IP address 10.1.1.2. When the packet enters R2's Eth1/2 interface, R2 compares the packet to ACL 1's first statement, and does not make a match (10.1.1.1 is not equal to 10.1.1.2). R2 then moves to the second statement, which requires some clarification. The ACL pseudocode, back in Figure 22-4, shows 10.1.1.x, which is meant to be shorthand that any value can exist in the last octet. Comparing only the first three octets, R2 decides that this latest packet does have a source IP address that begins with first three octets 10.1.1, so R2 considers that to be a match on the second statement. R2 takes the listed action (deny), discarding the packet. R2 also stops ACL processing on the packet, ignoring the third line in the ACL.

Finally, consider a packet sent by host C, again to server S1. The packet has source IP address 10.3.3.3, so when it enters R2's Eth1/2 interface, and drives ACL processing on R2, R2 looks at the first command in ACL 1. R2 does not match the first ACL command (10.1.1.1 in the command is not equal to the packet's 10.3.3.3). R2 looks at the second command, compares the first three octets (10.1.1) to the packet source IP address (10.3.3), still no match. R2 then looks at the third command. In this case, the wildcard means ignore the last three octets, and just compare the first octet (10), so the packet matches. R2 then takes the listed action (permit), allowing the packet to keep going.

This sequence of processing an ACL as a list happens for any type of NX-OS ACL: IP and other protocols.

Finally, if a packet does not match any of the items in the ACL, the packet is discarded. The reason is because every IP ACL has a deny all statement implied at the end of the ACL. It does not exist in the configuration, but if a router keeps searching the list, and no match is made by the end of the list, IOS considers the packet to have matched an entry that has a deny action.

Matching Logic and Command Syntax

NX-OS IP ACLs use the following global command:

```
Switch(config)# ip access-list name
Switch(config-ip-acl)# [sequence-number] {permit | deny} protocol source destination
```

Each NX-OS IPv4 ACL has one or more access list entry commands, with an associated sequence number for each entry so they can be reordered if needed (whole number between 1 and 4,294,967,295).

Besides the ACL sequence number, each **ip access-list** subcommand also lists the action (**permit** or **deny**), plus the matching logic. The rest of this section examines how to configure the matching parameters for NX-OS IPv4 ACLs.

To match a specific source IP address, all you have to do is type that IP address with a /32 mask at the end of the command. For example, the previous example uses pseudocode for "permit if source = 10.1.1.1." The following command configures that logic with correct syntax using an ACL named sample-acl:

```
Switch(config)# ip access-list sample-acl
Switch(config-ip-acl)# permit ip 10.1.1.1/32 any
```

Matching the exact full IP address is that simple. Another option is to use the **host** keyword instead of using the /32, as seen in the following example ACL sample-acl-host:

```
Switch(config)# ip access-list sample-acl-host
Switch(config-ip-acl)# permit ip host 10.1.1.1 any
```

NOTE An important thing to understand from this example is that all ACLs in NX-OS have what is referred to as an *explicit deny*. If you applied this ACL to an interface only, host 10.1.1.1 would be able to communicate because at the end of each ACL is an implicit deny statement of **ip any any**, which denies anything that has not been permitted using the ACL entries.

Matching TCP and UDP Port Numbers

Cisco Nexus ACLs can also examine parts of the TCP and UDP headers, particularly the source and destination port number fields. The port numbers identify the application that sends or receives the data.

The most useful ports to check are the well-known ports used by servers. For example, web servers use well-known port 80 by default. Figure 22-6 shows the location of the port numbers in the TCP header, following the IP header.

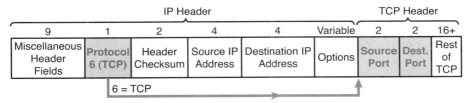

Figure 22-6 *IP Header, Followed by a TCP Header and Port Number Fields*

When a Cisco Nexus ACL command includes either the **tcp** or **udp** keyword, that command can optionally reference the source/destination port. To make these comparisons, the syntax uses keywords for equal, not equal, less than, greater than, and for a range of port numbers. In addition, the command can use either the literal decimal port numbers, or more convenient keywords for some well-known application ports. Figure 22-7 shows the positions of the source and destination port fields in the **access-list** command and these port number keywords.

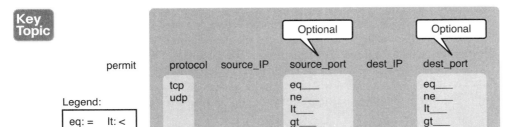

Figure 22-7 *Cisco Nexus ACL Syntax with Port Numbers Enabled Using Protocol TCP or UDP*

For example, consider the simple network shown in Figure 22-8. The FTP server sits on the right, with the client on the left. The figure shows the syntax of an ACL that matches the following:

- Packets that include a TCP header
- Packets sent from the client subnet
- Packets sent to the server subnet
- Packets with TCP destination port 21 (FTP server control port)

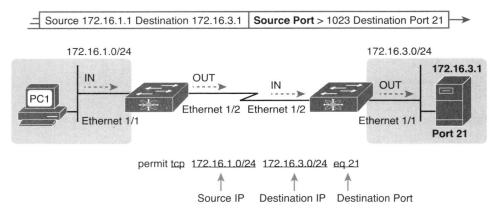

Figure 22-8 *Filtering Packets Based on Destination Port*

To fully appreciate the matching of the destination port with the **eq 21** parameters, consider packets moving from left to right, from PC1 to the server. Assuming the server uses well-known port 21 (FTP control port), the packet's TCP header has a destination port value of 21. The ACL syntax includes the **eq 21** parameters after the destination IP address. The position after the destination address parameters is important: That position identifies the fact that the **eq 21** parameters should be compared to the packet's destination port. As a result, the ACL statement shown in Figure 22-8 would match this packet, and the destination port of 21, if used in any of the four locations implied by the four dashed arrowed lines in the figure.

Conversely, Figure 22-9 shows the reverse flow, with a packet sent by the server back toward PC1. In this case, the packet's TCP header has a source port of 21, so the ACL must check the source port value of 21, and the ACL must be located on different interfaces. In this case, the **eq 21** parameters follow the source address field, but come before the destination address field.

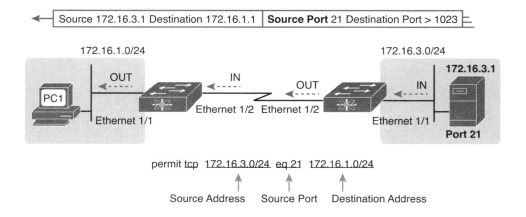

permit tcp 172.16.1.0/24 172.16.3.0/24 eq 21

Figure 22-9 *Filtering Packets Based on Source Port*

For exam questions that require ACLs and matching of port numbers, first consider the location and direction in which the ACL will be applied. That direction determines whether the packet is being sent to the server, or from the server. At that point, you can decide whether you need to check the source or destination port in the packet, assuming that you want to check the well-known port used by that service.

For reference, Table 22-2 lists many of the popular port numbers and their transport layer protocols and applications. Note that the syntax of the **access-list** commands accepts both the port numbers and a shorthand version of the application name.

Table 22-2   Popular Applications and Their Well-Known Port Numbers

Port Number(s)	Protocol	Application	access-list Command Keyword
20	TCP	FTP data	**ftp-data**
21	TCP	FTP control	**ftp**
22	TCP	SSH	—
23	TCP	Telnet	**telnet**
25	TCP	SMTP	**smtp**
53	UDP, TCP	DNS	**domain**
67, 68	UDP	DHCP	**nameserver**
69	UDP	TFTP	**tftp**
80	TCP	HTTP (WWW)	**www**
110	TCP	POP3	**pop3**
161	UDP	SNMP	**snmp**
443	TCP	SSL	—
16,384 – 32,767	UDP	RTP-based voice (VoIP) and video	—

Table 22-3 lists several example **access-list** commands that match based on port numbers. Cover the right side of the table, and try to characterize the packets matched by each command. Then, check the right side of the table to see if you agree with the assessment.

Table 22-3   Extended **access-list** Command Examples and Logic Explanations

access-list Statement	What It Matches
deny tcp any gt 1023 host 10.1.1.1 eq 23	Packets with a TCP header, any source IP address, with a source port greater than (gt) 1023, a destination IP address of exactly 10.1.1.1, and a destination port equal to (eq) 23.
deny tcp any host 10.1.1.1 eq 23	The same as the preceding example, but any source port matches, because that parameter is omitted in this case.

22

access-list Statement	What It Matches
deny tcp any host 10.1.1.1 eq telnet	The same as the preceding example. The **telnet** keyword is used instead of port 23.
deny udp 1.0.0.0 0.255.255.255 lt 1023 any	A packet with a source in network 1.0.0.0/8, using UDP with a source port less than (lt) 1023, with any destination IP address.

Implementing Cisco Nexus IPv4 ACLs

This chapter has already introduced all the configuration steps in bits and pieces. This section summarizes those pieces as a configuration process. The process also refers to the **access-list** command, whose generic syntax is repeated here for reference:

```
ip access-list name
```

Step 1.   Configure one or more **access-list** subconfiguration commands to create the ACL, keeping the following in mind:

    A.   The list is searched sequentially, using first-match logic.

    B.   The default action, if a packet does not match any of the **access-list** commands, is to deny (discard) the packet.

Step 2.   Enable the ACL on the chosen interface (port/routed/VACL), in the correct direction, using the **ip access-group/** *number* {**in | out**} interface subcommand.

> **NOTE**   IPv4 ACLs can be applied in three different manners: port for Layer 2 interfaces in the direction of in, as a standard Layer 3 ACL for both in and out, and as a VLAN access control list (VACL) by being a match in the VLAN access class list. The following example will show focus on routed interface applications.

The rest of this section shows a couple of examples.

ACL Example 1

The first example shows the configuration for the same requirements, demonstrated with Figure 22-4 and Figure 22-5. Restated, the requirements for this ACL are as follows:

    1.   Enable the ACL inbound on R2's Eth1/2 interface.

    2.   Permit packets coming from host A.

    3.   Deny packets coming from other hosts in host A's subnet.

    4.   Permit packets coming from any other address in Class A network 10.0.0.0.

    5.   The original example made no comment about what to do by default; so, simply deny all other traffic.

Example 22-1 shows a completed correct configuration, starting with the configuration process, followed by output from the **show running-config** command.

Example 22-1 *Standard ACL Example 1 Configuration*

```
R2# configure terminal
Enter configuration commands, one per line.  End with CNTL/Z.
R2(config)# ip access-list standard-acl
R2(config-ip-acl)#permit ip 10.1.1.1/32 any
R2(config-ip-acl)#deny ip  10.1.1.0/24 any
R2(config-ip-acl)#permit ip 10.0.0.0/8 any
R2(config)# interface Ethernet 1/2
R2(config-if)# ip access-group standard-acl in
R2(config-if)# ^Z
R2# show ip access-lists
! Lines omitted for brevity

   IP access list standard-acl
       10 permit ip 10.1.1.1 255.255.255.255 any
       20 deny ip 10.1.1.0 255.255.255.0 any
       30 permit ip 10.0.0.0 255.0.0.0 any
```

First, pay close attention to the configuration process at the top of the example. Note that the **ip access-list** command does change the command prompt from the global configuration mode prompt, because the **ip access-list** command enters a sub IP ACL configuration mode. Then, compare that to the output of the **show running-config** command: The details are identical compared to the commands that were added in configuration and subconfiguration mode. Finally, make sure to note the **ip access-group standard-acl in** command, under R2's Eth1/2 interface, which enables the ACL logic (both location and direction).

ACL Example 2

The second example, Example 22-2, shows the configuration for a slightly more advanced ACL configuration. This example configures an ACL named advanced-acl on R2 that only allows FTP from host 10.1.1.1 to anyone and HTTP from the 10.1.1.0/24 to anyone.

Example 22-2 *Advanced ACL Example 2 Configuration*

```
R2# configure terminal
Enter configuration commands, one per line.  End with CNTL/Z.
R2(config)# ip access-list advanced-acl
R2(config-ip-acl)# permit tcp 10.1.1.1/32 any eq ftp
R2(config-ip-acl)# permit tcp 10.1.1.1/32 any eq ftp-data
R2(config-ip-acl)# permit tcp 10.1.1.0/24 any eq http
R2(config-ip-acl)# permit tcp 10.1.1.0/24 any eq https
    R2(config)# interface Ethernet 1/2
R2(config-if)# ip access-group advanced-acl in
R2(config-if)# ^Z
```

22

This example shows a more advanced ACL configuration, using an ACL to only allow certain TCP ports out from a single host or subnet. In this case, you are limiting it to FTP traffic from host 10.1.1.1 and allowing 10.1.1.1.0/24 network the ability to use the Web. The example uses source, destination, port, and protocol to determine what can communicate in the advanced ACL. This example demonstrates the power you have to lock down communication using this type of ACL within your own network.

Practice Cisco Nexus IPv4 ACLs

Some CCNA-DC topics, like subnetting, simply require more drills and practice than others. You can also benefit from doing practice drills with ACLs in part because ACLs require you to think of parameters to match ranges of numbers, and that, of course, requires some use of math and some use of processes.

This section provides some practice problems and tips, from two perspectives. First, this section asks you to build one-line ACLs to match some packets. Second, this section asks you to interpret existing ACL commands to describe what packets the ACL will match. Both skills are useful for the exams.

Practice Building access-list Commands

This section provides some practice in getting comfortable with the syntax of the **ip access-list** command, particularly with choosing the correct matching logic. These skills will prove helpful when reading about ACLs.

First, the following list summarizes some important tips to consider when choosing matching parameters to any **access-list** command:

■ To match a specific address, just list the address.

■ To match any and all addresses, use the **any** keyword.

■ To match based only on the first one, two, or three octets of an address, use the subnet masks, respectively. Also, make sure that the source (address) parameter has correct subnet masks.

■ To match a subnet, use the subnet ID as the source, and find the subnet mask prefix by using the "/" prefix length.

Table 22-4 lists the criteria for several practice problems. Your job: Create a one-line standard ACL that matches the packets. The answers are listed in the section "Answers to Earlier Practice Problems," later in this chapter.

Table 22-4   Building IPv4 ACLs: Practice

Problem	Criteria
1	Packets from 172.16.5.4
2	Packets from hosts with 192.168.6 as the first three octets
3	Packets from hosts with 192.168 as the first two octets
4	Packets from any host

Problem	Criteria
5	Packets from subnet 10.1.200.0 255.255.248.0
6	Packets from subnet 10.1.200.0 255.255.255.224
7	Packets from subnet 172.20.112.0 255.255.255.254
8	Packets from subnet 172.20.112.0 255.255.255.192
9	Packets from subnet 192.168.9.64 255.255.255.240
10	Packets from subnet 192.168.9.64 255.255.255.252

22

Exam Preparation Tasks

Review All the Key Topics

Review the most important topics from this chapter, noted with the Key Topic icon. Table 22-5 lists these key topics and where each is discussed.

Table 22-5   Key Topics for Chapter 22

Key Topic Element	Description	Page Number
Figure 22-1	Locations to filter packets from hosts A and B going toward server S1	557
Paragraph	Summary of the general rule of the location and direction for an ACL	558
Figure 22-3	Summary of four main categories of IPv4 ACLs in Cisco IOS	560
Paragraph	Summary of first-match logic used by all ACLs	560
Figure 22-7	Cisco Nexus ACL syntax with port numbers enabled using protocol TCP or UDP	563
Table 22-2	Popular applications and their well-known port numbers	565
List	Steps to plan and implement a standard IP ACL	566
List	Tips for creating matching logic for the source address field in the **access-list** command	568

Definitions of Key Terms

After your first reading of the chapter, try to define these key terms, but do not be concerned about getting them all correct at that time. Chapter 23, "Final Preparation," directs you in how to use these terms for late-stage preparation for the exam.

standard access list, wildcard mask

Appendix H Practice Problems

DVD Appendix H, "Practice for Chapter 22: Basic IPv4 Access Control Lists on Cisco Nexus Switches," lists additional practice problems and answers.

Command Reference to Check Your Memory

Although you should not necessarily memorize the information in the tables in this section, this section includes a reference for the configuration and EXEC commands covered in this chapter. Practically speaking, you should memorize the commands as a side effect of reading this chapter and doing all the activities in this "Exam Preparation" section. To see how well you have memorized the commands as a side effect of your other studies, cover the left side of the table, read the descriptions on the right side, and see whether you remember the command.

Table 22-6 Chapter 22 Configuration Command Reference

Command	Description
ip access-list *name* (config-ip-acl)# [*sequence-number*] {**permit**	**deny**} *protocol source destination*	Global command for IPv4 access lists. Use subcommands for permit and deny functions
ip access-group name {**in**	**out**}	Interface subcommand to enable access lists

Table 22-7 Chapter 22 EXEC Command Reference

Command	Description
show ip interface [*type number*]	Includes a reference to the access lists enabled on the interface
show ip access-list [*access-list-number*	*access-list-name*]	Shows IP access lists

22

Part V Review

Keep track of your part review progress with the checklist shown in Table P5-1. Details on each task follow the table.

Table P5-1 Part V Review Checklist

Activity	First Date Completed	Second Date Completed
Repeat All DIKTA Questions		
Answer Part Review Questions		
Review Key Topics		
Create Command Mind Map by Category		

Repeat All DIKTA Questions

For this task, answer the "Do I Know This Already?" questions again for the chapters in this part of the book, using the PCPT software. Refer to the Introduction to this book, heading "How to View Only DIKTA Questions by Part," for help with how to make the PCPT software show you DIKTA questions for this part only.

Answer Part Review Questions

For this task, answer the Part Review questions for this part of the book, using the PCPT software. Refer to the Introduction to this book, heading "How to View Only Part Review Questions by Part," for help with how to make the PCPT software show you Part Review questions for this part only.

Review Key Topics

Browse back through the chapters and look for the Key Topic icons. If you do not remember some details, take the time to reread those topics.

Create Command Mind Map by Category

Part V of this book introduces many Layer 3 features on Nexus switches. As with several other parts of this book, the large number of commands can be intimidating. This mind map exercise attempts to help you move from the point of intimidation to being more comfortable with the command set as a whole.

For the exam, you do not necessarily have to memorize every command and every parameter. However, you should be able to remember all the categories of Layer 3 topics that can be configured in Nexus switches (at least those mentioned in the book), and at least remember the first word or two of most of the commands. This mind map exercise is designed to help you work on organizing these commands in your mind.

Create a mind map with the following categories of commands from this part of the book:

IPv4 addressing, static IPv4 routes, Layer 3 switching, RIP, OSPF, EIGRP, ACLs

For each category, think of all configuration commands and all EXEC commands (mostly **show** commands). Group the configuration commands separately from the EXEC commands. Figure P5-1 shows a sample for the switch IPv4 branch of the commands.

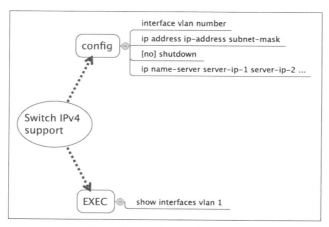

Figure P5-1   *Sample Mind Map from the Switch IPv4 Branch*

NOTE   For more information on mind mapping, refer to the Introduction, in the section "About Mind Maps."

Finally, keep the following points in mind when working on this project:

■ Learning happens when creating the mind map. Make an attempt; it truly does help your own brain organize the information.

■ Make your first attempt without notes and without looking at the book.

■ After your first attempt, then you can review notes, the book, and especially the command summary tables at the end of some chapters. Note which commands you did not remember so that you can focus on those commands when you review later.

■ Do not bother to record every single parameter of every command; just write down enough of the command to remember it.

■ Note which commands you feel you understand well, and which you feel less sure about.

■ Repeat this exercise later when you have 10 spare minutes, as a way to find out how much you recall.

DVD Appendix K, "Mind Map Solutions," shows a sample answer, but your mind map will likely differ.

Part VI

Final Preparation

Chapter 23: Final Review

Final Review

Congratulations! You made it through the book, and now it's time to finish getting ready for the exam. This chapter helps you get ready to take and pass the exam in two ways.

This chapter begins by talking about the exam itself. You know the content and topics. Now you need to think about what happens during the exam and what you need to do in these last few weeks before taking the exam. At this point, everything you do should be focused on getting you ready to pass so that you can finish up this hefty task.

The second section of this chapter gives you some exam review tasks as your final preparation for your DCICN exam.

Advice About the Exam Event

Now that you have finished the bulk of this book, you could just register for your Cisco DCICN exam, show up, and take the exam. However, if you spend a little time thinking about the exam event itself, learning more about the user interface of the real Cisco exams, and the environment at the Vue testing centers, you will be better prepared, particularly if this is your first Cisco exam. This first of three major sections in this chapter gives some advice about the Cisco exams and the exam event itself.

Learn the Question Types Using the Cisco Certification Exam Tutorial

In the weeks leading up to your exam, you should think more about the different types of exam questions and have a plan for how to approach those questions. One of the best ways to learn about the exam questions is to use the Cisco Exam Tutorial.

To find the Cisco Certification Exam Tutorial, go to www.cisco.com and search for "exam tutorial." The tutorial sits inside a web page with a Flash presentation of the exam user interface. The tutorial even lets you take control as if you were taking the exam. When using the tutorial, make sure that you take control and try the following:

- Try to click **Next** on the multichoice, single-answer question without clicking an answer, and see that the testing software tells you that you have too few answers.

- On the multichoice, multianswer question, select too few answers and click **Next** to again see how the user interface responds.

- In the drag-and-drop question, drag the answers to the obvious answer locations, but then drag them back to the original location. (You might do this on the real exam if you change your mind when answering the question.)

- On the simulation (sim) question, first just make sure that you can get to the command-line interface (CLI) on one of the routers. To do so, you have to click the PC icon for a PC connected to the router console; the console cable appears as a dashed line, and network cables are solid lines. (Note that the exam tutorial uses the IOS CLI, not NX-OS, but it is similar enough to get the idea.)

■ Still on the sim question, make sure that you look at the scroll areas at the top, at the side, and in the terminal emulator window.

■ Still on the sim question, make sure that you can toggle between the topology window and the terminal emulator window by clicking **Show Topology** and **Hide Topology**.

■ On the testlet question, answer one multichoice question, move to the second and answer it, and then move back to the first question, confirming that inside a testlet you can move around between questions.

■ Again on the testlet question, click the **Next** button to see the pop-up window that Cisco uses as a prompt to ask whether you want to move on. Testlets might actually allow you to give too few answers and still move on. After you click to move past the testlet, you cannot go back to change your answer for any of these questions.

Think About Your Time Budget Versus Numbers of Questions

On exam day, you need to keep an eye on your speed. Going too slowly hurts you because you might not have time to answer all the questions. Going too fast can hurt as well if your fast speed is because you are rushing and not taking the time to fully understand the questions. So, you need to be able to somehow know whether you are moving quickly enough to answer all the questions, while not rushing.

The exam user interface shows some useful time information, namely a countdown timer and question counter. The question counter shows a question number for the question you are answering, and it shows the total number of questions on your exam.

Unfortunately, treating each question as equal does not give you an accurate time estimate. For example, if your exam allows 90 minutes, and your exam has 45 questions, you would have 2 minutes per question. After answering 20 questions, if you had taken 40 minutes, you would be right on time. However, several factors make that kind of estimate difficult.

First, Cisco does not tell us beforehand the exact number of questions for each exam. For example, Cisco.com (at the time of this writing) listed DCICN as a 90-minute exam with 65 to 75 questions. So, you only know a range of questions. But you do not know how many questions are on your exam until it begins, when you go through the screens that lead up to the point where you click **Start Exam**.

Next, some questions (call them *time burners*) clearly take a lot more time to answer:

Normal-time questions: Multichoice and drag-and-drop, approximately 1 minute each

Time burners: Sims, simlets, and testlets, approximately 6 to 8 minutes each

Finally, the exam software counts each testlet and simlet question as one question in the question counter. For example, if a testlet question has four embedded multiple-choice questions, in the exam software's question counter that counts as one question.

NOTE   While Cisco does not tell us why you might get 65 questions and someone else taking the same exam might get 75 questions, it seems reasonable to think that the person with 65 questions might have a few more of the time burners, making the two exams equivalent.

You need a plan for how you will check your time, a plan that does not distract you from the exam. It might be worth taking a bit of a guess, to keep things simple, like this:

60 questions, 90 minutes, is exactly 1:30 per question. Then just guess a little based on how many time-burner questions you have seen so far.

No matter how you plan to check your time, think about it before exam day. You can even use the method listed under the next heading.

A Suggested Time-Check Method

You can use the following math to do your time check in a way that weights the time based on those time-burner questions. You do not have to use this method. But this math uses only addition of whole numbers, to keep it simple. It gives you a pretty close time estimate, in my opinion.

The concept is simple. Just do a simple calculation that estimates the time you should have used so far. Basically, this process gives you 1 minute for normal questions, and 7 minutes per time burner. Here's the math:

Number of Questions Answered So Far + 7 Per Time Burner

Then, you check the timer to figure out how much time you have spent:

- **You have used exactly that much time, or a little more:** Your timing is perfect.
- **You have used less time:** You are ahead of schedule.
- **You have used noticeably more time:** You are behind schedule.

For example, if you have already finished 17 questions, 2 of which were time burners, your time estimate is 17 + 7 + 7 = 31 minutes. If your actual time is also 31 minutes, or maybe 32 or 33 minutes, you are right on schedule. If you have spent less than 31 minutes, you are ahead of schedule.

So, the math is pretty easy: Questions answered, plus 7 per time burner, is the guesstimate of how long you should have taken so far if you are right on time.

NOTE   This math is an estimate, with no guarantees that the math will be an accurate predictor on every exam.

23

Miscellaneous Pre-Exam Suggestions

Here are just a few more suggestions for things to think about before exam day arrives:

- Get some earplugs. Testing centers often have some, but if you do not want to chance it, come prepared. The testing center is usually a room inside the space of a company that does something else as well, oftentimes a training center. So, there are people talking in nearby rooms and others office noises. Earplugs can help. (Headphones, as electronic devices, are not allowed.)

- Some people like to spend the first minute of the exam writing down some notes for reference. For example, maybe you want to write down the table of magic numbers for finding IPv4 subnet IDs. If you plan to do that, practice making those notes. Before each practice exam, transcribe those lists, just like you expect to do at the real exam.

- Plan your travel to the testing center with enough time so that you will not be rushing to make it just in time.

- If you tend to be nervous before exams, practice your favorite relaxation techniques for a few minutes before each practice exam, just to be ready to use them.

Exam-Day Advice

We hope the exam goes well for you. Certainly, the better prepared you are, the better chances you have on the exam. These small tips can help you do your best on exam day:

- Rest the night before the exam, rather than staying up late to study. Clarity of thought is more important than one extra fact, especially because the exam requires so much analysis and thinking rather than just remembering facts.

- If you did not bring earplugs, ask the testing center for some, even if you cannot imagine you would use them. You never know whether it might help.

- You can bring personal effects into the building and testing company's space, but not into the actual room in which you take the exam. So, take as little extra stuff with you as possible. If you have a safe place to leave briefcases, purses, electronics, and so on, leave them there. However, the testing center should have a place to store your things as well. Simply put, the less you bring, the less you have to worry about storing. (For example, I have even been asked to remove my analog wristwatch on more than one occasion.)

- The exam center will give you a laminated sheet and pen, as a place to take notes. (Test center personnel usually do not let you bring paper and pen into the room, even if supplied by the testing center.)

- Leave for the testing center with extra time so that you do not have to rush.

- Plan on finding a restroom before going into the testing center. If you cannot find one, you can use one in the testing center, of course, and test personnel will direct you and give you time before your exam starts.

- Do not drink a 64-ounce drink on the trip to the testing center. After the exam starts, the exam timer will not stop while you go to the restroom.

■ On exam day, use any relaxation techniques that you have practiced to help get your mind focused while you wait for the exam.

Exam Review

This exam review completes the Study Plan materials as suggested by this book. At this point, you have read the other chapters of the book, and you have done the chapter review Exam Preparation Tasks and Part Review tasks. Now you need to do the final study and review activities before taking the exam, as detailed in this section.

This section suggests some new activities and repeating some old ones. However, whether new or old, the activities all focus on filling in your knowledge gaps, finishing off your skills, and completing the study process. While repeating some tasks you did at chapter review and part review can help, you need to be ready to take an exam, so the exam review asks you to spend a lot of time answering exam questions.

The exam review walks you through suggestions for several types of tasks and gives you some tracking tables for each activity. The main categories are as follows:

■ Practicing for speed

■ Taking practice exams

■ Finding what you do not know well yet (knowledge gaps)

■ Configuring and verifying functions from the command-line interface (CLI)

■ Repeating the chapter and Part Review tasks

Practice Subnetting and Other Math-Related Skills

Like it or not, some of the questions on the DCICN exam require you to do some math. To pass, you have to be good at the math. You also need to know when to use each process.

The Cisco exams also have a timer. Some of the math crops up often enough so that if you go slow with the math, or if you have to write down all the details of how you compute the answers, you might well run out of time to answer all the questions. (The two biggest reasons we hear as to why people do not finish on time are: slow speed with the math-related work and slow speed when doing simulator questions using the CLI.)

However, look at these math processes and the time crunch as a positive instead of a negative. Right now, before the exam, you know about the challenge. You know that if you keep practicing subnetting and other math, you will keep getting faster and better. As exam day approaches, if you have spare minutes, try more practice with anything to do with subnetting in particular. Look at it as a way to prepare now so that you do not have to worry about time pressure so much on the day of the exam.

Table 23-1 lists the topics in this chapter that both require math and require speed. Table 23-2 lists items for which the math or process is important but speed is probably less important. By this point in your study, you should already be confident at finding the right answer to these kinds of problems. Now is the time to finish off your skills at getting the right answers, plus getting faster so that you reduce your time pressure on the exams.

23

> **NOTE**   The time goals in the table are goals chosen by the author to give you an idea of a good time. If you happen to be a little slower on a few tasks, that does not mean you cannot do well on the test. But if you take several times as much time for almost every task, know that the math-related work can cause you some time problems.

Table 23-1   DCICN Math-Related Activities That Benefit from Speed Practice

Chapter	Activity	Book's Excellent Speed Goal (Seconds)	Self-Check: Date/Time	Self-Check: Date/Time
13	From a unicast IPv4 address, find key facts about its classful network.	10		
14	From one mask in any format, convert to the other two mask formats.	10		
14	Given an IPv4 address and mask, find the number of network, subnet, and host bits, plus the number of hosts/subnet and number of subnets.	15		
15	Given an IPv4 address and mask, find the resident subnet, subnet broadcast address, and range of usable addresses.	30		

Table 23-2   DCICN Math-Related Activities That Can Be Less Time Sensitive

Chapter	Activity	Self-Check: Date/Time	Self-Check: Date/Time
17	Find the best abbreviation for one IPv6 address.		
17	Find the IPv6 address of one router interface when using EUI-64.		
22	Build an ACL command to match a subnet's addresses.		
22	List the addresses matched by one existing ACL command.		

To practice the math listed in both Tables 23-1 and 23-2, look at the end of the respective chapters for some suggestions. For example, for many subnetting problems, you can make up your own problems and check your work with any subnet calculator. In addition, all these chapters have matching DVD appendixes with additional practice. Finally, the author's blogs include extra practice problems, created just to give you another source from which to practice.

Take Practice Exams

One day soon, you need to pass a real Cisco exam at a Vue testing center. So, it's time to practice the real event as much as possible.

A practice exam using the Pearson IT Certification Practice Test (PCPT) exam software lets you experience many of the same issues as when taking a real Cisco exam. The software gives you a number of questions, with a countdown timer shown in the window. After you answer a question, you cannot go back to it. (Yes, that's true on Cisco exams.) If you run out of time, the questions you did not answer count as incorrect.

The process of taking the timed practice exams helps you prepare in three key ways:

- To practice the exam event itself, including time pressure, the need to read carefully, and the need to concentrate for long periods

- To build your analysis and critical thinking skills when examining the network scenario built in to many questions

- To discover the gaps in your networking knowledge so that you can study those topics before the real exam

As much as possible, treat the practice exam events as if you were taking the real Cisco exam at a Vue testing center. The following list gives some advice on how to make your practice exam more meaningful, rather than as just one more thing to do before exam day rolls around:

- Set aside 2 hours for taking the 90-minute timed practice exam.

- Make a list of what you expect to do for the 10 minutes before the real exam event. Then visualize yourself doing those things. Before taking each practice exam, practice those final 10 minutes before your exam timer starts. (The earlier section "Exam-Day Advice" lists some suggestions about what to do in those last 10 minutes.)

- You cannot bring anything with you into the Vue exam room, so remove all notes and help materials from your work area before taking a practice exam. You can use blank paper, a pen, and your brain only. Do not use calculators, notes, web browsers, or any other app on your computer.

- Real life can get in the way, but if at all possible, ask anyone around you to leave you alone for the time you will practice. If you must do your practice exam in a distracting environment, wear headphones or earplugs to reduce distractions.

- Do not guess, hoping to improve your score. Answer only when you have confidence in the answer. Then, if you get the question wrong, you can go back and think more about the question in a later study session.

Practicing Taking the DCICN Exam

To take a DCICN practice exam, you need to select one or both of the DCICN exams from PCPT. If you followed the study plan in this book, you will not have seen any of the questions in these two exam databases before now. After you select one of these two exams, you simply need to choose the **Practice Exam** option in the upper right and start the exam.

You should plan to take between one and three DCICN practice exams with these exam databases. Even people who are already well prepared should do at least one practice exam, just to experience the time pressure and the need for prolonged concentration. For those who want more practice exams, these two exam databases have enough questions for more than two exams. As a result, if you took a fourth practice exam with these exam databases, you will have seen almost all the questions before, making the practice exam a little too easy. If you are interested in purchasing more practice exams, check out the *DCICN 640-911 Official Cert Guide Premium Edition eBook and Practice Test* product at www.ciscopress.com/title/9780133787849 and be sure to use the 70 percent off coupon included in the DVD sleeve of this book.

Table 23-3 gives you a checklist to record your different practice exam events. Note that recording both the date and the score is helpful for some other work you will do, so note both. Also, in the Time Notes section, if you finish on time, note how much extra time you had. If you run out of time, note how many questions you did not have time to answer.

Table 23-3 DCICN Practice Exam Checklist

Exam	Date	Score	Time Notes
DCICN			
DCICN			
DCICN			
DCICN			

Advice on How to Answer Exam Questions

Open a web browser. Yes, take a break and open a web browser on any device. Do a quick search on a fun topic. Then, before you click a link, get ready to think where your eyes go for the first 5 to 10 seconds after you click the link. Now, click a link and look at the page. Where did your eyes go?

Interestingly, web browsers, and the content on those web pages, have trained us all to scan. Web page designers actually design content with the expectation that people will scan with different patterns. Regardless of the pattern, when reading a web page, almost no one reads sequentially, and no one reads entire sentences. They scan for the interesting graphics and the big words, and then scan the space around those noticeable items.

Other parts of our electronic culture have also changed how the average person reads. For example, many of you grew up using texting and social media, sifting through hundreds or thousands of messages, but each message barely fills an entire sentence. (In fact, that previous sentence would not fit in a tweet, being longer than 140 characters.)

Those everyday habits have changed how we all read and think in front of a screen. Unfortunately, those same habits often hurt our scores when taking computer-based exams.

If you scan exam questions like you read web pages, texts, and tweets, you will probably make some mistakes because you missed a key fact in the question, answer, or exhibits. It helps to start at the beginning and read all the words—a process that is amazingly unnatural for many people today.

> **NOTE**   I have talked to many college professors, in multiple disciplines, and Cisco Networking Academy instructors, and they consistently tell me that the number-one test-taking issue today is that people do not read the question well enough to understand the details.

For when you are taking the practice exams, and answering individual questions, let me make two suggestions. First, before the practice exam, think about your own personal strategy for how you will read a question. Make your approach to multiple-choice questions in particular be a conscious decision on your part. Second, if you want some suggestions on how to read an exam question, use the following strategy:

Step 1.   Read the question itself thoroughly from start to finish.

Step 2.   Scan any exhibit (usually command output) or figure.

Step 3.   Scan the answers to look for the types of information. (Numeric? Terms? Single words? Phrases?)

Step 4.   Reread the question thoroughly from start to finish to make sure that you understand it.

Step 5.   Read each answer thoroughly while referring to the figure/exhibit as needed. After reading each answer, before reading the next answer

  A. If correct, select as correct.

  B. If for sure it is incorrect, mentally rule it out.

  C. If unsure, mentally note it as a possible correct answer.

> **NOTE**   Cisco exams will tell you the number of correct answers. The exam software also helps you finish the question with the right number of answers noted. For example, the software prevents you from selecting too many answers. Also, if you try to move on to the next question but have too few answers noted, the exam software asks if you truly want to move on.

Use the practice exams as a place to practice your approach to reading. Every time you click to the next question, try to read the question following your approach. If you are feeling time pressure, that is the perfect time to keep practicing your approach, to reduce and eliminate questions you miss because of scanning the question instead of reading thoroughly.

Taking Other Practice Exams

Many people add other practice exams and questions other than the questions that come with this book. Frankly, using other practice exams in addition to the questions that come with this book can be a good idea, for many reasons. The other exam questions can use different terms in different ways, emphasize different topics, and show different scenarios that make you rethink some topics.

No matter where you get additional exam questions, if you use the exam questions for a timed practice exam, it helps to take a few notes about the results. Table 23-4 gives you a place to take those notes. Also, take a guess at the percent of questions you have seen before taking the exam, and note whether you think the questions are less, more, or the same challenge level as the questions that come with this book. And as usual, note whether you ran out of time or had extra time left over at the end.

Table 23-4   Checklist for Practice Exams from Other Sources

Exam Source	Other Exam Notes	% Questions Repeated (Estimate)	Challenging?	Date	Score	Time Notes

Note that the publisher does sell products that include additional test questions. The *DCICN 640-911 Official Cert Guide Premium Edition eBook and Practice Test* product is basically the publisher's eBook version of this book. It includes a soft copy of the book, in formats you can read on your computer or on the most common book readers and tablets. The product includes all the content you would normally get with the DVD that comes with the print book, including all the question databases mentioned in this chapter. This product also includes two more DCICN exam databases for extra exams.

NOTE   In addition to getting the extra questions, the Premium editions have links to every test question, including those in the print book, to the specific section of the book for further reference. This is a great learning tool if you need more detail than what you find in the question explanations. You can purchase the eBooks and additional practice exams at 70 percent off the list price using the coupon on the back of the activation code card in the DVD sleeve, making the Premium editions the best and most cost-efficient way to get more practice questions.

Find Knowledge Gaps Through Question Review

You just took a number of practice exams. You probably learned a lot, gained some exam-taking skills, and improved your networking knowledge and skills. But if you go back and look at all the questions you missed, you might be able to find a few small gaps in your knowledge.

One of the hardest things to find when doing your final exam preparation is to discover gaps in your knowledge and skills. In other words, what topics and skills do you need to know that you do not know? Or what topics do you think you know, but you misunderstand about some important fact? Finding gaps in your knowledge at this late stage requires more than just your gut feel about your strengths and weaknesses.

This next task uses a feature of PCPT to help you find those gaps. The PCPT software tracks each practice exam you take, remembering your answer for every question and whether you got it wrong. You can view the results and move back and forth between seeing the question and seeing the results page. To find gaps in your knowledge, follow these steps:

Step 1. Pick and review one of your practice exams.

Step 2. Review each incorrect question until you are happy that you understand the question.

Step 3. When finished with your review for a question, mark the question.

Step 4. Review all incorrect questions from your exam until all are marked.

Step 5. Move on to the next practice exam.

Figure 23-1 shows a sample Question Review page, in which all the questions were answered incorrectly. The results list a Correct column, with no check mark meaning that the answer was incorrect.

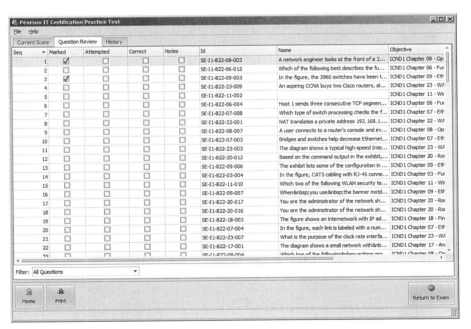

Figure 23-1 *PCPT Grading Results Page*

To perform the process of reviewing questions and marking them as complete, you can move between this Question Review page and the individual questions. Just double-click a question to move back to that question. From the question, you can click **Grade Exam** to move back to the grading results and to the Question Review page shown in Figure 23-1. The question window also shows the place to mark the question, in the upper left, as shown in Figure 23-2.

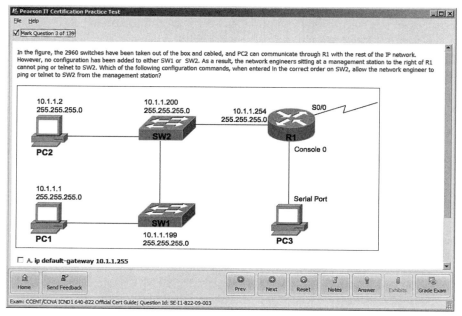

Figure 23-2   *Reviewing a Question, with Mark Feature in Upper Left*

If you want to come back later to look through the questions you missed from an earlier exam, start at the PCPT home screen. From there, instead of clicking the **Start** button to start a new exam, click the **View Grade History** button to see your earlier exam attempts and work through any missed questions.

Track your progress through your gap review in Table 23-5. PCPT lists your previous practice exams by date and score, so it helps to note those values in the table for comparison to the PCPT menu.

Table 23-5   Tracking Checklist for Gap Review of Practice Exams

DCICN Exam	Original Practice Exam Date	Original Exam Score	Date Gap Review Was Completed

Practice Hands-On CLI Skills

To do well on sim and simlet questions, you need to be comfortable with many Cisco NX-OS commands and how to use them from the CLI. As described in the Introduction to this book, sim questions require you to decide what configuration commands need to be configured to fix a problem or to complete a working configuration. Simlet questions require you to answer multichoice questions by first using the CLI to issue **show** commands to look at the status of routers and switches in a small network.

Appendix D, "Nexus Lab Guide," discusses some options for getting some hands-on skills with NX-OS.

Review Mind Maps from Part Review

During Part Review, you created different mind maps with both configuration and verification commands. To remember the specific mind maps, flip back to each part's "Part Review" section.

Other Study Tasks

If you get to this point, and still feel the need to prepare some more, this last topic gives you three suggestions.

First, the chapter review "Exam Preparation Tasks" and "Part Review" sections give you some useful study tasks.

Second, take more exam questions from other sources. You can always get more questions in the Cisco Press Premium Edition eBook and Practice Test products, which include an eBook copy of this book plus additional questions in additional PCPT exam banks. However, you can search the Internet for questions from many sources, and review those questions as well.

NOTE   Some vendors claim to sell practice exams that contain the literal exam questions from the exam. These exams, called brain dumps, are against the Cisco testing policies. Cisco strongly discourages using any such tools for study.

23

Finally, join in the discussions on the Cisco Learning Network. Try to answer questions asked by other learners; the process of answering makes you think much harder about the topic. When someone posts an answer with which you disagree, think about why and talk about it online. This is a great way to both learn more and build confidence.

Final Thoughts

You have studied quite a bit, worked hard, and sacrificed time and money to be ready for the exam. We hope your exam goes well, that you pass, and that you pass because you really know your stuff and will do well in your IT and networking career.

We encourage you to celebrate when you pass, and ask advice if you do not. The Cisco Learning Network is a great place to make posts to celebrate and to ask advice for the next time around. We (both authors) would love to hear about your progress through Twitter (@wendellodom and @chadh0517). We wish you well, and congratulations for working through the entire book!

Part VII

Appendices

Appendix A: Answers to the "Do I Know This Already?" Quizzes

Appendix B: DCICN Exam Updates

Appendix C: Numeric Reference Tables

Appendix D: Nexus Lab Guide

APPENDIX A

Answers to the "Do I Know This Already?" Quizzes

Chapter 1

1. D and F. Of the remaining answers, Ethernet defines both physical and data link protocols, PPP is a data link protocol, IP is a network layer protocol, and SMTP and HTTP are application layer protocols.

2. A and G. Of the remaining answers, IP is a network layer protocol, TCP and UDP are transport layer protocols, and SMTP and HTTP are application layer protocols.

3. B. Adjacent-layer interaction occurs on one computer, with two adjacent layers in the model. The higher layer requests services from the next lower layer, and the lower layer provides the services to the next higher layer.

4. B. Same-layer interaction occurs on multiple computers. The functions defined by that layer typically need to be accomplished by multiple computers—for example, the sender setting a sequence number for a segment, and the receiver acknowledging receipt of that segment. A single layer defines that process, but the implementation of that layer on multiple devices is required to accomplish the function.

5. A. Encapsulation is defined as the process of adding a header in front of data supplied by a higher layer (and possibly adding a trailer as well).

6. D. By convention, the term *frame* refers to the part of a network message that includes the data link header and trailer, with encapsulated data. The term packet omits the data link header and trailer, leaving the network layer header with its encapsulated data. The term segment omits the network layer header, leaving the transport layer header and its encapsulated data.

7. C. The network layer concerns itself with delivery of data over the complete end-to-end path. That requires a way to identify each device, using addresses, and the addresses must be logical addresses that are therefore not tied to the physical details of the network.

8. A. The OSI physical layer includes all standards that specify the shape of connectors, wiring in cabling, electrical details, and encoding that the electrical signals use to encode bits over a cable.

9. C and E. The layer names, from top to bottom, are application, presentation, session, transport, network, data link, and physical.

Chapter 2

1. **A.** The IEEE defines Ethernet LAN standards, with standard names that begin with 802.3, all of which happen to use cabling. The IEEE also defines wireless LAN standards, with standard names that begin with 802.11, which are separate standards from Ethernet.

2. **C.** The number before the word "BASE" defines the speed, in megabits per second (Mbps). 1000 Mbps equals 1 gigabit per second (1 Gbps). The "T" in the suffix implies twisted-pair or UTP cabling, so 1000BASE-T is the UTP-based Gigabit Ethernet standard name.

3. **B.** Crossover cables cross the wire at one node's transmit pin pair to the different pins used as the receive pins on the other device. For 10- and 100-Mbps Ethernet, the specific crossover cable wiring connects the pair at pins 1 and 2 on each end of the cable to pins 3 and 6 on the other end of the cable, respectively.

4. **B, D, and E.** Routers, wireless access point Ethernet ports, and PC NICs all send using pins 1 and 2, whereas hubs and LAN switches transmit on pins 3 and 6. Straight-through cables connect devices that use opposite pin pairs for sending, because the cable does not need to cross the pairs.

5. **B.** NICs (and switch ports) use the carrier sense multiple access collision detect (CSMA/CD) algorithm to implement half-duplex logic. While CSMA/CD attempts to avoid collisions, it also notices when collisions do occur, with rules about how the Ethernet nodes should stop sending, wait, and try again later.

6. **C.** The 4-byte Ethernet FCS field, found in the Ethernet trailer, allows the receiving node to see what the sending node computed with a math formula that is a key part of the error-detection process. Note that Ethernet defines the process of detecting errors (error detection), but not error recovery.

7. **B, C, and E.** The preassigned universal MAC address, given to each Ethernet port when manufactured, breaks the address into two 3-byte halves. The first half is called the organizationally unique identifier (OUI), which the IEEE assigns to the company that builds the product as a unique hex number only to be used by that company.

8. **C and D.** Ethernet supports unicast addresses, which identify a single Ethernet node, and group addresses, which can be used to send one frame to multiple Ethernet nodes. The two types of group addresses are the broadcast address and multicast addresses.

Chapter 3

1. **B.** OSI Layer 1, the physical layer, defines how to physically transmit bits using some kind of physical medium, like a cable or radio waves. OSI Layer 2, the data link layer, defines protocols that control and manage the transmission, including the definition of data link frames, which include addresses, and fields to help perform error detection.

2. **B.** The four-wire circuit cable supplied by the telco connects to the device acting as the CSU/DSU. That can be an external CSU/DSU or a CSU/DSU integrated into a router serial interface card. LAN switches do not have serial interfaces, and router serial interfaces do not have transceivers.

3. C. Leased lines can run at various preset speeds. These include multiples of 64 kbps, up through 24 times 64 kbps. The speeds can also be multiples of T1 speed (1.544 Mbps), up to 28 times that speed.

4. B. The standard HDLC header does not include a Type field, which identifies the type of packet encapsulated inside the HDLC frame.

5. B and D. The physical installation uses a model in which each router uses a physical Ethernet link to connect to some SP device in an SP facility called a point of presence (POP). The Ethernet link does not span from each customer device to the other. From a data link perspective, both routers use the same Ethernet standard header and trailer used on LANs; HDLC does not matter on these Ethernet WAN links.

6. B and C. Leased lines transmit data at the same speed in both directions, making it a symmetric service. DSL and cable Internet offer asymmetric speeds, with a faster downstream speed. BGP is a routing protocol and is not an Internet access technology.

7. C. With DSL, the requirements on the phone's wiring are unchanged. The phone can connect to any working telephone jack, as if the DSL modem and router did not exist.

Chapter 4

1. A and C. The network layer defines logical addressing, in contrast to physical addressing. The logical address structure allows easy grouping of addresses, which makes routing more efficient. Path selection refers to the process of choosing the best routes to use in the network. Physical addressing and arbitration typically are data link layer functions, and error recovery typically is a transport layer function.

2. C and E. Because PC1 and PC2 are separated by routers, the PCs must rely on the routers to use routing logic. With routing, the router discards the data link header of an incoming frame, making a decision of where to forward the packet de-encapsulated from the frame. As a result, the largest entity that passes from PC1 to PC2 is the IPv4 packet (or IPv6 packet), which goes by the more general name of L3 PDU.

3. B. 224.1.1.1 is a Class D address. 223.223.223.255 is the network broadcast address for Class C network 223.223.223.0, so it cannot be assigned to a host.

4. D. The first octet of Class A addresses ranges from 1 to 126, inclusive; Class B, 128 to 191, inclusive; and Class C, 192 to 223 inclusive. 127 is technically in the Class A range, but it is a reserved address used as a loopback.

5. D and F. Without any subnetting in use, all addresses in the same network as 10.1.1.1—all addresses in Class A network 10.0.0.0—must be on the same LAN. Addresses separated from that network by some router cannot be in network 10.0.0.0. So, the two correct answers are the only two answers that list a valid unicast IP address that is not in network 10.0.0.0.

6. A. PC1 will send an Ethernet frame to Router1, with PC1's MAC address as the source address and Router1's MAC address as the destination address. Router1 will remove the encapsulated IP packet from that Ethernet frame, discarding the frame header and trailer. Router1 will forward the IP packet by first encapsulating it inside an HDLC

A

frame, but Router1 will not encapsulate the Ethernet frame in the HDLC frame, but rather the IP packet. Router2 will deencapsulate the IP packet from the HDLC frame and forward it onto the Ethernet LAN, adding a new Ethernet header and trailer, but this header will differ. It will list Router2's MAC address as the source address and PC2's MAC address as the destination address.

7. C. Routers compare the packet's destination IP address to the router's IP routing table, making a match and using the forwarding instructions in the matched route to forward the IP packet.

8. B and C. IPv4 hosts generally use basic two-branch logic. To send an IP packet to another host on the same IP network or subnet that is on the same LAN, the sender sends the IP packet directly to that host. Otherwise, the sender sends the packet to its default router (also called the default gateway).

9. A and C. Routers do all the actions listed in all four answers. However, the routing protocol does the functions in the two listed answers. Independent of the routing protocol, a router learns routes for IP subnets and IP networks directly connected to its interfaces. Routers also forward (route) IP packets, but that process is called IP routing, or IP forwarding, and is an independent process as compared with the work of a routing protocol.

10. C. Address Resolution Protocol (ARP) does allow PC1 to learn information, but the information is not stored on a server. The **ping** command does let the user at PC1 learn whether packets can flow in the network, but it again does not use a server. With the Domain Name System (DNS), PC1 acts as a DNS client, relying on a DNS server to respond with information about the IP addresses that match a given host name.

Chapter 5

1. D. Three of the answers define functions of TCP: error recovery, flow control, and segmentation. The correct answer defines a function not done by TCP nor UDP, but instead done by application layer protocols.

2. D and E. Many headers include a field that identifies the next header that follows inside a message. Ethernet uses the Ethernet Type field, and the IP header uses the Protocol field. The TCP and UDP headers identify the application that should receive the data that follows the TCP or UDP header by using the port number field in the TCP and UDP headers, respectively.

3. A, B, C, and F. IP, not TCP, defines routing. Many other protocols define encryption, but TCP does not. The correct answers simply list various TCP features.

4. C. TCP, not UDP, performs windowing, error recovery, and ordered data transfer. Neither performs routing or encryption.

5. C and F. The terms *packet* and *L3PDU* refer to the header plus data encapsulated by Layer 3. *Frame* and *L2PDU* refer to the header (and trailer), plus the data encapsulated by Layer 2. Segment and L$PDU refer to header and data encapsulated by the transport layer protocol.

6. B. Note that the host name is all the text between the // and the /. The text before the // identifies the application layer protocol, and the text after the / represents the name of the web page.

7. A and D. VoIP flows need better delay, jitter, and loss, with better meaning less delay, jitter, and loss, as compared with all data applications. VoIP typically requires less bandwidth than data applications.

Chapter 6

1. C and D. 10BASE-5 and 10BASE-2 both used cabling that ran close to each device, much like a bus drives past each bus stop, so that these early Ethernet technologies were considered to be a physical bus topology. These technologies also used a single electrical circuit, so that a frame sent by a device passed to each other device on the bus, again mimicking a bus route, so that the network industry also referred to the logic as a logical bus topology.

2. B and D. Ethernet hubs act as Ethernet repeaters, which use Layer 1 logic. A hub immediately regenerates and repeats a new signal out all other ports, without waiting, and without using CSMA/CD. Both a hub and a bridge do not forward the data out the same port in which it was received. However, a bridge, and not a hub, separates the LAN into multiple collision domains, and uses CSMA/CD logic.

3. A. A switch compares the destination address to the MAC address table. If a matching entry is found, the switch knows out which interface to forward the frame. If no matching entry is found, the switch floods the frame.

4. B. Switches need to learn the location of each MAC address used in the LAN relative to that local switch. When a switch sends a frame, the source MAC identifies the sender. The interface in which the frame arrives identifies the local switch interface closest to that node in the LAN topology.

5. A and B. When the frame sent by PC3 arrives at the switch, the switch has learned a MAC address table entry for only 1111.1111.1111, PC1's MAC address. PC3's frame, addressed to 2222.2222.2222, is flooded, which means it is forwarded out all interfaces except for the interface on which the frame arrived.

6. A. A collision domain contains all devices whose frames could collide with frames sent by all the other devices in the domain. Bridges, switches, and routers separate or segment a LAN into multiple collision domains, whereas hubs and repeaters do not.

7. A, B, and C. A broadcast domain contains all devices whose sent broadcast frames should be delivered to all the other devices in the domain. Hubs, repeaters, bridges, and switches do not separate or segment a LAN into multiple broadcast domains, whereas routers do.

8. B and D. The IEEE Ethernet standards support 100-meter links when using UTP cabling. Most standards that use fiber-optic cabling, like the standards in the two correct answers, use lengths longer than 100 meters.

A

9. D. Full-duplex can be used on any Ethernet link between a switch and a PC. The IEEE autonegotiation process states that the two endpoints on a link should choose the best speed and the best duplex that both support, with full-duplex being better than half-duplex.

Chapter 7

1. D. NX-OS enables you to execute EXEC command from any level of the command structure as long as your role has the privileges to do this.

2. B. Network-admin is the only role listed that enables you to reload the switch.

3. B. SSH encrypts all passwords and data exchanges; telnet does not.

4. A. Volatile random-access memory (VRAM) located on a supervisor module is used for temporary or pending changes.

5. F. Nonvolatile random-access memory (NVRAM) located on a supervisor module is used for storing the startup-configuration file.

6. A and B. In configuration mode, you are one mode above EXEC mode. Using **exit** will bring you down one mode level, and **end** will always return you to EXEC mode.

Chapter 8

1. C. The command **username Fred password Cisco123 role network-operator** is correct because the default user role of network-operator has read-only access to the switch.

2. D. None of these answers are correct because the username admin password mypassword role network-admin works for both Telnet and SSH.

3. C. The banner text that is displayed starts and stops with a delimiter character; in this case, we are using # as this character, so the text to be displayed will be between the # symbols.

4. A. On a Nexus switch is correct. The management interface mgmt0 is in the management VRF by default.

5. E. Interface configuration mode is correct because to configure interface setting you must be in the interface configuration mode: (config-if)#.

Chapter 9

1. B. A VLAN is a set of devices in the same Layer 2 broadcast domain. A subnet often includes the exact same set of devices, but it is a Layer 3 concept. A collision domain refers to a set of Ethernet devices, but with different rules than VLAN rules for determining which devices are in the same collision domain.

2. D. Although a subnet and a VLAN are not equivalent concepts, the devices in one VLAN are typically in the same IP subnet and vice versa.

3.   B. 802.1Q defines a 4-byte header, inserted after the original frame's destination and source MAC address fields. The insertion of this header does not change the original frame's source or destination address. The header itself holds a 12-bit VLAN ID field, which identifies the VLAN associated with the frame.

4.   A. 802.1Q defines the native VLAN as one designated VLAN on a trunk for which the devices choose to not add an 802.1Q header for frames in that VLAN. The switches can set the native VLAN to any VLAN ID, but the switches should agree. The default native VLAN is VLAN 1. Note that only one such native VLAN is allowed on any one trunk; otherwise, that VLAN associated with untagged frames could not be discerned by the receiving switch.

5.   B and C. Each VLAN, a Layer 2 concept, is its own broadcast domain. A Layer 2 switch purposefully keeps broadcast domains separate, purposefully choosing to not forward traffic that enters in a port in one broadcast domain (VLAN) into a second broadcast domain (VLAN). Bridges use the same forwarding logic as a Layer 2 switch. Devices that perform IP routing, like routers and switches configured as Layer 3 switches, can route IP packets between the devices in different VLANs.

6.   B and C. Only VTP server and client modes allow a switch to learn new information with VTP. Transparent and off modes give switches a couple of ways to effectively not use VTP; switches using both these modes will not update their configuration based on receiving a VTP message.

7.   A and D. Of the listed answers, VTP distributes only the VLAN ID and VLAN name. VTP does not distribute configuration that ties to specific ports on any one switch.

Chapter 10

1.   B and C. **switchport access vlan 10** enables Ethernet 1/1 to participate in VLAN 10 and the interface must be in **no shutdown** mode for the interface to come up.

2.   A and B. Issuing the **vlan 22** command, followed by the **name Evans-VLAN** command, will configure VLAN 22, which will be shown in the output of the **show vlan brief** command as well as the **show running-config** command.

3.   B and C. **show interface switchport** and **show interface trunk** are valid commands for identifying switch interfaces as being trunking interfaces. **show interface** does not show whether the interface is trunking, and **show trunks** is not a valid command.

4.   A and C. **switchport mode trunk** and **no shutdown** are the valid responses here because switchport mode trunk or dot1q is the only supported protocol on Nexus for trunking, and the interface must be **no shutdown** for the interface to come up.

5.   A and D. **feature vtp** and **vtp mode client** are the correct answers because the **feature vtp** command will enable VTP, and VTP mode client will set the mode of the VTP service to client.

A

Chapter 11

1. A and B. Listening and learning are transitory port states, used only when moving from the blocking to the forwarding state. Discarding is not an 802.1D STP port state.

2. C and D. Listening and learning are transitory port states, used only when moving from the blocking to the forwarding state. Discarding is not an 802.1D STP port state. Forwarding and blocking are stable states.

3. C. The smallest numeric bridge ID wins the election.

4. B. Nonroot switches forward Hellos received from the root; the root sends these Hellos based on the root's configured Hello timer.

5. D. The PortFast feature enables STP to move a port from blocking to forwarding, without going through the interim listening and learning states. STP allows this exception when the link is known to have no switch on the other end of the link, removing the risk of a switching loop. BPDU Guard is a common feature to use at the same time as PortFast, because it watches for incoming bridge protocol data units (BPDU), which should not happen on an access port, and prevents the loops from a rogue switch by disabling the port.

6. D. RSTP has several improvements over STP for faster convergence, including waiting on three times the hello timer when a wait is necessary. However, when the root port actually fails, both 802.1D and 802.1w can react without waiting (a fact that rules out two answers). Another RSTP optimization is that an alternate port (that is, a port that can be used as root port when the root port fails) can be used immediately and be placed into a forwarding state, without first spending MaxAge time in learning state.

7. D. RSTP refers to potential root ports to use when the current root port fails, an alternate port. The backup port role is used when one switch connects two or more ports to the same collision domain (for example, when connecting to a hub). Blocking (802.1D) and discarding (802.1w) are names of port states, not port roles.

Chapter 12

1. B and C. To change a switch's bridge ID value you can use the **root primary** or **secondary** command or hard code this value with the **priority** command.

2. A. You can tell by looking at the priority and sys-id-ext output. The sys-id-ext is always the VLAN number, which in this case is 1.

3. A and D. Hard code a cost of 2, or using the default cost would also be 2 because it is a 10 Gbps interface.

4. D. To add interfaces to a PortChannel you must use the **channel-group** (*x*) command under the interfaces to add them to the PortChannel.

5. B. The switch will choose the interface with the lowest root cost as its root port.

6. A and D. Both commands will provide output that lists a nonroot switch's root cost.

Chapter 13

1. B and D. The general rule to determine whether two devices' interfaces should be in the same subnet is whether the two interfaces are separated from each other by a router. To provide a way for hosts in one VLAN to send data to hosts outside that VLAN, a local router must connect its LAN interface to the same VLAN as the hosts and have an address in the same subnet as the hosts. All the hosts in that same VLAN on the same switch would not be separated from each other by a router, so these hosts would also be in the same subnet. However, another PC, connected to the same switch but in a different VLAN, will require its packets to flow through a router to reach Host A, so Host A's IP address would need to be in a different subnet compared to this new host.

2. D. By definition, two address values in every IPv4 subnet cannot be used as host IPv4 addresses: the first (lowest) numeric value in the subnet for the subnet ID, and the last (highest) numeric value in the subnet for the subnet broadcast address.

3. B and C. At least 7 subnet bits are needed, because $2^6 = 64$, so 6 subnet bits could not number 100 different subnets. Seven subnet bits could, because $2^7 = 128 => 100$. Similarly, 6 host bits is not enough, because $2^6 - 2 = 62$, but 7 host bits is enough, because $2^7 - 2 = 126 => 100$.

   The number of network, subnet, and host bits must total 32 bits, making one of the answers incorrect. The answer with 8 network bits cannot be correct because the question states that a Class B network is used, so the number of network bits must always be 16. The two correct answers have 16 network bits (required because the question states the use of a Class B network), and at least 7 subnet and host bits each.

4. A and C. The private IPv4 networks, defined by RFC 1918, are Class A network 10.0.0.0, the 16 Class B networks from 172.16.0.0 to 172.31.0.0, and the 256 Class C networks that begin with 192.168.

5. A, D, and E. The private IPv4 networks, defined by RFC 1918, are Class A network 10.0.0.0, the 16 Class B networks from 172.16.0.0 to 172.31.0.0, and the 256 Class C networks that begin with 192.168. The three correct answers are from the public IP network range, and none are reserved values.

6. A and C. An unsubnetted Class A, B, or C network has two parts: the network and host parts.

7. B. An unsubnetted Class A, B, or C network has two parts: the network and host parts. To perform subnetting, the engineer creates a new subnet part by borrowing host bits, shrinking the number of host bits. The subnet part of the address structure exists only after the engineer chooses a nondefault mask. The network part remains a constant size.

8. C and D. Subnet ID (short for subnet identifier), subnet address, and subnet number are all synonyms and refer to the number that identifies the subnet. The actual value is a dotted-decimal number, so the term *subnet name* does not apply. The term *subnet broadcast*, a synonym for the subnet broadcast address, refers to the last (highest) numeric value in a subnet.

A

Chapter 14

1. B and C. Class A networks have a first octet in the range of 1–126, inclusive, and their network IDs have a 0 in the last three octets. 130.0.0.0 is actually a Class B network (first octet range 128–191, inclusive). All addresses that begin with 127 are reserved, so 127.0.0.0 is not a Class A network.

2. E. Class B networks all begin with values between 128 and 191, inclusive, in their first octets. The network ID has any value in the 128–191 range in the first octet, and any value from 0–255 inclusive in the second octet, with decimal 0s in the final two octets. Two of the answers show a 255 in the second octet, which is acceptable. Two of the answers show a 0 in the second octet, which is also acceptable.

3. B and D. The first octet (172) is in the range of values for Class B addresses (128–191). As a result, the network ID can be formed by copying the first two octets (172.16) and writing 0s for the last two octets (172.16.0.0). The default mask for all Class B networks is 255.255.0.0, and the number of host bits in all unsubnetted Class B networks is 16.

4. A and C. The first octet (192) is in the range of values for Class C addresses (192–223). As a result, the network ID can be formed by copying the first three octets (192.168.6) and writing 0 for the last octet (192.168.6.0). The default mask for all Class C networks is 255.255.255.0, and the number of host bits in all unsubnetted Class C networks is 8.

5. D. To find the network broadcast address, first determine the class, and then determine the number of host octets. At that point, convert the host octets to 255 to create the network broadcast address. In this case, 10.1.255.255 is in a Class A network, with the last three octets as host octets, for a network broadcast address of 10.255.255.255. For 192.168.255.1, it is a Class C address, with the last octet as the host part, for a network broadcast address of 192.168.255.255. Address 224.1.1.255 is a Class D address, so it is not in any unicast IP network, so the question does not apply. For 172.30.255.255, it is a Class B address, with the last two octets as host octets, so the network broadcast address is 172.30.255.255.

6. B. To find the network ID, first determine the class, and then determine the number of host octets. At that point, convert the host octets to 0 to create the network ID. In this case, 10.1.0.0 is in a Class A network, with the last three octets as host octets, for a network ID of 10.0.0.0. For 192.168.1.0, it is a Class C address, with the last octet as the host part, for a network ID of 192.168.1.0. Address 127.0.0.0 looks like a Class A network ID, but it begins with a reserved value (127), so it is not in any Class A, B, or C network. 172.20.0.1 is a Class B address, with the last two octets as host octets, so the network ID is 172.20.0.0.

Chapter 15

1. C. Thinking about the conversion one octet at a time, the first two octets each convert to 8 binary 1s. 254 converts to 8-bit binary 11111110, and decimal 0 converts to 8-bit binary 00000000. So, the total number of binary 1s (which defines the prefix length) is 8+8+7+0 = /23.

2. B. Thinking about the conversion one octet at a time, the first three octets each convert to 8 binary 1s. 240 converts to 8-bit binary 11110000, so the total number of binary 1s (which defines the prefix length) is 8+8+8+4 = /28.

3. C. /24 is the equivalent of the mask that in binary has 24 binary 1s. To convert that to DDN format, write down all the binary 1s (24 in this case), followed by binary 0s for the remainder of the 32-bit mask. Then take 8 bits at a time, and convert from binary to decimal (or memorize the nine possible DDN mask octet values and their binary equivalents). Using the /24 mask in this question, the binary mask is 11111111 11111111 11111111 00000000. Each of the first three octets is all binary 1s, so each converts to 255. The last octet, all binary 0s, converts to decimal 0, for a DDN mask of 255.255.255.0. See Appendix C, "Numeric Reference Tables," for a decimal/binary conversion table.

4. B. /30 is the equivalent of the mask that in binary has 30 binary 1s. To convert that to DDN format, write down all the binary 1s (30 in this case), followed by binary 0s for the remainder of the 32-bit mask. Then take 8 bits at a time, and convert from binary to decimal (or memorize the nine possible DDN mask octet values and their binary equivalents). Using the /30 mask in this question, the binary mask is 11111111 11111111 11111111 11111100. Each of the first three octets is all binary 1, so each converts to 255. The last octet, 11111100, converts to 252, for a DDN mask of 255.255.255.252. See Appendix C for a decimal/binary conversion table.

5. C. The size of the network part is always either 8, 16, or 24 bits, based on whether it is Class A, B, or C, respectively. As a Class A address, N=8. The mask 255.255.255.0, converted to prefix format, is /24. The number of subnet bits is the difference between the prefix length (24) and N, so S=16 in this case. The size of the host part is a number that, when added to the prefix length (24), gives you 32, so H=8 in this case.

6. A. The size of the network part is always either 8, 16, or 24 bits, based on whether it is Class A, B, or C, respectively. As a Class C address, N=24. The number of subnet bits is the difference between the prefix length (27) and N, so S=3 in this case. The size of the host part is a number that, when added to the prefix length (27), gives you 32, so H=5 in this case.

7. B and D. Classless addressing rules define a two-part IP address structure: the prefix and the host part. The host part is defined the same way as with classful IP addressing rules. The classless address rules' prefix length is the length of the combined network and subnet parts when using classful IP addressing concepts. Mathematically, the prefix length is equal to the number of binary 1s in the mask. In this case, with a mask of 255.255.255.0, the prefix length is 24 bits. The host length is the number of bits added to 24 to total 32, for 8 host bits.

8. D. Classless addressing rules define a two-part IP address structure: the prefix and the host part. This logic ignores Class A, B, and C rules, and can be applied to the 32-bit IPv4 addresses from any address class. By ignoring Class A, B, and C rules, classless addressing ignores any distinction as to the network part of an IPv4 address.

A

9. A and B. The masks in binary define a number of binary 1s, and the number of binary 1s defines the length of the prefix (network + subnet) part. With a Class B network, the network part is 16 bits. To support 100 subnets, the subnet part must be at least 7 bits long. Six subnet bits would supply only 2^6 = 64 subnets, while 7 subnet bits supply 2^7 = 128 subnets. The /24 answer supplies 8 subnet bits, and the 255.255.255.252 answer supplies 14 subnet bits.

Chapter 16

1. D. When using classful IP addressing concepts as described in Chapter 15, "Analyzing Subnet Masks," addresses have three parts: network, subnet, and host. For addresses in a single classful network, the network parts must be identical for the numbers to be in the same network. For addresses in the same subnet, both the network and subnet parts must have identical values. The host part differs when comparing different addresses in the same subnet.

2. B and D. In any subnet, the subnet ID is the smallest number in the range, the subnet broadcast address is the largest number, and the usable IP addresses sit between those. All numbers in a subnet have identical binary values in the prefix part (classless view) and network + subnet part (classful view). To be the lowest number, the subnet ID must have the lowest possible binary value (all 0s) in the host part. To be the largest number, the broadcast address must have the highest possible binary value (all binary 1s) in the host part. The usable addresses do not include the subnet ID and subnet broadcast address, so the addresses in the range of usable IP address never have a value of all 0s or 1s in their host parts.

3. C. The mask converts to 255.255.255.0. To find the subnet ID, for each octet of the mask that is 255, you can copy the IP address's corresponding values. For mask octets of decimal 0, you can record a 0 in that octet of the subnet ID. As such, copy the 10.7.99 and write a 0 for the fourth octet, for a subnet ID of 10.7.99.0.

4. C. First, the resident subnet (the subnet ID of the subnet in which the address resides) must be numerically smaller than the IP address, which rules out one of the answers. The mask converts to 255.255.255.252. As such, you can copy the first three octets of the IP address because of their value of 255. For the fourth octet, the subnet ID value must be a multiple of 4, because 256 – 252 (mask) = 4. Those multiples include 96 and 100, and the right choice is the multiple closest to the IP address value in that octet (97) without going over. So, the correct subnet ID is 192.168.44.96.

5. C. The resident subnet ID in this case is 172.31.77.192. You can find the subnet broadcast address based on the subnet ID and mask using several methods. Following the decimal process in the book, the mask converts to 255.255.255.224, making the interesting octet be octet 4, with magic number 256 – 224 = 32. For the three octets where the mask = 255, copy the subnet ID (172.31.77). For the interesting octet, take the subnet ID value (192), add magic (32), and subtract 1, for 223. That makes the subnet broadcast address be 172.31.77.223.

6. C. To answer this question, you need to find the range of addresses in the subnet, which typically then means you need to calculate the subnet ID and subnet broadcast address. With subnet ID/mask of 10.1.4.0/23, the mask converts to 255.255.254.0. To find the subnet broadcast address, following the decimal process described in this chapter, you can copy the subnet ID's first two octets because the mask's value is 255 in each octet. You write a 255 in the fourth octet because the mask has a 0 on the fourth octet. In octet 3, the interesting octet, add the magic number (2) to the subnet ID's value (4), minus 1, for a value of 2 + 4 − 1 = 5. (The magic number in this case is calculated as 256 − 254 = 2.) That makes the broadcast address 10.1.5.255. The last usable address is 1 less: 10.1.5.254. The range that includes the last 100 addresses is 10.1.5.155–10.1.5.254.

7. B. To answer this question, you do not actually need to calculate the subnet broadcast address, because you only need to know the low end of the range of addresses in the subnet. The first IP address in the subnet is 1 more than the subnet ID, or 192.168.9.97. The first 20 addresses then include 192.168.9.97–192.168.9.116.

Chapter 17

1. D. The most compelling reason was the address-exhaustion problem. The rest of the motivations are true motivations and benefits of IPv6 as well.

2. D. If following the steps in the book, the first step removes up to three leading 0s in each quartet, leaving FE80:0:0:100:0:0:0:123. This leaves two strings of consecutive all-0 quartets; by changing the longest string of all 0s to ::, the address is FE80:0:0:100::123.

3. B. This question has many quartets that make it easy to make a common mistake: removing trailing 0s in a quartet of hex digits. To abbreviate IPv6 addresses, only leading 0s in a quartet should be removed. Many of the quartets have trailing 0s (0s on the right side of the quartet), so make sure to not remove those 0s.

4. C. The /64 prefix length means that the last 64 bits, or last 16 digits, of the address should be changed to all 0s. That process leaves the unabbreviated prefix as 2000:000 0:0000:0005:0000:0000:0000:0000. The last four quartets are all 0s, making that string of all 0s be the longest and best string of 0s to replace with ::. After you remove the leading 0s in other quartets, the answer is 2000:0:0:5::/64.

5. A. Global unicast addresses can begin with many different initial values, but most commonly, they begin with either a hex 2 or 3.

6. D. The global routing prefix is the address block, represented as a prefix value and prefix length, given to an organization by some numbering authority. All IPv6 addresses inside the company have the same value in these initial bits of their IPv6 addresses. Similarly, when a company uses a public IPv4 address block, all the addresses have the same value in the network part.

7. B. Subnetting a global unicast address block, using a single prefix length for all subnets, breaks the addresses into three parts. The parts are the global routing prefix, subnet, and interface ID.

A

8. B and D. With SLAAC, the host learns the prefix from a router using NDP RS/RA messages, and then the host builds the rest of the address (the interface ID). The host can use EUI-64 rules, or use a defined process to randomly generate the interface ID value. The host does not learn the interface ID from any other device, which helps make the process stateless, because no other device needs to assign the host its full address.

Chapter 18

1. B. The PC will send packets to its default gateway when the device it is trying to communicate with is on a different network.

2. A and C. The router will compare the subnet via the mask and subnet ID to determine which route is in the table it matches.

3. A. To disable Layer 2 protocols on an individual interface you must use a routed interface on a Cisco Nexus switch.

4. C. If you want to have Layer 2 and Layer 3 functionality simultaneously on a Cisco Nexus switch you would use a switched virtual interface (SVI).

5. B. When dealing with link down detection for Layer 3 peering a routed interface is faster than an SVI because an SVI is a logical interface.

Chapter 19

1. A. To disable Layer 2 functionality on a Cisco Nexus Switch you must use a routed interface, which is enabled by the **no switchport** command.

2. B. To add an interface to a VLAN you use the command **switchport access vlan** *vlan number*.

3. B. To add an IP address to an SVI, you enter interface configuration mode using the **interface vlan** *vlan number* command. Then enter the **ip address** command with the address and mask.

4. C. You would see Interface VLAN in the routing table as a connected/direct route.

5. D. You do not need the next hop router's subnet mask to configure a static route to that router.

6. D. To configure a static route you must use the **ip route** statement followed by the route subnet and mask and either the outgoing interface or the next hop router's IP address.

Chapter 20

1. D. Split horizon causes a router to not advertise a route out of the same interface on which the router was learned. It also causes the router to not advertise about the connected route on an interface in updates sent out that interface. Route poisoning also helps prevent loops, although it does not affect how many routes a router advertises about on an interface. The other two answers are unrelated to loop prevention.

2. D. Route poisoning means advertising the failed route with an "infinite" metric, as opposed to simply ceasing to advertise the route. Of the incorrect answers, SPF defines how link-state protocols calculate and choose routes; hello refers to the messages some routing protocols use to discover and monitor neighboring routers; and split horizon limits what routes a router advertises to help avoid routing loops.

3. A and D. RIPv2 continues to use several features like RIPv1 in an effort to allow easier migration from RIPv1 to RIPv2. The features include using the same hop-count metric and using split horizon as one of the loop prevention mechanisms. The other two answers are true about RIPv2, but not RIP1.

4. B. RIPv1 and RIPv2 both use hop-count as the metric, so the two answers referencing the bandwidth are incorrect. Both RIPv1 and RIPv2 consider a route with metric 16 to be a poisoned (bad) route, and the metric value 16 to be infinite, but a route with metric 15 is a usable route. So, R1 adds the route for 10.1.1.0/24 to its IP routing table.

5. A. EIGRP separates the function of monitoring neighbor state into the hello message process, relying on the receipt of a hello message. If a router does not receive an EIGRP hello within the configured EIGRP hold time, the local router believes the neighbor has failed.

6. A and B. EIGRP uses bandwidth and delay by default. Load and reliability can be added to the mix with configuration, but Cisco recommends against adding these to the metric calculation.

7. D. Both versions of RIP use distance vector logic, and EIGRP uses a different kind of logic, characterized either as advanced distance vector or a balanced hybrid.

8. B. Link-state protocols do not exchange data that lists routes. They do list metric information, but it is per-interface information, and it is not tied to a subnet. Link-state protocols do require the SPF algorithm to take the varied pieces of information and create routes based on that information.

Chapter 21

1. C. RIP is a distance vector routing protocol.

2. B. To show all of the RIP-specific configuration, the **show running-config rip** command should be used.

3. C. The default OSPF interface type for an Ethernet interface is broadcast.

4. A and C. Bandwidth and delay are the two default enabled K values for EIGRP.

5. C. To configure a router ID for EIGRP, the configuration command is **router-id** *address*.

A

Chapter 22

1. **A and C.** An IP ACL can be configured to match the exact IP address by using the host keyword or using a /32 subnet mask for the source address. This can be done in one entry.

2. **D.** When creating an IOS ACL, you use the wildcard mask to match the ACL entry. The wildcard mask for 255.255.255.0 is 0.0.0.255.

3. **E.** When creating an IOS ACL, you use the wildcard mask to match the ACL entry. The wildcard mask for 255.255.240.0 is 0.0.15.255.

4. **A.** In an ACL the first match is used; in this case, 1.1.1.1 would match 1.0.0.0/8.

5. **A.** To permit only host 10.1.1.1 to host 192.168.1.3 on port 80 or the Web, you must use the host keyword or a /32 subnet address. Using the host keyword will only allow a host to talk to a host on a particular port, in this case, port 80.

DCICN Exam Updates

Over time, reader feedback allows Cisco Press to gauge which topics give our readers the most problems when taking the exams. Additionally, Cisco might make small changes in the breadth of exam topics or in the emphasis of certain topics. To assist readers with those topics, the author creates new materials clarifying and expanding upon those troublesome exam topics.

The document you are viewing is Version 1.0 of this appendix and there are no updates. You can check for an updated version at www.ciscopress.com/title/9781587204548.

Numeric Reference Tables

This appendix provides several useful reference tables that list numbers used throughout this book. Specifically:

Table C-1: A decimal-binary cross reference, useful when converting from decimal to binary and vice versa.

Table C-1 Decimal-Binary Cross Reference, Decimal Values 0–255

Decimal Value	Binary Value	Decimal Value	Binary Value	Decimal Value	Binary Value	Decimal Value	Binary Value
0	00000000	32	00100000	64	01000000	96	01100000
1	00000001	33	00100001	65	01000001	97	01100001
2	00000010	34	00100010	66	01000010	98	01100010
3	00000011	35	00100011	67	01000011	99	01100011
4	00000100	36	00100100	68	01000100	100	01100100
5	00000101	37	00100101	69	01000101	101	01100101
6	00000110	38	00100110	70	01000110	102	01100110
7	00000111	39	00100111	71	01000111	103	01100111
8	00001000	40	00101000	72	01001000	104	01101000
9	00001001	41	00101001	73	01001001	105	01101001
10	00001010	42	00101010	74	01001010	106	01101010
11	00001011	43	00101011	75	01001011	107	01101011
12	00001100	44	00101100	76	01001100	108	01101100
13	00001101	45	00101101	77	01001101	109	01101101
14	00001110	46	00101110	78	01001110	110	01101110
15	00001111	47	00101111	79	01001111	111	01101111
16	00010000	48	00110000	80	01010000	112	01110000
17	00010001	49	00110001	81	01010001	113	01110001
18	00010010	50	00110010	82	01010010	114	01110010
19	00010011	51	00110011	83	01010011	115	01110011
20	00010100	52	00110100	84	01010100	116	01110100
21	00010101	53	00110101	85	01010101	117	01110101
22	00010110	54	00110110	86	01010110	118	01110110
23	00010111	55	00110111	87	01010111	119	01110111
24	00011000	56	00111000	88	01011000	120	01111000
25	00011001	57	00111001	89	01011001	121	01111001
26	00011010	58	00111010	90	01011010	122	01111010
27	00011011	59	00111011	91	01011011	123	01111011
28	00011100	60	00111100	92	01011100	124	01111100
29	00011101	61	00111101	93	01011101	125	01111101
30	00011110	62	00111110	94	01011110	126	01111110
31	00011111	63	00111111	95	01011111	127	01111111

Table C-1   Decimal-Binary Cross Reference, Decimal Values 0–255

Decimal Value	Binary Value	Decimal Value	Binary Value	Decimal Value	Binary Value	Decimal Value	Binary Value
128	10000000	160	10100000	192	11000000	224	11100000
129	10000001	161	10100001	193	11000001	225	11100001
130	10000010	162	10100010	194	11000010	226	11100010
131	10000011	163	10100011	195	11000011	227	11100011
132	10000100	164	10100100	196	11000100	228	11100100
133	10000101	165	10100101	197	11000101	229	11100101
134	10000110	166	10100110	198	11000110	230	11100110
135	10000111	167	10100111	199	11000111	231	11100111
136	10001000	168	10101000	200	11001000	232	11101000
137	10001001	169	10101001	201	11001001	233	11101001
138	10001010	170	10101010	202	11001010	234	11101010
139	10001011	171	10101011	203	11001011	235	11101011
140	10001100	172	10101100	204	11001100	236	11101100
141	10001101	173	10101101	205	11001101	237	11101101
142	10001110	174	10101110	206	11001110	238	11101110
143	10001111	175	10101111	207	11001111	239	11101111
144	10010000	176	10110000	208	11010000	240	11110000
145	10010001	177	10110001	209	11010001	241	11110001
146	10010010	178	10110010	210	11010010	242	11110010
147	10010011	179	10110011	211	11010011	243	11110011
148	10010100	180	10110100	212	11010100	244	11110100
149	10010101	181	10110101	213	11010101	245	11110101
150	10010110	182	10110110	214	11010110	246	11110110
151	10010111	183	10110111	215	11010111	247	11110111
152	10011000	184	10111000	216	11011000	248	11111000
153	10011001	185	10111001	217	11011001	249	11111001
154	10011010	186	10111010	218	11011010	250	11111010
155	10011011	187	10111011	219	11011011	251	11111011
156	10011100	188	10111100	220	11011100	252	11111100
157	10011101	189	10111101	221	11011101	253	11111101
158	10011110	190	10111110	222	11011110	254	11111110
159	10011111	191	10111111	223	11011111	255	11111111

C

Table C-2: A hexadecimal-binary cross reference, useful when converting from hex to binary and vice versa.

Table C-2   Hex-Binary Cross Reference

Hex	4-Bit Binary
0	0000
1	0001
2	0010
3	0011
4	0100
5	0101
6	0110
7	0111
8	1000
9	1001
A	1010
B	1011
C	1100
D	1101
E	1110
F	1111

Table C-3: Powers of 2, from 2^1 through 2^{32}.

Table C-3   Powers of 2

X	2^x	X	2^x
1	2	17	131,072
2	4	18	262,144
3	8	19	524,288
4	16	20	1,048,576
5	32	21	2,097,152
6	64	22	4,194,304
7	128	23	8,388,608
8	256	24	16,777,216
9	512	25	33,554,432
10	1024	26	67,108,864
11	2048	27	134,217,728
12	4096	28	268,435,456
13	8192	29	536,870,912
14	16,384	30	1,073,741,824
15	32,768	31	2,147,483,648
16	65,536	32	4,294,967,296

C

Table C-4: Table of all 33 possible subnet masks, in all three formats.

Table C-4   All Subnet Masks

Decimal	Prefix	Binary
0.0.0.0	/0	00000000 00000000 00000000 00000000
128.0.0.0	/1	10000000 00000000 00000000 00000000
192.0.0.0	/2	11000000 00000000 00000000 00000000
224.0.0.0	/3	11100000 00000000 00000000 00000000
240.0.0.0	/4	11110000 00000000 00000000 00000000
248.0.0.0	/5	11111000 00000000 00000000 00000000
252.0.0.0	/6	11111100 00000000 00000000 00000000
254.0.0.0	/7	11111110 00000000 00000000 00000000
255.0.0.0	/8	11111111 00000000 00000000 00000000
255.128.0.0	/9	11111111 10000000 00000000 00000000
255.192.0.0	/10	11111111 11000000 00000000 00000000
255.224.0.0	/11	11111111 11100000 00000000 00000000
255.240.0.0	/12	11111111 11110000 00000000 00000000
255.248.0.0	/13	11111111 11111000 00000000 00000000
255.252.0.0	/14	11111111 11111100 00000000 00000000
255.254.0.0	/15	11111111 11111110 00000000 00000000
255.255.0.0	/16	11111111 11111111 00000000 00000000
255.255.128.0	/17	11111111 11111111 10000000 00000000
255.255.192.0	/18	11111111 11111111 11000000 00000000
255.255.224.0	/19	11111111 11111111 11100000 00000000
255.255.240.0	/20	11111111 11111111 11110000 00000000
255.255.248.0	/21	11111111 11111111 11111000 00000000
255.255.252.0	/22	11111111 11111111 11111100 00000000
255.255.254.0	/23	11111111 11111111 11111110 00000000
255.255.255.0	/24	11111111 11111111 11111111 00000000
255.255.255.128	/25	11111111 11111111 11111111 10000000
255.255.255.192	/26	11111111 11111111 11111111 11000000
255.255.255.224	/27	11111111 11111111 11111111 11100000
255.255.255.240	/28	11111111 11111111 11111111 11110000
255.255.255.248	/29	11111111 11111111 11111111 11111000
255.255.255.252	/30	11111111 11111111 11111111 11111100
255.255.255.254	/31	11111111 11111111 11111111 11111110
255.255.255.255	/32	11111111 11111111 11111111 11111111

Nexus Lab Guide

This guide shows you how to deploy Nexus 1000v on VMware Workstation or VMware Fusion for Mac. You will learn the two steps required to provide you with a virtual machine running NX-OS to help with your certification studies. You can purchase VMware Fusion and Workstation at www.vmware.com.

The workstation requirements are as follows:

- Java installed
- Approximately 8 GB of memory
- Minimum 50 GB of available storage
- VMware Workstation 9 or VMware Fusion 6 installed

Step 1. Download Nexus 1000v.

 a. VMware workstation should be previously installed and working. You'll want at least 50 GB of storage on your workstation for VMs.

 b. Go to www.cisco.com/go/support.

 c. Click the **Download** tab.

 d. Type **Nexus 1000v** in the search field and press **Enter** (see Figure D-1).

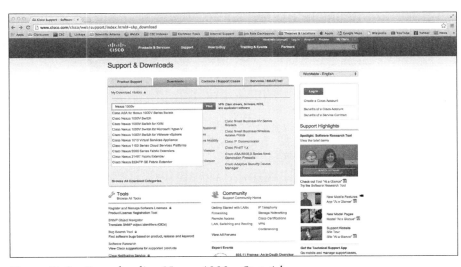

Figure D-1 *Downloading Nexus 1000v: Step 1d*

    e. Click **Nexus 1000v.**

    f. Click **NX-OS System Software** (see Figure D-2).

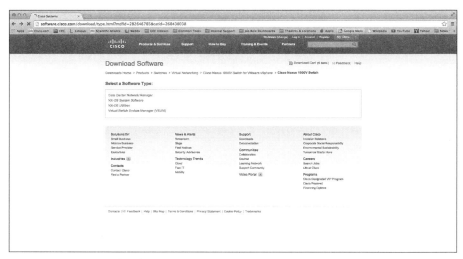

Figure D-2 *Downloading Nexus 1000v: Step 1f*

    g. Click **Download** (see Figure D-3).

Figure D-3 *Downloading Nexus 1000v: Step 1g*

    h. Click **Login to download software** and use your Cisco.com login information (see Figure D-4).

NOTE You must have sufficient rights tied to your Cisco.com login account to download the Nexus 1000v software.

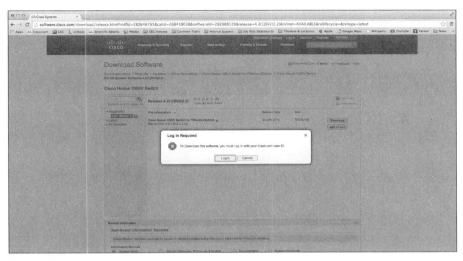

Figure D-4   *Downloading Nexus 1000v: Step 1h*

    i. Click the **Accept License Agreement** button (see Figure D-5).

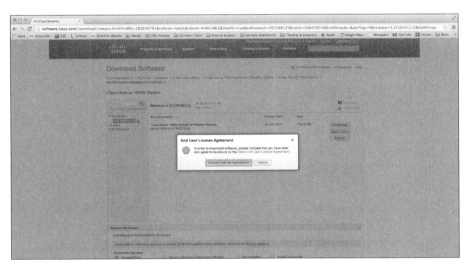

Figure D-5   *Downloading Nexus 1000v: Step 1i*

    j. Save the Zip file to a local destination and unzip the file (see Figure D-6).

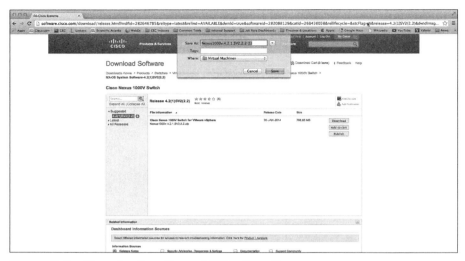

Figure D-6   *Downloading Nexus 1000v: Step 1j*

    k. Navigate to the local directory where the file has been unzipped and browse the file directory and find the .iso file under the VSM folder (see Figure D-7).

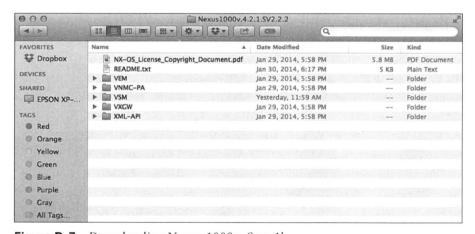

Figure D-7   *Downloading Nexus 1000v: Step 1k*

Step 2.   Install the VM for Nexus 1000v.

    a. In VM Fusion or Workstation, click **File, New**.

    b. Choose **Install from disc or image** and click **Continue** (see Figure D-8).

Figure D-8   *Installing Nexus 1000v: Step 2b*

    c. Click **Use another disc or disc image** (see Figure D-9).

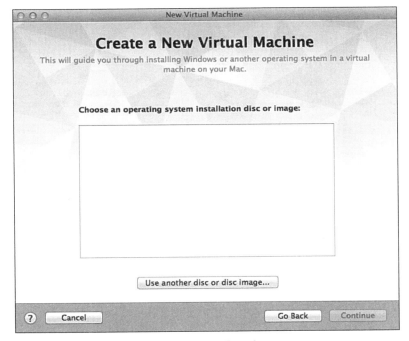

Figure D-9   *Installing Nexus 1000v: Step 2c*

d. Browse to the 1000v directory under the VSM/Install folder and choose the .iso file (see Figure D-10).

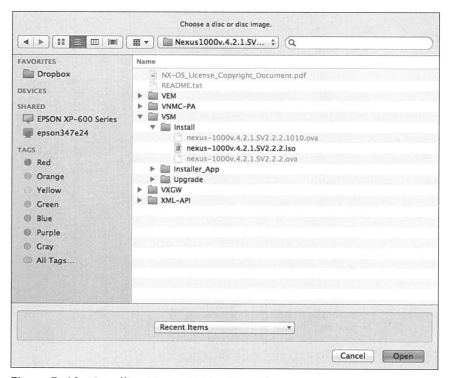

Figure D-10   *Installing Nexus 1000v: Step 2d*

e. Click **Continue** (see Figure D-11).

Figure D-11 *Installing Nexus 1000v: Step 2e*

      f.   Under Choose Operating System, select **Linux and Other Linux 3.x Kernel 64-bit** (see Figure D-12).

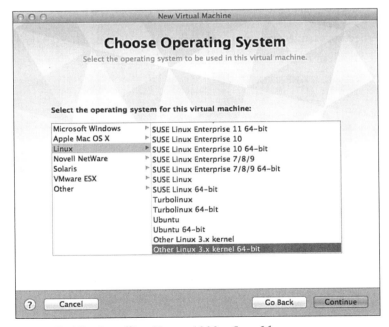

Figure D-12 *Installing Nexus 1000v: Step 2f*

g. In the Finish window, click **Customize Settings** (see Figure D-13).

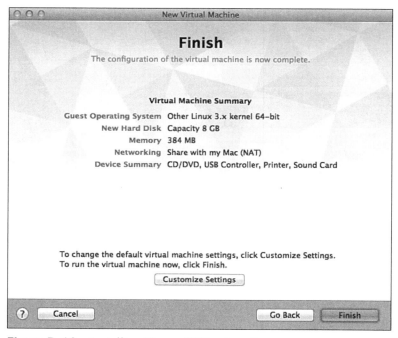

Figure D-13 *Installing Nexus 1000v: Step 2g*

h. Give your VM a name and save.

i. Click **Processors and Memory**, choose two processor cores and 2 GB on memory (see Figure D-14 and Figure D-15).

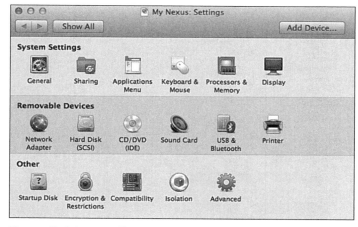

Figure D-14 *Installing Nexus 1000v: Step 2i (Part 1)*

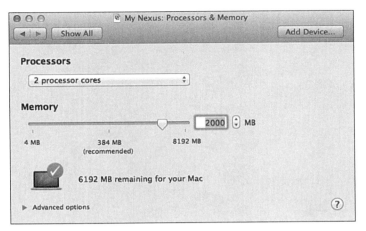

Figure D-15 *Installing Nexus 1000v: Step 2i (Part 2)*

j. Click **Show All.**

k. Click **Network Adapters,** and then click **Add Device, Network Adapter, Add.** Do this twice to create three total network adapters (see Figure D-16 and Figure D-17).

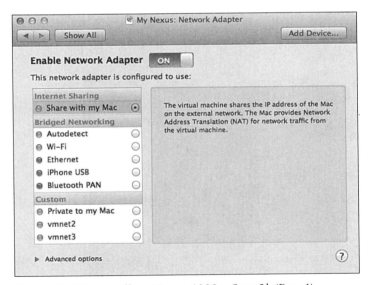

Figure D-16 *Installing Nexus 1000v: Step 2k (Part 1)*

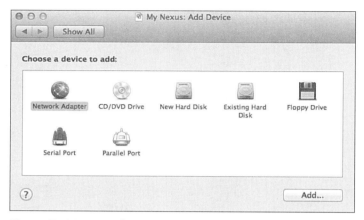

Figure D-17   *Installing Nexus 1000v: Step 2k (Part 2)*

      l. Close the Settings window.

      m. Click the **Play** button to start your VM.

      n. Press **Enter** for "install Nexus1000v and bring up the new image."

      o. Enter a password for admin.

      p. Choose **standalone** for the HA role (see Figure D-18).

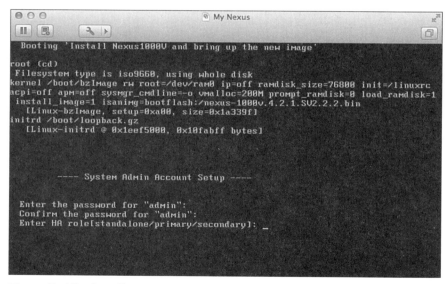

Figure D-18   *Installing Nexus 1000v: Step 2p*

      q. Choose a domain ID and press **Enter**.

      r. Type **No** to enter basic configuration dialog (see Figure D-19).

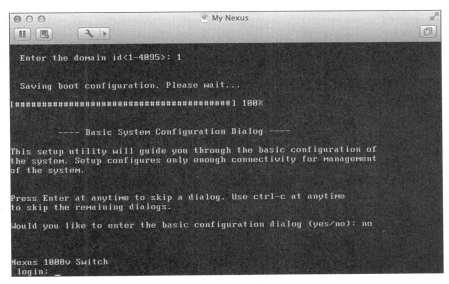

Figure D-19   *Installing Nexus 1000v: Step 2r*

        s. Log in to your Nexus 1000v (see Figure D-20).

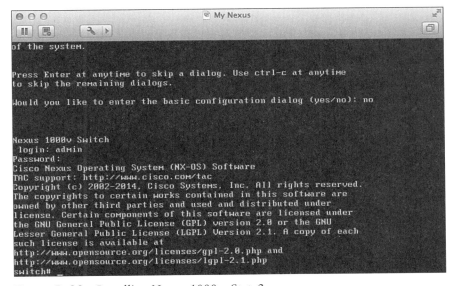

Figure D-20   *Installing Nexus 1000v: Step 2s*

You now have a Nexus 1000v that you can use to validate commands and to familiarize yourself with the operating system. The Nexus 1000v is a virtual switch that can help you become familiar with NX-OS as a whole. Figure D-21 demonstrates some navigation through the command-line interface (CLI).

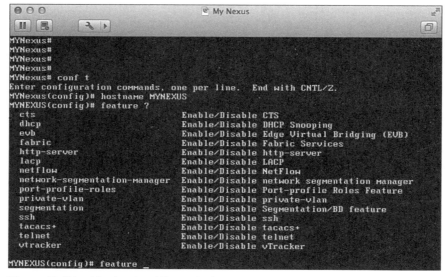

Figure D-21 *Navigating Through the Nexus 1000v CLI*

Index

Numerics

10BASE-T, 46
  bridges, 157
  switches, 158
10GBASE-T, 46
10 Gig Ethernet, 46
100BASE-LX, 46
100BASE-T, 46
404 return codes (HTTP), 137
802.1D, 288-290
802.1Q, 247-248
802.3, 46
802.3ab, 46
802.3an, 46
802.3u, 46
802.3z, 46
802.11, 42-43
1000BASE-T, 46

Symbols

/ (slash), 393

A

AAA (authentication, authorization, and accounting) servers, 217-218
abbreviating IPv6 addresses, 443-444

ABRs (Area Border Routers), 526
Accept License Agreement button, 625
access interfaces, 264-267
access-list command
  eq parameter, 564
  syntax, 562
accessing Nexus 5500 switch CLIs, 186
  debug/show commands, 196
  NX-OS, 186, 191-192
  user settings, 192-195
ACLs (access control lists)
  applying, 568-569
  extended numbered IP ACLs, 562-565
  IPv4, 557-559
  matching packets, 558
  placement of, 557-558
  standard numbered IPv4, 560-568
Address field (HDLC), 75
addresses
  address-exhaustion problem, 440
  classes, 99-103
  conventions for Class A, Class B, and Class C, 380-381
  fields, 75
  IP. *See* IP
  IPv4. *See* IPv4
  IPv6. *See* IPv6
  MAC. *See* MAC addresses
  SLAAC, 459

adjacent-layer interactions, 22

administrative mode (trunking), 269

alternate ports, 305

analyzing

Layer 2 forwarding path, 227

practicing, 403-404

subnet masks, 423

answering exam questions, 586-587

application layer

HTTP overview, 19-21

OSI models, 32

TCP/IP networking model, 19

WWW

DNS resolution, 135-137

URLs, 134-136

applications

receiving application, 138-139

TCP/IP, 132

DNS, 125

QoS requirements, 132-133

SNMP, 125

TFTP, 125

well-known port numbers, 125

WWW, 125

applying IPv4 ACLs, 568-569

APs (access points), 43

areas, OSPF, 526

ARP (Address Resolution Protocol), 95, 112-113

caches, 113

Reply messages, 113

requests, 113

ARPANET, 440

ASICs (Application Specific Integrated Circuits), 483

assigning

IP addresses, 348-349

IPv6

addresses, 457-460

prefixes, 447-448

subnets to different locations, 367

VLANs to access interfaces, 264-267

asymmetric speeds, 84

authentication, 218-219

authentication, authorization, and accounting. See AAA

autonegotiation, 175-176

disabling, 176

duplex mismatches, 178

failure of, 177

on hubs, 178

autonomous system ID, 545

availability (HA), Cisco NX-OS, 199

B

backup ports, 305-307

balancing load with PSVT+ (Per-VLAN Spanning Tree Plus), 316

bandwidth, 132

banner motd global configuration command, 220

banners, configuring on Cisco Catalyst switches, 220

batch applications, QoS requirements, 132-133

Berners-Lee, Tim, 20

best path selection, Dijkstra SPF algorithm, 524

BIA (burned-in address), 57

BID (bridge ID), 291

binary math

memorization versus calculation, 430-431

practice problems, 419-420

range of usable subnet addresses, 422

subnet broadcast addresses, 418-422

subnet IDs, calculating, 416-421

binary subnet mask formats, 392

DDN, 394-396

prefix formats, 393-394

binary-to-hexadecimal conversion, 618

blocking state (STP), 169, 288-291

Boolean math, 422

borrowing bits from host part for subnetting, 361

BPDU (bridge protocol data units), 291-292

BPDU Guard, 303-304, 324-326

brain dumps, 591

Bridge Assurance, 324

bridge ID (BID), 291, 316-317

bridge protocol data units (BPDU), 291-292

bridges, 157

broadcast addresses, 56, 165

of Class B networks, 380

Ethernet, 57

subnet broadcast addresses, 415-422, 428-430

broadcast domains, 171, 244

design concepts, 245

impact on LAN design, 173

broadcast storms, 286-288

budgeting your time during exams, 580-584

building lists of all subnets in internetwork, 365

C

cable Internet, 84-85

cabling

coaxial, 152

consoles, connecting, 187

crossover cables, 53

distance limitations on campus LANs, 174

EMI, 48

Ethernet, 42, 45-46

for leased lines, 72

connectors, 73

CPE, 73

CSU/DSU, 73

data link layer protocols, 74-76

DCE, 73

DTE, 73

serial cable, 73

UTP, 48-55

WAN links, creating in labs, 73-74

calculating

EIGRP, 518

IPv6 prefixes, 445-447

number of hosts

for classful networks, 377-378

per subnets, 353, 401-403

number of subnets per internetwork, 351

powers of 2, numeric reference table, 620

ranges of usable subnet addresses, 422

subnet broadcast address

with binary math, 418-422

with Boolean math, 422

with decimal math, 428-430

versus memorization, 430-431

subnet broadcast addresses, 415, 430

subnet IDs

    with binary math, 416-421

    with Boolean math, 422

    with decimal math, 425-427

    practice problems, 427-428

    versus memorization, 430-431

    total subnets in network, 401-403

CAM (Content Addressable Memory), 166

campus LANs, maximum cable lengths, 174

carrier sense multiple access with collision detection. *See* CSMA/CD

CDP (Cisco Discovery Protocol), 331

CEF (Cisco Express Forwarding, 483-484

channel-group commands, 326-331

channel-group number(i) mode on command, 327, 334

CIDR (classless interdomain routing), 393

Cisco Binary Game, 394

Cisco Catalyst switches

    banners, 220

    CLI, 217, 221

    interfaces, 225-227

    IP address, 223-224

    SSH, 219-220

Cisco.com login account, 624

Cisco Discovery Protocol. *See* CDP

Cisco Exam Tutorials, 579-580

Cisco IOS, comparing to Cisco NX-OS, 201

Cisco Learning Network, 591

Cisco NX-OS. *See* NX-OS

Cisco-proprietary version of HDLC, 75

Cisco routers. *See* routers

Cisco switches. *See* switches

Class A networks

    default mask, 375

    hosts per network, 375

    loopback address, 380

    octets in host and network address part, 375

    total networks provisioned for, 375

    unicast IP addresses, 374

    valid network numbers, 375

Class B networks

    broadcast address, 380

    default mask, 375

    hosts per network, 375

    octets in host and network address part, 375

    total networks provisioned for, 375

    unicast IP addresses, 374

    valid network numbers, 375

Class C networks

    default mask, 375

    hosts per network, 375

    network IDs, 381

    octets in host and network address part, 375

    total networks provisioned for, 375

    unicast IP addresses, 374

    valid network numbers, 375

classes of IPv4 networks, 99-103

classful addressing, 401

classful IP networks, 103

classful networks, 374-375

    Class A networks, loopback addresses, 380

    default masks, 377

    first usable addresses, deriving, 378-380

hosts
  part, 376
  per network, calculating number of, 377-378
  last usable addresses, deriving, 378-380
  multicast addresses, 374
  networks
    broadcast addresses, deriving, 378-380
    IDs, deriving, 378-380
    parts, 376
  private IP networks, 359-360
  public classful IP networks, 357-358
  subnetting, 360-365, 413. *See also* subnetting
  unicast IP addresses, 374
classful routing protocols, 401
classless addressing, 401
classless interdomain routing (CIDR), 441
classless routing protocols, 401
CLIs (command-line interfaces)
  banners, 220
  hands-on practice, 591
  history buffer commands, 221
  Nexus 5500 switch, 186
    debug/show commands, 196
    NX-OS, 186, 191-192
    user settings, 192-195
  securing, 217
  security, 217
clients, VTP, 253
clock rate command, 74
clocking, 74
clouds, 15
coaxial cabling, 152
coexistence, IPv6, 461-463

collision domains, 61, 157-158, 170-173
command-line interfaces. *See* CLIs
commands
  access-list, 562-564
  banner motd global configuration, 220
  channel-group, 330
  clock rate, 74
  configure terminal EXEC, 202
  copy, 194-195
  debug, 196
  description, 225
  exec-timeout, 222
  feature ssh, 192
  feature telnet, 192
  history buffer commands, 221
  interface, 202, 265
  interface range, 226
  ip address, 494-496
  ip route, 500-501
  ip router rip enterprise, 538
  line vty configuration, 192
  logging console global, 222
  logging synchronous, 222
  mode trunk, 269
  no shutdown, 224, 227
  no switchport, 496
  ping, 113-114
  reload, 192
  show, 189, 194-196
    show interfaces status, 226
    show interfaces trunk, 272
    show ip eigrp, 545
    show ip eigrp neighbors, 545
    show ip ospf 1, 550
    show ip rip, 541
    show ip rip neighbor, 541

show ip route, 495

show running-config, 567

show running-config eigrp, 545

show running-config ospf, 549

show running-config rip, 541

show spanning-tree root, 320

show spanning-tree vlan 10, 322

show spanning-tree vlan 10 bridge, 320

show ssh, 220

show version, 209

show vlan brief, 267

shutdown, 224, 272

shutdown vlan, 272

spanning-tree

    spanning-tree mode mst, 314

    spanning-tree mode rapid-pvst, 314

    spanning-tree vlan vlan-id priority value, 322

ssh key, 219

switchport

    switchport access vlan, 267

    switchport mode, 269

    switchport mode trunk, 271

    switchport trunk encapsulation, 269

vlan vlan-id global config, 268

comparing

Cisco IOS/NX-OS, 201

EIGRP/OSPF, 521

Ethernet and HDLC header fields, 75

IGPs, 509-510

internal routing logic, types of, 484

LANs and WANs, 67

memorization and calculation for subnetting, 430-431

networks and subnets, 414

operational and design views of subnetting, 347

original and modern TCP/IP models, 28

OSI and TCP/IP networking models, 30-31

TCP and UDP, 120

competition, Ethernet, 162-164

computer networking before TCP/IP, 16

configuration commands, standard numbered IPv4 ACLs, 560-562

configure terminal EXEC command, 202

configuring

BPDU Guard, 324-326

Cisco Catalyst switches, 217-220, 223-226

Cisco NX-OS, 202-208

connected routes, 494

consoles, terminal emulators, 188

contexts, 202-204

EIGRP, 517-521, 541-545

EtherChannel, 326-332

files

    copying, 206-207

    erasing, 206-207

    storing, 204-206

IP routing, 475

    examples, 478-481

    internal processing (Cisco routers), 482

    Nexus switches, 484-487

IPv4 routing, 475-477

LANs, 170-178

Layer 3 switching, 497-498

management interfaces, 191

Nexus 5500 switches, 222-229
debug/show commands, 196
user settings, 192-195
OSPF, 521-526, 546-550
PortFast, 324-326
RIPv2 on NX-OS, 536-541
routes on Nexus switches, 494-501
SLAAC, 459
standard numbered IPv4 ACLs, 566-568
static routes, 499-501
STP, 298-301, 314-329
submodes, 202-204
subnetting, 346-349
implementing, 366-367
Layer 3, 349-350
sizing, 354-356
trunks, 270
verification, 270
VLANs, 264-274
VTP, 252-257, 275-279
connected routes
configuring, 495
VLANs, routing between subnets, 497-498
connecting
connection establishment, 126
consoles, cabling, 187
Ethernet links, 49
LANs with WANs, 70
termination (TCP), 127
connectionless protocols, 127
connection-oriented protocols, 127
connectivity, testing with ping command, 113-114
connectors for CSU/DSU, 73

consoles
connecting, cabling, 187
inactivity timeouts, defining, 222
terminal emulators, configuring, 188
contexts, configuring, 202-204
conventions, addressing conventions for Class A, Class B, 380-381
convergence, 508
EIGRP, 519-521
STP, 289, 300-301
converting
binary to hexadecimal, 618
binary subnet masks to DDN, 393-396
DDN
to binary, 394-396
subnet masks to prefix formats, 396-397
decimal to binary, 615-617
hexadecimal to binary, 618
prefix subnet masks
to binary, 393-394
to DDN, 396-397
copy command, 194-195
copying switch configuration tiles, 206-207
COs (central offices), 72, 83
CPE (customer premises equipment), 73
CPUs (central processing units), troubleshooting, 483
crossover cable pinouts, 53
CSMA/CD (carrier sense multiple access with collision detection), 61-62
CSU/DSU (channel service unit/data service unit), 73-74

D

data applications, 134. *See also* applications

data encapsulation, 28-30

data link layer

error detection, 120

Ethernet, 46, 58-62, 160

frames, 46-47

HDLC, 74

data transmission through, 75-76

header fields, 75

OSI models, 33

protocols, 55-56

role in IP routing, 95

TCP/IP networking model, 26-28

data segmentation, 121

databases, LSDB, 522

DataDirect Networks. *See* DDN

DCE (data communications equipment), 73

DDN (DataDirect Networks), 25, 98

binary conversions, 394-396

octets, 98

subnet masks, 392

prefix format conversions, 396-397

debug command, 196

debug spanning-tree events command, 335

decimal math

memorization versus calculation, 430-431

subnet broadcast address, calculating, 428-430

subnet IDs, calculating, 425-427

decimal-to-binary conversions

Cisco Binary Game, 394

numeric reference tables, 615-617

deencapsulation, 76, 480

default gateways, 94, 105, 476

default masks, 377

for Class A networks, 375

for Class B networks, 375

for Class C networks, 375

default routers, 93

default routes, 501

defining

sizes of planned subnets, 354-356

subnets, 412

delay, 132

delete vtp command, 280-281

delimited hexadecimals, 443

deriving

first usable addresses from classful networks, 378-380

last usable addresses from classful networks, 378-380

network broadcast addresses from classful networks, 378-380

network IDs from classful network addresses, 378-380

describing protocols by referencing OSI layers, 31

description command, 225

design. *See also* configuring

LANs, 170-178

OSPF, 525

subnetting, 346-349, 357-365

implementing, 366-367

Layer 3, 349-350

sizing, 354-356

designated ports (DPs)

choosing, 296-297

explained, 290

destination hosts, 476

Destination MAC Address field (Ethernet frames), 56

destination ports

numbers, 123

as packet filtering criteria, 562-564

destination unicast MAC addresses, 57

development of TCP/IP, 17

devices

Ethernet, 154

hubs, 60-62

routers, 43

DHCP (Dynamic Host Configuration Protocol)

IP addresses

configuring on Cisco Catalyst switches, 223-224

verifying on Cisco Catalyst switches, 224

static and dynamic ranges per subnet, selecting, 367-368

DHCPv6 (Dynamic Host Configuration Protocol version 6), 460-461

difficult masks, 423

interesting masks, 424-425

interesting octets, 424

memorization versus calculation, 430-431

subnet broadcast addresses, calculating with, 428-430

subnet IDs, calculating with decimal math, 425-427

Digital Equipment Corp. (DEC), 159

Dijkstra SPF (Shortest Path First) algorithm, 524

directed broadcast address, 365

disabling

autonegotiation, 176

VTP, 256

discarded packets, deny all keyword (ACL), 561

discovering knowledge gaps through practice exam question, 588-590

distance, maximum cabling, 154

distance vector (DV) routing protocols

explained, 511-512

full update messages, 512

route poisoning, 514-515

split horizon, 513-514

DNS (Domain Name System), 125

ARP cache, viewing contents of, 113

name resolution, 111-113

resolution, 135-137

domains, broadcast, 244-245

dotted decimal format, 377

downloading Nexus 1000v, 623-625

DPs (designated ports)

choosing, 296-297

explained, 290

DSL (digital subscriber line), 82-84

DSLAM (DSL Access Multiplexer), 84

DTE (data terminal equipment), 73

DTP (Dynamic Trunking Protocol), 269

dual stacks, 462

duplex mismatches, 178

DV (distance vector) routing protocols

explained, 511-512

full update messages, 512

route poisoning, 514-515

split horizon, 513-514

dynamic EtherChannels, configuring, 328-329

dynamic port numbers, 123

dynamic ranges per subnet, selecting, 367-368

E

easy masks, 423

edge ports, 324

EIGRP (Enhanced Interior Gateway Routing Protocol), 508, 517-521

   compared to other routing protocols, 510

   hello packets, 518

   NX-OS, configuring, 541-545

   OSPF, comparing, 521

electing root switches, 292-294

electrical circuits over Ethernet LANs, 48

EMI (electromagnetic interference), 48

enabling

   EIGRP on NX-OS, 541-545

   OSPF on NX-OS, 546-550

   RIPv2 on NX-OS, 536-541

   VTP, 275-276

encapsulation, 28-30, 76, 481-482

encoding schemes, data transmission over Ethernet LANs, 48

Enhanced Interior Gateway Routing Protocol. *See* EIGRP

enterprise LANs, 43-45

enterprise networks, 15

EoMPLS (Ethernet over MPLS), 78-79

eq parameter (access-list command), 564

erasing switch configuration tiles, 206-207

error

   detection, 59, 120

   recovery, 21, 120, 127-129

estimating time needed to finish exam, 581

EtherChannel, 302-303

   configuring, 326-332

   troubleshooting, 329-332

Ethernet, 42

   10BASE-T, 51-54, 157-158

   100BASE-T, 51-54

   1000BASE-T, 55

   addressing, 56-59

   autonegotiation, 175-178

   broadcast domains, 171-173

   cabling, 48

   collision domains, 158, 170-171

   data link layer standard, 46-47

   data link protocols, 55-56, 160

   data transmission over, 48

   electrical circuits, creating, 48

   emulation, 79

   EoMPLS, 78-79

   frames, 247

   full-duplex data transmission, 59-60

   half-duplex data transmission, 60-62

   history of, 152-164

   LANs, 42-45, 170-178

   links, 48

      connecting, 49

      RJ-45 connectors, 49

      RJ-45 ports, 49

   physical layer standards, 45-46, 161-162

   standards, 159

   as WAN technology, 77

EtherType field, 58

exams

   brain dumps, 591

   Cisco Exam Tutorial, 579-583

   exam-day advice, 582-583

   hands-on CLI practice, 591

knowledge gaps, discovering through, 588-590

math-related skills, practicing for, 583-584

practicing for, 381-383, 585-587

pre-exam suggestions, 582

preparing for, 587-588

questions, 586-587

suggested time-check method, 581

EXEC mode, 192, 195

exec-timeout command, 222

exhaustion of public IP address spaces, 358

expanding IPv6 addresses, 444-445

explicit deny, 562

extended numbered IP ACLs

packet filtering, 562-564

packet filtering criteria, 565

external authentication servers, 218-219

F

failure of autonegotiation, rules for, 177

Fast Ethernet, 46

fast switching, 483-484

FCS (Frame Check Sequence) fields, 56, 59, 75

feature ssh command, 192

feature telnet command, 192

fiber-optic cabling, 46

fields in Ethernet frames, 55-56

files

configuration

copying, 206-207

erasing, 206-207

storing, 204-206

transferring with HTTP, 137

filtering

packets, 557

by destination port, 562-564

by source port, 565

versus forwarding, 165-166

FIN bit, 127

first-match logic, standard numbered IPv4 ACLs, 560-561

first usable addresses, deriving from classful network, 378-380

Flag field (HDLC), 75

flooding, 167, 522-524

flow control, 120, 130-131

formats of subnet masks, 364-365, 392

binary, 392

DDN conversions, 394-396

Prefix conversions, 393-394

DDN, 392

binary conversions, 394-396

prefix format conversions, 396-397

prefix format, 393

binary conversions, 393-394

DDN conversions, 396-397

forward acknowledgment, 128

Forward Delay timers (STP), 299-300

forward-versus-filter decisions, 166

forwarding

data between VLANs, 248, 251

versus filtering, 165-166

logic in IP routing, 92, 105-107

delivering data to end, 94

example of, 107-108

routing across the network, 94

transmitting packets to, 93

packets, 480-481

state (STP), 169, 288-289

    DPs (designated ports), 290, 296-297

    reasons for, 290-291

    root switches, 290-294

    RPs (root ports), 290

frames, 286

  encapsulation, 29

  Ethernet, 46-47, 247

    EtherType field, 58

    FCS field, 59

    header and trailer fields, 55-56

  forwarding logic on switches, 165-169

  host routing, 106-107

  multiple frame transmission, 288

  router processing for IP routing, 479-480

  transmitting via IP routing process, 482

  unknown unicast, 168

FTP (File Transfer Protocol), 125

full-duplex

  data transmission

    collisions, 61

    duplex mismatches, 178

    on Ethernet LANs, 59-60

  WANs, 71

full update messages, 512

functions of routing protocols, 508

G

GBIC (gigabit interface converter), 50

Gigabit Ethernet, 46

global routing prefixes, 447

global unicast addresses, 449-452

goals of routing protocols, 109

graceful restarts, 199

group addresses, 57

grouping IP addresses into networks, 98-99

growth

  of internetworks, 353

  of IP addresses, 358

guaranteed delivery, 21

H

HA (high availability), Cisco NX-OS, 199

half duplex

  collisions, 61

  duplex mismatches, 178

  on Ethernet LANs, 60-62

hands-on CLI practice, 591

HDLC (High-Level Data Link Control), 74, 477

  Cisco-proprietary version of, 75

  data transmission, 75-76

  header fields, 75

headers, 20, 27

  encapsulation, 28-30

  fields

    for Ethernet frames, 55-56

    HDLC, 75

    TCP, 121-122

  HDLC, 477

  TCP, 22

hello packets (EIGRP), 518

hello timers (STP), 299-300

help features, NX-OS, 194-195

hexadecimal-to-binary conversion, 618

hierarchical OSPF design

  multiarea OSPF, 526

  single-area OSPF, 525

high availability. *See* HA

high-speed Internet connections, 14

history

of Ethernet, 152-162

of OSI, 17

of TCP/IP

comparing original and modern networking, 28

pre-TCP/IP computer networking, 16

history buffer commands, 221

home page, 19

hosts

calculating, 353, 401-403

destination, 476

forwarding logic in IP routing, 92

delivering data to, 94

routing across the, 94

transmitting packets, 93

per network

Class A networks, 375

Class B networks, 375

Class C networks, 375

parts

classful network addresses, 376

of subnet addresses, 399

receiving application, identifying, 138-139

role in IP routing, 105-107

routing, 107-108

how spanning-tree vlan 10 command, 322

HTTP (Hypertext Transfer Protocol), 19-21, 135

files, transferring between web servers and web, 137

GET requests, 137

GET responses, 137

requests, 137

TCP error recovery, 21

hubs

autonegotiation, 178

Ethernet, 155

half-duplex data transmission, 60-62

LANs, 59

I

IANA (Internet Assigned Numbers Authority), 358

ICANN (Internet Corporation for Assigned Names and Numbers), 440

ICMP (Internet Control Message Protocol), 113-114

ICND1 practice exams, 586

IDs

BID (bridge ID), 316-317

system ID extension, 316-317

identifying classes of IPv4 networks, 101-103

IEEE (Institute of Electrical and Electronics Engineers), 42

802.1D, 288-290

802.1Q, 247-248

802.3, 46

802.3ab, 46

802.3an, 46

802.3u, 46

802.3z, 46

802.11, 42-43

autonegotiation, 175-176

disabling, 176

duplex mismatches, 178

failure of, 177

on hubs, 178

history of Ethernet standards, 159

standards naming conventions, 46

STP, 288-290, 311

IGPs (Interior Gateway Protocols), 509-510

IGRP (Interior Gateway Routing Protocol), 508

implementing. *See also* configuring

EIGRP, 517-521

IP routing, 475

examples, 478-481

internal processing (Cisco routers), 482

Nexus switches, 484-487

IPv4 routing, 475-477

IPv6, 457-463

OSPF, 521-526

standard numbered IPv4 ACLs, 566-568

subnetting, 366-367

inactivity timers, 167

inbound ACLs, 557

inferior hello (STP), 292

infinity, 514

initial configuration of Cisco NX-OS, 208. *See also* configuring

in-service software upgrades (ISSUs), 199

installing

Nexus 1000v, 623-625, 630-633

workstation requirements, 623

Institute of Electrical and Electronics Engineers. *See* IEEE

Intel, 159

interactive applications. *See also* applications

QoS requirements, 132-133

WWW, 134

DNS resolution, 135-137

URLs, 134-136

interesting octets, 424-425

interface command, 202, 265

interface range command, 226

interfaces. *See also* CLIs

access, 265

configuring on Cisco Catalyst switches, 225-226

management (Nexus switches), 190-191

OSPF, 524

STP, modifying, 300

SVIs, 538

unused, securing, 226-227

Interior Gateway Protocols. *See* IGPs

interleaving 1s and 0s, binary subnet mask rules, 392

internal processing (Cisco routers), 482

internal routing logic, 483

CEF, 483

comparing types of, 484

fast switching, 483

performance issues, 483

Internet

always on service, 85

cable Internet, 84-85

DSL, 82-84

high-speed connections, 14

Internet core, 81

ISPs, 80

service providers, 71

Internet Assigned Numbers Authority. *See* IANA

Internet Corporation for Assigned Names and Numbers. *See* ICANN

internetworks, 96, 365

ip commands

ip address command, 494-496

ip route command, 500-501

ip router rip enterprise command, 538

IP (Internet Protocol), 23-24

addressing

binary-to-hexadecimal conversion, 618

decimal-to-binary conversion, 615-617

hexadecimal-to-binary conversion, 618

growth of, 358

phones, 133

configuring on Cisco Catalyst switches, 223-224

IPv4. *See* IPv4

IPv6. *See* IPv6

routing

connected routes, 494-495

examples, 107-108, 478-481

host routing, 105-107

internal processing on Cisco, 483

internal processing on Cisco routers, 482

internal routing logic, 483

Nexus switches, 484-487

routing logic, 476-478

static routes, 499-501

tables, 94

subnetting

Layer 3, 349-350

overview of, 346-349

sizing, 354-356

telephony, 133

verifying on Cisco Catalyst switches, 224

IPv4 (Internet Protocol version 4)

ACLs

extended numbered IP ACLs, 562-565

matching packets, 558

placement of, 557-558

standard numbered ACLs, 560-562

addresses, 24-25, 98, 401-403

ACLs, 557-559

address classes, 99--103

address-exhaustion problem, 440

classful addressing, 401

classful IP networks, 103

classful networks, 374-380

classless addressing, 401

DDN, 98

DNS resolution, 135-137

grouping into IP networks, 98-99

IPv4 header, 96

role in IP routing, 95-96

subnet addresses, 398-399

subnet masks, 393-399

subnetting, 103-105, 346-356, 412-430

routing, 475-477

DV (distance vector) routing protocols, 511-515

EIGRP, 510, 518

IGRP, 508

OSPFv2, 510

RIP-2, 510

tunneling IPv6 inside, 462

IPv6 (Internet Protocol version 6), 358, 440-447

address conventions, 443

assigning, 447-448

implementing, 457-463

subnetting, 449-456

ISL (Inter-Switch Link), 247-248

ISO (International Organization for Standardization), 75

ISPs (Internet service providers), 80

access technologies

cable Internet, 84-85

DSL, 82-84

Internet core, 81

ISSUs (in-service software upgrades), 199

J-K-L

jitter, 132

knowledge gaps, discovering through question review, 588-590

L3PDUs, 34, 95

L4PDUs, 122

LANs (local area networks)

campus LANs, 174

comparing with WANs, 67

connecting with WANs, 70

design, 170-178

enterprise, 15

enterprise LANs, 43-45

Ethernet, 45-49, 55-62, 157-158, 170-173

history of, 152-164

hubs, 59

IP telephony, 133

SOHO, 42-43

subnets, 349

switches, 164-170

DPs (designated ports), 290, 296-297

frame forwarding logic, 165-169

root switches, 290-294

RPs (root ports), 290, 294-295

STP (Spanning Tree Protocol). See STP

switch reactions to changes with STP, 299-300

wired LANs, 39

last usable addresses, deriving from classful network, 378-380

Layer 1, 32-33, 74. See also application layer; physical layer

Layer 2, 164-170, 223. See also data link layer

analyzing, 227

forwarding data between VLANs, 251

Layer 3. See also network layer

routing between VLANs, 250-251

switches, 223, 251

configuring, 497-498

sizing, 354-356

subnet rules, 349-350

Layer 4. See also transport layer

TCP, 121

connections, 126-127

error recovery and reliability, 127-129

flow control with windowing, 130-131

header fields, 121-122

multiplexing, 122-124

port numbers, 124

well-known port numbers, 125

UDP, 131

header format, 131

multiplexing, 122-124

port numbers, 124

well-known port numbers, 125

Layer 5, 32. *See also* Session layer

Layer 6, 32. *See also* presentation layer

layers, 18. *See also* specific layer

adjacent-layer interactions, 22

encapsulation, 34

of networking models, 28-30

of OSI models, 31-34

same-layer interactions, 22

Learning state (STP), 301

leased circuits, 72

leased lines

cabling, 72

COs, 72

connectors, 73

CSU/DSU, 73

DCE, 73

DTE, 73

serial cables, 73

CPE, 73

data link layer protocols, 74-76

Ethernet as WAN technology, 77-79

full-duplex operation, 71

Internet access technologies, 81

cable Internet, 84-85

DSL, 82-84

Layer 1 service, 74

links, 72

point-to-point links, 72

private lines, 72

serial links, 72

service providers, 71

T1, 72

length of IPv6 prefixes, 445

licenses

Accept License Agreement button, 625

Cisco NX-OS, 200

limiting VTP, 278-279

line vty configuration command, 192

link layer, TCP/IP networking model, 18, 26-28

link local addresses, IPv6, 454-455

link-state database (LSDB), 522

link-state routing protocols, OSPF, 522-526

links, 72

broadcast storms, 286

UTP Ethernet, 48-49

WAN links, creating in lab, 73-74

list logic, standard numbered IPv4 ACLs, 560

Listening state (STP), 301

load balancing with PSVT+ (Per-VLAN Spanning Tree Plus), 316

local usernames, 217-218

log messages, displaying, 222

logging console global commands, 222

logging synchronous command, 222

login authentication, 217. *See also* passwords

loop avoidance, STP, 168-169

loopback address, 380

looping

broadcast storms, 286

frames, 286

loss, 132

LSDB (link-state database), 522-524

M

MAC addresses, 56, 165
  address table
    Layer 2 forwarding path, analyzing, 227
    STP, 288
  BIA, 57
  OUI, 57
  role in frame forwarding process, 167
  switching table, 166
magic numbers, 426, 430
management interfaces (Nexus switches), 190-191
manual EtherChannels, configuring, 326-328
masks, selecting for planned subnet, 360-365
matching logic, 562
matching packets, 558-561
math-related skills, practicing for speed, 583-584
Max Age timers (STP), 299-300
maximum cabling distance, 154
Media Access Control addresses. *See* MAC addresses
memorization versus calculation, 430-431
Message of the Day. *See* MOTD
messages
  full update, 512
  TCP/IP, 30
metric calculations (EIGRP), 518
mind maps, 591
mode trunk command, 269
modes
  EXEC, 192, 195
  Setup (Cisco NX-OS), 208

modifying
  Cisco NX-OS, 202-208
  Consoles, terminal emulators, 188
  contexts, 202-204
  EIGRP, 517-521, 541-545
  files
    copying, 206-207
    erasing, 206-207
    storing, 204-206
  interfaces, 300
  IP routing, 475
    examples, 478-481
    internal processing (Cisco routers), 482
    Nexus switches, 484-487
  IPv4 routing, 475-477
  LANs, 170-178
  management interfaces, 191
  Nexus 5500 switches, 222-229
    debug/show commands, 196
    user settings, 192-195
  OSPF, 521-526, 546-550
  RIPv2 on NX-OS, 536-541
  routes on Nexus switches, 494-501
  SLAAC, 459
  STP, 298-301
  submodes, 202-204
  subnetting, 346-349
    implementing, 366-367
    Layer 3, 349-350
    sizing, 354-356
  trunks, 270
  verification, 270
  VTP, 252-257, 275-279
modularity in Cisco NX-OS, 197
monitoring neighbor state, 513
MOTD (Message of the Day), 220

MPLS (Multiprotocol Level Switching), 78

multiarea OSPF, 526

multicast addresses, 56, 165, 374

Ethernet, 57

IPv6, 455-456

multilayer switches, 223

multiple frame transmission, 288

multiplexing, 120-123

destination port number, 123

dynamic port numbers, 123

sockets, 123-124

multiswitch VLANs, 245-247

N

name resolution (DNS), 111-113

naming conventions (IEEE), 46

NAT/PAT (Network Address Translation / Port Address Translation), 358-359, 441

native VLAN, 248

neighbors, monitoring, 513

Network Address Translation / Port Address Translation (NAT/PAT), 441

network broadcast address, deriving from classful network, 378-380

network layer, 32

IP routing, 94

delivering data to end, 94

logic over LANs and WANs, 76

routing across the network, 94

transmitting packets to default, 93

IP routing logic over LANs and WANs, 76

Layer 3 switches, 251

role in DNS resolution, 111-113

routing

example of, 107-108

host routing, 105-107

IP addressing role in, 95-96

TCP/IP networking model, 22-26

network part (classful network addresses), 376

network part of IPv4 address prefix, 400

networking, 15

diagrams, 15, 27

encapsulation, 28-30

IDs, 101-103

within Class C networks, 381

deriving from classful network addresses, 378-380

layers, 18. *See also* network layer

OSI models

application layer, 32

comparing with TCP/IP, 30-31

data link layer, 33

encapsulation, 34

history of, 17

layers, 33-34

network layer, 32

PDUs, 34

physical layer, 33

presentation layer, 32

session layer, 32

transport layer, 32

parts, 376, 400

ports, 374

versus subnets, 414

TCP/IP, 17-19

application layer, 19-21

comparing, 28-31

development of, 17

link layer, 26-28

network layer, 22-26

RFCs, 17-18

transport layer, 21-22

Nexus 1000v switches

downloading, 623-625

installing, 626-633

Nexus 5500 switches

CLIs, 186-192

configuring, 222-229

debug/show commands, 196

user settings, 192-195

Nexus Operating System. *See* **NX-OS**

Nexus switches

IP routing, 484-487

routes, 494-501

NIC (network interface card), **49**

no shutdown command, **224, 227, 332**

no switchport command, **496**

normal ports, **324**

number of hosts per network, calculating for classful, 377-378

numeric patterns, predictability within interesting octets, **424-425**

numeric reference table

binary-to-hexadecimal conversion, 618

decimal-to-binary conversion, 615-617

hexadecimal-to-binary conversion, 618

NX-OS (Nexus Operating System), 196

accessing, 186-192

Cisco IOS, comparing, 201

configuring, 202-208

EIGRP, configuring, 541-545

HA, 199

licensing, 200

OSPF, configuring, 546-550

reloading, 209-210

RIPv2, configuring, 536-541

service restart in, 198

software modularity in, 197

O

objects, **137**

octets, **98**

in Class A network addresses, 375

in Class B network addresses, 375

in Class C network addresses, 375

decimal-to-binary conversion, 394

interesting octets, predictability in numeric, 424-425

subnet broadcast address, 422

subnet IDs, 420-423

one-size-fits-all design philosophy, **355-356.** *See also* **VLSMs**

Open Shortest Path First. *See* **OSPF**

operating systems

NX-OS. *See* NX-OS

selecting, 629

optimizing STP, **321**

organizationally unique identifier (OUI), **57**

OSI networking models, **17**

application layer, 32

comparing with TCP/IP, 30-31

data link layer, 33, 95

history of, 17

layers, 33-34

network layer, 32

forwarding logic, 92-94

IP routing logic over LANs and, 76

role in DNS resolution, 111-113

routing, 94

PDUs, 34

physical layer, 33

presentation layer, 32

session layer, 32

transport layer, 32

OSPF (Open Shortest Path First), 521-526, 546-550

ABRs, 526

best route selection, 524

flooding process, 522-524

LSDB, 522-524

multiarea OSPF, 526

NX-OS, configuring, 546-550

OSPFv2, 510

single-area OSPF, 525

OUI (organizationally unique identifier), 57

outbound ACLs, 557

P

packets

deencapsulation, 480

encapsulation, 29, 481-482

filtering

ACLs, 557-558

matching packets, 558

standard numbered IPv4 ACLs, 566-568

forwarding routing logic, 480-481

IP routing, 475-487

IPv4

ACLs, 557

routing, 475-477

types of ACLs, 559

loss, 132

packet switching, 484

routing, 249-251

VLANs, routing with routers, 249

passwords, 191-192, 217

path selection, 93

PCPT (Pearson IT Certification Practice Test) exam, 585-587

PDUs (protocol data units), 34

performance

Cisco routers during IP routing process, 483

pps, 482

periodic updates, 513

permanent keyword (ip route command), 501

Persistent Storage Service. *See* PSS

physical layer

OSI model, 33

standards, 45-46, 161-162

TCP/IP networking model, 26-28

pinouts

for 10BASE-T, 51-53

for 100BASE-T, 51-53

for 1000BASE-T, 55

for IEEE autonegotiation, 175

selecting, 54

pins, 49

placement of ACLs, 557-558

planning

internetwork growth, 353

subnets, 348-356, 366-368

point-to-point links, 72

policies (HA), 199

port numbers, 124-125

PortFast, 303, 324-326

ports, 186

alternate, 305

backup, 305-307

on Cisco switches, 50

destination ports, 562-564

DPs (designated ports), 290, 296-297

numbers, 124-125

port costs, 298

RJ-45 ports, 49

root

    STP, 305-307

    tiebreakers for, 296

RPs (root ports), 290, 294-295

source ports, 565

STP, 321-324

postal code example of subnetting, 349

powers of 2 numeric reference table, 620

pps (packets per second), 482

predefined user roles, 193

predictability within interesting octets, 424-425

prefixes, 393-397

global routing, 447

IPv6, 445

network part, 400

notation, 365

subnet mask format, 393

    converting to binary format, 393-394

    converting to DDN, 396-397

subnets

    addresses, 398-399

    parts, 400

presentation layer (OSI model), 32

pre-TCP/IP computer networking, 16

preventing collisions on Ethernet LANs, 61

priority of switches, 322-324

private IP networks, 357-360

private lines, 72

processes

IDs, 548

process switching, 482-484

RSTP, 306-307

protocols, 15

CDP, 331

data-link, 160

describing with OSI layers, 31

DV routing protocols, 511-515

EIGRP, 517-521, 541-545

headers, 20, 27-30

IGPs, 509-510

IGRP, 508

IP. *See* IP

IPv4. *See* IPv4

IPv6. *See* IPv6

layered protocols, 33-34

OSPF, 521-526, 546-550

RIP, 515-516

RIPv2, 536-541

STP, 286

    alternate ports, 305-307

    need for, 286

    optional features, 301-303

trailers, 27

VTP, 252-257, 275-279

pruning VTP, 278-279

PSS (Persistent Storage Service), 199

public classful IP networks, 357

public IP networks, 357-358

PVST+ (Per-VLAN Spanning Tree Plus), 315

Q

QoS (quality of service), 132

bandwidth, 132

data application requirements, 132-133

delay, 132

jitter, 132

loss, 132

video application requirements, 133

voice application requirements, 133

quartets, 443

R

range of usable subnet addresses, 415, 422

Rapid Spanning Tree Protocol. *See* RSTP

recalling commands, 221

receiving applications, identifying, 138-139

Regional Internet Registries (RIR), 440

registered public IP networks, 357-358

reliability, 127-129

reload command, 192

reloading Cisco NX-OS, 209-210

repeaters, Ethernet, 154-155

requirements

single-size subnets, 355-356

VLSMs, 356

workstation, 623

reserved IP addresses, 380

resident addresses, memorization versus calculation, 430-431

resident subnets, 412-414, 427-428

resolving URL host name to IP address, 135-137

restarting Cisco NX-OS, 198

reviews, exam, 583

rfc-editor.org, 124

RFCs, 17

RFC 1122, 18

RFC 1918, 359

topics, searching, 124

RIP (Routing Information Protocol), 512, 515-516

RIPv2 (Routing Information Protocol, version 2), 510, 536-541

RIRs (Regional Internet Registries), 440

RJ-45 ports, 49

roles

NX-OS, 193

of subnet broadcast address, 415

root cost, 290

root ports (RPs)

choosing, 294-295

explained, 290

STP, 305-307

tiebreakers for, 296

root switches, electing via STP, 292-294

route learning process for routing protocols, 109-110

route poisoning, 514-515

router-on-a-stick, 250

routers, 42

ACLs, 557-559

ASICs, 483

data transmission using HDLC, 75-76

default router, 93

IP routing, 482-483

LANs, connecting with WANs, 70

Layer 3 switches, 251

router-on-a-stick, 250

routing logic, 476-482

serial interface cards, 73

subnets, 349

VLANs, routing packets with, 249

wireless, 43

routing, 25-26
    data link layer role in, 95
    EIGRP, 517-521
    EoMPLS, 79
    example of, 107-108
    forwarding logic, 92
        delivering data to end, 94
        routing across the network, 94
        transmitting packets to default, 93
    global prefixes, 447
    IGPs, comparing, 509-510
    IP, 475
        addresses, 95-96
        examples, 478-481
        internal processing (Cisco routers), 482
        Nexus switches, 484-487
        roles, 23-24
    IPv4. *See* IPv4
    IPv6. *See* IPv6
    Layer 3 switches, 251
    network layer, 94
    OSPF, 521-526
    path selection, 93
    protocols, 97. *See also* protocols
        ABRs, 526
        classful, 401
        classless, 401
        convergence, 508
        goals of, 109
        OSPF, 522-526
        route learning process, 109-110
    routes, configuring, 494-501
    tables, 94
Routing Information Protocol. *See* RIP
routing tables, 94

RPs. *See* root ports
RSTP (Rapid Spanning Tree Protocol), 302-305
    backup ports, 307
    processes, 306-307
    states, 306-307
rules, Layer 3 subnet, 349-350

S

same-layer interactions, 22
scaling OSPF
    multiarea OSPF, 526
    single-area OSPF, 525
Secure Shell. *See* SSH
security
    CLIs, 217
    passwords, 191-192, 217
segmentation, 121, 152
    broadcast domains, 171-173
    collision domains, 170-171
    encapsulation, 29
    impact on LAN design, 173
selecting
    classful network for subnet design, 357-360
    mask for planned subnet, 360-365
    operating systems, 629
    pinouts for Ethernet UTP cabling, 54
    static and dynamic ranges per subnets, 367-368
sending frames via IP routing process, 482
SEQ (sequence number), 22
serial cables, 73
serial interface cards, 73
serial links, 72

servers

AAA, 217

VTP, 253

service providers, 71

Ethernet as WAN technology, 77-79

Internet access technologies

cable, 84-85

DSL, 82-84

service restart in Cisco NX-OS, 198

session layer (OSI model), 32

Setup mode (Cisco NX-OS), 208

SFD (Start Frame Delimiter) field, 56

SFP (small form-factor pluggables), 50

shortcuts for calculating subnets

broadcast addresses with, 422

IDs with binary math, 420-421

show commands, 189, 194-196

show etherchannel command, 327, 335

show etherchannel summary command, 330

show interfaces command, 495

show interfaces status command, 226

show interfaces trunk command, 272

show ip eigrp command, 545

show ip eigrp neighbors command, 545

show ip ospf 1 command, 550

show ip rip command, 541

show ip rip neighbor command, 541

show ip route command, 495, 499

show ip route static command, 500

show running-config command, 326, 567

show running-config eigrp command, 545

show running-config ospf command, 549

show running-config rip command, 541

show spanning-tree bridge command, 324, 335

show spanning-tree command, 320, 328, 335

show spanning-tree interface command, 335

show spanning-tree root command, 320, 324, 335

show spanning-tree vlan command, 319-320, 335

show ssh command, 220

show version command, 209

show vlan brief command, 267

shutdown command, 224, 272, 332

shutdown vlan command, 272

Sim questions, 580

Simlet questions, 591

single-area OSPF, 525

single-building enterprise LAN, 44-45

single-size subnets, 355-356

size

broadcast domains, 173

subnets, 354-356

defining, 354

one-size-fits-all design philosophy, 355-356

VLSMs, 356

SLAAC (stateless address autoconfiguration), 459

slash mask, 393

SNA (Systems Network Architecture), 16

SNMP (Simple Network Management Protocol), 125

software modularity in Cisco NX-OS, 197

SOHO LANs, 42-43

Source MAC Address field (Ethernet frames), 56

source MAC addresses, 167

source ports as packet filtering criteria, 565

spanning tree algorithm (STA), 290

spanning-tree commands

    spanning-tree bpduguard default command, 326

    spanning-tree bpduguard disable command, 326, 334

    spanning-tree bpduguard enable command, 325-326, 334

    spanning-tree mode command, 334

    spanning-tree mode pvst command, 314

    spanning-tree portfast bpduguard default command, 334

    spanning-tree portfast command, 325-326, 334

    spanning-tree portfast default command, 326, 334

    spanning-tree portfast disable command, 326, 334

    spanning-tree vlan command, 317, 321-323, 334

Spanning Tree Protocol. *See* STP

split horizons, 512-514

SSH (Secure Shell), 189-190, 218-220

ssh key command, 219

STA (spanning tree algorithm), 290

stacks, dual, 462

standard numbered IPv4 ACLs

    command syntax, 562

    example configuration, 566-568

    first-match logic, 560-561

    implementing, 566

    list logic, 560

    practice problems, 568-569

standards, Ethernet, 159-162

state, neighbors, 513

stateful restarts, 199

stateless address autoconfiguration. *See* SLAAC

states (RSTP), 306-307

static default routes, 501

static ranges per subnet, selecting, 367-368

static routes, configuring, 499-501

status (SSH), 220

steady-state networks, 298-299

steady-state operations (RIP), 512

storing switch configuration tiles, 204-206

STP (Spanning Tree Protocol), 283, 286, 311

    BID (bridge ID), 291

    blocking state, 288-291

    BPDU (bridge protocol data units), 291-292, 303-304

    broadcast storms, 287-288

    configuring, 314-318, 321-329

    convergence, 289, 300-301

    EtherChannel, 302-303

    forwarding state, 288-294

    interface state changes, 300-301

    Learning state, 301

    Listening state, 301

    loop avoidance, 168-169

    MAC table instability, 287-288

    multiple frame transmission, 288

    need for, 286-288

    optional features, 301-303

    PortFast, 303

ports
  alternate ports, 305-307
  DPs (designated ports), 290, 296-297
  port costs, 298
  RPs (root ports), 290, 294-295
  types of, 324
root switches, 292-294
RSTP (Rapid Spanning Tree Protocol), 302-305
STA (spanning tree algorithm), 290
state comparison table, 301
steady-state networks, 298-299
timers, 299-300
topology, 288-289, 298-301
troubleshooting, 329-332
verifying
  default operation, 320
  STP operation, 318-321
straight-through cable pinouts, 51-53
submodes, configuring, 202-204
subnet addresses
  host part, 399
  prefix part, 398-399
subnet bits, calculating requirements for, 362-363
subnet broadcast address, 365, 415
  calculating
    with binary math, 418-422
    with Boolean math, 422
    with decimal math, 428-430
  memorization versus calculation, 430-431
  practice problems, 430

subnet IDs, 414
  calculating
    with binary math, 416-421
    with Boolean math, 422
    with decimal math, 425-427
  practice problems, 427-428
subnet masks
  analysis, practicing, 403-404
  binary format, 392
    converting to DDN, 394-396
    converting to prefix format, 393-394
  conversion, practicing, 397-398
  DDN, 392
    converting to binary, 394-396
    converting to prefix format, 396-397
  difficult masks
    subnet broadcast address, 428-430
    subnet ID, calculating, 425-427
  easy masks, 423
  formats, 392
  host part of subnet addresses, 399
  prefix format, 393
    converting to binary format, 393-394
    converting to DDN, 396-397
    parts of subnet addresses, 399-400
  slash mask, 393
  total subnets in network, calculating, 401-403
subnetting, 103-105
  binary math, 419-420
  classful network, selecting, 357-360
  connected routes, 494-495
  defining subnets, 412

example of, 346, 364

host part of IP address, 361

hosts per subnet, calculating, 353

interesting octets, predictability within, 424-425

IP address assignment, rules for, 348-349

IPv6, 447-456

Layer 3, 349-350

masks

easy masks, 423

mask format, 364-365

selecting, 360

networks and subnets, comparing, 414

overview of, 346-349

planning the implementation, 366-368

postal code example, 349

practice problems, 430

practicing for speed, 583-584

range of usable addresses, 415, 422

sizing, 354-356

subnet bits, calculating requirements for, 362-363

subnet broadcast addresses, 418-419, 422, 428-430

subnet IDs, calculating, 414

binary math, 416-421

Boolean math, 422

decimal math, 425-427

subnets of equal size, 413

subnets per internetwork, calculating, 351

unicast IP addresses, 412

VLANs, routing between, 497-498

superior hello (STP), 292

SVIs (switched virtual interfaces), 497, 538

switches, 158

banners, 220

CLI security, 217

collision domains, 158

configuration files

copying, 206-207

erasing, 206-207

storing, 204-206

Ethernet, 42

external authentication servers, 218-219

forward-versus-filter decisions, 166

frame forwarding logic, 165-169

inactivity timer, 167

installing, 623-633

interfaces, 226-227

IP address, 223-224

LANs, 164-170

Layer 2, 223

Layer 3

sizing, 354-356

subnet rules, 349-350

Nexus

configuring routes on, 494-501

IP routing, 484-487

Nexus 1000v. *See* Nexus 1000v switches

Nexus 5500, 186

configuring, 222-229

debug/show commands, 196

NX-OS, 186, 191-192

user settings, 192-195

NX-OS

EIGRP, 541-545

OSPF, 546-550

RIPv2, 536-541

priority of, 322-324

SSH, 219-220

VLANs, 244, 248, 251, 264-268

switching table, 166

switching VLANs, 173

switchport access vlan command, 267

switchport administrative mode commands, 269

switchport mode command, 269

switchport mode trunk command, 271

switchport trunk encapsulation command, 269

switchports, 324

symmetric speeds, 84

system ID extension, configuring, 316-317

T

T1 leased lines, 72

tables, MAC address tables, 287

tagging (VLAN), 245

TCP (Transmission Control Protocol), 121

comparing with UDP, 120

connections, 126-127

error recovery, 21, 127-129

flow control with windowing, 130-131

header fields, 121

multiplexing, 122-124

port numbers, 124-125

receiving applications, identifying, 138-139

segments, 122

SEQ, 22

source port, 565

TCP/IP (Transmission Control Protocol/Internet Protocol), 17-19

application layer, 19-21

applications, 132

HTTP, 137

video applications, 133

voice applications, 133

WWW, 134-137

comparing, 28-31

data applications (QoS requirements), 132-133

development of, 17

DNS, 125

encapsulation, 28-30

layers, 18

link layer, 26-28

messages, 30

network layer, 22-24

IP addressing, 24-25

routing, 25-26

pre-TCP/IP computer networking, 16

RFCs, 17-18

SNMP, 125

TFTP, 125

transport layer, 21-22, 120

WWW, 125

telcos

COs, 72

CSU/DSU connectors, 73

Internet core, 81

leased lines, cabling, 72

Telnet, 189-190, 218

terminal emulators, 188

testing connectivity with ping command, 113-114

Testlet questions, preparing for, 580

TFTP (Trivial File Transfer Protocol), 125

third-party practice exams, 587-588

three-area OSPF, 526

three-way handshake, 126

tiebreakers for root ports, 296

time needed for exam completion, estimating, 581

timed practice exams, 585-587

topics of RFCs, searching, 124

topologies

EIGRP, 518

STP, 298-301

total networks provisioned

for Class A networks, 375

for Class B networks, 375

for Class C networks, 375

trailer fields for Ethernet frames, 55-56

trailers, 27

transferring files with HTTP, 137

transitions, IPv6, 461-463

transport layer, 120

OSI model, 32

receiving applications, identifying, 138-139

TCP, 121

connection establishment, 126

connection termination, 127

error recovery and reliability, 127-129

flow control with windowing, 130-131

header fields, 121-122

multiplexing, 122-124

well-known port numbers, 125

TCP/IP, 21, 120, 124

adjacent-layer, 22

same-layer, 22

TCP error recovery, 21

UDP, 131

multiplexing, 122-124

well-known port numbers, 124-125

troubleshooting

EIGRP, 543

EtherChannel, 329-332

OSPF, 548

STP, 329-332

trunking, 245-247

802.1Q, 247-248

administrative mode options, 269

allowed VLAN list, 271-274

configuring, 268-269

IPv6 inside IPv4, 462

ISL, 247-248

VTP, 275

two-phase practice approach, 381-383

Type field

Ethernet frames, 56

HDLC, 75

types

of Ethernet, 46

of IP ACLs, 559

of STP ports, 324

U

UDP (User Datagram Protocol), 131

comparing with TCP, 120

header format, 131

multiplexing, 122-123

destination port number, 123

dynamic port numbers, 123

sockets, 123-124

port numbers, 124-125

receiving applications, identifying, 138-139

unicast addresses, 56, 165, 374, 412

uninteresting octets, 427

unique local unicast addresses, 453-454

universal addresses, 57

unknown unicast frames, 168

unused interfaces, securing, 226-227

updating

IPv6, 442

periodic updates, 513

URLs (Uniform Resource Locators), 20, 134-136

usernames, local, 217

UTP (unshielded twisted-pair), 45

10BASE-T, 51-54

100BASE-T, 51-54

1000BASE-T, 55

data transmission on Ethernet LANs, 48

electrical circuits, creating on Ethernet LANs, 48

EMI, 48

Ethernet links, 48-49

V

VACLs (VLAN access control list), 566

valid network numbers

for Class A networks, 375

for Class B networks, 375

for Class C networks, 375

validating

EIGRP, 543

OSPF, 548

verification

configuring, 270

Cisco Catalyst switches, 224

RIPv2, 539

STP, 318-321

VTP, 275-279

video applications, QoS requirements, 133

viewing contents of ARP cache, 113

virtual routing and forwarding. See VRF

VLAN access control lists. See VACLs

VLAN Trunking Protocol. See VTP

vlan vlan-id global config command, 268

VLANs (virtual LANs), 172-173

broadcast domains, 244-245

configuring, 266-268, 271-274

forwarding data between, 248-251

Layer 3 switching, 497-498

packet routing, 249

STP (Spanning Tree Protocol) configuration, 315-317

subnet requirements, calculating, 352

subnets, routing between, 497

tagging, 245

trunking, 245-248, 268-274

VLAN ID (VLAN identifiers), 245

VLSMs, 356

voice applications, QoS requirements, 133

VoIP, 133

VRF (virtual routing and forwarding), 190

VTP (VLAN Trunking Protocol), 252-257

configuring, 275-279

enabling, 275-276

pruning, 278-279

W

WANs (wide area networks), 70
  cabling, 72
    connectors, 73
    COs, 72
    DCE, 73
    DTE, 73
    serial cable, 73
  comparing with LANs, 67
  CPE, 73
  CSU/DSU, 73
  data link layer protocol, 74-76
  Ethernet, 77-79
  full-duplex operation, 71
  Internet access technologies, 81
    cable Internet, 84-85
    DSL, 82-84
  LANs, connecting, 70
  leased circuits, 72
  leases, 67
  links, 72-74
  point-to-point links, 72

private lines, 72
serial links, 72
service providers, 71
web browsers, 134
  DNS resolution, 135-137
  home page, 19
  HTTP, 19-21
  URLs, 134-136
web clients, 134, 137
web pages, 134
  links, 135
  objects, 137
web servers, 134
websites, rfc-editor.org, 124
well-known port numbers, 124-125
windowing, 130-131
wired LANs, 39
wireless enterprise LANs, 44-45
wireless LANs, 42-43
workstation requirements, 623
WWW (World Wide Web), 125, 134
  DNS resolution, 135-137
  URLs, 134-136

ciscopress.com: Your Cisco Certification and Networking Learning Resource

Subscribe to the monthly Cisco Press newsletter to be the first to learn about new releases and special promotions.

Visit **ciscopress.com/newsletters.**

While you are visiting, check out the offerings available at your finger tips.

–Free Podcasts from experts:
- OnNetworking
- OnCertification
- OnSecurity

Podcasts

View them at **ciscopress.com/podcasts.**

–Read the latest author **articles** and **sample chapters** at ciscopress.com/articles.

–Bookmark the Certification Reference Guide available through our partner site at **informit.com/certguide.**

Connect with Cisco Press authors and editors via Facebook and Twitter, visit informit.com/socialconnect.